Index to Handicraft Books, 1974–1984

INDEX TO

Handicraft Books

1974–1984

Compiled by the staff of the
Science and Technology Department,
Carnegie Library of Pittsburgh

University of Pittsburgh Press

Published by the University of Pittsburgh Press, Pittsburgh, Pa. 15260

Copyright © 1986, University of Pittsburgh Press

Feffer and Simons, Inc., London

Manufactured in the United States of America

Library of Congress Cataloging-in-Publication Data

Main entry under title:

Index to handicraft books, 1974–1984.

    1. Handicraft—Indexes.   2. Handicraft—Bibliography.
I. Carnegie Library of Pittsburgh. Science and Technology Dept.
Z6151.I5 1986   [TT145]   016.7455   85-40857
ISBN 0-8229-3532-5

Contents

Preface

This craft index is a subject guide to projects in how-to-do-it books. It is intended to supplement such publications as *Make It*[1] and the *Index to Handicrafts*[2] series (last published in 1975), by providing quick access to craft projects in books more recent than these sources have indexed. The books included in this index have publication dates of 1974 or later and are a part of the collection at the Carnegie Library of Pittsburgh, mainly in the Library of Congress classification TT section.

Subjects covered are as diverse as furniture construction and repair, needlework projects, making toys and games, and crafting jewelry. During the past ten years, crafts have gone through several fads; many of these projects are included in the index. Macrame, doll house construction and furnishing, and quilting have been popular subjects for books, while fewer books were published about such projects as furniture construction and boat building.

Most citations are for specific projects such as plans for a picnic table, how to build a chair, installation of patios, making a particular desk accessory, or knitting a sweater. Each entry in the index consists of the name of the project as listed in the original book, at times some additional description in parentheses, the author and title of the book, and the page numbers on which the project can be found. The author and title listed correspond to those in the List of Works Cited section. The index aids in locating a specific craft project in a book. In addition to actual projects, this book also lists various ways to accomplish a particular task, such as how to use a lathe, remodel a basement, and make lace.

The index was started in 1983 as a card file and has grown rapidly with the efforts of the librarians in the Science and Technology Department at the Carnegie Library of Pittsburgh. The librarians who helped with this index are: Joan Anderson, Sandra Janicki, Elizabeth Lee, Robert Matlack, Dorothy Melamed, and David Murdock. Marilyn Macevic did most of the typing of the file cards from which the book was assembled.

Martha E. Lyle
Editor

1. Joyce Shields, *Make It* (Metuchen, New Jersey: Scarecrow Press, 1975).
2. Pearl Turner, *Index to Handicrafts, Model Making, and Workshop Projects* (Westwood, Massachusetts: F. W. Faxon Company, 1975 and previous volumes).

Index to Handicraft Books, 1974–1984

List of Books Indexed

Abrams, A. Jay. Building craft equipment: an illustrated manual. Praeger, 1976

Adams, Florence. Make your own baby furniture. M. Evans. 1980

Adams, Jeannette T. Arco's complete woodworking handbook. Arco, 1981

Adams, John Duncan. How to make mission style lamps and shades. Dover, 1982

Adkins, Jan. Wood book. Little, Brown & Co., 1980

Aiken, Joyce. Total tote bag book. Taplinger, 1977

Albers, Vernon M. How to use woodworking tools effectively and safely. A. S. Barnes, 1975

Alth, Max. Do-it-yourself roofing and siding. Hawthorn Books, 1977

———. Making plastic pipe furniture. Everest House, 1981

———. Rattan furniture. Hawthorn Books, 1979

Ambuter, Carolyn. Carolyn Ambuter's needlepoint celebrations. New York Times Book Co., 1976

———. Open canvas. Workman Publishing, 1982

American School of Needlework. Great Christmas crochet book. Sterling, 1981

———. Great crochet bazaar book. Sterling, 1982

Ammen, C. W. Constructing & using wood patterns. Tab Books, 1983

Andersen, Gretchen M. Creative exploration in crafts. Reston, 1976

Anderson, Barbara. Costume design. Holt, Rinehart & Winston, 1984

Anderson, Enid. Crafts and the disabled. B. T. Batsford, 1982

Anderson, Fay. Tie dyeing and batik. Chartwell Books, 1977

Anderson, Marilyn. Guatemalan textiles today. Watson-Guptill, 1978

Andes, Eugene. Far beyond the fringe: three-dimensional knotting techniques using macrame & nautical ropework. Van Nostrand Reinhold, 1973

Andrews, Denison. How to make your own hammock and lie in it. Workman Publishing, 1972

Appel, Ellen. Sand art: materials, techniques, terrariums, sandpainting, sculpture, projects. Crown, 1976

Araki, Chiyo. Origami for Christmas. Kodansha International Ltd., 1983

Arnold, Dennis M. Needlepoint pattern book. Morrow, 1974

Ashurst, Elizabeth. Collage. Marshall Cavendish, 1976

Auld, Rhoda L. Molas: what they are, how to make them, ideas they suggest for creative applique. Van Nostrand Reinhold, 1977

————. Tatting: the contemporary art of knotting with a shuttle. Van Nostrand Reinhold, 1974

Avery, Virginia. Quilts to wear. Scribner's, 1982

Bacon, Lenice Ingram. American patchwork quilts. Morrow, 1973

Badzinski, Stanley. House construction: a guide to buying, building and evaluating. Prentice-Hall, 1976

Baker, Muriel L. Stumpwork: the art of raised embroidery. Scribner's, 1978

Bakke, Karen. Sewing machine as a creative tool. Prentice-Hall, 1976

Baldwin, Ed. Old fashioned wooden toys. Hearst Books, 1982

————. Scrap fabric crafts. HP Books, 1982

————. Weepeeple. Putnam's Sons, 1983

Ball, Richard. Master pieces. Hearst Books, 1983

Ballinger, Raymond A. Design with paper in art and graphic design. Van Nostrand Reinhold, 1982

Banov, Abel. Book of successful painting. Structures Publishing, 1975

Banzhof, Robert A. Screen process painting. McKnight Publishing, 1983

Bard, Rachel. Successful wood book. Structures Publishing, 1978

Barnes, Charles. 120 needlepoint design projects. Crown, 1974

Barrett, Clotilde. Boundweave. Colorado Fiber Center, 1982

Barrett, Timothy. Japanese papermaking. Weatherhill, 1983

Bass, Charlotte Christiansen. Applique quiltmaking. Arco, 1984

Batchelder, Martha. Art of hooked-rug making. Down East Books, 1983

Bath, Virginia C. Needlework in America: history, designs, and techniques. Viking, 1979

Bausert, John. Complete book of wicker and cane furniture making. Drake Publishers, 1976

Bealer, Alex W. Art of blacksmithing. Funk & Wagnalls, 1976

————. Tools that built America. Bonanza Books, 1976.

Beard, Betty J. Fashions from the loom: handwoven clothing made easy. Interweave Press, 1980

Beatty, Alice. Hook book. Stackpole Books, 1977

Beckman, Bob. Building and flying giant scale radio control aircraft. Kalmbach Books, 1983

Beiderman, Charles. Beginner's handbook of woodcarving. Prentice-Hall, 1983

Belfer, Nancy. Designing in batik and tie dye. Prentice-Hall, 1977

Benton, Kitty. Sewing classic clothes for children. Hearst Books, 1981

Bergan, Hans R. Lingore paper airplane folding manual. Lingore Press, 1981

Berry, Jane. How to make party and holiday decorations. Chilton Book Co., 1976

Better Homes and Gardens. Deck and patio projects you can build. Meredith Corp., 1977

————. Step-by-step masonry and concrete. Meredith Corp., 1982

Better Homes & Gardens applique. Meredith Corp., 1978

Better Homes and Gardens easy bazaar crafts. Better Homes and Gardens, 1981

Better Homes & Gardens embroidery. Meredith Corp., 1978

Better Homes & Gardens holiday decorations you can make. Meredith Corp., 1974

Better Homes and Gardens sewing for your home. Meredith Corp., 1974

Better Homes and Gardens step-by-step cabinets and shelves. Meredith Corp., 1983

Better Homes and Gardens treasury of Christmas crafts & foods. Meredith Corp., 1980

Better Homes and Gardens treasury of needlecrafts. Meredith Corp., 1982

Beveridge, June. Warp/weft/sett: a reference manual for handweavers. Van Nostrand Reinhold, 1980

Beyer, Jinny. Quilter's album of blocks & borders. EPM Publications, 1980

Biegeleisen, Jacob I. Screen printing. Watson-Guptill, 1971

Bjerregaard, Lena. Techniques of Guatemalan weaving. Van Nostrand Reinhold, 1977

Bird, Adren J. Craft of Hawaiian lauhala weaving. University of Hawaii Press, 1982

Black, Mary E. Key to weaving: a textbook of hand weaving for the beginning weaver. Macmillan, 1980

Black and Decker power tool carpentry. Van Nostrand Reinhold, 1978

Blackburn, Charles. Needlepoint designs for traditional furniture. Vanguard Press, 1980.

Blackwell, Johnny. Johnny Blackwell's poor man's catalog. St. Martin's Press, 1981

Blair, Margot Carter. Banners and flags: how to sew a celebration. Harcourt Brace Jovanovich, 1977

Blandford, Percy W. Building better beds. Tab Books, 1984

———. Constructing outdoor furniture, with 99 projects. Tab Books, 1983

———. Do-it-yourselfer's guide to furniture repair and refinishing. Tab Books, 1977

———. 53 space-saving built-in furniture projects. Tab Books, 1983

———. Giant book of wooden toys. Tab Books, 1982

———. How to make early American & colonial furniture. Tab Books, 1979

———. How to make your own built-in furniture. Tab Books, 1976

———. Practical handbook of blacksmithing and metalworking. Tab Books, 1980

———. 66 children's furniture projects. Tab Books, 1979

———. Upholsterer's bible. Tab Books, 1978

Blandford book of traditional handicrafts. Blandford Press, 1981

Bliss, Anne. Handbook of dyes from natural materials. Scribner's, 1981

Blizzard, Richard E. Making wooden toys. Sterling, 1982

Boberg, Anne-Marie. Macrame. Arco, 1975

Boeschen, John. Successful playhouses. Structures Publishing, 1979

Borssuck, B. Needlework monograms. Arco, 1982

Botermans, Jack. Paper flight. Holt, Rinehart & Winston, 1984

Botsford, Shirley J. Between thimble & thumb. Holt, Rinehart & Winston, 1979

Bovin, Murray. Jewelry making. Bovin Publishing, 1979

Bowen, Kernochan. Four-harness weaving. Watson-Guptill, 1978

Bowen, Marjorie. Designing with dye resists, batik and tie-and-dye. Stephen Hope Books, 1974

Bowie, Hamish. Jewelry making. Regnery, 1976

Boye, David. Step-by-step knifemaking: you can do it! Rodale Press, 1977

Boyles, Margaret. Bargello: an explosion in color. MacMillan, 1974

————. Margaret Boyles book of needle art. Harcourt Brace Jovanovich, 1978

————. Needlework gifts for special occasions. Simon & Schuster, 1981

Brack, Edith. Modern flower arranging. B. T. Batsford, 1982

Bradley, Duane. Design it, sew it, and wear it. Crowell, 1979

Bragdon, Allen D. Homeowner's complete manual of repair & improvement. Arco, 1983

Bramson, Ann. Soap. 2nd ed. Workman Publishing, 1975

Brann, Donald R. How to build a kayak. Directions Simplified, 1978

————. How to build colonial furniture. Directions Simplified, 1976

————. How to build kitchen cabinets, room dividers, and cabinet furniture. Directions Simplified, 1976

————. How to build outdoor furniture. Directions Simplified, 1976

————. How to build outdoor projects. Directions Simplified, 1975

————. How to build patios and sundecks. Directions Simplified, 1974

————. How to build pet housing. Directions Simplified, 1975

————. How to build workbenches, sawhorse tool chest and other build-it-yourself projects. Directions Simplified, 1974

————. How to construct built-in and sectional bookcases. Directions Simplified, 1974

————. How to modernize an attic. Directions Simplified, 1974

————. How to modernize a kitchen. Directions Simplified, 1967

————. How to repair, refinish, reupholster. Easi-bild Directions Simplified, 1982

Braren, Ken. Homemade: 101 easy-to-make things for your garden, home, or farm. Garden Way Publishing, 1977

Bray, Bonita. Afghans: traditional & modern. Crown, 1977

Breckenridge, Muriel. Lap quilting: How to make beautiful quilted projects, large & small. Sterling, 1980

Bridgewater, Alan. A treasury of woodcarving designs. Van Nostrand Reinhold, 1981

Brightman, Robert. 101 practical uses for propane torches. Tab Books, 1977

Briney, Doug. Home machinist's handbook. Tab Books, 1983

Broadwater, Elaine. Woodburning, art and craft. Crown, 1980

Brock, Delia. Gladrags; redesigning, remaking, refitting all your old clothes. Simon & Schuster, 1974

Brodie, Regis C. Energy efficient potter. Watson-Guptill, 1982

Bronson, J. Early American weaving and dyeing: the domestic manufacturer's assistant and family directory in the arts of weaving and dyeing. Dover, 1977

Brooke, Margaret L. Lace in the making with bobbins and needle. Robin and Russ Handweavers, 1975

Brostoff, Laya. Professional handweaving on the fly-shuttle loom. Van Nostrand Reinhold, 1978

Brown, Gail. Super sweater idea book: hundreds of new and exciting ways to turn sweater fabrics into unique fashions, home accessories, and gifts. Butterick, 1978

Brown, Margery. Cane and rush seating. Larousse, 1976

———. Complete book of rush and basketry techniques. Larousse, 1983

Brown, Rachel. Weaving, spinning and dyeing book. Knopf, 1978

Brown, Raymond D. 44 terrific woodworking plans & projects. Tab Books, 1984

Brumbaugh, James E. Wood furniture finishing, refinishing, repairing. T. Audel, 1974

Brunner, Marguerite Ashworth. Pass it on: how to make your own family keepsakes. Sovereign Books, 1979

Bubel, Mike. Working wood. Rodale Press, 1977

Buckland, Ralph S. Toymaker's book of wooden vehicles. Van Nostrand Reinhold, 1984

Buckwalter, Len. Easy speaker projects. H. W. Sams, 1974

———. Homeowner's handbook of power tools. Funk and Wagnalls, 1976

Built-ins. Time-Life Books, 1979

Bumper book of things a boy can make. Tab Books, 1978

Bumper book of things a girl can make. Tab Books, 1977

Burch, Mary Lou. Making leaf rubbings. S. Greene Press, 1979

Burch, Monte. Building small barns, sheds, and shelters. Garden Way Publishing, 1983

———. Tile: indoors and out, every kind and use. Creative Homeowner Press, 1981

Burchette, Dorothy. More needlework blocking and finishing. Scribner's, 1979

———. Needlework: blocking and finishing. Scribner's, 1974

Burns, Marjorie A. Altering ready-to-wear. Lippincott, 1976

———. Shirt look. Lippincott, 1976

———. Super sewing; the new Bishop/Arch book. Lippincott, 1974

Buxton, Gail. Craftmaking: for love or money. Executive Communications, 1983

Cabrera, Roberta. Classic tailoring techniques. Fairchild Publications, 1983

Calhoun, Elizabeth. 20 simple solar projects. Rodale Press, 1983

Campbell, Donald. Using the potter's wheel. Van Nostrand Reinhold, 1978

Campbell, Stu. Home water supply. Garden Way Publishing, 1983

Cane, rush and straw. Excalibur Books, 1977

Capotosto, Rosario. Woodworking techniques and projects. Van Nostrand Reinhold, 1982

———. Woodworking wisdom. Popular Science Books, 1983

Carbo, Dorothy. Fix-it guide for women. Arco, 1976

Carroll, David. Make your own chess set. Prentice-Hall, 1974

Carty, Sally Clarke. How to make braided rugs. McGraw-Hill, 1977

Cary, Jane Randolph. Storage: cabinets, closets, and wall systems. Harper & Row, 1979

Cary, Jere. Building your own kitchen cabinets. Taunton Press, 1983

Cary, Mara. Basic baskets. Houghton Mifflin, 1975

Casselman, B. J. Crafts from around the world. Creative Home Library, 1975

Casselman, Karen Leigh. Craft of the dyer: colour from plants and lichens of the Northeast. University of Toronto Press, 1980

Casson, Michael. Craft of the potter. Barron's, 1977

Cauro, Roland. Stringcraft. Sterling, 1976

Ceramics. Excalibur Books, 1977

Chadwick, Eileen. Craft of hand spinning. Scribner's, 1980

Challenging projects in stained glass. Arco, 1983

Chamberlain, Marcia. Beyond weaving. Watson-Guptill, 1974

———. Metal jewelry techniques. Watson-Guptill, 1976

Chamberlain, Susan. Fences, gates & walls. HP Books, 1983

Chappell, James. Potter's complete book of clay and glazes. Watson-Guptill, 1977

Chatterton, Pauline. Coordinated crafts for the home. Marek Publishers, 1980

Chatterton, Pauline. Patchwork & applique. Dial Press, 1977

———. Scandinavian knitting designs. Scribner's, 1977

Chesneau, Roger. Scale models in plastic. Scribner's, 1979

Chisholm, K. Lomneth. Candlemaker's primer. E.P. Dutton, 1973

Christensen, Jo Ippolito. Needlepoint: the third dimension. Prentice-Hall, 1979

———. Needlepoint and bargello stitchery. Sterling, 1980

———. Needlepoint book. 303 stitches with patterns & projects. Prentice-Hall, 1976

———. Teach yourself needlepoint. Prentice-Hall, 1978

Christmas crafts book. Search Press, 1979

Christmas decorations from Williamsburg's folk art collection. Holt, Rinehart & Winston, 1976

Chroman, Eleanor. Potter's primer. Hawthorn Books, 1974

Churchill, James E. Backyard building book. Bryn Mawr Press, 1976

———. Backyard building book II. Stackpole Books, 1978

———. Big backyard building book. Stackpole Books, 1983

———. Complete book of tanning skins and furs. Stackpole Books, 1983

Clark, Christine L. The make-it-yourself shoe book. Knopf, 1977

Clarke, Mary Washington. Kentucky quilts and their makers. University Press of Kentucky, 1976

Clifford, Jerrold R. Basic woodworking and carpentry with projects. Tab Books, 1980

Coffey, Francine. Francine Coffey's celebrity sewing bee. Harper & Row, 1974

Coker, Alec. Craft of straw decoration. Dryad Press, 1971

Colby, Averil. Pincushions. Scribner's, 1975

Collection of designs for cross-stitch. Ondorisha Publishers, 1980

Colletti, Jack D. Art of woodcarving. Prentice-Hall, 1977

Collier, Ann. Creative design in bobbin lace. Charles T. Branford Co., 1982

Collingwood, Peter. Techniques of sprang: plaiting on stretched threads. Watson-Guptill, 1974

———. Techniques of tablet weaving. Watson-Guptill, 1982

Colson, Frank A. Kiln building with space-age materials. Van Nostrand Reinhold, 1975

Complete book of baby crafts. Arco, 1981

Complete guide to blacksmithing. Bonanza Books, 1981

Complete guide to needlework. Chartwell Books, 1982

Complete handyman do-it-yourself encyclopedia. H. S. Stuttman Co., 1975

Compton, Rae. Complete book of traditional knitting. Scribner's, 1983

Conner, Anna Thomas. Corncraft. A. S. Barnes, 1980

Conrad, John W. Contemporary ceramic formulas. Macmillan, 1980

————. Contemporary ceramic techniques. Prentice-Hall, 1979

Cook, Harold C. Decorating for the holidays. Castle Books, 1976

Cooper, Emmanuel. Potter's book of glaze recipes. Scribner's, 1980

Cooper, Patricia. Quilters. Anchor Press/Doubleday, 1978

Cope, Dwight W. Plastics. Goodheart-Willcox Co., 1982

Cornelius, Rosemary. Teaching needlecraft: a handbook for the beginning instructor. Van Nostrand Reinhold, 1979

Corrigan, Barbara. How to make pants and jeans that really fit. Doubleday, 1978

Coskey, Evelyn. Christmas crafts for everyone. Abingdon, 1976

Couldridge, Alan. Hat book. Prentice-Hall, 1980

Cowan, Sally. Left-handed sewing. Van Nostrand Reinhold, 1984

Coyne, John. How to make upside-down dolls. Bobbs-Merrill, 1977

————. Penland School of Crafts book of jewelry making. Bobbs-Merrill, 1975.

————. Penland School of Crafts book of pottery. Bobbs-Merrill, 1975

Creager, Clara. Weaving: a creative approach for beginners. Doubleday, 1974

Creative Crafts yearbook: an exciting new collection of needlework and crafts. Columbia House, 1979

Creative sewing. Mason/Charter, 1977

Creekmore, Betsey B. Your world in miniature; a guide to making smallscale rooms and scenes. Doubleday, 1976

Critchley, Paula. Step by step guide to making artificial flowers. Hamlyn, 1973

Crochet: by the editors of Ladies' Home Journal. Mason/Charter, 1976

Crockett, Candace. Complete spinning book. Watson-Guptill, 1977

Crown, Fenya. How to recycle old clothes into new fashions. Prentice-Hall, 1977

Cudlipp, Edythe. Furs. Hawthorn Books, 1978

Dal Fabbro, Mario. How to make children's furniture and play equipment. 2nd. ed. McGraw-Hill, 1975

D'Amato, Janet. Italian crafts. M. Evans, 1977

Daniele, Joseph W. Building early American furniture. Stackpole Books, 1974

————. How to build 35 great clocks. Stackpole Books, 1984

Daniels, George E. Decks, porches, and patios. Creative Home Library, 1974

Davidson, Margaret. Successful studios and work centers. Structures Publishing, 1977

Davies, Natalie. Beads as jewelry. Chilton Book Co., 1975

Davis, Dee. Step-by-step decoupage. Golden Press, 1976

Davis, Kenneth. Restoring furniture. Arco, 1978

Davis, Mary Kay. Needlework doctor: how to solve every kind of needlework problem. Prentice-Hall, 1982

Day, Jere. Complete book of rock crafting. Drake Publishers, 1976

Day, Richard. How to build patios and decks. Popular Science Books, 1976

Decks and patios. Creative Homeowner Press, 1980

DeCristoforo, R. J. Build your own wood toys, gifts and furniture. Popular Science Books, 1981

DeLeon, Sherry. Basketry book. Holt, Rinehart & Winston, 1978

DeLynn, Eileen. Secrets of how to have the latest pant styles. Seagulls Artistic Publications, 1981

Dendel, Esther Warner. Basic book of fingerweaving. Simon & Schuster, 1974

DeRodriguez, Judy Ziek. Weaving on a backstrap loom: pattern designs from Guatemala. Hawthorn, 1978

Design crochet. Hawthorn Books, 1978

Designing apparel through the flat pattern. Rev. 5th ed. Fairchild Publications, 1982

Dickerson, John. Pottery making: a complete guide. Viking, 1974

Dieringer, Beverly. Paper bead book. David McKay, 1977

Dillmont, Therese de. Complete encyclopedia of needlework. Running Press, 1978

Dittrick, Mark. Hard crochet. Hawthorn Books, 1978

Dodge, Jane. Step-by-step new macrame. Golden Press, 1979

Dodge, Venus. Dolls' house do-it-yourself book. Sterling, 1983

Doeser, Linda. Paper. Excalibur Books, 1978

Doherty, Anna Marie. Family Circle book of 429 great gifts-to-make all year round for just 10¢ to $10.00. Rawson Associates, 1977

Do-it-yourself flooring. Lane, 1982

Dreher, Denise. From the neck up: an illustrated guide to hatmaking. Madhatter Press, 1981

Dudley, Taimi. Strip patchwork: quick and easy patchwork using the Seminole technique. Van Nostrand Reinhold, 1980

Duncan, Alastair. Leaded glass. Watson-Guptill, 1975

Duncan, Thomas. How to buy and restore wicker furniture. Duncan-Holmes, 1983

Duthie, Arthur L. Decorative glass processes. Dover, 1982

Dyeing & printing. Excalibur Books, 1977

Dyer's art: ikat, batik, plangi. Van Nostrand Reinhold, 1976

Earnshaw, Pat. Dictionary of lace. Shire Publications, 1982

Easy-to-make tables and chairs. Lane, 1976

Edson, Nicki Hitz. Creative crochet. Watson-Guptill, 1973

Edwards, Keith. Lost wax casting of jewelry. Regnery, 1974

Egge, Ruth Stearns. Recycled with flair. Coward, McCann & Geoghegan, 1980

Elbert, Virginie. Paperworks: colorful crafts from picture eggs to fish kites. Prentice-Hall, 1982

————. Shell craft. Bobbs-Merrill, 1977

Ellen, Aunt. Aunt Ellen's quilting handbook. Modern Handcraft, 1982

Elliot, Zena. Working with copper. Drake Publishers, 1976

Ellis, Chris. Scale modeler's handbook. Chartwell Books, 1979

Embroidery. Van Nostrand Reinhold, 1978

Embroidery of roses. Ondorisha Publishers, 1980

Emlyn-Jones, Gwen. Make your own gloves. Scribner's, 1974

Encyclopedia of crafts. Exeter Books, 1982

Endacott, G. W. Fine furniture making and woodworking. Sterling, 1982

Epple, Anne O. Something from nothing crafts. Chilton Book Co., 1976

Erlandsen, Ida-Merete. Bead book. Van Nostrand Reinhold, 1974

Evans, Hilary. Ribbonwork. Bobbs-Merrill, 1976

Evrard, Gwen. Homespun crafts from scraps. New Century, 1982

———. Twinkletoes: footwear to make and wear. Scribner's, 1976

Fairfield, Helen. Patchwork. Octopus, 1980

Family handyman handbook of carpentry plans/projects. Tab Books, 1980

Family handyman handbook of home improvement and remodeling. Tab Books, 1979

Fanning, Robbie. Complete book of machine quilting. Chilton Book Co., 1980

Farlie, Barbara L. All about doll houses. Bobbs-Merrill, 1975

———. Pennywise boutique. Creative Home Library, 1974

Farmer, Bonnita M. Concepts of fit: an individualized approach to pattern design. Macmillan, 1982

Farnworth, Warren. Creative work with plaster. B. T. Batsford, 1975

Farrell, Peg. Counted cross-stitch patchwork design. Van Nostrand Reinhold, 1980

Favorite easy-to-make toys. Sedgewood Press, 1982

Favorite knitting & crochet patterns. Sedgewood Press, 1982

Feder, Carol. Candlemaking design book. F. Watts, 1974

Fee, Jacqueline. Sweater workshop. Interweave Press, 1983

Feirer, John L. Cabinetmaking and millwork. Rev. 2nd ed. Bennett, 1982

Felcher, Cecelia. Complete book of rug making: folk methods and ethnic designs. Hawthorn, 1975

Feldman, Annette. Big book of afghans. Van Nostrand Reinhold, 1981

———. Handmade lace and patterns. Harper and Row, 1975

———. Needlework boutique. Rutledge Books, 1977

Fine woodworking techniques 1. Taunton Press, 1978

Fine woodworking techniques 2. Taunton Press, 1980

Fine woodworking techniques 3. Taunton Press, 1981

Fine woodworking techniques 4. Taunton Press, 1982

Fine woodworking techniques 5. Taunton Press, 1983

Finegold, Rupert. Silversmithing. Chilton Book Co., 1983

Firestein, Cecily Barth. Rubbing craft: how to rub doors, letterboxes, gravestones, manhole covers and how to use these designs to make jewelry, T-shirts, needlepoint and more. Quick Fox, 1977

Firsoff, Valdemar Axel. Working with gemstones. Arco, 1974

Fischer, Pauline. Egyptian designs in modern stitchery. E.P. Dutton, 1979

Fischman, Walter Ian. Decks. Grosset & Dunlap, 1975

Fisher, Katharine. Craft of smocking. Scribner's, 1979

———. Quilting in squares. Scribner's, 1978

Fletcher, Edward. Rock and gem polishing. Blandford Press, 1973

Flick, Pauline. Dollhouse idea book: furniture and decoration. Hawthorn Books, 1976

Flower, Cedric. Puppets, methods and materials. Davis Publications, 1983

Foose, Sandra L. More scrap saver's stitchery. Doubleday, 1981

————. Scrap saver's stitchery book. Doubleday, 1978

Foote, Estelle J. Mender's manual: repairing and preserving garments and bedding. Harcourt Brace Jovanovich, 1976

Foote, Theodore P. Jewelry making. Davis Publications, 1981

44 string and nail art projects. Crown, 1974

Foss, Mildred B. Creative embroidery with your sewing machine. Prentice-Hall, 1976

Fournier, Robert L. Electric kiln construction for potters. Van Nostrand Reinhold, 1977

Fowler, Earl P. Can crafts. Chilton Book, Co., 1977

Frager, Dorothy. Book of sampler quilts. Chilton Book Co., 1983

————. Quilting primer. Chilton Book Co., 1974

Frame, Mary. Tie-dyeing and batik. Octopus, 1974

Francini, Audrey A. Crewel embroidery, with texture & thread variations. Van Nostrand Reinhold, 1979

Frary, Dave. How to build realistic model railroad scenery. Kalmback Books, 1982

Fraser, B. Kay. Modern stitchery: stitches, patterns, free-form designing. Crown, 1976

Fraser, Henry. Glazes for the craft potter. Watson-Guptill, 1974

Frid, Tage. Tage Frid teaches woodworking. Vol 2. Taunton Press, 1981

Funaro, Diana. Yestermorrow clothes book: how to remodel second hand clothes. Chilton Book Co., 1976

Gadney, Alan. How to enter and win fabric and fiber crafts contests. Facts on File Publications, 1983

————. How to enter and win jewelry and metal crafts contests. Facts on File Publications, 1983

Garage, attic and basement storage. Lane, 1982

Gardner, Andrew B. Artist's silkscreen manual. Grosset & Dunlap, 1976.

Gardner, John. Building classic small craft. International Marine Publishing Co., 1977

Gardner, Pat. Dough creations. Chilton Book Co., 1977

Gault, Carol. Needlework dragons and other mythical creatures. Van Nostrand Reinhold, 1983

Gault, Elizabeth. Crafts for the disabled. Crowell, 1979

Geary, Don. Complete handbook of home exterior repair and maintenance. Tab Books, 1982

————. How-to book of floors & ceilings. Tab Books, 1978

————. How to design and build your own workspace—with plans. Tab Books, 1981

Geary, Ida. Plant prints and collages. Viking, 1978

Gehret, Ellen J. Rural Pennsylvania clothing. Liberty Cap Books, 1976

Giant book of crafts. Sterling, 1975

Giant book of metalworking projects. Tab Books, 1983

Gilbert, Laura S. Needlepoint designs from Amish quilts. Scribner's, 1977

Gilby, Myriam. Free weaving. Scribner's, 1976

Gill, Ann E. Beadwork: the technique of stringing, threading, and weaving. Watson-Guptill, 1976

Gillies, Jean. Patterns for applique and pieced work—and ways to use them. Doubleday, 1982

Gilmurray, Susan. Weaving tricks. Van Nostrand Reinhold, 1981

Gladstone, Bernard. Hints and tips for the handy-person. Cornerstone Library, 1975

Gladstone, Meredith. Kids' clothes by Meredith Gladstone: a sewing book. Morrow, 1976

Glashausser, Suellen. Plaiting step-by-step. Watson-Guptill, 1976

Glick, Ruth. Dollhouse furniture you can make. A. S. Barnes, 1977

Goldberg, Rhoda O. New knitting dictionary: 1000 stitches and patterns. Crown, 1984

Golden book of colonial crafts. Golden Press, 1975

Golden book of hand and needle arts. Golden Press, 1977

Goldman, Phyllis W. Decorate with felt. Crowell, 1973

Goldsworthy, Maureen. Clothes for disabled people. B. T. Batsford, 1981

———. Mend it! a complete guide to clothes repair. Stein & Day, 1980

Gordon, Lesley. Complete guide to drying and preserving flowers. Chartwell Books, 1982

Gordon, Theron L. How to build, customize, & design plastic models. Tab Books, 1982

Gorham, Georgia L. Charted designs for holidays and special occasions. Dover, 1981

———. Treasury of charted designs for needleworkers. Dover, 1977

Gostelow, Mary. Complete international book of embroidery. Simon & Schuster, 1977

———. Cross stitch book. Van Nostrand Reinhold, 1982

———. Embroidery of all Russia. Scribner's, 1977

———. Mary Gostelow's embroidery book. E.P. Dutton, 1978

Gotshall, Franklin H. Provincial furniture design and construction. Crown, 1983

———. Wood carving and whittling for everyone. Scribner's, 1977

Gould, Marilyn. Skateboards, scooterboards, and seatboards you can make. Lothrop, Lee & Shepard, 1977

Gould, Zack. Owner-built fireplace. Van Nostrand Reinhold, 1978

Grafton, Carol Belanger. Traditional patchwork patterns: full-size cut-outs and instructions for 12 quilts. Dover, 1974

Graham, Boyd. Engraving glass. Van Nostrand Reinhold, 1982.

Grainger, Stuart E. Creative papercraft. Blandford Press, 1980

———. Creative ropecraft. Norton, 1975

———. Making aids for disabled living. B. T. Batsford, 1981

Grainger, Sylvia. How to make your own moccasins. Lippincott, 1977

Great cross-stitch. Sedgewood Press, 1984

Great granny crochet book. American School of Needlework. Columbia House, 1979

Grebanier, Joseph. Chinese stoneware glazes. Watson-Guptill, 1975

Green, H. D. Carving realistic birds. Dover, 1977.

Green, Suzie. Sand art book: a complete course in creating sand art. New American Library, 1976

Greenhowe, Jean. Costumes for nursery tale characters. Plays, 1976

———. Dolls in national and folk costume. Charles T. Branford Co., 1978

———. Making minature toys and dolls. Van Nostrand Reinhold, 1977

Grime, Kitty. Illustrated guide to furniture repair & restoration. Arco, 1980.

Grotz, George. Furniture doctor. Doubleday. 1983

Guide to wallpaper and paint. McGraw-Hill, 1980

Guild, Vera P. Dollmaker's workshop. Hearst Books, 1981

Guth, Phyllis. Sewing with scraps. Tab Books, 1977

Guy, Gary V. Easy-to-make candles. Dover, 1979

Hackleman, Michael A. Waterworks: an owner-builder guide to rural water systems. Doubleday, 1983

Hagans, Marilyn Todd. All good gifts. Paulist Press, 1983

Hagerty, Francis W. Make your own antiques. Little, Brown & Co., 1975

Halevy, Robyne. Knitting and crocheting pattern index. Scarecrow Press, 1977

Hall, Carolyn V. Sewing machine craft book. Van Nostrand Reinhold, 1980

———. Soft sculpture. Davis Publications, 1981

———. Teddy bear craft book. Van Nostrand Reinhold, 1983

Halliday, Anne. Decorating with crochet. Houghton Mifflin, 1975

Hamilton, Katie. Build it together. Scribner's, 1983

Hana, Nora. Embroidery. Two Continents, 1977

Handtools of arts and crafts: the encyclopedia of the fine decorative and applied arts. St. Martin's Press, 1981

Handyman. Banner Press, 1975

Hanley, Hope. Hope Hanley's patterns for needlepoint. Scribner's, 1976

———. Needlepoint. Scribner's, 1975

Haraszty, Eszter. Embroiderer's portfolio of flower designs. Liveright, 1981

———. Needlepainting, a garden of stitches. Liveright, 1974

Harmon, Allen Jackson. Porches & terraces. Grosset & Dunlap, 1975

Harvey, Roger. Building pottery equipment. Watson-Guptill, 1975

Harvey, Virginia I. Techniques of basketry. Van Nostrand Reinhold, 1974

Hauser, Priscilla. Priscilla Hauser book of tole & decorative painting. Van Nostrand Reinhold. 1977.

Hawkesworth, Eric. Paper cutting: making all kinds of paper shapes and figures. S. G. Phillips, 1977

Haynie, Paul J. Cabinetmaking. Prentice-Hall, 1976

Hayward, Charles H. Antique furniture repairs. Scribner's, 1976

Heard, Audrey. Complete guide to quilting. Creative Home Library, 1974

Hedden, Jay W. Successful shelves and built-ins. Structures Publishing, 1979

Hedin, Solweig. Knit sweaters the easy way. Doubleday, 1981

Held, Shirley E. Weaving: a handbook for fiber craftsmen. Holt, Rinehart & Winston, 1973

Helm, Harvey E. Making wood banks. Sterling, 1983

Henderson, Jacqueline. Woman's Day book of designer crochet. Bobbs-Merrill, 1980

Hetzer, Linda. Fancy folds. Hearst Books, 1980

Hibbs, Ruth. Straw sculpture. Drake Publishers, 1974

Higgins, Alfred. Common-sense guide to refinishing antiques. Funk & Wagnalls, 1976

Hilts, Len. Furniture repair & restoration. Creative Home Owner Press, 1981

Hilts, Leonard Finley. Popular Mechanics complete book of furniture. Hearst Corp., 1976

Hinson, Dolores A. Quilts for babies & children. Arco, 1983

Hirst-Smith, Ann. Complete candlemaker. Van Nostrand Reinhold, 1974

Hobbs, Harry J. Veneer craft for everyone. Scribner's, 1976

——. Veneering simplified. Albert Constantine and Sons, 1975

Hochberg, Bette. Handspindles. Straw into Gold, 1977

Hodges, Lewis H. 46 step-by-step wooden toy projects. Tab Books, 1984

——. How to build your own fine doll houses and furnishings. Tab Books, 1979

——. Woodturning handbook—with projects. Tab Books, 1984

Hogbin, Stephen. Wood turning. Van Nostrand Reinhold, 1980

Holderness, Esther R. Peasant chic: a guide to making unique clothing using traditional folk designs. Hawthorn Books, 1977

Holkeboer, Katherine Strand. Patterns for theatrical costumes. Prentice-Hall, 1984

Holland, Nina. Weaving primer: a complete guide to inkle, back-strap, and frame looms. Chilton Book Co., 1978

Hollander, Harry. Plastics for jewelry. Watson-Guptill, 1974

Hollingworth, Shelogh. Complete book of traditional Aran knitting. B. T. Batsford, 1982

Holtje, Adrienne. Cardcraft. Chilton Book Co., 1978

Holz, Loretta. How-to book of international dolls. Crown, 1980

——. Mobiles you can make. Lothrop, Lee & Shepard, 1975

Hopf, Claudia. Scherenschnitte, traditional papercutting. Applied Arts, 1977

Horwitz, Elinor. Mountain people, mountain crafts. Lippincott, 1974

Houck, Carter. American quilts and how to make them. Scribner's, 1975

——. Big bag book. Scribner's, 1977

——. 101 folk art designs for counted cross-stitch and other needlecrafts. Dover, 1982

——. Patchwork pattern book. E. P. Dutton, 1981

Howard, Joyce. New tole & folk art designs. Chilton Book Co., 1979

Howell, Frank. Craft of pottery: a problem-solving approach to the fundamentals of pottery making. Harper & Row, 1975

Howell-Koehler, Nancy. Soft jewelry: design, techniques and materials. Prentice-Hall, 1977

——. Step-by-step furniture finishing. Golden Press, 1975

Hubert, Margaret. Weekend knitting projects. Van Nostrand Reinhold, 1979

Huckleberry, E. R. How to make your own wooden jewelry. Tab Books, 1979

Hulbert, Anne. Creative beadwork. Two Continents, 1977

Hundley, Joyce D. Folk art toys and furniture for children. Doubleday, 1975

Hutchings, Margaret. Big book of stuffed toy and doll making. Dover, 1982

Hyde, Christopher S. Complete book of rock tumbling. Chilton Book Co., 1977.

Hylton, William H. Handcrafted shelves & cabinets. Rodale Press, 1984

Ickis, Marguerite. Weaving as a hobby. Adams, 1974

Illes, Robert E. Men in stitches. Van Nostrand Reinhold, 1975

Ingham, Rosemary. Costumer's handbook: how to make all kinds of costumes. Prentice-Hall, 1980

Introduction to repairing and restoring: books, clocks, furniture, pottery, porcelain, prints, painting, frames, silver, pewter, brass. Arco, 1981

Ireys, Katharine. Encyclopedia of canvas embroidery stitch patterns. Crowell, 1977

Isenberg, Anita. Crafting in glass. Chilton Book Co., 1981

———. How to work in beveled glass. Chilton Book Co., 1982

———. How to work in stained glass. 2nd ed. Chilton Book Co., 1983

Ives, Suzy. Ideas for patchwork. Charles T. Branford Co., 1974

Jablonski, Ramona. Folk art designs to color or cut: from Polish wycinanki and Swiss and German Scherenschnitte. Stemmer House, 1978

Jackson, Albert. Modelmaker's handbook. Knopf, 1981

Jacobs, Shanie. Crochet book. Bobbs-Merrill, 1979

James, Michael. Quiltmaker's handbook: a guide to design and construction. Prentice-Hall, 1978

———. Second quiltmaker's handbook: creative approaches to contemporary quilt design. Prentice-Hall, 1981

Janitch, Valerie. All made from paper. Viking, 1974

———. Candlemaking and decorations. Hamlyn, 1973

———. Collage: a step by step guide. Hamlyn, 1974

———. Paper flowers. Chilton Book Co., 1976

Jarnow, Jill. (Re)do it yourself: a guide to decoration and renovation with stencil, folk art painting, decoupage, collage, and mosaic. Dial Press, 1977

Jarvey, Paulette S. You can dough it! Hot Off the Press, 1980

Jensen, Gerald E. Building in miniature. Chilton Book Co., 1982

Jensen, Tom. Skylights. Running Press, 1983

Jerdee, Rebecca. Fabric applique for worship. Augsburg Publishing House, 1982

Johnson, Bruce E. Knock on wood. Putnam's Sons, 1984

Johnson, Cathy A. Quiltwear. Van Nostrand Reinhold, 1984

Johnson, Edwin. Old house woodwork restoration. Prentice-Hall, 1983

———. Restoring antique furniture. Sterling, 1982

Johnson, Lorraine. How to restore, repair and finish almost everything. Macmillan, 1977

Johnson, Mary E. Nature crafts. Oxmoor House, 1980

Johnston, David Robert. Craft of furniture making. Scribner's, 1979.

Jones, Iris S. Early North American dollmaking: a narrative history and craft instructions. 101 Productions, 1976

Jones, Jan. Clothing—your way. Prentice-Hall, 1977

Jones, Peter. Fixing furniture. Butterick, 1979

——. Plan and build more storage space. Butterick, 1979

Jones, Robert. Fireplaces. Creative Homeowner Press, 1980

Joyner, Nina Glenn. Dollhouse construction and restoration. Chilton Book Co., 1977

——. Furniture refinishing at home. Chilton Book Co., 1975

Kadar, Wayne Louis. Clock making for the woodworker. Tab Books, 1984

Kaestner, Dorothy. Designs for needlepoint and latch hook rugs. Scribner's, 1978

——. Four way bargello. Scribner's, 1974

Kalish, Susan Schoenfeld. Oriental rugs in needlepoint: ten chartered designs. Van Nostrand Reinhold, 1982

Kampmann, Lothar. Creating with found objects. Van Nostrand Reinhold, 1973

Kangas, Robert. By hand: low-cost, no-cost decorating. Prentice-Hall, 1983

Katz, Ruth J. Footwear: shoes and socks you can make yourself. Van Nostrand Reinhold, 1979

Kauffman, Henry J. Easy-to-make wooden candlesticks, chandeliers and lamps. Dover, 1982

Kellogg, Kathy. Home tanning. Williamson Publishing, 1984

Kenny, Carla. Creative design in sand casting. Crown, 1978

Ketchum, William C. Hooked rugs: a historical and collector's guide: how to make your own. Harcourt Brace Jovanovich, 1976

Kicklighter, Clois E. Crafts, illustrated designs and techniques. Goodheart-Wilcox Co., 1980

Kinney, Jean. How to make 19 kinds of American folk art. Atheneum, 1974

Kinney, Ralph Parsons. Complete book of furniture repair and refinishing. New rev. ed. Scribner's, 1981

Kinser, Charleen. Sewing sculpture. Lippincott, 1977

Kluger, Phyllis. Needlepoint gallery of patterns from the past. Knopf, 1975

——. Victorian designs for needlepoint. Holt, Rinehart & Winston, 1978

Kmit, Ann. Ukrainian embroidery. Van Nostrand Reinhold, 1978

Knitting techniques and projects. Lane, 1976

Kopp, Ernestine. Designing apparel through the flat pattern. Rev. 4th ed. Fairchild Publications, 1975

Kozaczka, Grazyna J. Polish cross stitch folk patterns. 1983

——. Polish embroidery workbook with patterns. Cambridge Springs, 1982

Kozlowski, Lawrence G. Paper cuts—Polish style. L. G. Kozlowski, 1981

Knitting: by the Editors of Ladies Home Journal Needle and Craft. Mason/Charter, 1977

Kramer, Jack. Outdoor garden build-it book. Scribner's, 1977

——. Wirecraft. Houghton Mifflin, 1978

Krenov, James. Impractical cabinetmaker. Van Nostrand Reinhold, 1979

Krevitsky, Nik. Shaped weaving: making garments and accessories with simple needle and finger-weaving techniques. Van Nostrand Reinhold, 1974

Kriwanek, Franz F. Keramos. Kendall/Hunt Publishing, 1978

Kronenberg, Bud. Spinning wheel building and restoration. Van Nostrand Reinhold, 1981

Krotz, David. How to hide almost anything. Morrow, 1975.

Kurita, Valerie. Second big book of afghans. Van Nostrand Reinhold, 1982

Kurten, Nancy Noland. Needlepoint in miniature. Scribner's, 1979

La Barge, Lura. Pet house book. Butterick, 1977

LaBelle, Judith. Patchworking: a quilt design & coloring book. New Century, 1983

Lammer, Jutta. Making samplers. Sterling, 1984

Lamoreaux, Marcia. Outdoor gear you can make yourself. Stackpole Books, 1976

Lampshades to make. Quality Books, 1976

Landis, Michael. Patios and decks: how to plan, build and enjoy. HP Books, 1983

Lane, Maggie. Gold and silver needlepoint. Scribner's, 1983

———. Maggie Lane's oriental patchwork. Scribner's, 1978

———. Rugs and wall hangings. Scribner's, 1976

Lane, Victor H. Building in your backyard. Workman Publishing, 1979

Langsner, Drew. Country woodcraft. Rodale Press, 1978

LaPlante, Jerry G. Plastic furniture for the home craftsman. Drake Publishers, 1978

Larsen, Judith LaBelle. Patchwork quilt design & coloring book. Butterick, 1977

Latham, Sidney. Knifecraft. Stackpole Books, 1978

———. Leathercraft. Winchester Press, 1977

Laury, Jean Ray. Handmade toys and games. Doubleday, 1975

———. Quilted clothing. Oxmoor House, 1982

———. Treasury of needlecraft gifts for the new baby. Taplinger, 1976

Layton, Reber B. 30 birds that will build in bird houses. Nature Book Publishers, 1977

Learoyd, Stan. Conservation and restoration of antique furniture. Sterling, 1983

Leavy, Herbert T. Bookshelves and storage units. Grosset & Dunlap, 1977

———. Successful small farms. Structures Publishing, 1978

Lee, Jerry. Making wood and stone jewelry. Taplinger, 1975

Lep, Annette. Crocheting patchwork patterns. Dover, 1981

Lewis, Alfred Allan. Everybody's weaving book. Macmillan, 1976

Lewis, Diehl. Patternless fashions: how to design and make your own fashions. Acropolis Books, 1981

Lewis, Gaspar J. Cabinetmaking, patternmaking, and millwork. Van Nostrand Reinhold, 1981

Ley, Sandra. Russian & other Slavic embroidery designs. Scribner's, 1976

Lindberg, Jana Hauschild. Counted cross-stitch designs for all seasons. Scribner's, 1983

Linderman, Earl W. Crafts for the classroom. Macmillan, 1977

Lindsley, E. F. Metalworking in the home shop. Van Nostrand Reinhold, 1983

Linsley, Leslie. America's favorite quilts. Delacorte Press, 1983

———. Custom made. Harper & Row, 1979

———. Decoupage on glass, wood, metal, rocks, shells, wax, soap, plastic, canvas, ceramic. Chilton Book Co., 1977

———. Fabulous furniture decorations. Crowell, 1978

———. Great bazaar. Delacorte Press, 1981

———. Lesley Linsley's Christmas ornaments and stockings. Marek Publishers, 1982

———. New ideas for old furniture. Lippincott & Crowell, 1980

———. Scrimshaw. Hawthorn Books, 1976

Lithgow, Marilyn. Quiltmaking & quiltmakers. Funk & Wagnalls, 1974

Loeb, Jo. Leather book. Prentice-Hall, 1975

Logan, Elizabeth D. Shell crafts. Scribner's, 1974

Longhurst, Denise. Vanishing American needle arts. Putnam's Sons, 1983

Lorant, Tessa. Hand & machine knitting. Scribner's, 1980

———. Yarns for textile crafts. Van Nostrand Reinhold, 1984

Lovesey, Nenia. Technique of needlepoint lace. Larousse, 1980

Lubkemann, Ernest C. Carving twigs and branches. Sterling, 1981

Luciano. Stained glass lamp art. Hidden House, 1976

Luxton, Elsie. Technique of Honiton lace. Charles T. Branford Co., 1979

Lydecker, Garrit D. Sign carving. Tab Books, 1983

Lyon, Jean. Arts and crafts objects children can make for the home. Parker, 1976

Lytle. R. J. Book of successful fireplaces. Structures Publishing, 1977

———. Farm builder's handbook, with added material for pole type industrial buildings. 3rd ed. McGraw-Hill, 1982

Maginley, C. J. America in miniatures: how to make models of early American houses, furniture, and vehicles. Harcourt Brace Jovanovich, 1976

———. Toys to make and ride. Harcourt Brace Jovanovich, 1977

———. Trains and boats and planes and . . . Hawthorn, 1979

Major, Connie. Contemporary patchwork quilts: a stitch in our time. Sterling, 1982

Make it! don't buy it. Rodale Press, 1983

Makris, Dimetra. First prize quilts. Simon & Schuster, 1984

Malone, Maggie. 115 classic American patchwork quilt patterns. Sterling, 1984

Manners, John. Country crafts today. Gale, 1974

Mansfield, Evelyn A. Clothing construction. 2nd ed. Houghton Mifflin, 1974

Marein, Shirley. Creating rugs and wall hangings: a complete guide. Viking, 1975

———. Stitchery, needlepoint, applique and patchwork: a complete guide. Viking, 1974

Marks, Fred M. Basics of radio control modeling. Kalmbach Books, 1975

Marlow, Andrew W. Classic furniture projects. Stein & Day, 1977

———. Early American furnituremaker's manual. Macmillan, 1973

Marshall, Cyril Leek. Foilcraft. Stackpole Books, 1977

Marshall, Mel. How to repair, reupholster, and refinish furniture. Harper & Row, 1979

———. Yard buildings. Doubleday, 1981

Marsten, Barbara. Step-by-step dollmaking. Van Nostrand Reinhold, 1981

Martensson, Alf. Woodworker's bible. Bobbs-Merrill, 1979

Matcham, Jonathan. Techniques of glass engraving. Larousse, 1982

Mattera, Joanne. Navajo techniques for today's weaver. Watson-Guptill, 1975

Mayes, Jim. How to make your own knives: knifemaking for the home hobbyist. Everest House, 1978

Maynard, Barbara. Modern basketry from the start. Scribner's, 1973

McBaine, Susan. Miniature needlepoint rugs for dollhouses: charted for easy use. Dover, 1976

McCall's big book of country needlecrafts. Chilton Book Co., 1983

McCall's big book of knit & crochet for home & family. Chilton Book Co., 1982

McCall's big book of needlecrafts. Chilton Book Co., 1982

McCall's book of America's favorite needlework and crafts. Simon & Schuster, 1976

McCall's book of Christmas. Simon & Schuster, 1975

McCall's book of rugmaking. Simon & Schuster, 1976

McCall's sewing for your home. Simon & Schuster/McCall Pattern Co., 1977

McCullough, Lorene. Clay flower techniques, vol. 1. Scott Publications, 1981

McCunn, Donald H. How to make sewing patterns. Design Enterprises of San Francisco, 1977

MacDonald, Jessie. Let's make a patchwork quilt—using a variety of sampler blocks. Farm Journal; distributed by Doubleday, 1980

McDonald, Robert J. Modern upholstering techniques. Scribner's, 1981

————. Upholstery repair and restoration. Scribner's, 1977

McEntee, Howard G. Radio control handbook. 4th ed. Tab Books, 1979

McKellips, Art. Practical pattern manual for woodcarving and other crafts. Timber Press, 1981

McNair, Don. Building & outfitting your workshop. Tab Books, 1983

McNeill, Moyra. Quilting. Octopus, 1980

McRaven, Charles. Country blacksmithing. Harper & Row, 1981

Meilach, Dona Z. Decorative and sculptural ironwork. Crown, 1977

————. Macrame gnomes and puppets: creative patterns and ideas. Crown, 1980

————. Modern approach to basketry with fibers and grasses, using coiling, twining, weaving, macrame, crocheting. Crown, 1974

————. Weaving off-loom. Contemporary Books, 1978

Mensinga-Biasiny, Nan. Beautiful baby clothes to crochet, knit, sew and embroider. Simon & Schuster, 1977

Meras, Phyllis. Vacation crafts. Houghton Mifflin, 1978

Mercer, Eileen. Let's make doll furniture. Schocken, 1975

Metal and enamel. Excalibur Books, 1978

Metalcrafting encyclopedia. Sterling, 1975

Meulenbelt-Nieuwburg, Alberta. Embroidery motifs from old Dutch samplers. Scribner's, 1974

Meyer, Carolyn. Christmas crafts. Harper & Row, 1974

————. Rock tumbling. Morrow, 1975

Meyers, Belle. Knitting know-how: an illustrated encyclopedia. Harper & Row, 1981

Meyers, L. Donald. Furniture repair and refinishing. Reston, 1974

————. Furniture repair and refinishing, Reston, 1978

Midkiff, Pat. Complete book of stenciling. Sterling, 1978

Miles, Bebe. Designing with natural materials. Van Nostrand Reinhold, 1975

Milinaire, Caterine. Cheap chic. Harmony Books, 1975

Millett, Sandra. Quilt-as-you-go. Chilton Book Co., 1982

Mills, Sonya. The book of presents. Pantheon Books, 1979

Milstein, Jeff. Building cardboard toys. Harper & Row, 1979

Mitton, Bruce H. How to make your own lamps and lampshades. Tab Books, 1979

Modern general shop. Goodheart-Wilcox Co., 1982

Moeller, Misse. Charted decorative initials. Dover, 1984

Mon Tricot. Knitting dictionary: stitches and patterns. Crown, 1975

Mordle-Barnes, Mollie. Good housekeeping making children's clothes. Good House-keeping Books, 1977

Morgan, Gwyn. Traditional knitting patterns of Ireland, Scotland, and England. St. Martin's Press, 1981

Morgan, Mary. Trapunto and other forms of raised quilting. Scribner's, 1977

Morrison, James W. Complete energy-saving home improvement guide. Arco, 1978

Morrison, Winifrede. Drying and preserving flowers. B. T. Batsford, 1973

Morton, Brenda. Sleeve puppets. Taplinger, 1978

Moser, Thomas. How to build shaker furniture. Sterling, 1980

————. Windsor chairmaking. Sterling, 1982

Mosesson, Gloria R. Jewelry craft for beginners. Bobbs-Merrill, 1974

————. New clothes from old. Bobbs-Merrill, 1977

Moshimer, Joan. Complete rug hooker. New York Graphic Society, 1975

Moyer, Roger A. Solar heat-n-grow window. Rodale Press, 1982

Muka, Angela. Creative designs for children, pretty, practical and young styles. Herrmann Printing and Litho, 1982

————. French touch: a unique method on how to alter effectively the printed patterns with perfect fit for all sizes. Wolfson, 1977

————. French touch II . . . the elegance of personal design for adults and teenagers. Muka, 1980

Murphy, Bruce W. Lampmaking. Sterling, 1976

Murray, Rosemary. Essential handbook of weaving. St. Martin's Press, 1982

Musheno, Elizabeth J. Sewing big; fashion advice and sewing tips for larger sizes. Van Nostrand Reinhold, 1982

Needlework nostalgia: a collection of authentic needlework designs from the Butterick archives. Butterick, 1975

Neighbors, Jane. Reversible two-color knitting. Scribner's, 1974

Nesovich, Peter. Reupholstering at home. Crown, 1979

Newman, Jay Hartley. Wire art. Crown, 1975

Newman, Lee Scott. Electroplating and electroforming for artists and craftsmen. Crown, 1979

Newman, Thelma. Contemporary African arts and crafts. Crown, 1974

————. Contemporary southeast Asian arts and crafts. Crown, 1977

————. Creative candlemaking. Crown, 1972

————. Quilting, patchwork, applique and trapunto. Crown, 1974

————. Sewing machine embroidery stitchery. Crown, 1980

Nickey, J. M. Stoneworker's bible. Tab Books, 1979

Nicole, Louis. Designer accessories to make for your home: 35 easy, inexpensive ways to complement any room. Butterick, 1978

Nicoletti, Sally. Japanese motifs for needlepoint. Morrow, 1981

Nielsen, Edith. Scandinavian embroidery, past and present. Scribner's, 1978

Nish, Dale L. Creative woodturning. Brigham Young University Press, 1975

Norbeck, Oscar. Book of authentic Indian life crafts. Galloway Corp., 1974

Nottingham, Pamela. Techniques of bobbin lace. Larousse, 1976

Nunn, Richard V. Home improvement, home repair. Creative Homeowner Press, 1980

————. Home paint book. Galahad Books, 1976

Oberrecht, Kenn. Plywood projects illustrated. Scribner's, 1983

O'Connor, Paul R. Twill of your choice. Interweave Press, 1981

Old, Leila S. Personalized apparel design: drafting and designing for the individual female figure. University Press of Idaho, 1977

Olin, Harold Bennett. Construction: principles, materials, and methods. 4th ed. Institute of Financial Education, 1980

Olsen, Don. Nature's candles. A. S. Barnes, 1976

101 do-it-yourself projects. Reader's Digest Association, 1983

101 folk art designs for counted cross-stitch and other needlecrafts. Dover, 1982

O'Neill, Jeanne Lamb. Make-it-merry Christmas book. Morrow, 1977

Ormond, Brande. American primitives in needlepoint. Houghton Mifflin, 1977

Orr, Jan. Now needlepoint; a joyous new approach to creative designing. Van Nostrand Reinhold, 1975

Osburn, Burl N. Measured drawings of early American furniture. Dover, 1975

Osler, Dorothy. Machine patchwork: technique and design. B. T. Batsford, 1980

Oughton, Frederick. Complete manual of wood finishing. Stein & Day, 1983

Outdoor projects for home and garden. Tab Books, 1979

Paak, Carl E. Decorative touch: how to decorate, glaze, and fire your pots. Prentice-Hall, 1981

Painting & wallpapering. Sharon Publications, 1976

Palmer, Bruce. Making children's furniture and play structures. Workman Publishing, 1974

Parker, Page. Upholstering for everyone. Reston, 1976

Parker, Xenia Ley. Beginner's book of off-loom weaving. Dodd, Mead, 1978

————. Creative handweaving. Dial Press, 1976

————. Mosaics in needlepoint. Scribner's, 1977

Parry, Megan. Stenciling. Van Nostrand Reinhold, 1977

Patera, Charlotte. Cutwork applique. New Century, 1983

Patton, Albert Brace. Furniture finishing. Drake Publishers, 1975

Payne, Chris. Furniture finishing & refinishing. Lane, 1977.

Pearce, D. W. Aviary design and construction. Blandford Press, 1983

Pelisser, Jaime. Jeweler's craft. Van Nostrand Reinhold, 1981

Perry, Margaret Curtiss. Holiday magic: the art of making decorations for eventful days throughout the year. Doubleday, 1978

Petersen, Grete. Stitches and decorative seams. Van Nostrand Reinhold, 1983

Peterson, Franklynn. Children's toys you can build yourself. Prentice-Hall, 1978

Philbin, Tom. Cabinets, bookcases & closets. Creative Homeowner Press, 1980

Phillips, Janet. Weaver's book of fabric design. St. Martin's Press, 1983

Picturemaking. Ed. Yvonne Deutch. Butterick, 1978

Pictures with pins. Arco, 1978

Pittaway, Andy. Traditional English country crafts and how to enjoy them today. Pantheon Books, 1975

Planning and remodeling bathrooms. Lane, 1975

Platt, Charles. T-shirting: a do-it-yourself guide to getting it on your chest. Hawthorn Books, 1975

Platt, John. Step-by-step woodcraft. Golden Press, 1978

Plewes, John. Repairing & restoring pendulum clocks. Sterling, 1984

Popular Mechanics do-it-yourself encyclopedia. Hearst Corp., 1982

Porches and patios. Time-Life Books, 1981

Pottery step-by-step. Macmillan, 1976

Powers, Bob. Crafting turquoise jewelry. Stackpole Books, 1978

Practical needlework. Chartwell Books, 1980

Preston, Doris Campbell. Needle-made laces and net embroideries. Dover, 1984

Price, Brick. Model-building handbook: techniques professionals use. Chilton Book Co., 1981

Priolo, Joan B. Ceramics by coil. Sterling, 1976

Probert, Christina. Knitting in Vogue. Viking, 1982

Proulx, Annie. Plan and make your own fences and gates, walkways, walls and drives. Rodale Press, 1983

Pucci, Cora. Pottery: a basic manual. Little, Brown & Co., 1974

Quick, Lelande. Gemcraft. 2nd ed. Chilton Book Co., 1977

Quirke, Lillian Mary. Rug book: how to make all kinds of rugs. Prentice-Hall, 1979

Rainey, Sarita R. Weaving without a loom. Prentice-Hall, 1977

Ramsey, Dan. Building a log home from scratch or kit. Tab Books, 1983

Rath, Erna. Splendid soft toy book. Sterling, 1981

Reader's Digest complete guide to needlework. Reader's Digest, 1979

Reader's Digest complete guide to sewing. Reader's Digest, 1976

Redman, Jane. Frame-loom weaving. Van Nostrand Reinhold, 1976

Restoring and reupholstering furniture. Rodale Press, 1982

Rhinehart, Jane. How to make men's clothes. Doubleday, 1975

Rhodes, Daniel. Pottery form. Chilton Book Co., 1976

Rhodes, Mary. Dictionary of canvas work stitches. Scribner's, 1980

———. Small woven tapestries. B. T. Batsford, 1973

Richards, Alison. Handmade jewelry. Funk & Wagnalls, 1976

Richardson, Milton Thomas. Practical blacksmithing. Weathervane Books, 1978

Riegger, Hal. Electric kiln ceramics. Litton Educational Publishing Co., 1978

Risinger, Hettie. Innovative machine quilting. Oak Tree Press, 1980

Rissell, Willetta R. Craftwork the handicapped elderly can make and sell. Charles C. Thomas Publisher, 1981

Roberts, Nadine H. Illustrated handbook of upholstery. Tab Books, 1982

Rockland, Mae Shafter. Hanukkah book. Schocken Books, 1975

Roda, Janet E. Fabric decorating for the home. Oxmoor House, 1976

Rodd, John. Repairing and restoring antique furniture. Van Nostrand Reinhold, 1976

Rogers, Gay Ann. Needlepoint designs from Asia. Doubleday, 1983

Romaniuk, Anna. Pants: how to do your own measuring, pattern drafting, fabric selection, cutting and sewing for a perfect fit. Crown, 1974

Romberg, Jenean. Let's discover papier-mâché. Center for Applied Research in Education, 1976

Rome, Carol Cheney. Needlepoint letters and numbers. Doubleday, 1977

Rose, Grace Berne. Illustrated encyclopedia of crafts and how to master them. Doubleday, 1978

Rosen, Selma. Children's clothing. Fairchild Publications, 1983

Rosenthal, Iris. Not-so-nimble needlework book. Grosset & Dunlap, 1977

Ross, Robert Horace. Ancient Persian designs in needlepoint. St. Martin's Press, 1982

Roth, Charlene Davis. Making original dolls of composition, bisque, and porcelain. Crown, 1980

Roth, Sandra. Creative gift wrapping. East Woods Press, 1982

Rothenberg, Polly. Decorating glass. Crown, 1977

Rowland, Amy Zaffarano. Handcrafted doors & windows. Rodale Press, 1982

Rubin, Jerome. Mission furniture: making it, decorating with it, its history and place in the antique market. Chronicle Books, 1980

Ruggieri, Lorraine. Woman's Day book of no-pattern sewing. Fawcett Columbine, 1981

Rush, Peter. Papier mâché. Farrar, Straus & Giroux, 1980

Russell, James E. Garages and carports. Creative Homeowner Press, 1981

———. Walks, walls and fences. Creative Homeowner Press, 1981

Rutan, Jackie. The perfect fit: easy pattern alterations. Prentice-Hall, 1977

Ruthberg, Helen. Book of miniatures: furniture and accessories. Chilton Book Co., 1977

Ryan, Mildred G. Complete encyclopedia of stitchery. Doubleday, 1979

Safford, Edward L. Advanced radio control: including rockets and robots. 2nd ed. Tab Books, 1980.

———. Model radio control. 3rd ed. Tab Books, 1979

———. Radio control hobbyist's handbook. Tab Books, 1984

Sainsbury, John. Craft of woodturning. Sterling, 1984

———. Sainsbury's woodturning projects for dining. Sterling, 1981

————. Woodworking projects with power tools. Sterling, 1983

Salazar, Tristan. Complete book of furniture restoration. St. Martin's Press, 1982

Sanders, Herbert H. Glazes for special effects. Watson-Guptill, 1974

Sanders, Herbert H. (Sunset ceramics book.) How to make pottery. Watson-Guptill, 1974

Sara, Dorothy. Sewing made easy. Doubleday, 1977

Saunders, Janice S. Speed sewing; 103 sewing machine shortcuts. Van Nostrand Reinhold, 1982

Saunders, Richard. Collecting and restoring wicker furniture. Crown, 1976

Savage, Jessie. Professional furniture refinishing for the amateur. Harper & Row, 1975

Sayer, Chloe. Crafts of Mexico. Doubleday, 1977

Sayles, Shirley. Step-by-step stitchery: a complete introduction to the craft of stitchery. Golden Press, 1976

Scharf, Bella. Butterick's fast and easy needlecrafts: over 50 fashion and decorating projects you can make in less than a day. Butterick, 1977

————. Illustrated patchwork crochet. Butterick, 1976

Scherer, John L. Complete handbook of home painting. Tab Books, 1975

Scheuer, Nikki. Designs for Holbein embroidery: 110 new geometric patterns. Doubleday, 1976

Schnitzler, Jeanne. New dimensions in needlework. Prentice-Hall, 1977

Schuler, Stanley. How to fix almost every thing: the standard A to Z guide to 1001 household fix-it problems. M. Evans, 1975

Schultz, Walter E. How to attract, house and feed birds. Collier Books, 1974

Schuman, Jo Miles. Art from many hands. Prentice-Hall, 1981

Schwebke, Phyllis W. Sewing with the new knits. Macmillan, 1975

Scobey, Joan. Decorating with needlepoint. Meredith Corp, 1975

————. First easy-to-see needlepoint workbook. Rawson Associates, 1977

————. Gifts from your garden. Bobbs-Merrill, 1975

————. Rugmaking: 3 quick and easy ways. Bobbs-Merrill, 1977

————. Rugs & wall hangings: period designs and contemporary techniques. Dial Press, 1974

Scurlock, William H. Muzzleloader Magazine's book of buckskinning II. Rebel Publishing Co., 1983

Seagroatt, Margaret. Basic textile book. Van Nostrand Reinhold, 1975

Self, Charles R. Woodworking tools and hardware. Tab Books, 1983

————. Working with plywood, including indoor/outdoor projects. Tab Books, 1979

Selfridge, Gail. Patchwork knitting. Watson-Guptill, 1977

77 furniture projects you can build. Tab Books, 1980

Shafer, Thomas. Pottery decoration. Watson-Guptill, 1976

Shea, John G. Pennsylvania Dutch and their furniture. Van Nostrand Reinhold, 1980

Sheldon, Emily S. Washable and dryable needlepoint. Arco, 1981

Sibbett, Ed. Art nouveau stained glass pattern book: 104 designs for workable projects. Dover, 1978

Siegele, Herman Hugo. Cabinets and built-ins. Drake Publishers, 1961

Silverstein, Mira. Mira Silverstein's guide to looped and knotted stitches. David McKay, 1977

Simmons, Paula. Spinning for softness and speed. Madrona Publishers, 1982

Simons, Violet K. Very basic book of sewing, altering, and mending: 999 pictures show you how. Sterling, 1976

Sjoberg, Jan. Working with copper, silver and enamel. Van Nostrand Reinhold, 1974

Skowronski, Hella. Sprang; thread twisting, a creative textile technique. Van Nostrand Reinhold, 1974

Slater, Elaine. Elaine Slater's book of needlepoint projects. Holt, Rinehart & Winston, 1978

———. New York Times book of needlepoint for left-handers. Quadrangle/New York Times Book Co., 1974

Smith, Edward Brinton. Gemcutting. Prentice-Hall, 1980

Smith, Glenora. Needlery. Butterick, 1978

Smith, Joyce Ronald. Taaniko, Maori hand weaving. Scribner's, 1975

Smith, Nancy Adaskovich. Old furniture. Little, Brown & Co., 1975

Snook, Barbara. Embroidery designs from the sea. Taplinger, 1977

Sommer, Elyse. Contemporary costume jewelry. Crown, 1974

———. Wearable crafts: creating clothing, body adornments, and jewelry from fabrics and fibers. Crown, 1976

Southard, Doris. Bobbin lacemaking. Scribner's, 1977

Speer, Michael L. Put your best foot forward. Broadman Press, 1977

Spence, William P. General carpentry. Prentice-Hall, 1983

———. Woodworking tools, materials, processes. American Technical Publishers, 1981

Spencer, Carl W. Designing and building your own stereo furniture. Tab Books, 1981

Spencer, David J. Knitting technology. Pergamon Press, 1983

Spielman, Patrick E. Making wood signs. Sterling/Oak Tree Press, 1981

———. Working green wood with PEG. Sterling, 1980

Sprintzen, Alice. Jewelry, basic techniques and design. Chilton Book Co., 1980

Staples, Caroline M. Yarn animal book. Simon & Schuster, 1976

Starmore, Alice. Scandinavian knitwear. Van Nostrand Reinhold, 1982

Starr, George Ross. Decoys of the Atlantic flyway. Winchester Press, 1974

Stearns, Ann. Batsford book of crochet. Anchor Press, 1981

———. Macrame. Arco, 1975

Step by step to better knitting and crochet. Arco, 1981

Stephan, Barbara B. Creating with tissue paper. Crown, 1973

Sterbenz, Carol Endler. Decorated tree: recreating traditional Christmas ornaments. Henry N. Abrams, Inc., 1982

Stevenson, Robert Presley. How to build and buy cabinets for the modern kitchen. Arco, 1974

Stiles, David R. Easy-to-make children's furniture. Pantheon Books, 1980

Stillwell, Alexandra. Technique of teneriffe lace. Charles T. Branford Co., 1980

Stine, George Harry. Handbook of model rocketry. Rev. 5th ed. Arco, 1983

Stone, Patricia. Portugese needlework rugs. EPM Publications, 1981

Stoneman, Milton. Easy-to-make wooden sundials. Dover, 1982

Stribling, Mary Lou. Crafts from North American Indian arts. Crown, 1975

Sullivan, William L. Cart book, with plans & projects. Tab Books, 1983

Sutton, Ann. Structure of weaving. Lark Books, 1982

Svinicki, Eunice. Old-fashioned crochet. Van Nostrand Reinhold, 1981

————. Step-by-step spinning and dyeing. Golden Press, 1974

Swanson, Karen. Rigid heddle weaving. Watson-Guptill, 1975

Syvanen, Bob. Interior finish: more tricks of the trade. East Woods Press, 1982

Tangerman, E. J. Carving flora and fables in wood. Sterling, 1981

————. Carving the unusual. Sterling, 1982

Taylor, Gertrude. America's knitting book. Rev. ed. Scribner's, 1974

Taylor, V. J. How to build period country furniture. Bonanza Books, 1978

Teal, Peter. Hand woolcombing and spinning: a guide to worsteds from the spinning wheel. Blandford Press, 1976

Termini, Maria. Silkscreening. Prentice-Hall, 1978

Thiebault, Andre. Kites and other wind machines. Sterling, 1982

Thompson, Ginnie. John James Audubon's birds in cross stitch. Scribner's, 1982

Thorpe, Azalea Stuart. Elements of weaving. Doubleday, 1978

Tie-dye, batik and candlemaking step-by-step. Macmillan, 1976

Tillett, Leslie. American needlework, 1776–1976: needlepoint and crewel patterns adapted from historic American images. New York Graphic Society, 1975

Time-Life Books. Boutique attire. Time-Life Books, 1975

————. Decorative techniques. Time-Life Books, 1975

————. Exotic styling. Time-Life Books, 1974

————. Floors and stairways. Time-Life Books, 1978

————. New living spaces. Time-Life Books, 1977

————. Novel materials. Time-Life Books, 1974

————. Personal touch. Time-Life Books, 1974

————. Repairing furniture. Time-Life Books, 1980

————. Separates that travel. Time-Life Books, 1975

————. Space and storage. Time-Life Books, 1976

————. Sporting scene. Time-Life Books, 1975

————. Traditional favorites. Time-Life Books, 1974

————. Working with wood. Time-Life Books, 1979

Toale, Bernard. Art of papermaking. Davis Publications, 1983

Tod, Osma Palmer Gallinger. Joy of hand weaving. Dover, 1977

Torbet, Laura. Macrame you can wear. Watson-Guptill, 1972

————. T-shirt book. Bobbs-Merrill, 1976

Torelli, Michael E. Reupholstering for the home craftsman. Chilton Book Co., 1977

Traister, John E. All about chimneys. Tab Books, 1982

Treasury of things to make. Grosset & Dunlap, 1977

Troy, Jack. Salt-glazed ceramics. Watson-Guptill, 1977

Turner, Katy. Legacy of the great wheel: myths, history and traditions, with practical lessons. Select Books, 1980

Tyler, Christopher. Raku. Watson-Guptill, 1975

Tyler, Mabs. Big book of dolls. Dial Press, 1976

————. Big book of soft toys. McGraw-Hill, 1972

Underhill, Roy. Woodwright's companion. University of North Carolina Press, 1983

Upton, John. Woodcarver's primer. Drake Publishers, 1976

Vaitses, Allen H. Covering wooden boats with fiberglass. International Marine Publishing Co., 1981

Vanderbilt, Gloria. Gloria Vanderbilt designs for your home. Simon & Schuster, 1975

Vane, Peter K. Pebble people, pets & things. Butterick, 1977

Villiard, Paul. Art and craft of sand casting. Funk & Wagnalls, 1975

Vogue sewing book. Vogue Patterns, 1975

Vor Tids Korssting. Contemporary Danish cross-stitch design. Hastings House, 1982

Wagner, Willis H. Modern woodworking. Goodheart-Wilcox Co., 1980

Wainwright, John. Discovering lapidary work. Mills and Boon, 1971

Wald, Robert. Introduction to jewelry casting. Association Press, 1975

Walke, Nancy. All about stained glass. Tab Books, 1982

Walker, Barbara G. Mosaic knitting. Scribner's, 1976

Walker, Irene. Tatting. Regnery, 1974

Waller, Irene. Knots and netting. Taplinger, 1977

Walters, James. Crochet. Octopus Books, 1980

Wargo, Stephanie. Soft crafts for special occasions. Dorison House, 1982

Warring, Ronald H. Balsa wood modelling. Sterling, 1973

Warwick, James F. Beginning jewelry. Scribner's, 1979

Water systems handbook. 7th ed. Water Systems Council, 1980

Waterford, Van. Microcomputer-controlled toys & games & how they work. Tab Books, 1983

Watson, Aldred Auld. Village blacksmith. Crowell, 1977

Waugh, Andrew. Handyman's encyclopedia. Drake Publishers, 1976

Weaving and spinning. Excalibur Books, 1977

Weiss, Rita. Crocheting afghans. Dover, 1979

Weiss, Rita. Crocheting placemats. Dover, 1978

Weldon and Company. Victorian crochet. Dover, 1974

Weller, Mary Anne. Complete manual of rapid sewing techniques. Rubric Press, 1982

Wells, Andy J. Building stereo speakers. McGraw-Hill, 1983

Wells, Kenneth. Wooden puzzles and games. Sterling, 1983

Wenn, Leslie. Restoring antique furniture. Watson-Guptill, 1974

Westcott, Linn H. How to build model railroad benchwork. Kalmbach Books, 1979

Wettlaufer, George. Getting into pots: a basic pottery manual. Prentice-Hall, 1976

Weygers, Alexander G. Modern blacksmith. Van Nostrand Reinhold, 1974

————. Recycling, use, and repair of tools. Van Nostrand Reinhold, 1978

Whatnot. Morrow, 1977

Wheeler, Gershon. Interior painting, wallpapering & paneling. Reston, 1974

Whitney, Alex. American Indian clothes and how to make them. David McKay, 1979

Wiita, Betty Smith. Dried flowers for all seasons. Van Nostrand Reinhold, 1982

Wilder, Edna. Secrets of Eskimo skin sewing. Alaska Northwest, 1976

Wiley, Jack. Woodcarving with projects. Tab Books, 1984

Wilkinson, Jan. Flower fabrications. Butterick, 1977

Williams, Arthur D. Spanish colonial furniture. Gibbs M. Smith, 1982

Williams, Barbara. Cookie craft: no-bake designs for edible party favors and decorations. Holt, Rinehart & Winston, 1977

Williams, Gary. Designing and building a grandfather clock. A. S. Barnes, 1980

Williams, Janice. Lettering in embroidery. B. T. Batsford, 1982

Williams, Ron. Building and flying indoor model airplanes. Peregrine Smith Books, 1984

Wilson, Erica. Ask Erica. Scribner, 1977

————. Erica Wilson's Christmas world. Scribner's, 1980

————. More needleplay. Scribner's, 1979

————. Needleplay. Scribner's, 1975

————. Needlework to wear. Oxmoor House, 1982

Wilson, Jean. Joinings, edges, and trims. Van Nostrand Reinhold, 1983

Wilson, Jean Verseput. Weaving you can use. Van Nostrand Reinhold, 1975

Windeknecht, Margaret B. Color-and-weave. Van Nostrand Reinhold, 1981

Windows and skylights. Lane, 1982

Winter, William J. World of model airplanes. Scribner's, 1983

Wiseman, Ann. Bread sculpture. Scribner's, 1975

————. Cuts of cloth: quick classics to sew and wear, shells for the body. Little, Brown & Co., 1978

Witt, Susan. Classics for needlepoint. Oxmoor House, 1981

Woman's Day bazaar best sellers. Sedgewood Press, 1983

Woman's Day book of gifts to make. Simon & Schuster, 1976

Woman's Day book of weekend crafts. Houghton Mifflin, 1978

Woman's Day creative stitchery from scraps. Columbia House, 1980

Woman's Day crochet showcase. Columbia House, 1980

Woman's Day decorative needlework for the home. Columbia House, 1980

Woman's Day prize-winning quilts, coverlets and afghans. Sedgewood Press, 1982

Wood, Louise. Make your own jewelry. Grosset & Dunlap, 1975

Wood, Paul W. Working with stained glass. Sterling, 1981

Wood finishing and refinishing. Creative Homeowner Press, 1982

Wood projects for the garden. Ortho Book Division, Chevron Chemical Co., 1979

Woodgate, Ralph W. Handbook of machine soldering. John Wiley & Sons, 1983

Woods, Pamela. Flowers from fabrics. Regnery, 1976

Woody, Elsbeth S. Handbuilding ceramic forms. Farrar, Straus & Giroux, 1978

———. Pottery on the wheel. Farrar, Straus & Giroux, 1975

Wooldridge, W. J. Woodturning techniques. Sterling, 1982

Wooster, Ann-Sargent. Quiltmaking: the modern approach to a traditional craft. Drake Publishers, 1972

Working with metal. Time-Life Books, 1981

Worst, Edward Francis. Weaving with foot-power looms. Dover, 1974

Wright, Dorothy. Complete book of baskets and basketry. Scribner's, 1977

Yoder, Ray A. Sculpture and modeling for the elementary school. Parker, 1976

Zechlin, Katharina. Games you can build yourself. Sterling, 1975

Zegel, Jon. Fast furniture. Running Press, 1978

———. Shelf book. Running Press, 1977

Zimmerman, Eric. Carving horses in wood. Sterling, 1983

Znamierowski, Nell. Step-by-step rugmaking. Golden Press, 1972

Zorza, Rosemary. Pottery: creating with clay. Doubleday, 1974

Zukerman, Dianne. Get hooked: creative crocheting. Tab Books, 1977

Index to Handicraft Books

A

Abacus
Abacus. Peterson. Children's toys you can build yourself. 109–14.

Acrylic materials. *See* **Plastics**

Acoustical materials. *See* **Soundproofing**

Adhesives
Adhesives for furniture repairs. Kinney. Complete book of furniture repair and refinishing. 10–22
A glue press. Fine woodworking techniques 4. 202
Glues. Sainsbury. Woodworking projects with power tools. 130–31
Gluing and clamping. Wagner. Modern woodworking. 85–97
Gluing and fastening. Gladstone. Hints and tips for the handyperson. 43–45
Removing epoxy. Brightman. 101 practical uses for propane torches. 131
Stick with the right glue. Popular Mechanics do-it-yourself encyclopedia. Vol. 1, 35–40
Tape up your repair problems. Popular Mechanics do-it-yourself encyclopedia. Vol. 18, 2842–44

Adobe
Working with adobe and stabilized-earth blocks. Leavy. Successful small farms. 98–101

Aerials. *See* **Antennas**

Afghans
Embroidered American Indian motifs throw, wildflower, crewel throw. Better Homes and Gardens treasury of needlecrafts. 329–31, 362–65
Flower trimmed afghan (crocheted flowers). Scharf. Butterick's fast and easy needlecrafts. 122
Gloria's favorite afghan glows with two techniques (crocheted & embroidered). Vanderbilt. Gloria Vanderbilt designs for your home. 84–89
Peruvian flat black afghan. Dendel. Basic book of fingerweaving. 29
Wildflower pillow & crewel throw. Better Homes & Gardens embroidery. 36–39
Woven afghan. Ickis. Weaving as a hobby. 12
Woven afghans. Wilson. Weaving you can use. 102

Afghans. *See also* **Lap Robes**

Afghans, Crocheted
Afghan and matching pillow (crocheted). Mills. The book of presents. 12–13
Afghan in Tunisian crochet. Reader's Digest complete guide to needlework. 402
Afghans. Henderson. Woman's Day book of designer crochet. 162–82
Aran-style afghan. Step by step to better knitting and crochet. 237–39
Baby blocks afghan, popcorn crochet on afghan stitch, "milk glass" design afghan with giant monogram, pineapples and diamonds, bridal rose afghan. McCall's big book of country needlecrafts. 85, 195–203, 257–58, 264–65
"Barn raising" afghan. Design crochet. 80–83
Crib coverlets. Better Homes and Gardens treasury of needlecrafts. 216–17
Confetti, textured, multi-striped, & triangle afghans. Woman's Day bazaar best sellers. 146–49
Christmas afghan. Great granny crochet book. 83
Crocheted afghans. Feldman. Big book of afghans. 74–123
Crocheted and hairpin lace afghans. Feldman. Handmade lace and patterns. 112–13
Crocheted baby blankets: fiesta, pandas on parade and baby's bouquet. Kurita. Second big book of afghans. 134–44
Crocheted designs. Woman's Day prize-winning quilts, coverlets and afghans. 134–99
Delphinium dream, autumn daisy, crests and emblems, Roman stripe, and fenced fields crocheted afghans. Woman's Day decorative needlework for the home. 14–15, 17–23
Flower striped afghan, couch cover, mohair granny squares, blue tiles afghan, Aran afghan in crochet. McCall's big book of knit & crochet for home & family. 159–62, 252–54
Freedom ripple & granny rainbow afghans. American School of Needlework. Great crochet bazaar book. 48–51
Granny square afghan. Rosenthal. Not-so-nimble needlework book. 132–33
Granny square afghan. Svinicki. Old-fashioned crochet. 38–41
Granny square afghans in many variations. Great granny crochet book. 8–22
Granny square picture afghans. Great granny crochet book. 23–43.
Granny square sampler afghan, crocheted star motif afghan, grandmother's flower garden, classic Americana pattern, brilliant flower patch afghan. Better Homes and Gardens treasury of needlecraft. 170–86
Granny squares cover afghan. Crochet. 13
Heirloom afghan is lighthearted "granny." Vanderbilt. Gloria Vanderbilt designs for your home. 91–93
Irish patch & log cabin afghans. Chatterton. Patchwork & applique. 78–82
Jewel of an afghan, stained-glass afghan and pillows, rainbow afghan, rising sun afghan, she loves me she loves me not afghan, & galaxy afghan. Woman's Day crochet showcase. 138–49
Log cabin afghan. Lep. Crocheting patchwork patterns. 35
Log cabin, Missouri puzzle and crazy quilt afghans. Crochet. 99–106
Marshmallow fluff baby afghan, gingham baby afghan, traditional granny afghan for baby. Great granny crochet book. 97, 99–101
Modern afghans. Bray. Afghans: traditional & modern. 19–26
Multipatched or star-patched afghan or wall hanging. Chatterton. Patchwork & applique. 84–86
Neon granny, Victorian openwork, woven pastel plaid, berry stitch, get-together, flowers at the crossroads, grapevine, lightning strikes, parrot motifs ahoy, colonial ripples, blue willow, crayon stripes. Kurita. Second big book of afghans. 74–120
Patchwork afghans. Scharf. Illustrated patchwork crochet. 157
Patchwork and African designs. Chatterton. Coordinated crafts for the home. 122–23, 130–31, 136–37, 143–45, 152–53, 156–58, 162–63, 184–85, 196–98
Poinsettia afghan, snow clusters, baby afghan, Christmas granny. American School of Needlework. Great Christmas crochet book. 104–09
Popcorn-and-leaf afghan (afghan stitch). Golden book of hand and needle arts. 13

Special interest afghans. Bray. Afghans: traditional & modern. 43–71
Striped afghan and square afghan. Halliday. Decorating with crochet. 40–47
Traditional afghans. Bray. Afghans: traditional & modern. 73–95
Variations on the granny patch. Time-Life Books. Traditional favorites. 157–59
Victorian afghan. McCall's big book of needlecrafts. 276–79
Victorian carriage robe, Victorian floral afghan, jewel-tone afghan, baby afghan, pattern-bands afghan. McCall's book of America's favorite needlework and crafts. 217–32
Weiss. Crocheting afghans.

Afghans, Knitted
Afghan of bands, lacy afghan. Knitting techniques and projects. 20–21
African checkers and African blanket coordinates. Chatterton. Coordinated crafts for the home. 186–87, 192–93
Brilliant colors & golden afghans. Chatterton. Patchwork & applique. 114–19
Cozy quilt patterned throw, quick knit patchwork afghan, old-fashioned "windowpane" knitted afghan, honeycomb throw and basket stitch pillow, embroidered knitted throw. Better Homes and Gardens treasury of needlecrafts. 187–93, 218–19
Diamond afghan, ripple runner. Knitting. 102
Garter stitch afghan, woven plaid afghan, pinwheel afghan, lily pond, rose afghan, plaid afghan, honeycomb blocks. McCall's big book of knit & crochet for home & family. 31, 67–71
Indian afghan. Knitting. 95
Inishmore, patch panels, nosegay Aran afghan, Irish fisherman, nautical stars and bars. McCall's big book of country needlecrafts. 215–18, 256–57, 259–60, 267–68
Irish fisherman afghans. Bray. Afghans: traditional & modern. 29–40
Knitted afghans. Chatterton. Scandinavian knitting designs. 206–21
Knitted afghans. Feldman. Big book of afghans. 16–50
Knitted baby blankets: ribbons and bows, patchwork hearts and baby smocking. Kurita. Second big book of afghans. 62–72
Knitted designs. Woman's Day prize-winning quilts, coverlets and afghans. 202–32
Lacy knitted afghan. Woman's Day book of gifts to make. 186–87
Modern afghans. Bray. Afghans: traditional & modern. 15–21
Navajo afghans, flag afghan. McCall's book of America's favorite needlework and crafts. 232–34
Patchwork afghan. Selfridge. Patchwork knitting. 132–33
Plaid baby afghan. Hubert. Weekend knitting projects. 20–21
Rosebud pattern and black and ombre knitted afghans. Woman's day decorative needlework for the home. 24–25
Sampler square afghan. Walker. Mosaic knitting. 198
Scandinavian rose, windblown snowflakes, enclosed flowers, fleur-de-lys, heart motif, diamond dazzler, diamond and stripes afghans. Chatterton. Coordinated crafts for the home. 23–25, 34–37, 48–51, 62–64, 68–69, 81–82, 88–89
Seascape, log cabin, all points, Irish knit updated, squares in the round, fan and feather, Icelandic accent, flowing lace, snowflakes, harlequin, chevron stripes and rattan. Kurita. Second big book of afghans. 20–52
Special interest afghans. Bray. Afghans: traditional & modern. 44–45
Traditional afghans. Bray. Afghans: traditional & modern. 75–93
Window pane afghan. Knitting. 106

Air compressors
Build your own air compressor. Popular Mechanics do-it-yourself encyclopedia. Vol. 6, 826–29

Air conditioning equipment
Air cleaner. Giant book of metalworking projects. 227–30
Air conditioner framing. Brann. How to modernize an attic. 13–14
Air conditioning fix-ups and maintenance. Nunn. Home improvement, home repair. 97–98, 135–37
Build in a room air conditioner, how to troubleshoot your air conditioner, quick checks on your car's air conditioner. Popular Mechanics do-it-yourself encyclopedia. Vol. 1, 43–57
Room air conditioner maintenance. Bragdon. Homeowner's complete manual of repair & improvement. 381

Airplane models
Aircraft. Chesneau. Scale models in plastic. 104–17
Aircraft. Ellis. Scale modeler's handbook. 54–65
Airplane models. Jackson. Modelmaker's handbook. 266–302
Three dimensional needlepoint airplane. Christensen. Needlepoint. 74–77
Williams. Building and flying indoor model airplanes.
Winter. World of model airplanes.

Airplanes, Toy
Airplane. Milstein. Building cardboard toys. 51–55
Bergan. Lingore paper airplane folding manual.
Biplane. Better Homes and Gardens treasury of Christmas crafts & foods. 277
Biplane flying machine. Baldwin. Old fashioned wooden toys. 80–83
Botermans. Paper flight.
Chuck gliders. Warring. Balsa wood modelling. 15–20
Crochet airplanes. Favorite easy-to-make toys. 116–17
Flying scale-model aeroplane, the jet fighter. Bumper book of things a boy can make. 116–18, 140–47
Indoor aircraft. Palmer. Making children's furniture and play structures. 135
Monoplane, space shuttle, propeller toy, helicopter. Hodges. 46 step-by-step wooden toy projects. 103–15
Terminal, control tower, monoplane, biplane, twin-engine airplane, helicopter, jet, tow tractors, and trailers, hangar. Maginley. Trains and boats and planes and . . . 135–66
Toy plane for mini-pilots. Popular Mechanics do-it-yourself encyclopedia. Vol. 19, 2921

Alarms. *See* **Burglar alarms**

Albums
Baby album cover. McCalls's big book of needlecrafts. 66–67
Butterfly album cover. Better Homes & Gardens embroidery. 40
Chinese albums. Whatnot. 90–91
Embroidered rose album. Embroidery of roses. 102–03
Keepsakes album. Better Homes and Gardens easy bazaar crafts. 14, 20
Lace photo album. Better Homes and Gardens treasury of Christmas crafts & foods. 175
Needlepoint free design for photo album. Smith. Needlery. 58–62
Padded album cover. Roda. Fabric decorating for the home. 96
Photo album. Laury. Treasury of needlecrafts gifts for the new baby. 93–95
Photo album. Scobey. First easy-to-see needlepoint workbook. 43–45
Plywood album cover; fabric appliqued. Doherty. Family Circle book of 429 great gifts-to-make all year round for just 10¢ to $10.00. 11–12, 45
Winged lion-griffin, Japanese Kabuki dancer. Scheuer. Designs for Holbein embroidery. 24–25, 34–35

Alphabets. *See* **Lettering**

Aluminum Foil. *See* **Metal foil**

Amusement Rooms. *See* **Basements; Recreation rooms**

Anemometers
Wind gauge. Complete handyman do-it-yourself encyclopedia. 3087–99

Angels
Angel dolls. Woman's Day bazaar best sellers. 139
Angel ornaments of baker's clay. McCall's book of Christmas. 105–06
Angels. Tangerman. Carving the unusual. 56–57
Angels, construction paper. Lyon. Arts and crafts objects children can make for the
    home. 86–87
Carved cherubs. Colletti. Art of woodcarving. 114–15
Christmas angel. Jarvey. You can dough it! 72–75
Christmas tree or angel (pom-poms glued on styrofoam or cardboard). Rissell. Craft-
    work the handicapped elderly can make and sell. 31–32
Clothespin angels, treetop angel in needlepoint. Wilson. Erica Wilson's Christmas
    world. 52–59
Corn husk and lacy angels. O'Neill. Make-it-merry Christmas book. 74–75
Cornhusk, yarn, and lace angel, pinecone angel. Christmas decorations from Williams-
    burg's folk art collection. 26, 28
Crocheted Christmas angel. Linsley. Great bazaar. 100–03
Cross-stitch angels on aida cloth. Wilson. Erica Wilson's Christmas world. 14–15
Flying angels. Miles. Designing with natural materials. 90–91
Gingham and lace angels. Better Homes and Gardens treasury of Christmas crafts &
    foods. 228–29
Golden angel. O'Neill. Make-it-merry Christmas book. 10–15
Golden angel for golden wedding anniversary. Janitch. Candlemaking and decorations.
    60–61
Little angel (crocheted). Linsley. Lesley Linsley's Christmas ornaments and stockings.
    162–64
Patchwork angels. McCall's book of Christmas. 181–82
Straw and metal foil angels. Christmas crafts book. 58–63
Straw angel and child; skater, peasant girl, lady with broom. Hibbs. Straw sculpture.
    50–51
Stuffed Christmas angel. Baldwin. Scrap fabric crafts. 71–73
Tin can angel. O'Neill. Make-it-merry Christmas book. 57, 59
Tree top angel. American School of Needlework. Great Christmas crochet book. 12–15

Animal traps. *See* **Traps**

Animals
Animal characters from pine cones: mouse, rabbit, cat and owl. Miles. Designing with
    natural materials. 123–25
Cardboard, fur-trimmed, pinch pot, ceramic, rock, crayon on wood, wooden and papier
    mâché animals. Lyon. Arts and crafts objects children can make for the home.
    22–24, 34–37, 43, 102–03, 115–16, 172–76
Eight small felt animals. Greenhowe. Making miniature toys and dolls. 76–79
Garden goblins, pinch pot animals, small pinch pot turtle. Chroman. Potter's primer.
    69–73
Horse, camel, bison, cow, elephant, Brahman bull, bear, hippopotamus, bull moose,
    eagle. Gottshall. Wood carving and whittling for everyone. 102–33
Papier mâché; tissue paper. Giant book of crafts. 389–90; 430–34

Papier mâché animals. Rush. Papier mâché. 87–94
Papier mâché pets: owl and pussy cat. Encyclopedia of crafts. 207
Pipe cleaner animals; paper animals. Bumper book of things a girl can make. 33–34, 41–42
Rooster, game cock, horse, sea gull. Metalcrafting encyclopedia. 92–95
Stuffed paper creatures. Linderman. Crafts for the classroom. 88–90
Wooden deer. Better Homes and Gardens treasury of Christmas crafts & foods. 134, 140

Animals, Crocheted
Crochet snail and alligator, lamb. Favorite easy-to-make toys. 118–19, 124–25
Crocheted animals. Staples. Yarn animal book. 195–223
Cuddly crocheted lambs. Woman's Day book of weekend crafts. 107–10
Kangaroo, panda, alligator & lion. McCall's big book of knit & crochet for home & family. 138–43
Piggy, baby elephant, Vincent van gator, Shelly turtle, Leonardo da lion, Bonita burro, Ginny giraffe, granny's cat, doodle bug, Barker family of dogs. Great granny crochet book. 47–57

Animals, Embroidered
Crewel-embroidered animals. Staples. Yarn animal book. 100–23

Animals, Knitted
Basketful of kittens and bunnies, lion. Woman's Day bazaar best sellers. 72–73
Garter stitch puppy & pussy cat. McCall's big book of knit & crochet for home & family. 28–29
Knitted animals. Staples. Yarn animal book. 162–92
Knitted playmates. Complete book of baby crafts. 153–55
Springtime lamb. Encyclopedia of crafts. 86

Animals, Needlepoint
Needlepoint animals. Staples. Yarn animal book. 128–58

Animals, Toy
Animal sculpture with boxes. Yoder. Sculpture and modeling for the elementary school. 160–61
Babies' cuddly toys: duckling, ducks, penguin, owl, squirrel; jointed toys: teddy bear, rabbit, poodle. Hutchings. Big book of stuffed toy and doll making. 58–66, 112–24
Beatrix Potter animals. Wilson. Erica Wilson's Christmas world. 115, 118–21
Camel, forest fawn, fairy reindeer, red reindeer, baby fawns for Christmas, rhinoceros, giraffe, sailor crab, butterfly, wasp & dragon. Hutchings. Big book of stuffed toy and doll making. 146–96
Cat and dog (felt). Favorite easy-to-make toys. 26–27
Chicken, horse, pig, cow, mouse & cat. Foose. Scrap saver's stitchery book. 8–11
Clara cow. Creative crafts yearbook: an exciting new collection of needlework and crafts. 74–76
Cuddly crocheted toys. Woman's Day crochet showcase. 129–33
Dilly duck, Olly owl and Clara chick. Creative crafts yearbook: an exciting new collection of needlework and crafts. 106–10
Dog and rabbit (stuffed). Complete book of baby crafts. 150–51
Felt menagerie. Mills. Book of presents. 94–95
Furry teddy; pompom penguin, chick, mouse, bunny sock dolls. Doherty. Family Circle book of 429 great gifts-to-make all year round for just 10¢ to $10.00. 18–19, 32–36, 178
Lily pads, frog, snails and walrus. Creative sewing. 107–10
Little lamb. Mills. The book of presents. 64–65

Menagerie. Laury. Treasury of needlecraft gifts for the new baby. 116–20
Mother goose. Baldwin. Scrap fabric crafts. 9–12
Owl and pussycat (corduroy and felt). Favorite easy-to-make toys. 78–85
Patchwork animals: dog, cat, horse & doll. Favorite easy-to-make toys. 74–77
Primitive wooden animals, soft muslin bunnies and bears. Better Homes and Gardens
  treasury of Christmas crafts & foods. 107, 270–71
Pup, bunny, and bear cuddlers, red-nosed reindeer, patchwork sitting duck. Woman's
  Day creative stitchery from scraps. 42–44, 112–14, 124–26
Quick-and-easy animal toys. Better Homes and Gardens applique. 18–19
Quick-and-easy animal toys. Better Homes and Gardens treasury of needlecrafts. 86–
  87
Soft animals from material scraps (cat, dog, rabbit, pig). Gault. Crafts for the disabled.
  32–36
Soft toy making: frog, owl, mother duck, elephant, puppy, ducklings, rabbit, and mother
  chicken. Anderson. Crafts and the disabled. 71–85
Stuffed animals. Laury. Handmade toys and games. 53–88
Stuffed animals. Linderman. Crafts for the classroom. 181–85
Stuffed animals, sock bunnies. Better Homes and Gardens easy bazaar crafts. 28, 29,
  35–37
Stuffed octopus, turtle, no-animal, spider, elephant, lion, giraffe. McCall's sewing for
  your home. 176–81
Swiveling crocodile. DeCristoforo. Build your own wood toys, gifts and furniture. 144–
  47
Wacky Willie puppet. Meilach. Macrame gnomes and puppets. 36–41
Wooden animal toys with wheel. Hodges. 46 step-by-step wooden toy projects. 34–74

Animals, Yarn
Latchet hooking, needle rya. Staples. Yarn animal book. 56–96
Mouse, worm, ladybug and owl. Wilson. Erica Wilson's Christmas world. 128–31
Yarn moppet, yarn dog and pom-pom variations. Rissell. Craftwork the handicapped
  elderly can make and sell. 9–11, 27–30, 79–84

Animation
Animating films without a camera. Giant book of crafts. 437–52

Anklets (jewelry)
Four foot jewelry designs. Katz. Footwear. 80–81
Rose petal anklet. Katz. Footwear. 62–63

Antennas
How to buy the right antenna, how to put up TV antennas. Popular Mechanics do-it-
  yourself encyclopedia. Vol. 1, 82–89
Install your own television antenna. Outdoor projects for home and garden. 46–56
Restore your TV antenna. Popular Mechanics do-it-yourself encyclopedia. Vol. 18,
  2848–50

Anvils
Anvils and anvil tools. Richardson. Practical blacksmithing. Vol. 1, 99–130
Making a small anvil from a railroad rail. Weygers. Modern blacksmith. 86–88

Apartments, Remodeled
Apartment plans. Siegele. Cabinets and built-ins. 89–92

Appliance covers. See **Dust covers**

Appliances. See **Kitchen appliances**

Applique
About applique. Newman. Quilting, patchwork, applique and trapunto. 125–92
Americana, florals, animals, alphabets, art deco and potpourri of designs. Needlework nostalgia. 8–72
Apple patch. Rosenthal. Not-so-nimble needlework book. 66–67
Applique. Frager. Quilting primer. 25–36
Applique. Marein. Stitchery, needlepoint, applique and patchwork. 185–201
Applique. Millett. Quilt-as-you-go. 95–130
Applique. Wooster. Quiltmaking. 77–103
Applique and patchwork. Bakke. Sewing machine as a creative tool. 11–47
Applique and raised work. Complete guide to needlework. 48–67
Applique and reverse applique, appliqued quilts. Giant book of crafts. 11–20, 134–39
Applique basics, reverse applique, turtle and alphabet appliques. Reader's Digest complete guide to needlework. 192–206, 263
Applique designs: Jean's rose, sunbonnet Sue and farmer boy, Dresden plate and aster, honey bee, and grandmother's flower garden. MacDonald. Let's make a patchwork quilt—using a variety of sampler blocks. 45–60, 69–72
Applique (Indian). Bath. Needlework in America. 70–71
Applique T-shirts, designs. Linsley. Custom made. 15–21
Applique with a sewing machine. Saunders. Speed sewing; 103 sewing machine short-cuts. 100–07
Applique work. Dillmont. Complete encyclopedia of needlework. 186–96
Appliqued vest and skirt. Better Homes and Gardens treasury of Christmas crafts & foods. 153–54
Art of applique. McCall's big book of needlecrafts. 74–87
Artistry of applique. Time-Life Books. Traditional favorites. 114–17
Auld. Molas.
Bass. Applique quiltmaking.
Cheap, quick fun (appliqued). Houck. Big bag book. 133–41
Designs for applique. Loeb. Leather book. 184–211
Fish & rabbit motif molas. Gostelow. Complete international book of embroidery. 16–17
Fruit & vegetables to applique. Embroidery. 18–19
Gillies. Patterns for applique and pieced work—and ways to use them.
Jerdee. Fabric applique for worship.
Lady bug applique. Baldwin. Scrap fabric crafts. 139–40
Learning to applique. Better Homes and Gardens Treasury of needlecrafts. 73
Machine applique Charlie Chaplin. Golden book of hand and needle arts. 21–22
Medium-sized and larger crocheted appliques. Chatterton. Patchwork & applique. 92–105
Molas—reverse applique designs. Golden book of hand and needle arts. 26–29
Paper molas. Schuman. Art from many hands. 167–70
Paper work applique: baby blocks and clamshell. MacDonald. Let's make a patchwork quilt—using a variety of sampler blocks. 116–18
Patera. Cutwork applique.
Personalized appliqued emblem. Linsley. Custom made. 112–14
Planning, cutting and sewing appliques. Chatterton. Patchwork & applique. 36–42
Reverse and shadow applique. Time-Life Books. Decorative techniques. 41–45
Reverse applique. Hall. Sewing machine craft book. 88–89
Rubbings for applique. Firestein. Rubbing craft. 62–63

Aprons
Ace of an apron. Botsford. Between thimble & thumb. 52–59
Apron. Gehret. Rural Pennsylvania clothing. 57–63
Apron with crochet motifs, smocked aprons. Encyclopedia of crafts. 99, 112
Apron with filet-radish insert. Svinicki. Old-fashioned crochet. 88–89
Apron with plenty of pockets, apron with decorated bib. Creative sewing. 47, 50

Baker's apron with trim. Svinicki. Old-fashioned crochet. 120–23
Barbecue apron. Mills. Book of presents. 83
Barbecue chef apron, tuxedo apron. Farlie. Pennywise boutique. 179–81
Bias-cut apron-shawl. Golden book of hand and needle arts. 54
Bobbin lace-trimmed apron. Reader's Digest complete guide to needlework. 432–34
Calico hostess apron with peace rose on bib. Gostelow. Cross stitch book. 130–34
Carpenter's apron. Coffey. Francine Coffey's celebrity sewing bee. 94
Checked tabard apron. Woman's Day bazaar best sellers. 71
Chef's apron and hat. Creative crafts yearbook: an exciting new collection of needle-
  work and crafts. 150–51
Child's apron. Evans. Ribbonwork. 59–62
Child's paint apron. Coffey. Francine Coffey's celebrity sewing bee. 116
Child's plastic pinafore, glamorous aprons for women, trio of aprons for men, gingham
  apron, child's Santa apron and pillow toy, cover-up play aprons for boys and girls.
  Doherty. Family Circle book of 429 great gifts-to-make all year round for just 10¢
  to $10.00. 18–19, 64–67, 120–21, 132, 165, 170–71
Christmas towel apron. Coffey. Francine Coffey's celebrity sewing bee. 152
Craft apron. Anderson. Crafts and the disabled. 55–57
Crayon; tea towel. Better Homes and Gardens easy bazaar crafts. 54–55, 61–62
Cross stitch adds a bright touch to aprons, huck embroidery and teneriffe embroidery.
  McCall's big book of needlecrafts. 196–97, 206–07, 228–29
Easy-as-pie aprons, all-occasion apron. Woman's Day book of gifts to make. 79–81,
  88–89
Embroidered apron. D'Amato. Italian crafts. 18–21
Embroidered apron. Treasury of things to make. 58–61
Gardening coverall. Reader's Digest complete guide to sewing. 494–97
Handkerchief apron, dish towel apron and child's party apron. Linsley. Great bazaar.
  82–84, 122, 123
Heart apron. Goldman. Decorate with felt. 41–42
Hostess apron. Mills. The book of presents. 58–59
Lacy pinafore apron, instant hostess apron, and butterfly hostess jumper. Farlie,
  Pennywise boutique. 44–47
Leather apron (men's). Gehret. Rural Pennsylvania clothing. 166–67
Little helper's tool apron. Evrard. Homespun crafts from scraps. 124–27
Long apron. Ley. Russian & other Slavic embroidery designs. 34–37
Mother-daughter aprons. Guth. Sewing with scraps. 155–57
Out-of-the-ordinary aprons. Crown. How to recycle old clothes into new fashions. 71–
  76
Party apron. Beard. Fashions from the loom. 87
Party apron. Linsley. Custom made. 128–30
Romanian apron. Gostelow. Complete international book of embroidery. 132–33
Santa, cookie and house. Foose. Scrap saver's stitchery book. 86–95
Seminole patchwork aprons and skirts. Dudley. Strip patchwork: quick and easy patch-
  work using the Seminole technique. 25–28
Seminole stitched apron. Treasury of things to make. 25–27
Sewing apron. Coffey. Francine Coffey's celebrity sewing bee. 82
Simple apron. Scurlock. Muzzleloader Magazine's book of buckskinning II. 64
Smocked apron. Fisher. Craft of smocking. 25–26
Smocked, double-pocket, handywoman, & appliqued aprons. Woman's Day bazaar
  best sellers. 96–98
Tie-dyed apron. Frame. Tie-dyeing and batik. 62–65
Toll-pocket apron. Woman's Day creative stitchery from scraps. 27–29
Transfer printed apron. Encyclopedia of crafts. 158
Variable star and tunic aprons. Laury. Quilted clothing. 129
Waisted apron. Evans. Ribbonwork. 57–59
Woman's apron. Walters. Crochet. 48–49

Aprons, Children
Victorian style apron. Step by step to better knitting and crochet. 232–33

Aquariums
Aquariums (repair). Schuler. How to fix almost everything. 12
Cabinet for tank. La Barge. Pet house book. 135–44
Coffee-table aquarium. Popular Mechanics do-it-yourself encyclopedia. Vol. 6, 810–15
Goldfish bowl sling. Doherty. Family Circle book of 429 great gifts-to-make all year round for just 10¢ to $10.00. 13
Home-made aquarium. Bumper book of things a boy can make. 217–18
Macrame swing and holder (fishbowl). Treasury of things to make. 168–71
Seaweed gardens and marine aquariums. Geary. Plant prints and collages. 92–93
Shell design for a fishbowl. Appel. Sand art. 93–96
Stone aquarium. Nickey. Stoneworkers bible. 195–97

Arc welding. *See* **Welding**

Architectural models
Architectural projects. Linderman. Crafts for the classroom. 298–300
Buildings. Jackson. Modelmaker's handbook. 216–26
Fairytale castle. Janitch. All made from paper. 37–41
Meetinghouse; an old district schoolhouse; an old stone barn. Maginley. America in miniatures. 24–31, 36–39
Plastic buildings and structures, card models. Ellis. Scale modeler's handbook. 104–21.

Armoires. *See* **Wardrobes**

Art from scraps, discards, and waste materials. *See* **Waste materials**

Art trade
Business of pottery. Howell. Craft of pottery. 133–41
Gadney. How to enter and win jewelry and metal crafts contests.

Artists easels. *See* **Easels**

Ashtrays
Ashtray. Fowler. Can crafts. 15–17
Ashtray and matchbox holder; armchair ashtrays. Bumper book of things a boy can make. 124–29
Deep bodied ash receptacle with hammered copper tray. Wooldridge. Woodturning techniques. 52–53
Mosaic ashtray base holder. Anderson. Crafts and the disabled. 37

Asphalt tiles. *See* **Tiles**

Audio systems
Amplifier for a transistor radio. Popular Mechanics do-it-yourself encyclopedia. Vol. 1, 74–75
Build a great wall of sound. Popular Mechanics do-it-yourself encyclopedia. Vol. 4, 488–90
Build a swivel hi-fi-center, open hi-fi rack. Popular Mechanics do-it-yourself encyclopedia. Vol. 10, 1444–49
Finishing radio cabinets, speaker boxes, etc. Patton. Furniture finishing. 152–57

Mix your way to better sound. Popular Mechanics do-it-yourself encyclopedia. Vol. 12, 1856–57
Mobile hi-fi for music outdoors or in. Popular Mechanics do-it-yourself encyclopedia. Vol. 12, 1878–82
Spencer. Designing and building your own stereo furniture.
Stereo hi-fi cabinet. 77 furniture projects you can build. 130–34
Stereo-hi-fi cabinet, music center, speaker system cabinets, TV hi-fi console cabinet. Family handyman handbook of carpentry plans/projects. 36–55

Automobile models
Miniature car, papier mâché. Epple. Something from nothing crafts. 70–72
Stutz bearcat made from tin cans. Popular Mechanics do-it-yourself encyclopedia. Vol. 18, 2875–80
Vehicles. Chesneau. Scale models in plastic. 163–74
Vechicles, cars. Jackson. Modelmaker's handbook. 109–32, 330–39

Automobile models, Racing
Hideaway track for model cars. Complete handyman-do-it-yourself encyclopedia. Vol. 11, 1694–1700
Racer. Milstein. Building cardboard toys. 35–37
Tin lizzie racer. Baldwin. Old fashioned wooden toys. 178–85

Automobile service stations, Toy
Garage. Blandford. Giant book of wooden toys. 237–43
Service station, gasoline service island. Maginley. Trains and boats and planes and . . . 27–30, 58–59

Automobile trailers, Toy
Boat trailer, travel trailer. Maginley. Trains and boats and planes and . . . 62–65

Automobiles, Body repair and refurbishing
Car care inside and out. Popular Mechanics do-it-yourself encyclopedia. Vol. 3, 384–88
How to repair rust. Popular Mechanics do-it-yourself encyclopedia. Vol. 16, 2480–81
Removing a dent. Brightman. 101 practical uses for propane torches. 85–87

Automobiles, Racing
Downhill racer. 101 do-it-yourself projects. 346–49
Go kart. Blandford. Giant book of wooden toys. 270–76
The gocart. Bumper book of things a boy can make. 122–23
Go-cart and trailer. Blizzard. Making wooden toys. 60–63
Peterson. Children's toys you can build yourself. 134–36
Toy racetrack. Popular Mechanics do-it-yourself encyclopedia. Vol. 19, 2922–23

Automobiles, Toy
Auto, race car, jeep. Buckland. Toymaker's book of wooden vehicles. 46, 74–77, 83–87
Block cars. Popular Mechanics do-it-yourself encyclopedia. Vol. 9, 1354
Board racer. Maginley. Toys to make and ride. 80–83
Bug, sports car, bus. DeCristoforo. Build your own wood toys, gifts and furniture. 162–69
Cars, trains, and wheels. Lawry. Handmade toys and games. 101–15
Compact auto, hatchback auto, automobile boat trailer and racer. Maginley. Trains and boats and planes and . . . 10–13, 60–62, 181–82
Fleet of blockmobiles. Popular Mechanics do-it-yourself encyclopedia. Vol. 19, 2911–13

Horseless carriage. Better Homes and Gardens treasury of Christmas crafts & foods. 276–77
Pillow car. Foose. Scrap saver's stitchery book. 56–57
Racing car. Palmer. Making children's furniture and play structures. 134
Scrap wood fleet of vehicles. Baldwin. Old fashioned wooden toys. 121–26
Sports car, rumble seat rambler modern racer, early racer. Hodges. 46 step-by-step wooden toy projects. 75–88

Automobiles, Toy. *See also* **Trucks, Toy**

Automobiles, Upholstery
Automobile upholstery. Roberts. Illustrated handbook of upholstery. 315–34

Awnings
Mini-awnings. McCall's sewing for your home. 138–39

Axes
Broadaxe. McRaven. Country blacksmithing.

B

Baby carriers. *See* **Infant slings**

Baby vehicles
(How to repair) a baby carriage. Schuler. How to fix almost everything. 17

Back packs. *See* **Packs**

Backgammon
Backgammon graphics. Sheldon. Washable and dryable needlepoint. 90–91
Marquetry backgammon board. Capotosto. Woodworking techniques and projects. 147–52
Woodburned backgammon table. Broadwater. Woodburning: art and craft. 110–12

Backyard playgrounds. *See* **Playground equipment**

Badminton
Badminton racket repair. Schuler. How to fix almost everything. 17–18

Baggage
Leather portmanteau. Scurlock. Muzzleloader Magazine's book of buckskinning II. 211–15
Suit case repair. Schuler. How to fix almost everything. 157

Baggage racks
Abstract luggage-rack straps. Scobey. Decorating with needlepoint. 137–39
Luggage rack straps. Roda. Fabric decorating for the home. 71
Net car-top carrier. Giant book of crafts. 100–04

Baggage tags. *See* **Labels**

Bags
Afrique tote bag. Sheldon. Washable and dryable needlepoint. 104–05
Aiken. Total tote bag book.
Applique shoulder bag, quilted calico holdall. Encyclopedia of crafts. 22–23, 37

Appliqued tote bags: big sun, peeping cat, bouquet, will-o'-the-wisp, signs of spring. Gillies. Patterns for applique and pieced work—and ways to use them. 28–41
Appliqued zoo sleeping bag and monkey tote. Better Homes and Gardens applique. 86–87
Aran textured tote (needlepoint). Boyles. Needlework gifts for special occasions. 53–55
Bag in Chinese braid. Dendel. Basic book of fingerweaving. 77
Bag, mountain. Latham. Leathercraft. 56–65
Bandanna bag. Coffey. Francine Coffey's celebrity sewing bee. 154
Bargello hosiery case. Christensen. Needlepoint and bargello stitchery. 75
Bargello tote bag (needlepoint). Rosenthal. Not-so-nimble needlework book. 107–12
Barrel bag. Reader's Digest complete guide to sewing. 500–01
Basic basketweave bag in two colors. Walker. Mosaic knitting. 250
Basic tote. Fanning. Complete book of machine quilting. 265–66
Basic tote bag, zipper bag, string bag. Hagans. All good gifts. 31–36
Beach bag; stenciled lunch bags; collector's tote bag. Linsley. Custom made. 29–30, 53, 149–50
Binca canvas shoulder bag. Anderson. Crafts and the disabled. 129–30
Cable-cord tote-all, minibag quartet in crochet, satin-and-lace evening pouch, doggy hot-water-bottle cover. Woman's Day bazaar best seller. 52, 54–56, 114
Carryall. Fairfield. Patchwork. 41
Carry-all. Romberg. Let's discover papier-mâché. 24–25
Carry-all barrel bag. Woman's Day creative stitchery from scraps. 137–39
Cat tote bag (reverse applique). Golden book of hand and needle arts. 31–32
Catchall bag. Laury. Treasury of needlecraft gifts for the new baby. 56–58
Churn dash and oddfellow's cross bags. Houck. Patchwork pattern book. 58–59, 62–63
Colonial sampler tote. Boyles. Margaret Boyles book of needle art. 46–49
Colorful crochet bags, smocked lally bag. Blandford. Book of traditional handicrafts. 24–25, 61–62
Cradle diaper bag with teddy toy. Foose. More scrap saver's stitchery. 59–63
Crayon bag. Foose. More scrap saver's stitchery. 48–53
Crazy patchwork tote bag. Breckenridge. Lap quilting. 57–58
Crochet bag on wooden handles. Gault. Crafts for the disabled. 110
Denim tote. Hall. Sewing machine craft book. 52–53
Diaper bag. Better Homes and Gardens easy bazaar crafts. 55, 63
Diet birthday cake bag for hair curlers, cotton puffs, or whatever. Coffey. Francine Coffey's celebrity sewing bee. 78
Duffle bag. Lamoreaux. Outdoor gear you can make yourself. 73–78
Duffle bag. Reader's Digest complete guide to sewing. 516–17
Durable duffle (patchwork). Botsford. Between thimble & thumb. 81–85
East African beaded bag. Hulbert. Creative beadwork. 88
Easy-to-make tote bag (patchwork). Crown. How to recycle old clothes into new fashions. 108–12
Everything is fair game (unusual bags). Houck. Big bag book. 142–50
Fabric lunch bags and velvet tote bags. Linsley. Great bazaar. 49, 73–75
Fat mushroom, three mushrooms, and clown face, needlepoint panels for a tote bag. Barnes. 120 needlepoint design projects. 91, 96, 120–21
Father-to-be-bag. Coffey. Francine Coffey's celebrity sewing bee. 90
Finnish pouch bag. Gostelow. Complete international book of embroidery. 83
Flat, round, boxed. Houck. Big bag book. 25–34
Flower trimmed drawstring bag. Creative crafts yearbook: an exciting new collection of needlework and crafts. 113
From Grandma's scrap bag (patchwork). Houck. Big bag book. 113–21
Granny and basketweave-stitch bags. Hubert. Weekend knitting projects. 25–27

Granny square tote bag (crocheted). Rosenthal. Not-so-nimble needlework book. 131–32

Handy tote bag. MacDonald. Let's make a patchwork quilt—using a variety of sampler blocks. 90–91

Handy woven bag. Tod. Joy of hand weaving. 302–04

Hieroglyphs initialed totebag. Fischer. Egyptian designs in modern stitchery. 136–41

Indian needlepoint bag. Gostelow. Complete international book of embroidery. 56–57

Jute bag with leno pattern. Swanson. Rigid heddle weaving. 112–17

Knitted patchwork bags. Selfridge. Patchwork knitting. 146–47

Knitted shopping bag, knitted bag on wooden handles. Gault. Crafts for the disabled. 69, 110–11

Knitted sisal bag, netting a bag. Encyclopedia of crafts. 238–39

Log cabin bags. Breckenridge. Lap quilting. 39–42

Making the duffle bag. Time-Life Books. Sporting scene. 127–29

Mesh back-tote. Woman's Day book of weekend crafts. 172–73

Mola tote bag, net tennis bag, camping bag, shopping bag. Giant book of crafts. 20, 104–08, 112–13, 118–20

Mosaic-patterned basket-weave bag. Walker. Mosaic knitting. 253–56

Needlepoint tote bag. Christensen. Needlepoint and bargello stitchery. 82–83

Netting bag. DeLeon. Basketry book. 124–26

Nine beige bags. Creative sewing. 95–98

Oriental tote and slipper. Jacobs. Crochet book. 120–22

Overnight bag. Burchette. More needlework blocking and finishing. 43–50

Paper shopping bags decorated with stenciled designs. Elbert. Paperworks. 32–34

Patchwork Abby tote bag. Scheuer. Designs for Holbein embroidery. 36–37

Patchwork tote bag. Scharf. Illustrated patchwork crochet. 158

Patchwork tote or pillow: project. Hall. Sewing machine craft book. 72–73

Pattern for tote bag with tree of life design (embroidered). Fraser. Modern stitchery: stitches, patterns, free-form designing. 87–89

Pencil duffle bag. Foose. Scrap saver's stitchery book. 38–41

Plastic toybag; pomander bag; drawstring gift bags; scarf needlework bag; awning cloth shopping bag; felt appliqued shopping bag. Doherty. Family Circle book of 429 great gifts-to-make all year round for just 10¢ to $10.00. 19, 52, 56, 132, 142–43, 152–56

Practical shopping bag, small shopping bag. Practical needlework. 136–38

Purses, bags and pillows in double weave. Dendel. Basic book of fingerweaving. 88–91

Quilted carryall. Laury. Treasury of needlecrafts gifts for the new baby. 100–01

Quilted Christmas tote bag. Foose. More scrap saver's stitchery. 122–24

Quilted cotton shoulder bag, envelope clutch bag, tote bag. Woman's Day book of gifts to make. 42–43, 50–51, 52, 90–91

Quilted workbag. McNeill. Quilting. 28

Rainbow tote bag in plaidpoint. Wilson. Needlework to wear. 90–91

Rainy day grab bag. Coffey. Francine Coffey's celebrity sewing bee. 119

Reversible kerchief bag. Rosenthal. Not-so-nimble needlework book. 38–39

Roomy pouch. Ruggieri. Woman's Day book of no-pattern sewing. 106

Santa gift tote. American School of Needlework. Great Christmas crochet book. 110–13

Schoolhouse bags. Houck. Patchwork pattern book. 32–33

Schoolhouse diaper bag. Baldwin. Scrap fabric crafts. 16–18

Shopping bag. Design crochet. 189–92

Shopping bag. Evans. Ribbonwork. 106–10

Shopping bag in broomstick crochet. Anderson. Crafts and the disabled. 123–24

Shopping bags. Mills. The book of presents. 76–77

Shopping/laundry bag. Jacobs. Crochet book. 168

Smocked cotton ball holder. Creative crafts yearbook: an exciting new collection of needlework and crafts. 41, 43

Sport your own bag (for games or sport equipment). Houck. Big bag book. 57–67

Square root of all bags (bags made from a square of materials). Houck. Big bag book. 48–52

Sturdy tote bag. Jacobs. Crochet book. 53–54

Suede applique bag. Gostelow. Complete international book of embroidery. 78–79

Tag-along tote (patchwork). Botsford. Between thimble & thumb. 73–77

Take-along. Burchette. More needlework blocking and finishing. 61–65

Tamboui tote bag. D'Amato. Italian crafts. 28–32

Textured totebag, needlework bag. Great granny crochet book. 126–27

Tooth fairy bag. Fanning. Complete book of machine quilting. 270, 272–73

Tote and duffle bags. Crochet. 67

Tote bag. Burchette. More needlework blocking and finishing. 70–73

Tote bag. Dittrick. Hard crochet. 115–19

Tote bag. Guth. Sewing with scraps. 54–55

Tote bag. Scobey. First easy-to-see needlepoint workbook. 114–16

Tote bag. Swanson. Rigid heddle weaving. 103–08

Tote-bag construction. Houck. Big bag book. 34–47

Tote bag (embroidered upholstery webbing). Rissell. Craftwork the handicapped elderly can make and sell. 70–72

Tote bag to crochet. Reader's Digest complete guide to needlework. 367

Tote bag with shell print. Elbert. Shell craft. 270–80

Tote bags. Christensen. Teach yourself needlepoint. 147–49

Tote bags. Sayles. Step-by-step stitchery. 60–61, 78

Tote bags and purses in center-to-edge braiding. Dendel. Basic book of fingerweaving. 57

Totes: stenciled denim in four sizes; quilted birdwatcher, quilted Indian print, red print, burlap; appliqued shoulder super-sized strip. Doherty. Family Circle book of 429 great gifts-to-make all year round for just 10¢ to $10.00. 139–40, 144–45, 150–58, 188–89

Travel pal tote bag. Baldwin. Scrap fabric crafts. 34–37

Weed bags, tapestry bag. Holland. Weaving primer. 112, 135–37

Wooden-handled fabric bag. Scharf. Butterick's fast and easy needlecrafts. 62–65

Woodlands, voyageur, & small Indian shooting bags. Scurlock. Muzzleloader Magazine's book of buckskinning II. 51–54

Woven bag. Tod. Joy of hand weaving. 296–97

Woven tote bag. Weaving and spinning. 52–53

Bags. See also **Infants, Equipment**

Bags, Felt
Drawstring bag in felt. Tyler. Big book of soft toys. 241–42

Bags, Laundry
Crazy patchwork laundry bag. Breckenridge. Lap quilting. 63–64

Decorated laundry bag. Wargo. Soft crafts for special occasions. 82–84

Drawstring bag for laundry or books. Coffey. Francine Coffey's celebrity sewing bee. 102

Hang-up hamper. Wargo. Soft crafts for special occasions. 136–38

Patchwork bag for rags, laundry. Goldman. Decorate with felt. 85

Piggy laundry bag. Foose. More scrap saver's stitchery. 19–23

Sliding clothespin bag or dirty laundry bag. Coffey. Francine Coffey's celebrity sewing bee. 66

Sunbonnet Sue or overall Sam laundry bags. Breckenridge. Lap quilting. 61–63

Swag bag laundry bag. Roda. Fabric decorating for the home. 206

Bags, Macrame
Drawstring bag. Torbet. Macrame you can wear. 86–87
Sisal bag. Brown. Complete book of rush and basketry techniques. 127–28

Bags, Shoe
Child's shoe bag. Goldman. Decorate with felt. 125
Child's shoe caddy. Woman's Day creative stitchery from scraps. 63–65
Shoe bag. Wargo. Soft crafts for special occasions. 140–41
Shoe bags. Breckenridge. Lap quilting. 58–60
Traveling shoe bag. Coffey. Francine Coffey's celebrity sewing bee. 103

Balancing toys
Equilibrist or balancing man. Blandford. Giant book of wooden toys. 169–72
Motion and balance toy. Dal Fabbro. How to make children's furniture and play equipment. 132

Ball bearings. See **Bearings**

Balls
Baby ball (crocheted). Creative crafts yearbook: an exciting new collection of needlework and crafts. 144
Fabric baby ball. Better Homes and Gardens treasury of Christmas crafts & foods. 105
Giant floor ball. Great granny crochet book. 138–40
Harlequin ball. Practical needlework. 257
Making little wooden balls. Fine woodworking techniques 4. 7
Simple felt ball, Easter ball, Christmas ball, ball from eight sections, bedfellow ball, Sputnik the rattly ball, tumbling Tommy, nodding mandarin. Hutchings. Big book of stuffed toy and doll making. 30–47
Wooden ball, fabric or leather ball, juggling balls, texture ball or "story ball." Hagans. All good gifts. 86–91

Bandsaws. See **Saws**

Banks, Toy
Bank. Romberg. Let's discover papier-mâché. 26–27
Banks for Hanukkah gift. Rockland. Hanukkah book. 139–42
Helm. Making wood banks.
Papier mâché piggy bank. Brunner. Pass it on. 130–31
Wheel-thrown piggy bank. Chroman. Potter's primer. 165–66

Banners. See **Wall hangings; Flags**

Barbecues
Backyard storage for barbecue equipment. Philbin. Cabinets, bookcases & closets. 108–10
Barbecue cart. Burch. Tile: indoors and out, every kind and use. 93
Barbecue pantry. Capotosto. Woodworking wisdom. 318–22
Barbecue repairs. Outdoor projects for home and garden. 67–68
Barbecue tools. Modern general shop. Metalworking. 104
Brick barbecue. Decks and patios. 128–29
Brick barbecue. 101 do-it-yourself projects. 314–16
Center-stage barbecue center. Better Homes and Gardens. Step-by-step masonry & concrete. 90–91
Clambake cooking. Golden book of colonial crafts. 59–67
Cookout bar. Popular Mechanics do-it-yourself encyclopedia. Vol. 6, 862–66
Cookout equipment. Daniels. Decks, porches, and patios. 98–105

Cut stone, concrete, masonry, and field stone barbecues. Decks and patios. 130
Firepit. Traister. All about chimneys. 83–84
Garden group with firebox. Fischman. Decks. 80–83
Hibachi table. Wood projects for the garden. 43
Installing a barbecue in concrete. Outdoor projects for home and garden. 272–76
Making a charcoal brazier and screening scoop. Weygers. Recycling, use, and repair of tools. 12–13
Mobile cook-center. Popular Mechanics do-it-yourself encyclopedia. Vol. 12, 1865–73
Open firepit cooking areas. Decks and patios. 126–28
Outdoor barbecue. Nickey. Stoneworker's bible. 238–41
Outdoor cooking tables, trolleys and benches. Blandford. Constructing outdoor furniture, with 99 projects. 227–44
Outdoor fireplaces. Traister. All about chimneys. 77–83
Portable electric grill, weather proof house for your grill. Popular Mechanics do-it-yourself encyclopedia. Vol. 9, 1370–77
Solar barbeque, solar oven. Calhoun. 20 simple solar projects. 62–87
Starting the charcoal. Brightman. 101 practical uses for propane torches. 130
Warm up to a patio firepit. Popular Mechanics do-it-yourself encyclopedia. Vol. 8, 1222–23
Wrap a table around your barbecue, how to install a gas-fired barbecue. Popular Mechanics do-it-yourself encyclopedia. Vol. 2, 174–78

Bargello
Bargello. Gostelow. Mary Gostelow's embroidery book. 27–33
Bargello techniques. Witt. Classics for needlepoint. 37–38, 109–20
Basic bargello. Chatterton. Patchwork & applique. 140–54
Boyles. Bargello.
Designing and working bargello. Reader's Digest complete guide to needlework. 173–82
Kaestner. Four ways bargello.
Kaleidoscope bargello. Wilson. More needleplay. 156–59

Bark
Bark rubbings. Burch. Making leaf rubbings. 45–47

Barns and stables
Barns. Burch. Building small barns, sheds, and shelters. 140–51, 155–58
Building a homestead barn. Buble. Working wood. 163–83
Dairy and beef cattle housing. Lytle. Farm builder's handbook, with added material for pole type industrial buildings. 89–99
Family cow barn. Burch. Building small barns, sheds, and shelters. 162–63
Horse barns. Burch. Building small barns, sheds, and shelters. 152–54, 158–61, 164–65
Horse housing. Lytle. Farm builder's handbook, with added material for pole type industrial buildings. 101–05
Housing for horses. Leavy. Successful small farms. 134–48
Pony shed. Churchill. Backyard building book. 121–25
Red barn garage. Churchill. Backyard building book. 166–87

Barns and stables, Toy
Barn. Maginley. Trains and boats and planes and . . . 44–46
Old stone barn. Maginley. America in minatures. 35–39
Stable. Hundley. Folk art toys and furniture for children. 60–66

Barometers
Accurate water barometer, handsome banjo barometer. Popular Mechanics do-it-your-self encyclopedia. Vol. 2, 180–84
Barometer repair and maintenance. Rodd. Repairing and restoring antique funiture. 152–58
Boy's barometer. Bumper book of things a boy can make. 209–10
Build a colonial weather station. Popular Mechanics do-it-yourself encyclopedia. Vol. 20, 3060–61
Miss Frescatti (cookie) barometer. Casselman. Crafts from around the world. 67–68
Sheraton-style barometer, name sign plaque-style weather station, strip-style weather station. Daniele. How to build 35 great clocks. 178–85
Wiggins tavern barometer. Daniele. Building early American furniture. 94–95

Bars (refreshment)
Bar. Waugh. Handyman's encyclopedia. 418–19
Bar cabinet. Complete handyman do-it-yourself encyclopedia. Vol. 2, 166–70
Bookcase/bar divider. Family handyman handbook of carpentry plans/projects. 161–64
Breakfast bar, mobile dry bar. 101 do-it-yourself projects. 136–38, 224–27
Build a patio appliance center. Popular Mechanics do-it-yourself encyclopedia. Vol. 11, 1622–25
Dry sink bar. Capotosto. Woodworking techniques and projects. 188–95
Family room bar, rec room service bar. Family handyman handbook of carpentry plans/projects. 101–09
Family room bar, hospitality cabinet and serving bar. 77 furniture projects you can build. 193–210
Handsome space-saving bar, "antiqued" bar, used whiskey barrel bar, cabinet bar. Popular Mechanics do-it-yourself encyclopedia. Vol. 2, 185–97
Lunch counter/bar. Zegel. Fast furniture. 70–73
Lunch counter/bar. Zegel. Shelf book. 86–88
Pass through breakfast bar, swing down table for a tight kitchen, snack bar. Family handyman handbook of home improvement and remodeling. 24–37
Roll-around wet bar with running water, service bar. Popular Mechanics do-it-yourself encyclopedia. Vol. 12, 1874–77, 1898–99
Simple bar, corner bar. Blandford. 53 space-saving built-in furniture projects. 308–13, 316–23
Snack bar. Family handyman handbook of carpentry plans/projects. 96–97
Snack bar and stools. Feirer. Cabinet-making and millwork. 710–13
Snack counter, colonial tavern look bar. Popular Mechanics do-it-yourself encyclope-dia. Vol. 8, 1180, 1183–84
Summer bar. Jarnow. (Re)do it yourself. 143–44

Baseboards
Baseboard. Syvanen. Interior finish: more tricks of the trade. 68–73

Basements
Basement remodeling ideas, finish your basement like a pro, stairwell to your base-ment, basement waterproofing. Popular Mechanics do-it-yourself encyclopedia. Vol. 2, 198–213
Basement room for children. Family handyman handbook of home improvement and remodeling. 136–39
Concrete floor for a basement. Time-Life Books. Floors and stairways. 56–63
Framing a basement room. Family handyman handbook of carpentry plans/projects. 265–72
Moisture and drainage repairs. Nunn. Home improvement, home repair. 43–44
Painting masonry basement walls. Scherer. Complete handbook of home painting. 115–20

Basket making

Arm's-length baskets. Johnson. Nature crafts. 21
Basket patterns. Dittrick. Hard crochet. 88–114
Basketry, fruit basket, plaited flower basket, cane shopping basket. Encyclopedia of crafts. 234–37, 243–44
Basketry process. Newman. Contemporary African arts and crafts. 127–46
Basketry techniques. Meilach. Weaving off-loom. 174–81
Basketry with a sewing machine. Hall. Sewing machine craft book. 68–69
Baskets. Treasury of things to make. 91–95
Bird basket. Kramer. Wirecraft. 80–82
Blackberry basket in buff willow. Maynard. Modern basketry from the start. 152–53
Braided paper baskets. Stephan. Creating with tissue paper. 230–32
Braided-straw basket. Hibbs. Straw sculpture. 94–95
Bread basket. Gardner. Dough creations. 75–79
Bread or fruit bowl. Wright. Complete book of baskets and basketry. 101–02
Brown. Complete book of rush and basketry techniques.
Cary. Basic baskets.
Cherry basket. Wright. Complete book of baskets and basketry. 50
Child's small round cane basket. Maynard. Modern basketry from the start. 134–35
Clam baskets. Platt. Step-by-step woodcraft. 28–29
Coiled baskets. Meilach. Modern approach to basketry. 65–147
Coiling, rope basket, Deerfield dish basket, Indian basket. DeLeon. Basketry book. 17–46
Crochet a natural jute basket. Vanderbilt. Gloria Vanderbilt designs for your home. 138–40
Crocheted baskets. Meilach. Modern approach to basketry. 221–35
Double-layer ribbon basket. Glashausser. Plaiting step-by-step. 103–09
Flower basket; large bowl; shopping basket. Cane, rush and straw. 94–106
Flower basket with ribbon insert. Svinicki. Old-fashioned crochet. 90–91
Fruit basket. Jacobs. Crochet book. 155
Harvey. Techniques of basketry.
Hexagonal plaited basket. Glashausser. Plaiting step-by-step. 112–33
Indian basketry. Norbeck. Book of authentic Indian life crafts. 90–93
Indian coil basket, hanging basket and shopping basket. Golden book of colonial crafts. 18–25
Large oval work basket (grass). Wilder. Secrets of Eskimo skin sewing. 122
Lauhala baskets. Bird. Craft of Hawaiian lauhala. 127–50
Making a basket from a tree. Fine woodworking techniques 4. 196–99
Making shaped platters. Cane, rush and straw. 21–27
Meilach. Modern approach to basketry.
Oval and round shopping basket in buff, white willow. Maynard. Modern basketry from the start. 159–62
Oval garden or agricultural basket. Wright. Complete book of baskets and basketry. 55
Oval shopping basket. Maynard. Modern basketry from the start. 140–42
Oval tray and baskets. Cane, rush and straw. 34–40
Owl basket. Casselman. Crafts from around the world. 180–83
Picnic baskets. Cane, rush and straw. 10–14
Picnic hamper with lid. Cane, rush and straw. 67–70
Pine cone basket. Johnson. Nature crafts. 132
Pine needle basket. Johnson. Natural crafts. 124–25
Pine needle basket, pomo basket, miniature beaded basket, yarn basket, basket over a bottle. Stribling. Crafts from North American Indian arts. 61–114
Pine needle baskets, honeysuckle basket. Meras. Vacation crafts. 121–26
Plain weaving wood-base baskets, plain woven-base baskets, coiled basketry. Kicklighter. Crafts, illustrated designs and techniques. 15–23
Plaiting mats and baskets (weaving without a loom). Newman. Contemporary Southeast Asian arts and crafts. 119–24

Plates. Wright. Complete book of baskets and basketry. 94
Round basket. Horwitz. Mountain people, mountain crafts. 99–108
Round basket (grass). Wilder. Secrets of Eskimo skin sewing. 119–22
Round flower basket in buff willow. Maynard. Modern basketry from the start. 154–55
Round linen basket. Wright. Complete book of baskets and basketry. 97–98, 105–06
Round workbaskets. Wright. Complete book of baskets and basketry. 91–92
Shopping baskets. Wright. Complete book of baskets and basketry. 54, 92–93, 98, 125
Single-layer plaited basket. Glashausser. Plaiting step-by-step. 84–89
Sisal tub. DeLeon. Basketry book. 101–02
Small oval, round eared rush baskets. Wright. Complete book of baskets and basketry. 113
Splint basket. DeLeon. Basketry book. 86–87
Straw basket. Hibbs. Straw sculpture. 110–11
Toy cat or dog basket. Maynard. Modern basketry from the start. 156–58
Twined baskets. Meilach. Modern approach to basketry. 147–75
Twined baskets, coiled Indian baskets, crocheted dried-flower basket and vegetable storer. McCall's book of America's favorite needlework and crafts. 378–84
Twining, fiesta basket, fish bags, banana basket. DeLeon. Basketry book. 47–75
Two baskets. Cane, rush and straw. 28–33
Violet basket, bell basket, Easter basket, fruit basket, heart basket, birdcage flower basket. Fowler. Can crafts. 91–103
Weaving baskets. Meilach. Modern approach to basketry. 177–87
Weaving rag or yarn baskets. Linderman. Crafts for the classroom. 241–44
White oak basketry. Langsner. Country wood craft. 225–40
Willow basket. Johnson. Nature crafts. 20
Wire basket, bread basket. Kramer. Wirecraft. 74–77
Workbasket with lid. Wright. Complete book of baskets and basketry. 114–15
Wright. Complete book of basket and basketry.

Basketball courts
Basketball hoop. Popular Mechanics do-it-yourself encyclopedia. Vol. 14, 2198
Basketball net. Giant book of crafts. 109

Baskets
Basket cover. Creative crafts yearbook: an exciting new collection of needlework and crafts. 126
Basket (repair). Schuler. How to fix almost everything. 20
Basket doll cradle. Evrard. Homespun crafts from scraps. 119–23
Berry baskets. Linsley. Great bazaar. 108–10
Bread dough baskets. Jarvey. You can dough it! 59–62
Calico baskets. Baldwin. Scrap fabric crafts. 143–45
Calico-lined basket. Evrard. Homespun crafts from scraps. 21–24
Care and repair of baskets. Wright. Complete book of baskets and basketry. 150–54
Cover and lining for baskets. Vanderbilt. Gloria Vanderbilt designs for your home. 134–35
Crocheted basket. Woman's Day book of gifts to make. 99–100
Crocheted cord baskets. Better Homes and Gardens treasury of needlecrafts. 228–29
Decorated straw baskets with homemade goodies. Coffey. Francine Coffey's celebrity sewing bee. 153
Dyeing natural basketry materials. Bliss. Handbook of dyes from natural materials. 153–57
Egg carton, plastic bottle, & styrofoam baskets. Epple. Something from nothing crafts. 41–43, 111–13
Garden basket. Linsley. Custom made. 156–57
Oval basket, striped basket with cover. Design crochet. 200, 202–05
Padded basket. Woman's Day bazaar best sellers. 108

Paint a basket with posies. Vanderbilt. Gloria Vanderbilt designs for your home. 136–37

Painting baskets. Jarnow. (Re)do it yourself. 67

Plastic canvas little yellow baskets and yellow basket pincushion lid. Wilson. Needle-play. 174–75

Repairing baskets. Johnson. How to restore, repair and finish almost everything. 66–70

Round, pedestal, square cane baskets. Nicole. Designer accessories to make for your home. 152–56, 158–59

Shaped crochet basket. Encyclopedia of crafts. 84

Single-layer lidded basket. Glashausser. Plaiting step-by-step. 92–95

Woven fabric baskets, bargello baskets, fabric bowls. Better Homes and Gardens treasury of Christmas crafts & foods. 36–37, 39, 108

Woven paper basket with lid. Woman's Day book of weekend crafts. 27–28

Baskets. See also **Easter baskets; Waste baskets; Wood baskets and boxes**

Bassinets

Bassinet. Dal Fabbro. How to make children's furniture and play equipment. 30

Bassinet set—2 sheets and 1 pillowcase. Mensinga-Biasiny. Beautiful baby clothes to crochet, knit, sew and embroider. 53–55

Quilted and ruffled liner. Mensinga-Biasiny. Beautiful baby clothes to crochet, knit, sew and embroider. 130–31

Bathing suits

Bandana bikini, diaper sunsuit. Wiseman. Cuts of cloth. 28–29, 58–59.

Bare bikini and a cover up. Time-Life Books. Separates that travel. 130, 137–41

Beach outfit. Complete book of baby crafts. 35

Bikini. Torbet. Macrame you can wear. 109–11

Bikini (crocheted). Time-Life Books. Sporting scene. 175–77

Bikini in a bag. Woman's Day crochet showcase. 63–65

Crocheted jet set bikinis. Favorite knitting & crochet patterns. 80–82

For fun at the beach (crocheted). Feldman. Needlework boutique. 49–52

Girl's bikini and cape (crocheted). Creative crafts yearbook: an exciting new collection of needlework and crafts. 28–29

Heart rimmed bikini and skirt. Knitting. 21–22

Knitted two-piece bathing suit. Knitting techniques and projects. 70–71

Making swim wear. Burns. Super sewing. 281–87

Playsuit. Crochet. 75–78

90 minute swim easy. Ruggieri. Woman's Day book of no-pattern sewing. 94–95

Racy ribbed bikini, sunset bathing suit. Henderson. Woman's Day book of designer crochet. 100–01, 105–06

Ribbed bikini. Knitting. 18

Swimsuit with flower cutout. Crochet. 74

Two-piece bikini. Jacobs. Crochet book. 105–07

Bathrooms

Basic vanity. Philbin. Cabinets, bookcases & closets. 136–37

Bathroom. Siegele. Cabinets and built-ins. 68–70

Bathroom cabinets. Family handyman handbook of carpentry plans/projects. 143–50

Bathroom shelves. Zegel. Shelf book. 84–85

Bathroom storage. Jones. Plan and build more storage space. 129–35

Built-in vanity. Philbin. Cabinets, bookcases & closets. 100–01

Ceramic tile and the bathroom. Burch. Tile: indoors and out, every kind and use. 68–80

Gathered sink skirt. Roda. Fabric decorating for the home. 214–15

Bathroom cupboard adaptation. Moser. How to build shaker furniture. 198–99
Bathroom vanity. 101 do-it-yourself projects. 162–65
Fixing bathroom plumbing problems. Popular Mechanics do-it-yourself encyclopedia. Vol. 1, 157–60
Illusion of a sunken tub, vanity hamper, medicine cabinet, towel and utility closet, prefab bath installation, remodeling, ladder shelves over toilet, caulk a bathtub. Popular Mechanics do-it-yourself encyclopedia. Vol. 2, 214–31
Inexpensive bath enclosure. Family handyman handbook of home improvement and remodeling. 84–88
Pebble covered sink cabinet. Jarnow. (Re)do it yourself. 160–62
Planning and remodeling bathrooms.
Recycling old bathroom fixtures. Kangas. By hand. 194–98
Refurbishing old tile around the bathtub. Family handyman handbook of home improvement and remodeling. 78–84
Shower and bathrooms. Siegele. Cabinets and built-ins. 32–41
Sleek bathroom vanity. Better Homes and Gardens step-by-step cabinets and shelves. 86–87
Soap dish holder. Brown. 44 terrific woodworking plans & projects. 137–39
Two handsome shaving cabinets, early American shaving console. Popular Mechanics do-it-yourself encyclopedia. Vol. 17, 2612–17
Vertical bathroom storage. Philbin. Cabinets, bookcases & closets. 116–18

Bathrooms, Accessories
Bathmat (crocheted). Step by step to better knitting and crochet. 249
Bath set (crocheted appliques and edgings for towels and covered bath mat). McCall's big book of knit & crochet for home & family. 157–59
Bathroom seat cover. Burchette. Needlework. 36–37
Cabinet/towel rack. Family handyman handbook of carpentry plans/projects. 154–56
Tissue covers, toilet. Linsley. Great bazaar. 141
Toilet lid cover. Roda. Fabric decorating for the home. 183
Toilet tank and seat covers, bath rugs. Better Homes and Gardens sewing for your home. 168–69
Toilet tissue covers. Goldman. Decorate with felt. 111–12
Toilet-tissue-roll cover to crochet. Woman's Day decorative needlework for the home. 147
Toothbrush holder. Cope. Plastics. 60

Bathtubs
Bathtubs. Parry. Stenciling. 110
Sunken Roman tub. Burch. Tile: indoors and out, every kind and use. 76–80

Batik
Batik. Dyer's art. 77–128
Batik. Kicklighter. Crafts, illustrated designs and techniques. 25–29
Batik. Linderman. Crafts for the classroom. 149–61
Batik. Rose. Illustrated encyclopedia of crafts and how to master them. 292–97
Batik. Seagroatt. Basic textile book. 80–81
Batik: hot wax and cool dye. Time-Life Books. Boutique attire. 64–69
Batik process. Newman. Contemporary Southeast Asian arts and crafts. 18–36
Batik—the unusual gift. Guth. Sewing with scraps. 193–202
Batik work. Sommer. Wearable crafts. 30–39
Batiking a gourd calabash. Mordecai. Gourd craft. 122–26
Batiking process. Schuman. Art from many hands. 144–49
Bowen. Designing with die resists, batik and tie-and-dye.
How to batik. Anderson. Tie dyeing and batik. 56–63
How to make your own batik. Belfer. Designing in batik and tie dye. 23–77
Introduction to batik. Tie-dye, batik and candlemaking step-by-step. 19–32

Making batik cards. Holtje. Cardcraft. 37–40
Methods, procedures. Andersen. Creative exploration in crafts. 33–43
Variations in batik process using starch paste resists, cold wax emulsions, and polymer emulsions. Belfer. Designing in batik and tie dye. 78–87

Beach bags. *See* **Bags**

Beads
Baker's beads, large beads, beads made from breadcrumb dough. Gardner. Dough creations. 61–69, 132–36
Beads from papier-mâché. Sommer. Contemporary costume jewelry. 180–81
Beads made from breadcrumb dough. Gardner. Dough creations. 132–36
Clay beads. Chroman. Potter's primer. 43–45
Enamelling beads. Sommer. Contemporary costume jewelry. 71–72
Handmade and dyed wooden beads. Sommer. Contemporary costume jewelry. 74–76
Handmade wooden beads. Huckleberry. How to make your own wooden jewelry. 113–17
Making a bead. Sprintzen. Jewelry basic techniques and design. 47–50
Making beads and buttons. Priolo. Ceramics by coil. 25
Making ceramic beads. Sprintzen. Jewelry, basic techniques and design, 171
Making clay beads. Sommer. Contemporary costume jewelry. 128–32
Making rolled paper, bamboo, wooden, salt, raffene-covered, papier mâché, clay and button beads. Hulbert. Creative beadwork. 121–28
Paper beads. Sommer. Contemporary costume jewelry. 163–66
Paper jewelry beads. Epple. Something from nothing crafts. 65–66
Super quick and easy wood beads. Sommer. Contemporary costume jewelry. 79

Beads. *See also* **Jewelry**

Beadwork
Art of beadweaving. Encyclopedia of crafts. 180–85
Bead mosaic, beadwork on wire. Whatnot. 79–81
Beaded bottles, beaded armband. Stribling. Crafts from North American Indian arts. 188–220
Beaded bouquet. McCall's big book of country needlecrafts. 54–58
Beading. Practical needlework. 224–25
Beadwork. Kicklighter. Crafts, illustrated designs and techniques. 31–39
Beading on a frame and attaching beading. Time-Life Books. Decorative techniques. 47–53.
Indian beadwork. Schuman. Art from many hands. 214–17
Ring, daisy chain medallion and loom beading. Golden book of colonial crafts. 106–11
Beadweaving. Gill. Beadwork: the technique of stringing, threading, and weaving. 113–22
Beadwork (Indian). Bath. Needlework in America. 53–66
Beadwork on printed fabric. Hulbert. Creative beadwork. 85
Dieringer. Paper bead book.
Erlandsen. Bead book.
Hanging decorations. Hulbert. Creative beadwork. 94–96
Hulbert. Creative beadwork.
Indian beadwork. Norbeck. Book of authentic Indian life crafts. 73–78
Oya patterns. Stearns. Batsford book of crochet. 147–52
Patterns of beads. Newman. Contemporary African arts and crafts. 212–23
Persian donkey beads of clay. Mosesson. Jewelry craft for beginners. 100–03
Stringing beads and bead weaving. Davies. Beads as jewelry. 25–32
Trimming with beads and sequins. Time-Life Books. Boutique attire. 112–14
Ways of assembling beads, weaving beads. Newman. Contemporary Southeast Asian arts and crafts. 264–69

Bean bags
Beanbags. Buxton. Craftmaking: for love or money. 122–23
Bean bag bunnies. Greenhowe. Making miniature toys and dolls. 82–84
Lady bird and frog. Christmas craft book. 108–09

Beans. *See* **Seeds, berries, etc.**

Bearings
Makeshift bearings. Weygers. Recycling, use, and repair of tools. 58–60

Bears
Bear. Day. Complete book of rock crafting. 78–84
Bear (lifesize). Kinser. Sewing sculpture. 94–99
Bear nap mat. Foose. More scrap saver's stitchery. 3–5
Big bear. American School of Needlework. Great Christmas crochet book. 122–27
Cuddly panda and koala (knit). Mills. The book of presents. 102–03
Hall. Teddy bear craft book.
Honeybears. Baldwin. Scrap fabric crafts. 13–15
Pine cone teddy bear. Better Homes and Gardens treasury of Christmas crafts & foods. 332
Tedda bear and four friends. Marsten. Step-by-step dollmaking. 58–64
Teddy bear. Benton. Sewing classic clothes for children. 63–67
Teddy bear. Hutchings. Big book of stuffed toy and doll making. 117–19
Teddy bear, crayon rubbed. Lyon. Arts and crafts objects children can make for the home. 179–81
Teddy bear family. Complete book of baby crafts. 145–49
Teddy bear (jointed). Practical needlework. 265
Teddy bears' picnic. Greenhowe. Making miniature toys and dolls. 55–57
Teddy or panda. Gault. Crafts for the disabled. 47–54
Traditional teddy bear. Favorite easy-to-make toys. 70–73

Bed pockets
Bedside caddy pocket. Woman's Day creative stitchery from scraps. 142–43
Bedside holder. Rosenthal. Not-so-nimble needlework book. 33
Saturday morning sackhound. Foose. More scrap saver's stitchery. 54–58

Bed trays. *See* **Furniture for the sick**

Bedclothes
Drunkard's path bed linen and tray cloth. Houck. Patchwork pattern book. 18–19
Embroidered sheet and pillowcase. Complete book of baby crafts. 84–85
Embroidered sheet and pillowcases. Boyles. Needlework gifts for special occasions. 106–09
Gingham trimmed sheet and matching pillowcase. Great cross-stitch. 53–54
Making pillow cases and bed linens. Better Homes and Gardens sewing for your home. 100–01
Morning glory embroidered sheet and pillowcase. Woman's Day decorative needlework for the home. 153–54
Sleepy-time sheep embroidered sheet & pillow case. Embroidery. 62–65
Thousand pyramids bed linen and matching picture. Houck. Patchwork pattern book. 12–13

Bedroom furniture

Multiple unit. Blandford. How to make your own built-in furniture. 299–303

Bunk bed over desk combination. Popular Mechanics do-it-yourself encyclopedia. Vol. 5, 668–70

Youth room for two with built-in beds, closet, and divider. Family handyman handbook of carpentry plans/projects. 127–29

Beds

Bed. Zegel. Fast furniture. 85–87

Basic bed. Brown. 44 terrific woodworking plans & projects. 178–81

Bed that flips into a wall. Built-ins. 95

Bedstead. Rubin. Mission furniture. 106–07

Blandford. Building better beds.

Built-in beds. Hedden. Successful shelves and built-ins. 71–80

Bunk bed group (single bed with bookshelf modules). Capotosto. Woodworking techniques and projects. 196–204

"Cannonball" four-poster bed, four-poster bed with tester top. Shea. Pennsylvania Dutch and their furniture. 204–07

Deacon Justinian's platform bed, ready-made bed, Madame Recamier's bed. Ball. Master pieces. 34–41, 58–65, 84–91

Double bed. Make it! don't buy it. 132–45

Eighteenth century four-poster bed. Taylor. How to build period country furniture. 169–72

Folding Revolutionary War camp cot, willow rod bed. Scurlock. Muzzleloader Magazine's book of buckskinning II. 199–203

Four-poster bed. Black and Decker power tool carpentry. 141–44

Four-poster bed, couch. Osburn. Measured drawings of early American furniture. 56–58, 68–69

Four-poster beds. McCall's sewing for your home. 94–98

Lightweight folding cots (covers). Better Homes and Gardens sewing for your home. 200–01

Loft bed. Black and Decker power tool carpentry. 128–32

Low post bed frame. Marlow. Early American furnituremaker's manual. 102–08

Low-post bed, trundle bed. Moser. How to build shaker furniture. 174–77

Platform bed. Oberrecht. Plywood projects illustrated. 125–29

Platform bed, low bed and trundle bed kits. 101 do-it-yourself projects. 180–84, 369–71

Pole furniture, queensize homestead bed. Churchill. Backyard building book II. 50–53

Queensize homestead bed. Churchill. Big backyard building book. 170–73

Shaker bed, twin beds with shelves, bookcases and desk. 77 furniture projects you can build. 217–28

Single bed. Fine woodworking techniques 5. 130–32

Standard bed. Waugh. Handyman's encyclopedia. 426–28

Studio bed with a woven cord spring. Brann. How to repair, refinish, reupholster. 96–108

Three handsome platform beds. Popular Mechanics do-it-yourself encyclopedia. Vol. 2, 252–57

Trundle bed. Dal Fabbro. How to make children's furniture and play equipment. 53–56

Twin beds, double bed. Williams. Spanish colonial furniture. 94–97

Under eaves rope bed. Brann. How to build colonial furniture. 201–22

Beds. *See also* **Children's furniture; Beds**

Beds, Bunk
Built-in bunk beds, bunk beds for 2 youngsters, twin bunks, closet bunk combo. 77 furniture projects you can build. 236–39, 260–63, 270–74, 274–76
Bunk bed and room divider. Time-Life Books. Space and storage. 68–83
Bunk bed/desk combination, bunk bed with a built-in chest. Popular Mechanics do-it-yourself encyclopedia. Vol. 5, 668–70, 674–75
Bunk beds. Black and Decker power tool carpentry. 123–27
Bunk beds. Brown. 44 terrific woodworking plans & projects. 179–88
Bunk beds. McCall's sewing for your home. 195–96
Bunk beds. 101 do-it-yourself projects. 354–57
Bunk beds, wallbed unit. Complete handyman do-it-yourself encyclopedia. Vol. 2, 235–49
Bunk beds with storage drawers. Make it! don't buy it. 48–57
Double-decker bed. Built-ins. 92–94
Double-decker bunk. Churchill. Big backyard building book. 102–03, 107
Stacking beds, built-in double decker with storage units. Dal Fabbro. How to make children's furniture and play equipment. 44–52
Stacking bunk beds, low stacking beds, simple bunk beds, turned bunk bed, bunk bed with drawers, corner bunk beds. Blandford. Building better beds. 175–213
Tree-house bunk beds. McCall's sewing for your home. 170–72
Twin bunks and closet combo, built-in bunk. Family handyman handbook of carpentry plans/projects. 119–26
Wall-edged bunk cushions; bunk seat. Blandford. Upholsterer's bible. 134–40; 306–08

Beds, Folding
Cabinets for a Murphy bed. Cary. Storage: cabinets, closets, and wall systems. 116–20

Beds, Headboards
Accenting the attached headboard. Roberts. Illustrated handbook of upholstery. 262–66
Appliqued headboard, soft brass appliqued headboard. Better Homes and Gardens treasury of needlecrafts. 60–61, 112–13
Bedhead with cabinets. Blandford. 53 space-saving built-in furniture projects. 277–81
Bed head with linen-fold carving. Taylor. How to build period country furniture. 166–68
Bookcase headboard. Blandford. How to make your own built-in furniture. 292–94
Cabinet headboard unit, mission-style headboard. 101 do-it-yourself projects. 185–89
Child's bookcase headboard. Blandford. How to make your own built-in furniture. 294–97
Combination, wall and bookcase headboard. Blandford. 66 children's furniture projects. 320–38
Curved headboard, headboard and footboard, fabric headboard, "diamond" headboard. McCall's sewing for your home. 98–100, 102–04
Deep-buttoned headboard. Grime. Illustrated guide to furniture repair & restoration. 118–23
Draped "headboard". McCall's sewing for your home. 61
Fabric panel for bed without headboard. Roberts. Illustrated handbook of upholstery. 260–62
Head panels. Blandford. Upholsterer's bible. 317–28
Headboard. Cane, rush and straw. 62–63
Headboard panels. Scobey. First easy-to-see needlepoint workbook. 63–67
Headboards. McDonald. Modern upholstering techniques. 100–08
High storage. Blandford. How to make your own built-in furniture. 297

Padded headboard. Roda. Fabric decorating for the home. 162–63
Quilted applique—a soft brass headboard. Better Homes and Gardens applique. 48–49
Spindle headboard. Moser. Windsor chairmaking. 92–94
Woven headboards. Wilson. Weaving you can use. 103

Beds, Repairing
Beds and other frames. Marshall. How to repair, reupholster and refinish furniture. 132–45
Joints for beds. Time-Life Books. Repairing furniture. 22–25

Bedside furniture. *See* **Furniture for the sick; Tables, Bedside**

Bedspreads
Antique bedspread. Svinicki. Old-fashioned crochet. 42–45
Aran Isle crocheted bedspread. Crochet. 90
Basic bedspread styles and variations. Better Homes and Gardens sewing for your home. 76–91
Bed drapery and bedspread. McCall's sewing for your home. 72–73
Bed of roses crocheted coverlet. Woman's Day decorative needlework for the home. 12–13
Bed throw. Goldman. Decorate with felt. 44–45
Bedspread. Reader's Digest complete guide to sewing. 454–56, 464–65
Bedspread. Reader's Digest complete guide to sewing. 477–78
Bedspread and bolster cover. McCall's sewing for your home. 78–79
Bedspread in Osage and other braids. Dendel. Basic book of fingerweaving. 65–67
Bedspread with "Kimono" cording. McCall's sewing for your home. 58–59
Bedspread woven in strips. Brown. Weaving, spinning, and dyeing book. 186–87
Bedspreads. Roberts. Illustrated handbook of upholstery. 233–41
Bedspreads. Sara. Sewing made easy. 382–84
Begin with a basic throw bedspread, make a handsome tailored bedspread. McCall's sewing for your home. 45–52
Calico bedspread with patchwork motif. Ives. Ideas for patchwork. 32–36
Children's bedspread with pennant decoration. Goldman. Decorate with felt. 52–58
Coverlet made from sheets, embroidered heirloom coverlet, crocheted popcorn square bedspread, star knitted bedspread, water lily crocheted bedspread, colonial crocheted bedspread. McCall's big book of country needlecrafts. 224–26, 252–53, 255–56, 260–67
Crochet bedspread. Treasury of things to make. 49–51
Crocheted and knitted bedspreads. Feldman. Handmade lace and patterns. 110–11
Crocheted leaves and trellis bedspread. Encyclopedia of crafts. 87
Crocheted rosette bedspread. McCall's book of America's favorite needlework and crafts. 234–36
Daybed covers. McCall's sewing for your home. 101–02
Design for bedspread in tatting and crochet. Dillmont. Complete encyclopedia of needlework. 361–64
Design for a cot cover worked in bands. Dillmont. Complete encyclopedia of needlework. 300–03
Diamond spread, double spread, and single blanket. Chatterton. Patchwork & applique. 119–26
Double-width bedspread with heavy homespun weft. Brown. Weaving, spinning, and dyeing book. 183–84
Embroidered rose bedspreads. Embroidery of roses. 111–13, 139–41
Flower basket bedspread. Walters. Crochet. 70–72
Flowered bedspread (crocheted). Step by step to better knitting and crochet. 286–88

Medieval art bedspread, popcorn bedspread. Woman's Day crochet showcase. 149–51, 160–61

Night spread. Roda. Fabric decorating for the home. 124

Op-art bedspread/wall hanging. Jacobs. Crochet book. 156–59

Patch-quilt bedspread. Halliday. Decorating with crochet. 30–32

Patchwork spread and pillows. Woman's Day creative stitchery from scraps. 154–57

Patchwork sweater craft projects. Brown. Super sweater idea book. 171–72

Pinwheel knitted bedspread. Woman's Day decorative needlework for the home. 26–27

Plaid and white sheet bedroom ensemble. Woman's Day decorative needlework for the home. 33–34

Pouf coverlet, happy-face coverlet, memory coverlet, family coverlet. Brunner. Pass it on. 38–46

Quick-and-easy coverlet and pillowcases. Better Homes and Gardens applique. 20–21

Quick-and-easy coverlet and pillowcases, knitted bed cover and pillows, crocheted filet-patterned bed coverlet, crocheted bed throw. Better Homes and Gardens treasury of needlecrafts. 88–89, 208, 210–13, 220–21

Quilted coverlet. Golden book of hand and needle arts. 63

Quilted spread. McCall's sewing for your home. 194

Ruffled bedspread. Roda. Fabric decorating for the home. 132–33

Scalloped coverlet. McCall's sewing for your home. 196–97

Simple counterpane. Practical needlework. 171–73

Straight furrow pattern bedspread. Osler. Machine patchwork. 108–09

Sunshine patchwork bedspread. Baldwin. Scrap fabric crafts. 91–95

Rosette, trellis, jiffy, Irish rose, motif for bedspread or tablecloth, popcorn, fringed & popcorn squares. McCall's big book of knit & crochet for home & family. 196–215

Tailored bedspread and canopy. Roda. Fabric decorating for the home. 146–47

Tapestry bedspread. Wilson. Weaving you can use. 97–101

Throw spread and bolster. Reader's Digest complete guide to sewing. 472–73

Trapunto bedspread. Casselman. Crafts from around the world. 92–96

Bell pulls

Bell pull. Burchette. Needlework. 42–44

Birds-on-ivy bellpull. Scobey. Decorating with needlepoint. 112–13

Borders, banding and bell pulls. Wilson. Needleplay. 138–39

Butterfly bell-pull. Gostelow. Cross stitch book. 97–98

Chinese garden & butterflies bell pulls. Rogers. Needlepoint designs from Asia. 102–14

Crewel bell pull. Boyles. Margaret Boyles book of needle art. 118–24

Five appliqued and embroidered bellpulls. Woman's Day decorative needlework for the home. 148–53

Floral bell-pull. Christensen. Teach yourself needlepoint. 135–37

Four seasons bell pull. Christensen. Needlepoint. 56–60

French stitch bellpull. Orr. Now needlepoint. 182–85

Hangings. Miles. Designing with natural materials. 113–16

Hans Christian Anderson bell pull. Nielsen. Scandinavian embroidery, past and present. 68–69

Heralding angel bellpull. Lindberg. Counted cross-stitch designs for all seasons. 83–84

Macrame klockstrang. Meyer. Christmas crafts. 18–24

Norwegian eight-point rose bell pull. Nielsen. Scandinavian embroidery, past and present. 64–65

Peacock bell pull. Scobey. First easy-to-see needlepoint workbook. 52–56

Plum blossoms on pine-bark lattice bellpull, tortoiseshell lattice bellpull, joined-circle lattice bellpull. Nicoletti. Japanese motifs for needlepoint. 39–40, 55–58

Purple foxglove bell pull. Nielsen. Scandinavian embroidery, past and present. 86–87

Bellows
Bellows. Scurlock. Muzzleloader Magazine's book of buckskinning II. 204–06
Building leather lung bellows. Watson. Village blacksmith. 128–46
Goodwife bellows. Daniele. Building early American furniture. 69–70

Bells
Ceramic bell. Rockland. Hanukkah book. 62–64
Clay bells. Chroman. Potter's primer. 66–68
Melodious bells. Metalcrafting encyclopedia. 90–91

Belt clasps, ornaments, etc.
Belt buckles. Bovin. Jewelry making. 246–48
Belt buckles or nué (Italian shading). Wilson. Needlework to wear. 126–27
Buckles. Gehret. Rural Pennsylvania clothing. 216–21
Buckles. Giant book of metalworking projects. 207, 209–10
Enamelled belt buckle. Brightman. 101 practical uses for propane torches. 114–15
Enamelled rooster belt buckle. Mosesson. Jewelry craft for beginners. 255
Hopi Indian buckle. Powers. Crafting turquoise jewelry. 188–90
Making a belt buckle. Sprintzen. Jewelry basic techniques and design. 31–37
Pewter belt buckle. Mosesson. Jewelry craft for beginners. 184–88
Reinforcing a pewter belt buckle with fiberglass. Hollander. Plastics for jewelry. 175–81
Turquoise maiden belt buckles. Powers. Crafting turquoise jewelry. 185–87
Wooden belt buckle. Lee. Making wood and stone jewelry. 27–29
Wooden belt buckles. Huckleberry. How to make your own wooden jewelry. 118

Belts
Adjustable ribbon, man's stretch, striped canvas. Doherty. Family Circle book of 429 great gifts-to-make all year round for just 10¢ to $10.00. 63, 105, 116
Bangle belt, chain-latch belt, cupboard-hinge belt, macrame evening belt, felt flower cummerband, fancy fish belt, seashell belt, suede-cloth belt and scalloped evening belt. Farlie. Pennywise boutique. 88–97
Beaded belt. Auld. Tatting; the contemporary art of knotting with a shuttle. 95–96
Beadwork belt. Gostelow. Complete international book of embroidery. 44
Belt bazaar. Mills. The book of presents. 38–41
Belt made from six-pack holders. Epple. Something from nothing crafts. 108–09
Belts. Wilder. Secrets of eskimo skin sewing. 118
Belts: pink and black, striped velvet and plaited. Evans. Ribbonwork. 49–53
Bias tube belt. Brown. Super sweater idea book. 171
Bobbin lace sash. Golden book of hand and needle arts. 151–52
Braided belts. Giant book of crafts. 32
Bug belt, paper punch felt belt and "embroidered" belt. Farlie. Pennywise boutique. 161–65
Cross stitch butterfly belt. Encyclopedia of crafts. 114
Cummerbund. Burchette. More needlework blocking and finishing. 89–90
Cummerbund tie belt. Woman's Day bazaar best sellers. 47
Lace belt. Southard. Bobbin Lacemaking. 182–83
Ladder belt. Gill. Beadwork: the technique of stringing, threading, and weaving. 100–01
Leather belts. Latham. Leathercraft. 36–47
Leather belts. Rose. Illustrated encyclopedia of crafts and how to master them. 95–99
Leather belts. Time-Life Books. Novel materials. 60–69
Limpet belt. Logan. Shell crafts. 143–45
Lupe knot belt. Stearns. Macrame. 76–80
Making a leather belt with stones. Meyer. Rock tumbling. 84–85
Mexican bag-belt. Gostelow. Cross stitch book. 108–09

Patchwork belt. Wooster. Quiltmaking. 131
Pocket-packing belt. Woman's Day creative stitchery from scraps. 150–51
Rainbow belt in Osage braiding. Dendel. Basic book of fingerweaving. 53–54
Soft belts. Ruggieri. Woman's Day book of no-pattern sewing. 102–04
Spiralled flat wire belt and armband, wire-and-bead-decorated belt. Metalcrafting ency-
    clopedia. 175–76
Strips for belts and head-bands. Erlandsen. Bead book. 73
Suede and leather belt. Encyclopedia of crafts. 247
Threaded bead belts. Hulbert. Creative beadwork. 13, 32, 35
Tube belt or necklace; cords, twists, and braids; pop-in flower belts and jewelled belt.
    Wilson. Needlework to wear. 115–19, 130
Tunic belt. Stearns. Macrame. 26–29
Ultrasuede belt. Creative sewing. 15
Western belt. Latham. Leathercraft. 79–83
Wooden bead hip belt. Hulbert. Creative beadwork. 64–65
Wooden block belt. Huckleberry. How to make your own wooden jewelry. 117–18
Woven bead belt. Gill. Beadwork: the technique of stringing, threading, and weaving.
    144–46

Belts, Crocheted
Belt patterns. Dittrick. Hard crochet. 85–87
Belts. Henderson. Woman's Day book of designer crochet. 139–47
Crochet buckle belt. Woman's Day book of gifts to make. 33–34
Medieval belt and choker. Jacobs. Crochet book. 100–01
Three-pouch belt. Jacobs. Crochet book. 79–80

Belts, Embroidered
Kismet cummerbund. Woman's Day book of gifts to make. 199–200
Squares, clover leaf, diamonds, butterflies alight, & elegance at hand belts. Great
    cross-stitch. 110–15

Belts, Knitted
Belt made of coils knitted on a spool. Knitting techniques and projects. 42
Knitted belt. Feldman. Needlework boutique. 58, 60
Knitted belts. Selfridge. Patchwork knitting. 148
Reversible belts. Neighbors. Reversible two-color knitting. 158

Belts, Macrame
Adjustable belt. Golden book of hand and needle arts. 138–39
Bag and belt from one knot (macrame). Time-Life Books. Boutique attire. 140–41
Belt. Boberg. Macrame. 96
How to make the macrame belt. Scharf. Butterick's fast and easy needlecrafts. 68
Macrame belt. Kinney. How to make 19 kinds of American folk art. 55
Macrame belts. Stearns. Macrame. 34–42
Silver sash, beaded belt, man's belt, bib apron. Torbet. Macrame you can wear. 76–
    77, 80–81, 84–85, 104–05
Woman's macrame belt. Reader's Digest complete guide to needlework. 459

Belts, Metal
Coiled belt is twisted copper wire. Elliot. Working with copper. 67–68

Belts, Needlepoint
Apple belt. Arnold. Needlepoint pattern book. 156–59
Bargello belts. Christensen. Needlepoint and bargello stitchery. 60–63
Belt (needlepoint). Christensen. Needlepoint book. 115–16
Belts. Burchette. Needlework. 45–48
Canvas work belt. Encyclopedia of crafts. 74

Checkerboard bargello belt, diamond-pattern bargello belt. Farlie. Pennywise boutique. 182–84
Embroidered belt on rug canvas. Rosenthal. Not-so-nimble needlework book. 91–92
Hieroglyphs belt and beltbag. Fischer. Egyptian designs in modern stitchery. 142–48
How to make the bargello belt. Scharf. Butterick's fast and easy needlecrafts. 69–72
Man's belt. Reader's Digest complete guide to needlework. 189
Mod needlepoint-by-the-inch belt. Arnold. Needlepoint pattern book. 162–63
On the green and rainbow geometrics. Sheldon. Washable and dryable needlepoint. 106–07
Pre-finished belt. Christensen. Teach yourself needlepoint. 76
Tulip belt, heart sash, smiling face belt, sailboat belt and folded ribbon belt. Barnes. 120 needlepoint design projects. 54, 74, 106–07, 153
Zig zag chain belt with buckle & fringe and fly stitch chevron belt with cords. Orr. Now needlepoint. 191–92

Belts, Woven
Basic diagonal, double face or double weave belt. Brown. Weaving, spinning, and dyeing book. 40–44
Belt in Mexican double weaving. Dendel. Basic book of weaving. 84–85
Belts woven on the inkle loom, weft-faced belt. Holland. Weaving primer. 20–34, 39, 41, 177
Decorative woven band for a hat or belt. Weaving and spinning. 20
Double cloth sash (Bolivian). Brown. Weaving, spinning, and dyeing book. 81–86
Pick-up belt. Golden book of hand and needle arts. 133
Sash based on panajachel weaving. DeRodriguez. Weaving on a backstrap loom. 63–77
Sash with warp-face stripes and weft-face bands. Brown. Weaving, spinning, and dyeing book. 77–78
Taaniko belt. Smith. Taaniko, Maori hand-weaving. 34–53
Traditional Hopi belt. Brown. Weaving, spinning, and dyeing book. 63–64
Warp-face and warp-face with pickup pattern belts. Brown. Weaving, spinning, and dyeing book. 52–54
Weaving a belt. Thorpe. Elements of weaving. 22–35
Woven bead belt. Hulbert. Creative beadwork. 59
Woven ties and belts. Krevitsky. Shaped weaving. 90–91

Bench cushions
Art deco bench cushion. Scobey. Decorating with needlepoint. 63–65
Bargello hall-bench pad. Scobey. Decorating with needlepoint. 60–62
Bench pad. Burchette. More needlework blocking and finishing. 104–06
Easy-to-stitch bargello bench. Better Homes and Gardens treasury of needlecrafts. 252–53
Flowered-plaid vanity seat. Scobey. Decorating with needlepoint. 66–69
Piano bench cushion. Roda. Fabric decorating for the home. 83
Rose Kennedy's piano bench cover. Tillett. American needlework, 1776–1976. 90–93
Upholstered bench. Halliday. Decorating with crochet. 63–66

Benches
Antique bench. Spence. Woodworking tools, materials, processes. 604
Bathroom bench. DeCristoforo. Build your own wood toys, gifts and furniture. 362–65
Bench. Blandford. How to make early American and colonial furniture. 110–13
Benches to build for your deck: movable bench, potting bench. Popular Mechanics do-it-yourself encyclopedia. Vol. 2, 264–67
Block bench. Kangas. By hand. 129–31
Brick and redwood bench. Better Homes and Gardens. Step-by-step masonry & concrete. 75

Brick bench or table for outdoors. Decks and patios. 129–31
Build a handsome pine and maple bench. Popular Mechanics do-it-yourself encyclopedia. Vol. 1, 90–94
Built in benches. Built-ins. 74–83
Butcher block parson bench. Decks and patios. 133–34
Common bench. Moser. How to build Shaker furniture. 108–09
Contour deck bench. Better Homes and Gardens. Deck and patio projects you can build. 84
Dining bench. Langsner. Country woodcraft. 269–71
Fireplace bench, patio bench. Williams. Spanish colonial furniture. 74–81
Fireside bench, cobblers bench. Brann. How to build colonial furniture. 25–33, 89–122
Foyer bench. 101 do-it-yourself projects. 86–87
Garden benches, firepit benches, and deck-top bench. Wood projects for the garden. 58–61
Garden or folding bench. Braren. Homemade. 128–31
Hexagonal tree bench. Capotosto. Woodworking techniques and projects. 171–77
Making a patio bench. Outdoor projects for home and garden. 267–70, 447–58
Mudroom boot bench. Make it! don't buy it. 68–77
Non-sprung stool upholstery. Restoring and reupholstering furniture. 92–99
Oak high-backed settle. Taylor. How to build period country furniture. 155–59
Other seating. Blandford. Constructing outdoor furniture, with 99 projects. 91–128
Outdoor bench that converts to a table. 77 furniture projects you can build. 302–09
Outdoor benches. Family handyman handbook of carpentry plans/projects. 367–70
Park bench. Capotosto. Woodworking wisdom. 110–13
Pine side bench. Shea. Pennsylvania Dutch and their furniture. 160
Rattan bed bench. Alth. Rattan furniture. 105–18
Redwood patio bench. Better Homes and Gardens. Deck and patio projects you can build. 81
Seats around trees. Blandford. Constructing outdoor furniture, with 99 projects. 301–07
Settee, Eastward settee, continuous arm bench, inverted arm bench, love seat, and alienation bench. Moser. Windsor chairmaking. 81–91, 95
Settle, piano bench. Rubin. Mission furniture. 62–63, 77
Shaker bench. 77 furniture projects you can build. 29–36
Simple seats. Blandford. Constructing outdoor furniture, with 99 projects. 41–57
Stone bench. Proulx. Plan and make your own fences and gates, walkways, walls and drives. 118
Storage bench/cabinet. Philbin. Cabinets, bookcases & closets. 90–91
Storage couch. 77 furniture projects you can build. 92–95
Tote bench. Wood projects for the garden. 69
Trestle bench, bench. Brown. 44 terrific woodworking plans & projects. 189–90, 192
Wagon seat bench, love seat. Blandford. How to make early American and colonial furniture. 332–40
Wagon seat storage bench, Virginia wagon seat bench. Daniele. Building early American furniture. 154–55; 218–19
Water bench. Make your own antiques. 82
Wooden outdoor bench. Decks and patios. 131–33
Wraparound bench for a deck. Porches and patios. 128–30
Wrap-around seating. Popular Mechanics do-it-yourself encyclopedia. Vol. 8, 1181

Benches. *See also* **Children's furniture, Benches; Settees; Workbenches;**

Bending, Wood. *See* **Wood bending**

Berries. *See* **Seeds, berries, etc.**

Beverage holders
Beverage glass holder. Modern general shop. Metalworking. 102
Drink server, automobile pop caddy. Cope. Plastics. 46–47, 74

Bibs
Appliqued bib. Benton. Sewing classic clothes for children. 26–27
Appliqued bib with case. Golden book of hand and needle arts. 19
Appliqued bibs. Complete book of baby crafts. 94–97
Baby bib, burp bib. Gillies. Patterns for applique and pieced work—and ways to use them. 90–94
Baby's maxibib. Farlie. Pennywise boutique. 139–40
Baby's Santa bib. American School of needlework. Great Christmas crochet book. 117–18
Bandana bib. Coffey. Francine Coffey's celebrity sewing bee. 134
Bib. Practical needlework. 111–12
Cloth, bibs and pillows (egg yolk in center). Creative crafts yearbook: an exciting new collection of needlework and crafts. 150
Feeding bib for the bedfast. Goldsworthy. Clothes for disabled people. 93
Feeding set. Laury. Treasury of needlecraft gifts for the new baby. 85–87
Gifts for the baby to wear. Laury. Treasury of needlecraft gifts for the new baby. 33–39
I'm a Christmas angel bib. Wilson. Erica Wilson's Christmas world. 142–45
Presto baby bibs. Linsley. Great bazaar. 120–21
Quilted bib. Benton. Sewing classic clothes for children. 22–25
Tortoise and hare place mat and bib. Coffey. Francine Coffey's celebrity sewing bee. 139
Trims for the stretch-suit. Complete book of baby crafts. 90–93
Turtle bib; reversible bibs. Doherty. Family Circle book of 429 great gifts-to-make all year round for just 10¢ to $10.00. 161

Bicycle racks
Bicycle bag. Lamoreaux. Outdoor gear you can make yourself. 78–85
Bicycle bag. Ruggieri. Woman's Day book of no-pattern sewing. 107
Bicycle-basket carryall. Farlie. Pennywise boutique. 134–35
Bicycle bulk (storage racks). Garage, attic and basement storage. 14–15
Bike panniers. Houck. Big bag book. 71–73
Carrier transports family bikes, cart for your bike. Popular Mechanics do-it-yourself encyclopedia. Vol. 2, 300–03
PVC bicycle rack. 101 do-it-yourself projects. 276–77
Trail-bike carrier for your car. In Popular Mechanics do-it-yourself encyclopedia. Vol. 12, 1915
Wood-frame bike cart, freighter, bike wagon, covered wagon, buggy, touring cart, mini-wagon, booth. Sullivan. Cart book, with plans and projects. 139–203
Build a bicycle built for two. Popular Mechanics do-it-yourself encyclopedia. Vol. 2, 296–99

Billboards. See **Signs**

Billfolds. See **Wallets**

Billiard and pool tables
Cue-and-ball rack. Popular Mechanics do-it-yourself encyclopedia. Vol. 20, 3063
Pool cue and ball rack. Spence. Woodworking tools, materials, processes. 591
Pool table, space-saving bumper-pool table. Popular Mechanics do-it-yourself encyclopedia. Vol. 15, 2256–68

Bins
Dough bin. Shea. Pennsylvania Dutch and their furniture. 177
Stacking storage bins. Oberrecht. Plywood projects illustrated. 53–55
Storage bins. 101 do-it-yourself projects. 152–55
Tilting bins. Blandford. 53 space-saving built-in furniture projects. 142–45
Wire vegetable bin, swinging bin cabinet. Stevenson. How to build and buy cabinets
    for the modern kitchen. 130–31

Bird baths
Bird bath. Churchill. Backyard building book II. 99–101
Cement bird bath. Churchill. Big backyard building book. 208–10
Concrete birdbath. Schultz. How to attract, house and feed birds. 108–11

Bird cage
Bird cages in white willow & palembang. Maynard. Modern basketry from the start.
    163–66
Flight cages. La Barge. Pet house book. 112–19
Parakeet cage. Brann. How to build pet housing. 153–71
Pearce. Aviary design and construction.
Pedro's night "cover-up" (crocheted bird cage cover). Feldman. Needlework boutique.
    76–78
Perch tree. La Barge. Pet house book. 120–21

Bird feeders
Aluminum bird feeder. Metalcrafting encyclopedia. 156
Bird feeder. Brown. 44 terrific woodworking plans & projects. 201
Bird feeder. Churchill. Backyard building book II. 101–05
Bird feeder. Churchill. Big backyard building book. 210–14
Bird feeder. Hamilton. Build it together. 140–47
Bird feeder. Modern general shop. Metalworking. 111
Bird feeder. 101 do-it-yourself projects. 282–83
Bird feeders. Braren. Homemade. 139
Bird feeders. Schutz. How to attract, house and feed birds. 68–102
Bird feeding stations. Complete handyman do-it-yourself encyclopedia. 270–75
Bird houses and feeders. Blandford. Constructing outdoor furniture, with 99 projects.
    271–86
Cage feeder. La Barge. Pet house book. 122–25
Four-station bird feeder. automatic bird feeder, birdhouse replica of your house, barn
    birdhouse. Popular Mechanics do-it-yourself encyclopedia. Vol. 3, 331–37
Hanging bird table. Mills. The book of presents. 120–21
Pill bottle, plastic bottle, net bag bird feeders. Epple. Something from nothing crafts.
    118–22, 136–38, 195–96

Bird houses
Birdhouse. Braren. Homemade. 135–38
Birdhouse. Brown. 44 terrific woodworking plans & projects. 200–01
Bird house. 101 do-it-yourself projects. 284–85
Bird house. Self. Working with plywood, including indoor/outdoor projects. 210–14
Birdhouse from a hollow log. Johnson. Nature crafts. 22
Bird houses and feeders. Constructing outdoor furniture, with 99 projects. 271–86
Building and mounting birdhouses, predator guards for birdhouses. Lane. Building in
    your backyard. 15–44
Eight family purple martin house, two family bluebird house, wren house. Churchill.
    Backyard building book II. 93–99
Eight-family purple martin house, two-family bluebird house, wren house. Churchill. Big
    backyard building book. 202–08

40 plans for bird houses. Layton. 30 birds that will build in bird houses. 165–205
Gourd bird house. Mordecai. Gourd craft. 200–03
Pigeon house. Churchill. Backyard building book II. 39–45
Shelters. Schutz. How to attract, house and feed birds. 115–82
Small-bird chalet, large-bird nesting box. Oberrecht. Plywood projects illustrated. 201–06
Wood duck house. Giant book of metalworking projects. 218–19
Wren house. Modern general shop. Woodworking. 107

Birds

Bird carving. Beiderman. Beginner's handbook of woodcarving. 109–27
Bird designs to applique, glue to board or embroider. Hana. Embroidery. 71–76
Bird-shaped models. Warring. Balsa wood modelling. 24–25
Cowrie bird. Elbert. Shell craft. 79–86
Duck. Day. Complete book of rock crafting. 94–107
Eagle. Villiard. Art and craft of sand casting. 73
Fluffy string bird (yarn). Lyon. Arts and crafts objects children can make for the home. 27–28
Gift ribbon bird. Grainger. Creative papercraft. 124
Macau (soft sculpture). Hall. Sewing machine craft book. 112–15
Owl, American eagle, alighting American eagle, baby owl. Colletti. Art of woodcarving. 69–73, 79–83, 111–13
Pair of little love birds. Janitch. Candlemaking and decorations. 34
Pair of turtle doves and bird of paradise collages. Janitch. Collage; a step by step guide. 42–47
Petey the peacock puppet. Meilach. Macrame gnomes and puppets. 71–79
Scarecrow. Casselman. Crafts from around the world. 160–62
Shell birds. Logan. Shell crafts. 165–69
Shell-sheathed swan. Vanderbilt. Gloria Vanderbilt designs for your home. 145–46
Small bird figures. Hibbs. Straw sculpture. 72–73
Starr. Decoys of the Atlantic flyway.
Stylized bird. Ormond. American primitives in needlepoint. 96–102
Swimming swan, perching parrot, standing robin. Hutchings. Big book of stuffed toy and doll making. 130–43
Turkey call. Underhill. Woodwright's companion. 72–75

Birds, Carved

American goldfinch. Green. Carving realistic birds. 67, 69
American robin. Green. Carving realistic birds. 54–61
Bald eagle. McKellips. Practical pattern manual for woodcarving and other crafts. 91–93
Bird wood carving. Green. Carving realistic birds. 1–46
Blue jay. Green. Carving realistic birds. 66–68, 72–73
Bremen eagle. Upton. Woodcarver's primer. 62–70
Broad eagle. Upton. Woodcarver's primer. 30–38
Cardinal. Green. Carving realistic birds. 61–64
Scarlet tanager. Green. Carving realistic birds. 13–19
Stylized birds. Tangerman. Carving the unusual. 48–50
Scissor-tailed flycatcher. Green. Carving realistic birds. 64–66

Birth announcements
Baby birth keepsake. Baldwin. Scrap fabric crafts. 149–51
Birth certificate of Anna Titus. Ormond. American primitives in needlepoint. 61–80
Birth record sampler (embroidered). Boyles. Needlework gifts for special occasions. 140–44
Birth sampler. Christensen. Teach yourself needlepoint. 130–31
Cross-stitch sampler. Creative crafts yearbook: an exciting new collection of needlework and crafts. 42–43
Name and birth date panels. Laury. Treasury of needlecraft gifts for the new baby. 13–24

Blackboards
Blackboard. Adams. Make your own baby furniture. 174–75
Chalkboard and easel. Blandford. Giant book of wooden toys. 266–70

Blacksmithing
Axles for carriages. Richardson. Practical blacksmithing. Vol. 4, 101–58
Basic blacksmithing. Fine woodworking techniques 2. 32–35
Bealer. Art of blacksmithing.
Blacksmith shears. Richardson. Practical blacksmithing. Vol. 2, 239–44
Blacksmith shop. Bealer. Art of blacksmithing. 46–73
Blacksmithing. Lindsley. Metalworking in the home shop. 270–86
Blacksmithing. In make it! don't buy it. 238–57
Blandford. Practical handbook of blacksmithing and metalworking.
Building a forge. Watson. Village blacksmith. 101–27
Carriage-ironing, spring-making, and tire-welding. Complete guide to blacksmithing. 153–82
Complete guide to blacksmithing.
Dog head carving in hot steel. Meilach. Decorative and sculptural ironwork. 136–38
Erecting animals in iron. Meilach. Decorative and sculptural ironwork. 131–49
Horseshoeing. Complete guide to blacksmithing. 47–149
Lamination of Damascus steel. Meilach. Decorative and sculptural ironwork. 221
Making a log cabin swivel. Richardson. Practical blacksmithing. Vol. 3, 241–55
McRaven. Country blacksmithing.
Meilach. Decorative and sculptured ironwork.
Richardson. Practical blacksmithing.
Shoeing a horse. Watson. Village blacksmith. 69–79
Shoeing mules and oxes. Complete guide to blacksmithing. 150–52
Shop forge you can build. Popular Mechanics do-it-yourself encyclopedia. Vol. 12, 1819
Weygers. Modern blacksmith.

Blankets
Bindings worn, torn, frayed (repairing). Schuler. How to fix almost everything. 23
Blanket pattern. Murray. Essential handbook of weaving. 153
Blanket quilting. Frager. Quilting primer. 92–124
Crewel embroidered wool coverlet. McCall's big book of country needlecrafts. 218–20
Diamond twill and double-face saddle blankets. Brown. Weaving, spinning, dyeing book. 112–16
Double-width weft-face blanket. Brown. Weaving, spinning, and dyeing book. 187–88
Embroidered throw & floor pillows. Better Homes & Gardens embroidery. 16–18
Knitted patch blankets. Chatterton. Patchwork & applique. 138–40
Navajo blanket. Dudley. Strip patchwork: quick and easy patchwork using the Seminole technique. 78–80
Peasant embroidered robe. Casselman. Crafts from around the world. 110–11

Play sheet. Morgan. Trapunto and other forms of raised quilting. 191–94
Scintillating blanket/wall hanging. Jacobs. Crochet book. 163–65
Sweater blankets. Brown. Super sweater idea book. 199–200
Twill reversible throw, brushed and fulled double-width mohair blanket, basket weave throw. Brown. Weaving, spinning, and dyeing book. 190–92

Blankets, Electric
Electric blanket (repair). Schuler. How to fix almost everything. 23

Blankets, Infants
Baby blanket. Brown. Super sweater idea book. 191
Baby carriage cover. Scobey. First easy-to-see needlepoint workbook. 136–38
Baby coverlet (woven on mesh). Rosenthal. Not-so-nimble needlework book. 78–79
Baby shawl. Mensinga-Biasiny. Beautiful baby clothes to crochet, knit, sew and embroider. 100–01
Baby's birth-date blanket. Coffey. Francine Coffey's celebrity sewing bee. 122
Baby's blanket. Step by step to better knitting and crochet. 20–21
Bicentennial baby carriage blanket. Scheuer. Designs for Holbein embroidery. 74–75
Crocheted bold baby blanket. Woman's Day bazaar best sellers. 149
Crocheted crib blankets. Feldman. Big book of afghans. 138–46
Crocheted sleeping bag and blanket. Favorite knitting & crochet patterns. 18–21
Delicate air: a soft and simple child's shawl (crocheted). Feldman. Needlework boutique. 32–33
Eyelet-bound carriage blanket. Benton. Sewing classic clothes for children. 36–39
Knitted crib blankets. Feldman. Big book of afghans. 64–72
Mosaic-patterned baby blanket. Walker. Mosaic knitting. 194
Peasant blanket (crocheted). Mensinga-Biasiny. Beautiful baby clothes to crochet, knit, sew and embroidery. 41–42
Reversible baby blanket. Hubert. Weekend knitting projects. 18–19
Traditional choice. Favorite knitting & crochet patterns. 133–34

Blinds. See **Window shades**

Block printing
Block printing. Kicklighter. Crafts, illustrated designs and techniques. 40–47
Block printing. Treasury of things to make. 52–55
Block printing designs. Lyon. Arts and crafts objects children can make for the home. 188–90
Linocut: rubbing designs transfixed onto linoleum blocks. Firestein. Rubbing craft. 52–56
Linoleum block printing. Buxton. Craftmaking: for love or money. 77–83
Printmaking. Schuman. Art from many hands. 224–27
Wood-block printing. Rose. Illustrated encyclopedia of crafts and how to master them. 111–17

Blocks, Toys
Babies building blocks. Coffey. Francine Coffey's celebrity sewing bee. 140
Blocks, blocks, blocks. Peterson. Children's toys you can build yourself. 25–31
Boats and blocks. Laury. Handmade toys and games. 120–23
Building blocks. Adams. Make your own baby furniture. 154–55
Building blocks. Blandford. Giant book of wooden toys. 37–40
Building blocks. DeCristoforo. Build your own wood toys, gifts and furniture. 280–81
Cloth blocks. Hagans. All good gifts. 92
Crocheted blocks. Better Homes and Gardens easy bazaar crafts. 55, 61
Foam baby blocks. Reader's Digest complete guide to sewing. 491

Newspaper building blocks. Yoder. Sculpture and modeling for the elementary school. 65–66

Soft baby blocks. Wargo. Soft crafts for special occasions. 49–55

Soft blocks. Laury. Treasury of needlecraft gifts for the new baby. 120–22

Soft nursery blocks. Woman's Day creative stitchery from scraps. 144–45

Standard construction blocks. Dal Fabbro. How to make children's furniture and play equipment. 133–34

Swedish blocks. Boeschen. Successful playhouses. 97–98

Village blocks. Hundley. Folk art toys and furniture for children. 67–68

Wooden blocks with tray. Better Homes and Gardens treasury of Christmas crafts & foods. 251

Blouses

Afghanistan bodice. Wiseman. Cuts of cloth. 48–49

Barbary coast halter. Jacobs. Crochet book. 75–76

Basic cover-up. Morgan. Trapunto and other forms of raised quilting. 180–82

Batik peasant blouse. Anderson. Tie dyeing and batik. 72–75

Batik peasant blouse. Frame. Tie-dyeing and batik. 102–05

Bavarian blouse. Gostelow. Complete international book of embroidery. 114–15

Beaded lace blouse. Hulbert. Creative beadwork. 86

Becoming serious about fit: a tailored shirt with darts. Bradley. Design it, sew it and wear it. 62–72

Birds and bees, traditional charm, Balkan beauty, south of the border, Grecian doll. Great cross-stitch. 70–87

Blouse alterations. Goldsworthy. Clothes for disabled people. 60–72

Blouses (alterations & remodeling). Brock. Gladrags, redesigning, remaking, refitting all your old clothes. 110–49

Blouses to dresses. Zukerman. Get hooked. 95–115

Boat neck topper. Heard. Complete guide to quilting. 258–59

Bulgarian peasant blouse, floral display, & the delicate beauty of a rose-embroidery on blouses. Embroidery. 88–97

Crocheted tank top, lace shell. Woman's Day book of gifts to make. 82–83, 193–194

Crocheted tank top with applique hearts. Chatterton. Patchwork & applique. 108–09

Camisole. Ruggieri. Woman's Day book of no-pattern sewing. 85–86

Closer fit: a basic blouse and a tennis shirt. Bradley. Design it, sew it and wear it. 40–55

Crochet together peasant shirt. Holderness. Peasant chic. 52–57

Cross your tees with lace: scoop neck, split sleeve, camisole, jacket & blouson. Ruggieri. Woman's Day book of no-pattern sewing. 59–62

Dainty V-neck tee, flower-border tee, scallop-edge camisole, tank-type camisole, shell-pattern camisole. Woman's Day crochet showcase. 33–40

Danish cape dress/top. Holderness. Peasant chic. 122–28

Doily camisole. Jacobs. Crochet book. 107–10

Double dip t-shirt. Laury. Quilted clothing. 140–42

Drafting blouse patterns. Lewis. Patternless fashions. 87–103

Drawstring blouse, T-top blouse, everyone's bog shirt, butterfly blouse, Macedonian shirt, Mallory's blouse, peasant blouse. Beard. Fashions from the loom. 59, 62–63, 66–71

Egyptian kaftan. Gostelow. Complete international book of embroidery. 202–03

Folk art patchwork blouse. Baldwin. Scarp fabric crafts. 129–31

Front-lace blouse crocheted. Crochet. 18

Glamor enfolded in a tunic. Time-Life Books. Boutique attire. 28–31

Gold leaf camisole. Wilson. Needlework to wear. 74–75

Grand gesture of an overblouse. Time-Life Books. Boutique attire. 32–37

Halter top. Morgan. Trapunto and other forms of raised quilting. 178–79

Halter top, wool blouse. Holland. Weaving primer. 41, 112–13

Holiday overblouse. Farlie. Pennywise boutique. 59–61
Huipil blouse. Gostelow. Complete international book of embroidery. 20–21
Huipil with brocade design. Brown. Weaving, spinning, and dyeing book. 79–81
Improvising with shirts (restyling blouses). Time-Life Books. Personal touch. 74–85
Instructions for making the feather blouse. Time-Life Books. Boutique attire. 126–27
Japanese kapogi. Holderness. Peasant chic. 38–44
Kite. Lane. Maggie Lane's oriental patchwork. 64–68
Knitted body tube & sizzling sun tops. Favorite knitting & crochet patterns. 184, 197–200
Lulu overblouse. Holderness. Peasant chic. 45–48
Making a bodice. Scurlock. Muzzleloader Magazine's book of buckskinning II. 67–68
Making an embroidered blouse. Kmit. Ukrainian embroidery. 102–08
Mexican embroidered blouse. Holderness. Peasant chic. 58–63
Mexican juipil. Holderness. Peasant chic. 36–37
Mini-tank halter. Jacobs. Crochet book. 86–87
Multi-color bra top. Crochet. 79–82
Patchwork halter top. Scharf. Illustrated patchwork crochet. 165
Pattern for Mexican folk blouse (embroidered). Fraser. Modern stitchery: stitches, patterns, freeform designing. 82–83
Rainbow-sleeved, Irish lace, camisole and lacy white tops. Crochet. 54–59
Ribbed knit top and softly draped culottes. Time-Life Books. Separates that travel. 122–25
Russian blouses. Ley. Russian & other Slavic embroidery designs. 76–79
Scarf top. Time-Life Books. Decorative techniques. 86–89
Sew-easy chiffons (sheer). Ruggieri. Woman's Day book of no-pattern sewing. 52–56
Shapeless crocheted top; t-shirt trimmed with ribbons, nailheads, rhinestones, and crocheted yoke. Doherty. Family Circle book of 429 great gifts-to-make all year round for just 10¢ to $10.00. 59–61, 70–72
Shisha blouse. Gostelow. Complete international book of embroidery. 230–32
Short gown. Gehret. Rural Pennsylvania clothing. 33–44
Spring bouquets for a blouse, reembroidered lace, ruffled cameo, cutwork sailor collar, wisteria branch yoke and victorian lace blouse. Wilson. Needlework to wear. 66–70
Striped big-top, drawstring-top, aloha pop top, camisole and eyelet top. Ruggieri. Woman's Day book of no-pattern sewing. 39–44
Swirling capelet for a collar. Time-Life Books. Boutique attire. 42–44
Tank top. Evans. Ribbonwork. 35–37
Tie-dyed blouse and skirt. Anderson. Tie dyeing and batik. 32–35
Tie-dyed blouse and skirt. Frame. Tie-dyeing and batik. 38–41
Tie-dyed T-shirt. Anderson. Tie dyeing and batik. 40–43
Tie top. Ruggieri. Woman's Day book of no-pattern sewing. 83
Top and pinny, circle blouse, and handkerchief tops. Wiseman. Cuts of cloth. 18–19, 22–23, 32–33
Top from rectangles: a simple peasant blouse. Bradley. Design it, sew it and wear it. 1–15
Top of the evening. Ruggieri. Woman's Day book of no-pattern sewing. 57–58
Tops. Crown. How to recycle old clothes into new fashions. 5–20
Simple paddle wheeler. Complete handyman do-it-yourself encyclopedia. 1800–05
Victorian blouse. Jacobs. Crochet book. 125–28
Woman's textured top. Design crochet. 76–79
Woven halters. Krevitsky. Shaped weaving. 67–69
Wraparound halter, tieback halter, free and easy dashiki, blouse from a swirl of paisleys. Time-Life Books. Exotic styling. 55–59, 120–31, 169–71
Yugoslavian blouse. Gostelow. Complete international book of embroidery. 126–27

Blowers. *See* **Bellows**

Boat models
Acrylic sailboat. Cope. Plastics. 54–56
Boats. Jackson. Modelmaker's handbook. 304–28
Challenge of modeling fine ships. Popular Mechanics do-it-yourself encyclopedia. Vol. 17, 2642–46
A first-rate sailing yacht. Bumper book of things a boy can make. 147–49
Ships. Chesneau. Scale models in plastic. 150–62
Simple ship models. Warring. Balsa wood modelling. 26, 28–29, 32–39
Steamship. Milstein. Building cardboard toys. 39–43
Tugboat, sailboat, raft. Williams. Cookie craft: no-bake designs for edible party favors and decorations. 89–97

Boats
Boat building. Wagner. Modern woodworking. 385–91
Brann. How to build a kayak.
Build a simple plywood kayak. Popular Mechanics do-it-yourself encyclopedia. Vol. 10, 1588–92
Gardner. Building classic small craft.
How to repair a fiberglass boat, sailboat from a pram. Popular Mechanics do-it-yourself encyclopedia. Vol. 16, 2442–45, 2494–97
Pick the right propeller. Popular Mechanics do-it-yourself encyclopedia. Vol. 15, 2345–47
Pontoon boats, fun raft. Popular Mechanics do-it-yourself encyclopedia. Vol. 15, 2252–55
River raft. Bumper book of the things a boy can make. 83–84
Successful winter layup. Popular Mechanics do-it-yourself encyclopedia. Vol. 3, 370–72
Trailers, RVs and boats storage. Garage, attic and basement storage. 50–51
Vaitses. Covering wooden boats with fiberglass.

Boats, Painting
Painting your wooden boat. Scherer. Complete handbook of home painting. 163–69

Boats, Toys
Boats and blocks. Laury. Handmade toys and games. 117–20
Cabin cruiser, paddle wheel, sailboat, catamaran, super-sailor. Peterson. Children's toys you can build yourself. 57–67
Candle-powered boats. 101 do-it-yourself projects. 350–53
Paddle boat. Blizzard. Making wooden toys. 18–19
Paddle wheel boat, ocean liner, x-panded play sub, jet-powered underwater sled. Hodges. 46 step-by-step wooden toy projects. 116–36
Paddle wheel steamer, sailing sloop, ferryboat & cars. Baldwin. Old fashioned wooden toys. 54–64, 69–78
Solar electric toy boat. Calhoun. 20 simple solar projects. 224–33
Steamboat. Peterson. Children's toys you can build yourself. 137–38
Tugboat, speedboat, houseboat, pontoon boats, freighter. Maginley. Trains and boats and planes and . . . 119–34
Wheeled freighter. Blandford. Giant book of wooden toys. 94–99
Wooden submarines, sail boat. Favorite easy-to-make toys. 155–58, 176–82

Bola ties. *See* **Neckties**

Bolsters
Big striped bolster. Step by step to better knitting and crochet. 188–89
Bolsters. Jones. Fixing furniture. 172–73
Cylinder bolster cover. Rosenthal. Not-so-nimble needlework book. 34–35
Firecracker bolster. Slater. Elaine Slater's book of needlepoint projects. 152–53

Bolts and nuts
Bolt and rivet clippers. Richardson. Practical blacksmithing. Vol. 2, 59–78
Forging a hexagon bolt head. Weygers. Modern blacksmith. 31
Making a carriage bolt heading plate, decorative bolt heads. Weygers. Modern blacksmith. 35
Upsetting steel into bolt heads with an upsetting matrix. Weygers. Modern blacksmith. 34
What you should know about bolts. Popular Mechanics do-it-yourself encyclopedia. Vol. 3, 393–96

Bones
Carving bones. Tangerman. Carving the unusual. 102–04

Book binding. *See* **Bookbinding**

Book covers
Address book. Scobey. First easy-to-see needlework workbook. 46–48
Address book cover. Reader's Digest complete guide to needlework. 190
Bargello eyeglass case and checkbook cover. Christensen. Needlepoint and bargello stitchery. 72
Bargello paperback book cover. Scharf. Butterick's fast and easy needlecrafts. 181–83
Book cover. Breckenridge. Lap quilting. 70–71
Book cover (needlepoint). Christensen. Needlepoint book. 118–19
Book covers. Burchette. Needlework. 49–51
Book covers. Roda. Fabric decorating for the home. 69
Checkbook cover. Burchette. Needlework. 108–09
Checkbook cover. Christensen. Teach yourself needlepoint. 90–91
Decorated loose-leaf folders. Elbert. Paperworks. 17–19
Design binder for embroidery. Gostelow. Cross stitch book. 65–66
Embroidered notebook cover, bead embroidered book cover. Encyclopedia of crafts. 109, 133
Fabric book covers. Hagans. All good gifts. 21–23
Magazine cover. Cane, rush and straw. 60–61
Nostalgic bouquet album cover (embroidered). McCall's book of America's favorite needlework and crafts. 85–86
Old notebook covers. Romberg. Let's discover papier-mâché. 48
Paperback book cover. Coffey. Francine Coffey's celebrity sewing bee. 156
Patchwork cover. Evans. Ribbonwork. 102–05
Photo album cover and paperback book cover. Linsley. Great bazaar. 67, 118–19
Prayer book cover. Christensen. Needlepoint and bargello stitchery. 88–89
Recipe-book cover, telephone book cover. Coffey. Francine Coffey's celebrity sewing bee. 79–80
Rose baby cross-stitch book cover. Gault. Needlepoint dragons and other mythical creatures. 72–74
Rose scroll memory book. Ambuter. Carolyn Ambuter's needlepoint celebrations. 34–35
Scrapbook cover (needlepoint). Christensen. Needlepoint book. 111–13
Stars and stripes, tulips, cherries, paisley, zebra skin, dog, pink elephant & turtle checkbook covers. Barnes. 120 needlepoint design projects. 22, 53, 90, 146, 158–60
Telephone book cover. Goldman. Decorate with felt. 96
Telephone book cover. Vanderbilt. Gloria Vanderbilt designs for your home. 111–12
Unpadded scrap book cover. Roda. Fabric decorating for the home. 97
Woven guest book. Tod. Joy of hand weaving. 293–96
Yellow pad cover. Burchette. More needlework blocking and finishing. 138–42

Book covers. *See also* **Albums**

Book rests. *See* **Bookracks**

Book shelves. *See* **Bookcases**

Bookbinding
Binding a paperback. Paper. 107–09
Binding magazines. Paper. 111–14
Bookbinding. Treasury of things to make. 86–90
Bookbinding. Whatnot. 92–93
Books. Introduction to repairing and restoring. 10–55
How to bind books: bookbinder's press. Bumper book of things a boy can make. 22–31
Japanese way to make a booklet. Schuman. Art from many hands. 117–20
Making a booklet. Geary. Plant prints and collages. 62–63
Making a sewing frame for binding. Paper. 114
Note pad binding. Linsley. Great bazaar. 71–72

Bookcases
All kinds of book shelves, inside-the-wall bookcase, walk-in bookcase closet. Popular Mechanics do-it-yourself encyclopedia. Vol. 3, 396–405
Book trough, bookcase. Rubin. Mission furniture. 83–85
Bookcase. Adams. Make your own baby furniture. 178–83
Bookcase. Alth. Making plastic pipe furniture. 123–28
Bookcase. Blandford. 66 children's furniture projects. 208–14
Bookcase. Brown. 44 terrific woodworking plans & projects. 156–61
Bookcase/bar divider, floating bookwall. Family handyman handbook of carpentry plans/projects. 161–70
Bookcase for paperbacks and tapes. Philbin. Cabinets, bookcases & closets. 130–31
Bookcase on a stone planter. Family handyman handbook of carpentry plans/projects. 237–39
Bookcase plus. Philbin. Cabinets, bookcases & closets. 122–23
Book case plus magazine display shelves. Philbin. Cabinets, bookcases & closets. 124–25
Bookcase with desk. Brann. How to build colonial furniture. 157–73
Bookcases. Leavy. Bookshelves and storage units. 72–77
Bookcases. Syvanen. Interior finish: more tricks of the trade. 114–15
Bookcases and bookshelves. Hedden. Successful shelves and built-ins. 29–43
Bookcases to frame a mirror or window. Brann. How to construct built-in and sectional bookcases. 56–65
Bookshelf projects. Clifford. Basic woodworking and carpentry . . . with projects. 200–08
Coffee table/bookcase; bookcase and shelves. Waugh. Handyman's encyclopedia. 408–09, 412–13
Corner bookcase. Brann. How to construct built-in and sectional bookcases. 52–55
Corner bookcase/cabinet, unit glass-door bookcase. Blandford. 53 space-saving built-in furniture projects. 168–74, 179, 182–88
Early American bookcase, jointed hardwood bookcase, built-in bookcase. 101 do-it-yourself projects. 62–71, 214–17
Easy-up bookshelves, bookcase/entertainment center. Oberrecht. Plywood projects illustrated. 130–33, 155–59
Free standing bookcase. Brann. How to construct built-in and sectional bookcases. 27–40
Large composite bookcase. Egge. Recycled with flair. 163–65

Modular bookcase, bookcase cabinet. Dal Fabbro. How to make children's furniture and play equipment. 66–69
Open end case. Brann. How to construct built-in and sectional bookcases. 45–51
Paperback shadowbox. Oberrecht. Plywood projects illustrated. 79–81
Plans for a bookcase. Geary. How to design and build your own workspace—with plans. 26–32
Poor man's dowel furniture. Blackwell. Johnny Blackwell's poor man's catalog. 125
Portable lectern bookcase. Complete handyman do-it-yourself encyclopedia. 344–47
Rejuvenate bookcase with woodburning. Broadwater. Woodburning: art and craft. 101–03
Sectional bookcases. Brann. How to construct built-in and sectional bookcases. 41–44
Sentinel bookcase, open bookcase, and bookcase. Williams. Spanish colonial furniture. 24–29
Seventeenth century book press. Taylor. How to build period country furniture. 85–90
Traditional bookcase. Spence. Woodworking tools, materials, processes. 599
Wall-to-wall bookcase with drawers. Brann. How to construct built-in and sectional bookcase. 79–95
Wall-to-wall bookcases. Brann. How to construct built-in and sectional bookcases. 7–26

Bookends. *See* **Bookracks**

Bookmarks
Amour bookmark. Svinicki. Old-fashioned crochet. 63–64
Bookmark (hardanger embroidery). Golden book of hand and needle arts. 82
Bookmark I and II. Burchette. More needlework blocking and finishing. 107–09
Bookmark pattern (embroidered). Fraser. Modern stitchery: stitches, patterns, free-form designing. 93
Bookmarks. Evans. Ribbonwork. 20–26
Bride's prayer book marker. Janitch. Candlemaking and decorations. 49
Cherries galore. Great cross-stitch. 129
Christian bookmarks. Hagans. All good gifts. 24–25
Crochet, felt, assisi, cross-stitch and needlepoint bookmarks. Creative crafts yearbook: an exciting new collection of needlework and crafts. 110–12
Decorative borders for cards, bookmarks and table match-boxes. Gordon. Complete guide to drying and preserving flowers. 73–77
Dried flower bookmark. O'Neill. Make-it-merry Christmas book. 43
Embroidered rose bookmarker. Embroidery of roses. 104
Four strand plaited bookmark. Grainger. Creative papercraft. 114
Granny bookmark. American School of Needlework. Great crochet bazaar book. 123
Hair-clip bookmark (felt mitten shape). Coffey. Francine Coffey's celebrity sewing bee. 157
Lace bookmark. Southard. Bobbin lacemaking. 184–85
Novel bookmark. Bumper book of things a girl can make. 151
Pressed-flower bookmark. Linsley. Great bazaar. 53
Rosebud bookmark. Lindberg. Counted cross-stitch designs for all seasons. 43
Weaving a bookmark. Tod. Joy of weaving. 24–34
Woven bookmarks. Encyclopedia of crafts. 54–55

Bookracks
Book cradle, cookbook/recipe holder. Capotosto. Woodworking techniques and projects. 89–94
Book rack. Cope. Plastics. 40–41
Book rack. Hamilton. Build it together. 90–97
Book rest. Mills. The book of presents. 128
Book trough. Blandford. 66 children's furniture projects. 94–96

Bookends. Burchette. More needlework blocking and finishing. 80–83
Bookends. Goldman. Decorate with felt. 91
Bookends. Hagans. All good gifts. 26–28
Bookends. Miles. Designing with natural materials. 118–19
Bookends. Modern general shop. Woodworking 105
Book ends. Romberg. Let's discover papier-mâché. 39
Bookends (needlepoint). Christensen. Needlepoint book. 120–21
Bookends, wine labeled wooden brick bookends. Doherty. Family Circle book of 429
  great gifts-to-make all year round for just 10¢ to $10.00. 3–4, 51
Bookrack. Blandford. 66 children's furniture projects. 92–94
Bookrack. Modern general shop. Woodworking 91–92
Botanical-print bookends. Scobey. Decorating with needlepoint. 175–77
Carved bookend. Gottshall. Wood carving and whittling for everyone. 40–47
Carved rooster bookends. Lubkemann. Carving twigs and branches. 83
Cookbook caddy. Popular Mechanics do-it-yourself encyclopedia. Vol. 10, 1597
Cookbook rack with drawer. Brown. 44 terrific woodworking plans & projects. 143–46
Chunky resin bookends. Encyclopedia of crafts. 212
Cookbook stand. Doherty. Family Circle book of 429 great gifts-to-make all year round
  for just 10¢ to $10.00. 134–35
Doll-face bookends. Woman's Day creative stitchery from scraps. 48–50
Dowel book rack. Blackwell. Johnny Blackwell's poor man's catalog. 122
Folding booklet rack. Blandford. 66 children's furniture projects. 104–06
Lighted dictionary stand, desktop book trough, pair of bookends, workshop plan stand.
  Oberrecht. Plywood projects illustrated. 49–52, 210–12, 216–17, 223–25
Metal tabletop bookrack. Popular Mechanics do-it-yourself encyclopedia. Vol. 15, 2364
Novel bookends. Bumper book of things a girl can make. 117–18
Page turner, page restrainer, book rest. Grainger. Making aids for disabled living. 20–
  25
Paper book-end. Grainger. Creative papercraft. 116–18
Personalized bookends, initial bookends, colonial bookrack, book-go-round for your
  desk, tabletop bookrack. Popular Mechanics do-it-yourself encyclopedia. Vol. 3,
  406–15
Pine book rack. Woman's Day book of gifts to make. 178–80
Plexiglas cookbook holder. Popular Mechanics do-it-yourself encyclopedia. Vol. 14,
  2210
Reading stand, book stand with metal legs, tall pedestal-base book stand. Egge.
  Recycled with flair. 176–82
Rock bookends. Vane. Pebble people, pets & things. 156–58
Shell bookends. Meras. Vacation crafts. 73
Veneer overlay: bird bookends. D'Amato. Italian crafts. 85–87
Woodburned bookend. Broadwater. Woodburning, art and craft. 104–05
Wooden initial bookends. Dal Fabbro. How to make children's furniture and play equip-
  ment. 86

Books
Child's quilt book. Baldwin. Scrap fabric crafts. 38–50
Counting book, picture book (fabric). Laury. Treasury of needlecraft gifts for the new
  baby. 126–31
Fabric book. Favorite easy-to-make toys. 86–90

Books. See also **Albums**

Boomerangs
Boomerang construction. Blackwell. Johnny Blackwell's poor man's catalog. 151–54

Booties
Baby booties (leather and fur). Wilder. Secrets of Eskimo skin sewing. 41–46
Bunny booties. Woman's Day bazaar best sellers. 66
Little Mary Janes (crocheted). Evrard. Twinkle-toes. 55–57
Pastel pixie, bold, jolly green giant, elf, & furry booties. Woman's Day crochet show-
case. 122–25
Trims for the stretch suit. Complete book of baby crafts. 90–93

Boots. *See* **Shoes**

Boring machinery. *See* **Drilling and boring machinery**

Bottle covers
Bottle corner. Burchette. More needlework blocking and finishing. 84–88
Crocheted bottle cover, macrame bottle cover. Scharf. Butterick's fast and easy
needlecrafts. 112–17
Crocheted bottle covers. McCall's book of America's favorite needlework and crafts.
382–83
Gift-wrapped wine and dressed-up bottle. Linsley. Great bazaar. 93, 139–40
Hot water bottle cover. Bumper book of things a girl can make. 133–34
Papier mâché over bottles and cans. Giant book of crafts. 391–95
Raffia basket for wine bottle. Encyclopedia of crafts. 240
Ropecraft cover for bottles and jars. Blandford book of traditional handicrafts. 11–14
Rosebud cover, rose cover. McCall's big book of country needlecrafts. 203–04

Bottle racks
Aid to hold bottles for mosaic application. Anderson. Crafts and the disabled. 40–41
Baby's bottle holder. American School of Needlework. Great crochet bazaar book. 15–
16
Easy way to store bottles. Family handyman handbook of home imporvement and
remodeling. 15–16
Urine bottle rack. Grainger. Making aids for disabled living. 45–47
Wine rack has a handy tray. Popular Mechanics do-it-yourself encyclopedia. Vol. 3,
424

Bottles
Building houses in bottles. Popular Mechanics do-it-yourself encyclopedia. Vol. 3,
422–23
Bottle cutting. Kicklighter. Crafts, illustrated designs and techniques. 48–55
Bottles. Rhodes. Pottery form. 49–53
Bottles that blossom. Linsley. Great bazaar. 138
Making a bottle shape. Ceramics. 72–77
Making a large bottle. Howell. Craft of pottery. 54–56, 66
Papier mâché bottle shapes. Elbert. Paperworks. 103–05
Pottery bottles. Campbell. Using the potter's wheel. 64–67
Sauce-bottle holder with lid. Sainsbury. Sainsbury's woodturning projects for dining.
76–80
Throwing a bottle. Howell. Craft of pottery. 33–35, 45
Turning a bottle stopper. Sainsbury. Craft of woodturning. 167–68
Wine-bottle. Sainsbury. Sainsbury's woodturning projects for dining. 89–91

Bow and arrow
Feathers off or damaged arrows (repair). Schuler. How to fix almost everything. 12
Flatbow and arrow making. Norbeck. Book of authentic Indian life crafts. 220–25
Making a bow and arrows. Bumper book of things a boy can make. 42–44
Miniature bows and arrows. Lubkemann. Carving twigs and branches. 68–69

Bow and arrow. *See also* **Quivers**

Bowls
Blue champleve dish. Metal and enamel. 128–30
Bowl: basic processes. Howell. Craft of pottery. 56–57, 66
Bowls. Rhodes. Pottery form. 67–80
Bowls. Romberg. Let's discover papier-mâché. 36
Carved wood snack dish. Popular Mechanics do-it-yourself encyclopedia. Vol. 4, 605
Decorative bowls. Cope. Plastics. 87–89
Flat based. outward curving and wide-topped thrown bowls, dish with vertical sides.
    Ceramics. 54–56, 58
Fruit bowl. Rockland. Hanukkah book. 153–54
Glass bottle, snack, papier mâché, plastic bottle. condiment server. Epple. Something
    from nothing crafts. 19, 22–23, 76–79, 125–26
Hand-formed bowl. Marshall. Foilcraft. 115
Hors d'oeuvre dishes. Ceramics. 32–33
Huichol beaded bowls. Sayer. Crafts of Mexico. 88–91
Make a coil bowl inside a plaster mold. Priolo. Ceramics by coil. 36
Making a soldered ring bowl. Newman. Wire art. 110–12
Papier mâché bowls. Giant book of crafts. 383, 387–88
Starfish dish. Elbert. Shell craft. 234–35
Nut bowl. DeCristoforo. Build your own wood toys, gifts and furniture. 326–28
Pottery bowls and trimming. Campbell. Using the potter's wheel. 22–31
Serving dish. Campbell. Using the potter's wheel. 80–81
Throwing deep and flat plates. Woody. Pottery on the wheel. 180–85
Thrown bowl. Howell. Craft of pottery. 40–41, 45
Thrown bowl. Pottery step-by-step. 27–28
Turning a bowl. Ceramics. 59–63
Wax-lined gourd bowl. Johnson. Nature crafts. 117
Yarn bowls dipped in a glue glaze. Doherty. Family Circle book of 429 great gifts-to-
    make all year round for just 10¢ to $10.00. 6–7

Bowls, Metal
Beating a copper bowl. Elliot. Working with copper. 31–38
Brass bowl. Metalcrafting encyclopedia. 161–62
Free-form metal dishes. Giant book of metalworking projects. 201–02
Sinking a bowl, making a bowl by raising with crimping, making a bowl by raising
    without crimping, stretching a gravy boat. Finegold. Silversmithing. 297–307, 330–
    71, 415–27
Swan dish. Kramer. Wirecraft. 68–69

Bowls, Wooden
Carved fruit bowl. Gottshall. Wood carving and whittling for everyone. 97–99
Checkered bowls, bowl gouge, bowl turning, green bowls. Fine woodworking tech-
    niques I. 134–44, 149–51
Contemporary salad bowl. Hodges. Woodturning handbook—with projects. 192–94
Fruit bowl and dish. Sainsbury. Sainsbury's woodturning projects for dining. 92–97
Grapefruit dish. Sainsbury. Sainsbury's woodturning projects for dining. 28–33
Laminated bowls. Fine woodworking techniques II. 140–41
Making PEG-treated wood bowls. Spielman. Working green wood with PEG. 80–90
Nut bowl with waste rim. Sainsbury. Sainsbury's woodturning projects for dining. 112–
    16
Nut dish with pick container. Sainsbury. Sainsbury's woodturning projects for dining.
    117–21
Segmented ring construction, laminated bowls, stave construction. Nish. Creative
    woodturning. 148–71

Side salad bowls in teak. Sainsbury. Sainsbury's woodturning projects for dining. 52–58

Soup bowl in teak. Sainsbury. Sainsbury's woodturning projects for dining. 34–36

Striped bowl. Popular Mechanics do-it-yourself encyclopedia. Vol. 11, 1655

Sugar bowl. Sainsbury. Sainsbury's woodturning projects, for dining. 133–35

Turned bowls and trays. Modern general shop. Woodworking 107

Turning a bowl, shallow dish. Sainsbury. Craft of woodturning. 105–10, 118–23

Turning a bowl with edge-decorated plugs, with plugs on the face and edges, or with plugs inserted into plugs. Sainsbury. Woodworking projects with power tools. 81–84

Turning a deep bowl, turning a shallow bowl. Nish. Creative woodturning. 116–27

Boxes

Antler box. Johnson. Nature crafts. 20

Bark boxes. Langsner. Country woodcraft. 217–22

Bead-covered box (glued). Hulbert. Creative beadwork. 90

Beaded boxes. Hulbert. Creative beadwork. 86

Beaded trinket box lid. Hulbert. Creative beadwork. 62–63

Beribboned band boxes. Evrard. Homespun crafts from scraps. 151–54

Beveled box. Isenberg. How to work in beveled glass. 199–201

Black and gilded boxes, shell box, bonbonnieres. Whatnot. 52–59, 99–101, 156–59

Calico baskets. Woman's Day decorative needlework for the home. 144–45

Candle box. Shea. Pennsylvania Dutch and their furniture. 186

Cardboard storage box. Palmer. Making children's furniture and play structures. 12–13

Carved boxes. Gottshall. Wood carving and whittling for everyone. 48–58

Carved wood trinket box. Popular Mechanics do-it-yourself encyclopedia. Vol. 4, 605–06

Clay boxes, papier mâché gift egg. Encyclopedia of crafts. 205–06

Collage top box, rickrack striped box. Creative sewing. 82

Compartments for boxes. Paper. 90

Constructing a box. Finegold. Silversmithing. 377–91

Decorated cube. Vanderbilt. Gloria Vanderbilt designs for your home. 172–73

Decorating a covered box. Marshall. Foilcraft. 56–59

Decoupaging a wooden box. Paper. 95–97

Early American band boxes, fancy gift boxes. Perry. Holiday magic. 82–89, 182

Early American fruit box. Woman's Day book of weekend crafts. 29–31

Enamelled box. Elliot. Working with copper. 95–96

Fabric boxes. Encyclopedia of crafts. 120–21

Fabric covered; fabric appliqued; pine tissue boxes. Doherty. Family Circle book of 429 great gifts-to-make all year round for just 10¢ to $10.00. 6, 45, 128

French fitting, bandsaw boxes, flip-open box from one piece of wood. Fine woodworking techniques 4. 179–81, 184–87, 191

Geometric marquetry box (straw). Johnson. Nature crafts. 98

Gold-leafed dragon box and bird tray. McCall's book of America's favorite needlework and crafts. 363–66

Hanging boxes. Blandford. How to make early American and colonial furniture. 138–43

How to make a box of plywood. Waugh. Handyman's encyclopedia. 388–95

Jody's needlepoint box. Christensen. Needlepoint. 53–56

Lace applique-gift box. Better Homes and Gardens applique. 54

Lace applique gift box. Better Homes and Gardens treasury of needlecrafts. 125

Lace boxes. Better Homes and Gardens treasury of Christmas crafts & foods. 173–74

Lacquered wooden box. Sayer. Crafts of Mexico. 72–75

Landis Valley candle box. Daniele. Building early American furniture. 131–32

Leather; wooden decoupage. Giant book of crafts. 286–87, 356–65

Lidded, covered box, padded plaid box. Woman's Day bazaar best sellers. 108, 119

Lyre and cross box top and griffin box top. Barnes. 120 needlepoint design projects. 136–37

Making a box and cover. Elbert. Paperworks. 135–36

Making a slab box. Howell. Craft of pottery. 76–77

Metal foil decorated boxes. Metalcrafting encyclopedia. 156–58

Molding chest (wooden box made from common crown molding). Capotosto. Woodworking techniques and projects. 114–18

Mosaic, floral table, gift wrap covered boxes. Epple. Something from nothing crafts. 54–55, 79–81, 85–86

Padded fabric boudoir boxes, bandboxes, embroidered chest. McCall's big book of country needlecrafts. 60–61, 270–72, 281–84

Paper patchwork boxes. Encyclopedia of crafts. 28

Patchwork box. Blandford book of traditional handicrafts. 109–13

Patchwork covered box. Ives. Ideas for patchwork. 82–85

Recipe box. Daniele. Building early American furniture. 127–28

Recipe box. Linsley. Custom made. 63–65

Sea serpent and pegasus cross-stitch fabric boxes. Gault. Needlework dragons and other mythical creatures. 100–05

Sequin-covered gift boxes. Doherty. Family Circle book of 429 great gifts-to-make all year round for just 10¢ to $10.00. 52–53

Sheet-metal shell tote. Giant book of metalworking projects. 69–72

Shell boxes, stick-on cache-pot made from shells cast in plastic resin, slab box or container. Elbert. Shell craft. 90–103, 188–91, 229–31

Show-off boxes. Elbert. Paperworks. 149–52

Slab boxes. Chroman. Potter's primer. 95

Small embossed aluminum or tin box. Schuman. Art from many hands. 163–67

Small turned wooden boxes. Fine woodworking techniques 2. 125–27

Stenciled boxes, ribbon box and paper patchwork box. Linsley. Great bazaar. 68–70, 162–63, 168–69

Straw marquetry box. D'Amato. Italian crafts. 96–98

Stuffed fabric box with patchwork top. Newman. Sewing machine embroidery stitch. 169–72

Sunburst box, Victorian medallion box, round plaster box. Logan. Shell crafts. 63–69

Sunflower box (straw). Johnson. Nature crafts. 99

Tiny patchwork boxes. Creative crafts yearbook: an exciting new collection of needlework and crafts. 135–36

Treasure chest. Popular Mechanics do-it-yourself encyclopedia. Vol. 9, 1355

Tricket box. Elbert. Paperworks. 138–40

Trinket box. Romberg. Let's discover papier-mâché. 44–46

Veneered and decorated boxes. Hobbs. Veneer craft for everyone. 133–35

Wall boxes and spoon rack. Shea. Pennsylvania Dutch and their furniture. 188–89

Wire in epoxy decorative box. Newman. Wire art. 148–50

Wooden glove box. Gotshall. Provincial furniture design and construction. 1–6

Woven fabric covered box for trinkets. Tod. Joy of hand weaving. 298–300

Boxes, Cardboard

Boxes with separate flopped lids, petal boxes. Paper. 85–87

Making round boxes with covering. Paper. 91

Making your own boxes. Paper. 82–83

Square boxes with lids, decorative paper cover, and lining. Paper. 89–90

Boxes, Decoupage

Davis. Step-by-step decoupage. 29–34

Decoupage boxes. Mills. The book of presents. 57

Decoupage doily box. Jarnow. (Re)do it yourself. 130–31
Decoupage treasures. McCall's book of America's favorite needlework and crafts. 406–09
Decoupage trinket box. Jarnow. (Re)do it yourself. 133
Pressed-rose box, recipe file and trinket boxes. Linsley. Great bazaar. 50–52, 54–56
Wooden baby box. Linsley. Decoupage on glass, wood, metal, rocks, shells, wax, soap, plastic, canvas, ceramic. 44–49

Boxes, Embroidered
Cross-stitch boxes. Better Homes and Gardens easy bazaar crafts. 15, 21
"Embroidered" embroidery box. Doherty. Family Circle book of 429 great gifts-to-make all year round for just 10¢ to $10.00. 50
Little girl's needlework box, embroidered trinket or jewel box. Tyler. Big book of soft toys. 253–56

Boxes, Needlepoint
Bargello boxes. Wilson. Needleplay. 127
Box top (needlepoint). Christensen. Needlepoint book. 121–23
Embroidered box. Evans. Ribbonwork. 72–75
Inlaid boxes. Scobey. First easy-to-see needlepoint workbook. 132–35
Mosaic-pattern jewel box, metal thread and inlay box, raffia stitching bargello-basket. Better Homes and Gardens treasury of needlecrafts. 278–79, 292–97
Needlework box. Ambuter. Carolyn Ambuter's needlepoint celebrations. 154–55

Boxes, Wood
Colonial trinket cabinet. Spence. Woodworking tools, materials, processes. 594
Gift boxes. Hamilton. Build it together. 134–39
How to veneer small boxes. Hobbs. Veneering simplified. 77–81
Making boxes. Warring. Balsa wood modelling. 7–8
Ornamented wooden box. Hibbs. Straw sculpture. 80
Small round boxes. Nish. Creative woodturning. 140–43
Stenciled wood boxes. Better Homes and Gardens treasury of Christmas crafts & foods. 106–07
Trinket box. Modern general shop. Woodworking 89. 90
Turned miniature boxes, layered boxes. Sainsbury. Woodworking projects with power tools. 31–48
Turning a box, ring box. Sainsbury. Craft of woodturning. 111–17, 146–47

Bracelets
Bangle bracelets of married metals. Sprintzen. Jewelry, basic techniques and design. 110–11
Bead and leather bangle bracelet. Hulbert. Creative beadwork. 87–88
Beaded wrist strap. Hulbert. Creative beadwork. 64
Bracelet construction. Bovin. Jewelry making. 235–43
Bracelet forming. Powers. Crafting turquoise jewelry. 114–16
Bracelets and napkins rings. Bird. Craft of Hawaiian lauhala weaving. 71–79
Bracelets (infants). Laury. Treasury of needlecraft gifts for the new baby. 47–48
Button bracelet. Mosesson. Jewelry craft for beginners. 48–49
Cabochon bracelet. Mosesson. Jewelry craft for beginners. 222–24
Climbing rope and ribbon bracelets. Wilson. Needlework to wear. 24–25
Coiled bracelet in 16 gauge copper wire. Elliot. Working with copper. 62, 67
Copper wire bracelet. Elliot. Working with copper. 69–71
Cube bead bracelet. Davies. Beads as jewelry. 92

Decorating a springy fiberglass bracelet with epoxy and pewter. Hollander. Plastics for jewelry. 183–91

Enamel bangle. Metal and enamel. 95

Flower silver bracelet. Powers. Crafting turquoise jewelry. 179–81

Fringed woven bead bracelet. Hulbert. Creative beadwork. 54

How to make an etched copper bracelet. Elliot. Working with copper. 78

Large center bracelet, bead bracelet, three-row bracelets using rocaille beads and different centers, woven bracelet with center cord, chevron bracelet with looped edge, bracelets with shaped fringe. Gill. Beadwork: the technique of stringing, threading, weaving. 52–54, 78–79, 101–04, 164–72

Looped-wire and bead bracelet. Metalcrafting encyclopedia. 167–68

Macrame bracelet. Torbet. Macrame you can wear. 69

Magazine & papier mâché bracelets. Epple. Something from nothing crafts. 65–66, 72–74

Making a bangle bracelet. Sprintzen. Jewelry, basic techniques and design. 23–28

Making a forged bracelet. Meilach. Decorative and sculptural ironwork. 238–39

Metal bracelet. Brightman. 101 practical uses for propane torches. 110–12

Multistrand bracelet. Mosesson. Jewelry craft for beginners. 24

Multistrand threaded bracelet. Mosesson. Jewelry craft for beginners. 28–29

Needlepoint rose bracelet and earring. Embroidery of roses. 109

Old White china bead bracelet. Hulbert. Creative beadwork. 32

One-piece wooden bracelet. Huckleberry. How to make your own wooden jewelry. 118–23

Open-ended bracelet with stone. Mosesson. Jewelry craft for beginners. 215–16

Papier mâché bracelet. Elbert. Paperworks. 105–07

Papier mâché bracelets. Sommer. Contemporary costume jewelry. 177–79

Pewter or silver open-ended bracelet. Mosesson. Jewelry craft for beginners. 160–63

Plexiglass bracelets. Sommer. Contemporary costume jewelry. 110–13

Ring bracelet. Mosesson. Jewelry craft for beginners. 63–65

Round and cube bead bracelet, dangle bracelet. Davies. Beads as jewelry. 142–44

Round bangle. Richards. Handmade jewelry. 69–70

Sawing, piercing and bending a bracelet. Sommer. Contemporary costume jewelry. 55–56

Seed-bead bracelet. Mosesson. Jewelry craft for beginners. 36

Silver bracelet. Metal and enamel. 66–67

Silver triangular bracelet. Coyne. Penland School of crafts book of jewelry making. 21–52

Simple round bracelet. Pelisser. Jeweler's craft. 55–59

Soft-hard: petit point and silver. Sommer. Wearable crafts. 87–89

Stencil-decorated plexiglass bracelet. Sommer. Contemporary costume jewelry. 115–16

Stretchy pearl bracelet. Hulbert. Creative beadwork. 32

Wire bracelet with bead. Metal and enamel. 7

Wire bracelet with stones. Meyer. Rock tumbling. 80–81

Woodburned bracelet. Broadwater. Woodburning: art and craft. 94

Wooden turned bracelets and bangles. Sainsbury. Woodworking projects with power tools. 17–23

Woven bead bracelet. Erlandsen. Bead book. 82

Woven bead Zulu wrist band. Hulbert. Creative beadwork. 88

Bracelets. See also **Jewelry**

Braiding
Braided-straw designs. Hibbs. Straw sculpture. 82–85
Braiding and plaiting; sprang; frame braiding; twisted braiding. Chamberlain. Beyond weaving. 119–44
Braiding rugs. Brunner. Pass it on. 50–53
Braiding three to seven strands. Reader's Digest complete guide to needlework. 486–93
Braiding wire. Newman. Wire art. 60
Carty. How to make braided rugs.
Center-to-edge weaving—the Osage Indian braid. Dendel. Basic book of fingerweaving. 48–53
Chinese braid. Dendel. Basic book of fingerweaving. 71–76
Diagonal braiding, chevron braiding, arrow design. Stribling. Crafts from North American arts. 124–30
Indian corn braid. Conner. Corncraft. 39–41
Peruvian flat braid weaving. Dendel. Basic book of fingerweaving. 21–29
Plaiting and splint basket, ribbon envelope, leather folder. DeLeon. Basketry book. 77–89
Rug, coasters and placemats. Golden book of colonial crafts. 150–57
Shuckery craft. Conner. Corncraft. 73–76
Single-layer-plaited bird and rocket shapes for use as a mat, wall hanging or mobile. Glashausser. Plaiting step-by-step. 63–71
Single-layer rectangular cube. Glashausser. Plaiting step-by-step. 98–102
Square and round braids. Dendel. Basic book of fingerweaving. 94–110

Braiding. See also **Rugs**

Brazing
Brazing. Brightman. 101 practical uses for propane torches. 19–26
Hard soldering or brazing. Metalcrafting encyclopedia. 34–35
Soldering and brazing. Blandford. Practical handbook of blacksmithing and metalworking. 361–75

Bread boards. See **Cutting boards**

Bread boxes
Antique bread box. Spence. Woodworking tools, materials, processes. 607
Bread dish with handle. Sainsbury. Sainsbury's woodturning projects for dining. 37–38
Tray and bread cabinets; aluminum-foil bread box. Stevenson. How to build and buy cabinets for the modern kitchen. 134–36; 148–49

Brick construction
Breaking through bricks. Time-Life Books. New living spaces. 92–94
Brick driveway, patio, or walk, brick screening wall, brick barbecue, brick-and-wood steps. 101 do-it-yourself projects. 306–07, 310–19
Brick patterns to set in sand or cement. Porches and patios. 80–87
Create your own bricks on a wall. Family handyman handbook of home improvement and remodeling. 275–78
How to apply artificial brick. Nunn Home paint book. 93–94
Laying bricks and patio blocks. Kramer. Outdoor garden build-it book. 27–37
Simulated brick walls. Popular Mechanics do-it-yourself encyclopedia. Vol. 3, 450–51

Brick construction. See also **Masonry**

Brick covers
Brick doorstop. Burchette. Needlework. 64–66
Brick doorstop (needlepoint). Christensen. Needlepoint book. 119
Doorstep. Parker. Mosaics in needlepoint. 104–08
Embroidered fabric brick cover. Silverstein. Mira Silverstein's guide to looped and knotted stitches. 92–95
Fabric covered brick door stop. Roda. Fabric decorating for the home. 26–27
Quickpoint bricks. Treasury of things to make. 127

Bricks
Applying artificial brick and stone. Nunn. Home paint book. 93–94
Refractory formulas. Conrad. Contemporary ceramic formulas. 65–83

Bridges
Building a small bridge. Russell. Walks, walls and fences. 67–68
Small bridge. Proulx. Plan and make your own fences and gates, walkways, walls and drives. 140–41
Stone bridge. Nickey. Stoneworker's bible. 197–98

Briefcases
Attache case. Dittrick. Hard crochet. 140–45
Briefcase. Burchette. More needlework blocking and finishing. 24–29
Briefcase. Endacott. Fine furniture making and woodworking. 92–93

Bronze
Bronzing. Brumbaugh. Wood furniture finishing, refinishing, repairing. 315–18
Manipulating and forging bronze. Meilach. Decorative and sculptural ironwork. 244–47

Brooches
Beaded flower brooch. Hulbert. Creative beadwork. 97–98
Bread-dough flower brooch. Sommer. Contemporary costume jewelry. 141
Brooch fastenings. Edwards. Lost wax casting of jewelry. 123–24
Brooches from tin foil. Janitch. All made from paper. 43–44
Embroidered brooches, pearl flower brooch, beaded butterfly, copper or silver brooches cut with a piercing saw. Encyclopedia of crafts. 137, 182, 192, 200
Fastenings for brooches. Richards. Handmade jewelry. 109–10
Inlaid silver brooch. Powers. Crafting turquoise jewelry. 175–78
Making a brooch with a stone. Meyer. Rock tumbling. 84
Needlepoint flower and bird brooches. Christensen. Teach yourself needlepoint. 93
Needlepoint rose brooch. Embroidery of roses. 109
Scrolled enamel brooch. Metal and enamel. 102–04
Transparent enamel brooch. Metal and enamel. 87–88
Small enamelled silver brooch. Metal and enamel. 133–35
Cut metal bird brooch. Metal and enamel. 28

Brooches. See also **Jewelry**

Brooms
Broom-making. Horwitz. Mountain people, mountain crafts. 94–96
Broom tying. Langsner. Country woodcraft. 211–15
Fireplace broom (cornhusk). Conner. Corncraft. 76–77
Gingham fireside broom. Nicole. Designer accessories to make for your home. 174–76

Buckets, Ice. See **Ice buckets**

Buckets (pails)
Antiqued wooden bucket (painted). McCall's book of America's favorite needlework and crafts. 350–53
(How to repair a) bucket. Schuler. How to fix almost everything. 31

Buckles. See **Belt clasps, ornaments, etc.**

Building blocks. See **Blocks, Toy**

Buffets
Sideboard, buffet. Zegel. Fast furniture. 83–84
Sideboard. Endacott. Fine furniture making and woodworking. 146–55
Dutch buffet. Leavy. Bookshelves and storage units. 78–80
Dining-table buffet. Leavy. Bookshelves and storage units. 88–92
Buffet. Williams. Spanish colonial furniture. 130–31
Buffet. Rubin. Mission furniture. 74–76

Building, Model. See **Architectural models**

Buildings (small). See **Garden houses, shelters, etc.; Tool houses**

Bulletin boards
Bulletin board. Christensen. Needlepoint. 88–90
Bulletin board. Hamilton. Build it together. 70–77
Bulletin board. Oberrecht. Plywood projects illustrated. 186–88
Bulletin board. Scobey. First easy-to-see needlepoint workbook. 72–75
Bulletin board or chalkboard. Dal Fabbro. How to make children's furniture and play equipment. 72–73
Bulletin or chalkboard. Blandford. 66 children's furniture projects. 89–91
Chalk reminder board, peg appointment board, apple chalkboard. Family Circle book of 429 great gifts-to-make all year round for just 10¢ to $10.00. 9, 128–29, 159–60
Cork message board. 101 do-it-yourself projects. 158–59
Framed bulletin boards, bulletin board frame with shelf. Egge. Recycled with flair. 75–79, 82–84
Locked glass door bulletin board. Brann. How to build outdoor projects. 109–23
Message board. Goldman. Decorate with felt. 80–81
Outdoor bulletin board. Brann. How to build outdoor projects. 79–107

Bunks. See **Beds, Bunk**

Buntings
Bunting and mittens. Complete book of baby crafts. 20–21
Bunting in geometric design (crocheted). Mensinga-Biasiny. Beautiful baby clothes to crochet, knit, sew and embroider. 66–70
Bunting. Benton. Sewing classic clothes for children. 52–57
Baby bunting. Crochet. 114
Baby bunting. McCall's big book of knit & crochet for home & family. 242
Crocheted bunting. Great granny crochet book. 98
Crocheted sleeping bag & blanket. Favorite knitting & crochet patterns. 18–21
Embossed bunting (knit). Mensinga-Biasiny. Beautiful baby clothes to crochet, knit, sew and embroider. 113–16
Embroidered bunting. Mensinga-Biasiny. Beautiful baby clothes to crochet, knit, sew and embroider. 152–55
Flower baby bunting. Johnson. Quiltwear. 55–60
Matching bunting and afghan. Woman's Day crochet showcase. 106–07

Quilted bunting, yellow bunting, wrap-up & velour bunting. Laury. Treasury of needle-craft gifts for the new baby. 132–40
Quilting blanket and bunting. Better Homes and Gardens easy bazaar crafts. 52, 56
Red plaid baby bunting. Evrard. Homespun crafts from scraps. 133–38
Royal blue bunting (knit). Mensinga-Biasiny. Beautiful baby clothes to crochet, knit, sew and embroider. 109–12
Snuggle-ups (baby, child & adult). Ruggieri. Woman's Day book of no-pattern sewing. 108
Tweed bunting. Mensinga-Biasiny. Beautiful baby clothes to crochet, knit, sew and embroider. 145–46
Two-piece bunting. Woman's Day bazaar best sellers. 65–66
Woven baby bunting. Beard. Fashions from the loom. 91
Woven baby bunting. Holland. Weaving primer. 187–89

Bureaus. See **Chests of drawers**

Burglar alarms
Protect your home from burglars. Popular Mechanics do-it-yourself encyclopedia. Vol. 16, 2547–56

Buses, Toy. See **Motorbuses, Toy**

Butter servers
Butter dish. Sainsbury. Sainsbury's woodturning projects for dining. 105–08

Butterflies
Beaded butterfly. Encyclopedia of crafts. 191
Butterfly mirror. Challenging projects in stained glass. 55–64
Coquina shell fluttering butterflies. Elbert. Shell craft. 65–67
Needle lace butterfly. Reader's Digest complete guide to needlework. 411–12
Needlepoint butterfly picture. Smith. Needlery. 63–64, 89–90
Stained glass butterfly. Wood. Working with stained glass. 28–31
Straight-wing butterfly, bent-wing butterfly. Isenberg. How to work in beveled glass. 187–89, 197–99
Wired imaginative butterfly. Hutchings. Big book of stuffed toy and doll making. 177–82

Buttons
Beaded buttons. Hulbert. Creative beadwork. 88
Buttons. Gehret. Rural Pennsylvania clothing. 183–89
Chinese ball buttons. Time-Life Books. Exotic styling. 75–77
Clay buttons. Chroman. Potter's primer. 45–46
Crochet buttons. Step by step to better knitting and crochet. 196–97
Crochet buttons and cross-stitch buttons. Wilson. Needlework to wear. 137, 139
Dorset crosswheel buttons. Encyclopedia of crafts. 144
Embroidered buttons. Woman's Day book of weekend crafts. 162–66
Embroidered buttons. Silverstein. Mira Silverstein's guide to looped and knotted stitches. 78–79
Making beads and buttons. Priolo. Ceramics by coil. 25
Ornamental buttonwork on tea cosies, egg baskets, mats. Whatnot. 94–98
Shell buttons. Logan. Shell crafts. 79–81
Singleton, bird's-eye, old dorset, crosswheel, basket, Blandford cartwheel. Blandford book of traditional handicrafts. 127–35
Wooden buttons and toggles. Huckleberry. How to make your own wooden jewelry. 125–35

C

Cabanas. *See* **Garden shelters, houses, etc.**

Cabinets
Basic pine cabinet. Clifford. Basic woodworking and carpentry . . . with projects. 224–29
Built-in hospitality cabinet. Family handyman handbook of carpentry plans/projects. 116–18
Built-in twin china cabinets. Philbin. Cabinets, bookcases & closets. 98–99
Built-in wall cabinet. Leavy. Bookshelves and storage units. 52–53
Cabinet construction. Martensson. Woodworker's bible. 234–41
Cabinet doors and hinges. Cary. Storage: cabinets, closets, and wall systems. 50–58
Cabinet frames. Cary. Storage: cabinets, closets, and wall systems. 41–46
Cabinetmaking. Fine woodworking techniques 2. 70–78
Cabinets (Plain and fancy). Built-ins. 7–72
Corner cabinet. Endacott. Fine furniture making and woodworking. 115–23
Corner cabinets. Philbin. Cabinets, bookcases & closets. 138–39
Corner display cabinet. Complete handyman do-it-yourself encyclopedia. 384–89
Counter, hall locker. Blandford. 53 space-saving built-in furniture projects. 311, 314–50
Curved cabinet. Krenov. Impractical cabinetmaker. 86–99
Early American server. Popular Mechanics do-it-yourself encyclopedia. Vol. 17, 2564–69
Filing cabinet, wall cabinet. Williams. Spanish colonial furniture. 118–19
Hinges and drawers. Siegele. Cabinets and built-ins. 14–18, 80–84
Home storage bar. Family handyman handbook of plans/projects. 157–60
Hutch cabinet. Brann. How to build colonial furniture. 43–74
Lewis. Cabinetmaking, patternmaking, and millwork.
Medicine cabinet, wall case. Rubin. Mission furniture. 116–18
Metal-tooled cabinet, Mexican design. Casselman. Crafts from around the world. 56–59
Movable twin storage cabinets. Family handyman handbook of home improvement and remodeling 184–87
Pendleton sideboard. Osburn. Measured drawings of early American furniture. 19–21
Recessed cabinet, wall cabinet. Brann. How to build colonial furniture. 137–56
Roll-around utility cabinet. Oberrecht. Plywood projects illustrated. 111–17
Server with china top. Feirer. Cabinetmaking and millwork. 723–28
Spencer. Designing and building your own stereo furniture.
Stenciled fruit cabinet. Jarnow. (Re)do it yourself. 85–88
Still life sideboard. Ball. Master pieces. 124–31
Swinging storage cabinet. Capotosto. Woodworking wisdom. 323–28
Take-apart cabinets. Philbin. Cabinets, bookcases & closets. 104–06
Three-way sports cabinets. Leavy. Bookshelves and storage units. 65–69
Two-drawer file cabinet, a vertical storage cabinet. Geary. How to design and build your own workspace—with plans. 12–17, 288–90
Two-part cabinet. McCall's big book of country needlecrafts. 89–90
Typewriter cabinet. Hedden. Successful shelves and built-ins. 85
Utility cabinet. Philbin. Cabinets, bookcases & closets. 120–21
Wall cabinet. Capotosto. Woodworking techniques and projects. 99–102
Wall cabinets, cabinet desk combo. 77 funiture projects you can build. 229–36

Cabinets. *See also* **Commodes; Kitchen cabinets**

Cabinets, Repairing
Balky cabinet door repair. Time-Life Books. Repairing furniture. 29–30
Cabinet pieces. Marshall. How to repair, reupholster, and refinish furniture. 122–31
Caseworks. Jones. Fixing furniture. 67–71
New life for old built-ins. Built-ins. 121–34

Cabinets, Tool. *See* **Tool boxes, racks, etc.**

Cages
Gerbil cage and gym. La Barge. Pet house book. 177–84
Guinea pig cage with table and bungalow and tunnel. La Barge. Pet house book. 148–60
Guinea pig, cavy, hamster or gerbil house. Brann. How to build pet housing. 172–73
Hamster cage with house, outhouse, rocker stair, and slide/tunnel toy. La Barge. Pet house book. 161–76
Rabbit hutch. Brann. How to build pet housing. 82–113
Twig possum home. Johnson. Nature crafts. 18

Cages. *See also* **Bird cages**

Cake
Wedding cake. Treasury of things to make. 98–104

Calendars
A silent night advent calendar. Mills. The book of presents. 54–55
Advent banner with glued on or appliqued houses. Meyer. Christmas crafts. 1–8
Advent calendar. Coffey. Francine Coffey's celebrity sewing bee. 148
Advent calendar. Lindberg. Counted cross-stitch designs for all seasons. 85–91
Advent calendar made from gift wrapping paper. Anderson. Crafts and the disabled. 130–31
Advent calendars. Coskey. Christmas crafts for everyone. 31–34
Birthday calendar. Linsley. Decoupage on glass, wood, metal, rocks, shells, wax, soap, plastic, canvas, ceramic. 111–16
Christian calendar, weekly calendar. Hagans. All good gifts. 118–22
Christmas Advent calendar. Perry. Holiday magic. 157–59
Christmas calendar (embroidered upholstery webbing). Rissell. Craftwork the handicapped elderly can make and sell. 66–67
Everlasting wall calendar. Elbert. Paperworks. 68–72
Felt decorated calendar. Goldman. Decorate with felt. 100
Forever calendar. Baldwin. Scrap fabric crafts. 99–107
Perpetual calendar made with blocks. Doherty. Family Circle book of 429 great gifts-to-make all year round for just 10¢ to $10.00. 8–9
Perpetual desk calendars. Bumper book of things a girl can make. 121–22
Pressed-flower decorated calendar. Scobey. Gifts from your garden. 143

Calking
How and what to caulk. Popular Mechanics do-it-yourself encyclopedia. Vol. 4, 614–15
Using caulk. Outdoor projects for home and garden. 70–73

Cameras
Make your own camera harness, two ways to make a custom camera bag, camera cleaning, telephoto gunstock. Popular Mechanics do-it-yourself encyclopedia. Vol. 4, 512–20
Photographing close-ups. Popular Mechanics do-it-yourself encyclopedia. Vol. 5, 785–87
Pinhole camera. Linderman. Crafts for the classroom. 456–62
Pinhole camera. Warring. Balsa wood modelling. 9

Camping outfits.
Poor man's mini kitchen, portable field cooler. Blackwell. Johnny Blackwell's poor man's catalog. 106, 114
Travelpod: compact cartop carrier, sleeping area, and outboard; camp/work conversion for a van; hi-lo camper for your pickup; sew your own camping gear; how to pick a pack. Popular Mechanics do-it-yourself encyclopedia. Vol. 4, 526–42

Can openers
Electric can opener (repair). Schuler. How to fix almost everything. 34
Hand operated wall type can opener (repair). Schuler. How to fix almost everything. 35

Canalware
Canalware. Mills. Book of presents. 52–53

Candelabra. *See* **Candlesticks**

Candles
Beeswax candle: simple, rolled, rose and cube. Hirst-Smith. Complete candlemaker. 39–44
Candle lantern. Wiita. Dried flowers for all seasons. 54–56
Candle log. Miles. Designing with natural materials. 104–05
Candlemaking. Janitch. Candlemaking and decorations. 5–24
Candlesmaking. Kicklighter. Crafts, illustrated designs and techniques. 64–71
Candlemaking basics. Better Homes and Gardens holiday decorations you can make. 122–25
Candles. Treasury of things to make. 101–12
Carved candles: fish, mushroom, seahorses, and owl. Olsen. Nature's candles. 173–83
Chisholm. Candlemaker's primer.
Crab candle. Olsen. Nature's candles. 195–97
Decorating candles with tissue paper. Stephan. Creating with tissue paper. 237–38
Decorating your candle. Hirst-Smith. Complete candlemaker. 88–113
Decoration candles. Tie-dye, batik and candlemaking step-by-step. 56–62
Decorative candles. Mills. The book of presents. 30–32
Decoupage effect. Newman. Creative candlemaking. 56–58
Dirt candles. Olsen. Nature's candles. 157–58
Feder. Candlemaking design book.
Flame colors. Chisholm. Candlemaker's primer. 38–40
Floating candles. Olsen. Nature's candles. 198–201
Get started in candlemaking, candles molded in snow. Popular Mechanics do-it-yourself encyclopedia. Vol. 4, 554–61
Guy. Easy-to-make candles.
Hand-dipped, wild-flower, beeswax honeycomb, confectionary and molded candles. Golden book of colonial crafts. 26–37
Jack-o-lantern candle. Kinney. How to make 19 kinds of American folk art. 50–51
Layered multi-colored, corrugated carved, fir cone, tin foil, hurricane, snowman, bottle, egg, & balloon candles. Hirst-Smith. Complete candlemaker. 64–87
Making candles, dipping and molding. Christmas craft book. 23–28
Making tapers and twisted tapers. Hirst-Smith. Complete candlemaker. 60–64
Marbled, perfumed, floating, layer, applique, ice candles, water, hurricane, dipped, rolled beeswax candles. Blandford book of traditional handicrafts. 120–26
Newman. Creative candlemaking.
Parrafin wax rose, free-form wax block, free-form foil and ice candles. Hirst-Smith. Complete candlemaker. 44–48
Plaited candles. Christmas crafts book. 29
Pressed flower decorated candle. Linsley. Decoupage on glass, wood, metal, rocks, shells, wax, soap, plastic, canvas, ceramic. 103–05.

Rock candles. Olsen. Nature's candles. 112–28
Sand candles. Hirst-Smith. Complete candlemaker. 46–55
Sand candles. Olsen. Nature's candles. 19–94
Sand candles. Woman's Day book of gifts to make. 116–18
Sand makeshift mold, watermelon, and rose candles. O'Neill. Make-it-merry Christmas
  book. 82–89
Sand-cast candles. Giant book of crafts. 316–23
Sandcast candles. Villiard. Art and craft of sand casting. 97–101
Sea shell and coral candles. Olsen. Nature's candles. 95–111
Simple molded, whipped wax, carved, sand, rolled beeswax, free-form wax, swirled
  wax, and taper candles. Tie-dye, batik and candlemaking step-by-step. 35–55
Snow candles. Olsen. Nature's candles. 159–86
Sprigged, pumpkin, imprinted, petaled, column, and sand candles. McCall's book of
  America's favorite needlework and crafts. 320–26
Water sculpture candle. Olsen. Nature's candles. 166–72
Wax candles. Pittaway. Traditional English country crafts and how to enjoy them to-
  day. 94–98
Whipped wax, in a glass and in a nutshell candles. Hirst-Smith. Complete candle-
  maker. 56–59

Candlesnuffers
Candle snuffer. Kramer. Wirecraft. 65–67

Candlestands. *See* **Stands**

Candlesticks
Adjustable candle stand. Shea. Pennsylvania Dutch and their furniture. 182
Bottle, jar, margarine tub candlesticks. Woman's Day book of gifts to make. 119–21
Bottle, leaded bottle, papier mâché floor, plastic bottle, spray can candlesticks. Epple.
  Something from nothing crafts. 9–15, 83–85, 123–24, 155
Brass candleholder. Metalcrafting encyclopedia. 108–11
Candelabra. Kramer. Wirecraft. 83–87
Candelabra. Modern general shop. Woodworking 98
Candelabra. Romberg. Let's discover papier-mâché. 40–41
Candelabra from Chinese ideograms. Fine woodworking techniques 4. 188
Candle garden (stained glass). Vanderbilt. Gloria Vanderbilt designs for your home.
  179–80
Candle holder. Modern general shop. Metalworking 107
Candleholder frame. Egge. Recycled with flair. 79–82
Candleholder, Russian folk art design. Casselman. Crafts from around the world. 41–
  44
Candleholders. Cope. Plastics. 65
Candle holders. Modern general shop. Metalworking 117
Candleholders. Scurlock. Muzzleloader Magazine's book of buckskinning II. 206–07
Candle holders. Spielman. Working green wood with PEG. 96–97
Candle holders. Yoder. Sculpture and modeling for the elementary school. 54–56
Candle lamps. Nish. Creative woodturning. 190–201
Candle or toothpick holder, candlestands. Fowler. Can crafts. 112–18
Candlestick. Weygers. Recycling, use, and repair of tools. 15
Candlestick I, II, III, IV. DeCristoforo. Build your own wood toys, gifts and furniture.
  314–25
Candlesticks. Sainsbury. Sainsbury's woodturning projects for dining. 6–10
Candlesticks from found objects. Cook. Decorating for the holidays. 52
Carved candlestick. Gottshall. Wood carving and whittling for everyone. 85–87
Carved dolphin candlestick. Gottshall. Wood carving and whittling for everyone. 87
Chandelier. Make it! don't buy it. 218–25

Classy candleholders. Better Homes and Gardens holiday decorations you can make. 126–33

Columnar candlesticks made from short dowels. Woman's Day bazaar best sellers. 105

Decorative candle holder. Wargo. Soft crafts for special occasions. 117–19

Driftwood candleholders and bases. Olsen. Nature's candles. 129–41

Early American candlestick. Hodges. Woodturning handbook—with projects. 209–13

Early American sixteen arm tin chandelier. Murphy. Lampmaking. 174–81

Early American tin chandelier. Murphy. Lampmaking. 159–68

Flaming candle jars, hanging barbecue light. Janitch. Candlemaking and decorations. 68–69

Flower candlesticks. Scobey. Gifts from your garden. 137–38

Fluted aluminum candle holder, pipe joint candelabra; wooden finial candlesticks; elegant wooden candle holders. Doherty. Family Circle book of 429 great gifts-to-make all year round for just 10¢ to $10.00. 4–5, 11–12, 39, 133

Four-arm and six-arm chandeliers. Kauffman. Easy-to-make wooden candlesticks, chandeliers and lamps. 28–32

Garden candle-holder. Encyclopedia of crafts. 208

Hanukkah lights. Rockland. Hanukkah book. 23–51

Holiday candle stand, flamed candle stand. Popular Mechanics do-it-yourself encyclopedia. Vol. 4, 562–64

Metal foil candleholder. Metalcrafting encyclopedia. 154

Metal foil, curled wood, flower, cross, and spiral candlesticks. Christmas crafts book. 31–33

Milk can candleholder. Fowler. Can crafts. 19–21

Mortise marking gauge candle holder. Murphy. Lampmaking. 183–86

Multilevel candlestand. Capotosto. Woodworking techniques and projects. 153–58

Natural candle holders. Spielman. Working green wood with PEG. 57

Nature's wooden candle holders. Olsen. Nature's candles. 142–56

Papier mâché candlestick. O'Neill. Make-it-merry Christmas book. 99–100

Patchwork decoupaged wooden candlestick. Berry. How to make party and holiday decorations. 110

Pottery tree of life candle bearing sculpture. Sayer. Crafts of Mexico. 104–06

Seashell table accessories. Johnson. Nature crafts. 37

Set of metal candlesticks, three candle holder. Giant book of metalworking projects. 186–89, 193

Silver candelabrum. Wilson. Erica Wilson's Christmas world. 80–85

Sphagnum moss and cones, nuts and pods candle rings. Miles. Designing with natural materials. 95–104

Stained glass candle dazzlers. McCall's book of America's favorite needlework and crafts. 329–30

Stained glass candlestick holder. Wood. Working with stained glass. 46–51

Tree of life, Mexican. Casselman. Crafts from around the world. 176–79

Water-lily candle holder. Paper. 64–65

Wood and brass chandelier. Murphy. Lampmaking. 168–72

Wood and brass hanging reflector chandelier. Murphy. Lampmaking. 153–58

Woodburned flower on a candlestick. Broadwater. Woodburning: art and craft. 57–59

Wooden candlesticks. Kauffman. Easy-to-make wooden candlesticks, chandeliers and lamps. 4–15

Wood-ring candlesticks, star candleholders, bird candleholders, tree of life candleholder, tree candleholder centerpiece, candy cane candleholder. Popular Mechanics do-it-yourself encyclopedia. Vol. 5, 700, 705–06

Wrought iron nail candleholders, wreath-shaped candleholder. Metalcrafting encyclopedia. 64

Wrought-iron table candelabra. Bealer. Art of blacksmithing. 307–09

Yarn spool and macrame knot candle holders, wooden candlesticks. Better Homes and Gardens treasury of Christmas crafts & foods. 32, 109, 151

Candlesticks. *See also* **Sconces**

Candy dishes
Candy dish. Cope. Plastics. 28–29
Candy dish, mint dish. Epple. Something from nothing crafts. 18, 180–81
Candy tray. Modern general shop. Woodworking 109
Shell candy dish. Linsley. Decoupage on glass, wood, metal, rocks, shells, wax, soap, plastic, canvas, ceramic. 128–31

Cane weaving
Cane chair. Restoring and reupholstering furniture. 46–53
Cane chair restoration. Davis. Restoring furniture. 48–55
Cane chair seating. Cane, rush and straw. 78–84
Cane chair seats, prewoven cane seating. Roberts. Illustrated handbook of upholstery. 280–93
Cane reseating. Jones. Fixing furniture. 104–11
Cane seating. Brown. Cane and rush seating. 9–47
Cane seats. Kinney. Complete book of furniture repair and refinishing. 181–88
Cane secting. Blandford. Upholsterer's bible. 393–97
Caning. Bragdon. Homeowner's complete manual of repair & improvement. 220–21
Caning. Grime. Illustrated guide to furniture repair & restoration. 67–72
Caning. Johnson. Restoring antique furniture. 87–94
Caning. Meyers. Furniture repair and refinishing. 200–07
Caning simplified. Brann. How to repair, refinish, reupholster. 46–68
Chair caning. Blandford. Do-it-yourselfer's guide to furniture repair and refinishing. 262–72
Hand caning. Bausert. Complete book of wicker and cane furniture making. 17–32
Hand caning a chair seat. Time-Life Books. Repairing furniture. 72–75
How to cane a chair. Popular Mechanics do-it-yourself encyclopedia. Vol. 4, 568–72
How to cane antique chairs. Handyman. 495–96
How to recane. Hilts. Popular mechanics complete book of furniture. 247–64
Installing a set-in cane seat. Saunders. Collecting and restoring wicker furniture. 104–05
Prewoven or machine caning. Bausert. Complete book of wicker and cane furniture making. 33–41
Process, patterns and cane a square stool. Gault. Crafts for the disabled. 84–97
Recaning a chair seat. Golden book of colonial crafts. 144–46
Repairing cane seats. Encyclopedia of crafts. 174–75
Repairing caning. Hilts. Furniture repair & restoration.
Six millimeter binding cane weaving. Bausert. Complete book of wicker and cane furniture making. 62–67
Working woven cane. Fine woodworking techniques 4. 159–61

Canisters
Canister cover-ups. Baldwin. Scrap fabric crafts. 66–68
Canisters. Romberg. Let's discover papier-mâché. 34–35
Cracker barrel. Sainsbury. Sainsbury's woodturning projects for dining. 108–11
Grocery-store bin five-in-one canister. Popular Mechanics do-it-yourself encyclopedia. Vol. 10, 1595
Hexagonal coffee-canister. Woman's Day bazaar best sellers. 99
Paper snax stuffers. Linsley. Decoupage on glass, wood, metal, rocks, shells, wax, soap, plastic, canvas, ceramic. 116–21
Shortening can canister. Epple. Something from nothing crafts. 161–62

Canoe paddles
Canoe paddle (repair). Schuler. How to fix almost everything. 34

Canoes
Repairing fiberglass and aluminum canoes. Golden book of colonial crafts. 48–49

Canopies
Bed and canopy, crocheted net canopy. McCall's big book of country needlecrafts. 175–77, 222–24
Canopies for all bed styles. Better Homes and Gardens sewing for your home. 94–99
Canopy frame and ruffled bed curtains. McCall's sewing for your home. 194–95
Crocheted bed canopy or valance. Better Homes and Gardens treasury of needlecrafts. 214–15
Easy to build canopy. Brann. How to build outdoor projects. 57–73
Ruffled bed canopy, mini canopy. McCall's sewing for your home. 74–78

Capes
A cloak for a sweeping flourish. Time-Life Books. Boutique attire. 22–27
A hooded cape of quadrates (crocheted). Time-Life books. Traditional favorites. 160–65
Aberdeen circle cape, circle cape-coat style. Beard. Fashions from the loom. 44–45
Bold-striped beach cape. Crochet. 70
Bridesmaids trailing coverlet. Jacobs. Crochet book. 66–67
Burnoose. Brown. Weaving, spinning, and dyeing book. 184–85
Fun fur caplet. Farlie. Pennywise boutique. 59
Garter-stitch cape. Knitting. 51
Gypsy four-way cape. Holderness. Peasant chic. 27–33
Half-moon wrap skirt or cape, blanket cape. Wiseman. Cuts of cloth. 16–17, 20–21
Hanky top for toddlers. Great granny crochet book. 108–09
Knitted capelet and cap. Knitting techniques and projects. 50
Making a cape. Scurlock. Muzzleloader Magazine's book of buckskinning II. 69–71
Mohair cape. Favorite knitting & crochet patterns. 49–51
Patchwork cape. Lane. Maggie Lane's oriental patchwork. 51–54
Portuguese cape (sewn). Holderness. Peasant chic. 21–23
Quilted cape and quilted coat. Creative sewing. 14
Rainbow hooded cape. Jacobs. Crochet book. 130–32
Semicircular cape with hood. Golden book of hand and needle arts. 60–61
Wind or rain cape (quilted). Laury. Quilted clothing. 78
Woven capes and ponchos. Krevitsky. Shaped weaving. 77–80

Card cases
Bargello credit card case. Christensen. Teach yourself needlepoint. 80–81
Bridge cards and accessories holder. Popular Mechanics do-it-yourself encyclopedia. Vol. 3, 452
Bridge set. Modern general shop. Woodworking. 96
Card box. Modern general shop. Woodworking. 6–8
Card boxes. Silverstein. Mira Silverstein's guide to looped and knotted stitches. 80–85
Playing card box. Marlow. Classic furniture projects. 22–29

Card weaving. *See* **Weaving, Card**

Cardboard work
Geometric shapes. Palmer. Making children's furniture and play structures. 99–109
Milstein. Building cardboard toys.

Carousels. *See* **Merry-go-rounds**

Carpet beaters
Carpet beater. Wright. Complete book of baskets and basketry. 100–01

Carpets
Carpet and carpet square installation. Family handyman handbook of home improve-
ment and remodeling. 410–18
Carpet construction and selection. Olin. Construction. 226
Carpeting for comfort. Built-ins. 109–11
Installing carpet tiles and seamless carpet. Carbo. Fix-it guide for women. 54–55
Installing wall to wall carpet. Time-Life Books. Floors and stairways. 98–115
Repairs for unsightly stains and tears. Time-Life Books. Floors and stairways. 116–22

Carpets. See also **Rugs**

Carports
Carport roof installation. Time-Life Books. New living spaces. 18–19
Constructing a carport. Russell. Garages and carports. 114–15

Carports. See also **Garages**

Carts
Cart for your bicycle. Popular Mechanics do-it-yourself encyclopedia. Vol. 2, 302–03
Chef's cart, garden cart planter. Complete handyman do-it-yourself encyclopedia.
487–94
Kitchen storage cart. Leavy. Bookshelves and storage units. 93–95
Multi-purpose foundry cart. Giant book of metalworking projects. 245–47
Pony cart and sleigh. Churchill. Backyard building book II. 128–29
Pooch power wagon, summer training cart for dog teams. Churchill. Backyard building
book II. 130–36
Sullivan. Cart book, with plans and projects.
Tractor cart. Bubel. Working wood. 83–86

Carts, miniature
Three-dimensional needlepoint golf cart. Christensen. Needlepoint. 77–83
Flower cart. Fowler. Can craft. 157–63

Carving
Carving plaster. Farnworth. Creative work with plaster. 61–74
Internal carving in clear plastic. Popular Mechanics do-it-yourself encyclopedia. Vol.
10, 1546–47

Casseroles
Casserole rims and lids. Howell. Craft of pottery. 58–59
Jute baskets for casseroles. Woman's Day crochet showcase. 162
Making a flat casserole with fitted lid. Ceramics. 85–92
Making a round stew pot. Ceramics. 93–97
Pottery casserole. Campbell. Using the potter's wheel. 76–77

Casters
Installing casters. Kinney. Complete book of furniture repair and refinishing. 70–71
Repairing casters. Time-Life Books. Repairing furniture. 30–31
Retractable casters for your tool stands. Popular Mechanics do-it-yourself encyclope-
dia. Vol. 15, 2321

Casting
Ammen. Constructing & using wood patterns.
Cast forms. Sanders. (Sunset ceramics book) How to make pottery. 125–29
Cast forms in plaster. Farnworth. Creative work with plaster. 12–37
Cast plastic jewelry. Sommer. Contemporary costume jewelry. 117–20
Casting. Bowie. Jewelry making. 112–27
Casting in charcoal, cuttlebone. Foote. Jewelry making. 97–100
Casting methods. Rose. illustrated encyclopedia of crafts and how to master them.
341–79
Casting of sterling silver. Warwick. Beginning jewelry. 71–81
Casting techniques. Price. Model-building handbook. 121–35
Casting with commercial made molds. Cope. Plastics. 75–79
Casting with polyester resin. Encyclopedia of crafts. 209
Centrifugal casting. Sprintzen. Jewelry, basic techniques and design. 84–85
Centrifical casting: spruing, investing, and burnout. Wald. Introduction to jewelry cast-
ing. 58–88
Charcoal casting. Sprintzen. Jewelry, basic techniques and design. 68
Cleaning the casting. Edwards. Lost wax casting of jewelry. 105–07
Cuttlebone casting. Sprintzen. Jewelry, basic techniques and design. 63–67
Cuttlefish bone casting. Richards. Handmade jewelry. 134–36
Cuttle fish bone casting. Wald. Introduction to jewelry casting. 23–32
Dies, patterns, and casting. Giant book of metalworking projects. 110–81
Hollow casting. Kenny. Creative design in sand casting. 55–63
Investment molds for lost-wax casting. Sprintzen. Jewelry, basic techniques and de-
sign. 72–83
Investment process. Edwards. Lost wax casting of jewelry. 73–80
Jewelry making from a wax casting. Sommer. Contemporary costume jewelry. 62–66
Kenny. Creative design in sand casting.
Lost-wax casting. Newman. Wire art. 177–85
Lost wax casting. Sprintzen. Jewelry, basic techniques and design. 68–73
Lost wax casting. Wood. Make your own jewelry. 127–44
Lost wax process. Newman. Contemporary African arts and crafts. 227–42
Lost wax process. Wald. Introduction to jewelry casting. 33–57
Lost-wax sand casting. Richards. Handmade jewelry. 138–41
Make your own metal castings. Popular Mechanics do-it-yourself encyclopedia. Vol.
12, 1786–89
Making cast shell forms from molds. Elbert. Shell craft. 209–42
Metal casting. Blandford. Practical handbook of blacksmithing and metalworking. 403–
14
Metalworking process. Newman. Contemporary Southeast Asian arts and crafts. 218–
29
Molten metal cast in a mold of moist sand. Working with metal. 106–10
Mounting techniques. Edwards. Lost wax casting of jewelry. 67–72
Moulded dishes and pots, slip cast forms. Pottery step-by-step. 16–21
Pattern construction. Edwards. Lost wax casting of jewelry. 47–64
Planning an object in cast wax. Meilach. Decorative and sculptural ironwork. 194
Plaster casting, cast plastic. Linderman. Crafts for the classroom. 328–33, 362–63
Sand casting. Richards. Handmade jewelry. 137–38
Sand casting. Treasury of things to make. 35–37
Sand, cuttle fish, tufa and centrifugal casting. Bovin. Jewelry making. 139–66
Sprueing. Edwards. Lost wax casting of jewelry. 65–67
Steam casting. Sprintzen. Jewelry, basic techniques and design. 86–87
Steam pressure casting. Wald. Introduction to jewelry casting. 89–92
Tufa channel casting, cuttlebone casting, sand casting, core casting, lost wax casting,
steam casting, centrifugal casting. Chamberlain. Metal jewelry techniques. 79–101

Using a mold to capture natural forms. Sommer. Contemporary costume jewelry. 120–22
Vacuum-assisted casting. Wald. Introduction to jewelry casting. 93–95
Villiard. Art and craft of sand casting.
Wax elimination and burnout. Edwards. Lost wax casting of jewelry. 81–88

Castles, Toy
Fairy tale castles. Greenhowe. Making miniature toys and dolls. 10–13

Cats
Bashful lion. Knitting. 127
Bendy cat. Hulbert. Creative beadwork. 96–97
Carved wood cat. Popular Mechanics do-it-yourself encyclopedia. Vol. 4, 607–08
Cat in a window. Ormond. American primitives in needlepoint. 89–95
Cat toy; pillows for cat lovers. Doherty. Family Circle book of 429 great gifts-to-make all year round for just 10¢ to $10.00. 13, 40–41
Christmas kittens embroidered in outlined stitches on muslin. Better Homes and Gardens easy bazaar crafts. 64–65, 76–78
Crochet lion. Favorite easy-to-make toys. 122–23
Cuddly cat family. American School of Needlework. Great crochet bazaar book. 101–04
Cuddly kitten. Guild. Dollmaker's workshop. 115
Kitten. Practical needlework. 257–58
Leather cat. Laury. Treasury of needlecraft gifts for the new baby. 115–16
Lion and the tiger. Marsten. Step-by-step dollmaking. 65–68
Lion cubs in needlepoint. Wilson. More needleplay. 174–75
Lion's head. McKellips. Practical pattern manual for woodcarving and other crafts. 1–3
Lovable lions-pillow and door or wall hanging. Foose. More scrap saver's stitchery. 8–13
Mohair kitten. McCall's big book of knit & crochet for home & family. 82
Seated cat embroidered pillow. Scheuer. Designs for Holbein embroidery. 50–51
Soft sculpture needlepoint lion. Better Homes and Gardens treasury of needlecrafts. 316–20
Stuffed lion toy. Better Homes and Gardens treasury of Christmas crafts & foods. 35–36

Cats, Equipment
All weather cat entry. Brann. How to build pet housing. 29–40
Bed/carrier. La Barge. Pet house book. 84–91
Cat bed. Woman's Day book of gifts to make. 72
Cat castles. Burch. Tile: indoors and out, every kind and use. 117
Catnip kitty bag. Fanning. Complete book of machine quilting. 266–70
Catpartment. Brann. How to build pet housing. 41–66
Cat's sweater. Feldman. Needlework boutique. 64–65
Lumber cattrees. La Barge. Pet house book. 92–105
Mouse toy. American School of Crochet. Great Christmas crochet book. 142–43
Natural cattrees. La Barge. Pet house book. 106–11
Pet bed/carrier. Family handyman handbook of carpentry plans/projects. 130–33
Pet nest. Hamilton. Build it together. 112–17
Pup and cat palace. Churchill. Backyard building book II. 86–89
Pups' and kitten's flea collars. Sheldon. Washable and dryable needlepoint. 82–83
Sasha sleeper, scratch post and ball posy kitty collar. Woman's Day book of weekend crafts. 145–47, 154–55
Window seat. La Barge. Pet house book. 77–83

Cats, Toy
Little kitten in a mitten. Greenhowe. Making miniature toys and dolls. 14–15

Caulking. *See* **Calking**

Cedar chests. *See* **Chests**

Ceilings
Building a celing. Time-Life Books. New living spaces. 68–71
Ceiling frames, suspended ceilings, wallboard ceilings. Clifford. Basic woodworking & carpentry . . . with projects. 177–83
Ceiling framing. Spence. General carpentry. 212–16
Ceilings. Parry. Stenciling. 94–95
How to install ceiling tile, simulated ceiling beams, make your own beams. Popular Mechanics do-it-yourself encyclopedia. Vol. 4, 616–27
Installing a suspended ceiling. Handyman. 231–33
Installing ceiling beams. Handyman. 228–30
Installing ceiling tile and suspended ceilings. Spence. General carpentry. 396–403
Installing gypsum ceilings. Geary. How-to book of floors & ceilings. 100–07
Installing suspended and ordinary tile ceilings. Family handyman handbook of home improvement and remodeling. 203–20
Installing suspended ceilings. Geary. How-to do floors and ceilings. 123–30
New ceilings. Bragdon. Homeowner's complete manual of repair & improvement. 46–51
Repairing gypsumboard and tile ceilings. Nunn. Home improvement, home repair. 40–42
Suspended ceiling headers. Time-Life Books. New living spaces. 11–13
Suspended tiles and wallboard ceilings. Clifford. Basic woodworking and carpentry . . . with projects. 177–82
Textured ceilings—plastered and tile. Geary. How-to book of floors & ceilings. 108–22
Wood ceilings. Geary. How-to book of floors & ceilings. 131–37

Cellars. *See* **Basements**

Cement. *See* **Concrete**

Ceramics. *See* **Pottery**

Cesspools. *See* **Septic tanks**

Chains
Chain breaker (for repairing chains). Giant book of metalworking projects. 220–23
Chain making. Edwards. Lost wax casting of jewelry. 124–26
Chain making, chain hook. Blandford. Practical handbook of blacksmithing and metalworking. 122–28
Chain with square wire. Pelisser. Jeweler's craft. 48–50
Chains. Richards. Handmade jewelry. 96–101
Chains and chain making. Bovin. Jewelry making. 231–35
Chains carved from solid wood. Huckleberry. How to make your own wooden jewelry. 137–39
Clover chains. Johnson. Nature crafts. 46
Making jump rings. Sprintzen. Jewelry, basic techniques and designs. 132
Paper chains. Christmas crafts book. 91–99
Silver chains & rings. Encyclopedia of crafts. 187–88
Soft sculpture garland and treetop ornament. Better Homes and Gardens treasury of Christmas crafts & foods. 82
Two simple chains. Sprintzen. Jewelry, basic techniques and design. 132–34
Wooden chains made of individual links. Huckleberry. How to make your own wooden jewelry. 139–44

Chair caning. *See* **Cane weaving**

Chair pads. *See* **Cushions**

Chair seats
Bargello director's chair. Scobey. Decorating with needlepoint. 51–53
Butterfly patch for chair seats. Meyers. Furniture repair and refinishing. 108
Chair cushion. Reader's Digest complete guide to needlework. 494
Chair seat on a multiharness loom. Make it! don't buy it. 396
Circular chair seat and chair cushion. Halliday. Decorating with crochet. 53–60
Cloud gong on tortoise shell lattice, director's chair. Nicoletti. Japanese motifs for
    needlepoint. 51–54
Director's chair. Burchette. More needlework blocking and finishing. 118–21
Director's chair. Halliday. Decorating with crochet. 49–52
Director's chair. McCall's sewing for your home. 56
Director's chair cover. Roda. Fabric decorating for the home. 226–27
Director's chairs. Loeb. Leather book. 43–55
Drop-in dining-chair seat. Grime. Illustrated guide to furniture repair & restoration. 85–
    88
Fabric covered slip seats. Roda. Fabric decorating for the home. 43
Fleur-de-lis motif chair cover. Christensen. Needlepoint and bargello stitchery. 84–85
Florentine chair seat. Encyclopedia of crafts. 65
Geometric-repeat chair seat. Scobey. Decorating with needlepoint. 48–50
Heart design needlepoint chair seat. Smith. Needlery. 91–94
Medley of musical chairs. (needlepoint seats). Time-Life books. Traditional favorites.
    180–83
Needlepointed chair covers. Hana. Embroidery. 69–70
Needlepoint take-offs (director's chair seat and back). Time-Life Books. Personal
    touch. 155
Pastel chair seat. Boyles. Margaret Boyles book of needle art. 38–41
Peonies with butterflies, lady's rocker, fans and scrolls chair seat. Nicoletti. Japanese
    motifs for needlepoint. 23–30
Pomegranate and tulip motif upholstered chair (needlepoint). McCall's book of Amer-
    ica's favorite needlework and crafts. 145–47
Quick and easy patchwork chair pad. Better Homes and Gardens treasury of needle-
    crafts. 19
Seating with willows, seagrass, and cord. Brown. Cane and rush seating. 64–75
Sewing-machine bargello chair seat. Better Homes and Gardens treasury of needle-
    crafts. 290–91
Shaped chair pads. Wilson. Weaving you can use. 68–75
Side chairs—upholstered and slip seat. Scobey. First easy-to-see needlepoint work-
    book. 81–89
Splint seat, cane seat and rush chair seat. Golden book of colonial crafts. 138–49
Stenciled director's chair. Creative sewing. 31
Textured needlepoint pillow and chair seat. Woman's Day decorative needlework for
    the home. 41–45
Upholstering chair bottoms. Johnson. Restoring antique furniture. 94–102
Webbing repair. Kinney. Complete book of furniture repair and refinishing. 202–06

Chairs
Armchair, curved-back armchair, side chair, Morris chair. Rubin. Mission furniture. 48–
    53, 56–57
Backbone beanbag. Easy-to-make tables and chairs. 9
Balloon chair. Easy-to-make tables and chairs. 19–20
Bannister-back chair, vase-back chair, shield-back chair, wing chair. Osburn. Mea-
    sured drawings of early American furniture. 24–26, 46–47, 66–67, 76–77

Casual armchairs. Easy-to-make tables and chairs. 35–36

Caterpillar lounge. Easy-to-make tables and chairs. 6–9

Chair braided on frame of steel tubing. Dendel. Basic book of fingerweaving. 59–61

Chair construction. Martensson. Woodworker's bible. 228–33

Chairs for stacking. Easy-to-make tables and chairs. 40–41

Colonial chair. Capotosto. Woodworking techniques and projects. 304–09

Colonial chair in solid cherry. Popular Mechanics do-it-yourself encyclopedia. Vol. 1, 102–11

Contemporary chair. Spence. Woodworking tools, materials, processes. 605

Contemporary plywood chair. Easy-to-make tables and chairs. 38–41

Drop-in seat. McDonald. Modern upholstering techniques. 78–81

Dual seat/chest. Blandford. 53 space-saving built-in furniture projects. 203–08

Early Georgian-style corner chair, Farthingale chair, Sheraton-style chair, ladder-back chair, Windsor chairs. Taylor. How to build period country furniture. 91–94, 103–05, 114–17, 126–30, 134–41

Easy chair; deep-sprung armchair; period wing chair. McDonald. Modern upholstering techniques. 123–36

Easy chair, straight chairs. Zegel. Fast furniture. 48–49, 66–69

Fireside chair, carver chair, recliner. Endacott. Fine furniture making and woodworking. 123–46

Foam roll chair. Easy-to-make tables and chairs. 30–32

Frame chair and a sofa. Fine woodworking techniques 4. 153–56

Hitchcock chair (painted). McCall's book of America's favorite needlework and crafts. 353–56

Indoor/outdoor chair. Waugh. Handyman's encyclopedia. 428–31

Inner-tube seats. Easy-to-make tables and chairs. 21

Machine-embroidered chair. Treasury of things to make. 140–42

Martha Washington chair frame. Marlow. Classic furniture projects. 80–95

Muffler-pipe chair. Easy-to-make tables and chairs. 32–33

Nest chair (stuffed fabric). Kinser. Sewing sculpture. 65–66, 71

On designing chairs, two-board chairs. Fine woodworking techniques 5. 122–28

One-piece chair. Fine woodworking techniques 4. 200–01

PVC and canvas chair. 101 do-it-yourself projects. 274–75

Pair of plywood chairs. Easy-to-make tables and chairs. 24–25

Peasant chair, ladderback chair, ladderback armchair, spindle chair, shaped chair, fire-house armchair, Windsor chair. Blandford. How to make early American and colonial furniture. 291–332

Peasant's chair. Daniele. Building early American furniture. 129–30

Side chair, arm chair. Alth. Making plastic pipe furniture. 106–22

Spanish armchairs and armchairs. Williams. Spanish colonial furniture. 34–43

Strawberry and shell deck chairs. Jarnow. (Re) do it yourself. 94–97

Swing chair with a rope frame. Dendel. Basic book of fingerweaving. 61–65

Tree trunck chair. Churchill. Big backyard building book. 178–80

2-by-2 lounge chair. Easy-to-make tables and chairs. 22–24

Two-slat ladderback chair. Moser. How to build Shaker furniture. 144–45

Unit chair. McDonald. Modern upholstering techniques. 109–13, 114–22

Upholstered occasional chair, square arm chair, buttoned wing-chair. Restoring and reupholstering furniture. 108–51

Vincent's chair, acrobat's, cat's chair, red studio chair, Saint Augustine's armchair, chair in the valley. Ball. Master pieces. 14–21, 92–97, 110–15, 132–44

Wooden chairs with loose pillows. Black and Decker power tool carpentry. 71–86

Wedding chair, Austrian design. Casselman. Crafts from around the world. 48–52

Chairs. *See also* **Children's furniture, Chairs**

Chairs, Dining
Abe Lincoln's hickory splint chair with woven seat. Popular Mechanics do-it-yourself encyclopedia. Vol. 5, 650–55
Antique Hitchcock chair with bronze powders. Midkiff. Complete book of stenciling. 41–43
Cafe table and chairs. 101 do-it-yourself projects. 139–43
Cheerful breakfast chair. Easy-to-make tables and chairs. 37
Continuous arm, bowback, fanback, inverted arm, and eastward side and arm chairs. Moser. Windsor chairmaking. 58–70
Curved-back chair. Capotosto. Woodworking techniques and projects. 267–80
Dining chair seat reupholstering. Grime. Illustrated guide to furniture repair & restoration. 105–10
Dining chairs. Black and Decker power tool carpentry. 99–104
Dining chairs. Williams. Spanish colonial furniture. 30–33
Dining chairs with upholstered seats. Make it! don't buy it. 120–31
Dining-room chair. Feirer. Cabinetmaking and millwork. 680–81
Four-slat ladderback chair, armchair. Moser. How to build Shaker furniture. 142–43, 148–49
Late plank bottom chair. Marlow. Early American furnituremaker's manual. 51–59
Painted kitchen chair, "judge's" chair, "Moravian" chair. Shea. Pennsylvania Dutch and their furniture. 156–58
Rattan dining room chairs. Alth. Rattan furniture. 166–79
Recovering a kitchen chair with vinyl plastic. Torelli. Reupholstering for the home craftsman. 119–23
Shaker armchair. 77 furniture projects you can build. 11–25
Step-down Windsor chair, Chippendale upholstered side chair. Gottshall. Provincial furniture design and construction. 137–46
Two chairs (restoration), chair with drop-in seat upholstery project, sprung dining chair. Restoring and reupholstering furniture. 40–53, 84–91, 100–07

Chairs, Folding
Folding seat for a fire surround. Blandford. How to make your own built-in furniture. 267–69
Jumbo director's chair. Capotosto. Woodworking techniques and projects. 205–13

Chairs, Outdoor
Briarcliff lawn chair. Brann. How to build outdoor furniture. 17–31
Casual chairs, covers for butterfly and director's & lawn chairs. Better Homes and Gardens sewing for your home. 194–96
Chairs. Blandford. Constructing outdoor furniture, with 99 projects. 59–89
Folding deck chair. Creative sewing. 55
Lawn chair. Braren. Homemade. 46–47
Matching settee. Brann. How to build outdoor furniture. 32–37
Patio rocking chair. Complete handyman do-it-yourself encyclopedia. 1187–90
Redwood chairs from aluminum frames. 77 furniture projects you can build. 296–302
Replacing webbing on outdoor chairs. 77 furniture projects you can build. 291–97, 312–17
Willow rod back rest. Scurlock. Muzzleloader Magazine's book of buckskinning II. 197–99

Chairs, Repairing
Bamboo chair seat. Johnson. How to restore, repair, and finish almost everything. 41–75
Chair repair. Rodd. Repairing and restoring antique furniture. 69–87
Chairs. Hayward. Antique furniture repairs. 27–45
Chairs. Marshall. How to repair, reupholster, and refinish furniture. 77–95

Chairs and stools. Salazar. Complete book of furniture restoration. 74–85
Loose chair parts. Meyers. Furniture repair and refinishing. 95–100
Making and installing new chair parts. Kinney. Complete book of furniture repair and refinishing. 50–53
Mending chairs. Jones. Fixing furniture. 55–58
Recovering worn seats, fixing cane seats. Carbo. Fix-it guide for women. 57–61
Renovating an old chair. Handyman. 493–94
Repairing chairs. Wenn. Restoring antique furniture. 58–59
Repairing wobbly and broken chairs. Fine woodworking techniques 4. 157–58
Reseating. Howell-Koehler. Step-by-step furniture finishing. 18–34
Restoring old chairs to renewed beauty. 77 furniture projects you can build. 25–29
Three chairs. Davis. Restoring furniture. 42–63
Windsor chair repairs. Moser. Windsor chairmaking. 23–29
Wooden chairs. Time-Life Books. Repairing furniture. 8–17

Chairs, Rocking
Armless rocking chair. Moser. How to build Shaker furniture. 146–47
Bottomless rocking chairs, reupholstery. Torelli. Reupholstering for the home craftsman. 168–69
Continuous arm rocker. Moser. Windsor chairmaking. 73–74
Lancaster rocker. Daniele. Building early American furniture. 142–43
Painted rocking chair. Linsley. Fabulous furniture decorations. 85–90
Rocking chair. Rubin. Mission furniture. 56–57
Rocking chair. Taylor. How to build period country furniture. 150–54
Rocking chair (adult). Adams. Make your own baby furniture. 206–09
Rocking chair. Zegel. Fast furniture. 76–79

Chairs, Upholstered
Armchair reupholstery. Grime. Illustrated guide to furniture repair & restoration. 97–100
Chair seats. Blandford. Upholsterer's bible. 92–111
Channel back chairs. Torelli. Reupholstering for the home craftsman. 149–54
Colonial chair. Torelli. Reupholstering for the home craftsman. 145–48
Crewel upholstery for wing chair. Wilson. More needleplay. 136–37
Deep-bottomed chair upholstering. Grime. Illustrated guide to furniture repair & restoration. 124–28
Enclosed chair frames. Blandford. Upholsterer's bible. 450–62
Fireside chair upholstering. Grime. Illustrated guide to furniture repair & restoration. 88–95
Forming a roll edge, traditional armchair re-upholstered. Grime. Illustrated guide to furniture repair & restoration. 111–17
Fully upholstered chairs. Blandford. Upholsterer's bible. 181–305
Gold chair. Boyles. Margaret Boyles book of needle art. 42–44
Lounge chairs. Blandford. Upholsterer's bible. 149–64
Office chair. Blandford. Upholsterer's bible. 125–28
Open chair frames. Blandford. Upholsterer's bible. 440–49
Overstuffed chair. Torelli. Reupholstering for the home craftsman. 125–34
Recliner upholstery. Torelli. Reupholstering for the home craftsman. 164–65
Thinking big. Wilson. Needleplay. 160–61
Torelli. Reupholstering for the home craftsman.
Tufted-backed chair. Torelli. Reuphostering for the home craftsman. 155–59
Wing chair. Torelli. Reupholstering for the home craftsman. 130–44

Chaise lounges
Chaise lounge. Alth. Making plastic pipe furniture. 129–37
Deck lounge. Wood projects for the garden. 44–46
Easy to build chaise. Brann. How to build outdoor furniture. 59–80
Quick and easy patchwork lounging mat. Better Homes and Gardens treasury of needlecrafts. 18
Rattan chaise longue. Alth. Rattan furniture. 132–42
Renovating a chaise lounge. Grime. Illustrated guide to furniture repair & restoration. 130–33
Restoring a chaise-longue. Davis. Restoring furniture. 88–99
Seat/bed/lounger. Blandford. Constructing outdoor furniture, with 99 projects. 170–72
Sun lounger. Blandford. Constructing outdoor furniture, with 99 projects. 307–18
Swiveling lounger. Capotosto. Woodworking techniques and projects. 128–33

Chalkboards. See **Blackboards**

Champlevé. See **Enamel and enameling**

Chaps
Chaps. Latham. Leathercraft. 95–101

Charcoal
Charcoal burning. Manners. Country crafts today. 32–36

Cheese boards
Cheeseboard. Sainsbury. Sainsbury's woodturning projects for dining. 99–100
Cheese board. Scobey. First easy-to-see needlepoint workbook. 126–28
Cheese board and dome. Hodges. Woodturning handbook—with projects. 176–78, 180–82

Cheese boards. See also **Cutting boards**

Chess and checkers
Basic monogram, painted and container wooden chess sets. Carroll. Make your own chess set. 55–72
Bridge table checker board. Coffey. Francine Coffey's celebrity sewing bee. 96
Building knights from nuts and bishops from bolts, chessboard. Giant book of metalworking projects. 206–07
Checker box. Dal Fabbro. How to make children's furniture and play equipment. 140
Chess board. Wells. Wooden puzzles and games. 102–07
Chess pieces made from moulding powder. Encyclopedia of crafts. 222
Chess set. Grainger. Creative papercraft. 99–103
Chess set fit for a king. Popular Mechanics do-it-yourself encyclopedia. Vol. 5, 658–61
Clothespin chess set. Doherty. Family Circle book of 429 great gifts-to-make all year round for just 10¢ to $10.00. 40
Cornstarch figure, plastic cube, cork and bottle cap, thread spool, and pill and capsule chess sets. Carroll. Make your own chess set. 113–40
Coin chess sets. Carroll. Make your own chess set. 105–12
Dual-function chessboard. Capotosto. Woodworking wisdom. 231–41
Electronic and electronic components chess sets. Carroll. Make your own chess set. 47–54
Figurine, kitchen, rocks and stones, and anything can be made into a chess set. Carroll. Make your own chess set. 141–48
Gumdrop, cookie and nut edible chess sets. Carroll. Make your own chess set. 93–104

Hooked on chess (rug board and chess pieces). Creative crafts yearbook: an exciting new collection of needlework and crafts. 6–13
Inlaid checker or chess board, acrylic chess set. 101 do-it-yourself projects. 238–41
King-size chess set. Hobbs. Veneer craft for everyone. 139–42
Marquetry chess board. Favorite easy-to-make toys. 188–91
Metal chessmen. Lindsley. Metalworking in the home shop. 300
Needlepoint American revolutionary chessmen. Wilson. More needleplay. 124–27
Screw, nail, ball bearing, plumbing parts, hook and eye, lag bolt and hose fixture metal chess sets. Carroll. Make your own chess set. 19–45
Playing card, paper cutout, and aluminium foil paper chess sets. Carroll. Make your own chess set. 73–92
Woodburned chess board. Brightman. 101 practical uses for propane torches. 93–95

Chess and checkers. *See also* **Game boards and tables**

Chests
"Anything" chest, storage chest. Self. Working with plywood, including indoor/outdoor projects. 229–35, 251–55
Apothecary chest; bride's chest, Shaker drawerless chest, Canaan storage chest, North family blanket chest. Daniele. Building early American furniture. 115–16, 124–26, 190–91, 192–93, 196–98
Blanket chest. Brann. How to build colonial furniture. 123–36
Blanket chest. Waugh. Handyman's encyclopedia. 397–99
Carved Gother chest. Gottshall. Wood carving and whittling for everyone. 59–65
Cedar chest. Rubin. Mission furniture. 112–13
Cedar-lined blanket chest. Make it! don't buy it. 146–61
Chest with curved sides. Fine woodworking techniques 3. 167–70
Chest with sawed-off legs. Egge. Recycled with flair. 137–39
Decorating a hope chest. Golden book of colonial crafts. 90–91
Decorative cedar chest. Oberrecht. Plywood projects illustrated. 82–86
Decorative trunk, cedar chest. Spence. Woodworking tools, materials, processes. 595, 600
Dowry chest, Romanian wood carving. Casselman. Crafts from around the world. 78–82
Early Spanish chest, chest, Spanish colonial chest. Williams. Spanish colonial furniture. 84–89, 110–11
Finishing cedar chests. Patton. Furniture finishing. 137–41
Foot locker slipcover to sew. Woman's Day decorative needlework for the home. 142
Footlocker/wooden-chest coffee table. Evrard. Homespun crafts from scraps. 25–29
How to reproduce a Pennsylvania Dutch dower chest, dower chest, dower chest with drawers. Shea. Pennsylvania Dutch and their furniture. 120–26, 168–71
Linen chest. Taylor. How to build period country furniture. 173–76
Linen chest. Black and Decker power tool carpentry. 145–49
Miser's chest. Ball. Master pieces. 72–77
Paper patchwork blanket chest. Linsley. Fabulous furniture decorations. 99–106
Period piece from stock moldings, chest in the Spanish style. Popular Mechanics do-it-yourself encyclopedia. Vol. 5, 662–67
Pine chest. Osburn. Measured drawings of early American furniture. 36–37
Restoring and decorating a trunk. Howard. New tole & folk art designs. 86–93
Shaker storage chest and linen chest. 77 furniture projects you can build. 83–89
Simple chest, chest with trays, small chest, chest with extended sides, seat chest, paneled chest. Blandford. How to make early American and colonial furniture. 148–79
Six-board chest. Hagerty. Make your own antiques. 96–97
Six-board chest, two-drawer blanket box. Moser. How to build Shaker furniture. 106–07, 170–71

Small dovetailed chest. Shea. Pennsylvania Dutch and their furniture. 196
Stenciled blanket chest. McCall's big book of country needlecrafts. 169–71
Stenciled blanket chest. 101 do-it-yourself projects. 176–79
Terry covered foot locker. Roda. Fabric decorating for the home. 203–05
Three-drawer Pennsylvania walnut chest, north European carved chest, small tulip and
   aster chest. Gottshall. Provincial furniture design and construction. 77–92
Wood burned storage chest. Brightman. 101 practical uses for propane torches. 96–97
Wooden storage chest with variations. Scurlock. Muzzleloader Magazine's book of
   buckskinning II. 191–95

Chests of drawers
Basket weave dresser. Linsley. Fabulous furniture decorations. 128–31
Building block fronts. Fine woodworking techniques 4. 167–69
Built-in dresser. Hylton. Handcrafted shelves & cabinets. 182–85
Bureau-chest, dresser, high-boy. Osburn. Measured drawings of early American furni-
   ture. 32–33, 60–62, 73–75
Chest of drawers. Marlow. Classic furniture projects. 122–37
Chest of drawers. Marlow. Early American furnituremaker's manual. 109–18
Chests of drawers. Zegel. Fast furniture. 89–91
Chest of drawers, chest of drawers kit. 101 do-it-yourself projects. 170–75, 374–76
Chest of drawers, decoupage. Giant book of crafts. 358–59
Chest of drawers restoration. Restoring and reupholstering furniture. 60–67
Chest of drawers. Shea. Pennsylvania Dutch and their furniture. 208–11
Early eighteenth century chest of drawers. Taylor. How to build period country furni-
   ture. 177–81
Four-drawer chest. Oberrecht. Plywood projects illustrated. 149–54
Five-drawer chest. Brown. 44 terrific woodworking plans & projects. 152–56
Five-drawer chest, ten-drawer chest. Moser. How to build Shaker furniture. 164–67
Hearts and ticking dresser. Linsley. Fabulous furniture decorations. 91–98
Hepplewhite chest of drawers. Gotshall. Provincial furniture design and construction.
   71–76
Highboy, Spanish highboy, Spanish lowboy and chest of drawers. Williams. Spanish
   colonial furniture. 98–103, 108–09
Painted folk art chest. Jarnow. (Re)do it yourself. 115–17
Painted trellis chest. McCall's big book of country needlecrafts. 226–27
Shaker chest of drawers and clothes bureau. 77 furniture projects you can build. 79–
   84
Three-drawer chest. Feirer. Cabinetmaking and millwork. 704

Chest of drawers, Repairing
Chest of drawers. Davis. Restoring furniture. 70–77
Mahogany chest of drawers. Wenn. Restoring antique furniture. 47–51

Chewing gum
Painted gum ball machine. Jarnow. (Re)do it yourself. 145

Chickens
Hen and eggs (stuffed). Laury. Treasury of needlecraft gifts for the new baby. 118–20
Laying hen. Favorite easy-to-make toys. 192–97
Rooster carved from a branch. Lubkemann. Carving twigs and branches. 26–54

Children's furniture
Baby seat. Adams. Make your own baby furniture. 71–75
Basement happy room for two children: sleeping, work & play areas. Family handbook
   of carpentry plans/projects. 27–29
Bureau from changing table. Adams. Make your own baby furniture. 50–67

Cabinet from changing table. Adams. Make your own baby furniture. 50–61, 68–69
Chairs and couch, coffee and end tables, dining tables and chairs, bed, chest of
    drawers. Brown. 44 terrific woodworking plans & projects. 193–98
Combination sleep, play and storage area. Leavy. Bookshelves and storage units. 41–
    42
Combined unit. Blandford. 66 children's furniture projects. 247–58
Love seat, bookcase, desk, and table made from plywood. Bragdon. Homeowner's
    complete manual of repair & improvement. 95
Play corner. Blandford. 66 children's furniture projects. 276–82
Sidestep storage. Leavy. Bookshelves and storage units. 22–23
Table chair. Adams. Make your own baby furniture. 95–105
Working board. Blandford. 66 children's furniture projects. 81–83

Children's furniture, Beds
Bed suspended from the ceiling, multilevel bed, children's bed alcove. Roberts. Illus-
    trated handbook of upholstery. 254–60
Bunk beds; climb-on-it superbed. Zegel. Fast furniture. 93–98
Carton and door bed. Palmer. Making children's furniture and play structures. 40–41
Children's unit. Blandford. 66 children's furniture projects. 312–20
Child's bed. Stiles. Easy-to-make children's furniture. 34–38
Junior bed with headboard. Dal Fabbro. How to make children's furniture and play
    equipment. 57–60
Loft bed. Stiles. Easy-to-make children's furniture. 40–44
Plain bed, two-part bed, stacking bunk beds, low stacking beds, trundle beds, and
    bunk beds. Blandford. Building better beds. 165–213
Sleeping tube bunks. Palmer. Making children's furniture and play structures. 44–45
Sleeping tubes. Palmer. Making children's furniture and play structures. 42–43
Tree-house bunk beds, flower headboard. McCall's sewing for your home. 170–74
Triple-wall bed. Palmer. Making children's furniture and play structures. 46–48

Children's furniture, Benches
Pouting bench. Hundley. Folk art toys and furniture for children. 107–12

Children's furniture, Cabinets
Particle board cabinet: storage cabinet. Blandford. 66 children's furniture projects.
    228–40

Children's furniture, Chairs
Bean bag cushion. Complete book of baby crafts. 127–31
Cardboard chairs for playhouse. Boeschen. Successful playhouses. 73
Child size chair. Brann. How to build outdoor furniture. 38–47
Child's director's chair. Slater. Elaine Slater's book of needlepoint projects. 128–33
Child's rocker. Moser. Windsor chairmaking. 71–72
Child's swivel desk chair. Popular Mechanics do-it-yourself encyclopedia. Vol. 5, 679
Corrugated wing chair. Palmer. Making children's furniture and play structures. 26–27
Decoupaged wooden child's chair. Linsley. Decoupage on glass, wood, metal, rocks,
    shells, wax, soap, plastic, canvas, ceramic. 35–40
Ephrata child's chair. Daniele. Building early American furniture. 148–49
Fiberboard barrel chair. Palmer. Making children's furniture and play structures. 20
First chair. Blandford. 66 children's furniture projects. 144–51
Flower-face chairs. McCall's sewing for your home. 175–76
High chair. Adams. Make your own baby furniture. 95–105
High chair. Blandford. How to make early American and colonial furniture. 340–44
High chair. Dal Fabbro. How to make children's furniture and play equipment. 37–39
High chair. Osburn. Measured drawings of early American furniture. 40–41
High chair. Stiles. Easy-to-make children's furniture. 50–53

Indian back rest. Boeschen. Successful playhouses. 125
Kit-kat rocker. Hundley. Folk art toys and furniture for children. 95–101
Ladderback chair. Blandford. 66 children's furniture projects. 198–206
Little folks rocker. Blackwell. Johnny Blackwell's poor man's catalog. 133
Low chair. Blandford. 66 children's furniture projects. 137–44
Nursing chair. Blandford. 66 children's furniture projects. 154–64
Plywood upholstered chair. Blandford. 66 children's furniture projects. 176–84
Rocking chair made from cradle. Adams. Make your own baby furniture. 34–42
Slot back chair. Palmer. Making children's furniture and play structures. 22–23
Standard chair, plywood chair, rocking chair, junior chair or high stool. Dal Fabbro.
    How to make children's furniture and play equipment. 95–102
Storage chair. Stiles. Easy-to-make children's furniture. 56–59
Tote chair. Hundley. Folk art toys and furniture for children. 116–20
Triple-wall lounger. Palmer. Making children's furniture and play structures. 24–25

Children's furniture, Chests
Chests. Blandford. 66 children's furniture projects. 202–14, 240–47, 258–62
Child's footlocker. Complete handyman do-it-yourself encyclopedia. Vol. 8, 1163–67
Low chest, high chest, chifforobe. Dal Fabbro. How to make children's furniture and
    play equipment. 107–15

Children's furniture, Chests. See also **Toys, Storage**

Children's furniture, Cribs
Baby crib (repair). Schuler. How to fix almost everything. 48
Bumper guards for crib. McCall's sewing for your home. 193–94
Colonial crib and rocker. Brann. How to build colonial furniture. 174–200
Cradle & crib. Churchill. Backyard building book II. 114–22
Crib. Stiles. Easy-to-make children's furniture. 28–31
Crib/desk. Adams. Make your own baby furniture. 77–93
Crib, portable crib. Dal Fabbro. How to make children's furniture and play equipment.
    31–36
Cribs. Blandford. 66 children's furniture projects. 288–98
Folding crib, paneled crib, drop-side crib, lift-side crib. Blandford. Building better beds.
    214–31
Wooden mechanism for dropside cribs. Fine woodworking techniques 5. 133

Children's furniture, Desks
Child's art desk. Stiles. Easy-to-make children's furniture. 78–82
Child's desk. DeCristoforo. Build your own wood toys, gifts and furniture. 366–70
Desk from a crib. Adams. Make your own baby furniture. 77–93
Desks. Blandford. 66 children's furniture projects. 117–21
Five-piece desk, triple wall desk. Palmer. Making children's furniture and play struc-
    tures. 34–37
Kneehole desk, built-in desk, typewriter desk. Dal Fabbro. How to make children's
    furniture and play equipment. 76–85
Rolltop desk for your child. Popular Mechanics do-it-yourself encyclopedia. Vol. 5,
    676–77

Children's furniture, Easels
Easel. Adams. Make your own baby furniture. 174–75

Children's furniture, Sofas
Crib becomes a couch. Stiles. Easy-to-make children's furniture. 31–32

Children's furniture, Stools
Turtle stool, a loverly stool. Hundley. Folk art toys and furniture for children. 121–31

Children's furniture, Tables
Adjust-table. Stiles. Easy-to-make children's furniture. 68–70
Book rack table. Blandford. 66 children's furniture projects. 184–93
Bookcase and table. Blandford. 66 children's furniture projects. 128–32
Built-in table. Blandford. 66 children's furniture projects. 114–17
Changing table. Adams. Make your own baby furniture. 49–69
Changing table. Stiles. Easy-to-make children's furniture. 62–66
Child's block table. Linsley. Fabulous furniture decorations. 159–66
Extending corner table. Blandford. 66 children's furniture projects. 170–76
Half-lapped table. Blandford. 66 children's furniture projects. 164–70
Pedestal table. Blandford. 66 children's furniture projects. 132–37
Small round table, play and work table. Dal Fabbro. How to make children's furniture
    and play equipment. 90–91
Standard table. Blandford. 66 children's furniture projects. 112–28
Table. Blandford. 66 children's furniture projects. 87–89
Tables and chairs for toddlers. Adams. Make your own baby furniture. 189–204
Toddler's table. Blandford. 66 children's furniture projects. 112–14
Tote table. Hundley. Folk art toys and furniture for children. 113–15
Tree trunk table, flower table. McCall's sewing for your home. 170, 174–75
Trestle table. Blandford. 66 children's furniture projects. 151–54
Work table. Dal Fabbro. How to make children's furniture and play equipment. 93–94

Children's vehicles
Cart and bookcase. Dal Fabbro. How to make children's furniture and play equipment.
    156
Handmobile, boxmobile. Maginley. Toys to make and ride. 64–69, 88–94
Kiddie car, no-gas car. DeCristoforo. Build your own wood toys, gifts and furniture.
    238–45, 262–79
Kiddie car, pedal car, scooter, castor car, jeep, bike trailer. Maginley. Toys to make
    and ride. 22–32, 40–57
Push tricycle. Blandford. Giant book of wooden toys. 146–51
Seatboards. Gould. Skateboards, scooterboards, and seatboards you can build. 55–65
Rocker/vehicle. Adams. Make your own baby furniture. 144–49
Tricycle. Stiles. Easy-to-make children's furniture. 92–93
Walker. Adams. Make your own baby furniture. 133–39
Walker truck. Blandford. 66 children's furniture projects. 409–10

Chimes. See **Bells; Door bells**

Chimneys
Building a chimney. Gould. Owner-built fireplace. 77–85
Building your own chimney. Traister. All about chimneys. 47–68
Chimney repair. Bragdon. Homeowner's complete manual of repair & improvement.
    495
Cleaning chimneys. Traister. All about chimneys. 19–46
How to cover those metal chimney pipes. Outdoor projects for home and garden. 20–
    22
Real-brick chimney. Better Homes and Gardens. Step-by-step masonry & concrete.
    88–89
Solar cooling chimney. Calhoun. 20 simple solar projects. 206–23

China cupboards. See **Cupboards**

China painting
Painting chinaware. Bumper book of things a girl can make. 29–31

Chisels
Chisels and chisel-shaped tools. Richardson. Practical blacksmithing. Vol. 2, 78–108
Chisels, and how to pare. Fine woodworking techniques 5. 53–57
Cold chisel. Make it! don't buy it. 249
Forging a cold chisel. Weygers. Modern blacksmith. 45
Forging woodcarving gouges. Weygers. Modern blacksmith. 75–77
Making a cold chisel. McRaven. Country blacksmithing. 145–47
Making chisels. Blandford. Practical handbook of blacksmithing and metalworking.
   180–92
Making chisels. Fine woodworking techniques 2. 60
Miniature chisel. Weygers. Recycling, use, and repair of tools. 52–55
Sharpening turning chisels. Nish. Creative woodturning. 13–21
Using a chisel. Waugh. Handyman's encyclopedia. 68–72
Woodturning chisels. Fine woodworking techniques 3. 142–45
Veining gouge. Weygers. Modern blacksmith. 78–79

Chokers
Beaded choker necklace. Auld. Tatting; the contemporary art of knotting with a shuttle.
   96–97
Beaded macrame choker. Scharf. Butterick's fast and easy needlecrafts. 78–79
Beadwork choker and bracelet. Encyclopedia of crafts. 181
Blackberry choker. Stearns. Macrame. 43–47
Choker strung on wire. Mosesson. Jewelry craft for beginners. 65–67
Choker woven in 2 colors, fringed choker, choker with front fastening and shaped
   ends, choker with woven fasteners, choker with partly-strung warps, chokers with
   wooden beads in several sizes, three-strand woven choker, choker with corded
   edge. Gill. Beadwork: the technique of stringing, threading, and weaving. 123–36,
   139–40, 147–50, 152–64
Feather chokers & earrings. Johnson. Nature crafts. 122–23
Flower choker. Ruggieri. Woman's Day book of no-pattern sewing. 109
Floweret chokers. Woman's Day crochet showcase. 76
Full choker, chokers using several sizes and shapes of wooden beads, double string
   choker, flower center chokers, two-color choker with a loop and bead fastener,
   choker with center patterns, flowered choker, arrow chokers. Gill. Beadwork: the
   technique of stringing, threading, and weaving. 18–22, 26–28, 33–37, 48–49, 56–
   59, 62–70
Half-circle choker, dangling-bead choker. Mosesson. Jewelry craft for beginners. 167–
   70
Heart-choker necklace. Dodge. Step-by-step new-macrame. 35–36
Irish crochet rose chokers. Svinicki. Old-fashioned crochet. 81
Making a wire choker. Sommer. Contemporary costume jewelry. 27
Medieval belt and choker. Jacobs. Crochet book. 100–01
Ring choker, feather choker, macrame choker. Torbet. Macrame you can wear. 66–67,
   71–72
Seed-bead choker. Mosesson. Jewelry craft for beginners. 39–41
Spiralled flat-wire and bead-choker. Metalcrafting encyclopedia. 173

Christening robes
Baptismal pillow. Laury. Treasury of needlecraft gifts for the new baby. 27–28
Christening dress. Woman's Day crochet showcase. 133–36
Christening dress and bonnet (knit). Mensinga-Biasiny. Beautiful baby clothes to
   crochet, knit, sew and embroider. 117–20
Christening dress and slip. Benton. Sewing classic clothes for children. 70–83

Christening gown and bonnet. Complete book of baby crafts. 79–83
Christening quilts. Laury. Treasury of needlecraft gifts for the new baby. 24–26
Christening robe. Practical needlework. 109
Crocheted christening coat and cap. Doherty. Family Circle of 429 great gifts-to-make all year round for just 10¢ to $10.00. 168–70
Crocheted christening robe. Favorite knitting & crochet patterns. 14–17
Cutwork or broderie anglaise christening dress. Embroidery. 98–103
Guardian angels. Great cross-stitch. 95–96

Christmas cards. *See* **Greeting cards**

Christmas decorations
Advent wreath. Cook. Decorating for the holidays. 4–5
Apple-head Christmas: night before Christmas in miniature. McCall's book of Christmas. 86–93
Beatrix Potter Christmas picture. Wilson. Erica Wilson's Christmas world. 109–13
Boxwood and bows hanging, pine cone boys and girls, creche in a seashell. Berry. How to make party and holiday decorations. 108–12
Calico doll swag. McCall's book of Christmas. 94–95
Christmas banner. Foose. Scrap saver's stitchery book. 112–18
Christmas bells in cane. Maynard. Modern basketry from the start. 142–45
Christmas doves in felt. McCall's book of Christmas. 95–96
Christmas elf. Gottshall. Wood carving and whittling for everyone. 134–38
Christmas ideas—patterns for Christmas. Fraser. Modern stitchery: stitches, patterns, free-form designing. 98
Christmas mobile. Christensen. Needlepoint. 71–72
Christmas sampler (embroidered). Wilson. Erica Wilson's Christmas world. 100–03
Christmas wall-hanging. Breckenridge. Lap quilting. 93–95
Coffee can Christmas boot. Coffey. Francine Coffey's celebrity sewing bee. 168
Coffee can Santa Claus. Coffey. Francine Coffey's celebrity sewing bee. 151
Cones for Christmas (paper figures). Creative crafts yearbook: an exciting new collection of needlework and crafts. 99–103
Counting ribbon (Advent). Cook. Decorating for the holidays. 49
Crocheted bells, crocheted snowmen, birds-of-a-feather tree and sleepy Santa pillow. Woman's Day book of weekend crafts. 78–90
Crocheted Christmas puppy, snowlady & snowman, Santa mouse, snowman, Mr. & Mrs. Claus, Christmas carolers. American School of Needlework. Great Christmas crochet book. 42–64, 81–93
Crocheted Santas, knitted beanbag elf and Santa, gift cover, terry Santa, furry Santa, tiny Santa. McCall's book of Christmas. 153–54, 164–70
Danish cake advent wreath, Lucia buns, Springerle, Berliner Kranze, gingerbread house, Nurnburg star cookies, stained-glass cookies. Coskey. Christmas crafts for everyone. 85–107
Decorated Santas and stars and snowflakes. Hawkesworth. Paper cutting: making all kinds of paper shapes and figures. 90–92
Decorations children can make. Better Homes and Gardens holiday decorations you can make. 166–83
Decorations from found objects. Cook. Decorating for the holidays. 51–58
A dozen decorating ideas to brighten the holidays. Vanderbilt. Gloria Vanderbilt designs for your home. 161–66
Edible ornaments: Lucia buns, Springerle, Berliner Kranze, gingerbread house, Nurnburg star cookies, stained glass cookies, breaddough ornaments and ice cream horns of plenty. Coskey. Christmas crafts for everyone. 91–110, 113–14
Evergreen swags and arches. Miles. Designing with natural materials. 77–81
Evergreens for the door. Meyer. Christmas crafts. 105–07
Father Christmas and sleigh. Janitch. All made from paper. 60–61

Father Christmas placesetting. Janitch. Candlemaking and decorations. 76–77

Felt vignettes (scenes of Christmas). McCall's book of Christmas. 93–94

Filet wall hanging—Christmas angel, nativity scene. American School of Needlework. Great Christmas crochet book. 38–41

Focus on your fireplace. Better Homes and Gardens holiday decorations you can make. 77–83

Fruit pyramid. Johnson. Nature crafts. 143

Garlands. Cook. Decorating for the holidays. 28–29

Ginger Santa, angel cookies. McCall's book of Christmas. 108–10

Gingerbread Hansel & Gretel house. Linsley. Custom made. 46–52

Gingerbread village. McCall's book of Christmas. 114–20

God Jul wall plaque. Nielsen. Scandinavian embroidery, past and present. 104–05

Holiday bells. Fowler. Can crafts. 24–26

Holiday greenery: decorating with native materials. Johnson. Nature crafts. 134–37

Holly garland. Wargo. Soft crafts for special occasions. 120–21

Inviting doorways. Better Homes and Gardens holiday decorations you can make. 134–47

Joy Christmas banner. Christensen. Teach yourself needlepoint. 87–88

Knitted Santa and elf. McCall's book of Christmas. 157–59

Luminarias. Coskey. Christmas crafts for everyone. 55–58

Making Christmas decorations. Marshall. Foilcraft. 107–11

Mantel decorations. Cook. Decorating for the holidays. 39

Mantelpieces. Miles. Designing with natural materials. 105–06

Musical centerpieces for Christmas. Popular Mechanics do-it-yourself encyclopedia. Vol. 4, 628–31

Needlepoint Xmas hanging. Smith. Needlery. 188–92

New England Christmas scene, felt tree wall hanging, Bethlehem glued-fabric panel, Bethlehem in applique, knitted Madonna, latch-hook Santa, crewel-embroidered Christmas creatures. McCall's book of Christmas. 58–71

Newspaper Christmas bells. Yoder. Sculpture and modeling for the elementary school. 54

Noel wall hanging. Great granny crochet book. 82

Ornamental hanging ball, cane and apple hanging. Christmas crafts book. 19–20

Outdoor decorations. Better Homes and Gardens holiday decorations you can make. 148–57

Pinecone drops. Miles. Designing with natural materials. 87–89

Quilted patchwork Noel banner. Foose. More scrap saver's stitchery. 103–13

Red-nosed reindeer. Woman's Day creative stitchery from scraps. 112–14

Reindeer and sleigh. Foose. Scrap saver's stitchery book. 120–25

Rejoice banner, soft-sculpture candles, patchwork package banner, soft fireplace, Christmas house, Christmas mountain, banners with symbols of peace and good-will. Better Homes and Gardens treasury of Christmas crafts & foods. 39, 101, 207–08, 224–26, 229, 308–23

Rustic, fir cone, red and gold and pine branch center pieces. Christmas crafts book. 10, 13–14, 18, 22

Santa Claus. Christmas crafts book. 106–07

Santa Claus and his reindeer. Araki. Origami for Christmas. 132–33

Santa Claus' special delivery. Greenhowe. Making miniature toys and dolls. 26–30

Santa Claus table decoration. Creative crafts yearbook: an exciting new collection of needlework and crafts. 104–05

Santa doorpiece, candle pot centerpiece, tinsel art Christmas tree, rainbow mobile, reindeer table decoration, Santa's candy cane boat. Popular Mechanics do-it-yourself encyclopedia. Vol. 5, 692–96

Santa in a balloon. Wilson. Erica Wilson's Christmas world. 138–41

Santa's boot. Cook. Decorating for the holidays. 48

Shell doorspray. Meras. Vacation crafts. 79–80

Stained glass Celtic cross. Janitch. All made from paper. 41–42
Stained-glass Christmas panel. McCall's book of Christmas. 99–101
Stained-glass snowflake. Janitch. Candlemaking and decorations. 78–79
Strip patchwork Christmas banner. Dudley. Strip patchwork: quick and easy patchwork
  using the Seminole technique. 115–23
Swags. Cook. Decorating for the holidays. 22–27
Table arrangements. Cook. Decorating for the holidays. 40–45
Table ornaments. Epple. Something from nothing crafts. 176
Table top magic: creches and table decorations. Better Homes and Gardens holiday
  decorations you can make. 84–99
Three kings by candlelight. Janitch. Candlemaking and decorations. 72–74
Tiny treasures—Santa, poinsettia, wreath & holly. American School of Needlework.
  Great Christmas crochet book. 119–21
Trapunto Christmas tree, Chinese fish and twenty-five cent eagle. Morgan. Trapunto
  and other forms of raised quilting. 154–55
Twelfth night circle. Janitch. Candlemaking and decorations. 32–33
Twelfth night scene. Cook. Decorating for the holidays. 62–63
Under-the-tree trims. Better Homes and Gardens holiday decorations you can make.
  14–15
Winter panoramas. McCall's book of Christmas. 96–99
Woodburned Christmas bell. Broadwater. Woodburning: art and craft. 121–24
Village and trees (needlepoint on plastic canvas). Wilson. Erica Wilson's Christmas
  world. 60–65

Christmas packages. *See* **Wrapping of packages**

Christmas stockings
Assorted Christmas stockings to sew. Woman's Day bazaar best sellers. 131–33
Cat, Santa, buttons and bows, pinecone stockings. Better Homes and Gardens easy
  bazaar crafts. 64, 70, 72, 74, 76, 78–79, 81
Christmas stocking. Christensen. Teach yourself needlepoint. 123–24
Christmas stocking. Christmas crafts book. 106
Christmas stocking. Linsley. Custom made. 1–3
Christmas stocking (felt). Coffey. Francine Coffey's celebrity sewing bee. 150
Christmas stockings. Great granny crochet book. 82
Christmas stockings. Scobey. First easy-to-see needlepoint workbook. 144–48
Crazy patchwork Christmas stocking. Breckenridge. Lap quilting. 84–87
Crazy quilt stocking. Fanning. Complete book of machine quilting. 227–30
Crocheted stocking trio snowman, Santa or gingerbread boy. McCall's book of Christ-
  mas. 160–62
Cross-stitch stockings: baby's first, little angel, prancing reindeer, Scandinavian snow-
  flakes and Christmas soldiers. Linsley. Lesley Linsley's Christmas ornaments and
  stockings. 129–31, 135–43, 146–48
Felt, fabric, and crocheted stockings. Better Homes and Gardens holiday decorations
  you can make. 63–75
Folk art stockings, crewel-embroidered stockings, country patchwork stockings, family
  satin stockings, yo-yo stocking, old-lady-in-the-shoe stocking. Better Homes and
  Gardens treasury of Christmas crafts & foods. 142, 154–55, 208, 210–11, 229
Fur-topped, cowboy, and embroidered felt boots, pair of stocking children, felt whimsy
  stockings, "patchwork" stockings paired with dolls. McCall's book of Christmas.
  172–81
Great big Christmas stocking. Baldwin. Scrap fabric crafts. 79–81
High button shoe, ice skate, cowboy boot, sneaker. Foose. Scrap saver's stitchery
  book. 96–104
Odalisk felt applique stockings. Heard. Complete guide to quilting. 280–81

Patchwork, buttons and bells and mouse stockings. Linsley. Lesley Linsley's Christmas ornaments and stockings. 152–57, 168–70

Peter rabbit stocking. Wilson. Erica Wilson's Christmas world. 114–17

Puppy dog stocking, giant ribbed Christmas stockings, Santa sock. American School of Needlework. Great Christmas crochet book. 94–103

Red candy-striped sock, green embroidered stocking, knitted dolls in stockings, striped knitted stocking, Granny stocking, needlepoint argyle and tree stockings. McCall's book of Christmas. 150–52, 156, 160, 170–72

Ribbon, knitted, black velvet, and family stockings. Better Homes and Gardens treasury of Christmas crafts & foods. 232–37

Santa stocking. Foose. More scrap saver's stitchery. 98–102

St. Nicholas day stocking. Meyer. Christmas Gifts. 29–35

Santa & tree Christmas stocking (needlepoint). Arnold. Needlepoint pattern book. 164–65

Striped Christmas stocking. Hubert. Weekend knitting projects. 24

Striped stocking, babes-in-toyland stocking, not a creature was stirring stocking, elf stocking and embroidered stockings. Linsley. Lesley Linsley's Christmas ornaments and stockings. 42–43, 51–52, 82–88, 112–24

Twelve days of Christmas sock. Ambuter. Carolyn Ambuter's needlepoint celebrations. 128–29

Christmas tree decorations

Acrylic decorations, glittering tree decorations, balloon ornaments, veneer ornaments, top ornament, ball and cup ornaments, zizzer, plastic tree ornaments, cookie cutter ornaments. Popular Mechanics do-it-yourself encyclopedia. Vol. 5, 701, 706–07

Alpine ornaments in cookie clay. McCall's book of Christmas. 102–03

Balls, metal foil, and tree top ornaments. Christmas crafts book. 45–53

Barnyard animal ornaments, snowflake frosting ornaments, hardanger embroidered ornaments, fabric bows. Better Homes and Gardens treasury of Christmas crafts & foods. 206–07, 212

Beaded multi-colored sphere and egg. Hulbert. Creative beadwork. 107–08

Beatrix Potter felt ornaments, crewel butterflies, Mr. and Mrs. Mouse, Chessie and playmates, golden birds and lace snowballs. Wilson. Erica Wilson's Christmas world. 20–25, 38–47, 50–51

Bird's nest made from margarine cups. Rissell. Craftwork the handicapped elderly can make and sell. 98–99

Birds' tree. Meyer. Christmas crafts. 125–29

Blown egg in macrame holder, gingham bag with cloves, clothespin doll, molded salt dough ornament. Christmas decorations from Williamsburg's folk art collection. 74–79

Braided straw ornaments, angels. Hibbs. Straw sculpture. 82

Bread dough ornaments, play clay ornaments. Coskey. Christmas crafts for everyone. 108–13

Cap and gown, birdcage, chandelier, stocking cap, drum, angel. Fowler. Can crafts. 124–32

Cat-stuffed, nametape, necktie. Better Homes and Gardens easy bazaar crafts. 64–65, 71, 73, 76, 79–80

Christmas balls. Gardner. Dough creations. 94–95

Christmas ornaments. Great granny crochet book. 85–87

Christmas package, ornaments, panda Christmas ornament, charted Christmas ornament. Christensen. Teach yourself needlepoint. 73–74, 88–89, 95, 127

Christmas snow flakes, Christmas crystals (needlepoint). Boyles. Needlework gifts for special occasions. 48–52

Christmas star and geometric ornament. Yoder. Sculpture and modeling for the elementary school. 28–31

Christmas tree candle holders. Weygers. Recycling, use and repair of tools. 49

Christmas tree floor skirt. Goldman. Decorate with felt. 24

Christmas tree ornament made from bottle, tin can winter stars, hanging spool ornament, ring ornament. Epple. Something from nothing crafts. 21–22, 181–82, 191, 197

Christmas tree ornaments. Breckenridge. Lap quilting. 80–84

Christmas tree ornaments. Burchette. More needlework blocking and finishing. 113–14

Christmas tree ornaments: snowman, box, bell, Santa tree, Jack-in-the-box. Scobey. First easy-to-see needlepoint workbook. 149–52

Christmas tree skirt. Christensen. Teach yourself needlepoint. 120–22

Christmas wreath ornament on plastic canvas. Christensen. Needlepoint. 48–49

Constructions from a triangle and octahedron, star-shaped ornaments. Stephen. Creating with tissue paper. 180–81, 188–89

Cookie-cutter Christmas tree ornaments. Chroman. Potter's primer. 125–27

Cornucopias, sugar plum cases, drums, lucky shoes, bonbon boxes. Whatnot. 176–83

Counted cross stitch stars, personalized sachet ornaments and initially hearts. Linsley. Lesley Linsley's Christmas ornaments and stockings. 125–28, 132–34, 144–45

Crochet covered tree ornaments, snowflakes, popcorn and cranberry garland. American School of Needlework. Great Christmas crochet book. 16–23

Crocheted boot; felt gingerbread men; Christmas stocking & Santa Claus-cap ornaments; crocheted boots with candy canes; Santa, mouse & elf felt ornaments; crocheted wreath, corkscrew, & circular ornaments; "strawberry" walnut ornaments; egg ornaments; soft-sculpture heart, star, and tree; ribbon star ornaments. Woman's Day bazaar best sellers. 132–36

Clay ornaments. Yoder. Sculpture and modeling for the elementary school. 47

Cornhusk ornaments. Conner. Corncraft. 97–109

Crocheted star chain. Meyer. Christmas crafts. 109–13

Decorations made from natural materials. Christmas decorations from Williamsburg's folk art collection. 27–45

Dried flower balls, seashell flower, walnut people, oyster shell, milkweed pod, glorified wishbone, bird's nest, gilded seashell, pod icicles, and dried doodad ornament. O'Neill. Make-it-merry Christmas book. 72–75

English walnut ornaments. Miles. Designing with natural materials. 89–90

Fabric decorations. Christmas decorations from Williamsburg's folk art collection. 9–25

Fabric ornaments. Heard. Complete guide to quilting. 278–79

Fairy on the tree. Janitch. Candlemaking and decorations. 74–76

Felt forum: penguin, contented cat, papa bear, mama bear, teddy pops, circus cat, angel cat, cool cats, folk doll, peasant girl, boys and girls together. Linsley. Lesley Linsley's Christmas ornaments and stockings. 59–81

Felt stuffed tree ornaments, stuffed doll tree ornaments; wooden crocheted Christmas baskets. Doherty. Family Circle book of 429 great gifts-to-make all year round for just 10¢ to $10.00. 46–49, 54–56

Four snowflakes. Henderson. Woman's Day book of designer crochet. 206–07

Gingerbread ornaments, train garland, horse ornament, punch-out ornament, heirloom rocker. Popular Mechanics do-it-yourself encyclopedia. Vol. 5, 693–95

Gingerbread sculptures. Meyer. Christmas crafts. 60–62

Gnomes (needlepoint). Wilson. Erica Wilson's Christmas world. 12–14

Gold filigree balls. Stephan. Creating with tissue paper. 176–77

Granny square jewels, crochet snowflakes, reindeer ornament, gingerbread puppets and house. Linsley. Lesley Linsley's Christmas ornaments and stockings. 150–51, 165–67, 171–75

Green carved ornament (gourds). Johnson. Nature crafts. 115

Handmade Christmas ornaments (stuffed). Baldwin. Scrap fabric crafts. 76–78

Ice-cream cone horns of plenty, Scandinavian yarn dolls, tomte, molded string cages, crocheted snowflakes, paper ornaments. Coskey. Christmas crafts for everyone. 113–40

Individual origami. Araki. Origami for Christmas. 22–122

Joy, angel, elf and dove. Jarvey. You can dough it! 69–81

Lace snowflake. Southard. Bobbin lacemaking. 185–86

Laminated paper ornaments. Romberg. Let's discover papier-mâché. 60

Lollipop Christmas tree ornaments, patchwork Christmas tree skirt. Evrard. Homespun crafts from scraps. 84–86, 89–91

Lunaria poinsettias, dusty miller snowflakes. Johnson. Nature crafts. 139–40

Metal foil Christmas ornaments. Metalcrafting encyclopedia. 152–53

Metal tree ornaments. Yoder. Sculpture and modeling for the elementary school. 133–34

Needlepoint ornaments. Treasury of things to make. 32–34

Needlepoint: shapes on plastic mesh, eight-point stars, babes-in-toyland, butterflies, antique cornucopia. Linsley. Lesley Linsley's Christmas ornaments and stockings. 45–58

Needlework decorations. Christmas decorations from Williamsburg's folk art collection. 46–54

Origami star and ball. Stephan. Creating with tissue paper. 148–54

Ornaments: Austrian foil, German star, and Mexican lanterns. Coskey. Christmas crafts for everyone. 50–55

Ornaments: bobbin lace, shell mosaic, leather tree, wood madonna, card & quillwork. D'Amato. Italian crafts. 139–47

Ornaments. Romberg. Let's discover papier-mâché. 49

Ornaments for the Christmas tree. Jerdee. Fabric applique for worship. 35–36

Ornaments from the garden. Scobey. Gifts from your garden. 140–42

Ornaments made from light bulbs, pie tins, walnut shells, sea shells. Brunner. Pass it on. 118–26

Owl family embroidered in turkey work. Wilson. Erica Wilson's Christmas world. 146–49

Paper and wood: paper patchwork stars, country animal charmers, boy or girl on swing, Christmas tree bores and Mexican ornaments made from clothespins. Linsley. Lesley Linsley's Christmas ornaments and stockings. 89–111

Paper decorations. Christmas decorations from Williamsburg's folk art collection. 55–62

Paper star. Meyer. Christmas crafts. 15–17

Pincushions & Christmas tree ornaments. Christensen. Needlepoint book. 109–10

Pine ornaments, fabric bows, bread-dough bird and butterfly ornaments, yarn-wrapped ornaments, calico bird and star ornaments, cross-stitch rose wreath ornaments, wooden angel ornaments, macrame snowflakes, log cabin ornaments, schoolhouse ornaments. Better Homes and Gardens treasury of Christmas crafts & foods. 16, 35, 82, 84

Plumed partridges in felt, silk baubles, wound thread ornaments, felt mini-figures, jumping jacks, needlepoint disks, pleated paper ornaments. McCall's book of Christmas. 4–19

Quilted Christmas tote bag and ornaments. Foose. More scrap saver's stitchery. 122–28

Ribbon and bead and egg carton ornament. O'Neill. Make-it-merry Christmas book. 66–70

Ring around angel, green garden, holly bead tree, satin puppy and kitty, golden ball, sweet memory, blue and green ball, pretty pink egg, velvet fruit, and wormy apple. Berry. How to make party and holiday decorations. 91–105

Salt dough ornament. O'Neill. Make-it-merry Christmas book. 46–48

Santa, angel, lion, lamb, Christmas tree, and God's eye. Sheldon. Washable and dry-able needlepoint. 86–89

Santa Claus & Christmas tree ornaments (needlepoint). Arnold. Needlepoint pattern book. 169–71

Seashore Christmas tree. Elbert. Shell craft. 77–78

Santa ornament. Fanning. Complete book of machine quilting. 195–98
Santa's helper ornament. Wargo. Soft crafts for special occasions. 109–10
Seminole patchwork tree ornaments. Dudley. Strip patchwork: quick and easy patchwork using the Seminole technique. 110
Sewn yarn, crocheted, needlepoint, felt, covered balls, cardboard, natural dough, and paper ornaments. Better Homes and Gardens holiday decorations you can make. 33–61
Shell Christmas tree ornaments. Logan. Shell crafts. 198–200
Silver stars and snowflakes, Beatrix Potter ornaments, noel boxes, diamond cubes, twinkle twinkle little star and stocking ornaments in needlepoint. Wilson. Erica Wilson's Christmas world. 16–19, 26–37
Snowflake, cornucopia, basket, pleated fan, chain and string of paper dolls. Elbert. Paperwork. 50–55
Snowflake tree ornament. Linsley. Great bazaar. 104
Spice tree ornaments. Johnson. Nature crafts. 141
Squirrel's christmas, Christmas candle (needlepoint). Needlework nostalgia. 66, 69–70
Stitch and stuff: pastel butterfly, bird of peace, fat cat, woolly mouse, big bear, piglet, stuffed heart, stars, magical mystical stars and moon, ribbon stars, miniature folk pillows and sleepy-time doll stocking. Linsley. Lesley Linsley's Christmas ornaments and stockings. 16–41
Sterbenz. Decorated tree.
Stuffed ornaments. Gillies. Patterns for applique and pieced work—and ways to use them. 113–29
Sugarplum baskets, porcupine, Danish pleated star, Danish reed ornament, Danish woven hearts, Polish heart ornament, Scandinavian mousetraps, Polish treetop angel. Coskey. Christmas crafts for everyone. 61–84
Terrarium tree ornaments. Johnson. Nature crafts. 131
Tin can ornaments: star, sunburst, fringed flower, Mexican star, hammered disk, Inca amulet, bell, bird, butterfly, fish, pinwheel, and flower holder. O'Neill. Make-it-merry Christmas book. 57–60
Tole painted Christmas tree ornaments. Howard. New tole & folk art designs. 77–85
Tree skirt. Great granny crochet book. 90–91
Treetop star, Mexican tin-can-top ornaments, Mexican yarn/clay figures, Ecuadorian bread ornaments, Mexican mirror ornaments, Pendo Christmas ball, painted delft ornaments, lace ornaments, satin angel ornaments. Better Homes and Gardens treasury of Christmas crafts & foods. 109, 138–39, 154–55, 163, 170
Trumpet, bell, drum, rocking horse, skate, cat in stocking, mouse and candy cane, teddy bear. Foose. Scrap saver's stitchery book. 106–14
Twelve-, eight-, sixteen-pointed and sunray decorations. Fowler. Can crafts. 119–24
Velvet Saint Nick. O'Neill. Make-it-merry Christmas book. 96–97
Victorian blue ornament. Nicole. Designer accessories to make for your home. 180–81
Wood decorations. Christmas decorations from Williamsburg's folk art collection. 63–74
Wood ornaments, bread dough ornaments. Buxton. Craftmaking: for love or money. 98–108, 115–17
Woodburned Christmas ornaments. Broadwater. Woodburning: art and craft. 38–54
Woodburned ornament (gourds). Johnson. Nature crafts. 112
Woodland animals Christmas tree ornaments. Wilson. Erica Wilson's Christmas world. 74–79

Christmas trees, Miniature

Beveled Christmas tree. Isenberg. How to work in beveled glass. 209
Calico Christmas tree. Baldwin. Scrap fabric crafts. 82–83
Calico tree, star pillow tree, star-topped felt tree, fringed tissue tree with fruits and vegetables, beaded tree, ruffled tree, teardrop tree, poinsettia tree. McCall's book of Christmas. 35–45

Celosia Christmas tree. Wiita. Dried flowers for all seasons. 95–96

Christmas tree. Janitch. All made from paper. 63

Christmas tree. Stephan. Creating with tissue paper. 172–73

Christmas tree. Wilson. Needleplay. 132–33

Christmas tree or angel (pom-poms glued on styrofoam or cardboard). Rissell. Craftwork the handicapped elderly can make and sell. 31–32

Christmas trees to make. Better Homes and Gardens holiday decorations you can make. 16–31

Construction paper trees. Lyon. Arts and crafts objects children can make for the home. 87–89

Crocheted tree. Henderson. Woman's Day book of designer crochet. 205–06

Happy Christmas tree. Janitch. Candlemaking and decorations. 77–78

Icy Christmas tree of shells embedded in clear casting resin. Elbert. Shell craft. 196–97

"Lace" Christmas trees, white origami tree. Araki. Origami for Christmas. 124–27

Macrame wall-hanging Christmas-tree, minitree centerpiece. Popular Mechanics do-it-yourself encyclopedia. Vol. 5, 701, 707

Macaroni tree. O'Neill. Make-it-merry Christmas book. 16–17

Make a tree for indoors. Miles. Designing with natural materials. 54–72

Patchwork tree. Berry. How to make party and holiday decorations. 109

Pine trees, corn husk tree. Better Homes and Gardens treasury of Christmas crafts & foods. 18, 332–33

Pinecone tree. Nicole. Designer accessories to make for your home. 99–101

Pod tree. Better Homes and Gardens easy bazaar crafts. 75, 81

Pom pom Christmas tree. Wargo. Soft crafts for special occasions. 107–08

Reader's Digest Christmas tree. Epple. Something from nothing crafts. 58–60

Salt dough topiary tree. O'Neill. Make-it-merry Christmas book. 50–53

Tree to remember . . . make it for keeps. Vanderbilt. Gloria Vanderbilt designs for your home. 158–60

Christmas wreaths. *See* **Wreaths**

Church furnishings
Church kneelers. Encyclopedia of crafts. 53

Church models
Rooftop church. Casselman. Crafts from around the world. 126–29

Church vestments
Ecclesiastical vestments (stole, cape). Blair. Banners and flags. 168–75

Jerdee. Fabric applique for worship.

Churns
Butter churn. Maginley. America in miniatures. 49–51

Cigarette holders
Cigarette box. Goldman. Decorate with felt. 22–23

Match-covered cigarette can, cigarette holder, ribbon trimmed bandage box, fabric cigarette case. Doherty. Family Circle book of 429 great gifts-to-make all year round for just 10¢ to $10.00. 5, 10–11, 63, 144–45

Cigarettes
El Placebo needlepoint cigarette. Sheldon. Washable and dryable needlepoint. 108

Ribbon trimmed lighter & matchbooks. Doherty. Family Circle book of 429 great gifts-to-make all year round for just 10¢ to $10.00. 39, 63

Circus models
Circus train, tent, and performing animals. Williams. Cookie craft: no-bake designs for edible party favors and decorations. 131–47

Circus, Toy
Circus wagon. Fowler. Can crafts. 145–53

Clamps
Bench clamp, wooden clamps. Fine woodworking techniques 2. 31, 42–49
Choose the right clamp, make a machine-vise clamp and bar clamps. Popular Mechanics do-it-yourself encyclopedia. Vol. 5, 738–44
Machinist's clamps. Briney. Home machinist's handbook. 238–44
Picture frame clamps. Fine woodworking techniques 4. 7

Clay
About clay and experimentation with local clay. Riegger. Electric kiln ceramics. 43–67
Clay coloring, engobes and stains. Chappell. Potter's complete book of clay and glazes. 117–39
Clays for salt glazing. Troy. Salt-glazed ceramics. 50–61
Digging your own clay. Chappell. Potter's complete book of clay and glazes. 17–24
Digging your own clay, buying clay, preparing and storing clay. Chroman. Potter's primer. 16–36
Earthenware, tableware, stoneware, ovenware, and porcelain formulas for clay. Conrad. Contemporary ceramic formulas. 2–64

Clay modeling. *See* **Modeling**

Clipboards
Clipboard. Cope. Plastics. 70–71
Telephone book and message clipboard. Coffey. Francine Coffey's celebrity sewing bee. 80

Clock cases, Grandfather
Grandfather clock. 77 furniture projects you can build. 134–40
Grandfather clock kit. 101 do-it-yourself projects. 366–68
Grandfather's clocks. Complete handyman do-it-yourself encyclopedia. 597–607
Handsome hall clock. Popular Mechanics do-it-yourself encyclopedia. Vol. 5, 754–64
Long case clock. Taylor. How to build period country furniture. 74–79
Molly pitcher clock (grandmother version). Capotosto. Woodworking techniques and projects. 299–303
Tall-case clock. Fine woodworking techniques 5. 147–51
Tall case clocks. Daniele. How to build 35 great clocks. 153–76
Tall clock. Moser. How to build Shaker furniture. 192–95
Williams. Designing and building grandfather clocks.

Clocks
Autumn leaves clock. Baldwin. Scrap fabric crafts. 64–65
Barn-board clock. Meras. Vacation crafts. 23–24
Child's wall clock. Coffey. Francine Coffey's celebrity sewing bee. 117
Clock case. Modern general shop. Metalworking. 112–13
Clock cases on the bench or lathe. Sainsbury. Woodworking projects with power tools. 100–109
Clock face. Cope. Plastics. 50–51
Clock face. Parker. Mosaics in needlepoint. 134–37
Clock medallions. Metalcrafting encyclopedia. 87
Clocks. Introduction to repairing and restoring. 58–103

Connecticut shelf clock, heirloom wall clock, simple clock from your lathe. Popular
    Mechanics do-it-yourself encyclopedia. Vol. 5, 750–53, 766–69
Daniele. How to build 35 great clocks.
Designing a foilcraft clock. Marshall. Foilcraft. 64–65
Floral clock. Challenging projects in stained glass. 102–18
Grandfather clock, schoolhouse clock, alarm clock, cuckoo clock decorations. Nicole.
    Designer accessories to make for your home. 107–35
Kadar. Clock making for the woodworker.
Mantel clock. Rubin. Mission furniture. 91
Miniature tall clock. Osburn. Measured drawings of early American furniture. 63–65
Plewes. Repairing & restoring pendulum clocks.
Poster clock. Hamilton. Build it together. 54–61
Sculpted dolphin clock. Capotosto. Woodworking wisdom. 275–81
Tell-time clock. Baldwin. Old fashioned wooden toys. 50–52
Toy clock. Hodges. 46 step-by-step wooden toy projects. 139–42
Wall clock. Moser. How to build Shaker furniture. 196–97
Wall clock; old Macdonald's tall clock; shelf clock. Daniele. Building early American
    furniture. 77–78, 103–07, 152–53
Wall clock in enamel and perspex. Elliot. Working with copper. 108–09
Wooden clockworks. Fine woodworking techniques 2. 110–17
Wooden slab clocks. Spielman. Working green wood with PEG. 59–60

Cloisonné
Art of cloisonné. Metal and enamel. 120–22
Cloisonné. Newman. Wire art. 130–38
Plique-a-jour and plastic plique-a-jour. Newman. Wire art. 139–47

Closets
Attic closet. Philbin. Cabinets, bookcases & closets. 154
Basement closet. Braren. Homemade. 16
Build an extra closet, make your closet work. Popular Mechanics do-it-yourself ency-
    clopedia. Vol. 5, 775–81
Building a cedar closet. Handyman. 170–71
Building a ceiling closet. Handyman. 171
Building new closets. Cary. Storage: cabinets, closets, and wall systems. 83–95
Built-in clothes closets. Blandford. 66 children's furniture projects. 382–84
Built-in storage closet. Kangas. By hand. 124–26
Cedar closets. Complete handyman do-it-yourself encyclopedia. Vol. 4, 609–14
Closet, recess hanging clothes closet, corner hanging clothes closet. Blandford. 53
    space-saving built-in furniture projects. 260–65, 267–73
Coping with all-weather wear (boot & coat storage), clothing hibernation for out-of-
    season wardrobes. Garage, attic and basement storage. 20–23
Closet extender. Zegel. Fast furniture. 111
Closet floor storage box. Family handyman handbook of home improvement and
    remodeling. 174–76
Closet shelves. Zegel. Shelf book. 64–67
Closets for bedrooms. Siegele. Cabinets and built-ins. 28–31
Closets. Jones. Plan and build more storage space. 156–62
Closet interiors. Philbin. Cabinets, bookcases & closets. 144–47
Closets construction. Black and Decker power tool carpentry. 133–36
Closet under the stairs. Philbin. Cabinets, bookcases & closets. 150–52
Corner closet. Philbin. Cabinets, bookcases & closets. 142–44
Creative closetry. Carbo. Fix-it guide for women. 111–12
Decorative closet panel. Goldman. Decorate with felt. 116–19
Designing and building a closet. Clifford. Basic woodworking and carpentry . . . with
    projects. 214–19

Dust/free closet. Philbin. Cabinets, bookcases & closets. 155
Entry closet. Leavy. Bookshelves and storage units. 24–25
Free standing closet casters. Brann. How to modernize an attic. 58–73
Free standing pegboard closet. Philbin. Cabinets, bookcases & closets. 153
Full-wall closet. Philbin. Cabinets, bookcases & closets. 141–42
His and her built-in closets. Family handyman handbook of carpentry plans/projects.
    139–41
Improving existing closets. Cary. Storage: cabinets, closets, and wall systems. 76–82
Internal corner closet, winter clothes closet, creative closetry, double corner closet.
    Family handyman handbook of carpentry plans/projects. 174–201
Linen closets. Siegele. Cabinets and built-ins. 51–55
Modular closets. Philbin. Cabinets, bookcases & closets. 149
Panelling closets with cedar. Family handyman handbook of carpentry plans/projects.
    202–07
Reorganizing closets. Time-Life Books. Space and storage. 114–23
Sliding broom and brush closet. Family handyman handbook of home improvement
    and remodeling. 20–22
Small closet. Blandford. How to make your own built-in furniture. 305–07
Walk-in bookcase closet. Popular Mechanics do-it-yourself encyclopedia. Vol. 3, 405
Winter clothes closet, convert a small room to a closet, double corner closet, built-in
    closets for two. Family handyman handbook of home improvement and remodel-
    ing. 149–64

Cloth toys

Baby's ball, clown, caterpillar, soft play-bricks using crochet circles or material rosettes
    or knitted squares. Gault. Crafts for the disabled. 105–08
Clown head crib toys, pig and beanbag piglets. Woman's Day book of weekend crafts.
    93–97
Octopus. Foose. Scrap saver's stitchery book. 25–31
Pillow toys. Foose. Scrap saver's stitchery book. 46–57
Pixies and toadstools; two roly poly toys: gnome and pirate; goldilocks and the three
    bears. Greenhowe. Making miniature toys and dolls. 34–39, 102–11
Rath. Splendid soft toy book.
Tyler. Big book of soft toys.

Cloth toys. See also **Animals, Toy; Dolls**

Clothes driers. See **Laundry equipment**

Clothes hangers. See **Coat hangers**

Clothes racks

Clothes rack. Blandford. 66 children's furniture projects. 100–02
Clothes tree. Dal Fabbro. How to make children's furniture and play equipment. 70–71
Coatrack. Egge. Recycled with flair. 38–44
Coat rack and mirror, man's valet. Brown. 44 terrific woodworking plans & projects.
    126–28, 140, 142
Coat rack, halved coat rack. Blandford. 53 space-saving built-in furniture projects.
    338–44
Coat tree. Hamilton. Build it together. 166–71
Coat tree. 101 do-it-yourself projects. 60–61
Coat tree and coat rack. Waugh. Handyman's encyclopedia. 420–21
Drip-dry airer. Blandford. 53 space-saving built-in furniture projects. 281–85
Fabric collage clothes rack. Jarnow. (Re)do it yourself. 139–41
Giraffe clothes tree. Popular Mechanics do-it-yourself encyclopedia. Vol. 19, 2916
Guardsman clothes rack. Roda. Fabric decorating for the home. 175–77

Hall tree. Williams. Spanish colonial furniture. 22–23
Laminated hat rack, clothes-drying rack. Make it! don't buy it. 58–67, 86–93
Moose cap rack. Better Homes and Gardens treasury of Christmas crafts & foods. 270
Owl hall butler. Capotosto. Woodworking wisdom. 248–64
Owl coat hook. Casselman. Crafts from around the world. 106–09
Rattan clothes tree. Alth. Rattan furniture. 97–104
Sepik coat hook. Casselman. Crafts from around the world. 112–14
Simple coatrack for a child. Popular Mechanics do-it-yourself encyclopedia. Vol. 5, 671
Totem pole clothes rack. Casselman. Crafts from around the world. 97–99
Wooden caterpillar coatrack. Woman's Day book of gifts to make. 133–34

Clothespin bags
Clothespin bag. Guth. Sewing with scraps. 55–56
Clothespin bag. Mills. The book of presents. 81

Clothing and dress
Patternless construction of garments—skirts, sweaters, vests, dresses, hats, bags, etc.
    Edson. Creative crochet. 84–95
Simple fitting (alterations). Burns. Super sewing. 182–207
Ski suits: a bright idea in overalls. Time-Life Books. Sporting scene. 131–49
Slick and colorful switch for warm-ups. Time-Life Books. Sporting scene. 89–101

Clothing and dress, Alterations and remodeling
About pants and what else you can make from them. Mosesson. New clothes from
    old. 98–111
Burns. Altering ready-to-wear.
Fashion-wise alterations. Musheno. Sewing big; fashion advice and sewing tips for
    larger sizes. 115–21
Goldsworthy. Clothes for disabled people.
How to lengthen practically anything. Mosesson. New clothes from old. 50–78
How to make it fit and how to outsmart wear and tear. Mosesson. New clothes from
    old. 79–97
Pocket crest. Parker. Mossaics in needlepoint. 84–88
Potpourri of ideas. Mosesson. New clothes from old. 161–84
Serendipity (shawls, jackets, halter, etc.). Brock. Gladrags; redesigning, remaking, re-
    fitting all your old clothes. 216–32, 234–37
Simons. Very basic book of sewing, altering and mending.
So you're expecting (altering regular clothes). Mosesson. New clothes from old. 112–
    21
When you have your figure back. Mosesson. New clothes from old. 122–38

Clothing and dress, Boys
Detective story shorts and t-shirt set. Farlie. Pennywise boutique. 178

Clothing and dress, Children
Applique decorations. Gladstone. Kids' clothes by Meredith Gladstone. 56–77
Bibbed overalls (sunsuit, jumper, pants, shorts, skirt). Gladstone. Kids' clothes by
    Meredith Gladstone. 35–42
Button shoulder dress and jumpsuit. Gladstone. Kids' clothes by Meredith Gladstone.
    25–34
Children's clothes. Crown. How to recycle old clothes into new fashions. 85–96
Children's clothes (quilted). Laury. Quilted clothing. 114–25
Child's skirt (afghan stitch). Golden book of hand and needle arts. 9–11
Cozy boot cuffs. Farlie. Pennywise boutique. 158
Embroidery decorations. Gladstone. Kids' clothes by Meredith Gladstone. 78–110
For the little girl in your life. Mosesson. New clothes from old. 139–60

Girls' button-front jumper. Crochet. 123
Jacket (tunic, coat, smock, bathrobe). Gladstone. Kids' clothes by Meredith Gladstone. 43–49
Knitwear for infants, toddlers and children. Selfridge. Patchwork knitting. 154–63
Little girl's pinafore, birthday gift apron, teeny-weeny bikini, old-fashioned skirt and stole ensemble, converted snowsuit jacket, little red riding hood cape, lion jumper, all-in-one jumper, toddler's holiday jumper and lacy party smock. Farlie. Pennywise boutique. 138–57
Mordle-Barnes. Good Housekeeping making children's clothes.
Muka. Creative designs for children.
Pockets. Gladstone. Kids' clothes by Meredith Gladstone. 111–28
Rosen. Children's clothing.
Short playsuit. Complete book of baby crafts. 108–10
Smocked romper. Benton. Sewing classic clothes for children. 124–29
Teddy bear top. Svinicki. Old-fashioned crochet. 64–65
Terrycloth tops for Independence Day. Creative crafts yearbook: an exciting new collection of needlework and crafts. 117–18
Toddlers' play clothes. Mills. The book of presents. 66–67
White-rimmed jumper and overalls. Crochet. 119–22
Wrap around skirt with tube top. Golden book of hand and needle arts. 62

Clothing and dress, Men

Cabrera. Classic tailoring techniques.
Rhinehart. How to make men's clothes.
Turtleneck (knit). Feldman. Needlework boutique. 86–87

Clothing and dress-mending

Foote. Mender's manual.
Mending. Practical needlework. 122–29
Repairing garments. Goldsworthy. Mend it! a complete guide to clothes repair. 73–123
Repairing specialized materials. Goldsworthy. Mend it! a complete guide to clothes repair. 63–70

Clothing and dress, Women

Burns. Altering ready-to-wear.
Caftan. Treasury of things to make. 146–47
Chenille bedspreads (caftan). Funaro. Yestermorrow clothes book. 51–52
Cloud-day vest and skirt (quilted). Golden book of hand and needle arts. 50–51
Engaging puffery for a sleeve. Time-Life Books. Traditional favorites. 68–85
Embroidered shirt. Treasury of things to make. 105
Caftans. Crown. How to recycle old clothes into new fashions. 82–83
Feminine ways with ruffles and edgings. Time-Life Books. Traditional favorites. 32–45
Flattery of demure necklines. Time-Life Books. Traditional favorites. 52–67
Jumpsuits, coveralls and romper suits. Crown. How to recycle old clothes into new fashions. 76–82
Lace-and-denim patio ensemble. Farlie. Pennywise boutique. 73–74
One-piece sunsuit. Jacobs. Crochet book. 81–83
Pants in variety. Corrigan. How to make pants and jeans that really fit. 141–43
Patchwork and other bits and pieces. Crown. How to recycle old clothes into new fashions. 105–12
Perky peplum. Time-Life Books. Traditional favorites. 86–91
Rutan. Perfect fit: easy pattern alterations.
Transforming lingerie and loungewear into street clothes. Funaro. Yestermorrow clothes book. 103–19
Trapunto tassel top. Creative sewing. 43
Tunic and bloomers. Creative sewing. 38
Wrapped tops. Funaro. Yestermorrow clothes book. 46–47

Clothing and dress. *See also* **Individual items of clothing**

Clothing, Secondhand
Crown. How to recycle old clothes into new fashions.
Funaro. Yestermorrow clothes book.
New clothes from old ones. Jones. Clothing-your way. 102–07

Coasters
Braided coaster. Golden book of colonial crafts. 153
Christmas tree coasters. Neighbors. Reversible two-color knitting. 162–65
Circular mold for mat or coaster. Hulbert. Creative beadwork. 46
Coaster mats. Ley. Russian & other Slavic embroidery designs. 64–65
Coaster set. Cope. Plastics. 45
Coaster set. Modern general shop. Woodworking. 97
Coasters. Hobbs. Veneering simplified. 73–76
Coasters cut from tree limbs. Meras. Vacation crafts. 24–25
Coasters in black walnut. Sainsbury. Sainsbury's woodturning projects for dining. 17
Felt covered coasters. Goldman. Decorate with felt. 12–17
Felt playing card coasters. Roda. Fabric decorating for the home. 103–04
Flowers in plastic coasters. O'Neill. Make-it-merry Christmas book. 93–94
Four glass jackets (needlepoint). Feldman. Needlework boutique. 119–20
Glass coasters. Linsley. Decoupage on glass, wood, metal, rocks, shells, wax, soap, plastic canvas, ceramic. 88–89
Jigsaw puzzle tray and coasters. Doherty. Family circle book of 429 great gifts-to-make all year round for just 10¢ to $10.00. 12
Needlepoint coasters and trivets. Burchette. Needlework. 52–53
Needlepoint mushroom coaster and rainbow coaster. Barnes. 120 needlepoint designs projects. 89, 158
Oriental heraldry coasters. Sheldon. Washable and dryable needlepoint. 116–17
Pattern for coasters (embroidered). Fraser. Modern stitchery: stitches, patterns, free-form designing. 94
Plastic ornaments and coasters, tin can lid coasters. Epple. Something from nothing crafts. 142–44, 166–67
Round coasters. Roda. Fabric decorating for the home. 65
Strawberry patch coasters. Wargo. Soft crafts for special occasions. 90–91
Wood burned coasters. Brightman. 101 practical uses for propane torches. 91–93

Coat hangers
Boutique bath hanger. Evrard. Homespun crafts from scraps. 30–32
Coat-hanger covers. Woman's Day book of gifts to make. 37–38
Covered hanger. Wargo. Soft crafts for special occasions. 139
Crocheted hanger covers, denim hanger covers. Doherty. Family Circle book for 429 great gifts-to-make all year round for just 10¢ to $10.00. 63, 76–77
Dress hanger covers to crochet. Woman's Day decorative needlework for the home. 147
Embellished hangers. Wargo. Soft crafts for special occasions. 84–85
Hanger covers (knitted). Rosenthall. Not-so-nimble needlework book. 140
Needlepoint covered coat hanger. Burchette. Needlework. 54–55
Padded coathangers. Creative crafts yearbook: an exciting new collection of needle-work and crafts. 65
Padded hangers. Laury. Treasury of needlecraft gifts for the new baby. 59–62
Personalized coat hanger. Broadwater. Woodburning; art and craft. 38–39

Coat tree. *See* **Clothes racks**

Coats
About face coat for all climes. Time-Life Books. Separates that travel. 92–100
Applique coat. Loeb. Leather book. 213–17
Bedouin coat. Wiseman. Cuts of cloth. 50–51
Burnoose. Blair. Banners and flags. 180
Capote. Scurlock. Muzzleloader Magazine's book of buckskinning II. 45–48
Coats (quilted). Laury. Quilted clothing. 76–89
Detachable fake fur lining for coat. Time-Life Books. Novel materials. 124–31
Rich Turkish coat. Johnson. Quiltwear. 137–44

Coats, Children
Child's appliqued coat. Creative sewing. 26
Loop stitch coat (knit). Complete book of baby crafts. 26–28
Suomi child's coat, hat & dress (Finland). Starmore. Scandinavian knitwear. 89–94
Toddler's coat (crocheted). Mills. The book of presents. 15–16
Toddler's hooded coat. Jacobs. Crochet book. 139–41

Coats, Girls
Girl's car coat. Hubert. Weekend knitting projects. 80–81
Girl's classic coat and hat set. Hubert. Weekend knitting projects. 38–39

Coats, Women
Basic women's patchwork and Magyar coats. Lane. Maggie Lane's oriental patchwork. 20–39
Classic wrap coat. Crochet. 46
Coats and waistcoats. Probert. Knitting in Vogue. 138–62
Coats, jackets and other outerwear. Crown. How to recycle old clothes into new fashions. 45–58
Crochet-look fall ensemble. Farlie. Pennywise boutique. 69–72
Crocheted coat sleeves and collar. Crochet. 35
Crocheted cold weather friend. Favorite knitting & crochet patterns. 73–75
Crocheted evening star coat. Lep. Crocheting patchwork patterns. 47–50
Crocheted fantasy coat. Design crochet. 117–21
Dalarna woman's mohair coat (Sweden). Starmore. Scandinavian knitwear. 61–63
Hooded coat and matching skirt. Knitting. 58
How to make a thrifty coat. Guth. Sewing with scraps. 44–47
Impressionist garden coat, alpaca coat, rainbow striped coat with matching hat, Mayan figure coat. Design crochet. 9–12, 18–22, 30–34, 62–67
Joseph's coat. Henderson. Woman's Day book of designer crochet. 76–84
Lady's full length Aran pattern coat. Hollingworth. Complete book of traditional Aran knitting. 119–23
Patchwork coat. Creative sewing. 19
Quilted cape and quilted coat. Creative sewing. 14
Quilted cire coat. McNeill. Quilting. 60–61
Quilted coat with crocheted sleeves. Creative sewing. 22
Reworking coats and jackets. Funaro. Yestermorrow clothes book. 133–44
Sherpa coat, simplicity coat, hooded parka, 19th century Ottoman Empire coat. Beard. Fashions from the loom. 46–48, 50
Short and three-quarter coats. Ruggieri. Woman's Day book of no-pattern sewing. 72–73
Sweaters to coats. Zukerman. Get hooked. 116–25
3-way coat. Ruggieri. Woman's Day book of no-pattern sewing. 70–71
Trapunto coat. Creative sewing. 46
Woman's mohair coat, hat and scarf set. Hubert. Weekend knitting projects. 56–57
Your own quilted coat. Ruggieri. Woman's Day book of no-pattern sewing. 74–76

Coffee cosies
Coffee pot covers. Creative crafts yearbook: an exciting new collection of needlework and crafts. 18–19

Coffee pots, percolators, etc.
Coffee grinder. Sainsbury. Sainbury's woodturning projects for dining. 149–56
Coffee mill. Capotosto. Woodworking techniques and projects. 95–98
Coffee mill. Family handyman handbook of carpentry plans/projects. 65–69
Finger-joint coffee mill. Capotosto. Woodworking wisdom. 265–74
How to repair your coffee percolator. Popular Mechanics do-it-yourself encyclopedia. Vol. 5, 782–84
Making a coffee pot. Ceramics. 79–84

Coin purses. *See* **Purses**

Cold Frames
Cold frames. Braren. Homemade. 75–83
Cold frames. Family handyman handbook of carpentry plans/projects. 474–77
Cold frame. Kramer. Outdoor garden build-it book. 173–74
Cold frame. Outdoor projects for home and garden. 430–32
Cold frame. Self. Working with plywood, including indoor/outdoor projects. 176–77
Cold frames. Popular Mechanics do-it-yourself encyclopedia. Vol. 6, 820–23
Hotbed. Popular Mechanics do-it-yourself encyclopedia. Vol. 19, 3034–37
Hotbed gardening. Churchill. Backyard building book. 25–28

Collages
Bead butterfly collage. Hulbert. Creative beadwork. 91–92
Beaded and embroidered collage. Hulbert. Creative beadwork. 97
Calico collage. Evrard. Homespun crafts from scraps. 147–50
Collage picture. Creative sewing. 82
Collages. Kicklighter. Crafts, illustrated designs and techniques. 78–83
Coloured tissue collage. Paper. 48–51
Fabric collages. Ashurst. Collage. 68–84
Flowers with wallpaper collage, pansies collage, hands collages. Vanderbilt. Gloria Vanderbilt designs for your home. 18–26
Frottage-collage. Geary. Plant prints and collages. 68–70
Janitch. Collage.
Kitchen things collages. Ashurst. Collage. 88–89
Making a collage. Paper. 38–47
Making pictures with scraps and found objects. Hana. Embroidery. 78–80
Metal collage. Ashurst. Collage. 44–50
Natural objects collage. Ashurst. Collage. 50–55
Open road, nesting bird, and September garden collages. Janitch. All made from paper. 13–19
Paper collage. Stephan. Creating with tissue paper. 90–107
Paper collage from rubbings. Firestein. Rubbing craft. 85
Paper collage pictures, mixed media collage pictures. Picturemaking. 31–37
Photomontage. Ashurst. Collage. 56–61
Red engine and finger mice puppet holder. Anderson. Crafts and the disabled. 62–70
Repousse collage. Linsley. Decoupage on glass, wood, metal, rocks, shells, wax, soap, plastic, canvas, ceramic. 138–46
Tissue collage of a bouquet of flowers. Rose. Illustrated encyclopedia of crafts and how to master them. 8–12
Wood base collage. Ashurst. Collage. 97–102
Yarn and fibers collages. Ashurst. Collage. 14–19

Collars

Band boxes. Buxton. Craftmaking: for love or money. 93–97
Bandboxes. McCall's big book of country needlecrafts. 270–72
Bead collars. Gill. Beadwork: the technique of stringing, threading, and weaving. 79–90
Beaded Bertha collar. Hulbert. Creative beadwork. 84
Beaded collar. Stearns. Macrame. 52, 55–57
Beribboned band boxes. Evrard. Homespun crafts from scraps. 151–54
Bobbin lace collar and cuffs. Golden book of hand and needle arts. 153–55
Collar with lace trim. Svinicki. Old-fashioned crochet. 118–19
Crochet collar. Dillmont. Complete encyclopedia of needlework. 336–44
Early American band boxes. Perry. Holiday magic. 82–89
Gold crochet collar, crochet ruffle collar and cuffs. Wilson. Needlework to wear. 138, 140
Irish crochet collar. Svinicki. Old-fashioned crochet. 75–76
Knitted turtleneck collars, lacy crochet collar. Woman's Day bazaar best sellers. 31, 48
Lace and granny square collars. American School of Needlework. Great crochet bazaar book. 31–34
Lace collar & cuffs. Design crochet. 112–13
Lacy collar. Walters. Crochet. 45
Making a decorative collar out of added strands. Dendel. Basic book of fingerweaving. 112–15
Mandarin collars, standing bias collar. Time-Life Books. Exotic styling. 41–47
Neckpieces. Henderson. Woman's Day book of designer crochet. 132–38
Patchwork collars. Sommer. Wearable crafts. 60–61
Raised flower petal collar, beaded lace collar, organza cutwork collar and lotus petal collar. Wilson. Needlework to wear. 120–25, 128–29
Strung bead collars. Gill. Beadwork: the technique of stringing, threading, and weaving. 106–09
Teneriffe lace collar. Encyclopedia of crafts. 92
Touch of lace. Ruggieri. Woman's Day book of no-pattern sewing. 110–12
Woven collar. Krevitsky. Shaped weaving. 22–23
Woven collars and other neckpieces. Krevitsky. Shaped weaving. 59–65
Woven sample made into collar. Dendel. Basic book of fingerweaving. 55–57

Combs

Colonial comb box. Popular Mechanics do-it-yourself encyclopedia. Vol. 6, 824
Sawed and carved wooden combs. Sommers. Contemporary costume jewelry. 83

Comforters

Pioneer knot comforter. Roda. Fabric decorating for the home. 128–29

Compost bins

Compost bin. 101 do-it-yourself projects. 292–93
Compost bin. Wood projects for the garden. 74–75
Compost materials. Braren. Homemade. 68–74

Concrete

Building concrete foundation and footings. Russell. Walks, walls and fences. 69–76
Concrete. Olin. Construction. 203–28
Concrete driveway, patio, or walk, concrete steps. 101 do-it-yourself projects. 268–69, 320–22
Concrete for patios. Landis. Patios and decks. 108–13
Concrete forms, slabs, & steps. Bragdon. Homeowner's complete manual of repair & improvement. 538–45
Concrete paving. Kramer. Outdoor garden build-it book. 21–23

Footings and foundations. Burch. Building small barns, sheds, and shelters. 38–55
Footings and foundations. Spence. General carpentry. 131–65
Forms for concrete. Adams. Arco's complete woodworking handbook. 302–18
How to color concrete. Brann. How to build patios and sundecks. 51
How to make attractive concrete, soil-cement, cast your patio indoors. Day. How to
    build patios and decks. 69–109
How to work with concrete, concrete slabs, how to color concrete, how to patch walks
    and driveways, how to lay concrete blocks. Popular Mechanics do-it-yourself ency-
    clopedia. Vol. 6, 830–53
Making individual paving blocks. Porches and patios. 73
Painting concrete. Geary. Complete handbook of home exterior repair and mainte-
    nance. 157–65
Patching concrete basement floor. Time-Life Books. Floors and stairways. 34–35
Removing the flaws from existing paving. Porches and patios. 78–79
Repairing cracks in concrete. Outdoor projects for home and garden. 255–57
Working with concrete. Outdoor projects for home and garden. 249–54

Containers
Ash-dried fruit. Johnson. Nature crafts. 7
Candy container. Linsley. Custom made. 12–14
Catchall paper buckets. Linsley. Decoupage on glass, wood, metal, rocks, shells, wax,
    soap, plastic, canvas, ceramic. 108–11
Coil pots for the kitchen, handles and lips. Ceramics. 42–43
Colorful origami containers. Paper. 122–23
Copper container. Metal and enamel. 61–63
Gourd containers. Mordecai. Gourd craft. 101–38
Happy Birthday container. Linsley. Decoupage on glass, wood, metal, rocks, shells,
    wax, soap, plastic, canvas, ceramic. 70–73
Large pots, pots with lids. Rhodes. Pottery form. 109–26
Make a container and lid in a cardboard box. Priolo. Ceramics by coil. 20–21
Making a slab cylinder. Howell. Craft of pottery. 78–79
Mustard pot. Sainsbury. Sainsbury's woodturning projects for dining. 71–73
Putting designs on tin cans. Brunner. Pass it on. 138
Sisal covered herb pots, flower pots, vases, and desk tidies. Encyclopedia of crafts.
    241
Staved containers. Fine woodworking techniques 3. 162–63
Utensil holders and a train design. Appel. Sand art. 97–101
Woven paper cylindrical container. Grainger. Creative papercraft. 115

Cookie jars and containers
Decoupaged gourd cookie jar. Mordecai. Gourd craft. 118–21
Fabric covered cookie tin. Jarnow. (Re)do it yourself. 137–38
Folk art painted cookie tin. Jarnow. (Re)do it yourself. 104–08
Metal cookie cannister. Linsley. Decoupage on glass, wood, metal, rocks, shells, wax,
    soap, plastic, canvas, ceramic. 73–82

Coolers
Camp cooler (repair). Schuler. How to fix almost everything. 33
Ice chests. Scurlock. Muzzleloader Magazine's book of buckskinning II. 195–96

Copper work
Cleaning copper. Elliot. Working with copper. 39
Copper crafting. Copper crafts. Giant book of crafts. 175–84
Copper wall panel. Metal and enamel. 29–34
Filling and backing copper shim. Elliot. Working with copper. 48–50
How to twist wire using a drill. Elliot. Working with copper. 67

Liver of sulphur for oxidizing copper. Elliot. Working with copper. 44–45
Making a bowl. Sjoberg. Working with copper, silver and enamel. 33–40
Oxidizing and coloring copper. Elliot. Working with copper. 43–46
Pattern copper shim. Elliot. Working with copper. 23–28
Tooling and enameling. Linderman. Crafts for the classroom. 364–72

Corn husks
Corn dollies. Brown. Complete book of rush and basketry techniques. 95–117
Corn husk crafting. Giant book of crafts. 253–66
Corn husks: nature's wrapping. Johnson. Nature crafts. 64–73
Cornhusk flowers. Conner. Corncraft. 117–21
Maize craft (mat, baskets, masks, dolls). Conner. Corncraft. 39–59
Making corn shuck dollies. Cane, rush and straw. 130–34
Three corn dollies. Pittaway. Traditional English country crafts and how to enjoy them today. 19–21

Cornices. *See* **Valances**

Cornucopias
Cornucopia. Colletti. Art of woodcarving. 115–16
Cornucopia. Maynard. Modern basketry from the start. 145

Corsages
Scallop corsage. Meras. Vacation crafts. 78

Cosmetics accessories
Child's bathroom "house" for holding toilet articles. Goldman. Decorate with felt. 108–09
Cosmetic bag. Fairfield Patchwork. 40
Cosmetic bag. Mills. Book of presents. 80
Cosmetic bow box. Linsley. Great bazaar. 64–66
Cosmetic case. Christensen. Teach yourself needlepoint. 107–08
Cosmetic cases. Burchette. Needlework. 105–07
Double butterfly vanity bag. Houck. Patchwork pattern book. 24
Hair-roller container. Goldman. Decorate with felt. 106–07
Jewelry or cosmetic bag. Breckenridge. Lap quilting. 68–70
Lips cosmetic bag. Woman's Day bazaar best sellers. 115
Lockets and lipstick holders. Woman's Day crochet showcase. 75
Needlepoint atomizer cover. Embroidery of roses. 108
Powder jar and lid. Wooldridge. Woodturning techniques. 38–39
Ribbon makeup basket. Jarnow. (Re)do it yourself. 141–42
Roll-up make up case. Coffey. Francine Coffey's celebrity sewing bee. 69
Smocked dressing-table set. Encyclopedia of crafts. 107
Tatted compact cover. Encyclopedia of crafts. 101

Costumes
Aladdin. Greenhowe. Costumes for nursery tale characters. 76–78
Anderson. Costume design.
Children's costumes. Coffey. Francine Coffey's celebrity sewing bee. 142–43
Cinderella and the Fairy Godmother. Greenhowe. Costumes for nursery tale characters. 25–32
Cowboy outfit. Creative crafts yearbook: an exciting new collection of needlework and crafts. 84–87
Crepe-paper costumes: buttercup, clown, Indian. Giant book of crafts. 345–54
Crowd of ogres. Kinser. Sewing sculpture. 105–115

Dutch girl, red Indian squaw, desert island girl. Bumper book of things a girl can make. 127–31

Frog prince and the princess. Greenhowe. Costumes for nursery tale characters. 55–59

Gehret. Rural Pennsylvania clothing.

Goldilocks and baby bear. Greenhowe. Costumes for nursery tale characters. 63–69

Costume leotard. Jacobs. Crochet book. 68–69

Holkeboer. Patterns for theatrical costumes.

Hot cross buns. Greenhowe. Costumes for nursery tale characters. 34–37

Indian maid outfit. Creative crafts yearbook: an exciting new collection of needlework and crafts. 88–90

Ingham. Costumer's handbook.

Little Bo-Peep. Greenhowe. Costumes for nursery tale characters. 70–74

Little Miss Muffet. Greenhowe. Costumes for nursery tale characters. 20–24

Little Red Riding Hood and the wolf. Greenhowe. Costumes for nursery tale characters. 38–46

Lucia celebration. Coskey. Christmas crafts for everyone. 34–35

Mary, Mary, quite contrary. Greenhowe. Costumes for nursery tale characters. 80–81

Mexican Huipil and Quechquemitl. Sayer. Crafts of Mexico. 46–47

Period costumes and paper costumes. Golden book of colonial crafts. 130–37

Puss in Boots. Greenhowe. Costumes for nursery tale characters. 82–85

Queen and knave of hearts. Greenhowe. Costumes for nursery tale characters. 48–54

Redskin chief; gipsy; cowboy costume. Bumper book of things a boy can make. 87–90

Robin Hood and Friar Tuck. Greenhowe. Costumes for nursery tale characters. 14–19

Wee Willie Winkie. Greenhowe. Costumes for nursery tale characters. 61–62

Costumes. *See also* **Indian costumes**

Couches. *See* **Sofas**

Counting toys
Learn-to-count chart (needlepoint). Feldman. Needlework boutique. 12–14

Covered wagon models. *See* **Prairie schooner models**

Cradles
Cradle. Gottshall. Provincial furniture design and construction. 15–18

Cradle. Zegel. Fast furniture. 101–04

Cradle–Plimoth plantation, New Jersey hooded cradle. Daniele. Building early American furniture. 67–68, 85–87

Cradle that can be transformed into toy box and a rocking chair. Adams. Make your own baby furniture. 34–42

Plywood cradle. Complete handyman do-it-yourself encyclopedia. 1160–62

Seventeenth century oak cradle. Taylor. How to build period country furniture. 182–85

Shaker cradle. Adams. Make your own baby furniture. 43–47

Spindle cradle. Fine woodworking techniques 5. 134–35

Traditional rocking cradle, swing cradle, turned swinging cradle. Blandford. Building better beds. 231–46

Traditional rocking, take-down and swing cradles. Blandford. 66 children's furniture projects. 298–312

Walnut cradle, hooded cradle. Shea. Pennsylvania Dutch and their furniture. 202–03

Wooden cradle. Better Homes and Gardens treasury of Christmas crafts & foods. 250–51

Cradles. *See also* **Children's furniture, Cribs**

Cream pitchers. *See* **Pitchers**

Creches
Artisan's musical creche. Popular Mechanics do-it-yourself encyclopedia. Vol. 9, 1358–59
Bread-dough Christmas manger. Meyer. Christmas crafts. 95–99
Building a creche. Coskey. Christmas crafts for everyone. 39–45
Christmas card creche. Coskey. Christmas crafts for everyone. 37–39
Christmas creche. Perry. Holiday magic. 161–67
Cloth, metal foil, clay, pine cone, and straw nativity scene. Christmas crafts book. 65–80
Embroidered creche. Better Homes & Gardens embroidery. 12–13
Gingerbread creche. McCall's book of Christmas. 111–13
Living nativity scene. Coskey. Christmas crafts for everyone. 45–49
Machine appliqued creche banner. Better Homes and Gardens applique. 34–35
Machine appliqued creche banner, needlepoint creche, embroidered creche. Better Homes and Gardens treasury of needlecrafts. 100–101, 310–15, 336–37
Nativity. Tyler. Big book of dolls. 182–91
Nativity scene. Araki. Origami for Christmas. 128–29
Nativity swag. Cook. Decorating for the holidays. 6
Nativity wall hanging. Foose. Scrap saver's stitchery book. 78–85
Papier mâché madonna and child, crocheted creche figures, Mexican creche, storybook creche. McCall's book of Christmas. 72–85
Pine creche, appliqued creche banner, embroidered creche figures, grotto for creche, stained-glass nativity, needlepoint creche, wooden creche, simple manger scenes. Better Homes and Gardens treasury of Christmas crafts & foods. 19, 32–33, 141–42, 288–307
Presepio: the setting & figurines. D'Amato. Italian crafts. 128–38
Quilted nativity scene. Wilson. Erica Wilson's Christmas world. 92–99
Unusual nativity scenes. Tangerman. Carving the unusual. 58–65
Wooden creche. Better Homes and Gardens easy bazaar crafts. 71, 79

Cribs. *See* **Children's furniture, Cribs**

Crocheting
Aran-style crochet. Stearns. Batsford book of crochet. 81–83
Basic crochet stitches. Better Homes and Gardens treasury of needlecrafts. 230–31
Basic pattern arrangements of geometric shapes. Scharf. Illustrated patchwork crochet. 154–56
Crochet. Meilach. Weaving off-loom. 156–73
Crochet as an off-loom technique. Parker. Beginner's book of off-loom weaving. 173–88
Crochet basics, crochet stitches, Tunisian crochet stitches. Reader's Digest complete guide to needlework. 358–93
Crochet on canvas. Stearns. Batsford book of crochet. 68–71
Crochet on net. Stearns. Batsford book of crochet. 72–74
Crochet stitches and patterns. Mon tricot. Knitting dictionary. 116–210
Crochet worked over cords. Stearns. Batsford book of crochet. 64–67
Crocheted inserts and additions to fabric. Jacobs. Crochet book. 26–47
Crocheting. Ryan. Complete encyclopedia of stitchery. 1–147
Edson. Creative crochet.
Filet crochet. Stearns. Batsford book of crochet. 59–63
Hairpin crochet. Stearns. Batsford book of crochet. 88–93
Hairpin lace crocheting for one-handers. Rissell. Craftwork the handicapped elderly can make and sell. 49–57
Halevy. Knitting and crocheting pattern index.

Irish crochet. Stearns. Batsford book of crochet. 124–43
Lep. Crocheting patchwork patterns.
Patchwork crochet: squares, rectangles, triangles, miscellaneous shapes and joining
     patches. Chatterton. Patchwork & applique. 51–68
Tunisian crochet. Stearns. Batsford book of crochet. 100–04
Turkish crochet. Stearns. Batsford book of crochet. 144–56
Weldon and Company. Victorian crochet.
Wire crocheting. Newman. Wire art. 63
Working methods for garment construction. Stearns. Batsford book of crochet. 105–23

Croquet sets
Croquet mallet (repair). Schuler. How to fix almost everything. 49

Crosses
Straw-inlay cross. Casselman. Crafts from around the world. 211–16

Crowns
Crown. Grainger. Creative papercraft. 78–80

Cuff links
Button and bead cuff links. Mosesson. Jewelry craft for beginners. 270–71
Cuff links. Bovin. Jewelry making. 243–45
Cuff links. Grainger. Creative ropecraft. 123–24
Cull links. Pelisser. Jeweler's craft. 43–49
Cuff links. Richards. Handmade jewelry. 117–18
Molding and reinforcing cufflinks. Hollander. Plastics for jewelry. 151–56
Sterling cuff links. Pelisser. Jeweler's craft. 83–85
Wire cuff links with stone. Meyer. Rock tumbling. 79

Cup holders
Cup holder. Kramer. Wirecraft. 70–71
Holders for drinks. Grainger. Making aids for disabled living. 60–65
Mug holder. Modern general shop. Metalworking. 99

Cupboards
Charming colonial lowboy. Popular Mechanics do-it-yourself encyclopedia. Vol. 11,
     1739
China closet, another china closet. Rubin. Mission furniture. 78–81
Colonial cupboard for china. Popular Mechanics do-it-yourself encyclopedia. Vol. 6,
     888–91
Compact hutch. Capotosto. Woodworking techniques and projects. 134–38
Corner cupboard, server or sideboard. Blandford. 53 space-saving built-in furniture
     projects. 144–50, 209, 213–18
Cove cupboard. Marlow. Early American furnituremaker's manual. 45–50
Crockery cupboard, Romanian design. Casselman. Crafts from around the world. 53–
     55
Cupboard. Williams. Spanish colonial furniture. 122–25
Dutch cupboard of pine, cherry Dutch cupboard, large cherry Dutch cupboard, pine
     corner cupboard, walnut corner cupboard with paneled doors, cherry corner cup-
     board. Gottshall. Provincial furniture design and construction. 97–136
Four-door side chest, six-drawer side chest, four-drawer side chest, pewter cupboard,
     Dr. White's chest, double cupboard. Moser. How to build Shaker furniture. 120–
     31, 178–79
Giant cockleshell for corner cupboard. Fine woodworking techniques 2. 158–59
Glass-fronted cabinet restoration. Restoring and reupholstering furniture. 68–77
Hanging cupboard. Moser. How to build Shaker furniture. 116–17

How to build a cupboard. Clifford. Basic woodworking and carpentry . . . with projects. 199–200
Kitchen cupboard. Endacott. Fine furniture making and woodworking. 94–98
Kitchen cupboard. 101 do-it-yourself projects. 124–27
Log house wall cupboard, Philadelphia double cupboard; corner cupboard; dry sink with top cupboard; Hutch cupboard. Daniele. Building early American furniture. 156–60, 164–65, 223–26, 234–37
New Hampshire cupboard. Hagerty. Make your own antiques. 98
Pie safe with pierced tin panels, staghorn-hinged hanging cupboard, scrolled wall cupboard, hanging cupboard. Shea. Pennsylvania Dutch and their furniture. 191, 193–95
Queen Anne-style corner cupboard and display cabinet, Welsh dresser. Taylor. How to build period country furniture. 66–73, 142–49
Renovating and restyling cupboards, tall cupboards from an old TV cabinet. Egge. Recycled with flair. 149–50, 155–61
Restoring a glass-fronted cabinet. Davis. Restoring furniture. 78–87
Small wall cupboard, corner wall cupboard, standing cupboard, Welsh cupboard. Blandford. How to make early American and colonial furniture. 352–64, 371–87
Water bench, corner cupboards, open cupboards, Pennsylvania Dutch dresser. Shea. Pennsylvania Dutch and their furniture. 197, 212–17

Cupolas
Cupola/weathervane. Capotosto. Woodworking techniques and projects. 214–24
Installing a cupola as a vent. Outdoor projects for home and garden. 18–20

Cups
Ceramic cup. Linsley. Decoupage on glass, wood, metal, rocks, shells, wax, soap, plastic, canvas, ceramic. 125–27
Collaring a cylinder and adding a handle. Ceramics. 65–68
Cup and saucer. Campbell. Using the potter's wheel. 42
Cups and saucers. Sainsbury. Sainsbury's woodturning projects for dining. 126–32
Cups, tea bowls, and mugs. Rhodes. Pottery form. 127–34
Goblets. Campbell. Using the potter's wheel. 68–69
Horn cups. Scurlock. Muzzleloader Magazine's book of buckskinning II. 209–10
Throwing a cup off the mound: basic steps. Howell. Craft of pottery. 32
Thrown goblet. Howell. Craft of pottery. 38–39, 45
Turning a goblet. Sainsbury. Craft of woodturning. 133–39
Turning goblets. Nish. Creative woodturning. 172–89
Wine goblet in walnut. Sainsbury. Sainsbury's woodturning projects for dining. 59–63

Curtain rods
How to hang traverse rods. Popular Mechanics do-it-yourself encyclopedia. Vol. 7, 1034–35
(How to repair a) curtain rod. Schuler. How to fix almost everything. 49
Repairing drapery hardware. Nunn. Home improvement, home repair. 45–46

Curtain tiebacks
Bargello drapery tiebacks. Scobey. Decorating with needlepoint. 119–20
Drapery tie-back. Burchette. Needlework. 110

Curtains and draperies
Bed drapery and bedspread. McCall's sewing for your home. 72–73
Bedroom curtains with valence. Goldman. Decorate with felt. 48–49
Blue and white striped curtains. Tod. Joy of hand weaving. 119–21
Burlap drapery with pulled-thread pattern. Woman's Day decorative needlework for the home. 111

Cafe curtains. Halliday. Decorating with crochet. 133–34
Cafe curtains. Practical needlework. 158–61
Cafe curtains with pennant decorations. Goldman. Decorate with felt. 59–61
Cafe curtains with valance. Golden book of hand and needle arts. 64–65
Casement curtains. Roda. Fabric decorating for the home. 25–26
Closet curtain. Goldman. Decorate with felt. 114–15
Cornice cover and draperies to sew. Woman's Day decorative needlework for the home. 107–09
Create a wisp of a curtain-drawn fabric embroidery. Embroidery. 70–75
Creative cafe curtains (appliqued). Botsford. Between thimble & thumb. 116–19
Crocheted curtains. McCall's big book of knit & crochet for home & family. 228
Curtain pattern. Murray. Essential handbook of weaving. 152–53
Curtains. Practical needlework. 150–57
Curtains (tab top). Reader's Digest complete guide to sewing. 467–68
Curtains on a multiharness loom. Make it! don't buy it. 392–95
Curtains with filet-rose panels. Svinicki. Old-fashioned crochet. 92–94
Curtains with tiebacks. Roda. Fabric decorating for the home. 48–49
Decorating the windows. Sara. Sewing made easy. 348–81
Decorative window panel. Great granny crochet book. 136–37
Draperies and tablecloth adapted from sheets. Woman's Day decorative needlework for the home. 118–19
Drapery panels. McCall's sewing for your home. 34
Filet curtain. Walters. Crochet. 52–53
Filet lace curtains. Treasury of things to make. 122–23
Grid curtain. Jacobs. Crochet book. 160
How to make draperies. Better Homes and Gardens sewing for your home. 46–59
Leather curtains. Casselman. Crafts from around the world. 226–28
Lined draperies on a wooden pole. Roda. Fabric decorating for the home. 12–15
Machine-appliqued glass curtains. Woman's Day decorative needlework for the home. 116–17
Machine-embroidered curtains & pillowcase. Better Homes & Gardens embroidery. 74–75
Making draperies. Roberts. Illustrated handbook of upholstery. 218–34
Other kinds of curtains. Practical needlework. 165–68
Plaid and white sheet bedroom ensemble. Woman's Day decorative needlework for the home. 33–34
Ruffled tie back curtains. McCall's sewing for your home. 137
Scalloped cafe curtains. McCall's sewing for your home. 168–69
Sea shell curtain (applique). Hall. Sewing machine craft book. 83
Sheer curtains. Roda. Fabric decorating for the home. 5–7
Solomon's knot curtain. Walters. Crochet. 41
Star pattern curtains and pillow, swan curtains, machine-embroidered curtains. Better Homes and Gardens treasury of needlecrafts. 32–33, 98–99, 386–87
Sunflowers window cover. Svinicki. Old-fashioned crochet. 62–63
Swag curtain, ruffle curtain, easy panels. Guth. Sewing with scraps. 175–80
Swan pillow and curtains. Better Home and Gardens applique. 32–33
Tie-dyed curtain. Frame. Tie-dyeing and batik. 50–51
Window and pillow ensemble adapted from sheets. Woman's Day decorative needlework for the home. 120–21
Window "vine" with organdy leaves. Woman's Day decorative needlework for the home. 121–22
Yarn-woven-canvas window panel. Woman's Day decorative needlework for the home. 112–13

Cushions

Bargello child's-chair cushion. Scobey. Decorating with needlepoint. 57–59
Basket cushions for chairs, patchwork cushion, quick point cushion. McCall's big book of country needlecrafts. 61–62, 87, 117–18
Bon appetit cushions. Ambuter. Carolyn Ambuter's needlepoint celebrations. 156–57
Boy and girl chair cushions. Houck. Patchwork pattern book. 36–37
Carpet and cowhide floor cushion. Kinser. Sewing sculpture. 64
Chair seat cushions and chair back covers. Roda. Fabric decorating for the home. 105–07
Chair seat with border design. Morgan. Trapunto and other forms of raised quilting. 207–09
Crocheted floor cushions in squares, and rectangles. Chatterton. Patchwork & applique. 71–75
Crocheted hexagonal striped cushions. Chatterton. Patchwork & applique. 90–91
Crocheted square cushion. Blandford book of traditional handicrafts. 25
Cross stitch cushion cover (16 by 16). Hana. Embroidery. 20–22
Cushion cover in crewel (20 by 20). Hana. Embroidery. 22–25
Cushion cover patterns. Murray. Essential handbook of weaving. 153
Cushions. McDonald. Modern upholstering techniques. 51–58
Cushions. Practical needlework. 142–49
Cushions. Roberts. Illustrated handbook of upholstery. 204–18
Cushions for chair or sofa seats. Nesovich. Reupholstering at home. 109–31
Fitted cushions. Jones. Fixing furniture. 160–71
Floor couch. Roda. Fabric decorating for the home. 236
Floor cushion. Osler. Machine patchwork. 94–95
Floor foams. Palmer. Making children's furniture and play structures. 21
Floor mats. Roda. Fabric decorating for the home. 240
Flower basket chair cushion. Houck. Patchwork pattern book. 40–41
Foam pads. Reader's Digest complete guide to sewing. 448
French provincial chair pad. Scobey. Decorating with needlepoint. 45–47
Knitted squares and rectangle log cabin and checkerboard cushions. Chatterton. Patchwork & applique. 110–14
Loveseat pillows and seat cushions to sew. Woman's Day decorative needlework for the home. 76–77
Paisley rocking-chair pad. Scobey. Decorating with needlepoint. 54–56
Patchwork driedel. Rockland. Hanukkah book. 143–46
Pouf floor pillow. Reader's Digest complete guide to sewing. 474–75
Round pillow with a quilted boxing. Roda. Fabric decorating for the home. 218–19
Seat cover. Sayles. Step-by-step stitchery. 62–63
Springing and cushion making. McDonald. Upholstery repair and restoration. 62–80
Squab cushion with patchwork trim. Ives. Ideas for patchwork. 37–40
Tie-dyed cushion covers. Tie-dyed, batik and candlemaking step-by-step. 10–11
Turkish corner floor pillow. Roda. Fabric decorating for the home. 36–37
Upholstering cushions. Blandford. Upholsterer's bible. 129–48
Window seat cushion with shirred boxing. Roda. Fabric decorating for the home. 110–11

Cutlery. *See* **Knives**

Cutting boards

Breadboard. Moser. How to build Shaker furniture. 100–01
Breadboard. Popular Mechanics do-it-yourself encyclopedia. Vol. 11, 1655
Build a cutting board for your shop. Popular Mechanics do-it-yourself encyclopedia. Vol. 6, 900–03
Butcher block (table). Capotosto. Woodworking techniques and projects. 258–66
Carving board. Sainsbury. Sainsbury's woodturning projects for dining. 74–76

Chopping block and knife drawer. Stevenson. How to build and buy cabinets for the modern kitchen. 241–43
Cutting board. Gottshall. Wood carving and whittling for everyone. 35–36
Cutting board. Hodges. Woodturning handbook—with projects. 212–15
Cutting board. Modern general shop. Woodworking. 106
Cutting board, cheese board, bread board. Hagans. All good gifts. 57–59
Disappearing chopping board. Family handyman handbook of home improvement and remodeling. 13
Plexiglas cutting board. Popular Mechanics do-it-yourself encyclopedia. Vol. 14, 2212–13
Raised cutting board. Blackwell. Johnny Blackwell's poor man's catalog. 120
Turned handle cutting board. Popular Mechanics do-it-yourself encyclopedia. Vol. 10, 1596

D

Darrooms
Avoid these simple darkroom goofs. Popular Mechanics do-it-yourself encyclopedia. Vol. 7, 970–73
Bathroom to darkroom and back. Family handyman handbook of carpentry plans/projects. 151–54
Borrow space for a darkroom, roll-away bathroom darkroom, darkroom in a suitcase. Popular Mechanics do-it-yourself encyclopedia. Vol. 6, 904–13
Home darkroom. Geary. How to build your own workspace—with plans. 120–50
Inexpensive photo print dryer. Popular Mechanics do-it-yourself encyclopedia. Vol. 7, 1056–57
Mini portable dark room, poor man's darkroom easel. Blackwell. Johnny Blackwell's poor man's catalog. 89, 93
Observatory and photography darkroom. Churchill. Backyard building book. 136–38
Photographic darkrooms. Davidson. Successful studios and work centers. 85–94

Darning
Couched darn. Goldsworthy. Mend it! a complete guide to clothes repair. 56–57
Darning. Goldsworthy. Mend it! a complete guide to clothes repair. 15–25
Double weft knitting. Goldsworthy. Mend it! a complete guide to clothes repair. 57–58
Mending fabrics. Dillmont. Complete encyclopedia of needlework. 38–46
Stocking darn. Goldsworthy. Mend it! a complete guide to clothes repair. 47–55

Davenports. *See* **Sofas**

Decks
All about decks. Daniels. Decks, porches, and patios. 43–59
Backyard sun deck. Family Handyman handbook of carpentry plans/projects. 415–17
Building a deck. Time-Life Books. New living spaces. 120–26
Building a wood deck. Day. How to build patios and decks. 34–56
Building the basic balcony and stairs. Russell. Garages and carports. 116–25
Deck builder's guide. Landis. Patios and decks. 125–57
Deck building bases. Decks and patios. 66–85
Decks. Bragdon. Homeowner's complete manual of repair & improvement. 562–65
Decks. Kramer. Outdoor garden build-it book. 105–17
Decks, porches and patios. Nunn. Home improvement, home repair. 206–08
Decks that blend into their surroundings. Porches and patios. 30–47
Duckboards and a deck. Wood projects for the garden. 40–41
Elevated decks. Better Homes and Gardens. Deck and patio projects you can build. 4–23

Fischman. Decks.
Garden sun deck. Outdoor projects for home and garden. 381–82
How to build a deck. Brann. How to build patios and sundecks. 53–55
Large sundeck above grade. Brann. How to build patios and sundecks. 63–70
On grade decks. Better Homes and Gardens. Deck and patio projects you can build. 24–43
Open deck, simple details add beauty to your deck, two-level deck. Popular Mechanics do-it-yourself encyclopedia. Vol. 6, 914–30
Overhead cover for decks & patios. Decks and patios. 83–101
Two great decks you can build, deck and patio ideas you can borrow. Popular Mechanics do-it-yourself encyclopedia. Vol. 14, 2098–2104
Wood deck and patio. Self. Working with plywood, including indoor/outdoor projects. 204–09
Wood decks. Handyman. 287–90
Wooden decks. Clifford. Basic woodworking and carpentry . . . with projects. 170–77
Wooden deck. 101 do-it-yourself projects. 301–06

Decoupage
Art povero a small metal box, wood plaque & pendant. D'Amato. Italian crafts. 105–07
Davis. Step-by-step decoupage.
Decorating with decoupage. Wood finishing and refinishing. 89–91
Decoupage. Christmas crafts book. 119–23
Decoupage. Howell-Koehler. Step-by-step furniture finishing. 67–70
Decoupage. Johnson. How to restore, repair and finish almost everything. 99–100
Decoupage. Kicklighter. Crafts, illustrated designs and techniques. 85–89
Decoupage. Kinney. Complete book of furniture repair and refinishing. 176–77
Decoupage. Meyers. Furniture repair and refinishing. 189–91
Decoupage. Payne. Furniture finishing & refinishing. 61–64
Decoupage. Vanderbilt. Gloria Vanderbilt designs for your home. 28–45
Decoupage card. Holtje. Cardcraft. 118–23
Decoupage methods, decoupaged rock. Brunner. Pass it on. 65–72, 134–35
Decoupage on wood and tinware. Buxton. Craftmaking: for love or money. 84–92
Decoupage technique. Jarnow. (Re)do it yourself. 119–27
Decoupage; three-dimensional decoupage. Giant book of crafts. 355–68, 411–26
Decoupaged rocks. Vane. Pebble people, pets & things. 29–31
Decoupaging furniture. Brumbaugh. Wood furniture finishing, refinishing, repairing. 320–26
Flowered fabric dresser. Linsley. Fabulous furniture decorations. 136–44
Gourd print dresser. Linsley. Fabulous furniture decorations. 49–59
Introduction to decoupage. Paper. 93–97
Linsley. Decoupage on glass, wood, metal, rocks, shells, wax, soap, plastic, canvas, ceramic.
Potichomanie. Whatnot. 67
Three-dimensional decoupage. Davis. Step-by-step decoupage. 49–51
Tissue paper on metal, glass and wood. Stephan. Creating with tissue paper. 40–50

Decoys. *See* Birds, Carved; Ducks; Wood carving

Desk furnishings
Acrylic desk set. Treasury of things to make. 68–71
Bargello blotter and pot trim. Creative crafts yearbook: an exciting new collection of needlework and crafts. 63–64
Bargello-trimmed desk set. Woman's Day decorative needlework for the home. 141
Behind-desk rack, wall tidy. Blandford. 53 space-saving built-in furniture projects. 297–310
Calico-covered desk set. Evrard. Homespun crafts from scraps. 33–37

Checkered desk blotter. Scobey. Decorating with needlepoint. 171–72
Chintz desk set, decorative paper desk set. Woman's Day book of weekend crafts. 18–26
Compartment treasure box. Elbert. Paperwork 147–49
Corner-of-the desk organizer, pill bottle desk organizer. Epple. Something from nothing crafts. 16, 115
Covered desk accessories. Treasury of things to make. 172–75
Decorations for letter opener, stamp and clip holder. Goldman. Decorate with felt. 97–99
Desk blotter-covered corners. Burchette. More needlework blocking and finishing. 115–17
Desk blotter in wood. Bumper book of things a boy can make. 76–77
Desk blotter-covered ends. Burchette. More needlework blocking and finishing. 91–92
Desk caddy. Brown. 44 terrific woodworking plans & projects. 129–30
Desk catchall. Goldman. Decorate with felt. 95
Desk organizer. Modern general shop. Woodworking 109
Desk organizer. Spence. Woodworking tools, materials, processes. 590
Desk set. Evans. Ribbonwork. 18–19
Desk set for father. Perry. Holiday magic. 93–95
Desk set for paper, pen and pencils, calendar, box for note paper, dispenser for roll stamps. Cope. Plastics. 32–33, 38–39, 62
Desktop organizer and light, correspondence trays. Oberrecht. Plywood projects illustrated. 100–03, 198–200
Fabric covered desk pad with blotter. Roda. Fabric decorating for the home. 75
Fabric covered in/out box. Roda. Fabric decorating for the home. 76–77
His name plate with a coordinating desk set. Feldman. Needlework boutique. 95–97
Letter file and easel. Modern general shop. Woodworking. 102
Letter holders. Romberg. Let's discover papier-mâché. 43
Memo pad and address book. Elbert. Paperwork. 87–88
Modern mail organizer. Popular Mechanics do-it-yourself encyclopedia. Vol. 20, 3064
Needlepoint blotter ends. Parker. Mosaics in needlepoint. 130–33
Nine-patch star pen case. Houck. Patchwork pattern book. 24
Office desk place mat. Coffey. Francine Coffey's celebrity sewing bee. 67
Ornamental blotter. Bumper book of things a girl can make. 16–18
Painted tinware (desk set, wall candelabrum, collar box). McCall's book of America's favorite needlework and crafts. 346–50
Pine tree variation pen cases and phone set. Houck. Patchwork pattern book. 60–61
Silk desk set (embroidered). McCall's book of America's favorite needlework and crafts. 81–83
Stamp and pencil set. Popular Mechanics do-it-yourself encyclopedia. Vol. 6, 931
Stand for your calculator. Popular Mechanics do-it-yourself encyclopedia. Vol. 4, 511
Turpentine can desk organizers, pine in and out trays, peg appointment board, cane desk accessories, gift wrap fabric appliques desk accessories, pine organizer. Doherty. Family Circle book of 429 great gifts-to-make all year round for just 10¢ to $10.00. 4, 9, 14, 45, 56, 162–63
Tidy trough. Grainger. Making aids for disabled living. 38–39

Desks

Chest table, campaign desk and roll-top desk. Capotosto. Woodworking techniques and projects. 324–42
Colonial lap desk. Evrard. Homespun crafts from scraps. 38–40
Corner desk, reading desk. Blandford. 53 space-saving built-in furniture projects. 295–306
Desk. Waugh. Handyman's encyclopedia. 416–17
Desk and cabinet combo, storage desk combo, built-in storage desk. 77 furniture projects you can build. 229–36, 250–52, 283–86

Desk on frame. Marlow. Early American furnituremaker's manual. 119–30

Desk plus shelves. Philbin. Cabinets, bookcases & closets. 102–03

Desk, two-faced desk. Zegel. Fast furniture. 60–65

Desks and study corners. Blandford. How to make your own built-in furniture. 276–80

Desks for the kitchen. Stevenson. How to build and buy cabinets for the modern kitchen. 234–38

Do-anything desk. Blackwell. Johnny Blackwell's poor man's catalog. 121

Drafting table, wall-hung desk. Spence. Woodworking tools, materials, processes. 598, 601

Gold-tooled desk top. Capotosto. Woodworking wisdom. 242–47

Grow-along desk. Leavy. Bookshelves and storage units. 49

Handsome campaign desk. Popular Mechanics do-it-yourself encyclopedia. Vol. 7, 964–69

Home computer station. Hamilton. Build it together. 84–89

How to build a space saving desk. Clifford. Basic woodworking & carpentry . . . with projects. 200

Lady's writing desk, writing desk and roll-top desk. Rubin. Mission furniture. 86–90, 92–95

Modern desk. Complete handyman do-it-yourself encyclopedia. 1183–86

Modern pedestal desk, handy lap desk. Oberrecht. Plywood projects illustrated. 165–70, 194–97

Nazareth Hall school desk, schoolmaster's desk, drop-lid desk. Shea. Pennsylvania Dutch and their furniture. 198–201

Pedestal desk, desk and bookcase top. Brown. 44 terrific woodworking plans & projects. 171–77

Pennsylvania desk-table. Shea. Pennsylvania Dutch and their furniture. 165

Pine desk refinishing. Davis. Restoring furniture. 36–41

Pine desk restoration. Restoring and reupholstering furniture. 34–38

Plans for a compact desk, a plywood desk top and support cabinets. Geary. How to design and build your own workspace—with plans. 18–29

Plans for a pigeon hole desk. Fine woodworking techniques 4. 148–52

Plywood desk, rolltop desk, menu-planning center. 101 do-it-yourself projects. 49–57, 144–47

Portable desk, roll-top table desk, lady's desk, slope-top desk. Marlow. Classic furniture projects. 1–15, 138–93

President's desk, desk-on-frame. Osburn. Measured drawings of early American furniture. 50–51, 80–82

Schoolmaster's desk. Hagerty. Make your own antiques. 94–95

Shaker desk, Shaker sewing desk, Shaker desk and working table, antique merchant's desk, Queen Anne secretary desk, captain's desk, study desk, desk for boy's room and Shaker child's desk. 77 furniture projects you can build. 37–78

Slant-top curly maple desk. Gottshall. Provincial furniture design and construction. 63–70

Small desk, writing desk and typewriter desk. Williams. Spanish colonial furniture. 106–07, 114–17

Small pedestal desk, large flat-topped desk, rustic desk, painted wall desk. Egge. Recycled with flair. 117–27

Study center for three, study corner. Family handyman handbook of carpentry plans/ projects. 19–23

Study furniture. Ball. Master pieces. 50–57

Sturbridge desk; sea captain's desk; Sabbath day lake desk; Winterthur desk; printer's desk; North family blanket chest/desk. Daniele. Building early American furniture. 88–91, 111–14, 161–63, 196–98, 207–09, 238–41

Stylish computer center. Better Homes and Gardens step-by-step cabinets and shelves. 90–91

Tambours, cylinder desk and book-case. Fine woodworking techniques 2. 88–95

Tambours for roll top desk. Martensson. Woodworker's bible. 250–51

Trestle table desk, standing desk, kitchen desk, small writing desk. Moser. How to build Shaker furniture. 138–39, 180–91

Versatile work or hobby bench. Popular Mechanics do-it-yourself encyclopedia. Vol. 12, 1894–95

Wall-hugger desk, swing-wing desk, split-level desk, charming colonial trestle desk, rolltop desk. Popular Mechanics do-it-yourself encyclopedia. Vol. 6, 935–60

Wall-hung study center. Popular Mechanics do-it-yourself encyclopedia. Vol. 18, 2818–19

Wall mounted desk, rolltop desk for your youngster. Popular Mechanics do-it-yourself encyclopedia. Vol. 5, 672, 676–77

Writing box restoration. Davis. Restoring furniture. 100–09

Writing table. Krenov. Impractical cabinetmaker. 73–85

Desks. See also **Children's furniture, Desks**

Dice

Dice. Sainsbury. Woodworking projects with power tools. 90–91

Dodeca-dice. Grainger. Creative papercraft. 104

Dining tables. See **Tables, Dining**

Dinosaurs

Soft sculpture dinosaurs. Better Homes and Gardens treasury of Christmas crafts & foods. 37–38

Stuffed stegosaurus. Complete book of baby crafts. 141–45

Dioramas.

Dioramas. Ellis. Scale modeler's handbook. 176–83

Dioramas and displays. Price. Model-building handbook. 136–52

Dioramas and landscapes. Jackson. Modelmaker's handbook. 156–92

Model buildings. Yoder. Sculpture and modeling for the elementary school. 156–58

Portable scenes and shops. Creekmore. Your world in miniature. 140–64

Scenic bases and dioramas. Chesneau. Scale models in plastic. 180–90

Story telling box lid, shoe box home, medieval fortress, town, jungle, ocean life, cave. Yoder. Sculpture and modeling for the elementary school. 116–24

Discards. See **Waste materials**

Dishes. See **Candy dishes; Cups; Teapots; etc.**

Dispensers

Kitchen paper dispenser. Complete handyman do-it-yourself encyclopedia. 1891–93

Display racks

Building a showcase. Ellis. Scale modeler's handbook. 184–89

Collector's briefcase. Hamilton. Build it together. 98–105

Collector's cabinet. Brown. 44 terrific woodworking plans & projects. 142–44

Display cabinet. Dal Fabbro. How to make children's furniture and play equipment. 116–18

Display cabinet and drawer combination, display cabinet. Egge. Recycled with flair. 165–73

Display dome base. Hodges. Woodturning handbook—with projects. 170–73

Display shelving. LaPlante. Plastic furniture for the home craftsman. 80–89

Display table, display cabinet. Gottshall. Provincial furniture design and construction. 23–26, 93–96

Displaying pottery. Harvey. Building pottery equipment. 166–68
Displays for shells. Logan. Shell crafts. 39–57
Electronic game cartridge holder. Hamilton. Build it together. 78–83
Glass case for display. Rush. Papier mâché. 98–99
Glass-fronted cabinet. Blandford. 53 space-saving built-in furniture projects. 206–12
How to make displays for your shells: metal display stand, shadow boxes, display table, cabinet, casting resin shell stand. Elbert. Shell craft. 21–39, 192–93
Making display bases for art work. Kangas. By hand. 222–24
Outdoor display cabinets. Brann. How to build outdoor projects. 107–08
Plaster and wire display stand for shells. Logan. Shell crafts. 60–63
Plate holder. Blackwell. Johnny Blackwell's poor man's catalog. 140
Rack for pots and pans. Woman's Day book of weekend crafts. 32–39
Showcase cabinet. Krenov. Impractical cabinet-maker. 100–14, 129–51
Woodburned art frame. Broadwater. Woodburning: art and craft. 54–56

Divans. see **Sofas**

Dog harness
Dog leash (repair). Schuler. How to fix almost everything. 51
Dog leash and choke collar. Lamoreaux. Outdoor gear you can make yourself. 67–69
Macrame dog leash and collar. Mills. The book of presents. 50–51
Manila leash. Doherty. Family Circle book of 429 great gifts-to-make all year round for just 10¢ to $10.00. 13
Pet parade (macrame leash & collar). Feldman. Needlework boutique. 66–68

Dogs
Carving a dog. Wiley. Woodcarving with projects. 319–21
Dog. Day. Complete book of rock crafting. 59–65
Fido's bones in felt Christmas tree decoration. Linsley. Great bazaar. 105
Jointed poodle, wired dog. Hutchings. Big book of stuffed toy and doll making. 121–24, 144–46
Soap Staffordshire dogs. McCall's book of America's favorite needlework and crafts. 413–14
Terrier. Practical needlework. 258–59

Dogs, Equipment
A-frame doghouse. 101 do-it-yourself projects. 286–87
Arctic dog house, chateau de canine, dog pens. Churchill. Backyard building book. 104–21
Dog Christmas coat. American School of Needlework. Great Christmas crochet book. 114–15
Dog coat. Henderson. Woman's Day book of designer crochet. 158–60
Dog coat in crochet. Woman's Day bazaar best sellers. 31
Doghouse. Brown. 44 terrific woodworking plans & projects. 213, 227–28
Dog sulky. Sullivan. Cart book, with plans & projects. 233–41
Dog sweater, needlepoint name collar. Woman's Day book of weekend crafts. 148–53
Doggie coat. Johnson. Quiltwear. 15–19
Dog's rain cape. Doherty. Family Circle book of 429 great gifts-to-make all year round for just 10¢ to $10.00. 175
Finishing a needlepoint dog coat. Burchette. Needlework. 62–63
Outdoor water dish. La Barge. Pet house book. 39–41
Patchwork denim walking coat (knit). Feldman. Needlework boutique. 73–75
Patchwork dog coat. Woman's Day creative stitchery from scraps. 57–59
Pet bed. Burchette. More needlework blocking and finishing. 53–57
Pup and cat palace. Churchill. Backyard building book II. 86–89
Pups' and kitties' flea collars. Sheldon. Washable and dryable needlepoint. 82–83

Reversible fabric dog coat. Woman's Day book of gifts to make. 108–09
Shelf for dog supplies. La Barge. Pet house book. 34–38
Solar doghouse. Calhoun. 20 simple solar projects. 108–25
Solar heated dog house. Churchill. Backyard building book II. 27–38
Solar heated dog house, bear den, beagle pen. Churchill. Big backyard building book. 189–200
A special blanket and bed pillow for "our friend" (hooked). Feldman. Needlework boutique. 69, 72
Year-round-deck. La Barge. Pet house book. 42–49

Dogs, Equipment. *See also* **Kennels**

Doilies
Antique pinwheel doily with Irish crochet edging. Svinicki. Old-fashioned crochet. 72–75
Battenberg lace. McCall's book of America's favorite needlework and crafts. 411–12
Chrysanthemum mats, cornflower doily, gothic cobweb doily & knitted aster doily. McCall's big book of knit & crochet for home & family. 93–103
Crochet chairbacks. Encyclopedias of crafts. 85
Crochet dressing-table mat, hairpin table centre, geese table centre. Encyclopedia of crafts. 80, 95–96
Crocheted, knitted, tatted and hairpin lace centerpieces. Feldman. Handmade lace and patterns. 105–08
Daffodils centerpiece. Svinicki. Old-fashioned crochet. 60–61
Doilies. Southard. Bobbin lacemaking. 156–64
Filet crochet chair set. Better Homes and Gardens treasury of needlecrafts. 225–27
Knitted mimosa and pinwheel doilies. McCall's book of America's favorite needlework and crafts. 251–53, 256
Modern Norwegian hardanger doily. Nielsen. Scandinavian embroidery, past and present. 88–89
Pink pineapple doily. American School of Needlework. Great crochet bazaar book. 52–54
Rectangular doily. Svinicki. Old-fashioned crochet. 36–37
Rose embroidered doilies. Embroidery of roses. 86–89, 96, 99–101, 120–21, 123–28, 132–33
Shamrock & rice stitch doilies. McCall's big book of knit & crochet for home & family. 178–79
Swedish Advent cloth. Nielsen. Scandinavian embroidery, past and present. 98–99
Tatted doily, daisy doily, large doily. McCall's big book of knit & crochet for home & family. 271–72, 276
Tatting table centre, hairpin crochet table centre. Blandford book of traditional handicrafts. 28–29, 34

Doll accessories
Barbie doll sleeping bag, doll's patchwork quilt. Coffey. Francine Coffey's celebrity sewing bee. 130, 137
Postage stamp quilt. Better Homes and Gardens treasury of Christmas crafts & foods. 247

Doll buggies
Doll carriage. Blandford. Giant book of wooden toys. 124–29
Stroller and doll carriage. Maginley. Toys to make and ride. 33–39

Doll furniture

Basket doll cradle. Evrard. Homespun crafts from scraps. 119–23
Cardboard doll furniture from odds and ends. Brunner. Pass it on. 96–99
Carry-cot or bassinet and baby doll. Tyler. Big book of soft toys. 232–35
Doll furniture. Better Homes and Gardens treasury of Christmas crafts & foods. 246
Dollhouse furniture. Favorite easy-to-make toys. 216–21
Doll slide. Hamilton. Build it together. 154–59
Doll's playpen. Blandford. Giant book of wooden toys. 40–43
Dressing table, dressers. Mercer. Let's make doll furniture. 70–73
Felt and cardboard dollhouse furniture. Better Homes and Gardens easy bazaar crafts.
    22–23, 30–32
Flick. Dollhouse idea book.
Foot stove. Maginley. America in miniatures. 56–59
Furniture construction, sofas, chairs, and stools. Ruthberg. Book of miniatures. 165–82
Glick. Dollhouse furniture you can make.
Hitchcock mirror, Chippendale mirrors. Farlie. All about doll houses. 220–25
Kurten. Needlepoint in miniature.
Making doll furniture. Blandford. Giant book of wooden toys. 227–34
Milk-carton bedroom suite, living-room corner, baby buggy. Woman's Day book of gifts
    to make. 24–27
Miniatures: toys and games, beach accessories, toys for toy shop, florist shop, fish-
    monger, butcher, & baker. Hutchings. Big book of stuffed toy and doll making. 67–
    85
Painted doll dishes. Jarnow. (Re)do it yourself. 114–15
Playpen. Fowler. Can crafts. 58
Stroller. Fowler. Can crafts. 52–55
Swing for your doll. Bumper book of things a girl can make. 113–14
Tea cart. Fowler. Can craft. 70–74
Television sets and radios. Mercer. Let's make doll furniture. 52–59
Wooden clothes peg doll's furniture: cradle, rocking chair, bunk beds, and four poster
    bed. Anderson. Crafts and the disabled. 131–37

Doll furniture, Beds

Antique doll beds. Baldwin. Old fashioned wooden toys. 152–57
Basic bed, high beds. Glick. Dollhouse furniture you can make. 23–26
Bassinette, brass bed, curved tester bed, straight tester bed. Farlie. All about doll
    houses. 71–73, 76–79
Bed. Fowler. Can crafts. 80–83
Bed, bunk beds. Woman's Day book of weekend crafts. 132–33, 135–36
Bedroom suite. Anderson. Crafts and the disabled. 125–29
Beds. Mercer. Let's make doll furniture. 68–70
Beds, headboards and cradles. Ruthberg. Book of miniatures. 183–90
Bedspreads, canopy, pillows, etc. Farlie. All about doll houses. 187–89
Brass bedstead made from curtain rings. Flick. Dollhouse idea book. 50–54
Bundling bed, a tester bed, and a trundle bed. Maginley. America in miniatures. 72–79
Canopy doll bed. Egge. Recycled with flair. 65–74
Decoupage doll bed. Jarnow. (Re)do it yourself. 131–33
Doll's bed. Mills. The book of presents. 122–23
Doll's bunk bed unit. Blandford. Giant book of wooden toys. 82–87
Doll's pine bedstead. Doherty. Family Circle book of 429 great gifts-to-make all year
    round for just 10¢ to $10.00. 32
Four poster bed. Favorite easy-to-make toys. 220–21

Doll furniture, Benches
Deacon's bench, settle. Farlie. All about doll houses. 156–58
Dressing table bench. Fowler. Can craft. 87–90
Dressing table bench, Shaker, high stool, fireside. Farlie. All about doll houses. 80–83
Settle, trestle table benches. Maginley. America in miniatures. 46–48, 67

Doll furniture, Bookcases
Bookcases. Mercer. Let's make doll furniture. 34–42
Bookcases. Ruthberg. Book of miniatures. 210–17
Secretary bookcase, breakfront. Farlie. All about doll houses. 84–88

Doll furniture, Chairs
Balloon back chairs, belter parlor chair, ladderback chair, Sheraton arm chair, Windsor
    rocking chair, wing chair. Farlie. All about doll houses. 89–103
Chair, beanbag chair. Woman's Day book of weekend crafts. 129–30, 134.
Chairs. Creekmore. Your world in miniature. 47–53
Chairs, big chair, chaise longue. Mercer. Let's make doll furniture. 11–17, 21–23, 60–
    67
Chaise lounge. Fowler. Can crafts. 68–69
Doll chair. Elbert. Paperworks. 144–46
Doll's chair. Blandford. Giant book of wooden toys. 74–77
Doll's high chair. Blandford. Giant book of wooden toys. 164–68
Highchair. Fowler. Can craft. 48–51
Ice cream parlor chair. Fowler. Can craft. 76–78
Ladder-back rocker. Horwitz. Mountain people, mountain crafts. 54
Loose pillow chair, bucket chair. Glick. Dollhouse furniture you can make. 31–37
Rocking chair. Fowler. Can craft. 58–63
Straight-back chair. Fowler. Can crafts. 78–80
Victorian side chair. Hodges. How to build your own fine doll houses and furnishings.
    236–42

Doll furniture, Chests
Blanket chest, Victorian bureau, chest-on-chest, bow front dresser, Chippendale high-
    boy & lowboy. Farlie. All about doll houses. 104–14
Chest. Ruthberg. Book of miniatures. 191–96
Chest of drawers. Flick. Dollhouse idea book. 48–50
Doll trunk. Hundley. Folk art toys and furniture for children. 55–59
Drawer furniture. Mercer. Let's make doll furniture. 43–51
An early American chest. Maginley. America in miniatures. 70–71
Miniature chest of drawers. Shea. Pennsylvania Dutch and their furniture. 185

Doll furniture, Clocks
Clocks and other wall accessories. Ruthberg. Book of miniatures. 38–46
Grandfather clock, school clock, steeple clock. Farlie. All about doll houses. 115–19

Doll furniture, Cradles
Cradle. Fowler. Can crafts. 55–57
Cradle. Maginley. America in miniatures. 60–63
Doll's cradle. Cane, rush and straw. 41–47
Doll cradle. Hundley. Folk art toys and furniture for children. 48–54
Doll's cradle in buff willow. Maynard. Modern basketry from the start. 162–63
Doll's cradle, towne cradle. Hagerty. Make your own antiques. 78–79, 92–93
Dolls cribs. Blandford. Giant book of wooden toys. 47–50
Doll's rocking crib. Blandford. Giant book of wooden toys. 43–47
Hooded cradle. Farlie. All about doll houses. 74–75
Rocking doll cradle. Baldwin. Old fashioned wooden toys. 148–51
Woven miniature cradle. Wright. Complete book of baskets and basketry. 99–100

Doll furniture, Cupboards
Armoire, Victorian china cabinet, commode, dry sink, hutch cupboard, icebox. Farlie. All about doll houses. 120–33
Cupboards. Ruthberg. Book of miniatures. 191–99
Kitchen cabinets. Woman's Day book of weekend crafts. 123–25
Miniature hutch. Brown. 44 terrific woodworking plans & projects. 147–52
Pine cupboard. Maginley. America in miniatures. 80–83
Queen Anne hunt board, Hepplewhite sideboard, serving board. Farlie. All about doll houses. 140–46

Doll furniture, Desks
Davenport desk, partner's desk, slant top desk. Farlie. All about doll houses. 134–39
Roll-top desk. Fine woodworking techniques 5. 164–71

Doll furniture, Lamps
Floor lamp. Fowler. Can crafts. 63–65
Floor lamp and desk lamp. Woman's Day book of weekend crafts. 131, 136
Floor and table lamps. Mercer. Let's make doll furniture. 92–94
Lighting fixtures and appliances. Ruthberg. Book of miniatures. 50–60

Doll furniture, Sofas
Beltor Victorian sofa, Chippendale sofa (camelback). Farlie. All about doll houses. 147–55
Easy lounge-sleep sofa, loose pillow sofa, skirted sofa, curved back Victorian style sofa. Glick. Dollhouse furniture you can make. 26–31, 37–41
Love seat. Fowler. Can crafts. 65–67
Making a lounge suite. Anderson. Crafts and the disabled. 129
Sofas and chairs, love seat. Mercer. Let's make doll furniture. 11–17, 19–21, 23–25
Victorian sofa. Hodges. How to build your own fine doll houses and furnishings. 242–46

Doll furniture, Stands
Cloverleaf candle stand. Farlie. All about doll houses. 159

Doll furniture, Stoves
Cast-iron stove. Farlie. All about doll houses. 182–83
Kitchen stove. Woman's Day book of weekend crafts. 125

Doll furniture, Tables
Dressing table. Fowler. Can crafts. 85–87
Glass-top table. Fowler. Can crafts. 75–76
Inlay card, circular coffee, console, circular dining, two-pedestal dining, dressing, drop-leaf dining, drum, marble top kitchen, pembroke, sewing or bedside, tea, trestle. Farlie. All about doll houses. 160–77
Kitchen table and coffee table. Woman's Day book of weekend crafts. 126, 130
Nightstand. Fowler. Can crafts. 83–85
Sheraton console table, Shaker trestle table. Hodges. How to build your own fine doll houses and furnishings. 227–36
Tables. Mercer. Let's make doll furniture. 6–10
Tables. Ruthberg. Book of miniatures. 200–09
Trestle table and benches, hutch table, settle, and chest. Maginley. America in miniatures. 64–71

Doll houses

Authentic log cabin. Joyner. Dollhouse construction and restoration. 12–25

Building a dollhouse. Glick. Dollhouse furniture you can make. 145–60

Building a dollhouse. Hodges. How to build your own fine doll houses and furnishings. 79–211

Canadian log hut. Bumper book of things a boy can make. 13–14

Cardboard, Sierra Madre, modular, English bungalow, colonial, paper doll houses. Boeschen. Successful playhouses. 45–60

Colonial doll house. McCall's book of America's favorite needlework and crafts. 310–18

Colonial, Georgian, Victorian architectural details. Farlie. All about doll houses. 50–70

Contemporary dollhouse. Joyner. Dollhouse construction and restoration. 26–34

Curtains, cornices, shades, etc. Farlie. All about doll houses. 190–95

Dodge. Dolls' house do-it-yourself book.

Doll house. Dal Fabbro. How to make children's furniture and play equipment. 135–38

Dollhouse. Favorite easy-to-make toys. 183–87

Doll house decorations. Miles. Designing with natural materials. 124

Dollhouse. Treasury of things to make. 38–40

Doll house, town house. Hundley. Folk art toys and furniture for children. 36–47

Doll's playroom. Blandford. Giant book of wooden toys. 209–11

Easy to make cardboard dollhouse. Doherty. Family Circle book of 429 great gifts-to-make all year round for just 10¢ to $10.00. 24–25

Enchanting dollhouse. Popular Mechanics do-it-yourself encyclopedia. Vol. 12, 1830–34

Fireplace accessories. Farlie. All about doll houses. 196–98

Flower arrangements for miniature rooms. Creekmore. Your world in miniature. 91–111

Frames, artwork and sculpture, mirrors, clock and other accessories. Ruthberg. Book of miniatures. 29–49

How miniature gardens grow. Creekmore. Your world in miniature. 112–39

Jensen. Building in miniature.

Kitchens, walls and floors, patios. Mercer. Let's make doll furniture. 81–86, 95–105

Kurten. Needlepoint in miniature.

Landscaping. Dollhouse construction and restoration. 88–94

Lights and lighting accessories. Farlie. All about doll houses. 199–205

Log cabin. Better Homes and Gardens treasury of Christmas crafts & foods. 255–57

Log cabin. Maginley. America in miniatures. 14–17

Log cabin doll house. Platt. Step-by-step woodcraft. 30–31

Making balsa buildings. Warring. Balsa wood modelling. 13–15

Making miniature shingles. Fine woodworking techniques 4. 11

Modular dollhouses. 101 do-it-yourself projects. 344–45

New England saltbox. Joyner. Dollhouse construction and restoration. 78–87

19th century English farmhouse. Popular Mechanics do-it-yourself encyclopedia. Vol. 19, 2916–19

Paintings, flower prints, mottos, portraits, etc. Farlie. All about doll houses. 220–25

Plantation house. Joyner. Dollhouse construction and restoration. 49–65

Plastic canvas small and large houses. Wilson. Needleplay. 176–79

Portable doll house. Rissell. Craftwork the handicapped elderly can make and sell. 90–93

Restoration of old dollhouses. Joyner. Dollhouse construction and restoration. 95–111

Revolving dolls' house and zoo. Anderson. Crafts and the disabled. 44–46

Salt box house. Maginley. America in miniatures. 40–43

Small doll house. Blandford. Giant book of wooden toys. 211–18

Town house for rent: ready for occupancy December 25. Vanderbilt. Gloria Vanderbilt designs for your home. 190–94.

Toy shop circa 1900. Creative crafts yearbook: an exciting new collection of needlework and crafts. 92–96
Traveling dollhouse with furniture. Woman's day book of weekend crafts. 118–38
Two-floor doll house. Blandford. Giant book of wooden toys. 219–26
Victorian mansion. Joyner. Dollhouse construction and restoration. 66–77
Spanish hacienda. Joyner. Dollhouse construction and restoration. 35–48
Victorian mansion doll house. Baldwin. Old fashioned wooden toys. 128–47
Wall dollhouse. Blandford. 53 space-saving built-in furniture projects. 125–28
Window treatment. Ruthberg. Book of miniatures. 120–27

Doll house, Bathrooms
Bathrooms. Mercer. Let's make doll furniture. 74–80

Doll houses, Fireplaces
Fireplaces. Creekmore. Your world in miniature. 38–40
Fireplaces. Mercer. Let's make doll furniture. 26–33
Fireplaces and hearthside equipment. Ruthberg. Book of miniatures. 110–19
Free-standing fireplace, brick fireplace. Flick. Dollhouse idea book. 42–46

Doll houses, Rugs
Braided rugs, hooked rugs, needlepoint rugs, etc. Farlie. All about doll houses. 226–33
Chinese dollhouse rug. Better Homes and Gardens treasury of needlecrafts. 274–75
Floor coverings. Ruthberg. Book of miniatures. 138–43
Kitchen mat, large shag rug and braided rug. Woman's Day book of weekend crafts. 126, 130, 134, 137
McBaine. Miniature needlepoint rugs for dollhouses.

Dolls
All kinds of dolls. Tyler. Big book of soft toys. 153–82
Anklet, bandanna, babushka, country girl, heart-trimmed. Better Homes and Gardens easy bazaar crafts. 6, 16, 24–26, 29, 33–34, 37
Antique fashion doll, three sisters dolls, early American quartet. McCall's book of America's favorite needlework and crafts. 294–302
Apple head and corn shuck dolls. Horwitz. Mountain people, mountain crafts. 35–45
Baby doll. Wargo. Soft crafts for special occasions. 59–62
Baldwin. Weepeeple.
Banner dolls. Blair. Banners and flags. 158–62
Basic cone doll, male doll with legs, female doll with legs, dolls with needle-modelled faces and hands. Greenhowe. Dolls in national and folk costume. 11–23
Batik corn dolls. McCall's big book of country needlecrafts. 158–59
Bead and pipecleaner dolls. Dodge. Dolls' house do-it-yourself book. 205–14
Bisque dolls: Beauty and the Beast, Thumbelina, the Goose Girl. Roth. Making original dolls of composition, bisque, and porcelain. 88–142
Composition dolls: Rumpelstiltskin, Snow Queen, Hansel and Gretel. Roth. Making original dolls of composition, bisque, and porcelain. 16–86
Cupid pillow-dolls, flying angel pillow dolls, French sailor pillow-doll. Marsten. Step-by-step dollmaking. 81–86; 94–96
Cylinder people: happy pixie, totem the red Indian, Antonio the chef, Esmeralda the witch, and regiment of skittles. Janitch. All made from paper. 69–76
Darning egg dolls, nuthead dolls. Jones. Early North American dollmaking, a narrative history and craft instructions. 63, 123–27
Dolls and figures. Laury. Handmade toys and games. 17–43
Gnome puppets or dolls. Meilach. Macrame gnomes and puppets. 42–69
Grandmother pillow doll, pillow girl, Shaker woman. Guild. Dollmaker's workshop. 99–103, 106–07

Holz. How-to book of international dolls.
Learning sample made into doll. Dendel. Basic book of fingerweaving. 54
Little nut-head doll. Perry. Holiday magic. 122–23
Magazine Daphne doll, pill bottle doll. Epple. Something from nothing crafts. 60–62,
    114–15
"Me" dolls. Gardner. Dough creations. 144–45
Mexican, Sicilian, Japanese, Indian, Spanish, New Zealand, French, Lapland, Welsh,
    American cowboy, German, Scottish fishwife, London pearly queen and king, and
    Netherland costumes. Greenhowe. Dolls in national and folk costume. 28–111
Miniature dolls. Hutchings. Big book of stuffed toy and doll making. 72–76
Nuthead dolls. Jones. Early North American dollmaking. 126–27
Nutheads, beanhead dolls. Holz. How-to book of international dolls. 322–26
Parlor dolls, wax dolls. Better Homes and Gardens treasury of Christmas crafts &
    foods. 246–47, 252–55
Passion flower dolls. Johnson. Nature crafts. 46
Patterns for dolls' clothes. Favorite easy-to-make toys. 63–69
Pioneer dolls. Conner. Corncraft. 81–96
Pipecleaner miniature dolls, poupard dolls (wooden ball on a stick). Favorite easy-to-
    make toys. 32–41
Pocket-size dollmates. Woman's Day book of weekend crafts. 111–17
Porcelain dolls: Rapunzel, the Mermaid. Roth. Making original dolls of composition,
    bisque, and porcelain. 144–76
Primitive sun doll. Creative sewing. 126
Rubbing made into a doll or pillow. Firestein. Rubbing craft. 68–69
Six dolls in historical costume, Mary, a miniature dressing-up doll, three Victorian-style
    dolls. Greenhowe. Making miniature toys and dolls. 40–54, 63–75, 94–99
Stand-up boy doll, silly face-makers, bouncy funnel dolls. Woman's Day creative stitch-
    ery from scraps. 102–05, 118–20, 130–32
Stuffed dolls and spool dolls. Linderman. Crafts for the classroom. 181–89
Tenants for a doll's house. Flick. Dollhouse idea book. 79–92
Three felt dolls, Bo-Peep, Red Riding Hood and Miss Muffet. Greenhowe. Making
    miniature toys and dolls. 22–25
Tyler. Big book of dolls.
Walnut and egg, pieces, clothespin, apple-head cornhusk and cloth dolls. Golden book
    of colonial crafts. 69–77

Dolls, African
Dolls of Africa and the Near East. Holz. How-to book of international dolls. 30–62
Sierra Leone mother and baby. Guild. Dollmaker's workshop. 144–45

Dolls, Apple
Apple doll. Brunner. Pass it on. 100–02
Apple dolls. Meras. Vacation crafts. 134–36
Apple head dolls. Better Homes and Gardens treasury of Christmas crafts and foods.
    206
Apple-head doll. Golden book of colonial crafts. 73
Applehead dolls. Holz. How-to book of international dolls. 314–19
Applehead dolls. Jones. Early North American dollmaking. 118–25
Applehead dolls. Schuman. Art from many hands. 227–30
Apple-head grandma. McCall's book of America's favorite needlework and crafts. 308–
    09

Dolls, Clothespin
Clothes peg doll. Jones. Early North American dollmaking, a narrative history and craft
  instructions. 59
Clothespin doll. Golden book of colonial crafts. 72
Clothespin doll. Perry. Holiday magic. 120–21
Clothespin dolls. Holz. How-to book of international dolls. 320–21
Peg dolls. Evans. Ribbonwork. 45–48

Dolls, Corncob
Abigail and Ebenezer. Guild. Dollmaker's workshop. 104–05
Corncob doll. Jones. Early North American dollmaking. 41–43

Dolls, Cornhusk
Cornhusk doll. Golden book of colonial crafts. 74
Cornhusk doll. Meras. Vacation crafts. 137–39
Cornhusk dolls. Brunner. Pass it on. 102–06
Corn husk dolls. Buxton. Craftmaking: for love or money. 109–14
Cornhusk dolls. Creative crafts yearbook: an exciting new collection of needlework and
  crafts. 127–28
Cornhusk dolls. Holz. How-to book of international dolls. 306–11
Corn husk dolls. Jones. Early North American dollmaking. 110–17
Corn husk dolls. Linderman. Crafts for the classroom. 188–89
Cornhusk dolls. McCall's book of America's favorite needlework and crafts. 303–05
Corn husk pioneer women. Johnson. Nature crafts. 68–73
Grass doll, corn husk doll. Jones. Early North American dollmaking, a narrative history
  and craft instructions. 55, 111–17
Modern cornhusk dolls. Conner. Corncraft. 143–60

Dolls, crocheted
Baby Barbara Jean, high school sweethearts, him and her dolls. American School of
  Needlework. Great crochet bazaar book. 105–21
Baby blue eyes. American School of Needlework. Great crochet bazaar book. 91–93
Crochet Dutch doll. Favorite easy-to-make toys. 128–30
Jack and Jill dolls. Great granny crochet book. 63–64
Rosy doll. Walters. Crochet. 52
Sister Sue & her basket, too, brother & sister dolls. American School of Needlework.
  Great Christmas crochet book. 128–32, 137–41

Dolls, Czech
Czech couple. Guild. Dollmaker's workshop. 133–35

Dolls, East Indian
East Indian stick dolls. Guild. Dollmaker's workshop. 123–24

Dolls, German
Gretel. Guild. Dollmaker's workshop. 136–40

Dolls, Greek
Greek yarn doll. Guild. Dollmaker's workshop. 141–43

Dolls, Handkerchief
Hanky panky family. Jones. Early North American dollmaking. 64–68

Dolls, Indian (American)
American Indian costume Blackfoot. Greenhowe. Dolls in national and folk costume. 24–27
Dolls of North America. Holz. How-to book of international dolls. 270–95
Kachina dolls. McCall's book of America's favorite needlework and crafts. 305–07
Navaho woman. Guild. Dollmaker's workshop. 118–22

Dolls, Irish
Colleen from Kildare. Guild. Dollmaker's workshop. 131–32

Dolls, Knitted
Basic knitted doll in three sizes, knitted snowman, twin boy and girl, red Indian chief, witch. Tyler. Big book of dolls. 60–67
Knitted doll, pirate, doctor and nurse. Favorite easy-to-make toys. 104–06, 110–15
Knitted dolls. Mills. Book of presents. 92–93
Knitted dolls. Tyler. Big book of soft toys. 183–205
Knitted playmates. Complete book of baby crafts. 153–55
Punchinello doll. Knitting techniques and projects. 39
Striped knitted clown doll. McCall's book of Christmas. 154–56

Dolls, Needlepoint
Bride and groom dolls. Better Homes and Gardens treasury of needlecrafts. 280–82
Doll. Smith. Needlery. 95–99
Needlepoint doll. Laury. Treasury of needlecraft gifts for the new baby. 76–77

Dolls, Oriental
Chinese man. Day. Complete book of rock crafting. 121–23
Chinese man. Guild. Dollmaker's workshop. 146–49
Dolls of Asia and the Pacific. Holz. How-to book of international dolls. 63–119
Geisha. Day. Complete book of rock crafting. 124–25

Dolls, Paper
Cinderella walking doll. Elbert. Paperworks. 62–65
Felt paper doll. Coffey. Francine Coffey's celebrity sewing bee. 136
Real paper doll. Elbert. Paperworks. 72–75

Dolls, Peruvian
Peruvian girl. Guild. Dollmaker's workshop. 128–30

Dolls, Rag
Amy rag doll. Baldwin. Scrap fabric crafts. 19–23
Big and little sister rag dolls. Doherty. Family Circle book of 429 great gifts-to-make all year round for just 10¢ to $10.00. 28–31
Bouncing doll, flying trapeze man, woven doll, Bets' doll and sock dolls. Laury. Treasury of needlecraft gifts for the new baby. 104–15
Colonial doll, pioneer dolls, country girl doll, old-fashioned dolls, tea-party pillow dolls, rag dolls, brother and sister dolls, little miss doll. Better Homes and Gardens treasury of Christmas crafts & foods. 100–01, 105, 107–08, 170–73, 212–13, 251–52, 274–76
Coyne. How to make upside-down dolls.
Downcast Greg and contented Jenny. Creative sewing. 122
Farmer's boy and milkmaid. Creative crafts yearbook: an exciting new collection of needlework and crafts. 66–73
From the smallest scraps: a clown doll (yoyo). Crown. How to recycle old clothes into new fashions. 114–23

Girl with a straw hat, Sandy sneakers, colonial lady, Lillie longstockings, Appalachian mountain couple, day of the week dolls, waking-sleeping doll. Guild. Dollmaker's workshop. 33–43, 49–63
Granny (lifesize). Kinser. Sewing sculpture. 82–87, 91
Halloween boy, brother/sister dolls and batik doll. Laury. Treasury of needlecraft gifts for the new baby. 78–84
Little girl. Practical needlework. 260–62
Little people dolls. Foose. More scrap saver's stitchery. 14–18
Little Red Ridinghood story doll. Guild. Dollmaker's workshop. 108–12
Old fashioned rag doll. Complete book of baby crafts. 134–40
Orphan Annie doll. Kinser. Sewing sculpture. 117–20
Pillow dolls. Kinser. Sewing sculpture. 77–78
Rag doll family. Marsten. Step-by-step dollmaking. 69–79
Rag doll with wardrobe, topsy turvy doll. Favorite easy-to-make toys. 42–56
Rag dolls. Gault. Crafts for the disabled. 55–63
Rath. Splendid soft toy book.
Simple rag doll. Jones. Early North American dollmaking. 130–31
Simple Sam the shepherd and his lamb. Mills. The book of presents. 62–64
Six miniatures (for dollhouses). Marsten. Step-by-step dollmaking. 39–56
Soldier, clown, elf, old woman who lived in a shoe. Hutchings. Big book of stuffed toy and doll making. 89–111
Stitch a printed doll or cat. Rosenthal. Not-so-nimble needlework book. 28
Stocking dolls. Creative sewing. 118
Super sweaterman. Brown. Super sweater idea book. 197–98
Surprising tale of a remarkable rag doll. Vanderbilt. Gloria Vanderbilt designs for your home. 198–209
Three American couples: frontier, southern, New England sea captain. Marsten. Step-by-step dollmaking. 11–30
Three working men: engineer, policeman, lion tamer. Marsten. Step-by-step dollmaking. 31–38
Tiny Tim doll. Baldwin. Scrap fabric crafts. 86–88
Two-headed dolls. Holz. How-to book of international dolls. 331–32

Dolls, Repairing
Doll. Schuler. How to fix almost everything. 52–53

Dolls, Russian
Russian needlepoint dolls. Encyclopedia of crafts. 72
Stroganoff family. Creative sewing. 127

Dolls, Sock
Anklet dolls. Better Homes and Gardens easy bazaar crafts. 29, 37
Boy and girl dolls. Favorite easy-to-make toys. 57–61
Girl with a pocket doll, twins in a bunting, Eskimo boy, snow baby, Muggs monkey. Guild. Dollmaker's workshop. 9–31
Sock doll. Jones. Early North American dollmaking. 132–35

Dolls, Straw
Grass doll. Jones. Early North American dollmaking. 52–55
Harvest maiden. Johnson. Nature crafts. 96–97

Dolls, Swiss
Swiss grandma. Guild. Dollmaker's workshop. 125–27

Dolls, Wooden
Dowel dolls. Blackwell. Johnny Blackwell's poor man's catalog. 139
Spoon dolls. Baldwin. Old fashioned wooden toys. 158–60
Spoon dolls. Better Homes and Gardens treasury of Christmas crafts & foods. 8, 16–17
Stump doll. Jones. Early North American dollmaking. 47
Twig doll. Jones. Early North American dollmaking. 49–51
Wooden dolls. Adams. Make your own baby furniture. 156–57
Wooden spoon doll, a clothes peg doll, a darning egg doll. Jones. Early North American dollmaking. 56–63

Dolls, Yarn
Braided yarn dolls. Rissell. Craftwork the handicapped elderly can make and sell. 43–47
Crochet doll. Creative crafts yearbook: an exciting new collection of needlework and crafts. 138
Disk doll. Woman's Day book of weekend crafts. 102–03
Yarn couples, Victorian lady, knitted Nellie, kitchen duet, crocheted Jack and Jill, needlepoint farm family. Guild. Dollmaker's workshop. 65–91
Yarn doll. Favorite easy-to-make toys. 62
Yarn people for party favors. Perry. Holiday magic. 177–78

Dolls, Yoyo
Clown doll and pillow top. Guth. Sewing with scraps. 57–58
Clown made of fabric yo-yos. Gault. Crafts for the disabled. 107
Yo-yo Humpty Dumpty and monkey. Rissell. Craftwork the handicapped elderly can make and sell. 33–36
Yoyo lady. Creative sewing. 102

Domes
Domes. Boeschen. Successful playhouses. 101–02
Geodesic dome. Family handyman handbook of carpentry plans/projects. 461–68
Geodesic dome guest house. Churchill. Backyard building book. 70–76
Nine-way geodesic dome. Outdoor projects for home and garden. 347–50

Domes, Play
Wattle-and-daub playhouse. Lane. Building in your backyard. 129–31
Garden house dome. Palmer. Making children's furniture and play structures. 84–87
Penta-hex dome. Palmer. Making children's furniture and play structures. 73–77
Triangle house. Palmer. Making children's furniture and play structures. 70–71
Two-frequency dowel dome. Palmer. Making children's furniture and play structures. 88–90

Door bells
Chimes and door buzzers. Waugh. Handyman's encyclopedia. 65–67
Door chime. Modern general shop. Electricity 98–101
Door chime. Popular Mechanics do-it-yourself encyclopedia. Vol. 10, 1466
Doorbell maintenance and repair. Nunn. Home improvements, home repair. 145–46
Doorbell with knight. Bealer. Art of blacksmithing. 315–16
How to repair your doorbell. Popular Mechanics do-it-yourself encyclopedia. Vol. 7, 1018–22
Installation of doorbells and door chimes. Complete handyman do-it-yourself encyclopedia. Vol. 6, 815–26
Macrame doorbells. Better Homes and Gardens easy bazaar crafts. 69, 78

Door mats
Braided door mat, cornhusk coiled mat. Giant book of crafts. 260–63
Embroidery rose welcome mat. Embroidery of roses. 142–43
Macrame doormat. Casselman. Crafts from around the world. 29–31
Owl and mushroom door mat. Christensen. Needlepoint and bargello stitchery. 9–11
Practical and pretty doormats. Guth. Sewing with scraps. 109–16
Raffia mat. Casselman. Crafts from around the world. 172–73
Rush floor mats. Brown. Complete book of rush and basketry techniques. 84–87

Doors
Adding vinyl woodgrain cover to a plain door. Family handyman handbook of home improvement and remodeling. 296–303
Art nouveau panel door, warm door, carved doors, barnwood doors, flush doors with flair. Rowland. Handcrafted doors & windows. 66–89
Beaded door finger plate. Hulbert. Creative beadwork. 62, 75
Bifold doors for closets. Popular Mechanics do-it-yourself encyclopedia. Vol. 5, 770–74
Building overlay, flush, and lip doors. Philbin. Cabinets, bookcases & closets. 55–59
Constructing doors. Johnston. Craft of furniture making. 85–87
Converting a window to a door. Time-Life Books. New living spaces. 82–88
Door catches, latches, bolts, handles, hinges. Blandford. Practical handbook of blacksmithing and metalworking. 228–66
Door frames and casings. Syvanen. Interior finish: more tricks of the trade. 40–62
Door kick pad. LaPlante. Plastic furniture for the home craftsman. 77–78
Doors. Bragdon. Homeowner's complete manual of repair & improvement. 132–45
Doors and door frames. Lewis. Cabinetmaking, patternmaking, and millwork. 399–408
Entryways. Popular Mechanics do-it-yourself encyclopedia. Vol. 8, 1148–53
Fabrication of doors. Haynie. Cabinetmaking. 47–61
Front-entry face-lift. Better Homes and Gardens. Step-by-step masonry and concrete. 80–81
Hang doors. Brann. How to modernize an attic. 41
How to hang a door, installing your own back door, install your own combination storm door. Family handyman handbook of home improvement and remodeling. 291–95, 303–20
How to remove doors. Brann. How to build kitchen cabinets, room dividers, and cabinet furniture. 52
How to trim sticking doors. Popular Mechanics do-it-yourself encyclopedia. Vol. 7, 1024–25
Doors. Parry. Stenciling. 95
Glass doors. Windows and skylights. 84–85
Installing a factory fitted door. Time-Life Books. New living spaces. 42–45
Installing an accordian door. Time-Life Books. New living spaces. 14–16
Installing doors. Burch. Building small barns, sheds, and shelters. 104–09
Installing doors. Clifford. Basic woodworking and carpentry . . . with projects. 149–56
Installing doors. Ramsey. Building a log home from scratch or kit. 168–73
Insulated workshop doors. McNair. Building & outfitting your workshop. 37–46
Interior doors and trim. Adams. Arco's complete woodworking handbook. 490–506
Louvered doors, entry doors, hanging a door. Fine woodworking techniques 2. 96–104
Making a door where there was none. Time-Life Books. New living spaces. 88–91
Making door jambs. Clifford. Basic woodworking and carpentry . . . with projects. 150–56
Making of doors. Rowland. Handcrafted doors & windows. 2–53
Mosaic door. Fine woodworking techniques 5. 92–93
Paneled cabinet doors. Martensson. Woodworker's bible. 242–45
Reglazing your door with safe material. Family handyman handbook of home improvement and remodeling. 308–13
Replacing storm doors. Outdoor projects for home and garden. 107–12

Setting a door frame and hanging a door. Spence. General carpentry. 301–10
Solar basement door. Calhoun. 20 simple solar projects. 194–205
Storm vestibule. Brann. How to build outdoor projects. 74
Unmilled batten door, wood mosaic doors. Rowland. Handcrafted doors & windows. 94–103
Wood doors. Olin. Construction. 202–28

Doors, Repairing
Doors. Hayward. Antique furniture repairs. 75–80
Doors. Nunn. Home improvements, home repair. 50–51
Squeaky doors, hinge troubles, locks, weather stripping. Carbo. Fix-it guide for women. 88–103

Doors, Sliding
Framing and hanging a door, installing sliding glass doors. Handyman. 157–68
How to install a sliding glass door. Better Homes and Gardens. Deck and patio projects you can build. 59
Installing sliding doors. Time-Life Books. New living spaces. 17
Sliding glass doors. Popular Mechanics do-it-yourself encyclopedia. Vol. 17, 2706–08
Sliding glass door. Porches and patios. 120–27
Sliding doors. Blandford. How to make your own built-in furniture. 303–04

Doorstops
Brick doorstop. Doherty. Family Circle book of 429 great gifts-to-make all year round for just 10¢ to $10.00. 51
Dolly doorstop. Guild. Dollmaker's workshop. 94–95
Personalized brick doorstop. Coffey. Francine Coffey's celebrity sewing bee. 111
Rabbit, sailboat door stops. Brann. How to build workbenches, sawhorse tool chest and other build-it-yourself projects. 87–90
Rock stop. Linsley. Decoupage on glass, wood, metal, rocks, shells, wax, soap, plastic, canvas, ceramic. 134–36
Tic-Tac-Toe doorstop. Slater. Elaine Slater's book of needlepoint projects. 134–35

Doorstops. See also **Brick covers**

Dough
Bakers clay. Gardner. Dough creations. 55–57
Baker's clay. Hagans. All good gifts. 41
Baker's clay, sawdust modeling playdough. Linderman. Crafts for the classroom. 271–86
Bread dough animals. McCall's book of Christmas. 107
Bread dough for ornaments. Buxton. Craftmaking: for love or money. 115–16
Bread dough, play clay (ornaments). Coskey. Christmas crafts for everyone. 108–13
Breadcrumb dough. Gardner. Dough creations. 120–22
Cornstarch dough. Carroll. Make your own chess set. 116–19
Cornstarch dough. Gardner. Dough creations. 88–92
Creative clay recipe. Nicole. Designer accessories for your home. 145
Dough art recipe, baking & finishing. Jarvey. You can dough it! 7–10
Flour and salt doughs for basket and dough boy. Brunner. Pass it on. 115–17
Recipe for salt dough. O'Neill. Make-it-merry Christmas book. 46
Salt dough. Christmas decorations from Williamsburg's folk art collection. 79
Salt dough. Gardner. Dough creations. 111
Salt dough. Hulbert. Creative beadwork. 125
Uncooked play dough, cornstarch modeling mixture, bread sculpture, uncooked modeling mix, and relief map mixture. Yoder. Sculpture and modeling for the elementary school. 43–45
Wiseman. Bread sculpture.

Dough trough tables. *See* **Tables, Dough-trough**

Downspouts. *See* **Gutters (roof)**

Dowels
Dowel maker. Fine woodworking techniques 2. 45
How to make a dowel-cutting tool. Rubin. Mission furniture. 45

Dragons
Dragon. Grainger. Creative papercraft. 45–48
Gault. Needlework dragons and other mythical creatures.
Wired felt dragon. Hutchings. Big book of stuffed toy and doll making. 187–96

Drainage
Drainage system ends flooding, how to unclog drains. Popular Mechanics do-it-yourself encyclopedia. Vol. 7, 1030–33
Dry well for rain water runoff. Geary. Complete handbook of home exterior repair and
maintenance. 88–89

Draperies. *See* **Curtains and draperies**

Drawers
Add-on drawers. Blandford. 53 space-saving built-in furniture projects. 151, 153, 155,
158–61
Ball bearing drawers. Family handyman handbook of carpentry plans/projects. 212–13
Building & repairing drawers. Handyman. 172–78
Building drawers. Brann. How to modernize a kitchen. 29–30
Building overlay, lip, and flush style drawers. Philbin. Cabinets, bookcases & closets.
54–57
Constructing drawers. Johnston. Craft of furniture making. 88–91
Door and drawer faces, drawer construction. Cary. Building your own kitchen cabinets.
60–81
Drawer assembly, drawer bottoms. Fine woodworking techniques 2. 78–87
Drawer construction. Brann. How to build kitchen cabinets, room dividers, and cabinet
furniture. 48–50
Drawer construction. Martensson. Woodworker's bible. 246–49
Drawer construction. Lewis. Cabinetmaking, patternmaking, and millwork. 256–64
Drawer construction. Stiles. Easy-to-make children's furniture. 13–17
Drawer work. Rodd. Repairing and restoring antique furniture. 92–97
Drawers. Cary. Storage: cabinets, closets, and wall systems. 59–64
Drawers. Hayward. Antique furniture repairs. 64–74
Drawers. Roberts. Illustrated handbook of upholstery. 378–79
Fabrication of drawers. Haynie. Cabinetmaking. 62–71
Gluing a drawer back together, drawers that stick. Time-Life Books. Repairing furni-
ture. 27–28
How to make drawers. Popular Mechanics do-it-yourself encyclopedia. Vol. 7, 1036–
39
Removable plastic drawers. Family handyman handbook of home improvement and
remodeling. 13
Repairing drawers. Kinney. Complete book of furniture repair and refinishing. 49–50
Repairing sticky drawers. Meyers. Furniture repair and refinishing. 101–02
Rolling shelves and ballbearing drawers. Family handyman handbook of home im-
provement and remodeling. 61–67
Sticking drawers, drawer construction. Waugh. Handyman's encyclopedia. 95–100

Drawing boards and tables
Drawing table. Abrams. Building craft equipment. 49–57
Wall-hung drawing cabinet. McNair. Building & outfitting your workshop. 109–15

Dresses
Appliqued dress. Loeb. Leather book. 213–17
Basic dress. Beard. Fashions from the loom. 80
Beaded sun and halter-top dresses. Crochet. 50–51
Bias tent dress (sundress), split triangle stretch gown. Wiseman. Cuts of cloth. 44–45, 56–57
Blouses to dresses. Zukerman. Get hooked. 95–115
Caftan dress. Goldsworthy. Clothes for disabled people. 90–92
Drafting dress patterns. Lewis. Patternless fashions. 112–27, 138–45
Dresses. Henderson. Woman's Day book of designer crochet. 58–64
Dresses and jumpers. Selfridge. Patchwork knitting. 179–80
Evening skirt and matching top. Reader's Digest complete guide to needlework. 354–55
From blouse to dress: an A-line dress and a beach cover-up. Bradley. Design it, sew it and wear it. 56–61
How to knit Scandanavian motifs. Time-Life Books. Traditional favorites. 148–49, 152–55
Needlepoint yoke. Smith. Needlery. 193–97
Norse sweater dress. McCall's big book of knit & crochet for home & family. 78–79
Norska-woman's mini-dress (Norway). Starmore. Scandinavian knitwear. 14–17
One-piece dress. Holland. Weaving primer. 154–55
Paisley print dress, floral appliqued dress, Ohio star dress. Laury. Quilted clothing. 92, 98–99, 101
Samoa rip-off (sundress, wraparound), java wrap or sarong, bib wrap, and halter shift. Wiseman. Cuts of cloth. 26–27, 30–31, 34–37
Simple shaping. Step by step to better knitting and crochet. 132–33
Woodland Indian buckskin dress, Cheyenne dress, making a chemise. Scurlock. Muzzleloader Magazine's book of buckskinning II. 40–44, 60–61
Zanzibar (tunic dress) and other basic dresses made from rectangles. Ruggieri. Woman's Day book of no-pattern sewing. 22–32
Bishop dress (smocked). Benton. Sewing classic clothes for children. 92–97
Child's dress. Coffey. Francine Coffey's celebrity sewing bee. 126
Child's dress. Ley. Russian & other Slavic embroidery designs. 30–33
Child's dress. Torbet. Macrame you can wear. 73
Child's red A-line dress. Doherty. Family Circle book of 429 great gifts-to-make all year round for just 10¢ to $10.00. 176–78
Child's smock. Frame. Tie-dying and batik. 58–61
Daisy sundress. Great granny crochet book. 104–05
Dress and hat or headscarf (crocheted). Complete book of baby crafts. 66–69
Embroidered gingham dress. Benton. Sewing classic clothes for children. 133–37
Girl's Sunday-best dress and matching bloomers. Knitting. 110
Halsingland child's dress (Sweden). Starmore. Scandinavian knitwear. 68–71
Karelia child's dress (Finland). Starmore. Scandinavian knitwear. 109–11
Lace-trimmed corduroy dress. Benton. Sewing classic clothes for children. 130–32
Midnight sun child's dress and hat (Lapland). Starmore. Scandinavian knitwear. 36–40
Simple sundress. Complete book of baby crafts. 118–21
Smocked dress. Benton. Sewing classic clothes for children. 118–23
Smocked party dress. Step by step to better knitting and crochet. 46–47
Smocked sundresses. Creative sewing. 123
Suomi child's coat, hat & dress (Finland). Starmore. Scandinavian knitwear. 89–94
Two in cotton (crocheted). Favorite knitting & crochet patterns. 39–41
Velvet party dress. Benton. Sewing classic clothes for children. 140–45

Dresses, Infants
Daisy sundress, sunny day dresses. Favorite knitting & crochet patterns. 135–37, 145–48
Embroidered dresses (knit). Complete book of baby crafts. 22–23
Smocked dress. Complete book of baby crafts. 98–101
Summer dress for a baby. Practical needlework. 116–17

Dresses, Women
Afghan dress. Gostelow. Complete international book of embroidery. 224–25
African kutu. Holderness. Peasant chic. 96–101
Basic kaftan with variations. Holderness. Peasant chic. 108–21
Batik long dress. Anderson. Tie dyeing and batik. 80–83
Bias slip dress. Lane. Maggie Lane's oriental patchwork. 40–45
Butterfly muumuu. Holderness. Peasant chic. 76–82
Crocheted yoke dress. Doherty. Family Circle book of 429 great gifts-to-make all year round for just 10¢ to $10.00. 70–72
Dress. Torbet. Macrame you can wear. 106–08
Dress yoke and sash (macrame). Golden book of hand and needle arts. 140–41
Dresses. Probert. Knitting in Vogue. 130–35.
Fringed mohair dress or skirt. Knitting. 46
Gold macrame bodice for evening dress. Stearns. Macrame. 87–90
Greek Island dress. Gostelow. Complete international book of embroidery. 160–61
Harem-style filet dress. Time-Life Books. Exotic styling. 176–79
Holiday-dazzle cocktail dress. Farlie. Pennywise boutique. 40–42
Hostess gown. Farlie. Pennywise boutique. 77–78
Indian wraparound. Knitting. 95–98
Instructions for knitting the dress ensemble. Time-Life Books. Personal touch. 182–85
Kaftan with Middle Eastern motifs. Gostelow. Cross stitch book. 112–16
Keep cool two-piece middy dress. Ruggieri. Woman's Day book of no-pattern sewing. 36–38
Long batik dress. Frame. Tie-dyeing and batik. 114–17
Knitted and crocheted dresses. Feldman. Handmade lace and patterns. 124–25
Moroccan sundress. Gostelow. Complete international book of embroidery. 196–97
New life for the thrift shop special. Brown. Super sweater idea book. 170–71
Plaid dress. Knitting. 59
Plains Indian tunic. Knitting. 75
Portable pareau (Polynesian). Ruggieri. Woman's Day book of no-pattern sewing. 89–93
Rejuvenated jumper. Farlie. Pennywise boutique. 79–80
Remodeling dresses. Crown. How to recycle old clothes into new fashions. 59–70
Remodeling dresses. Funaro. Yestermorrow clothes book. 55–101
Rose wonder, drawstring, glamour & shirred-top tube evening gowns. Ruggieri. Woman's Day book of no-pattern sewing. 47–51
Sind dress. Gostelow. Complete international book of embroidery. 244–45
Sleeve overlay for evening dress. Stearns. Macrame. 30–33
Smocked nightgown, maternity dress or sundress. Fisher. Craft of smocking. 28
Stenciled caftan. Creative sewing. 34
Sue-sun dress. Beard. Fashions from the loom. 94
Tabard. Lane. Maggie Lane's oriental patchwork. 59–63
Tie-dyed dress, tie-dyed and painted dress. Creative sewing. 27, 30
Tunic dress. Ruggieri. Woman's Day book of no-pattern sewing. 87–88
Two shirt dresses: one basic, one feminine. Bradley. Design it, sew it and wear it. 102–18
Tye-dyed kimono. Anderson. Tie dying and batik. 16–19
Variations on a basic theme (restyling dresses). Time-Life Books. Personal touch. 59–73

Venezuelan dress and overskirt. Holderness. Peasant chic. 129–35
Woolen dress with beaded yoke. Hulbert. Creative beadwork. 85

Dressing tables
Bathroom vanity. Cary. Storage: cabinets, closets, and wall systems. 105–06
Bathroom vanity cabinet. Hedden. Successful shelves and built-ins. 64–70
Built in dressing table. Black and Decker power tool carpentry. 137–40
Built-in wall dressing table. Blandford. 66 children's projects. 384–90
Corner dressing table. Blandford. How to make your own built-in furniture. 288–92
Dresser set. Cope. Plastics. 43
Dressing chest. Blandford. 66 children's furniture projects. 356–63
Dressing table. Zegel. Fast furniture. 88
Dressing table and stool. Williams. Spanish colonial furniture. 112–13
Hair-grooming center. Cary. Storage: cabinets, closets, and wall systems. 107–09
Fold-flat dresser, wall dresser, unit dresser, clothes closet-dresser. Blandford. 53
    space-saving built-in furniture projects. 247–61
Kidney shaped. Blandford. 66 children's furniture projects. 362–68
Pigtail pol vanity. Woman's Day creative stitchery from scraps. 69–71
Princess dresser. Rubin. Mission furniture. 110–11
Ruffled dressing table skirt. Roda. Fabric decorating for the home. 166–67
Theatrical vanity mirror; combination vanity table and writing desk. Complete handy-
    man do-it-yourself encyclopedia. Vol. 20, 2957–64
Vanity center. Popular Mechanics do-it-yourself encyclopedia. Vol. 12, 1896–97
Wall dressing table. Blandford. How to make your own built-in furniture. 255–57

Drilling and boring machinery
Accessories for your drill. Popular Mechanics do-it-yourself encyclopedia. Vol. 15,
    2291–95
Drill bit holder made from L'eggs panty hose package. Popular Mechanics do-it-
    yourself encyclopedia. Vol. 6, 932–33
Drill, use and maintenance. Buckwalter. Homeowner's handbook of power tools. 16–
    33
End-boring jig. Fine woodworking techniques 2. 62–63
Get the most out of your drill press, portable drill basics. Popular Mechanics do-it-
    yourself encyclopedia. Vol. 7, 1040–49
Graduated drill bit holders. Doherty. Family Circle book of 429 great gifts-to-make all
    year round for just 10¢ to $10.00. 124–25
Hand drill. Modern general shop. Metalworking. 108
Making a multitude of holes. Time-Life Books. Working with wood. 61–75
Portable drill, drill press. Capotosto. Woodworking wisdom. 60–83
Sharpen twist drills. Popular Mechanics do-it-yourself encyclopedia. Vol. 19, 2976–78
Table lifter for your drill press. Popular Mechanics do-it-yourself encyclopedia. Vol. 11,
    1719–22

Driveways
Asphalt & concrete driveway repairs & renewal. Nunn. Home improvements, home
    repair. 197–200
Building a concrete driveway. Russell. Garages and carports. 152–53
Corduroy road. Proulx. Plan and make your own fences and gates, walkways, walls
    and drives. 142–43
Driveways—plan, construct and repair your own. Proulx. Plan and make your own
    fences and gates, walkways, walls and drives. 121–49
Enlarging a driveway. Russell. Garages and carports. 18–20
Laying a cold asphalt driveway. Russell. Garages and carports. 151–52
Repairing asphalt driveways. Outdoor projects for home and garden. 114–20
Resurface your asphalt drive. Popular Mechanics do-it-yourself encyclopedia. Vol. 1,
    112–15

Drums
Gourd drum. Johnson. Nature crafts. 118–19
Gourd drum. Mordecai. Gourd craft. 198–99
Indian drum. Norbeck. Book of authentic Indian life crafts. 107–09

Dry sinks
Colonial dry sink. Popular Mechanics do-it-yourself encyclopedia. Vol. 7, 1050–53
Dry sink. Blandford. How to make early American and colonial furniture. 364–73
Dry sink. Complete handyman do-it-yourself encyclopedia. Vol. 6, 893–99
Dry sink. Marlow. Early American furnituremaker's manual. 37–44
Dry sink. Philbin. Cabinets, bookcases & closets. 140
Dry sink hutch, small cherry dry sink. Gottshall. Provincial furniture design and construction. 39–48

Ducks
Carving a duck. Wiley. Woodcarving with projects. 322–25
Duck inn. Brann. How to build pet housing. 67–81
Felt duckling & duck, furry duck. Hutchings. Big book of stuffed toy and doll making. 58–64
Gingham ducks. Better Homes and Gardens treasury of Christmas crafts & foods. 268
Poplar and walnut duck. Popular Mechanics do-it-yourself encyclopedia. Vol. 11, 1656

Dust covers
Boy and girl toaster cover. Houck. Patchwork pattern book. 36–37
Dust covers (embroidered). Fraser. Modern stitchery: stitches, patterns, free-form designing. 97
Kitchen kittens appliance covers. Foose. More scrap saver's stitchery. 80–85
Mosaic-style letter-tray cover. Scobey. Decorating with needlepoint. 169–70
Plate protectors. Goldman. Decorate with felt. 84
Quilted appliance covers. Woman's Day bazaar best sellers. 95
Rectangular tea cozy/toaster cover. Morgan. Trapunto and other forms of raised quilting. 194–95
Sampler typewriter cover. Scobey. Decorating with needlepoint. 165–68
Shoo fly and pine tree variation phone covers. Houck. Patchwork pattern book. 20–21, 60–61
Spanish-motif spray-can cover. Scobey. Decorating with needlepoint. 162–63
Toaster cover. Goldman. Decorate with felt. 82–83
Toaster cover. Guth. Sewing with scraps. 120–21
Typewriter cover. Goldman. Decorate with felt. 94
Typewriter cover. Roda. Fabric decorating for the home. 78–79

Dust ruffles
Bed base cover. Practical needlework. 174–75
Dust ruffle. Roberts. Illustrated handbook of upholstery. 235–36
Dust ruffle. Roda. Fabric decorating for the home. 125–26
Dust ruffles. Sara. Sewing made easy. 384–86
Dust ruffles and tailored flounces. Better Homes and Gardens sewing for your home. 92–93
Easy dust ruffle. Fanning. Complete book of machine quilting. 309
Make a gathered dust ruffle, tiered dust ruffle. McCall's sewing for your home. 53, 57
Pleated dust ruffle with stenciled pattern, dust ruffle. McCall's big book of country needlecrafts. 182, 224–25

Dusters
Dustmops, window blind cleaner, and feather duster. Doherty. Family Circle book of 429 great gifts-to-make all year round for just 10¢ to $10.00. 138

Dyes and dyeing
African tie-dyeing. Schuman. Art from many hands. 16–22
Bliss. Handbook of dyes from natural materials.
Casselman. Craft of the dyer.
Cold water, direct and acid dyes for tie dyeing. Seagroatt. Basic textile book. 76–79
Dyeing fibers. Svinicki. Step-by-step spinning and dyeing.37–46
Dye plants. Casselman. Craft of the dyer. 83–222
Dye your own yarn with recipes for dyes. Brown. Weaving, spinning, and dyeing book. 246–71
Dyeing. Felcher. Complete book of rug making. 194–98
Dyeing for rugs. Znamierowski. Step-by-step rugmaking. 52–53
Dyeing, natural and synthetic. Chamberlain. Beyond weaving. 45–53
Dyeing of cotton. Bronson. Early American weaving and dyeing. 105–52
Dyeing with chemical dyes and vegetable recipes. Gilby. Free weaving. 139–45
Dyeing your own material. Ketchum. Hooked rugs. 103–05
Dyeing your yarns. Parker. Creative handweaving. 78–88
Dyes and dyeing. Dyer's art. 240–44
Dyes and dyeing. Worst. Weaving with foot-power looms. 248–72
Folded tie dye, sewn tie dye. Andersen. Creative exploration in crafts. 19–30
Home-made dyes. Dyeing & printing. 12–16
How to make your own tie-dye. Belfer. Designing in batik and tie dye. 93–135
Ikat. Dyer's art. 129–233
Introduction to tie-dye. Tie-dye, batik and candlemaking step-by-step. 6–18
Natural and synthetic dyes. Seagroatt. Basic textile book. 64–74
Natural & synthetic dyestuffs. Pittaway. Traditional English country crafts and how to enjoy them today. 63–66
Natural dye-making. Giant book of crafts. 303–15
Natural dyes. Bronson. Early American weaving and dyeing. 185–93
Natural dyes. Held. Weaving. 280–89
Natural dyes. Meras. Vacation crafts. 127–29
Natural dyes and tie-dye. Linderman. Crafts for the classroom. 134–61
Plangi. Dyer's art. 27–76
Random look from tie-dye. Time-Life Books. Boutique attire. 56–63
Resist processes. Newman. Contemporary African arts and crafts. 66–78
Tie-and-dye, marbling, circles, pleating, and folding. Seagroatt. Basic textile book. 74–76
Tie-and-dye, printing and painting. Murray. Essential handbook of weaving. 149–51
Tie dye or plangi process. Newman. Contemporary Southeast Asian arts and crafts. 36–41
Tie-dye. Treasury of things to make. 124–26
Tie-dye and related dye-resist techniques on fabric. Bliss. Handbook of dyes from natural materials. 163–67
Tie dyeing. Rose. Illustrated encyclopedia of crafts and how to master them. 297–301
Tie-dyeing, ikat, resist, tritik and batik. Dyeing & printing. 20–52
Wood dyeing. Bronson. Early American weaving and dyeing. 153–84
Yarn dyeing. Held. Weaving. 268–90

E

Earrings
Bead earrings. Mosesson. Jewelry craft for beginners. 12–14
Bead edgings and fringes. Hulbert. Creative beadwork. 111–17
Beaded hoop earrings. Hulbert. Creative beadwork. 105–06
Beaded drop earrings. Hulbert. Creative beadwork. 106–07
Bugle tubes and rounds. Davies. Beads as jewelry. 40–42

Button earrings. Mosesson. Jewelry craft for beginners. 49–50
Columella earrings, button earrings. Logan. Shell crafts. 78–81
Dainty petal earrings made from paper napkins. Janitch. All made from paper. 45
Decoupaged egg earrings. Sommers. Contemporary costume jewelry. 187
Domed earrings without soldering. Sprintzen. Jewelry, basic techniques and design.
    50–51
Ear drops using wooden and china beads. Hulbert. Creative beadwork. 41
Earring construction. Bovin. Jewelry making. 218–21
Earrings. Sommer. Contemporary costume jewelry. 62–66
Enameling wood plique-a-jour earrings. Hollander. Plastics for jewelry. 121–24
Forged earrings. Richards. Handmade jewelry. 71–72
Gold and pearl drops. Hulbert. Creative beadwork. 40
Horn ring earrings, agate chip earrings, spiral earrings, pearl earrings, dangle earrings.
    Davies. Beads as jewelry. 102, 111, 124, 136, 144
Mixed-media earrings. Hollander. Plastics for jewelry. 35–39
Night glow earrings. Davies. Beads as jewelry. 89
Quill work earrings. Encyclopedia of crafts. 186
Ring earrings. Mosesson. Jewelry craft for beginners. 64–65
Seed-bead earrings. Mosesson. Jewelry craft for beginners. 36–38
Silver earrings. Metal and enamel. 67
Spiral drop earrings. Hibbs. Straw sculpture. 104–06
Split-straw earrings. Hibbs. Straw sculpture. 70–72
Threaded earrings. Mosesson. Jewelry craft for beginners. 29–30
Threaded straw earrings. Hibbs. Straw sculpture. 68
Twisted and coiled earrings. Sommer. Contemporary costume jewelry. 28–31
Wire earrings. Metal and enamel. 7–8
Wire earrings. Powers. Crafting turquoise jewelry. 165–67
Woven bead earrings. Davies. Beads as jewelry. 69

Earrings. *See also* **Jewelry**

Easels
Art horse, studio box, table easel, convertible craft easel. Abrams. Building craft equip-
    ment. 58–105
Miniature easels. Popular Mechanics do-it-yourself encyclopedia. Vol. 12, 1889
Picture easel. Modern general shop. Metalworking 98
Table model easel. Anderson. Crafts and the disabled. 38–40

Easter baskets
Egg carton basket. Epple. Something from nothing crafts. 41
Small cane basket for Easter eggs or bridesmaids. Maynard. Modern basketry from
    the start. 132–34
Woven paper Easter basket. Yoder. Sculpture and modeling for the elementary school.
    168–70

Easter decorations
Easter eggs, rabbit, easter card. Lyon. Arts and crafts objects children can make for
    the home. 95–99

Easter eggs. *See* **Eggs, Decorated**

Edgings
Add a colored border. Embroidery. 20–25
Apple motifs. Great cross-stitch. 30
Binding garment edges with crochet. Time-Life Books. Boutique attire. 97–100
Blackwork hecuts and flowers. Scheuer. Designs for Holbein embroidery. 73

Borders. Ormond. American primitives in needlepoint. 129–39
Budding vine and garden border. Sheldon. Washable and dryable needlepoint. 118–19
Colorful crochet trimmings. Time-Life Books. Personal touch. 162–169
Crochet borders. Walters. Crochet. 44
Crochet trimmings, hairpin lace trimmings. McCall's big book of knit & crochet for home & family. 277, 280
Crochet trims. Svinicki. Old-fashioned crochet. 102–24
Crocheted edgings and insertions. Reader's Digest complete guide to needlework. 401
Decorative edges. Mansfield. Clothing construction. 363–68
Decorative trim and braid uses, fringes & tassels, embroidered border designs. Time-Life Books. Exotic styling. 70–73, 85–87, 152–53
Decorative trimmings for child's dress. Walters. Crochet. 48
Double looped edging. Step by step to better knitting and crochet. 198
Edgings. Southard. Bobbin lacemaking. 41–149, 169–71, 187
Edgings, insertions, and motifs. Feldman. Handmade lace and patterns. 95–103
Elegant edgings (pineapple designs). American School of Needlework. Great crochet bazaar book. 55–57
Embroidered edgings for curtains, sheets and pillow cases. Hana. Embroidery. 37–43
Filet-crochet rose-pattern edging. Better Homes and Gardens treasury of Christmas crafts & foods. 151, 157–58
Fringe, tassels, pompom and twisted cord. Rosenthal. Not-so-nimble needlework book. 151–54
Fringes. Stearns. Macrame. 90–100
Fringing. Reader's Digest complete guide to needlework. 456–58
Fringing. Rose. Illustrated encyclopedia of crafts and how to master them. 290–92
Galoons, clothing trims. Holland. Weaving primer. 45–46, 50
Gold braided fringe. Stearns. Macrame. 58–60
Handkerchief border. Walters. Crochet. 60
Insertions and braids. Stearns. Macrame. 80–85
Irish crochet lace edging for parasol. Stearns. Batsford book of crochet. 140–42
Knitted handkerchief edging from Scotland. Compton. Complete book of traditional knitting. 174
Knitted lace. Dillmont. Complete encyclopedia of needlework. 258–69
Lace edging in hairpin crochet. Dillmont. Complete encyclopedia of needlework. 304–08
Motif for woman's apron and child's dress. Walters. Crochet. 49
Needlework trimmings. Dillmont. Complete encyclopedia of needlework. 657–87
Nineteenth-century edging pattern. Auld. Tatting; the contemporary art of knotting with a shuttle. 56
Pillowcase and sheet edging. Crochet. 91–94
Plain, macrame & macrochet tassels; techniques for making fringe & cording. Orr. Now needlepoint. 194–202.
Potpourri of designs for embroidery or needlepoint. Needlework nostalgia. 65–72
Quick ribbon chic. Ruggieri. Woman's Day book of no-pattern sewing. 113–14
Restyling with trimmings. Crown. How to recycle old clothes into new fashions. 125–36
Shamrock edging, narrow filet edging (crocheted). McCall's book of America's favorite needlework and crafts. 254, 256
Self border with bluebell motif. Lindberg. Counted cross-stitch designs for all seasons. 42
Silken braids and fringe. Time-Life Books. Decorative techniques. 55–63
Small crochet edgings—some introducing picots, crochet braids, crochet fringes, decorative edgings using pompoms and covered polystyrene balls. Stearns. Batsford book of crochet. 48–52
Tatted edgings-handkerchief, collar, pillow case edgings. Blandford book of traditional handicrafts. 32–33

Teneriffe lace doily edging. Stillwell. Technique of teneriffe lace. 80–81
Teneriffe lace scalloped, straight & fringed edgings. Stillwell. Technique of teneriffe
  lace. 86–88
Wild rose & star flower tatted edgings, tatted squares, hairpin lace, tatted edging,
  towel insertion & edging. McCall's big book of knit & crochet for home & family.
  269–70, 276, 281
Wilson. Joinings, edges, and trims.

Egg cozies
Egg cozy. Mills. The book of presents. 96–97
Egg cosy woven in wooden beads. Hulbert. Creative beadwork. 54
New leaves for New Year's Day (paper egg cosies). Janitch. Candlemaking and deco-
  rations. 29–30
Patchwork egg cosy. Encyclopedia of crafts. 13

Egg cups
Egg cup. Hodges. Woodturning handbook—with projects. 190–92
Egg cup. Sainsbury. Sainsbury's woodturning projects for dining. 168–71
Nest of egg cups. Woolridge. Woodturning techniques. 69–72
Turning an egg-cup. Sainsbury. Craft of woodturning. 158–60

Eggs
Turning a wooden egg. Sainsbury. Craft of woodturning. 169–70

Eggs, Decorated
Chirpy chicks, dainty Easter eggs. Janitch. Candlemaking and decorations. 37–38
Christmas eggs. Meyer. Christmas crafts. 65–67
Crochet eggs. Treasury of things to make. 148–49
Decorated eggs, jumbo Easter eggs. Wargo. Soft crafts for special occasions. 125–28
Decorating eggs. Jarnow. (Re)do it yourself. 64–66
Easter egg. Romberg. Let's discover papier-mâché. 28–29
Easter eggs. Whatnot. 173–74
Easter eggs. Woman's Day book of weekend crafts. 139–41
Egg characters in fancy hats. Janitch. All made from paper. 56–60
Gold trimmed Easter eggs, ribbon trimmed eggs. Doherty. Family Circle book of 429
  great gifts-to-make all year round for just 10¢ to $10.00. 51
Making pysanky. Schuman. Art from many hands. 72–79
Natural dyes for Easter eggs. Johnson. Nature crafts. 4
Painted Easter eggs. Woman's Day book of gifts to make. 63–64
Picture egg of papier-mâché. Elbert. Paperworks. 119–23
Plastic multicolored eggs. Linsley. Decoupage on glass, wood, metal, rocks, shells,
  wax, soap, plastic, canvas, ceramic. 94–96
Pysanky eggs. Better Homes and Gardens treasury of Christmas crafts & foods. 139–
  40
Tissue paper egg decorations. Stephan. Creating with tissue paper. 51–59
Treasured egg-crafted heirlooms. Brunner. Pass it on. 109–14
Ukrainian eggs. McCall's book of Christmas. 3
Wax-resist eggs. Linderman. Crafts for the classroom. 158–61

Electric appliances. *See* **Kitchen appliances**

Electric blankets. *See* **Blankets, Electric**

Electric fans
How to install an attic fan. Nunn. Home improvement, home repair. 98

Electric flashers
Safety flasher. Modern general shop. Electricity. 110–11

Electric heaters. *See* **Furnaces; Heating; Heating pads, Electric; Water heaters**

Electric lamps. *See* **Lamps**

Electric motors
Guide to electric motors, how to repair home workshop motors, piggyback speed reducer. Popular Mechanics do-it-yourself encyclopedia. Vol. 13, 1924–29
Oscillating motor wig-wag, two-pole motor. Modern general shop. Electricity 105–08
Wind generator & motor. Churchill. Backyard building book. 89–103
Wind motor. Churchill. Big backyard building book. 123–28

Electric switch plate covers
Decorator light switch plates. Linsley. Great bazaar. 157
Finger plates and switch plates. Gordon. Complete guide to drying and preserving flowers. 78–81
Light switch covers. Romberg. Let's discover papier-mâché. 60
Metal switch plate. Modern general shop. Metalworking. 101

Electric switches
Elephant light-pull. Goldman. Decorate with felt. 126–27
Providing a wall switch. Time-Life Books. New living spaces. 73
Replacing switches. Waugh. Handyman's encyclopedia. 252–54

Electric testers
Battery "brain" to test and recharge most batteries, auto electrical-system tester. Popular Mechanics do-it-yourself encyclopedia. Vol. 2, 237–41
Electric outlet tester. Popular Mechanics do-it-yourself encyclopedia. Vol. 5, 657
Put a tester in your screwdriver. Popular Mechanics do-it-yourself encyclopedia. Vol. 18, 2860–61
Screwdriver test light. Modern general shop. Electricity. 111–12

Electric wiring
Audio oscillator. Modern general shop. Electricity. 94–96
Basics of home wiring. Popular Mechanics do-it-yourself encyclopedia. Vol. 7, 1060–74
Electrical fixtures, wiring and appliances. Bragdon. Homeowner's complete manual of repair & improvement. 292–383
Electrical updates and repairs. Nunn. Home improvements, home repair. 149–67
Electricity and wiring. Handyman. 389–420
Exterior electrical wiring for lighting. Decks and patios. 146–51
Home electric wiring. Family handyman handbook of home improvement and remodeling. 539–69
Installing electrical boxes for switches and lighting fixtures. Waugh. Handyman's encyclopedia. 45–48
Interior wiring. Leavy. Successful small farms. 102–12
Protect your family from outdoor electric shock. Popular Mechanics do-it-yourself encyclopedia. Vol. 20, 3082–86
Splicing wires, installing a plug. Carbo. Fix-it guide for women. 17–20
Switch & light circuits. Modern general shop. Electricity. 91–92
Tin-can reel for an extension cord. Popular Mechanics do-it-yourself encyclopedia. Vol. 8, 1165
Wiring. Burch. Building small barns, sheds, and shelters. 115–25
Wiring. Olin. Construction. 521–28

Electroplating
Electro-plating. Bowie. Jewelry making. 128–39
Electroplating and electroforming. Chamberlain. Metal jewelry techniques. 109–12
Newman. Electroplating and electroforming for artists and craftsmen.

Elephants
Elephant. Day. Complete book of rock crafting. 69–78

Embroidery
All about embroidery. McCall's big book of needlecrafts. 184–231
Baker. Stumpwork.
Blue jeans and skirt motifs. Wilson. More needleplay. 148–49
Borssuck. Needlework monograms.
Brilliant flight in embroidery (butterfly). Time-Life Books. Personal touch. 156–57
Card embroidery. Gostelow. Mary Gostelow's embroidery book. 50–52
Counted cross-stitch. Time-Life Books. Decorative techniques. 104–07
Crewel vegetables, field of flowers in crewel. Wilson. More needleplay. 152–55
Embroidered evenweave pocket. Encyclopedia of crafts. 64
Embroidered flower designs for window screen, fire screen, lamp shade, roller blinds, curtains and clothing. Hana. Embroidery. 53–63
Embroidered flower squares quilts. Haraszty. Embroiderer's portfolio of flower designs. 9–110
Embroidering. Ryan. Complete encyclopedia of stitchery. 150–357
Embroidery and crewel stitches. Marein. Stitchery, needlepoint, applique and patchwork. 9–81
Embroidery (Indian). Bath. Needlework in America. 66–69
Embroidery motifs. Sayer. Crafts of Mexico. 56–59
Embroidery of roses.
Embroidery on tulle. Practical needlework. 213–14
Embroidery on white materials. Dillmont. Complete encyclopedia of needlework. 47–84
Embroidery stitches. Reader's Digest complete guide to needlework. 8–55
Fishing for compliments—embroidery on a knitted tank top, gather ye rosebuds embroidery on a pullover, fresh as a daisy embroidery on cardigans. Embroidery. 82–87
Flower applique, circles within a circle mixed media. Golden book of hand and needle arts. 72–73
Flowers in various embroidery stitches. Embroidery. 116–26
Francini. Crewel embroidery.
Gadney. How to enter and win fabric and fiber crafts contests.
Gorham. Treasury of charted designs for needleworkers.
Gostelow. Embroidery of all Russia.
Haraszty. Needlepainting, a garden of stitches.
Hausa motif. Gostelow. Complete international book of embroidery. 183
Holding frame for handicapped. Rissell. Craftwork the handicapped elderly can make and sell. 73–74
Kmit. Ukrainian embroidery.
Kozaczka. Polish embroidery workbook with patterns.
Linen and gold embroidery. Dillmont. Complete encyclopedia of needlework. 85–185
Meulenbelt-Nieuwburg. Embroidery motifs from old Dutch samplers.
Motif revival from stencils, embroidery on patterned fabric, glossy leaves embroidered motif. Embroidery. 9–11, 30–33, 80–81
Net embroidery. Gostelow. Mary Gostelow's embroidery book. 190–93
Nielsen. Scandinavian embroidery, past and present.
Openwork on linen. Dillmont. Complete encyclopedia of needlework. 455–96
Orange and dogwood designs to decorate towels, potholders, and clothing. Hana. Embroidery. 45–52

Pattern for the rya knot squares. Hana. Embroidery. 25
Petersen. Stitches and decorative seams.
Reflections on the tree of life. Time-Life Books. Traditional favorites. 138–41
Rubbing for hand and machine embroidery. Firestein. Rubbing craft. 64–67
Shadow work. Practical needlework. 198
Shisha. Wilson. Needleplay. 180–82
Shisha stitchery-embroidered fish. Better Homes and Gardens embroidery. 87–89
Silk, metal thread & bead embroidery, machine embroidery, counted thread embroidery, crewel, whitework, cutwork, drawn and pulled work. Complete guide to needlework. 102–89
Tibetan motif. Gostelow. Complete international book of embroidery. 261
Tillett. American needlework, 1776–1976.
Using small motifs. Encyclopedia of crafts. 134
Whitework. Gostelow. Mary Gostelow's embroidery book. 235–39
Wilson. Ask Erica.
Wire embroidery. Newman. Wire art. 162–65

Embroidery, Assisi work
Assisi embroidery. Reader's Digest complete guide to needlework. 69
Assisi work. Gostelow. Mary Gostelow's embroidery book. 22–26
Birds and flowers. Great cross-stitch. 156–62

Embroidery, Blackwork
Blackwork. Gostelow. Mary Gostelow's embroidery book. 34–37
Blackwork embroidery. Reader's Digest complete guide to needlework. 56–65
Blackwork embroidery scroll. Better Homes & Gardens embroidery. 61–63
Blackwork embroidery scroll. Better Homes and Gardens treasury of needlecrafts. 379–81
Lady Margaret Peyton stitched from a brass rubbing. Gostelow. Cross stitch book. 134–37
Scheuer. Designs for Holbein embroidery.

Embroidery, Candlewicking
Candlewicking. Bath. Needlework in America. 144–47
Candlewicking. Practical needlework. 211

Embroidery, Cross stitch
Collection of designs for cross-stitch.
Counted cross-stitch coverlet. Woman's Day prize-winning quilts, coverlets and afghans. 126–31
Cross stitch embroidery, balloons and bear design for child's dress. Reader's Digest complete guide to needlework. 66–68, 109
Cross-stitch embroidery, floral bouquet. McCall's big book of needlecrafts. 192–97, 262–63
Cross-stitch rose wreaths. Better Homes and Gardens treasury of needlecrafts. 348–49
Farrell. Counted cross-stitch patchwork design.
Gorham. Charted designs for holidays and special occasions.
Gostelow. Cross stitch book.
Great cross-stitch.
Hoop-framed samplers. Golden book of hand and needle arts. 97–99
Houck. 101 folk art designs for counted cross-stitch and other needlecrafts.
Kozaczka. Polish cross stitch folk patterns.
Lammer. Making samplers.
Lindberg. Counted cross-stitch designs for all seasons.
Meulenbelt-Nieuwburg. Embroidery motifs from old Dutch samplers.

101 folk art designs for counted cross-stitch and other needlecrafts.
Six dog pictures in cross-stitch. McCall's book of America's favorite needlework and crafts. 46–48
Thompson. John James Audubon's birds in cross stitch.
Vor tids Korssting. Contemporary Danish cross-stitch design.

Embroidery, Cutwork
Cutwork. Gostelow. Mary Gostelow's embroidery book. 90–96
Cutwork. Longhurst. Vanishing American needle arts. 21–41
Cutwork. Practical needlework. 199–202
Openwork/cutwork embroidery, design on a caftan. Reader's Digest complete guide to needlework. 90–91, 108
Hedebo. Gostelow. Mary Gostelow's embroidery book. 127–32
Machine cutwork turkey. Hall. Sewing machine craft book. 46–47

Embroidery, Darning
Darning. Gostelow. Mary Gostelow's embroidery book. 97–99
Needleweaving. Ambuter. Open canvas. 79–102
Swedish darning embroidery. Nielsen. Scandinavian embroidery, past and present. 116–22

Embroidery, Drawn thread
Drawn-thread work. Gostelow. Mary Gostelow's embroidery book. 108–11
Drawn thread work. Practical needlework. 203–07
Drawnwork to enhance beautiful linens, space fillers (drawn thread work fillings). Embroidery. 34–37, 40–43
Hemstitching. Ambuter. Open canvas. 105–44
Openwork/pulled thread/drawn thread and embroidery. Reader's Digest complete guide to needlework. 74–85
Pulled-thread work. Gostelow. Mary Gostelow's embroidery book. 209–14

Embroidery, Hardanger
Hardanger. Ambuter. Open canvas. 195–217
Hardanger. Gostelow. Mary Gostelow's embroidery book. 122–26
Hardanger embroidery. Longhurst. Vanishing American needle arts. 43–59
Openwork/hardanger embroidery. Reader's Digest complete guide to needlework. 86–89

Embroidery, Machine
Drawing. Bakke. Sewing machine as a creative tool. 48–78
Foss. Creative embroidery with your sewing machine.
Free motion stitching. Hall. Sewing machine craft book. 46–61
Machine embroidery. Better Homes and Gardens treasury of needlecrafts. 382–91
Machine embroidery. McCall's big book of needlecrafts. 212–16
Machine embroidery. Reader's Digest complete guide to needlework. 98–102
Monogramming and machine embroidery. Saunders. Speed sewing; 103 sewing machine shortcuts. 107–26
Newman. Sewing machine embroidery and stitchery.

Enamel and Enameling
Art of champlevé. Metal and enamel. 126–28
Art of enameling. Metal and enamel. 77–135
Cloisonné. Sjoberg. Working with copper, silver and enamel. 88–89
Copper enameling. Rose. Illustrated encyclopedia of crafts and how to master them. 61–67
Copper enamelling; Sgraffito. Giant book of crafts. 185–92

Enamel. Chamberlain. Metal jewelry techniques. 142–43
Enamelling. Sainsbury. Woodworking projects with power tools. 113–17
Enameling. Wood. Make your own jewelry. 107–13
Enameling metal. Kicklighter. Crafts, illustrated designs and techniques. 90–95
Enameling techniques. Elliot. Working with copper. 86–98
Enamelling. Bowie. Jewelry making. 96–105
Enamelling. Metalcrafting encyclopedia. 46–50
Enamelling. Sjoberg. Working with copper, silver and enamel. 74–88
Enamels and beads. Pottery step-by-step. 60–62
How to enamel. Mosesson. Jewelry craft for beginners. 226–42
Metal enameling. Sommer. Contemporary costume jewelry. 67–71
Simple enameling. Marshall. Foilcraft. 127–31
Stencil enameling. Andersen. Creative exploration in crafts. 149–62

End tables. *See* **Tables, End**

Engine models
Electric engine. Modern general shop. Electricity. 109
Motors and engines. Jackson. Modelmaker's handbook. 227–52
Power sources. Winter. World of model airplanes. 119–45

Engraving
Engraving. Sjoberg. Working with copper, silver and enamel. 68–69
Engraving. Wood. Make your own jewelry. 102–05
Engraving and carving. Bowie. Jewelry making. 107–09
Engraving glass. Rothenberg. Decorating glass. 68–80
Engraving jewelry. Richards. Handmade jewelry. 124–28
Fun with a doodling engraver. Popular Mechanics do-it-yourself encyclopedia. Vol. 16,
    2544–46
Graham. Engraving glass.
Matcham. Techniques of glass engraving.
Niello work. Richards. Handmade jewelry. 128–30

Enlargers
Light box. Abrams. Building craft equipment. 21–43

Eskimos
Dolls. Wilder. Secrets of Eskimo skin sewing. 111–16
Eskimo. Day. Complete book of rock crafting. 127–28
Eskimo boy. Guild. Dollmaker's workshop. 20–25
Eskimo dolls. Holz. How-to book of international dolls. 296–99
Eskimos (clay). Lyon. Arts and crafts objects children can make for the home. 40–42

Etching
Electric pencil. Modern general shop. Electricity. 102–03
Etch solutions. Marshall. Foilcraft. 135
Etching. Bowie. Jewelry making. 110–11
Etching. Metalcrafting encyclopedia. 51–53
Etching. Sjoberg. Working with copper, silver and enamel. 72–73
Etching. Sprintzen. Jewelry, basic techniques and design. 101–04
Etching and coloring. Meilach. Decorative and sculptural ironwork. 192
Etching copper. Elliot. Working with copper. 73–78
Etching designs into a steel knife. Boye. Step-by-step knifemaking: you can do it!
    211–31
Etching glass. Rothenberg. Decorating glass. 68–80
Etching on metal. Richards. Handmade jewelry. 121–22

Etching with stop-out varnish (asphaltum). Elliot. Working with copper. 119–20
Glass etching. Matcham. Techniques of glass engraving. 144–50
Instruction for two etched plates using resist paint. Elliot. Working with copper. 81–83
Rose. Illustrated encyclopedia of crafts and how to master them. 127–36

Exercising equipment
Design for a home gym. Popular Mechanics do-it-yourself encyclopedia. Vol. 6, 854–59
Exercise mat. Coffey. Francine Coffey's celebrity sewing bee. 163
Jogging machine, rowing machine. Complete handyman do-it-yourself encyclopedia. Vol. 7, 1014–26
Ladder house, Stegel (balance beam and climbing structure). Beoschen. Successful playhouses. 69–72
Leg exerciser. Dal Fabbro. How to make children's furniture and play equipment. 141
Punching ball. Reader's Digest complete guide to sewing. 487
Weight bench for exercise. Popular Mechanics do-it-yourself encyclopedia. Vol. 8, 1162–63

Eyeglass cases. *See* **Spectacle cases**

F

Fabric printing. *See* **Textile printing**

Facial tissue box covers
Black work tissue covers (for pocket packs of tissues). Golden book of hand and needle arts. 74–75
Calico tissue holder, calico-covered trinket and tissue boxes. Woman's Day bazaar best sellers. 57, 109
Patchwork tissue box cover. Scharf. Illustrated patchwork crochet. 158
Pine tissue holders. Doherty. Family Circle book of 429 great gifts-to-make all year round for just 10¢ to $10.00. 128
Tissue box. Marlow. Classic furniture projects. 16–21
Tissue box cover. Christensen. Needlepoint and bargello stitchery. 90–91
Tissue box cover. Goldman. Decorate with felt. 104–05
Tissue box cover. Roda. Fabric decorating for the home. 182–83
Tissue covers to crochet. Woman's Day decorative needlework for the home. 146–47
Tissue holder. Cope. Plastics. 66
Tissue holders. Holland. Weaving primer. 39
Veneering a box. Hobbs. Veneering simplified. 81–84

Fagoting
Fagoting stitch. Mansfield. Clothing construction. 376–77
Narrow and wide faggoting. Saunders. Speed sewing; 103 sewing machine shortcuts. 90–91

Family trees
Applique family tree. Laury. Treasury of needlecraft gifts for the new baby. 30–32

Fans
Fans. Johnson. Nature crafts. 62
Feather fan, bouquet fan. Whatnot. 119–23
Lauhala fan. Bird. Craft of Hawaiian lauhala. 95–126
Summer fan. Elbert. Paperworks. 94–98

Farm equipment
Body of a farm wagon. Complete guide to blacksmithing. 203–07
Carriage and wagon painting. Complete guide to blacksmithing. 208–22
Drags (harrow). Langsner. Country woodcraft. 201–03
Goat milking stand. Braren. Homemade. 155
Hay rakes. Langsner. Country woodcraft. 135–43
Making a four-tined manure fork. Richardson. Practical blacksmithing. Vol. 3, 176–79
Spike-tooth A-harrow. Langsner. Country woodcraft. 197–99
Pitchforks. Langsner. Country woodcraft. 145–59
Watering trough. Braren. Homemade. 156–57

Farm equipment. See also **Plows; Yokes**

Farms, Toy
Model farm. Blandford. Giant book of wooden toys. 234–37

Favors (for parties)
Basic crepe crackers and clown crackers. Paper. 54–59
Egg carton cups, styrofoam drinking cup, planter favors, plastic coffee can measuring cup, & spool character favors. Epple. Something from nothing crafts. 41–44, 111–12, 154, 158–59, 192–93
Halloween witch's hat, cat, pumpkin and ghost. Creative crafts yearbook: an exciting new collection of needlework and crafts. 122–24
Miniature needlepoint Beatrix Potter tote bags. Wilson. Erica Wilson's Christmas world. 134–37
Perry. Holiday magic
Thanksgiving placecards. Connor. Corncraft. 63
Williams. Cookie craft: no-bake designs for edible party favors and decorations.

Feathers
Feather repair. Schuler. How to fix almost everything. 72
Feathers: nature's palette. Johnson. Nature crafts. 120–23
Trimming with feathers. Time-Life Books. Boutique attire. 114–15

Felt work
Basic animals. Rath. Splendid soft toy book. 64–65
Felt: nature's textile. Johnson. Nature crafts. 8–11
Felt repair. Schuler. How to fix almost everything. 72
Making wool felt. Chamberlain. Beyond weaving. 22–25

Fences
Baffles to deflect wind and prying eyes. Porches and patios. 116–19
Basket-weave garden fence, picket fence and gate. 101 do-it-yourself projects. 266–67, 290–91
Board fence, horizontal siding fence, contemporary screen fence. Complete handyman do-it-yourself encyclopedia. 1036–41
Board fencing and matching gate. Brann. How to build outdoor projects. 39–49
Breezy privacy fence. Better Homes and Gardens. Deck and patio projects. 86
Colonial picket fencing. Brann. How to build outdoor projects. 26–38
Construction of a wood fence or screen. Decks and patios. 117–25
Decorative outdoor screen. Family handyman handbook of carpentry plans/projects. 457–60
Down-home stone fence. Better Homes and Gardens. Step-by-step masonry & concrete. 92
Eight easy-to build fence designs. Popular Mechanics do-it-yourself encyclopedia. Vol. 8, 1202–05
Farm fences. Leavy. Successful small farms. 161–73

Fence yourself in and enjoy it. Outdoor projects for home and garden. 383–417
Fences. Bragdon. Homeowner's complete manual of repair & improvement. 558–61
Fences. Kramer. Outdoor garden build-it book. 59–84
Fences and gates plus trellises, arbors and pergolas. Proulx. Plan and make your own fences and gates, walkways, walls and drives. 1–36
Garden fence. Braren. Homemade. 108–15
Garden fence. Burch. Tile: indoors and out, every kind and use. 89–90
How to build fences. Chamberlain. Fences, gates & walls. 35–71
Hurdles. Underhill. Woodwright's companion. 79–84
Installing canvas, fiberglass, aggregate panels and prefabricated panels for fences. Russell. Walks, walls and fences. 116–17
Livestock fencing. Burch. Building small barns, sheds, and shelters. 213–25
Picket fence how-to. Capotosto. Woodworking wisdom. 282–303
Pickets and shutters. Spence. Woodworking tools, materials, processes. 613
Post and rail fence. Brann. How to build outdoor projects. 8–26
Privacy partition. Brann. How to build patios and sundecks. 71–76
Privacy screens, privacy fence attractive from both sides. Popular Mechanics do-it-yourself encyclopedia. Vol. 15, 2334–40
Unique fences made of wood. Family handyman handbook of carpentry plans/projects. 478–88
View divider, grille fence. Popular Mechanics do-it-yourself encyclopedia. Vol. 14, 2112–13
Wire fences. Russell. Walks, walls and fences. 115–16
Wood fences. Brown. 44 terrific woodworking plans & projects. 204, 206–09
Wood fences. Russell. Walks, walls and fences. 104–13
Wooden fences, fiberglass fence. Family handyman handbook of carpentry plans/projects. 371–87
Wrought iron fences, gates and rails. Bealer. Art of blacksmithing. 317–40

Figurines
Acrobats, contortionists and balanced figures. Tangerman. Carving the unusual. 51–53
Bakers clay figures. Gardner. Dough creations. 84
Bokota ancestor figure—Mluila-Ngula. Casselman. Crafts from around the world. 122–25
Bottle clowns and rock people. Lyon. Arts and crafts objects children can make for the home. 24–25, 42–43
Carton creatures, whoozits, animals, and people. Romberg. Let's discover papier-mâché. 47, 50, 54–57
Character heads. Romberg. Let's discover papier-mâché. 30
Figure painting and detailing. Price. Model-building handbook. 85–120
Figures. Chesneau. Scale models in plastic. 135–49
Figures. Jackson. Modelmaker's handbook. 134–54
Figurine repair. Schuler. How to fix almost everything. 74
Folk figures. Gardner. Dough creations. 128–32
Good-luck rooster. Casselman. Crafts from around the world. 72–75
Human form. Kramer. Wirecraft. 94–95
Leaded glass figurines: piano and pianist, cello and cellist. Wood. Working with stained glass. 52–63
Metal and plastic figures. Ellis. Scale modeler's handbook. 90–103
Pipe cleaner figures. Christmas crafts book. 100–07
Scottish warrior, caveman, Greek warrior, cowboy, sea captain, cowboy with cup, continental soldier. McKellips. Practical pattern manual for woodcarving and other crafts. 5–25, 79–81, 95–97
Straw animal and bird figures: chicken, three French hens, goat, giraffe, pony, sheep, horse, squirrel, rabbit, stork, parrot, and child figures. Hibbs. Straw sculpture. 32–63

Files and rasps
Flat filing and drilling. Weygers. Recycling, use, and repair of tools. 66–75

Filing cases
Accordion bill file. Coffey. Francine Coffey's celebrity sewing bee. 91
File cabinet. Goldman. Decorate with felt. 92–93
Two-drawer file cabinet, four-drawer file cabinet. Oberrecht. Plywood projects illustrated. 87–92, 160–64.

Film projection. *See* **Projection apparatus**

Finger painting
Finger painting. Linderman. Crafts for the classroom. 402–03
Rabbit, finger paint transparencies. Lyon. Arts and crafts objects children can make for the home. 96–97, 164–65

Finger puppets. *See* **Puppets, Finger**

Fire engine models
Fire engine. Williams. Cookie craft: no-bake designs for edible party favors and decorations. 57–63

Fire engines, Toy
Firehouse, pumper, ladder truck, ambulance. Maginley. Trains and boats and planes and . . . 31–42
Hook & ladder truck. Baldwin. Old fashioned wooden toys. 116–20
Pumper, ladder truck, fire chief's station wagon. Maginley. Trains and boats and planes and . . . 168–80

Fire screens
Autumn flowers on checked ground, fire screen. Nicoletti. Japanese motifs for needlepoint. 99–104
Draughtboard firescreen. Bumper book of things a boy can make. 132–34
Japanese fireplace screen. Scobey. Decorating with needlepoint. 134–36

Fireplace equipment
Copper hood for a fireplace or stove, fireplace set, brass ash or dust scoop. Lindsley. Metalworking in the home shop. 292–96
Energy-saving fireplace cover. Popular Mechanics do-it-yourself encyclopedia. Vol. 12, 1820
Fire dogs, andirons, hearth shovel, tongs, hearth cranes, pot hooks, trammels, trivets and utensils. Bealer. Art of blacksmithing. 245–81
Fire tool handler. Brown. 44 terrific woodworking plans & projects. 131, 135–36
Fireplace crane, forging an andiron. McRaven. Country blacksmithing. 115–16, 129–34
Fireplace front. Braren. Homemade. 27
Fireplace tools. Make it! don't buy it. 322–33
Forging a fireplace poker and fireplace tongs. Weygers. Modern blacksmith. 57–58
Making a fireplace shovel. Weygers. Modern blacksmith. 82–85
Simple poker, small tongs, campfire fork. Scurlock. Muzzleloader Magazine's book of buckskinning II. 227–33
Building a brick fireplace. Jones. Fireplaces. 65–74
Building a stone fireplace. Jones. Fireplaces. 51–64
Building your own fireplace. Traister. All about chimneys. 69–92
Built-in fireplace, free-standing fireplace. 101 do-it-yourself projects. 228–35
Ceramic tile hearth covering. Burch. Tile: indoors and out, every kind and use. 58–60

Fireplace. Churchill. Big backyard building book. 103–06, 108
Fireplace repairs. Nunn. Home improvements, home repair. 42–43
Gould. Owner-built fireplace
How to have a smokeless fireplace, give a prefab fireplace a custom look. Popular
    Mechanics do-it-yourself encyclopedia. Vol. 8, 1224–27
Installing prefabricated units. Jones. Fireplaces. 75–82
Lytle. Book of successful fireplaces.
Renovating the older fireplace. Jones. Fireplaces. 44–50
Rustic stone fireplace facade. Better Homes and Gardens. Step-by-step masonry &
    concrete. 84–85
Stone fireplace. Nickey. Stoneworker's bible. 173–93
Summer dressings for fireplaces: simple fire paper, shredded tarlatan with myrtle
    wreath, rustic fender. Whatnot. 129–31

Firewood
Basket of kindling cones. O'Neill. Make-it-merry Christmas book. 32–33
Choosing and using wood. Jones. Fireplaces. 98–103
Fireplace faggots. Scobey. Gifts from your garden. 142
Firewood brace, fuel sled. Braren. Homemade. 22, 24
Firewood dryer. Calhoun. 20 simple solar projects. 126–37
How to cut and stack firewood. Popular Mechanics do-it-yourself encyclopedia. Vol.
    11, 1736-38
How to cut firewood and use a fireplace. Popular Mechanics do-it-yourself encyclope-
    dia. Vol. 8, 1129–1231
How to split and store firewood. Outdoor projects for home and garden. 498–503
Newspaper fireplace logs. Epple. Something from nothing crafts. 86–88
Newspaper logs for a fire. Traister. All about chimneys. 142
Primer on firewood. Traister. All about chimneys. 137–62
Stashing firewood. Garage, attic and basement storage. 24–25

Fish
Carving a dolphin in the round. Upton. Woodcarver's primer. 39–47
Fish. Hana. Embroidery. 9–14
Fish pillow and sleepy santa pillow. Woman's Day book of weekend crafts. 104–06,
    88–90
Fish on a dowel. Gillies. Patterns for applique and pieced work—and ways to use
    them. 118, 123
Making a fish banner, fish prints. Schuman. Art from many hands. 120–24
Shisha stitchery—embroidered fish. Better Homes and Gardens treasury of needle-
    crafts. 394–96

Fish ponds, Garden. *See* **Garden pools**

Fishing equipment
Make your own take-along rod. Popular Mechanics do-it-yourself encyclopedia. Vol. 8,
    1234–36

Fishing lures, flies, etc.
Fisherman's box. Cope. Plastics. 42
Laminated fishing nets. Fine woodworking techniques 4. 203
Make your own fishing spoons, wobbler minnow lure. Popular Mechanics do-it-yourself
    encyclopedia. Vol. 11, 1752–57
Make your own poppers. Popular Mechanics do-it-yourself encyclopedia. Vol. 4, 609
Poor man's fish lures, poor man's fly-tying vise. Blackwell. Johnny Blackwell's poor
    man's catalog. 108, 112
Shad dort lure. Giant book of metalworking projects. 215–17

Flags
American flags. Blair. Banners and flags. 183–193
Banners and flowers. Treasury of things to make. 135–37
Blair. Banners and flags.
Festive rejoice banner. Better Homes and Gardens applique. 36–37
Flag (patchwork). Hall. Sewing machine craft book. 74
House banner. Foose. Scrap saver's stitchery book. 64–70
International numeral pennants. Rome. Needlepoint letters and numbers. 113
International alphabet flags. Rome. Needlepoint letters and numbers, 110–12

Floor mats. *See* **Rugs**

Floors
Broken tile mosaic floor. Jarnow. (Re)do it yourself. 155–60
Building floors. Clifford. Basic woodworking and carpentry with projects. 162–66
Building floors and decks. Ramsey. Building a log home from scratch or kit. 111–19
Do-it-yourself flooring.
Floor construction. Spence. General carpentry. 166–93
Floor construction, finish flooring. Badzinski. House construction. 44–58, 160–74
Floor framing. Adams. Arco's complete woodworking handbook. 255–72
Floor refinishing techniques. Scherer. Complete handbook of home painting. 131–44
Floor repair and refinishing. Nunn. Home improvement, home repair. 54–60
Floors. Parry. Stenciling. 93–94
Hardwood flooring. Syvanen. Interior finish: more tricks of the trade. 90–96
How to install underlayment, how to lay hardwood flooring, tile floors, how to patch a hole in sheet flooring. Popular Mechanics do-it-yourself encyclopedia. Vol. 8, 1237–49
Installation of wood strip, block and tile wood flooring. Geary. How-to book of floors & ceilings. 76–87
Installing a new floor. Nunn. Home improvement, home repair. 76–77
Installing a self-sticking wood tile floor. Handyman. 218–19
Installing a sheet vinyl floor. Family handyman handbook of home improvement and remodeling. 441–46
Installing a wood floor. Time-Life Books. Floors and stairways. 38–46
Installing hardwood parquet flooring. Family handyman handbook of home improvement and remodeling. 418–28
Installing vinyl and vinyl asbestos tile, sheet-type vinyl and wood flooring. Spence. General carpentry. 411–27
Layered flooring, subfloor and underlayment, hardwood floor. Time-Life Books. New living spaces. 60–67
Laying sheet vinyl floors. Geary. How-to book of floors & ceilings. 43–58
Lone star floor (painted). McCall's book of America's favorite needlework and crafts. 356–57
Pour a plastic floor. Family handyman handbook of home improvement and remodeling. 446–51
Refinishing a wood floor. Time-Life Books. Floors and stairways. 24–27
Repairing and refinishing floors. Do-it-yourself flooring. 86–111
Repairing floors, new floors and floor coverings. Bragdon. Homeowner's complete manual of repair & improvement. 72–93
Speedy installation of resilient flooring. Handyman. 211
Stenciled kitchen & dining room floor. Jarnow. (Re)do it yourself. 88–93
Terrazzo. Olin. Construction. 453.1–16
Wood flooring, wood framed floors, resilient flooring. Olin. Construction. 202.29–42, 321.1–17, 452.1–26

Floors, Repairing
Do your own floor refinishing. Johnson. Old house woodwork restoration. 149–60
Floor repair. Waugh. Handyman's encyclopedia. 123–26
Floors and steps. Gladstone. Hints and tips for the handyperson. 71–76
Quick cures for wood floor's ailments: patches, sagging, weak joists, failing post, tired girder. Time-Life Books. Floors and stairways. 8–23
Refinishing floors. Wood finishing and refinishing. 92–104
Refinishing wood floors. Family handyman handbook of home improvement and remodeling. 399–404
Repair of resilient and hard-surfaced tile floors. Time-Life Books. Floors and stairways, 28–33

Floors, Tile
Ceramic tile floors: surface preparation, laying, and grouting. Geary. How-to book of floors & ceilings. 59–75
How to lay tile floor. Brann. How to modernize an attic. 34–40
How to tile a floor. Popular Mechanics do-it-yourself encyclopedia. Vol. 18, 2866–68
Installing floor tiles. Brightman. 101 practical uses for propane torches. 61–68
Installing floor tiles. Carbo. Fix-it guide for women. 48–52
Installing tile floors. Family handyman handbook of home improvement and remodeling. 428–41
Laying a tile floor. Handyman. 216–18
Laying non-ceramic tile flooring. Geary. How-to book of floors & ceilings. 20–42
Laying patterns in tile. Time-Life Books. Floors and stairways. 46–55
Laying tile. Time-Life Books. New living spaces. 64–66
Quarry tile entry floor. Popular Mechanics do-it-yourself encyclopedia. Vol. 15, 2362–63
Tiling floors—resilient tile, self-stick tiles, wood tile, carpet tile. Burch. Tile: indoors and out, every kind and use. 94–117

Flower arrangements
Basket of flourettes, hearth basket. Nicole. Designer accessories to make for your home. 90–95
Brack. Modern flower arranging.
Containers, vases and arrangements. Gordon. Complete guide to drying and preserving flowers. 190–200
Golden harvest (flowers in brandy glass). Janitch. Candlemaking and decorations. 43–44
Herb bouquets. Johnson. Nature crafts. 52–53
"Old sack" with a new bag (burlap). Nicole. Designer accessories to make for your home. 69–71
Paper and lace bouquet, popcorn and cranberry nosegay. Nicole. Designer accessories to make for your home. 171–73, 190
Teasel bouquet. Nicole. Designer accessories to make for your home. 65–68
Wiita. Dried flowers for all seasons.

Flower boxes, planters, etc.
Appliqued flower pot. Scharf. Butterick's fast and easy needlecrafts. 149
Dried-flower container. Yoder. Sculpture and modeling for the elementary school. 137–38
Felt covered flowerpot. Goldman. Decorate with felt. 20–21
Log flower trough, flower boxes, plant pot. Blandford. Constructing outdoor furniture, with 99 projects. 321–32
Lucite flowerpot. Linsley. Decoupage on glass, wood, metal, rocks, shells, wax, soap, plastic, canvas, ceramic. 90–94
Patchwork flowerpots. Woman's Day creative stitchery from scraps. 146–47

Plant trough. Mills. Book of presents. 124–25
Rustic hanging baskets, fern cases. Whatnot. 199–203, 207–14
Sheet-music covered flower pot. Roda. Fabric decorating for the home. 84
Shell flower pot. Jarnow (Re)do it yourself. 162–63
Shell flowerpots. Logan. Shell crafts. 162–64
Woven dried weed holder. Svinicki. Step-by-step spinning and dyeing. 55

Flower pictures
Brushed wool pansies, raised bouquet. Wilson. More needleplay. 139–41
Cork pictures, tile pictures, waste-paper bins and mirrors. Gordon. Complete guide to
    drying and preserving flowers. 61–64
Collages from growing things. Ashurst. Collage. 26–31
Daisies. Janitch. Collage; a step-by-step guide. 51–52,54
Dried flower meadow scene, all-year bouquets. McCall's book of America's favorite
    needlework and crafts. 372–74
Designing larger pictures. Gordon. Complete guide to drying and preserving flowers.
    97–169
Embroidered daisies in a basket. Woman's Day book of weekend crafts. 60–63
Flower bouquet plaque. Jarvey. You can dough it!. 14–15
Frames and other available settings. Gordon. Complete guide to drying and preserving
    flowers. 61–64
Making flower pictures. Creative crafts yearbook: an exciting new collection of needle-
    work and crafts. 52–53
Pictures for children and pictures by children. Gordon. Complete guide to drying and
    preserving flowers. 89–96
Pressed flower pictures. Brunner. Pass it on. 54–61
Pressed flower pictures. Morrison. Drying and preserving flowers. 78–89
Stained glass tudor rose collage. Janitch. Collage; a step by step guide. 63–65
Summer garden. Janitch. Collage; a step by step guide. 38–40

Flower pot holders
Bead flower pot cover. Hulbert. Creative beadwork. 98, 103
Chintz cover; crocheted cover; glasscloth tie-on for; upholstered cover; wooden cover.
    Doherty. Family Circle book of 429 great gifts-to-make all year round for just 10¢
    to $10.00. 95, 102
Coiled flower pots. Better Homes and Gardens easy bazaar crafts. 7, 17
Crocheted striped flowerpot cover. Scharf. Butterick's fast and easy needlecrafts. 144–
    45
Egg carton flowerpot container, wire coat hanger flowerpot holders, graduated pill
    bottle plant container. Epple. Something from nothing crafts. 40–41, 89–91, 119–
    20
Flower pot holder. Cope. Plastics. 59
Grow a graceful indoor garden. Popular Mechanics do-it-yourself encyclopedia. Vol.
    10, 1496–98
Herb garden clay pots. McCall's book of America's favorite needlework and crafts.
    341–42
Indian baskets. McCall's big book of knit & crochet for home and family. 243
Landscape planter jacket. Scobey. Decorating with needlepoint. 143–45
Ornamental jardinieres. Whatnot. 68–71
Plant center. Hamilton. Build it together. 148–53
Plant containers and plant hangers. Halliday. Decorating with crochet. 107–16
Planter. Parker. Mosaics in needlepoint. 88–91
Wall plant holder. Modern general shop. Metalworking. 97

Flower vases. *See* **Vases**

Flowers
Cornhusk flowers. Conner. Corncraft. 117–21
Looped flowers (yarn). Silverstein. Mira Silverstein's guide to looped and knotted stitches. 69–73
Pine cone roses. Johnson. Nature crafts. 133
Seashell table accessories. Johnson. Nature crafts. 37

Flowers, Artificial
Anniversary rose. Janitch. Candlemaking and decorations. 54–57
Art nouveau plant form. Kinser. Sewing sculpture. 121–23
Basket of flowers. Christensen. Needlepoint. 67–70
Basket of pine cone flowers. O'Neill. Make-it-merry Christmas book. 28–31
Beaded bouquets bring back a touch of elegance. Vanderbilt. Gloria Vanderbilt designs for your home. 122–29
Beaded crochet flowers. Encyclopedia of crafts. 93
Beaded strawberry basket. McCall's book of America's favorite needlework and crafts. 402–04
Bouquet of zinnias. Gardner. Dough creations. 69–73
Bowl of flowers (clay), synthetic raffia flower spray. Encyclopedia of crafts. 224, 242
Canvas plants. Treasury of things to make. 152–54
Carnation. Halliday. Decorating with crochet. 135–36
Check-a-bloom flowers. Doherty. Family Circle book of 429 great gifts-to-make all year round for just 10¢ to $10.00. 190
Colorful paper flowers. Yoder. Sculpture and modeling for the elementary school. 31–32
Cookie flowers, gum drop garden. Williams. Cookie craft: no-bake designs for edible party favors and decorations. 31–35
Cornhusk flowers. Johnson. Nature crafts. 65–67
Cotton fabric flowers. Wilkinson. Flower fabrication. 51–67
Cotton, hessian, suede, and felt flowers. Woods. Flowers from fabrics. 80–92
Crepe paper: star-shaped, Christmas and white rose. Critchley. Step by step guide to making artificial flowers. 16–25
Crepe paper carnation, tulip, and rose. Grainger. Creative Papercraft. 124–26
Crepe paper yellow buttercup, daisy, dianthus. Wilkinson. Flower fabrications. 39–47
Crocheted cactus garden. American School of Needlework. Great crochet bazaar book. 128–30
Daisies in a pot, rose and bud, morning glory plant, bluebells, and giant dahlias. Janitch. All made from paper. 48–55
Egg carton flowers, magazine zippy zinnia. Epple. Something from nothing crafts. 46–53, 57–58
English nosegay. Gardner. Dough creations. 126–28
Fabric flowers, eggshell tulips and roses from aluminum cans. Woman's Day book of weekend crafts. 55–59, 64–68
Fabric sculptured flowers. Yoder. Sculpture and modeling for the elementary school. 184–88
Fancy flowers. Perry. Holiday magic. 171–72
Field buttercups, meadow daisies, daffodils, narcissi and gentians, anemones, marigolds. Janitch. Paper flowers. 12–29
Fingerprint roses and rose tree. Gardner. Dough creations. 122–26
Flower cone. Critchley. Step by step guide to making artificial flowers. 70–71
Flowers and bouquets. Fowler. Can crafts. 28–47
Flowers from waste materials. Wilkinson. Flower fabrication. 147–67
Foil flowers, plastic film flowers, feather flowers, fabric flowers. Kicklighter. Crafts, illustrated designs and techniques. 102–11
Gemstone flowers. Meyer. Rock tumbling. 91–93
Giant tissue chrysanthemum. Janitch. Candlemaking and decorations. 62, 64

Gift ribbon flowers. Grainger. Creative papercraft. 121–22
Lace flowers. Wargo. Soft crafts for special occasions. 79–80
How to carve a rose. Cope. Plastics. 91–93
Leaded & glass flower cart with glass flowers. Isenberg. Crafting in glass. 150–63
Leaves, berries and seeds. Woods. Flowers from fabrics. 93–109
Making flowers in crepe paper—artichoke flowers. Paper. 72–77
McCullough. Clay flower techniques, Vol. 1.
Metal flowers. Yoder. Sculpture and modeling for the elementary school. 139–41
Milk weed pod poinsettia, corn husk flower: peony and chrysanthemum, magnolia leaf daisy and galax leaf rose. O'Neill. Make-it-merry Christmas book. 76–81
Miniature roses. Linsley. Great bazaar. 129–31
Mod flowers (polyester resin). Cope. Plastics. 37
Morning glories. Hibbs. Straw sculpture. 108–09
Morning glory, moss roses, love-in-a-mist, carnations, asters, tiger lilies, canterbury bells, ranunculus, petunias, pin cushions, poppies, cornflowers. Janitch. Paper flowers. 30–62
Nearly natural flowers from beech masts, fir cones, honesty seed pods and preserved leaves. Critchley. Step by step guide to making artificial flowers. 48–52
Needlepoint flowers. Better Homes and Gardens treasury of needlecrafts. 276–77
Needlepoint flowers, yarn flowers. Better Homes and Gardens treasury of Christmas crafts & foods. 163, 175, 344–45
Needlepoint pansies. Smith. Needlery. 105–08
Organdie, net and chiffon flowers. Woods. Flowers from fabrics. 57–79
Organdy rose. Wilkinson. Flower fabrication. 108–11
Origami: flower fold, lily, iris, cube flowers. Stephan. Creating with tissue papers. 136–47
Paper flower making: cabbage rose, carnation, fuchsia, daisies. Whatnot. 124–28
Party flowers, button chrysanthemums, carnation, sixteen-petal flower, double petal flower, straw flower, pleated flower, daisy, circle flower, cosmos, half-moon, bachelor buttons, folded roses, party roses, cabbage rose, yardstick rose, curlicue flowers, posy, sweet pea, lily, peony, poppy and chrysanthemum. Stephan. Creating with tissue paper. 107–35
Potted plants: geraniums, hydrangea, violets, and begonia. Wilkinson. Flower fabrications. 183–95
Quilled floral bouquet. Paper. 35–36
Realistic crepe paper roses. Paper. 78–80
Ribbon and raffia: daisy, fuchsia, jonquil, rose bud, dahlia, chrysanthemum and imaginary. Woods. Flowers from fabrics. 28–41
Ribbon roses. Wilson. Needlework to wear. 138
Rick-rack "applique" rose bud, rose, daisy, forget-me-nots, baby mum and lilac. Wargo. Soft crafts for special occasions. 129–32
Rose. Evans. Ribbonwork. 30–34
Roses. Janitch. Paper flowers. 63–75
Roses, large flower (tin can). Metalcrafting encyclopedia. 88–90
Seaside bouquets (shells). McCall's book of America's favorite needlework and crafts. 368–69
Shell flowers. Logan. Shell crafts. 100–42
Silk flower-making. Giant book of crafts. 140–57
Silk, satin and velvet flowers. Woods. Flowers from fabrics. 42–55
Silk tulip, iris, day lilies, daffodils, johnny-jump-ups, and poppy. Wilkinson. Flower fabrication. 69–103
Splashy paper flowers. Elbert. Paperworks. 58–60
Stained glass bouquet with vase. Wood. Working with stained glass. 77–87
Stained glass window flower. Critchley. Step by step guide to making artificial flowers. 44–47

Starched fabric flowers: cream peony, primrose posy and checked gingham. Critchley. Step by step guide to making artificial flowers. 36–43
Sunflower, peonies, dahlias, chrysanthemums, helleborus niger, ivy. Janitch. Paper flowers. 76–90
Take some paper—roses and fuchsias. Creative crafts yearbook: an exciting new collection of needlework and crafts. 78–80
3-D spring flowers. In Lyon. Arts and crafts objects children can make for the home. 26–27
Tin can flowers. O'Neill. Make-it-merry Christmas book. 58, 61
Tissue and ribbon roses, ribbon poinsettia. Paper. 130–31
Tissue paper flowers, wild roses, chrysanthemums, carnations and daisy. Critchley. Step by step guide to making artificial flowers. 8–15
Tissue peonies. Paper. 69–71
Velvet tulip, pansy, gardenia, and poinsettia. Wilkinson. Flower fabrication. 123–44
Victorian dome flower arrangement. Critchley. Step by step guide to making artificial flowers. 34–35
Waxed flowers: harebell, leaves for roses, and ivy. Critchley. Step by step guide to making artificial flowers. 26–34
Waxen flowers from yesteryear. McCall's book of America's favorite needlework and crafts. 396–98
White lily. Wilkinson. Flower fabrication. 112–15
Wired-stem flowers. Jarvey. You can dough it!. 16–17
Wood and corn husk flowers. Horwitz. Mountain people, mountain crafts. 74–79

Flowers, Collection and preservation
Candied flowers and leaves. Scobey. Gifts from your garden. 89–91
Crystallized flowers. Gordon. Complete guide to drying and preserving flowers. 210–12
Drying, pressing and preserving flowers. Pittaway. Traditional English country crafts and how to enjoy them today. 172–77
Making pressed flower arrangements. Schuman. Art from many hands. 82–88
Porcelainized flowers. Better Homes and Gardens treasury of Christmas crafts & foods. 151
Pressing flowers. Scobey. Gifts from your garden. 39–62

Flowers, Dried
Art of drying flowers. Brunner. Pass it on. 62–64
Dried flower bouquet. Mills. The book of presents. 51
Dried flower cards. Holtje. Cardcraft. 141–47
Dried flowers. Johnson. Nature crafts. 38–41
Dried flowers. Kicklighter. Crafts, illustrated designs and techniques. 96–101
Dried flowers. McCall's big book of country needlecrafts. 43
Drying flowers. Scobey. Gifts from your garden. 17–37
Encasing pressed flowers and leaves. Johnson. Nature crafts. 61
Lavender spray. Evans. Ribbonwork. 90–92
Methods of preserving. Gordon. Complete guide to drying and preserving flowers. 171–89
Morrison. Drying and preserving flowers.
Preserved flowers. Treasury of things to make. 46–48
Preserving flowers. Wiita. Dried flowers for all seasons. 13–30
Pressed flower picture. Critchley. Step by step guide to making artificial flowers. 62–65
Pressed flowers. Blandford book of traditional handicrafts. 138–47
Pressing and preparing the materials. Gordon. Complete guide to drying and preserving flowers. 12–60
Pressing flowers. Wiita. Dried flowers for all seasons. 31–32
Skeleton leaves. Whatnot. 160–61

Food carts. *See* **Serving carts; Tea wagons**

Food, Drying
Fruit and vegetable dryer. Popular Mechanics do-it-yourself encyclopedia. Vol. 7, 1054–55
Solar drier. Braren. Homemade. 42
Stovepipe food dryer, solar window herb dryer. Calhoun. 20 simple solar projects. 88–107

Food processing
Food preservation and storage workshop. Geary. How to design and build your own workspace—with plans. 232–61
Food processing centers. Davidson. Successful studios and work centers. 51–58
Homemade cider press. Popular Mechanics do-it-yourself encyclopedia. Vol. 5, 710–15
Using propane torch to remove pin feathers from a fowl. Brightman. 101 practical uses for propane torches. 125

Food storage
Food . . . for next winter, next week. Garage, attic and basement storage. 26–27
Root cellar, outdoor storage bins. Braren. Homemade. 28–31, 33–38

Food warmers
Bun warmer. Roda. Fabric decorating for the home. 50
Dish warmer—uses candle for fuel. Modern general shop. Metalworking. 115
Felt yogurt warmer. Johnson. Nature crafts. 12–13
Henny-penny bun warmer. Woman's Day book of stitchery from scraps. 34–36
Pot holders and bun warmers. Frager. Quilting primer. 85
Solar cooker. Boeschen. Successful playhouses. 103–04
Stone cookery. Boeschen. Successful playhouses. 125

Foot scrapes
Foot scraper. Blandford. Practical handbook of blacksmithing and metalworking. 270–76

Footstools
Bargello stitch footstool. Christensen. Needlepoint and bargello stitchery. 20–21
Bores and ottomans. Blandford. Upholsterer's bible. 308–16
Box pouffe. McDonald. Modern upholstering techniques. 89–99
Country French footstool pad. Scobey. Decorating with needlepoint. 70–72
Covered foot stool. Holland. Weaving primer. 138
Covering a footstool with needlepoint. Burchette. Needlework. 69–72
Cricket-on-the-hearth. Shea. Pennsylvania Dutch and their furniture. 161
Drum hassock. Roda. Fabric decorating for the home. 173–74
Fancy footwork. Great cross-stitch. 16–19
Fiddle-back foot stool. Blackwell. Johnny Blackwell's poor man's catalog. 127
Footstool. Hagerty. Make your own antiques. 83
Footstool. Worst. Weaving with footpower looms. 230–31
Footstool covers worked in French stitch. Orr. Now needlepoint. 91–92
Footstool cushion. Halliday. Decorating with crochet. 61–62
Footstool, (needlepoint ring of strawberries). Christensen. Teach yourself needlepoint. 94
Footstool. Hamilton. Build it together. 118–25
Footstools. Torelli. Reupholstering for the home craftsman. 170–73
Generous ottoman. Easy-to-make tables and chairs. 17
Hassock. Christensen. Teach yourself needlepoint. 137–38

Hassock. Roberts. Illustrated handbook of upholstery. 266–76
Hassock and cushions. Reader's Digest complete guide to sewing. 450, 479–81
Ivy scrolls, footstool top. Nicoletti. Japanese motifs for needlepoint. 31–33
Leather-covered footstool, footstool. Rubin. Mission furniture. 96–97
Making a footstool. Grime. Illustrated guide to furniture repair & restoration. 101–04
Needlepoint-covered footstool. Woman's Day decorative needlework for the home.
    155–58
Oriental-design needlepoint footstool cover. Reader's Digest complete guide to needle-
    work. 188
Ottoman. Blandford. Upholsterer's bible. 435–39
Pine footstool. Woman's Day book of gifts to make. 207–09
Reverse applique hassock. Roda. Fabric decorating for the home. 232–33
Scenic needlepoint hassock. Better Homes and Gardens treasury of needlecrafts.
    283–85
Seashell and poppies footstool covers (needlepoint). McCall's book of America's favo-
    rite needlework and crafts. 131, 133–34
Slipcovered ottoman. Roda. Fabric decorating for the home. 69–71
Stools. McDonald. Modern upholstering techniques. 82–88
Three-cushion footstool. Roda. Fabric decorating for the home. 236
Unusual hassock (hairpin lace). Feldman. Needlework boutique. 104–05
Woodburned floral footstool with lady bugs. Broadwater. Woodburning: art and craft.
    118–20

Forks. *See* **Silverware**

Forts, Toy
Elevated play fort. Hamilton. Build it together. 188–97
Fort. Blandford. Giant book of wooden toys. 52–56
Kentuck kamp fort. Churchill. Backyard building book. 126–32

Found objects. *See* **Waste materials**

Fountains
Building a fountain. Handyman. 291–96
Garden fountain. 101 do-it-yourself projects. 296–97

Frames (for charts, pictures, etc.). *See* **Picture frames**

Frogs (for clothing)
Chinese ball buttons and frogs. Time-Life Books. Exotic styling. 75–77
Frogs. Mansfield. Clothing construction. 359–63

Frogs and toads
Bouncing frog or butterfly. Rosenthal. Not-so-nimble needlework book. 29–32
Coat-hanger wire frog. Kramer. Wirecraft. 57–58
Felt frog. Hutchings. Big book of stuffed toy and doll making. 86–88
Freddie frog. American School of Needlework. Great crochet bazaar book. 94–96
Frog. Day. Complete book of rock crafting. 65–69
A frog with top hat and umbrella. Scheuer. Designs for Holbein embroidery. 46–47
Jeremy Fisher stuffed felt frog. Wilson. Erica Wilson's Christmas world. 122–27
Toad. Kinser. Sewing sculpture. 92–93

Frogs and toads. *See also* **Animals** *Entries*

Fur
Care of furs. Cudlipp. Furs. 169–79
Churchill. Complete book of tanning skins and furs.
Recycling furs. Saunders. Speed sewing; 103 sewing machine shortcuts. 94–97
Sewing and caring for furs. Time-Life Books. Novel materials. 96–123
Sewing with fur. Kellogg. Home tanning. 141–63

Furnaces
Build a superhot furnace for metalworking. Popular Mechanics do-it-yourself encyclopedia. Vol. 6, 884–86
Filling a hot water heating system. Waugh. Handyman's encyclopedia. 121–22
Furnace fix-ups. Nunn. Home improvements, home repair. 93–95
Gas heating unit repairs, coal furnaces, electric furnaces, and hot water heating. Nunn. Home improvement, home repair. 129–35
Home heating—forced warm air, hot water, steam, and electric. Handyman. 318–31
How to troubleshoot furnace failure. Popular Mechanics do-it-yourself encyclopedia. Vol. 9, 1298–1301
Multifuel boiler. Popular Mechanics do-it-yourself encyclopedia. Vol. 3, 390–92

Furniture
Butcher block furniture: table, couch, chair. Popular Mechanics do-it-yourself encyclopedia. Vol. 3, 463–67
Cast resin furniture. LaPlante. Plastic furniture for the home craftsman. 119–54
Construction and design basics of rattan furniture. Alth. Rattan furniture. 3–77
Dozen ways to attach legs to furniture. Popular Mechanics do-it-yourself encyclopedia. Vol. 11, 1710–11
Fabric-covered furniture. Creative sewing. 63–66
Foam "furniture." Reader's Digest complete guide to sewing. 440–43
Furniture. Parry. Stenciling. 96, 105
Furniture decorated with chintz, leafwork on furniture. Whatnot. 82–89
Furniture painting and decorating using Pennsylvania Dutch designs. Shea. Pennsylvania Dutch and their furniture. 128–47
Hauser. Priscilla Hauser book of tole and decorative painting.
Mix and match living room furniture. Black and Decker power tool carpentry. 76–86
PVC furniture. Kangas. By hand. 126–29
Zegel. Fast furniture

Furniture, Built-in
Blandford. 53 space-saving built-in furniture projects.
Building into walls. Clifford. Basic woodworking and carpentry . . . with projects. 193–97
Built-in units (bed combos, wall storage, workbench etc.). 77 furniture projects you can build. 229–89
Modular entertainment center. Complete handyman do-it-yourself encyclopedia. Vol. 8, 1170–73

Furniture, Children's. *See* **Children's furniture**

Furniture, Doll. *See* **Doll furniture**

Furniture for the sick
Bed tray. Dal Fabbro. How to make children's furniture and play equipment. 61
Bed tray. Zegel. Fast furniture. 112
Folding bed table. Grainger. Making aids for disabled living. 80–86
Footboard bed table. Popular Mechanics do-it-yourself encyclopedia. Vol. 5, 673

Furniture Joints. *See* **Joints (carpentry)**

Furniture, Miniature. *See* **Doll furniture**

Furniture, Outdoor
Bench designs. Kramer. Outdoor garden build-it book. 142–50
Butcher block furniture. Blandford. Constructing outdoor furniture, with 99 projects. 245–70
Coffee table or table and stools. Popular Mechanics do-it-yourself encyclopedia. Vol. 6, 816–18
Double garden seat. Blandford. Constructing outdoor furniture, with 99 projects. 164–70
Ferro-furniture for outdoor living. Day. How to build patios and decks. 162–71
Flip-top deck mate (privacy screen/ storage bench). Better Homes and Gardens. Deck and patio projects you can build. 80
Folding furniture: stools, chairs, tables and footrest. Blandford. Constructing outdoor furniture, with 99 projects. 181–212
Free swinging patio glider. Better Homes and Gardens. Deck and patio projects you can build. 77
Garden bench. Black and Decker power tool carpentry. 150–53
Glider. Churchill. Backyard building book II. 106–09
Lawn glider. Brann. How to build outdoor furniture. 96–126
Lawn glider. Churchill. Big backyard building book. 215–18
New webbing for outdoor furniture. Time-Life Books. 76–79
Outdoor furniture. Marshall. How to repair, reupholster, and refinish furniture. 146–51
Outdoor furniture storage. Garage, attic and basement storage. 32–33
Outdoor furniture that's simply elegant (canvas stretched across bent aluminum tubing). Popular Mechanics do-it-yourself encyclopedia. Vol. 5, 644–48
Patio benches. Fischman. Decks. 76–83
Plastic furniture from lightweight tubing. Porches and patios. 133
Repair of outdoor furniture. Outdoor projects for home and garden. 64–67
Repairing lawn furniture webbing. Brann. How to build patios and sundecks. 91–92
Replacing webbing in old lawn furniture. Outdoor projects for home and garden. 458–67
Rustic furniture made from natural poles and logs. Blandford. Constructing outdoor furniture, with 99 projects. 213–26
Trestle table and benches, double decker bunk. Churchill. Backyard building book. 156–59
Wraparound redwood seating. Better Homes and Gardens. Deck and patio projects you can build. 82–83

Furniture, Refinishing
Acid treatment. Blandford. Do-it-yourselfer's guide to furniture repair and refinishing. 82
Age simulation. Blandford. Do-it-yourselfer's guide to furniture repair and refinishing. 303–08
Antique furniture refinishing. Higgins. Commonsense guide to refinishing antiques. 39–126
Antiquing. Blandford. Do-it-yourselfer's guide to furniture repair and refinishing. 308–10
Antiquing. Johnson. How to restore, repair, and finish almost everything. 92–93
Blond finishes. Blandford. Do-it-yourselfer's guide to furniture repair and refinishing. 82
Distressing gives aged look. Payne. Furniture finishing and refinishing. 52
Faux porphyry (spatter technique). Johnson. How to restore, repair, and finish almost everything. 95–96
Final finishing. Howell-Koehler. Step-by-step furniture refinishing. 48–66
Finish removal. Howell-Koehler. Step-by-step furniture finishing. 35–38
Finishing furniture. Egge. Recycled with flair. 185–202

Finishing furniture. Payne. Furniture finishing and refinishing. 4–75
Fixing furniture finishes. Jones. Fixing furniture. 76–93
Flocking. Brumbaugh. Wood furniture finishing, refinishing, repairing. 326–29
French polish. Brumbaugh. Wood furniture finishing, refinishing, repairing. 222–24
From touch-ups to refinishing. Time-Life Books. Repairing furniture. 81–95
Furniture patching. Johnson. Restoring antique furniture. 108–12
Furniture refinishing. Joyner. Furniture refinishing at home. 3–60, 99–113
Graining. Blandford. Do-it-yourselfer's guide to furniture repair and refinishing. 83
Grotz. Furniture doctor.
Hand-rubbed finishes. Jones. Fixing furniture. 91–93
Hilts. Furniture repair & restoration.
How to refinish furniture. Hilts. Popular Mechanics complete book of furniture. 137–246
Johnson. Knock on wood.
Kinney. Complete book of furniture repair and refinishing. New rev. ed.
Liming. Blandford. Do-it-yourselfer's guide to furniture repair and refinishing. 79–80
Loudspeaker cabinet refinishing. Buckwalter. Easy speaker projects. 91–94
Marbleizing. Higgins. Common-sense guide to refinishing antiques. 183
Marbling. Johnson. How to restore, repair, and finish almost everything. 93–95
Meyers. Furniture repair and refinishing.
Paint finishes. Blandford. Do-it-yourselfer's guide to furniture repair and refinishing. 31–44
Patton. Furniture finishing.
Physical distressing. Johnson. How to restore, repair, and finish almost everything. 98
Pickled or limed wood. Higgins. Common-sense guide to refinishing antiques. 181
Preparation of wood. Blandford. Do-it-yourselfer's guide to furniture repair and refinishing. 19–30
Preparing wood surfaces for finishing, the new finish, fancy painting techniques. Meyers. Furniture repair and refinishing. 127–66, 183–98
Professional cabinetmaker scrapers. Popular Mechanics do-it-yourself encyclopedia. Vol. 16, 2526–27
Pyrography. Blandford. Do-it-yourselfer's guide to furniture repair and refinishing. 89–91
Refinishing a dresser. Clifford. Basic woodworking and carpentry . . . with projects. 208–12
Refinishing all types of furniture. Linsley. New ideas for old furniture. 28–174
Refinishing furniture. Handyman. 477–514
Refinishing furniture. Marshall. How to repair, reupholster, and refinish furniture. 198–221
Refinishing furniture is easier than ever. Popular Mechanics do-it-yourself encyclopedia. Vol. 8, 1208–17
Refinishing old furniture. Blandford. Do-it-yourselfer's guide to furniture repair and refinishing. 275–79, 295–302
Restoring surface finishes. Learoyd. Conservation and restoration of antique furniture. 90–99
Renovating the finish. Hayward. Antique furniture repairs. 113–17
Restoration projects. Restoring and reupholstering furniture. 28–77
Restoring and refinishing antique furniture. Oughton. Complete manual of wood finishing. 226–37
Savage. Professional furniture refinishing for the amateur.
Shading. Blandford. Do-it-yourselfer's guide to furniture repair and refinishing. 80–82
Shellac. Blandford. Do-it-yourselfer's guide to furniture repair and refinishing. 59–65
Shellac finishes. Brumbaugh. Wood furniture finishing, refinishing, and repairing. 214–22
Spatterwork. Higgins. Common-sense guide to refinishing antiques. 179
Special opaque finishes. Blandford. Do-it-yourselfer's guide to furniture repair and refinishing. 83–86

Spray finishes. Blandford. Do-it-yourselfer's guide to furniture repair and refinishing. 75–78

Stained dresser. Linsley. Fabulous furniture decorations. 60–61

Staining. Brumbaugh. Wood furniture finishing, refinishing, repairing. 195–213

Stains and fillers. Blandford. Do-it-yourselfer's guide to furniture repair and refinishing. 45–52

Stripping. Blandford. Do-it-yourselfer's guide to furniture repair and refinishing. 287–93

Stripping and finishing. Johnson. Restoring antique furniture. 41–86

Stripping, sanding, staining, polishing, & painting furniture. Encyclopedia of crafts. 162–69

Stripping the finish. Hilts. Popular Mechanics complete book of furniture. 167–80

Surface prep, brushes, first coats, finishing, specialty finishes. Bragdon. Homeowner's complete manual of repair & improvement. 222–67

Surface preparation. Howell-Koehler. Step-by-step furniture finishing. 39–47

Treating wood well, restoring the glow to furniture. Grime. Illustrated guide to furniture repair and restoration. 33–56

Varnishing. Blandford. Do-it-yourselfer's guide to furniture repair and refinishing. 53–57

Wax finishes. Brumbaugh. Wood furniture finishing, refinishing, repairing. 278–81

Wicker furniture-refinishing. Patton. Furniture finishing. 147–51

Wood preparation. Brumbaugh. Wood furniture finishing, refinishing, repairing. 178–94

Wood refinishing. Blandford. Upholsterer's bible. 464–77

Furniture, Refinishing. See also **Wood finishing**

Furniture, Repairing

Bamboo furniture. Blandford. Do-it-yourselfer's guide to furniture repair and refinishing. 313

Bamboo repair and refinishing. Johnson. How to restore, repair, and finish almost everything. 64–65

Bandings. Hayward. Antique furniture repairs. 93–96

Chairs, drawer troubles, patching veneers, covering scratches. Carbo. Fix-it guide for women. 57–69

Cleaning furniture and other wood. Wood finishing and refinishing. 130–38

Dealing with minor damage. Blandford. Do-it-yourselfer's guide to furniture repair and refinishing. 113–70, 187–94, 281–85

Frame, spring, and upholstery repair. Roberts. Illustrated handbook of upholstery. 55–95

Furniture. Introduction to repairing and restoring. 106–49

Furniture beetle damage. Hayward. Antique furniture repairs. 111–12

Furniture repair. Bragdon. Homeowner's complete manual of repair & improvement. 196–221

General carcase repairs. Hayward. Antique furniture repairs. 18–26

Glass replacement. Wenn. Restoring antique furniture. 88–89

Glue blocks. Jones. Fixing furniture. 43

Grotz. Furniture doctor.

How to repair furniture. Hilts. Popular Mechanics complete book of furniture. 91–134

How to repair scratches in furniture. Popular Mechanics do-it-yourself encyclopedia. Vol. 9, 1302–03

Jones. Fixing furniture.

Kinney. Complete book of furniture repair and refinishing. New rev. ed.

Learoyd. Conservation and restoration of antique furniture.

Leg repairs. Hayward. Antique furniture repairs. 46–56

Lengthening legs. Kinney. Complete book of furniture repair and refinishing. 52–53

Marshall. How to repair, reupholster, and refinish furniture.

Metal furniture. Blandford. Do-it-yourselfer's guide to furniture repair and refinishing. 313–15

Meyers. Furniture repair and refinishing.

Plastic furniture repair. Marshall. How to repair, reupholster, and refinish furniture. 154–56

Rattan and wicker repair. Alth. Rattan furniture. 193–206

Rebuilding furniture. Blandford. Do-it-yourselfer's guide to furniture repair and refinishing. 195–218

Repairing and restyling frames. Blandford. Upholsterer's bible. 478–91

Repairing antiques. Higgins. Common-sense guide to refinishing antiques. 85–93

Repairing minor damage. Blandford. Upholsterer's bible. 329–54

Repairing, restoring, and stripping. Brumbaugh. Wood furniture, finishing, refinishing, repairing. 149–77

Repairs made easy. Johnson. Restoring antique furniture. 17–40

Replacing finials. Marshall. How to repair, reupholster, and refinish furniture. 158–61

Restoring furniture. Hilts. Popular Mechanics complete book of furniture. 303–17

Restoring furniture. Howell-Koehler. Step-by-step furniture finishing. 9–17

Rodd. Repairing and restoring antique furniture.

Rudiments of construction and structural repair, cosmetic repairs. Meyers. Furniture repair and refinishing. 79–125

Salazar. Complete book of furniture restoration.

Savage. Professional furniture refinishing for the amateur.

Simple repairs. Grime. Illustrated guide to furniture repair & restoration. 27–31

Smith. Old furniture.

Stripping old furniture finishes, glues, clamping chair rungs. 77 furniture projects you can build. 361–83

Time-Life Books. Repairing furniture.

Tips on repairing and preparing. Linsley. New ideas for old furniture. 13–27

Using wood dough, plastic, putty, stick shellac, etc. to repair broken corners, dents & bruises. Kinney. Complete book of furniture repair and refinishing. 27–34

Warping. Brumbaugh. Wood furniture finishing, refinishing, repairing. 170–71

Wood. Johnson. How to restore, repair, and finish almost everything. 24–45

G

Game boards and tables

Backgammon board. Popular Mechanics do-it-yourself encyclopedia. Vol. 20, 3047–48

Backgammon board and patchwork checkerboard. McCall's big book of needlecrafts. 64–66

Card and game tables. Oberrecht. Plywood projects illustrated. 46–48

Checkerboard table. Wood projects for the garden. 56

Checkerboard table and filling a tabletop with sand art. Appel. Sand art. 109–12

Chess table. Krenov. Impractical cabinetmaker. 115–27

Chessboard-topped game table, plastic tic-tac-toe board. Complete handyman do-it-yourself encyclopedia. Vol. 9, 1208–17

Cribbage board for your pocket. Popular Mechanics do-it-yourself encyclopedia. Vol. 6, 877

Cribbage board, tic-tac-toe. Cope. Plastics. 20–21, 26–27

Flip-flop table for backgammon and chess. Popular Mechanics do-it-yourself encyclopedia. Vol. 1, 146–49

Game table for your playroom. Popular Mechanics do-it-yourself encyclopedia. Vol. 9, 1304–07

Imitation ebony and ivory chessboard, illuminated backgammon board, picture checkerboards. Whatnot. 48–51, 106–10, 164–67

Jack card table and backgammon boards in needlepoint. Wilson. More needleplay. 118–23

Make your own board. Carroll. Make your own chess set. 149–50

Once-around cribbage board, triangle game. Oberrecht. Plywood projects illustrated. 189–91, 213–15
Parsons game table. Midkiff. Complete book of stenciling. 47–49
Quickie card tables, game dividers and screens, checkerboard top cube stool. Popular Mechanics do-it-yourself encyclopedia. Vol. 8, 1187, 1189–90
Ribbon chess/checker cloth. Roda. Fabric decorating for the home. 109–10
Round table game. Easy-to-make tables and chairs. 56–57
Shuffleboard table. Popular Mechanics do-it-yourself encyclopedia. Vol. 17, 2678–79

Game rooms. *See* **Basements; Recreation rooms**

Games
And for indoor sports (needlepoint backgammon, checkerboard). Feldman. Needlework boutique. 106–08
Ball game, table ball game. Blandford. Giant book of wooden toys. 186–91
Checker set. Gardner. Dough creations. 143–44
Checkerboard beach towel. Reader's Digest complete guide to sewing. 508–09
Chess board (needlepoint). Christensen. Needlepoint book. 110–11
Cup and ball. Blandford. Giant book of wooden toys. 159–61
Decorative board for backgammon (needlepoint). Time-Life Books. Traditional favorites. 184–87
Diabolo. Blandford. Giant book of wooden toys. 152–56
Felt games (checkers, tic-tac-toe, backgammon) Treasury of things to make. 82–85
Game of darts. Scobey. First easy-to-see needlepoint workbook. 31–35
Games built from wood; pegboard games. Giant book of crafts. 267–80
Giant checkerboard game. Great granny crochet book. 131
Hanukkah games. Rockland. Hanukkah book. 115–38
Horseshoes, croquet, badminton, volleyball, basketball, handball, shuffleboard, tennis, and putting green. Outdoor projects for home and garden. 438–45
How to light a game area. Popular Mechanics do-it-yourself encyclopedia. Vol. 20, 3149–52
Leaf-pattern backgammon board. Scobey. Decorating with needlepoint. 100–02
Marble game, up the hill-down the hill game, tic-tac-toe game. Hodges. 46 step-by-step wooden toy projects. 89–96
Mental arithmetic and alphabet soup games. Grainger. Creative papercraft. 91–94, 104
Patchwork pachisi design. Gostelow. Mary Gostelow's embroidery book. 206–08
Peg game box. Modern general shop. Woodworking. 103
Pegball game. Mills. The book of presents. 129
Pin table. Blandford. Giant book of wooden toys. 203–08
Quick-and-easy game banner. Better Homes and Gardens applique. 15
Skill game, dart board. Spence. Woodworking tools, materials, processes. 588–89
Sliding ball game. Blandford. Giant book of wooden toys. 193–94
Snooker (pool) game. Blizzard. Making wooden toys. 35–37
"Swiss-cheese" mountain game, baffling puzzle. Popular Mechanics do-it-yourself encyclopedia. Vol. 20, 3065–67
Tic-tac-toe game, peg game. Modern general shop. Woodworking. 111–12
Tic-tac-toe pillow. Golden book of hand and needle arts. 12
Tick-tack-toe board and men, spiral game, zig-zag traveler, marble ride, marble roller coaster. DeCristoforo. Build your own wood toys, gifts and furniture. 184–221
Waterford. Microcomputer-controlled toys & games & how they work.
Wells. Wooden puzzles and games.
Wooden tic-tac toe. Favorite easy-to-make toys. 153–54
World's greatest needlepoint Scrabble board. Sheldon. Washable and dryable needlepoint. 92–93
Zechlin. Games you can build yourself.

Garage doors
Fixing garage doors to look like new. Family handyman handbook of home improvement and remodeling. 320–26
Install your own garage door opener. Family handyman handbook of home improvement and remodeling. 187–201
Installing overhead garage doors. Spence. General carpentry. 315–17
Keep your garage door rolling. Popular Mechanics do-it-yourself encyclopedia. Vol. 9, 1308–11
Maintaining a garage door. Bragdon. Homeowner's complete manual of repair & improvement. 143
Planning and installing overhead garage doors. Russell. Garages and carports. 82–85
Attached carport. Burch. Building small barns, sheds, and shelters. 179–80
Building a concrete block garage. Russell. Garages and carports. 126–37
Building a metal garage. Russell. Garages and carports. 156
Building a two-story garage. Russell. Garages and carports. 104–13
Converting the garage for living space. Russell. Garages and carports. 142–49
Expanding a one-car garage. Russell. Garages and carports. 138–41
Garage cabinets. Family handyman handbook of carpentry plans/projects. 171–73
Garage ceiling storage. Family handyman handbook of home improvement and remodeling. 176–77
Garages. Adams. Arco's complete woodworking handbook. 418–23
Maximizing storage, yet leaving space for the car. Garage, attic and basement storage. 62–67
One car garage. Marshall. Yard buildings. 59–65
Red barn garage. Churchill. Backyard building book. 166–87
Red barn garage. Churchill. Big backyard building book. 48–69
Using garage kits. Russell. Garages and carports. 154–55
Willow chunk garage. Bubel. Working wood. 75–81
Work plans, materials, grading and drainage, footings and foundations, framing, and finishing. Russell. Garages and carports. 30–103

Garages. *See also* **Carports**

Garbage cans. *See* **Refuse receptacles**

Garden equipment
Berry box. Braren. Homemade. 95
Functional potting table. Geary. How to design and build your own workspace—with plans. 288, 291–93
Garden gadgetry, bulk supplies, heavy garden gear storage. Garage, attic and basement storage. 34–37
Garden kneeler. Blandford. Constructing outdoor furniture, with 99 projects. 318–21
Garden work center. Kramer. Outdoor garden build-it book. 175–76
Gardening bench. Lane. Building in your backyard. 170–71
How to choose good gardenshears. Popular Mechanics do-it-yourself encyclopedia. Vol. 17, 2618–19
Indoor storage bins. Braren. Homemade. 39
Knee pads. Wood projects for the garden. 68
Plant protectors. Braren. Homemade. 90–92
Plant supports. Braren. Homemade. 102
Portable gardening stove. Kramer. Outdoor garden build-it book. 150–52
Potting bench. Braren. Homemade. 18
Potting cart. 101 do-it-yourself projects. 288–89
Preparing lawn and garden furniture for storage. Outdoor projects for home and garden. 192–94
Repairing a shovel and mattock. Weygers. Recycling, use, and repair of tools. 8–11

Sifting screen. Bubel. Working wood. 99–100
Soil sifters. Braren. Homemade. 84–87
Wood-frame garden cart, steel-frame garden cart. Sullivan. Cart book, with plans & projects. 134–37, 205–12

Garden frames. *See* **Cold frames**

Garden gates. *See* **Gates**

Garden houses, shelters, etc.
Cabana. Creative sewing. 91
Cabana for your pool. Popular Mechanics do-it-yourself encyclopedia. Vol. 15, 2270–73
Chalet storage building, family bank, Irish shanty. Churchill. Backyard building book II. 61–77
Harvest kitchen and root cellar. Churchill. Backyard building book. 59–68
Hexagonal gazebo. Kramer. Outdoor garden build-it book. 179–81
Outdoor dining shelter. Marshall. Yard buildings. 85–91
Pergolas, gazebo. Marshall. Yard buildings. 144–49
Picturesque poolhouse. Popular Mechanics do-it-yourself encyclopedia. Vol. 3, 476–79
Polygonal gazebo. Lane. Building in your backyard. 200–04
Root cellar. Braren. Homemade. 28–31
Screened trail shelter. Churchill. Backyard building book. 139–46
Screenhouse. Churchill. Backyard building book. 153–57
Screenhouse, screened trail shelter. Churchill. Big backyard building book. 97–101, 181–88
Sheds for storage overflow. Garage, attic and basement storage. 42–43
Simple guest houses: geodesic dome & yurt; solar heated guest house or hideaway. Churchill. Big backyard building book. 9–24, 131–48
Storage/guest house. Marshall. Yard buildings. 47–58
Three gracious summer houses: screen house, garden gazebo, canopy gazebo. Popular Mechanics do-it-yourself encyclopedia. Vol. 18, 2821–25
Two attractive garden shelters, work center for your garden, handsome cookout gazebo. Popular Mechanics do-it-yourself encyclopedia. Vol. 9, 1330–34, 1347–50
Two-story round gazebo. Lane. Building in your backyard. 205–25

Garden lighting. *See* **Lighting, Outdoor**

Garden ornaments
Lawn ornaments. Brann. How to build workbenches, sawhorse tool chest and other build-it-yourself projects. 71–81

Garden pools
Forming a garden pool. Marshall. Foilcraft. 124–25
Garden pool and waterfall. Bragdon. Homeowner's complete manual of repair & improvement. 476–77
Making a garden pool and waterfall, waterfall rock garden. Outdoor projects for home and garden. 277–80, 303–06

Garden sprinklers. *See* **Sprinklers**

Garden tools
Cultivator and garden rake repair. Brightman. 101 practical uses for propane torches. 117–18
Hay rakes. Bubel. Working wood. 95–98
Hedge trimmer, rotary lawn mower. Buckwalter. Homeowner's handbook of power tools. 193–211

Poor man's hoe/weeder, dandelion cutter, etc. Blackwell. Johnny Blackwell's poor man's catalog. 71–79
Repair. Outdoor projects for home and garden. 198–99
Tools for potted plant gardeners. Modern general shop. Metalworking. 115
Trowel. Giant book of metalworking projects. 203–06

Garden walks
Brick and flagstone walks. Proulx. Plan and make your own fences and gates. Walkways, walls and drives. 65–66
Handsome garden paths and walkways. Popular Mechanics do-it-yourself encyclopedia. Vol. 14, 2084–89
Hard walks: concrete, brick, asphalt to flagstone. Russell. Walks, walls, and fences. 43–55
Soft walks: gravel, crushed stone and brick, bark and wood chips, and treated wood. Russell. Walks, walls and fences. 56–58
Walk patterns, finishes and edgings. Russell. Walks, walls and fences. 33–42
Walks and paths. Kramer. Outdoor garden build-it book. 118–25
Walks and paths. Nunn. Home improvements, home repair. 200–05

Garden walks. See also **Sidewalks**

Garment bags
Garment bag. Roda. Fabric decorating for the home. 138–39
Garment bags; shoulder guards, woman's carry-on garment bag & two pocket duffle. Doherty. Family Circle book of 429 great gifts-to-make all year round for just 10¢ to $10.00. 76–77, 148–49

Garters
Bridal garter. Wargo. Soft crafts for special occasions. 73–74
Garters. Gehret. Rural Pennsylvania clothing. 238–41

Gates
Building a simple gate. Russell. Walks, walls and fences. 118–21
Children's gate. Blandford. 66 children's furniture projects. 83–84
Corral gate. Braren. Homemade. 154
Entrance gate posts. Nickey. Stoneworker's bible. 243
Farm gates. Bubel. Working wood. 145–52
Foot-operated gate. Braren. Homemade. 118–19
Garden gates. Black and Decker power tool carpentry. 160–64
Gates. Braren. Homemade. 116–27
Gates, grilles, railings. Meilach. Decorative and sculptural ironwork. 153–83
Gates. Proulx. Plan and make your own fences and gates, walkways, walls and drives. 37–40
How to build a better gate. Capotosto. Woodworking wisdom. 304–17
How to build gates. Chamberlain. Fences, gates & walls. 130–45
Mailbox and name plate gate. Brann. How to build outdoor projects. 49–56

Gavels
Gavel. Hodges. Woodturning handbook—with projects. 178–85

Gazebos. See **Garden houses, shelters, etc.**

Gems
Gem tree. Encyclopedia of crafts. 199

Gesso.
How and when to use gesso. Upton. Woodcarver's primer. 144–45

Gift tags. *See* **Labels**

Gift wrapping. *See* **Wrapping of packages**

Gilding
Cleaning gold leaf. Popular Mechanics do-it-yourself encyclopedia. Vol. 4, 573
Damaged gilt work. Wenn. Restoring antique furniture. 63–64
Finishing candles with gold/silver leafing. Newman. Creative candlemaking. 64–66
Gilding. Brumbaugh. Wood furniture finishing, refinishing, repairing. 308–15
Gilding. Johnson. How to restore, repair, and finish almost everything. 100–02
Gilding. Marshall. Foilcraft. 132–34
Gilding. Meyers. Furniture repair and refinishing. 191–93
Gilding. Oughton. Complete manual of wood finishing. 110–18
Gilding. Payne. Furniture finishing and refinishing. 54, 59–60
Gilding a carving. Upton. Woodcarver's primer. 150–52
Gilding, silvering, and mosaic (glass). Duthie. Decorative glass processes. 193–206
Gold leafing. Johnson. How to restore, repair, and finish almost everything. 103–07
Using gold leaf. Blandford. Do-it-yourselfer's guide to furniture repair and refinishing. 312–13

Gingerbread
Gingerbread cottage. Meyer. Christmas crafts. 53–59
Gingerbread house. Boeschen. Successful playhouses. 59–60
No-bake "gingerbread" house made from graham crackers. Doherty. Family Circle book of 429 great gifts-to-make all year round for just 10¢ to $10.00. 204–05

Glass
Bending glass tubing. Brightman. 101 practical uses for propane torches. 75–76
Embossing glass. Rothenberg. Decorating glass. 45–67
Fire polishing a glass sheet. Brightman. 101 practical uses for propane torches. 76
Glass jewels. Metal and enamel. 104
Glassblowing. Rose. Illustrated encyclopedia of crafts and how to master them. 254–64
Isenberg. How to work in beveled glass.

Glass cutting
Brilliant cutting and bevelling. Duthie. Decorative glass processes. 156–74
From bottles to fancy glassware. Popular Mechanics do-it-yourself encyclopedia. Vol. 3, 418–21
Short course in glass cutting. Popular Mechanics do-it-yourself encyclopedia. Vol. 9, 1363–64
Technique, glasses, bottle, jar and jug projects. Epple. Something from nothing crafts. 6–25

Glass etching
Embossed glass. Duthie. Decorative glass processes. 127–55
Embossing on glass. Whatnot. 64–65
Glass etching. Rothenberg. Decorating glass. 68–80
Sand-blast. Duthie. Decorative glass processes. 175–92

Glass holders. *See* **Beverage holders**

Glass painting
Glass painting. Rothenberg. Decorating glass. 11–44
Glass painting, Noah's ark. Casselman. Crafts from around the world. 205–06
Painting. Duthie. Decorative glass processes. 206–08
Painting on glass. Isenberg. How to work in stained glass. 186–95
Potichomania: gluing paper cutouts to glass. Brunner. Pass it on. 73–75
Tinsel flowers (painted on glass). McCall's book of America's favorite needlework and
    crafts. 360–61

Glassware, Repairing
Repair and care of glass. Johnson. How to restore, repair, and finish almost every-
    thing. 144–47
Repairing chipped glassware. Brightman. 101 practical uses for propane torches. 75

Glazes and glazing
Art of glazing, nature of glazing, glaze firing. Dickerson. Pottery making. 93–117
Aventurine, crystal, and crystalline matt glazes. Conrad. Contemporary ceramic for
    mulas. 188–249
Clay and glazes. Tyler. Raku. 70–96
Composition of slips and glazes. Troy. Salt-glazed ceramics. 62–77
Cooper. Potter's book of glaze recipes.
Earthenware leadless glazes. Conrad. Contemporary ceramic formulas. 109–20
Formulas (glazes). Brodie. Energy efficient potter. 188–91
Fraser. Glazes for the craft potter.
Glass and clay as glazes. Conrad. Contemporary ceramic techniques. 43–56
Glaze. Casson. Craft of the potter. 81–93, 98–104
Glaze and experimenting with glazes. Riegger. Electric kiln ceramics. 68–107
Glaze calculation. Grebanier. Chinese stoneware glazes. 115–26
Glaze defects. Zorza. Pottery: creating with clay. 123–26
Glaze formulas for raku, earthenware and stoneware. Paak. Decorative touch. 113–24
Glazing with slate and concrete sealer. Priolo. Ceramics by coil. 37–38
Light-blue chun, kuan-chun, celadon, dark blue-and-brown mottled, copper red and
    peach bloom, turquoise, temmokee, TZ' U-Chou and combinations. Grebanier.
    Chinese stoneware glazes. 15–100
Low-temperature glazes. Conrad. Contemporary ceramic techniques. 1–42
Luster on glazes. Conrad. Contemporary ceramic techniques. 95–108
Luster ware glazes. Sanders. Glazes for special effects. 92–109
New concepts in glazes. Kriwanek. Keramos. 21–54
Oxides. Pottery step-by-step. 37–39
Raku wear. Sanders. Glazes for special effects. 118–23
Salt-glazing. Conrad. Contemporary ceramic techniques. 71–94
Salt glazing, Egyptian paste, Majolica and overglaze enamels. Dickerson. Pottery mak-
    ing. 125–29
Sanders. Glazes for special effects.
Simple glazes: Earthenware and stoneware. Zorza. Pottery; creating with clay. 106–22
Single-firing, wide-firing-range cup and spoon, measure, special effects, earthenware,
    soft stoneware, stoneware, porcelain, celadon, copper red, ash slip, salt and va-
    por, and colorants. Chappell. Potter's complete book of clay and glazes. 140–417
Sodium as a vapor glaze. Troy. Salt-glazed ceramics. 126–39
Stoneware glazes. Conrad. Contemporary ceramic formulas. 151–87
Synthetic wood ash. Grebanier. Chinese stoneware glazes. 127–31
Tests, color blends, applications, defects, and types of glazes. Paak. Decorative touch.
    45–80

Glider models
Making a glider. Bumper book of things a boy can make. 21–22

Gloves
Driving gloves (crocheted). Feldman. Needlework boutique. 93–94
Emlyn-Jones. Make your own gloves.
Fair Isle scarf, hat and gloves. Morgan. Traditional knitting patterns of Ireland, Scotland and England. 87–89
Felt trimmed gloves. Creative crafts yearbook: an exciting new collection of needlework and crafts. 115
Gloves from Fair Isle. Compton. Complete book of traditional knitting. 165–67
Gloves (leather). Practical needlework. 139–41
Guernsey fingerless gloves. Morgan. Traditional knitting patterns of Ireland, Scotland and England. 53–57
Ladies' three-season gloves. Jacobs. Crochet book. 146–47
Leather gloves. Rose. Illustrated encyclopedia of crafts and how to master them. 104–09
Leather gloves. Time-Life Books. Novel materials. 70–83
Lively stitched hand warmers (knitted). Time-Life Books. Boutique attire. 154–56
Men's winter gloves. Jacobs. Crochet book. 137–38
Movable gloves. Johnson. Quiltwear. 67–71
Snowflake pattern gloves. McCall's big book of knit & crochet for home & family. 89–90
Stenciled work gloves, knitted gloves for men & boys. Doherty. Family Circle book of 429 great gifts-to-make all year round for just 10¢ to $10.00. 104–05, 108–09

Glue. See **Adhesives**

Go karts. See **Automobiles, Racing**

Golf
Build a putting green from artificial turf. Popular Mechanics do-it-yourself encyclopedia. Vol. 15, 2356–59

Golf clubs
Golf club covers (knit). Feldman. Needlepoint. 128–29
Golf club mits. Brown. Super sweater idea book. 189–91
Golf club mitts. Doherty. Family Circle book of 429 great gifts-to-make all year round for just 10¢ to $10.00. 69
Golf club socks. Roda. Fabric decorating for the home. 114
Golf clubs (repair). Schuler. How to fix almost everything. 96

Gongs
Dinner gong. Woman's Day book of weekend crafts. 45

Gourds
Calabash decoration. Newman. Contemporary African arts and crafts. 147–64
Carved gourd designs. Schuman. Art from many hands. 170–74
Decorated gourds. Casselman. Crafts from around the world. 115–17
Gourd bird houses, dippers, bowls. Horwitz. Mountain people, mountain crafts. 92–93
Gourd containers. Scurlock. Muzzleloader Magazine's book of buckskinning II. 225–26
Gourd pots. Stribling. Crafts from North American Indian arts. 241–45
Gourds: clowns of the plant kingdom. Johnson. Nature crafts. 106–19
Mordecai. Gourd craft.
Oriental hollow gourd of papier mâché. Elbert. Paperworks. 115–19
Peruvian gourd lamp. Murphy. Lampmaking. 93–96

Grandfather clocks. See **Clock cases, Grandfather**

Grass cutters. *See* **Lawn mowers**

Greenhouses
A-frame bath house. Kramer. Outdoor garden build-it book. 182
Add a greenhouse—an elegant addition. Popular Mechanics do-it-yourself encyclope-
dia. Vol. 1, 30–33
Attached greenhouse. Brown. 44 terrific woodworking plans & projects. 212–26
Building greenhouses. Leavy. Successful small farms. 113–31
Combination greenhouse and storage shed. Lane. Building in your backyard. 172–80
Gazebos. Black and Decker power tool carpentry. 174–81
Greenhouse. Self. Working with plywood, including indoor/outdoor projects. 178–92
Greenhouse addition to house, window greenhouse. 101 do-it-yourself projects. 258–
63, 294–95
Greenhouse entry door. Rowland. Handcrafted doors & windows. 56–59
Greenhouses. Marshall. Yard buildings. 131–36
Guide to greenhouses. Outdoor projects for home and garden. 356–63
Lush greenhouse in your window. Popular Mechanics do-it-yourself encyclopedia. Vol.
10, 1492–94
Mobile greenhouses. Capotosto. Woodworking techniques and projects. 233–43
Moyer. Solar heat-n-grow window.
Shed/greenhouse combination. Famly handyman handbook of carpentry plans/
projects. 399–404
Window greenhouse. Braren. Homemade. 32
Window greenhouse. Calhoun. 20 simple solar projects. 50–61
Window greenhouse, A-frame greenhouse, excavated green house, full-size conven-
tional frame greenhouse. Churchill. Backyard building book. 22–25, 28–43
Window greenhouse, hotbed gardening, A-frame greenhouse, excavated greenhouse,
full-size conventional frame greenhouse. Churchill. Big backyard building book.
25–47

Greeting card holders
Reindeer Christmas card holder. American School of Needlework. Great Christmas
crochet book. 24–28

Greeting cards
Animated cards—dreaming dog and juggling clowns. Paper. 17–21
Birthday card for young adult. Janitch. Candlemaking and decorations. 53–57
Candleglow, I saw three ships, Christmas rose, Christmas tree, gold lace, falling
leaves, white puppy, birthday cake, tissue rose, three daisies, bird in a cage, and
rocking cradle. Janitch. All made from paper. 82–95
Christmas cards using collage, gummed paper cut-outs, stencils, lino-prints, and
pressed flowers. Christmas crafts book. 81–89
Christmas and general occasion greeting cards. Janitch. Collage; a step by step guide.
74–75
Cross-stitch Christmas cards. Doherty. Family Circle book of 429 great gifts-to-make
all year round for just 10¢ to $10.00. 42–43
Cross-stitch greeting cards, tatted note cards. Better Homes and Gardens bazaar
crafts. 14, 20, 69, 78
Designer greeting cards. Linsley. Custom made. 152–53
Easter & Christmas cards. Perry. Holiday magic. 64–65, 167–69
Greeting cards. Giant book of crafts. 369–80
Greeting cards (embroidered). Fraser. Modern stitchery: stitches, patterns, free-form
designing. 91
Greeting cards and envelopes. Gordon. Complete guide to drying and preserving
flowers. 64–73
Holtje. Cardcraft.

Making greeting cards from four photos. Popular Mechanics do-it-yourself encyclopedia. Vol. 5, 684–88
Making postcards. Holtje. Cardcraft. 115–17
Mirror border, floral border. Scharf. Butterick's fast and easy needlecrafts. 191–93
Needlepoint, cross-stitch, batik, quick cross-stitch, machine-embroidered, felt silhouettes, printed, and crackled glue cards. McCall's book of Christmas. 122–38
Permanent greeting card (rock). Vane. Pebble people, pets & things. 25–28, 135–38
Pressed flower valentine and Christmas cards. Scobey. Gifts from your garden. 132, 140
Rubbings for greeting cards. Firestein. Rubbing craft. 89
Simple pop-up cards, fan-folds and cut-outs. Paper. 6–16
Special gift cards. Elbert. Paperworks. 25–26
Spiral loop card, birdcage card, praying hands cards, chimney/crane card, Santa Claus card. Araki. Origami for Christmas. 136–41
Stenciled Christmas cards. Meyer. Christmas crafts. 43–48
Wild cards. Linsley. Decoupage on glass, wood, metal, rocks, shells, wax, soap, plastic, canvas, ceramic. 121–24

Greeting cards. See also **Stationery**

Grinding and polishing
Barrelling (finishing). Edwards. Lost wax casting of jewelry. 134–37
Bench grinder, hand-held grinder. Buckwalter. Homeowner's handbook of power tools. 94–108
Grinding. Fine woodworking techniques 5. 44
Grinding and grinding equipment. Sainsbury. Craft of woodturning. 57–61
Machine polishing. Edwards. Lost wax casting of jewelry. 137–40
Sand blast finishing. Edwards. Lost wax casting of jewelry. 133–34

Growth charts
Bunny growth chart. Roda. Fabric decorating for the home. 197–98
Child's growth chart. Scobey. First easy-to-see needlepoint workbook. 49–53
Giraffe growing chart. Coffey. Francine Coffey's celebrity sewing bee. 118
Monkey growth chart. Foose. Scrap saver's stitchery book. 33–37
Zip-up panel. Laury. Treasury of needlecraft gifts for the new baby. 28–29

Gun cabinets
Cabinet for your guns, custom-fit gun rack. Popular Mechanics do-it-yourself encyclopedia. Vol. 9, 1378–83
Economy gun cabinet. Blackwell. Johnny Blackwell's poor man's catalog. 104
Gun cabinet. Complete handyman do-it-yourself encyclopedia. 800–05
Gun case. Latham. Leathercraft. 162–69
Gun rack. Spence. Woodworking tools, materials, processes. 615
North Plains gun cover. Scurlock. Muzzleloader Magazine's book of buckskinning II. 55–56

Gun holsters. See **Holsters**

Gun models
Air cannons. Complete handyman do-it-yourself encyclopedia. 2280–85
Ship's cannon. Briney. Home machinist's handbook. 256–60
24-pounder cannon from the U. S. Constitution. Popular Mechanics do-it-yourself encyclopedia. Vol. 4, 574–80

Gutters (roof)
Gutters and downspouts. Bragdon. Homeowner's complete manual of repair & improvement. 498–503
How to install gutters and downspouts, how to keep your gutters and downspouts functioning. Popular Mechanics do-it-yourself encyclopedia. Vol. 9, 1384–93
Maintenance of gutters and downspouts. Geary. Complete handbook of exterior repair and maintenance. 65–87
Roof work. Brightman. 101 practical uses for propane torches. 49–60
Taking care of gutters and downspouts. Outdoor projects for home and garden. 88–100

Gymnastic equipment
Balance beams. Boeschen. Successful playhouses. 67
Parallel bars, high bar. Dal Fabbro. How to make children's furniture and play equipment. 166–69

H

Hair decorations
Bead hair tie. Hulbert. Creative beadwork. 34
Braided ribbon barrette, dragonfly hair comb, comb with ruffle and wrapped cord comb. Wilson. Needlework to wear. 137, 141
Brooches made of hair. Whatnot. 149–50
Butterfly hair ornament, fabric-covered barrettes, belt head band, and felt buttons and flowers. Farlie. Pennywise boutique. 103–09
Chignon net (crocheted). Creative crafts yearbook: an exciting new collection of needlework and crafts. 137
Cold weather headbands. Brown. Super sweater idea book. 186–87
Combs and barrettes. Linsley. Great bazaar. 41
Crochet trim for a comb. Creative crafts yearbook: an exciting new collection of needlework and crafts. 137
Hair decorations. Couldridge. The hat book. 108–17
Hair ornaments: crocheted lace flowers, ribbon flowers, embroidered. Woman's Day bazaar best sellers. 51
Hair ribbons, bows, rosettes, and stars and hairbands. Evans. Ribbonwork. 26–30
Personalized silver and bead barrette. Metalcrafting encyclopedia. 174–75
Woven cloth or copper wire barrettes. Krevitsky. Shaped weaving. 87–89

Halloween
Door decoration, window decorations. Lyon. Arts and crafts objects children can make for the home. 82–85
Witches on broomsticks for Halloween. Janitch. Candlemaking and decorations. 41–42

Hammers
Ball peen hammer. Briney. Home machinist's handbook. 225–31
Heavy stone hammer. McRaven. Country blacksmithing. 100
How to use a claw hammer. Popular Mechanics do-it-yourself encyclopedia. Vol. 5, 745

Hammocks
Hammock. Boeschen. Successful playhouses. 16
Hammock. DeLeon. Basketry book. 126–32
Hammock. Grainger. Creative ropecraft. 110–13
Hammock and pillow covers. Creative sewing. 54
Hammocks. Better Homes and Gardens sewing for your home. 197

Installing a hammock. Andrews. How to make your own hammock and lie in it. 93–96
Knitted hammock. Woman's Day book of gifts to make. 40–41
Making Brazilian, naval, twin oaks and sprang hammocks. Andrews. How to make your own hammock and lie in it. 26–91
Stenciled hammock. Creative sewing. 58
Woven hammock. Wilson. Weaving you can use. 76

Handbags. *See* **Purses**

Handicapped.
Adopting clothing designs for the handicapped. Farmer. Concepts of fit. 212–16
Grainger. Making aids for disabled living.
Playground for handicapped children. Boeschen. Successful playhouses. 80–81
Wheelchair cart. Sullivan. Cart book, with plans & projects. 243–48

Handkerchiefs
Crochet-edge hankies, personalized ironed on letters. Woman's Day bazaar best sellers. 53, 151
Handkerchief. Gehret. Rural Pennsylvania clothing. 205–07
Hankie with lace trim. Svinicki. Old-fashioned crochet. 117–18
Tie dyed large handkerchief. Frame. Tie-dyeing and batik. 52–53
Victorian handkerchief bag. Walters. Crochet. 60–61

Hanging baskets
Aluminum hanging planter. Woman's Day book of weekend crafts. 42–45
Bentwood planters. Capotosto. Woodworking techniques and projects. 103–08
Chives plant hanger. Dodge. Step-by-step new-macrame. 41–42
Flowerpot holders (macrame). McCall's book of America's favorite needlework and crafts. 391–94
Four-card macrame hanging planter, macrame doubledecker hanging planter. Scharf. Butterick's fast and easy needlecrafts. 142–43, 146–48
Hang it (macrame). Creative crafts yearbook: an exciting new collection of needlework and crafts. 14–16
Hang-up. Design crochet. 198–99
Hanging flower basket. Maynard. Modern basketry from the start. 139–40
Hanging plant holder. Hamilton. Build it together. 1–7
Hanging plant holders. Parker. Beginning book of off-loom weaving. 195–99
Hanging planter. Pottery step-by-step. 33
Hanging planter from squares. Scharf. Illustrated patchwork crochet. 158–60
Hanging planter made of crocheted rings. Scharf. Butterick's fast and easy needlecrafts. 138–39
Hanging planter using the Egyptian braid. Dendel. Basic book of fingerweaving. 107
Hanging planters. Braren. Homemade. 50–53
Jute plant hanger. DeLeon. Basketry book. 103–07
Jute planter. Jacobs. Crochet book. 169–70
Macrame plant holder. Casselman. Crafts from around the world. 27–28
Macrame plant-pot hangers. Blandford book of traditional handicrafts. 17–18
Macrame pot hangers. Encyclopedia of crafts. 232
Plant hammock in crochet. Woman's Day decorative needlework for the home. 143–45
Plant hanger. Feldman. Needlework boutique. 100–01
Plant hangers. Halliday. Decorating with crochet. 112–16
Queen conch hanging plant holder. Elbert. Shell craft. 48–49
Small plant hanger. Anderson. Crafts and the disabled. 117–18

Sparkling beaded plant hangers, plastic bowl, cutting board, fancy tube, coconut, and twig basket planters. Doherty. Family Circle book of 429 great gifts-to-make for 10¢ to $10.00. 98–102

Wooden sky gardens. Wood projects for the garden. 62–63

Woven plant hanger. Holland. Weaving primer. 38–39

Hanukkah decorations

Hanukkah menorah, Gucci ribbons Christmas arrangement, holiday swag, holiday sleigh decoration, Victorian winter display. Wiita. Dried flowers for all seasons. 91–95

Hardware

Doorknobs and handles, gearstick and walking stick knobs. Sainsbury. Woodworking projects with power tools. 55–72

Handmade door hardware. Rowland. Handcrafted doors & windows. 60–65

House hardware. McRaven. Country blacksmithing. 111–34

Inlaid brasswork and other furniture metal work. Wenn. Restoring antique furniture. 72–73

Miscellaneous carriage hardware. Richardson. Practical blacksmithing. Vol. 4, 1–40

Shaker pegboard. Moser. How to build shaker furniture. 202–03

Techniques of making hardware. Bealer. Art of blacksmithing. 204–44

Wall hooks and brackets. Blandford. Practical handbook of blacksmithing and metalworking. 264–70

Wooden hardware. Martensson. Woodworker's bible. 202–03

Hassocks. *See* **Footstools**

Hat boxes

Fabric covered round hat box. Roda. Fabric decorating for the home. 135–36

Felt hatbox. Goldman. Decorate with felt. 122–24

Round hat-box in cane. Maynard. Modern basketry from the start. 148–51

Hats

Baby's cap. Morgan. Trapunto and other forms of raised quilting. 185

Beach hat (sewn). Burns. Super sewing. 291

Beret for a child. Ickis. Weaving as a hobby. 13–14

Bonnet. Grainger. Creative papercraft. 77

Cap. Gehret. Rural Pennsylvania clothing. 64–71

Chef's apron and hat. Creative crafts yearbook: an exciting new collection of needlework and crafts. 150–51

Child's cane hat. Maynard. Modern basketry from the start. 149, 151

Dreher. From the neck up.

Dress-up hat, Mary Poppins hat and heirloom baby bonnet. Farlie. Pennywise boutique. 158–64

Fabric hat and visor cap. Ruggieri. Woman's Day book of no-pattern sewing. 115

Fabric hats from flat patterns. Couldridge. The hat book. 24–37

Fur hats, collars and cuffs. Time-Life Books. Novel materials. 134–43

Hat patterns. Dittrick. Hard crochet. 124–39

Instructions for the broomstick lace purse and hat. Time-Life Books. Decorative techniques. 158–63

Instructions for the trapunto stole and hat. Time-Life Books. Boutique attire. 122–23

Jacket and tam made of narrow-woven strips. Tod. Joy of hand weaving. 301–02

Lace cap (sewn). Benton. Sewing classic clothes for children. 29–31

Mad cap. Holderness. Peasant chic. 66–69

Making a mobcap, Canadian cap. Scurlock. Muzzleloader Magazine's book of buckskinning II. 73, 82

Making rush hats. Cane, rush and straw. 107–09
Men's hats for women. Couldridge. The hat book. 118–25
Packable rain hat. Reader's Digest complete guide to sewing. 498–99
Paper plate hat. Yoder. Sculpture and modeling for the elementary school. 40–41
Rejuvenated hat, floppy knit hat, felt brimmed hat and rainy day hat and umbrella.
    Farlie. Pennywise boutique. 127–31
Rosy and sunny cloches. Crochet. 83–86
Scarves as hats. Couldridge. The hat book. 38–47
Simple turbans. Couldridge. The hat book. 64–71
Slices of calico hat and patchwork hat. Heard. Complete guide to quilting. 255–57
Smocked bonnet. Benton. Sewing classic clothes for children. 32–35
Softest baby bonnet. Brown. Super sweater idea book. 192
String quilted snap-on hat. Fanning. Complete book of machine quilting. 231–32
Summer sun hats. Woman's Day book of gifts to make. 44–46, 48–49
Trapper's fur cap. Wilder. Secrets of Eskimo skin sewing. 84–92
Tube hat and scarf. Brown. Super sweater idea book. 183–84
Uzbek cap. Gostelow. Complete international book of embroidery. 146
Watermelon hat and pockets. Foose. More scrap saver's stitchery. 24–25
Wool cap. Holland. Weaving primer. 115–16

Hats, Crocheted
All in the family: caps and scarves. Feldman. Needlework boutique. 43–44
Baby bonnet. Great granny crochet book. 100
Baby's Santa hat. American School of Needlework. Great Christmas crochet book. 116
Basic brimmed hat. Jacobs. Crochet book. 83–84
Beret, hat with brim, and child's cap. Reader's Digest complete guide to needlework.
    371
Checked and flower-band caps. Crochet. 79–82
Children's hat, scarf and mitten sets. Henderson. Woman's Day book of designer
    crochet. 152–57
Child's hat. Walters. Crochet. 52
Child's red crochet hat. Rosenthal. Not-so-nimble needlework book. 126
Crocheted cap with earflaps, white crocheted cap. Better Homes and Gardens easy
    bazaar crafts. 41, 46
Crocheted hat. Creative sewing. 22
Crocheted hat, ombre beret, cartwheel hat, fluffy hat, houndstooth hat, popcorn
    trimmed hat, Juliet mesh cap, mother-daughter hats. Woman's Day crochet show-
    case. 27, 68–74, 77, 121
Crocheted hats. Crochet. 19–22, 30, 39, 42
Crocheted summer hats. Woman's Day book of gifts to make. 142–45
Deerstalker's cap. Feldman. Needlework boutique. 126–27
Dress and hat. Complete book of baby crafts. 66–67
Granny square hat (crocheted). Rosenthal. Not-so-nimble needlework book. 130
Hat. Design crochet. 107–08
Hat. Gault. Crafts for the disabled. 79–80
His-her country hats, natty cap. Woman's Day crochet showcase. 169–70
Hooded scarf. Feldman. Needlework boutique. 46–48
Looped hat. Encyclopedia of crafts. 100
Men's cossack hat. Jacobs. Crochet book. 129
Net hat. Jacobs. Crochet book. 48–50
Openwork brimmed hat. Crochet. 59
Openwork cloche hat, openwork hat with lacy brim, bulky brimmed hat with flower
    applique trim. Scharf. Butterick's fast and easy needlecrafts. 92–96, 101–05
Pretty smart choice: crochet hat in navy and white. Creative crafts yearbook: an excit-
    ing new collection of needlework and crafts. 155
Pull-on patchwork hat. Scharf. Illustrated patchwork crochet. 168

Sportsman's hat made from aluminum beer cans. Epple. Something from nothing crafts. 170–75

Stiff-brimmed hat. Scharf. Illustrated patchwork crochet. 168–69

Striped demi-cloche. Jacobs. Crochet book. 78–79

Studded cloche. Time-Life Books. Boutique attire. 167

Summer hats. Henderson. Woman's Day book of designer crochet. 107–12

Three crocheted hats. Step by step to better knitting and crochet. 216–17

Tricolor crocheted cap, cold weather cap for girls or boys, christening cap. Doherty. Family Circle book of 429 great gifts-to-make all year round for just 10¢ to $10.00. 58, 165, 170

Twist edge hat, rolled-brim hat and muff, cuffed hats. Woman's Day bazaar best sellers. 21–24

Two bonnets (crocheted). Complete book of baby crafts. 62–63

Winter hats. Henderson. Woman's Day book of designer crochet. 113–21

Hats, Decorations

Bargello hatband. Christensen. Needlepoint and bargello stitchery. 66–67

Feather hat band. Johnson. Nature crafts. 123

Hat band and bag handle (woven). Golden book of hand and needle arts. 130

Hat bands. Latham. Leathercraft. 36–47

Hatband. Burchette. More needlework blocking and finishing. 93–94

Roman stripe three-piece set (needlepoint hatband). Boyles. Needlework gifts for special occasions. 69

Whimsical hat trims. Woman's Day creative stitchery from scraps. 19–23

Hats, Embroidered

Flowered hat. Sayles. Step-by-step stitchery. 66–67

Hats, Felt

Felt hat. Creative sewing. 14

Flat hat. Gehret. Rural Pennsylvania clothing. 84–87

Winter felt hats. Couldridge. The hat book. 48–63

Hats, Knitted

Cable-stitched sweater, leggings, and cap. Knitting. 122

Cap from Sweden. Compton. Complete book of traditional knitting. 182–83

Child and adult hat, mittens and socks spiral knit set. Knitting. 123

Child's rainbow stocking cap. Evrard. Homespun crafts from scraps. 104–07

Fair Isle scarf, hat and gloves. Morgan. Traditional knitting patterns of Ireland, Scotland and England. 87–89

Fisherman's hat. Gladstone. Kid's clothes by Meredith Gladstone. 52–54

For his skiing, a cap and mittens. Feldman. Needlework boutique. 142–45

Honeycomb, striped, & mosaic pattern hats. Knitting techniques and projects. 63–65

Knit Aran hat. Hollingworth. Complete book of traditional Aran knitting. 131–33

Knitted hats. Chatterton. Scandinavian knitting designs. 222–27

Knitted hats. Couldridge. The hat book. 88–95

Mans' or boys' knitted cap, Cossack hat, collegiate striped hat, Fair Isle cap. Doherty. Family Circle book of 429 great gifts-to-make all year round for just 10¢ to $10.00. 103–04, 108–11, 114–15, 119

Midnight sun child's dress and hat (Lapland). Starmore. Scandinavian knitwear. 36–40

Patchwork hats. Selfridge. Patchwork knitting. 150–51

Peruvian hat. Knitting. 74

Rainbow-striped pullover and matching hat. Knitting. 50

Reversible hat and mittens. Neighbors. Reversible two-color knitting. 155–56

Rib-knit ski hoods, two-tone hats, rolled-brim hat & scarf, tasseled stocking cap and leg warmers. Woman's Day bazaar best sellers. 20–25

Seed-stitch and rib-stitch hat and scarf sets. Hubert. Weekend knitting projects. 16–17
Sequined jacket and cap. Knitting. 31
Spot sweater and cap. Knitting. 118
Striped garter stitch hat. Reader's Digest complete guide to needlework. 253
Suomi child's coat, hat & dress (Finland). Starmore. Scandinavian knitwear. 89–94
Toddler sweater, hat, mittens and socks spiral knit set. Knitting. 126
Toddler's hat and mittens. Mills. The book of presents. 116
Turkish hat. Time-Life Books. Boutique attire. 166–67
Two-tone helmet. Complete book of baby crafts. 30
Two-toned and scarf set. Hubert. Weekend knitting projects. 58
V-neck halter and hat. Knitting. 34
Various knitted hats. Step by step to better knitting and crochet. 126–27
Watch cap for child and adult. Rosenthal. Not-so-nimble needlework book. 142–43
Winter warmers. Mills. Book of presents. 114–15

Hats, Leather
Leather hats. Latham. Leathercraft. 158–62

Hats, Straw
Hat with batik scarf. Frame. Tie-dyeing and batik. 94–97
Straw hats. Hibbs. Straw sculpture. 88–94
Summer straw hats. Couldridge. The hat book. 72–87

Headbands
Batik headband. Anderson. Tie dyeing and batik. 64–67
Brow bands. Wilson. Needlework to wear. 137
Nihoniho and straight-edged headbands. Bird. Craft of Hawaiian lauhala weaving. 39–69
Woven beaded head band. Hulbert. Creative beadwork. 65

Headboards. See **Beds, Headboards**

Headdress
Masks and head-dresses. Tyler. Big book of soft toys. 69–70

Headscarves
After-swim cap and matching beach bag. Feldman. Needlework boutique. 133
Batik headband. Frame. Tie-dyeing and batik. 86–89
Braid-trimmed vest and head scarf. Knitting. 55
Head scarf. Ley. Russian & other slavic embroidery designs. 38–41
Lace wrap around (crocheted). Feldman. Needlework boutique. 61–62
Scarf (embroidered and beaded). Silverstein. Mira Silverstein's guide to looped and knotted stitches. 87, 68
Silk tie-dyed scarf. Anderson. Tie dyeing and batik. 24–27
Toddler's dress and headscarf (crocheted). Complete book of baby crafts. 68–69
Triangular head scarf (knitted). Rosenthal. Not-so-nimble needlework book. 141

Heating
Heating. Bragdon. Homeowner's complete manual of repair & improvement. 458–73
How to repair portable room heaters, how to choose the right space heater, get more heat from a space heater, how to save money on heating your home. Popular Mechanics do-it-yourself encyclopedia. Vol. 9, 1407–09, 1419–39
Installing a baseboard heater. Time-Life Books. New living spaces. 104–05
Tin-can space heater. Popular Mechanics do-it-yourself encyclopedia. Vol. 4, 543
Window heater, solar air heater. Calhoun. 20 simple solar projects. 164–93
Wood stove heater. Braren. Homemade. 21

Heating pads, Electric
Heating pad cover. Rosenthal. Not-so-nimble needlework book. 25

Helicopter models
Model helicopter. McEntee. Radio control handbook. 320–49

Hex signs
Hex signs. Shea. Pennsylvania Dutch and their furniture. 148–54
Pennsylvania Dutch barn signs. Daniele. Building early American furniture. 171–72

High chairs. *See* **Children's furniture, Chairs**

Hinges
Brass hinges, forged door hinges. Make it! don't buy it. 226–29, 278–83
Forging hinges. Weygers. Modern blacksmith. 52–54
Hinge pin cutout. McRaven. Country blacksmithing. 119
Hinge repairs & installations. Jones. Fixing furniture. 37–41
Installing hinges. Handyman. 161–63
Swing it on the right hinge. Popular Mechanics do-it-yourself encyclopedia. Vol. 10, 1450–53

Hobbyhorses
Basic horse, hobbyhorse, rocking pony. Peterson. Children's toys you can build yourself. 127–34
Elegant hobbyhorse, wooden rocking horse, stick reindeer. Better Homes and Gardens treasury of Christmas crafts & foods. 153, 247–49, 270
Hobby horse. Blandford. Giant book of wooden toys. 146
Hobby horse. Favorite easy-to-make toys. 91–94
Hobby horse, rocking horse. DeCristoforo. Build your own wood toys, gifts and furniture. 246–61
Hobbyhorse, rocking horse. Hundley. Folk art toys and furniture for children. 23–35
Hobby horse, rocking horse. Maginley. Toys to make and ride. 15–21
Rocking horse. Blandford. 66 children's furniture projects. 410–18
Rocking horse. Blizzard. Making wooden toys. 44–48
Rocking horse. Daniels. Building early American furniture. 166–67
Stick stallion, old-fashioned rocking horse, country rocking horse. Baldwin. Old fashioned wooden toys. 84–86, 162–67, 199–206
Trestle rocking horse. Blandford. Giant book of wooden toys. 62–68

Hockey
Build a tabletop hockey game. Popular Mechanics do-it-yourself encyclopedia. Vol. 1, 58–60
Hockey stick (repair). Schuler. How to fix almost everything. 103–04
Hockey table. Dal Fabbro. How to make children's furniture and play equipment. 144–45
Table hockey. Blandford. Giant book of wooden toys. 200–02

Holsters
Gun holster. Latham. Leathercraft. 84–92, 130–37

Homespun weaving. *See* **Weaving**

Hooked rugs. *See* **Rugs**

Horn work
Fur trade horn, French & Indian and Revolutionary War horns, minute-man horn, rum horn. Scurlock. Muzzleloader Magazine's book of buckskinning II. 117–48
Horn can be carved and formed. Tangerman. Carving the unusual. 113–15

Horses
American war horse. Ormond. American primitives in needlepoint. 81–88
Felt pony (stuffed). Complete book of baby crafts. 160–61
Portable horse stable. Braren. Homemade. 151–53

Horses, Model
Horse. Grainger. Creative papercraft. 49–52
Zimmerman. Carving horses in wood.

Hose holders
Hose box. Wood projects for the garden. 76
Hose reels. Outdoor projects for home and garden. 428–30
Hose storage. Braren. Homemade. 65

Hosiery. See **Stockings**

Hot dish mats. See **Table mats; Trivets**

Hot rods. See **Automobiles, Racing**

Hot water heaters. See **Water heaters**

Hotbeds. See **Cold frames**

Hour glasses. See **Timing devices**

House construction
Badzinski. House construction.
Carpentry. Wagner. Modern woodworking. 356–83
Coopered columns. Fine woodworking techniques 5. 112–17
Factory manufactured homes. Spence. General carpentry. 473–82
Frame carpentry. Fine woodworking techniques 3. 199–209
Framing dormers. Spence. General carpentry. 246–47
Housewrights. Underhill. Wood wright's companion. 179–89
Locating and leveling a building. Spence. General carpentry. 121–30
Post and beam construction. Spence. General carpentry. 462–72
Ramsey. Building a log home from scratch or kit.
Solar heated guest house. Churchill. Backyard building book II. 9–26
Spence. General carpentry
Stone house. Nickey. Stoneworker's bible. 199–243
Three bedroom A-frame house, geodesic dome, guest house, yurt guest house. Churchill. Backyard building book. 44–58, 69–84
Vacation homes, vacation home for your RV. Popular Mechanics do-it-yourself encyclopedia. Vol. 19, 3010–26

House numbers
House number lit up. Popular Mechanics do-it-yourself encyclopedia. Vol. 10, 1487
House number sign. Modern general shop. Metalworking. 95–96
Key house numbers. Popular Mechanics do-it-yourself encyclopedia. Vol. 20, 3067

House painting
Banov. Book of successful painting.
Brush cleaner. Braren. Homemade. 20
Fundamental purposes of painting, paints and equipment. Adams. Arco's complete
woodworking handbook. 509–69
Interior & exterior house painting. Handyman. 119–46
Painting. Bragdon. Homeowner's complete manual of repair & improvement. 52–61
Painting and preserving. Nunn. Home improvement, home repair. 216–28
Painting home interiors and exteriors. Family handyman handbook of home improve-
ment and remodeling. 353–97
Painting—preparation, sequence of and cleanup. Guide to wallpaper and paint. 66–98

House painting, Exterior
Exterior house painting. Nunn. Home paint book. 1–79
Exterior house painting. Scherer. Complete handbook of home painting. 103–14
Exterior painting. Bragdon. Homeowner's complete manual of repair & improvement.
518–27
Exterior painting of home. Geary. Complete handbook of home exterior repair and
maintenance. 91–152
House painting with a regional flavor. Popular Mechanics do-it-yourself encyclopedia.
Vol. 10, 1488–91
Paint your house with a roller, how to pick the right roller, right way to paint your
house. Popular Mechanics do-it-yourself encyclopedia. Vol. 13, 2029–38
Painting, blister and peel prevention, choosing paints, equipment and materials. Out-
door projects for home and garden. 125–72
Right way to paint a room, pick the right painting tools, how to paint with spray cans.
Popular mechanics do-it-yourself encyclopedia. Vol. 13, 2045–53

House painting, Interior
Interior house painting. Nunn. Home paint book. 1–79
Interior house painting. Painting & wallpapering. 3–54
Interior house painting. Scherer. Complete handbook of home painting. 91–102
Painting. Wheeler. Interior painting, wall-papering & paneling. 5–72

House restoration
Johnson. Old house woodwork restoration.

House wiring. *See* **Electric wiring**

I

Ice buckets
Floral ice bucket. Scobey. Decorating with needlepoint. 159–61
Needlepoint covered ice bucket. Burchette. Needlework. 75–76
Stave construction ice bucket. Nish. Creative woodturning. 164–71

Icons
Antique icon. Picturemaking. 14–17

Indian costume
Buffalo headdress, robe. Schuman. Art from many hands. 206–08
Indian breeches, shirts, dresses, belts, headdresses, armbands, anklets, jewelry.
Whitney. American Indian clothes and how to make them. 27–89
Indian head dress, shirt, vest, leggings, robe, blankets. Norbeck. Book of authentic
Indian life crafts. 19–64

Indian costume. *See also* **Moccasins**

Indian tepees. *See* **Tents**

Indians
Indian. Day. Complete book of rock crafting. 117–20
Indian maiden-hand puppet. Meilach. Macrame gnomes and puppets. 80–83

Infant clothing
Afghan coat with cross-stitch embroidery (crocheted). Mensinga-Biasiny. Beautiful
  baby clothes to crochet, knit, sew, and embroider. 71–75
Baby blue kimono and slippers. Mensinga-Biasiny. Beautiful baby clothes to crochet,
  knit, sew and embroider. 33–38
Baby gown. Practical needlework. 110–15
Baby shirt and soaker, hooded baby jacket, baby helmet and mittens. Woman's Day
  crochet showcase. 105–06, 108–09, 128–29
Baby's angel top. Evans. Ribbonwork. 81–85
Baby's cardigan (crocheted). Mills. The book of presents. 16
Baby's cardigan with Fair Isle borders. Morgan. Traditional knitting patterns of Ireland,
  Scotland and England. 97–99
Baby's dress (smocked). Creative crafts yearbook: an exciting new collection of
  needlework and crafts. 39–41
Baby's embroidered shirt & jacket. Doherty. Family Circle book of 429 great gifts-to-
  make all year round for just 10¢ to $10.00. 164–65
Baby's striped robe. Step by step to better knitting and crochet. 41–42
Bath cape and wash mitten. Mensinga-Biasiny. Beautiful baby clothes to crochet, knit,
  sew and embroider. 125–26
Bonnet and sacque. Mensinga-Biasiny. Beautiful baby clothes to crochet, knit, sew
  and embroider. 156–57
Bright bandanas (shirt, kimono, robe, sundress, dress). Mensinga-Biasiny. Beautiful
  baby clothes to crochet, knit, sew and embroider. 132–41
Cap and sacque and jumpsuit. Crochet. 115
Child's guernsey duffle jacket, baby's guernsey. Morgan. Traditional knitting patterns of
  Ireland, Scotland and England. 46–58
Cozy baby bag (crocheted). Step by step to better knitting and crochet. 152
Cozy hooded cape. Step by step to better knitting and crochet. 221–22
Crochet hat and sacque, surplice sweater and hat, two-tone helmet and mitts, no-
  thumbs mittens and bonnet. Woman's Day bazaar best sellers. 60–68
Crocheted baby's overalls. Favorite knitting & crochet patterns. 28–30
Cross-stitch shirt. Mensinga-Biasiny. Beautiful baby clothes to crochet, knit, sew and
  embroider. 149–51
Cute suit, junior jumpsuits. Favorite knitting & crochet patterns. 138–140
Dress and jacket (knit). Complete book of baby crafts. 15–17
Dress in variegated yarn (knit). Mensinga-Biasiny. Beautiful baby clothes to crochet,
  knit, sew and embroider. 95–96
For the little one: crocheted jacket and bonnet. Step by step to better knitting and
  crochet. 269–72
Fur trimmed jacket and bag. Laury. Treasury of needlecraft gifts for the new baby.
  141–43
Garter drop-stitch smock and slippers (knit). Mensinga-Biasiny. Beautiful baby clothes
  to crochet, knit, sew and embroider. 91–94
Gifts for the baby to wear (shirts, pants and gowns). Laury. Treasury of needlecraft
  gifts for the new baby. 40–42
Granny square sweater, poncho, and bonnet. Scharf. Illustrated patchwork crochet.
  172–73

Hat, mittens and booties set (knit). Mensinga-Biasiny. Beautiful baby clothes to crochet, knit, sew and embroider. 86–87

Irish lace yoke dress, bloomers and bonnet (crocheted). Mensinga-Biasiny. Beautiful baby clothes to crochet, knit, sew and embroider. 58–65

Kimono and booties (knit). Mensinga-Biasiny. Beautiful baby clothes to crochet, knit, sew and embroider. 102–05

Knitted baby caftan. Treasury of things to make. 16–17

Knitted baby sweater and hat. Reader's Digest complete guide to needlework. 351

Knitted baby wardrobe. Favorite knitting & crochet patterns. 126–32

Knitted lace pattern baby set & Aran baby set. McCall's big book of knit & crochet for home & family. 64–65, 72–73

Knitted layette sweater. McCall's big book of knit & crochet for home & family. 42

Lacy coat. Complete book of baby crafts. 56–57

Lacy layette (knit) (shawl, jacket, dress, cardigans, leggings, undershirt, bonnet, booties and mittens). Complete book of baby crafts. 10–14

Last-minute project (undershirt). Mensinga-Biasiny. Beautiful baby clothes to crochet, knit, sew and embroider. 159

Made to match: crocheted quilt, pillow, sweater, pants. Favorite knitting & crochet patterns. 22–24

Marshmallow fluff baby layette. Great granny crochet book. 94–97

Matinee coat (crocheted). Blandford book of traditional handicrafts. 27–28

Norwegian sleeper. Mensinga-Biasiny. Beautiful baby clothes to crochet, knit, sew and embroider. 106–08

Openwork top (crocheted). Complete book of baby crafts. 52–53

Overalls and pullover (knit). Complete book of baby crafts. 32–34

Pants and top (knit). Complete book of baby crafts. 18–19

Quilted baby's jacket. McNeill. Quilting. 44

Rabbit motif-trimmed playsuit (crocheted). Complete book of baby crafts. 39–41

Ribbon baby bonnet. American School of Needlework. Great crochet bazaar book. 13–14

Scallops of lace (hairpin lace layette). Feldman. Handmade lace and patterns. 115

Shell pattern outfit (crocheted) (jacket, bonnet). Complete book of baby crafts. 49–51

Sleeping bag. Mensinga-Biasiny. Beautiful baby clothes to crochet, knit, sew and embroider. 158

Snowsuit (knit). Mensinga-Biasiny. Beautiful baby clothes to crochet, knit, sew and embroider. 97–99

Stretchy top. Complete book of baby crafts. 105–07

Striped robe (knit). Complete book of baby crafts. 31–32

Striped sleeping bag (crocheted). Complete book of baby crafts. 38

Striped tank top and soakers (knit). Mensinga-Biasiny. Beautiful baby clothes to crochet, knit, sew and embroider. 83–85

Sunbonnet Sue or Sam baby hats. Woman's Day book of gifts to make. 11–13

Sunsuit (crocheted). Mensinga-Biasiny. Beautiful baby clothes to crochet, knit, sew and embroider. 39–40

Swiss smock. Mensinga-Biasiny. Beautiful baby clothes to crochet, knit, sew and embroider. 142–43

T-shirt and soakers (crocheted). Mensinga-Biasiny. Beautiful baby clothes to crochet, knit, sew and embroider. 43–45

Textured stitch layette (crocheted) (blanket, jacket, cardigan, dress, pullover, overalls, bonnet, booties and mittens). Complete book of baby crafts. 42–48

Three baby smocks. Step by step to better knitting and crochet. 165–67

Three-piece quilted calico set (jacket, hat & booties). Mensinga-Biasiny. Beautiful baby clothes to crochet, knit, sew and embroider. 127–29

Traditional baby layette. American School of Needlework. Great crochet bazaar book. 21–25

Two-piece suit (crocheted). Complete book of baby crafts. 58–59

Warm woolen jacket and booties (knit). Mensinga-Biasiny. Beautiful baby clothes to crochet, knit, sew and embroider. 88–90
Woven layette, knitted layette, crocheted layette. Better Homes and Gardens easy bazaar crafts. 50–53, 56–61
Wrap cardigan. Crochet. 118
Yellow jacket and bonnet. Mensinga-Biasiny. Beautiful baby clothes to crochet, knit, sew and embroider. 46–52

Infant clothing. See also **Blankets, Infants; Buntings; Christening robes**

Infant slings
Baby carrier. Laury. Treasury of needlecraft gifts for the new baby. 90–93
Baby carrier. Wilson. Weaving you can use. 118–19
Baby carrier or baby tote. Linsley. Great bazaar. 62–63
Baby-carrying sling. Complete book of baby crafts. 86–89
Baby sling. Coffey. Francine Coffey's celebrity sewing bee. 140–41
Infant carriers. Stiles. Easy-to-make children's furniture. 46–48
Quilted portable bed. Complete book of baby crafts. 72–74

Infants, Equipment
Baby basket. Better Homes and Gardens treasury of Christmas crafts & foods. 104
Nursery accessories: baby care basket, laundry bag, diaper holder, diaper bag, cotton ball bag, coat hanger and pincushion. Complete book of baby crafts. 75–79
Ruffled carriage set. Doherty. Family Circle book of 429 great gifts-to-make all year round for just 10¢ to $10.00. 167
Schoolhouse diaper bag. Baldwin. Scrap fabric crafts. 16–18

Ink
Marking pen needlepoint. Holtje. Cardcraft. 32–36

Inkle weaving. See **Weaving**

Inkstands
Sculptured inkwell and pen and pencil tray. Gottshall. 99–101

Inlay
Cloth tape inlay. Popular Mechanics do-it-yourself encyclopedia. Vol. 10, 1537
How inlay is made, inlaying mother-of-pearl. Fine woodworking techniques 5. 180–86
Inlaying. Brumbaugh. Wood furniture finishing, refinishing, repairing. 133–48
Inlays. Richards. Handmade jewelry. 131–33
Making inlaid designs. Schuman. Art from many hands. 128–34
Routing for inlays. Fine woodworking techniques 3. 114–15
Wood inlays. Sprintzen. Jewelry, basic techniques and design. 172–76
Wooden tray, cutting board and a box resurfaced with inlaid veneers. D'Amato. Italian crafts. 88–90

Inlay. See also **Marquetry**

Insect and pest control
Fly swatter. Burchette. Needlework. 67–68
Hanging bug trap. Popular Mechanics do-it-yourself encyclopedia. Vol. 10, 1538
Wasp removal. Outdoor projects for home and garden. 113–14
What to do about termites. Popular Mechanics do-it-yourself encyclopedia. Vol. 18, 2854–56

Insects
Ladybug, caterpillar, flying insects (fly, bee and butterfly). Day. Complete book of rock crafting. 43–55
Turkey work bee. Wilson. Needleplay. 154

Insulation, Doors and Windows
Draft stopper or windjammer filled with sand. Meras. Vacation crafts. 64
Stenciled draft stops. McCall's big book of country needlecrafts. 160
Weather stripping, caulking seams. Bragdon. Homeowner's complete manual of repair & improvement. 152–55
Weatherproofing; caulking, weatherstripping, replacing windows and doors. Outdoor projects for home and garden. 22–34
Window and door recommendations. Olin. Construction. 105. 21–105. 30

Insulation (Heat)
Adding insulation. Russell. Garages and carports. 97–103
Building insulation. Olin. Construction. 105. 11–105. 20
Home insulation. Clifford. Basic woodworking and carpentry . . . with projects. 121–32
Home insulation. Morrison. Complete energy-saving home improvement guide. 56–93
How to install insulation. Popular Mechanics do-it-yourself encyclopedia. Vol. 10, 1539–41
Installing insulation. Spence. General carpentry. 347–64
Insulating a home. Geary. How-to book of floors & ceilings. 159–84
Insulation. Bragdon. Homeowner's complete manual of repair & improvement. 146–63, 374–80
Insulation. Time-Life Books. New living spaces. 102–04
Insulation and ventilation. Geary. Complete handbook of home exterior repair and maintenance. 249–63
Insulation installation. Nunn. Home improvement, home repair. 81–91
Plugging leaks and drafts. Geary. Complete handbook of home exterior repair and maintenance. 169–204
10 worst heat thieves in your home. Popular Mechanics do-it-yourself encyclopedia. Vol. 20, 3078–81
Thermal insulation, vapor barriers. Adams. Arco's complete woodworking handbook. 573–86

Insulation (sound). *See* **Soundproofing**

Invalid's furniture. *See* **Furniture for the sick**

Ironing equipment
How to repair an electric iron. Popular Mechanics do-it-yourself encyclopedia. Vol. 10, 1548–51
Ironing board. Family handyman handbook of carpentry plans/projects. 248–49

Ironwork
Decorative ironwork: scrolls, collars, square corners, quatrefoils & leaves. Blandford. Practical handbook of blacksmithing and metalworking. 277–99
Finishing iron work. Blandford. Practical handbook of blacksmithing and metalworking. 301–07
Wrought iron railings. Outdoor projects for home and garden. 418–23

Ivory
Ivory carving. Tangerman. Carving the unusual. 116–23
Ivory repair. Schuler. How to fix almost everything. 110

J

Jack-in-the-boxes
Jack in the box. Bumper book of things a boy can make. 91–93
Jack-in-the-box in cane. Maynard. Modern basketry from the start. 146–48
Jack-in-the-box. Tyler. Big book of dolls. 146–50
Jolly jump up. Blackwell. Johnny Blackwell's poor man's catalog. 136

Jackets
Afghan jacket. Crochet. 38
Arctic parka. Lamoreaux. Outdoor gear you can make yourself. 120–37
Avery. Quilts to wear.
Coolie jacket. Wiseman. Cuts of cloth. 52–53
Fringed jacket. Latham. Leathercraft. 170–79
Greek sheepherder's jacket (sewn). Holderness. Peasant chic. 16–20
Happi coat. Bradley. Design it, sew it and wear it. 33–39
Jacket woven on a frame loom. Weaving and spinning. 93–96
Jackets. Loeb. Leather book. 125–49
Man's or woman's long jacket & scarf. Design crochet. 184–88
Norwegian fisherman's jacket (sewn). Holderness. Peasant chic. 3–10
Parkas. Wilder. Secrets of Eskimo skin sewing. 93–110
Reversible jacket. Time-Life Books. Sporting scene. 114–26
Shepherd jacket or coat. Simmons. Spinning for softness and speed. 60–68
Tunisian (afghan) jacket. Walters. Crochet. 57
Striped beach jacket. Crochet. 71
Utility jacket. Lamoreaux. Outdoor gear you can make yourself. 95–104

Jackets, Children
Bomber-style jacket. Step by step to better knitting and crochet. 250–51
Boy's parka. Crochet. 123
Child's jacket. Design crochet. 68–70
Child's Japanese jacket. Laury. Quilted clothing. 74–75
Crocheted kid's cozy jackets. Favorite knitting & crochet patterns. 25–27
Knitted zippered jackets and matching pompom hats. Woman's Day bazaar best
    sellers. 70–71
Nomad child's blouson jacket (Lapland). Starmore. Scandinavian knitwear. 41–43
Patchwork jacket. Knitting techniques and projects. 41
Quilted coat. Complete book of baby crafts. 102–04

Jackets, Men
Coat (men's jacket). Gehret. Rural Pennsylvania clothing. 168–79
Estonia man's jacket (Finland). Starmore. Scandinavian knitwear. 117–19
Man's western-style jacket. Knitting. 62
Men's lounge jacket. Jacobs. Crochet book. 102–04
Trøndelag man's jacket (Norway). Starmore. Scandinavian knitwear. 25–27

Jackets, Women
American Indian patchwork jacket. Creative sewing. 23
Crocheted cotton summer blazer. Favorite knitting & crochet patterns. 76–79
Delsbø woman's mohair jacket (Sweden). Starmore. Scandinavian knitwear. 76–78
Glitter coverlet. Jacobs. Crochet book. 98–99
Halland woman's jacket (Sweden). Starmore. Scandinavian knitwear. 57–60
Hooded jacket. Great granny crochet book. 111–13
Jacket. Design crochet. 140–47
Jacket and tam made of narrow-woven strips. Tod. Joy of hand weaving. 301–02
Jackets (quilted). Laury. Quilted clothing. 46–57, 61

Karate jacket. Lane. Maggie Lane's oriental patchwork. 69–73
Knitted jacket with fake fur. Time-Life Books. Novel materials. 180–81
Knitted loose and bulky jacket, evening sparkle, check jacket, t-shaped jacket, bell cluster jacket. Step by step to better knitting and crochet. 30–31, 52–55, 75, 101–02
Painted and quilted silk jacket. Wilson. Needlework to wear. 72–73
Potpourri jacket, basketweave hooded jacket. Design crochet. 23–26, 40–46
Seamless jacket. Walters. Crochet. 68–69
Sequined jacket and cap. Knitting. 31
Silk jacket with ruched sleeves. McNeill. Quilting. 56–57
Woman's Chanel-type tweed jacket, hat and scarf set. Hubert. Weekend knitting projects. 82–83
Woman's curly battle jacket. Hubert. Weekend knitting projects. 14–15
Woman's lace and ribbon jacket. Johnson. Quiltwear. 123–27
Woman's poncho jacket. Hubert. Weekend knitting projects. 62–63

Jars
Apothecary jar. Linsley. Decoupage on glass, wood, metal, rocks, shells, wax, soap, plastic, canvas, ceramic. 84–89
Bell jar made from wine or cider jug. Epple. Something from nothing crafts. 15
Decoupage a glass jar. Giant book of crafts. 360
Hexagon jars. Coyne. Penland School of Crafts book of pottery. 21–52
Jam jar covers. McCall's big book of country needlecrafts. 137–39
Jar lid covers. Jarvey. You can dough it! 66–68
Jars and vases. Rhodes. Pottery form. 43–48
Lids and jars. Campbell. Using the potter's wheel. 44–54
Man with blinders. Coyne. Penland School of Crafts book of pottery. 77–92
Marmalade or jampot top. Sainsbury. Sainsbury's woodturning projects for dining. 164–67
Millefiore pot: night garden with ladies. Coyne. Penland School of Crafts book of pottery. 57–70
Pot tops (gingham covers for jelly and preserve jars). Creative crafts yearbook: an exciting new collection of needlework and crafts. 126
Sensational apothecary jars. Doherty. Family Circle book of 429 great gifts-to-make all year round for just 10¢ to $10.00. 2–3
Squared, inverted square and jar with cut handles. Campbell. Using the potter's wheel. 86–91
Stoppered jar, ginger jar, flange jar with the knob lid. Wettlaufer. Getting into pots. 60–66
Throwing jars and covers. Woody. Pottery on the wheel. 133–58
Thrown form. Coyne. Penland School of Crafts book of pottery. 137–52
Thrown jar and lid. Howell. Craft of pottery. 37, 45

Jet planes, Toy. *See* **Airplanes, Toy**

Jewelry
Bending simple clasps. Metalcrafting encyclopedia. 27
Bovin. Jewelry making.
Bowie. Jewelry making.
Bread dough for jewelry. Sommer. Contemporary costume jewelry. 139–40
Chains. Powers. Crafting turquoise jewelry. 122–27
Chamberlain. Metal jewelry techniques.
Clasps. Richards. Handmade jewelry. 110–15
Clay costume jewelry. Yoder. Sculpture and modeling for the elementary school. 48–49

Clay jewelry: pendants, pins, and earrings. Chroman. Potter's primer. 47–51
Creating jewelry from the sea. Elbert. 104–58
Crochet jewelry. Encyclopedia of crafts. 98
Crocheting with wire. Sommer. Contemporary costume jewelry. 37–39
Dapping to shape domes. Sprintzen. Jewelry, basic techniques and design. 47
Decals on wooden jewelry. Huckleberry. How to make your own wooden jewelry. 86–89
Decorative tooling. Sommer. Contemporary costume jewelry. 57–61
Dumbell constructional toy for necklaces, pendants, belts. Grainger. Creative paper-craft. 92
Ear clips for earrings. Richards. Handmade jewelry. 115–17
Eggshell inlays for jewelry. Sommer. Contemporary costume jewelry. 186
Enamelled jewelry set in black, white and red. Elliot. Working with copper. 92
Eyeglass lens jewelry. Sommer. Contemporary costume jewelry. 102–06
Findings. Edwards. Lost wax casting of jewelry. 120–22
Finishing wood for jewelry. Huckleberry. How to make your own wooden jewelry. 79–92
Finishing wooden jewelry. Lee. Making wood and stone jewelry. 65–67
Finishing your jewelry. Hollander. Plastics for jewelry. 16–19
Foote. Jewelry making.
Gadney. How to enter and win jewelry and metal crafts contests.
Hand made jump-ring chains. Sommer. Contemporary costume jewelry. 35–36
Handcrafted veneer jewelry. Hobbs. Veneer craft for everyone. 130–31
Hardware for wooden jewelry. Huckleberry. How to make your own wooden jewelry. 96–112
Hearts and flowers jewelry. Woman's Day creative stitchery from scraps. 8–9
Howell-Koehler. Soft jewelry.
Inlaid metal jewelry. Sommer. Contemporary costume jewelry. 50–54
Jeweled cache (stained glass). McCall's book of America's favorite needlework and crafts. 335–36
Jewelry fastenings. Gill. Beadwork: the technique of stringing, threading, and weaving. 22–26
Jewelry from rubbings. Firestein. Rubbing craft. 78–79
Jewelry making. Brightman. 101 practical uses for propane torches. 105–12
Jewelry you can carve from wood. Popular Mechanics do-it-yourself encyclopedia. Vol. 10, 1556–61
Leather and bead jewelry. Sommer. Contemporary costume jewelry. 159
Making a chain. Sjoberg. Working with copper, silver and enamel. 41–48
Making chenier for hinges. Richards. Handmade jewelry. 104–09
Making clay jewelry. Mosesson. Jewelry craft for beginners. 83–97
Making jump rings. Foote. Jewelry making. 92
Making your own chains. Elliot. Working with copper. 68–69
Making your own jump rings. Meyer. Rock tumbling. 77–78
Metal and enamel.
Metal jewelry. 101 do-it-yourself projects. 334–36
Metalworking techniques for jewelry making. Mosesson. Jewelry craft for beginners. 135–52
Mixed-media clay jewelry. Sommer. Contemporary costume jewelry. 136–39
Mokume: Japanese lamination. Sprintzen. Jewelry, basic techniques and design. 120–22
Mounting & finishing pewter jewelry. Metal and enamel. 41
Necklace, bracelet and earrings (crocheted). Creative crafts yearbook: an exciting new collection of needlework and crafts. 136–37

Needlepoint rose jewelry box. Embroidery of roses. 104–05
Needlepoint Indian jewelry. Wilson. More needleplay. 166–67
Niello. Chamberlain. Metal jewelry techniques. 115
Paper costume jewelry. Yoder. Sculpture and modeling for the elementary school. 67–71
Perspex jewelry, foil and nail varnish jewelry, macrame jewelry, macrame miniature jewelry. Encyclopedia of crafts. 201, 203, 229, 233
Photo processes on metals. Chamberlain. Metal jewelry techniques. 105–08
Plastic jewelry. Linderman. Crafts for the classroom. 358–64
Pommels. Sjoberg. Working with copper, silver and enamel. 67
Powers. Crafting turquoise jewelry.
Richards. Handmade jewelry.
Rivets, cheniers and fastening for jewelry. Edwards. Lost wax casting of jewelry. 128–31
Seed-bead tassels. Mosesson. Jewelry craft for beginners. 38–39
Setting stones. Mosesson. Jewelry craft for beginners. 192–225
Setting stones into wood. Lee. Making wood and stone jewelry. 44–49
Shaping wood for jewelry. Huckleberry. How to make your own wooden jewelry. 53–77
Silver jewelry. Rose. Illustrated encyclopedia of crafts and how to master them. 39–53
Silver jewelry. Treasury of things to make. 20–24
Solder jewelry. Sommer. Contemporary costume jewelry. 43–45
Soldered wire cages. Sommer. Contemporary costume jewelry. 40–42
Sprintzen. Jewelry, basic techniques and design.
Sunburst pin and earring set. Hibbs. Straw sculpture. 22–23
Tissue paper jewels, string & yarn jewelry and aluminum foil. Linderman. Crafts for the classroom. 335–81
Trembling flowers. (brooch, pendant or metal sculpture). Metal and enamel. 49–52
Wald. Introduction to jewelry casting.
Warwick. Beginning jewelry.
Wire jewelry. Giant book of crafts. 230–42
Wire jump rings. Metalcrafting encyclopedia. 38–39
Wire spiral jewelry. Newman. Wire art. 126–27
Wire wrapping, sheet metal settings, and built-up settings for baroque stones. Hyde. Complete book of rock tumbling. 131–48
Wood. Make your own jewelry.
Wood and stone inlay. Lee. Making wood and stone jewelry. 68–77
Wood with other materials. Lee. Making wood and stone jewelry. 78–89
Wooden costume jewelry. Sainsbury. Woodworking projects with power tools. 9–16
Woven fabric jewelry on copper wire. Krevitsky. Shaped weaving. 80–87

Jewelry, Care and repair
Beads, string broken. Schuler. How to fix almost everything. 21
Jewelry repair. Schuler. How to fix almost everything. 110
String repair. Gill. Beadwork: the technique of stringing, threading, and weaving. 37–39

Jewelry cases
Antique look Victorian jewel box. Janitch. All made from paper. 45–46
Bargello jewelry case. Christensen. Needlepoint and bargello stitchery. 74
Beaded jewelry case. Hulbert. Creative beadwork. 66
Butterfly jewelry roll. Gostelow. Cross stitch book. 99–101
Dresser-top valet, ring caddy, heart-shaped jewelry box. Popular Mechanics do-it-yourself encyclopedia. Vol. 9, 1355, 1361–62
Earring rack. Cope. Plastics. 24–25

Jewelry banners. Woman's Day creative stitchery from scraps. 72–74
Jewel box. Brown. 44 terrific wood-working plans & projects. 121–25
Jewelry box. 101 do-it-yourself projects. 192–93
Jewel box. Scobey. First easy-to-see needlepoint workbook. 129–31
Jewelry box. Spence. Woodworking tools, materials, processes. 614
Jewelry box fit for a queen, two beautiful jewel boxes. Popular Mechanics do-it-yourself
    encyclopedia. Vol. 10, 1562–69
Jewelry boxes. Sainsbury. Woodworking projects with power tools. 26–30
Jewelry keeper tree. Popular Mechanics do-it-yourself encyclopedia. Vol. 20, 3066
Jewelry rack made from spools. Epple. Something from nothing crafts. 188–89
Jewelry roll. Burchette. Needlework. 77–80
Oriental gold. Wilson. Needleplay. 184–85
Receding forms. Scheuer. Designs for Holbein Embroidery. 58–59
Renaissance jewel box. D'Amato. Italian crafts. 21–24
Ring tray. Goldman. Decorate with felt. 50
Traveling jewelry case (felt). Farlie. Pennywise boutique. 102–03
Traveling treasure case. Botsford. Between thimble & thumb. 161–67
Trinket or jewel box. Bumper book of things a girl can make. 15–16
Zippered travelling jewel case and flowering garden jewel cabinet. Wilson. Needlework
    to wear. 40–45

Jigs

Box-joint jig. Fine woodworking techniques 3. 30–31
Plywood cutoff jig. Popular Mechanics do-it-yourself encyclopedia. Vol. 14, 2236–37
Router. Capotosto. Woodworking wisdom. 84–90
Wire-straightening tools. Weygers. Recycling, use, and repair of tools. 64–65

Joints (Carpentry)

Butt joints, lap joints, dado joints, mortise-and-tenons joints, dovetailed joints, miter
    joints. Meyers. Furniture repair and refinishing. 80–86
Butterfly joint, dowel joint, frame and panel, on dovetailing carcasses, on precision
    joinery. Fine woodworking techniques 4. 125–38. 142–45
Case joinery. Cary. Building your own kitchen cabinets. 34–41
Dado and other joints. Blandford. How to make your own built-in furniture. 103–16
Dado, rabbet, mortise and tenon joints. Time-Life Books. Working with wood. 128–33
Dovetail joints. Blandford. How to make your own built-in furniture. 97–102
Dovetail joints. Popular Mechanics do-it-yourself encyclopedia. Vol. 7, 1026–29
Dowelled, mortise and tenon, dado and lap, dovetail, and screwed joints. Blandford.
    Upholsterer's bible. 413–28
Furniture joints and fastenings. Kinney. Complete book of furniture repair and refinish-
    ing. 42–49
Glued and lapped joints. Blandford. How to make your own built-in furniture. 79–86
Gluing wood. Martensson. Woodworker's bible. 212–16
How to make joints. Philbin. Cabinets, bookcases & closets. 42–53
Joinery. Fine woodworking techniques I. 86–113
Joinery. Jones. Fixing furniture. 24–33
Joinery. Roberts. Illustrated handbook of upholstery. 363–69
Joints. Blandford. 66 children's furniture projects. 53–77
Joints. Brown. 44 terrific woodworking plans & projects. 76–92
Joints: edge, halving, mortise and tenon, shelf, dovetail, and others. Blandford. How to
    make early American and colonial furniture. 45–68
Mortise and tenon joinery. Langsner. Country woodcraft. 281–89
Mortise and tenon joint, haunched mortise and tenon, mortise and tenon by machine,
    locking the joint, tapered sliding dovetails. Fine woodworking techniques 3. 56–78,
    110
Mortice-and-tenon joints, dovetail joints. Johnston. Craft of furniture making. 56–72

Rabbet and dado, professional dowel joints, short course in wood joinery. Popular Mechanics do-it-yourself encyclopedia. Vol. 10, 1571–80
Repairing dowels. Kinney. Complete book of furniture repair and refinishing. 34–41
Repairing furniture joints. Hayward. Antique furniture repairs. 98–106
Spline-mitered joinery, routing mortises, cutting box joints on the radial-arm saw, template dovetails, decorative joinery, curved dovetails, curved seat-mortise and tenon, gluing up, pole-and-wire joinery. Fine woodworking techniques 5. 70–101
Tenon and dowel joints. Blandford. How to make your built-in furniture. 87–96
Wood joining. Handyman. 377–83
Woodworking joints. Martensson. Woodworker's bible. 166–207
Woodworking joints. Waugh. Handyman's encyclopedia. 299–319

Jugs
Beaded jug cover. Hulbert. Creative beadwork. 47
Rounded jugs from a cylinder. Ceramics. 69–71

Jumpers
Child's jumper. Step by step to better knitting and crochet. 176–77
Doily jumper, blue denim jumper. Laury. Quilted clothing. 96, 102
Free-floating tunic. Woman's Day book of gifts to make. 154–56
Tunic-jumper. Henderson. Woman's Day book of designer crochet. 53–57
Versatile wraparound jumper. Time-Life Books. Boutique attire. 38–41

Jumpers, Girls
Knitted family jumper. Knitting techniques and projects. 53–54
Molly's dream jumper. Johnson. Quiltwear. 87–94
Patch jumper. Complete book of baby crafts. 115–18
Striped jumper. Woman's Day crochet showcase. 113–14

Jumping jacks
Acrobat, hammering men. Blandford. Giant book of wooden toys. 88–93
Acrobat. Bumper book of things a boy can make. 151–52
Jumping jacks. Christmas crafts book. 102–03
Jumping jacks. McCall's book of Christmas. 13–14
Limber Jim. Holz. How-to book of international dolls. 326–31
Spinning clown. Hodges. 46 step-by-step wooden toy projects. 217–21
Twisting acrobat. Blandford. Giant book of wooden toys. 72–74

Jumpsuits, Children
One-piece suit (knit). Complete book of baby crafts. 24–25
Striped jumpsuit (knit). Complete book of baby crafts. 28–29

K

Karting. *See* **Automobiles, Racing**

Kennels
Animal accommodations. Marshall. Yard buildings. 125–30
Building a dog-run. Proulx. Plan and make your own fences and gates, walkways, walls and drives. 36
Doghouse. Brann. How to build pet housing. 17–28
Doghouse. La Barge. Pet house book. 50–74
Doghouses. Lane. Building in your backyard. 47–57
Lean-to dog kennel. Brann. How to build pet housing. 114–52
Making a dog kennel. Bumper book of things a boy can make. 182–83

Key holders
Bargello key case. Christensen. Needlepoint and bargello stitchery. 71–72
Cross-stitch flower motif key ring. Great cross-stitch. 119
Egyptian eye and the mouse takes the cheese key rings. Sheldon. Washable and dryable needlepoint. 109–11
Flat-wire key ring. Metalcrafting encyclopedia. 177
Hardanger key holder. Longhurst. Vanishing American needle arts. 52–53
Key chain. Giant book of metalworking projects. 217–19
Key chains and key holders. Romberg. Let's discover papier-mâché. 60–61
Key chain (needlepoint). Christensen. The needlepoint book. 125–26
Key chains. Burchette. Needlework. 81–82
Key holder. Woman's Day book of gifts to make. 56
Key holders. Bovin. Jewelry making. 248
Key/luggage tag. Fanning. Complete book of machine quilting. 264–65
Key rack. Hamilton. Build it together. 40–45
Key ring tag of wooden cube beads. Hulbert. Creative beadwork. 60
Key ring tags. Mills. The book of presents. 98–99
Pine key cupboard (3 corner). Shea. Pennsylvania Dutch and their furniture. 192
Plastic key chain. Christensen. Teach yourself needlepoint. 86
Plastic mesh key ring tag. Rosenthal. Not-so-nimble needlework book. 90–91
Roman stripe three-piece set (needlepoint). Boyles. Needlework gifts for special occasions. 69
Turning a key tag. Sainsbury. Craft of woodturning. 167
Veneered woman's purse key finder. Hobbs. Veneer craft for everyone. 128
Wire key ring with stone. Meyer. Rock tumbling. 79–80
Wooden key holder. Linsley. Decoupage on glass, wood, metal, rocks, shells, wax, soap, plastic, canvas, ceramic. 30–35
Wooden keyholders. Richards. Handmade jewelry. 145–47
Wooden-key key chains. Woman's Day bazaar best sellers. 57

Keys. *See* **Locks and keys**

Kilns
Barn for air-drying lumber, alternative wood-drying technologies: solar energy and dehumidification. Fine woodworking techniques 4. 2–6
Building and using a kiln. Encyclopedia of crafts. 218
Building kilns; insulating existing kilns. Brodie. Energy efficient potter. 24–92
Building and firing a gas kiln. Wettlaufer. Getting into pots. 144–54
Cast kiln. Colson. Kiln building with space-age materials. 90–98
Downdraft Roman-arch kiln. Colson. Kiln building with space-age materials. 32–47
Dry kiln, solar kiln. Fine woodworking techniques I. 29–34
Efficient firing. Brodie. Energy efficient potter. 111–14.
Electric, full-burning, Roman-style, and simple kilns. Dickerson. Pottery making. 118–24
Electric kiln. Riegger. Electric kiln ceramics. 13–42
Electric table kiln. Abrams. Building craft equipment. 198–208
Firing and kilns. Howell. Craft of pottery. 113–20
Firing and making your own kiln. Casson. Craft of the potter. 94–98
Firing pottery. Wettlaufer. Getting into pots. 118–40
Firing the kiln. Sanders. (Sunset ceramics book) How to make pottery. 131–35
Firing your pots. Paak. Decorative touch. 87–106
Fournier. Electric kiln construction for potters.
Indian kiln. Norbeck. Book of authentic Indian life crafts. 182–84
Introduction to kilns and firing techniques. Ceramics. 127–34
Kiln-dry your lumber with solar heat. Popular Mechanics do-it-yourself encyclopedia. Vol. 10, 1593

Kiln theory and practice. Colson. Kiln building with space-age materials. 10–19
Kilns and firing. Woody. Pottery on the wheel. 194–97
Kilns and firing equipment. Harvey. Building pottery equipment. 80–157
New concepts in kilns. Kriwanek. Keramos. 55–73
Packing and firing the kiln. Pottery step-by-step. 49–51
Packing the bisque kiln. Dickerson. Pottery making. 88–92
Portable Raku kiln. Colson. Kiln building with space-age materials. 63–72
Production kiln with two can beds. Colson. Kiln building with space-age materials. 72–89
Raku kiln. Fournier. Electric kiln construction for potters. 139
Requirements, construction and use of kilns. Tyler. Raku. 113–36
Safety regulations, and pollution control fuel systems. Colson. Kiln building with space-age materials. 115–22
Salt firing schedule. Troy. Salt-glazed ceramics. 140–49
Salt kiln. Troy. Salt-glazed ceramics. 106–19
Sawdust kiln. Pottery step-by-step. 58–59
Stacking and kiln setting for salt glazes. Troy. Salt-glazed ceramics. 120–25
Suspension drum kiln. Colson. Kiln building with space-age materials. 48–62
Trouble shooting kilns. Colson. Kiln building with space-age materials. 107–14
Updraft catenary kiln. Colson. Kiln building with space-age materials. 20–31
Use and care of the kiln. Zorza. Pottery creating with clay. 127–41

Kissing balls
Kissenbaum. Wilson. Erica Wilson's Christmas world. 68–69
Kissing ball. Gordon. Complete guide to drying and preserving flowers. 205, 208
Kissing ball. Meras. Vacation crafts. 50
Kissing ball (plant). Johnson. Nature craft. 142
Permanent, hoop and live kissing balls. Miles. Designing with natural materials. 84–87
Pom-pom kissing ball. Nicole. Designer accessories to make for your home. 142–43

Kitchen accessories
Handy rack for food-processor parts. Popular Mechanics do-it-yourself encyclopedia. Vol. 1, 99–101
Kitchen kuties: (towel sets and hot plate mats). American School of Needlework. Great crochet bazaar book. 61–62

Kitchen appliances
Built-in range and oven. Brann. How to modernize a kitchen. 47
How to fix a food freezer, install a garbage disposer yourself, how to repair a garbage disposer. Popular Mechanics do-it-yourself encyclopedia. Vol. 9, 1286–91, 1323–29
How to fix a vacuum cleaner, tip-proof vacuum dollies. Popular Mechanics do-it-yourself encyclopedia. Vol. 19, 3028–32
How to fix your dishwasher. Popular Mechanics do-it-yourself encyclopedia. Vol. 7, 1002–08
How to repair a pop-up toaster. Popular Mechanics do-it-yourself encyclopedia. Vol. 19, 2890–95
How to repair portable food mixers, what to do when your food processor stops. Popular Mechanics do-it-yourself encyclopedia. Vol. 8, 1260–63
How to troubleshoot a food mixer. Popular Mechanics do-it-yourself encyclopedia. Vol. 12, 1858–63
Modernize a kitchen refrigerator. Brann. How to modernize a kitchen. 61–64

Kitchen cabinets
ABC's of cabinet construction, spacesaving kitchen island. Better Homes and Gardens step-by-step cabinets and shelves. 36–61, 92–93
Barbecue bar for your family room. Popular Mechanics do-it-yourself encyclopedia. Vol. 2, 171–73
Base cabinet. Brann. How to build kitchen cabinets, room dividers, and cabinet furniture. 20–25
Basic kitchen cabinets. Philbin. Cabinets, bookcases & closets. 92–95
Basics of cabinet building. Stevenson. How to build and buy cabinets for the modern kitchen. 55–104
Build this kitchen island, tip-out bin, efficient kitchen in one weekend, more storage space in your kitchen, how to install kitchen cabinets. Popular Mechanics do-it-yourself encyclopedia. Vol. 11, 1604–20
Building base cabinets. Brann. How to modernize a kitchen. 25–34
Building extra space into kitchen cabinets. Time-Life Books. Space and storage. 102–09
Built-in for kitchen and laundry. Popular Mechanic do-it-yourself encyclopedia. Vol. 3, 454–55
Built-in kitchen cabinets. Siegele. Cabinets and built-ins. 9–13, 19–22, 46–50, 61–66, 71–79
Built-in oven and cooking tops. Stevenson. How to build and buy cabinets for the modern kitchen. 163–70
Built-in refrigerator enclosure. Brann. How to build kitchen cabinets, room dividers and cabinet furniture. 35–39
Built-in serving bar. Family handyman handbook of carpentry plans/projects. 98–100
Cabinets. Syvanen. Interior finish: more tricks of the trade. 105–13
Cary. Building your own kitchen cabinets.
Conventional kitchen cabinets. Brann. How to build kitchen cabinets, room dividers, and cabinet furniture. 79–96
Corner cabinets. Stevenson. How to build and buy cabinets for the modern kitchen. 173–88
Counter range cabinet. Feirer. Cabinetmaking and millwork. 209
Country kitchen sideboard. Gottshall. Provincial furniture design and construction. 35–38
Do-it-yourself kitchen counters. Family handyman handbook of home improvement and remodeling. 37–45
Door construction. Brann. How to build kitchen cabinets, room dividers, and cabinet furniture. 26–27
Doors and drawers, cabinets, corners, higher storage, shelves. Blandford. 53 spacesaving built-in furniture projects. 226–45
Double-up on appliances to save space. Family handyman handbook of home improvement and remodeling. 57–61
Drop-in sink cabinet. Brann. How to build kitchen cabinets, room dividers, and cabinet furniture. 29–30
Extra storage for kitchens. Cary. Storage: cabinets, closets, and wall systems. 101–04
Floor-to-ceiling cabinets. Stevenson. How to build and buy cabinets for the modern kitchen. 219–28
Free standing island. Brann. How to build kitchen cabinets, room dividers, and cabinet furniture. 40–48
Free standing refrigerator cabinet. Brann. How to build kitchen cabinets, room dividers, and cabinet furniture. 36–37
Haynie. Cabinetmaking.
How to build a cupboard, basic pine cabinets. Clifford. Basic woodworking & carpentry . . . with projects. 199–200, 224–29
How to build decorative doors. Brann. How to modernize a kitchen. 70–79
How to build wall cabinets. Brann. How to modernize a kitchen. 38–41

How to modernize wooden kitchen cabinets. Brann. How to modernize a kitchen. 64–70

Hylton. Handcrafted shelves & cabinets.

Installing cabinets. Spence. General carpentry. 452–61

Installing your cabinets. Stevenson. How to build and buy cabinets for the modern kitchen. 229–33

Island kitchen cabinet. Family handyman handbook of carpentry plans/projects. 70–72

Island kitchen cabinet. 77 furniture projects you can build. 111–12

Kitchen base cabinet, kitchen wall cabinet, kitchen cupboard, mobile work island, peninsula work center. 101 do-it-yourself projects. 115–35

Kitchen cabinet installation. Philbin. Cabinets, bookcases & closets. 85–88

Kitchen cabinets. Hedden. Successful shelves and built-ins. 7–28

Kitchen cupboard adaptation. Moser. How to build Shaker furniture. 200–01

Kitchen furniture. Blandford. How to make your own built-in furniture. 235–46

Kitchen organizer shelves. Family handyman handbook of carpentry plans/projects. 89–91

Kitchen sink cabinet. Family handyman handbook of home improvement and remodeling. 177–78

Kitchen storage. Jones. Plan and build more storage space. 111–28

Kitchen storage cabinet. Shea. Pennsylvania Dutch and their furniture. 172

Kitchen wall cabinet. Black and Decker power tool carpentry. 119–22

Made-to-measure kitchen cabinet. Black and Decker power tool carpentry. 108–13

Mobile mixing center, range counter unit, tall storage unit. Feirer. Cabinetmaking and millwork. 748–59

Paper plate and cup storage. Family handyman handbook of home improvement and remodeling. 12–13

Peninsula cabinets. Stevenson. How to build and buy cabinets for the modern kitchen. 189–201

Platter cabinet. Stevenson. How to build and buy cabinets for the modern kitchen. 144–46

Pop-up mixer cabinet. Stevenson. How to build and buy cabinets for the modern kitchen. 138–39

Range cabinet. Brann. How to build kitchen cabinets, room dividers, and cabinet furniture. 29–30

Refrigerator enclosure. Brann. How to modernize a kitchen. 37

Sink cabinets. Stevenson. How to build and buy cabinets for the modern kitchen. 113–26

Sliding shelves, cabinet with swing shelves, super pantry for storage of cans. Family handbook of home improvement and remodeling. 16, 22–24

Space adders for crowded kitchens, tailgate cabinet or auxiliary food center. Popular Mechanics do-it-yourself encyclopedia. Vol. 4, 492–500

Special-purpose base cabinets. Stevenson. How to build and buy cabinets for the modern kitchen. 127–49

Split level oven/cook top. Black and Decker power tool carpentry. 114–18

Tambour kitchen cabinets. Fine woodworking techniques 4. 182–83

Wall cabinet. How to build kitchen cabinets, room dividers, and cabinet furniture. 30–35

Wall oven cabinet. Brann. How to modernize a kitchen. 35–36

Wall oven enclosure. How to build kitchen cabinets, room dividers, and cabinet furniture. 40

Potrack. McRaven. Country blacksmithing. 122–25

Troubleshooting appliances. Bragdon. Homeowner's complete manual of repair & improvement. 374–80

Kitchen utensils
Bead toast rack. Hulbert. Creative beadwork. 92–94
Domestic tool rack, pan lid rack. Blandford. 53 space-saving built-in furniture projects. 220–26
Fish scaler, tongs, spatulas, whisk. Doherty. Family Circle book of 429 great gifts-to-make all year round for just 10¢ to $10.00. 131, 134–35
Kitchen tools. Spence. Woodworking tools, materials, processes. 612
Kitchen utensils (repair). Schuler. How to fix almost everything. 111
Laminated wood rolling pin. Popular Mechanics do-it-yourself encyclopedia. Vol. 11, 1654
Mortar and pestle. Sainsbury. Sainsbury's woodturning projects for dining. 142–43
Pine whisks. Langsner. Country woodcraft. 273–76
Potato masher. Sainsbury. Sainsbury's woodturning projects for dining. 159–63
Rolling pin. Sainsbury. Sainsbury's woodturning projects for dining. 157–58
Steak tenderizer. Sainsbury. Sainsbury's woodturning projects for dining. 140–41

Kitchen witches. See **Witches**

Kitchens
Butcherblock kitchen table. DeCristoforo. Build your own wood toys, gifts and furniture. 349–53
Counter tops. Syvanen. Interior finish: more tricks of the trade. 97–104
Installing tile on a new plywood countertop or plastic laminate. Burch. Tile: indoors and out, every kind and use. 63–67
Kitchen improvements. Nunn. Home improvement, home repair. 63–75

Kitchens, Play
Play kitchen with portable sink. Stiles. Easy-to-make children's furniture. 89–90
Small-fry kitchen appliances. Popular Mechanics do-it-yourself encyclopedia. Vol. 19, 2908–10

Kites
Japanese fish kite. Elbert. Paperworks. 20–23
Kite making, kite for windy weather. Bumper book of things a boy can make. 131, 204
Kite making, oriental kites. Favorite easy-to-make toys. 206–15
Kite (repair). Schuler. How to fix almost everything. 110–11
Kites. Linderman. Crafts for the classroom. 310–14
Making kites. Warring. Balsa wood modelling. 20–24
Thiebault. Kites and other wind machines.
Winged box, delta wing, flexible, fighter, nikko, and bird kites. Popular Mechanics do-it-yourself encyclopedia. Vol. 11, 1627–33

Knickers
Pants in variety. Corrigan. How to make pants and jeans that really fit. 135–39

Knife racks
Chopping block and knife drawer; knife rack. Stevenson. How to build and buy cabinets for the modern kitchen. 241–243, 246
Kitchen knife rack. Kangas. By hand. 187–88
Knife storage block. 101 do-it-yourself projects. 160–61

Knife sharpening. See **Knives, Sharpening**

Knights
Knight. Grainger. Creative papercraft. 52–55

Knitting
Basic knitting stitches. Better Homes and Gardens treasury of needlecrafts. 232–33
Borders. Chatterton. Scandinavian knitting designs. 123–65
Evolution of knitting technology. Spencer. Knitting technology. 6–10
Goldberg. New knitting dictionary.
Halevy. Knitting and crocheting pattern index.
Knitting. Ryan. Complete encyclopedia of stitchery. 360–559
Knitting basics, knitting stitches. Reader's Digest complete guide to needlework. 270–325
Knitting stitches and patterns. Mon Tricot. Knitting dictionary. 4–113
Knitwear for infants, toddlers and children. Selfridge. Patchwork knitting. 154–63
Meyers. Knitting know-how.
Neighbors. Reversible two-color knitting.
Rake knitting (enlarged version of spool knitting). Rissell. Craftwork the handicapped elderly can make and sell. 85–89
Repairing knitting. Dillmont. Complete encyclopedia of needlework. 239–45
Scandinavian patterns. Chatterton. Scandinavian knitting designs. 39–122
Spool and slot knitting. Held. Weaving. 239–40
Taylor. America's knitting book.
Variation of knitting. Rainey. Weaving without a loom. 77

Knitting, Machine
Lorant. Hand & machine knitting.
Spencer. Knitting technology.

Knives
Bowie knife. Latham. Knifecraft. 126–45
Boye. Step-by-step knifemaking: You can do it!
Blacksmithing for knives. Meilach. Decorative and sculptural ironwork. 199–203
Customize your hunting-knife handle. Popular Mechanics do-it-yourself encyclopedia Vol. 11, 1634–36
Damascus blades. Latham. Knifecraft. 146–69
Decorative pocketknife. Coyne. Penland School of Crafts book of jewelry making. 58–72
Drawknife. Fine woodworking techniques 4. 80–82
Folder and tapered-tang hunting knife. Latham. Knifecraft. 96–125
Kitchen knives. Family handyman handbook of carpentry plans/projects. 85–88
Knife block. Hamilton. Build it together. 24–31
Knife decoration. Latham. Knifecraft. 170–89
Knife handles. Latham. Knifecraft. 46–53
Making shaper knives. Fine woodworking techniques I. 60–62
Mayes. How to make your own knives.
Razor blade knife. Bumper book of things a boy can make. 19–20
Stick-handle and boot knife. Latham. Knifecraft. 66–95

Knives, Sharpening
Sharpening and maintenance. Boye. Step-by-step knifemaking: you can do it! 189–97
Sharpening knives. Latham. Knifecraft. 222–27

Knockers
Door knocker. Modern general shop. Metalworking. 106
Door knockers. Grainger. Creative ropecraft. 118, 121–22

Knots and splices
Basic and decorative knots. Waller. Knots and netting. 11–27
Grainger. Creative ropecraft.
Knots everyone should know. Popular Mechanics do-it-yourself encyclopedia. Vol. 11, 1640–43
Knots: overhand, Lark's head, square half, square knot sennet, alternate squareknots, double half hitch and weaver's. DeLeon. Basketry book. 93–98
Knotting. Chamberlain. Beyond weaving. 97–117

Knots and splices. *See also* **Macrame**

L

Labels
Christmas gift nametags. Janitch. Candlemaking and decorations. 79
Christmas package name tags. Coffey. Francine Coffey's celebrity sewing bee. 169
"Designer labels" for clothing. Hagans. All good gifts. 77–78
Felt gift tags. McCall's book of Christmas. 139–40
Gift tags. O'Neill. Make-it-merry Christmas book. 113–14
Gift tags cut from balsa wood. Linsley. Lesley Linsley's Christmas ornaments and stockings. 158–59
Labels. Elbert. Paperworks. 47–48
Making your own decals. Holtje. Cardcraft. 123–25
Many happy returns gift tags. Janitch. Candlemaking and decorations. 36
Nametag, key/luggage tag. Fanning. Complete book of machine quilting. 263–65
Sandwich labels; name labels for parties. Bumper book of things a girl can make. 20–23

Lace and lacemaking
Aemilia-ara lace, hedebo, netting, teneriffe. Longhurst. Vanishing American needle arts. 3–19, 61–91, 135–47
Bedfordshire or beds-Maltese and Cluny lace. Nottingham. Techniques of bobbin lace. 55–130
Bobbin lace. Blandford book of traditional handicrafts. 35–50
Bobbin lace (heavy threads). Chamberlain. Beyond weaving. 142–45
Braids and trimmings for modern use. Nottingham. Techniques of bobbin lace. 203–11
Brooke. Lace in the making with bobbins and needle.
Bucks point lace. Nottingham. Techniques of bobbin lace. 131–202
Collier. Creative design in bobbin lace.
Crochet chair back. Dillmont. Complete encyclopedia of needlework. 329–36
Crochet groend and/or lace. Dillmont. Complete encyclopedia of needlework. 309–29
Earnshaw. Dictionary of lace.
Embroidered laces. Dillmont. Complete encyclopedia of needlework. 497–544
Filet lace. Dillmont. Complete encyclopedia of needlework. 409–54
Honiton lace, patterns and techniques. Luxton. Technique of Honiton lace.
Instructions for the broomstick lace purse and hat. Time-Life Books. Decorative techniques. 158–63
Knitted lace. Dillmont. Complete encyclopedia of needlework. 258–76
Lace as an off-loom technique. Meilach. Weaving off-loom. 122–33
Lace bobbins. Sainsbury. Woodworking projects with power tools. 73–77
Lacemaking. Bath. Needlework in America. 303–25
Needle lace, filet netting, bobbin lace, lace weaves, hairpin lace. Reader's Digest complete guide to needlework. 404–12, 420–42
Needle made laces. Dillmont. Complete encyclopedia of needlework. 545–603
Needlepoint lace, patterns & techniques. Lovesey. Technique of needlepoint lace.

Point lace work, designs. Whatnot. 72–76
Pillow laces (bobbin lace). Dillmont. Complete encyclopedia of needlework. 604–56
Preston. Needle-made lace and net embroideries.
Southard. Bobbin lacemaking.
Stillwell. Technique of teneriffe lace.
Torchon lace. Nottingham. Techniques of bobbin lace. 23–54

Lacquer and lacquering
Burmese lacquerware. Schuman. Art from many hands. 124–25
Lacquer finishes. Johnson. How to restore, repair, and finish almost everything. 76–89
Lacquer: history, technique, practice. Oughton. Complete manual of wood finishing. 95–109
Lacquering metal. Metalcrafting encyclopedia. 43
Lacquerware-wood, woven or plaited forms. Newman. Contemporary Southeast Asian arts and crafts. 146–55
Repairing lacquer. Wenn. Restoring antique furniture. 68–71

Ladders
Build a mobile scaffold. Popular Mechanics do-it-yourself encyclopedia. Vol. 16, 2524–25
Long look at long ladders, how to work from ladders. Popular Mechanics do-it-yourself encyclopedia. Vol. 11, 1645–51
Using ladders. Waugh. Handyman's encyclopedia. 156–60

Ladles. *See* **Spoons**

Laminated construction
Applying plastic laminate. Hedden. Successful shelves and built-ins. 117–24
Applying plastic laminates. Spence. General carpentry. 458–60
Fine art of layering wood, how to apply plastic laminate. Popular Mechanics do-it-yourself encyclopedia. Vol. 11, 1652–56, 1658–61
Flexible plastic, repairing laminated surfaces. Marshall. How to repair, reupholster, and refinish furniture. 71–76
How to apply plastic laminate on a counter top. Brann. How to modernize a kitchen. 42–44
How to cut, glue, and trim plastic laminate. Stiles. Easy-to-make children's furniture. 6–9
Installing plastic laminate. Bragdon. Homeowner's complete manual of repair & improvement. 218
Laminated plastic tops. Haynie. Cabinetmaking. 79–92
Laminating. Platt. Step-by-step woodcraft. 62–63
Laminating. Wagner. Modern woodworking. 307–10
Plastic laminate application. Brann. How to build kitchen cabinets, room dividers, and cabinet furniture. 27–29
Plastic laminated tabletops. Meyers. Furniture repair and refinishing. 221–22
Plastic laminating. Lewis. Cabinetmaking, patternmaking, and millwork. 278–84
Tapered lamination. Fine woodworking techniques 3. 148–51

Lamp posts
How to install a yard light, mercury vapor lamp, shrubbery light. Popular Mechanics do-it-yourself encyclopedia. Vol. 15, 2296–2301
Lamppost for yard. Complete handyman do-it-yourself encyclopedia. Vol. 12, 1765–69
Lamppost for your yard. Popular Mechanics do-it-yourself encyclopedia. Vol. 10, 1467
Outdoor colonial lamp and sign post. Brann. How to build outdoor projects. 138–55
Post lamp. Popular Mechanics do-it-yourself encyclopedia. Vol. 14, 2112

Lamp shades
Art deco lampshade. Duncan. Leaded glass. 160–71
Basketry lampshades. Lampshades to make. 60–63
Batik lampshade. Tie-dye, batik and candlemaking step-by-step. 24–25
Bead lamp shade cover. Hulbert. Creative beadwork. 44
Beaded lampshades. Hulbert. Creative beadwork. 109–10
Butterfly design. Adams. How to make mission style lamps and shades. 106–09
Butterfly lamp shades. Paper. 65
Candle shades and wall light. Fishburn. Making lampshades. 63–64
Cane lampshades. Maynard. Modern basketry from the start. 135–39
Chequers, chu chin chow, space flight, ship's lantern, carousel, and toadstool village
    paper lampshade. Janitch. All made from paper. 20–28
Classic shades. Lampshades to make. 20–23
Coat-hanger wire lampshade. Kramer. Wirecraft. 60–61
Collage aquarium lampshade. Janitch. Collage; a step by step guide. 72–74
Collage lampshades. Elbert. Paperworks. 80–82
Cone lamp shades. Fishburn. Making lampshades. 84–87
Copper foil lampshades. Duncan. Leaded glass. 185–94
Craft aid to hold lamp frames for one-handed clients. Anderson. Crafts and the dis-
    abled. 41–42
Crochet lampshades. Lampshades to make. 48–49
Crocheted lamp shade. Halliday. Decorating with crochet. 38–39
Crocheted lamp shade cover. Scharf. Butterick's fast and easy needlecrafts. 119–20
Cylindrical base lampshades. Grainger. Creative papercraft. 107–11
Cylindrical lampshades; vase-shaped shade; open-worked shade. Cane, rush and
    straw. 72–77
Desk lamp shade. Adams. How to make mission style lamps and shades. 47–53
Droplights. Adams. How to make mission style lamps and shades. 15–19, 54–56
Embroidered lampshades. Lampshades to make. 81–83
Embroidered rose lampshades. Embroidery of roses. 92–93, 98
Embroidered tiffany lamp shade. Lampshades to make. 84–87
Etched lamp shade. Adams. How to make mission style lamps and shades. 75–97
Fabric covered pleated lampshade. Roda. Fabric decorating for the home. 68
Fabric covered smooth lampshade. Roda. Fabric decorating for the home. 54–55
Fiberglass lampshades. Lampshades to make. 76–77
Firm lampshades. Fishburn. Making lampshades. 78–79
Flat-paneled shades, iris lampshade. Challenging projects in stained glass. 1–48
Fringed lampshade. Lampshades to make. 78–80
Glass lamp shades. Lampshades to make. 68–70
Glass tiffany shade. Lampshades to make. 70–76
Hexagonal dome for library lamp. Adams. How to make mission style lamps and
    shades. 68–74
Knitted shade. Lampshades to make. 44–45
Knitted tiffany shade. Lampshades to make. 46–47
Lamp shade. Christensen. Needlepoint and bargello stitchery. 92–93
Lampshade. Andes. Far beyond the fringe. 69–75
Lampshade making. Murphy. Lampmaking. 53–54
Lampshade with patchwork edging. Ives. Ideas for patchwork. 50–53
Lampshades. Gordon. Complete guide to drying and preserving flowers. 85–89
Lamp shades of plastic. Cope. Plastics. 93–94
Lampshades with flowers and leaves. Stephan. Creating with tissue paper. 204–07
Lead came lampshades. Duncan. Leaded glass. 157–74
Luciano. Stained glass lamp art.
Macrame lampshade. Encyclopedia of crafts. 230
Macrame lampshade. Lampshades to make. 52–53
Making stained-glass lampshades. Isenberg. How to work in stained glass. 196–218

Near drum and oval shades. Fishburn. Making lampshades. 82–83
Panelled shades. Lampshades to make. 14–19
Paper lampshades. Lampshades to make. 31–35
Papier mâché lampshade. Mills. The book of presents. 28–29
Papier mâché lampshades. Stephan. Creating with tissue paper. 194–97
Parchment lampshade. Stephan. Creating with tissue paper. 198–203
Parchment lamp shades; a frilled lampshade. Bumper book of things a girl can make. 90–93, 233–34
Pleated and swathed lampshades. Fishburn. Making lampshades. 53–60
Pleated lampshade. Time-Life Books. Decorative techniques. 128–33
Pleated paper shades. Lampshades to make. 36–40
Pleated shades. Lampshades to make. 24–27
Pyramid design. Adams. How to make mission style lamps and shades. 111–14
Quick shade. Lampshades to make. 29–30
Raffia lampshades. Lampshades to make. 56–59
Rajah shade. Lampshades to make. 50–51
Sectional lampshades. Fishburn. Making lampshades. 61–62
Sewn lamp shades. Adams. How to make mission style lamps and shades. 98–105
Silhouette shades. Lampshades to make. 40–43
Smocked lampshade. Time-Life Books. Decorative techniques. 134–35
Square dining-room dome. Adams. How to make mission style lamps and shades. 36–38
Stained glass lampshade. Giant book of crafts. 226–29
Stained glass lampshades. Walke. All about stained glass. 217–31
Stained glass lighting fixture and lamp shade. Wood. Working with stained glass. 42–45, 64–75
Straight-sided drum lampshade. Fishburn. Making lampshades. 80–81
Table lamp shade (macrame). Lampshades to make. 54–55
Tailored shades with balloon lining. Fishburn. Making lampshades. 35–41
Tasseled lampshade cover. Crochet. 110
Textured lamp shade. Holland. Weaving primer. 116
Tiffany lampshades. Fishburn. Making lampshades. 42–49
Tiffany shades. Lampshades to make. 8–13
Wicker lampshade. Casselman. Crafts from around the world. 174–75
Wooden lampshade. Lampshades to make. 64–67
Wool lampshade. Design crochet. 214–16
Woven lampshade. Parker. Beginner's book of off-loom weaving. 191–95

Lamps
Angel weathervane lamp. Murphy. Lampmaking. 83–88
Antique bottle lamp. Murphy. Lampmaking. 89–92
Antique coffee grinder lamp. Murphy. Lampmaking. 105–10
Antique doll lamp. Murphy. Lampmaking. 67–70
Basket lamps. Treasury of things to make. 160–63
Beveled lamp. Isenberg. How to work in beveled glass. 208–09
Butcher block lamp. Mitton. How to make your own lamps and lampshades. 122–25
Candle holder lamp. Mitton. How to make your own lamps and lampshades. 66–68
Candle lamps, Japanese lantern, circus lamp. Women's Day book of gifts to make. 122–25
Carved wooden lamp. Lubkemann. Carving twigs and branches. 70–73
Ceramic lamp. Murphy. Lampmaking. 111–16
Ceramic monkey lamp. Mitton. How to make your own lamps and lampshades. 126–28
Chandeliers. Adams. How to make mission style lamps and shades. 57–60
Child's room lamp. Mitton. How to make your own lamps and lampshades. 88–90
Copper teapot lamp. Murphy. Lampmaking. 97–100

Cube lamp. Modern general shop. Woodworking. 92–93

Cylindrical swag lamp, monofilament swag lamp. Cope. Plastics. 30, 44

Driftwood lamp. Mitton. How to make your own lamps and lampshades. 105–09

Duck or snipe decoy lamps. Murphy. Lampmaking. 57–66

Early American corner lamp. Murphy. Lampmaking. 123–30

Early American lantern lamp. Murphy. Lampmaking. 117–22

Electric hurricane lamp. Murphy. Lampmaking. 102–03

Fire extinguisher lamp. Mitton. How to make your own lamps and lampshades. 91–94

Flower pot lamps. Mitton. How to make your own lamps and lampshades. 134–39

Ginger jar lamp. Murphy. Lampmaking. 79–82

Glass lamps decoupaged. Davis. Step-by-step decoupage. 45

Globe lamp, wall hung reading lamp, stained glass lamp. 101 do-it-yourself projects. 168–69, 190–91, 323–27

Gold leaf stenciled lamp. Murphy. Lampmaking. 130–38

Gourd lamps. Mordecai. Gourd craft. 171–79

Hanging basket lamp. Mitton. How to make your own lamps and lampshades. 99–101

Hanging lamps. Duncan. Leaded glass. 200–02

Hanging lampshade lamp. Mitton. How to make your own lamps and lampshades. 95–98

Hanging redwood patio lamp. Popular Mechanics do-it-yourself encyclopedia. Vol. 14, 2111

Hexagonal library lamp. Adams. How to make mission style lamps and shades. 61–67

Hurricane lamp, American lamp. Fowler. Can crafts. 108–12

Lamp making. Bumper book of things a boy can make. 60–65

Lamps from one-gallon oil tin or metal wastebasket. DeCristoforo. Build your own wood toys, gifts and furniture. 355–61

Lamp stand. Rubin. Mission furniture. 104

Lighted bottle lamp. Mitton. How to make your own lamps and lampshades. 61–65

Lighthouse lamp. Mitton. How to make your own lamps and lampshades. 78–83

Low-cost spotlight. Blackwell. Johnny Blackwell's poor man's catalog. 95

Macrame lamp with no frame members. Andes. Far beyond the fringe. 82–87

Macramed lamp base. Andes. Far beyond the fringe. 76–81

Make a hanging lamp in a cardboard container. Priolo. Ceramics by coil. 46–47

Make a lamp base in a paper container. Priolo. Ceramics by coil. 28–29

Making a lamp base. Ceramics. 22

Making a lamp base. Marshall. Foilcraft. 104–06

Making table lamps. Duncan. Leaded glass. 195–99

Mannequin floor lamp. Mitton. How to make your own lamps and lampshades. 147–53

Milk can lamp. Mitton. How to make your own lamps and lampshades. 84–87

Mirror frame with lamp. Coyne. Penland School of Crafts book of pottery. 177–88

Mission chandelier. Adams. How to make mission style lamps and shades. 40–45

Needlepoint lamp. Murphy. Lampmaking. 187–90

Night-light, table lamp. Cope. Plastics. 48–49, 58

Oak table lamp. Mitton. How to make your own lamps and lampshades. 161–66

Oriental basket lamp. Murphy. Lampmaking. 145–49

Painted deco desk lamp. Jarnow. (Re)do it yourself. 112–14

Picture frame lamp. Mitton. How to make your own lamps and lampshades. 140–43

Pin-up lamp, globe lamp. Giant book of metalworking projects. 192–94, 210–11

Quick bottle lamp. Mitton. How to make your own lamps and lampshades. 54–56

Ratlan covered lamp. Murphy. Lampmaking. 149–52

Reading lamps. Adams. How to make mission style lamps and shades. 22–33

Rooster lamp. McCall's big book of country needlecrafts. 172–73

Rope lamp. Murphy. Lampmaking. 75–78

Rose-pattern lamp base. Scobey. Decorating with needlepoint. 146–48

Sand cast lamps. Johnson. Nature crafts. 48–49

Sea fan and shells lamp. Murphy. Lampmaking. 139–44

Seashell lamp. Johnson. Nature crafts. 30
"Slipcover" lamp bases (needlepoint). McCall's book of America's favorite needlework and crafts. 147–48
Spanish-style lamp, candlestand lamp, cobbler's bench table lamp, spoonholder lamp, six-in-one lamp. Popular Mechanics do-it-yourself encyclopedia. Vol. 11, 1662–74
Square acrylic lamps. LaPlante. Plastic furniture for the home craftsman. 108–14
Stained-glass lamp base made from wine bottle or jug. Woman's Day book of weekend crafts. 14–15
Stained glass night light, terrarium lamp, lantern. Epple. Something from nothing crafts. 25–27, 34–37, 164–65
Table lamp. Feirer. Cabinetmaking and millwork. 188
Table lamp and shade. Make it! don't buy it. 306–15
Table lamps. Grainger. Creative ropecraft. 119–22
Table lamps, adjustable standard lamp. Endacott. Fine furniture making and woodworking. 86–91, 99–102
Tin can lamps. Mitton. How to make your own lamps and lampshades. 69–73
Tree-trunk lamp, scrap lumber lamp and nautical lamp. Capotosto. Woodworking techniques and projects. 124–27, 165–70, 296–98
Tripod based lamp, floor standard lamp. Wooldridge. Woodturning techniques. 63–69
Tripod lamp. Modern general shop. Woodworking. 104–05
Turned wood lamp. Mitton. How to make your own lamps and lampshades. 110–13
Turning lamp bases and heavy spindles. Spielman. Working green wood with PEG. 70–78
Two-basket lamp. Mitton. How to make your own lamps and lampshades. 102–04
Vase lamp. Mitton. How to make your own lamps and lampshades. 129–37
Wall and table lamps. Spielman. Working green wood with PEG. 58
Wall lamp. Mitton. How to make your own lamps and lampshades. 144–46
Wall lamps and rustic lamp. Family handyman handbook of carpentry plans/projects. 319–24
Whiskey bottle lamp. Mitton. How to make your own lamps and lampshades. 57–60
Wine bottle lamp. Murphy. Lampmaking. 71–74
Wiring a hanging lamp. Kangas. By hand. 155–57
Wiring lamps. Andes. Far beyond the fringe. 110–16
Wood and copper floor lamp. Mitton. How to make your own lamps and lampshades. 154–60
Wood and rope lamp. Mitton. How to make your own lamps and lampshades. 116–21
Woodburned lamp base. Broadwater. Woodburning: art and craft. 105–06
Wooden lamp bases. Kauffman. Easy-to-make wooden candlesticks, chandeliers and lamps. 16–25
Woven copper TV lamp. Elliot. Working with copper. 28–30
Wrought-iron mantel lamp. Mitton. How to make your own lamps and lampshades. 74–77

Lamps, Fluorescent
Fluorescent lamp. Modern general shop. Electricity. 114–16
What you should know about fluorescent lamps. Popular Mechanics do-it-yourself encyclopedia. Vol. 8, 1250–53

Lamps, Repairing
Restoring old lamps. Joyner. Furniture refinishing at home. 94–98
Rewiring older lamps and fixtures. Kangas. By hand. 151–75

Landscape models
City park. Christensen. Needlepoint. 137–47
Frary. How to build realistic model railroad scenery.
Landscape in miniature. Bumper book of things a girl can make. 51–52
Landscape table top. Christensen. Needlepoint. 107–17

Lanterns
Betty lamps with threaded standard (stand). Pennsylvania Dutch and their furniture.
  183
Decorative lantern. Metalcrafting encyclopedia. 155
Five-sided lantern. Grainger. Creative papercraft. 112–13
Japanese lanterns. Elbert. Paperworks. 44–47
Modeling a lantern. Marshall. Foilcraft. 42–44
Outdoor lighting fixture. 101 do-it-yourself projects. 254–55
Punched aluminum lantern. Sayer. Crafts of Mexico. 29–31

Lanterns. *See also* **Lighting, Outdoor**

Lanyards
Lanyard for knife or whistle. Grainger. Creative ropecraft. 110

Lap pads
Gifts for new parents or grandparents. Laury. Treasury of needlecraft gifts for the new
  baby. 97–100

Lap robes
Double-face lap robe with brushed mohair. Brown. Weaving, spinning, and dyeing
  book. 185
Lap hugger. Coffey. Francine Coffey's celebrity sewing bee. 97
Lap quilt or throw in log cabin pattern. Houck. Patchwork pattern book. 6–7
Stadium robe, Navajo pattern wool lap robe. Holland. Weaving primer. 120–21, 157
Yo-yos stitched together for a lap robe. Rissell. Craftwork the handicapped elderly can
  make and sell. 37–38

Lap robes, Crocheted
Crocheted lap robes. Feldman. Big book of afghans. 126–36
Gardenia lace and hexagon-motif crocheted lap throws. Woman's Day decorative
  needlework for the home. 16–17
Lap robe and pillow. Crochet. 98
Navajo symbols, portable lap robe, stitch sample. Kurita. Second big book of afghans.
  122–32

Lap robes, Knitted
Knitted lap robes. Feldman. Big book of afghans. 52–62
Tiny blossoms, arrowtip lace and argyle borders. Kurita. Second big book of afghans.
  54–60

Lapidary work
Combination machine for the do-it-yourself enthusiast. Wainwright. Discovering lapi-
  dary work. 65–121
Firsoff. Working with gemstones.
Gems, cabochon polishing, faceting. Rose. Illustrated encyclopedia of crafts and how
  to master them. 74–86
Grinding, prepolishing and polishing. Hyde. Complete book of rock tumbling. 57–89
How to carve and engrave gems. Quick. Gemcraft. 136–61
Hyde. Complete book of rock tumbling.

Lapidary. Kicklighter. Crafts, illustrated designs and techniques. 144–51
Meyer. Rock tumbling.
Setting of gemstones. Edwards. Lost wax casting of jewelry. 113–20
Smith. Gemcutting.
Stone grinding and polishing. Giant book of crafts. 324–42
Stone setting, cutting and polishing stones. Wood. Make your own jewelry. 114–26, 156–67
Triple-screen sorter for rockhounds. Popular Mechanics do-it-yourself encyclopedia. Vol. 11, 1686–87
Turquoise. Powers. Crafting turquoise jewelry. 36–74

Lapidary work, Faceting
Facet cutting. Wainwright. Discovering lapidary work. 51–64
Faceting. Smith. Gemcutting. 136–63
Gem faceting. Firsoff. Working with gemstones. 101–37
How to facet gems. Quick. Gemcraft. 75–124
Simple faceting. Fletcher. Rock and gem polishing. 76–81

Lapidary work, Polishing and tumbling
Polishing gems. Quick. Gemcraft. 25–63
Polishing gems. Wainwright. Discovering lapidary work. 30–39, 122–28, 156–71
Shop-built polisher. Popular Mechanics do-it-yourself encyclopedia. Vol. 11, 1682–84

Latches. *See* **Locks and keys**

Lathes
Boring-bar set for your lathe, king-size toolpost, lathe indexing attachment, setscrew chucks you can make, swing tool-holder for your lathe, turning rings on a lathe, filing on a lathe, fine finish on lathe projects, turn plastic on your lathe. Popular Mechanics do-it-yourself encyclopedia. Vol. 12, 1790–1818
Drill-driven lathe. Blackwell. Johnny Blackwell's poor man's catalog. 28
How to make a wood-turning lathe. Weygers. Recycling, use, and repair of tools. 24–26
How to recycle and operate a metal-turning lathe. Weygers. Recycling, use and repair of tools. 78–87
Lathe. Capotosto. Woodworking wisdom. 91–95
Lathe and its equipment, safety on the lathe, beginner's equipment. Sainsbury. Craft of woodturning. 1–37
Lathe operation. Briney. Home machinist's handbook. 81–126
Lathes. Buckwalter. Homeowner's handbook of power tools. 135–47
Lathe. Wagner. Modern woodworking. 232–51
Make a faceplate lathe from odds and ends, miniature tabletop lathe, wood lathe techniques. Popular Mechanics do-it-yourself encyclopedia. Vol. 20, 3100–17
Making lathe tools. Weygers. Recycling, use, and repair of tools. 27–31, 34–36, 61–63
Metal lathe. Modern general shop. Metalworking. 84–91
Reverse lathe. Weygers. Recycling, use, and repair of tools. 76–77
Spring-pole lathe. Langsner. Country woodcraft. 123–30
Treadle lathe, freewheel lathe drive. Fine woodworking techniques 3. 120–26
Shop-made bowl lathe. Fine woodworking techniques 5. 20–22
Short course in lathe work. DeCristoforo. Build your own wood toys, gifts and furniture. 295–308
Tuning up your lathe. Fine woodworking techniques 4. 114–15
Using the wood lathe. Ammen. Constructing & using wood patterns. 129–48

Lathes. *See also* **Wood turning**

Lattice work. *See* **Trellises**

Laundry equipment
Built in laundry room. Family handyman handbook of carpentry plans/projects. 241–51
Built-ins for kitchen and laundry. Popular Mechanics do-it-yourself encyclopedia. Vol. 3, 454–55
Clothes drying horse. Bumper book of things a girl can make. 107–08
Home laundry center. Geary. How to build your own workspace—with plans. 212–21
How to fix an automatic washer. Popular Mechanics do-it-yourself encyclopedia. Vol. 20, 3056–59
Installing a hamper within walls. Time-Life Books. Space and storage. 98–99
Laundry cart and sink cabinet. Feirer. Cabinetmaking and millwork. 760–61
Laundry center in a closet. Popular Mechanics do-it-yourself encyclopedia. Vol. 10, 1465
Laundry centers. Davidson. Successful studios and work centers. 59–67
Laundry needs: out-of-site ironing board, laundry chute, clothing sorter. Garage, attic and basement storage. 38–39
Laundry storage. Philbin. Cabinets, bookcases & closets. 110–11
Modular laundry center. Complete handyman do-it-yourself encyclopedia. Vol. 11, 1567–72

Lavatories. *See* **Bathrooms; Plumbing**

Lawn furniture. *See* **Chairs, Outdoor; Chaise lounges; Furniture, Outdoor; Outdoor rooms**

Lawn mowers
Get your power mower ready for spring, how to choose a riding mower, keep your power mower purring. Popular Mechanics do-it-yourself encyclopedia. Vol. 13, 1937–46
Hand mowers: keep your lawn and yourself in shape. Popular Mechanics do-it-yourself encyclopedia. Vol. 9, 1394–95
Repairing and storage of mowers. Outdoor projects for home and garden. 180–81, 184–97
Repairing lawn mowers. Outdoor projects for home and garden. 69–70

Lawn ornaments. *See* **Garden ornaments**

Lazy susans
Double lazy susan. McNair. Building & outfitting your workshop. 144–51
Hors d'oeuvre dish. Sainsbury. Sainsbury's woodturning projects for dining. 24–27
How to install a lazy susan. Brann. How to modernize a kitchen. 33–34
Lazy susan table server. Popular Mechanics do-it-yourself encyclopedia. Vol. 11, 1704–05
Rotating centerpiece server. Capotosto. Woodworking techniques and projects. 159–64

Leather
Restoring and replacing leather. Johnson. How to restore, repair, and finish almost everything. 124–130

Leather work
Burning on leather. Broadwater. Woodburning: art and craft. 133–34
Cutting sewing, embossing, and carving leather. Encyclopedia of crafts. 246–55
Gentlebeast. Kinser. Sewing sculpture. 124–37
Kellogg. Home tanning & leathercraft simplifed.

Lacing, stitches, procedure. Andersen. Creative exploration in crafts. 209–29
Latham. Leathercraft.
Leather. Chamberlain. Metal jewelry techniques. 152–157
Leather. Rose. Illustrated encyclopedia of crafts and how to master them. 87–110
Leather bank, encased bottles and petite patch pouch. D'Amato. Italian crafts. 62–75
Leather stitchery. Guth. Sewing with scraps. 79–86
Leather tooling. Giant book of crafts. 281–88
Leather tooling. Linderman. Crafts for the classroom. 374–76
Leathercraft. Kicklighter. Crafts, illustrated designs and techniques. 152–75
Loeb. Leather book.
Skin game (leather clothes). Time-Life Books. Novel materials. 18–59
Working with leather. Newman. Contemporary African arts and crafts. 177–88

Leaves
Glass leaf making. Isenberg. Crafting in glass. 140–49
How to make a leaf rubbing. Burch. Making leaf rubbings. 3–31
Leaf lace. Pittaway. Traditional English country crafts and how to enjoy them today. 177
Printing with plants: direct, offset and proof press. Geary. Plant prints and collages. 27–43
Skeleton leaf prints. Geary. Plant prints and collages. 86

Leg warmers
Child's rainbow legwarmers. Evrard. Homespun crafts from scraps. 108–12
Fleur-de-lis legwarmers (knitted). Evrard. Twinkletoes. 32–33
Leg warmers. Step by step to better knitting and crochet. 127
Neck and wrist warmers. Brown. Super sweater idea book. 185–86
Rib knit, extra-long, below-the-knee. Woman's Day bazaar best sellers. 24–26
Scandinavian leg and foot bundler (knitted). Evrard. Twinkletoes. 49–51
Woodland leggings, early 19th century leggings. Scurlock. Muzzleloader Magazine's book of buckskinning II. 33–34, 38–39

Letter files. *See* **Filing cases; Stationery holders**

Letter holders. *See* **Desk furnishings; Mail racks; Stationery holders;**

Lettering
ABC's and 123's. Torbet. T-shirt book. 113–25
Alphabet in various embroidery stitches. Embroidery. 104–15
Alphabet letters (embroidered). Gladstone. Kids' clothes by Meredith Gladstone: a sewing book. 95–107
Alphabet strip of woven letters. Gill. Beadwork: the technique of stringing, threading, and weaving. 176–78
Alphabets. Sayles. Step-by-step stitchery. 54–57
Alphabets and letters. Meulenbelt-Nieuwburg. Embroidery motifs from old Dutch samplers. 93–102
Alphabets (embroidered). Boyles. Needlework gifts for special occasions. 150–52.
Alphabets for cross stitch. Gostelow. Cross stitch book. 85–89
Beveled alphabet soup. Isenberg. How to work in beveled glass. 203–05
Borssuck. Needlework monograms.
Built-up decoration on box lid; raised letter poster. Bumper book of things a boy can make. 66–70
Calligraphy. Kicklighter. Crafts, illustrated designs and techniques. 58–63
Calligraphy. Treasury of things to make. 56–57
Chinese terrestrial signs. Rome. Needlepoint letters and numbers. 97–100
Cross stitch designs and alphabet. Wilson. Needleplay. 170–71

Cross-stitch, floral, and fancy block alphabets. Needlework nostalgia. 45–50
Cutout letters. Spielman. Making wood signs. 37–43
Granny square alphabet. Great granny crochet book. 60–61
Greek. Rome. Needlepoint letters and numbers. 105–07
Hebrew. Rome. Needlepoint letters and numbers. 101–04
Incised lettering. Fine woodworking techniques 3. 164–66
Infinite intrigue of monograms. Time-Life Books. Personal touch. 146–53
Letter shapes. Favorite easy-to-make toys. 21
Lettering. Linderman. Crafts for the classroom. 410–16
Lettering and dimensioning. Modern general shop. Drafting. 45–47
Letters. Jarvey. You can dough it! 82–91
Making foil letters. Marshall. Foilcraft. 61
Messages on cards. Holtje. Cardcraft. 148–56
Moeller. Charted decorative initials.
Monogram alphabets. Sheldon. Washable and dryable needlepoint. 122–27
Monogramming. McCall's big book of needlecrafts. 217–23
Monogramming/machine embroidery. Reader's Digest complete guide to needlework.
    103
Monograms or names: project (machine stitched). Hall. Sewing machine craft book.
    44–45
Mythical character cross-stitch alphabet projects. Gault. Needlework dragons and other
    mythical creatures. 78–97
Needlepoint alphabet. Slater. New York Times book of needlepoint for left-handers.
    235–47
Needlepoint initials. Smith. Needlery. 117–21
Rome. Needlepoint letters and numbers.
Sentiments in stitches/names in needlepoint. Wilson. Needleplay. 155
Wheel engraved lettering. Matcham. Techniques of glass engraving. 77–81
Williams. Lettering in embroidery.
Wooden name cutouts. Richards. Handmade jewelry. 148–53
Yours personally (monogrammed bags). Houck. Big bag book. 122–32

Lighting

Built-in lighting. Siegele. Cabinets and built-ins. 42–45
Ceiling fixtures, fluorescents, & track lighting. Bragdon. Homeowner's complete manual
    of repair & improvement. 350–71
Fabric covered chandelier cord. Roda. Fabric decorating for the home. 58
Hanging chandelier (candle). Bealer. Art of blacksmithing. 299–303
Hanging light fixture. Rubin. Mission furniture. 102–03
Inserting a fluorscent light fixture in a ceiling. Time-Life Books. New living spaces. 72–
    73
Installing a new chandelier. Family handyman handbook of home improvement and
    remodeling. 220–28
Kitchen lighting. Stevenson. How to build and buy kitchen cabinets for the modern
    kitchen. 258–61
Making a light box. Kangas. By hand. 85–88
Recessing a light fixture. Time-Life Books. New living spaces. 77
Shell night light. Elbert. Shell craft. 44–45
Simple kitchen lights you can make. Popular Mechanics do-it-yourself encyclopedia.
    Vol. 11, 1728–30
Track lighting. Geary. How-to book of floors & ceilings. 141–51

Lighting. *See also* **Lamps; Lanterns; Lighting, Outdoor**

Lighting, Outdoor
Aluminum yard lamp. Giant book of metalworking projects. 186–92
Lighting systems and units. Kramer. Outdoor garden build-it book. 132–41
Low-voltage lighting systems. Outdoor projects for home and garden. 432–37
Outdoor lighting. Bragdon. Homeowner's complete manual of repair & improvement.
382–83
Outdoor lighting. Day. How to build patios and decks. 126–32
Rustic lamp. Outdoor projects for home and garden. 437–38
Transform your yard with night lighting, how to light a game area. Popular Mechanics
do-it-yourself encyclopedia. Vol. 20, 3144–52

Linen chests. *See* **Chests**

Lingerie
Easy lingerie budget sewing. Guth. Sewing with scraps. 87–99
Lingerie cases. Vanderbilt. Gloria Vanderbilt designs for your home. 184–85
Lingerie pouch. Gostelow. Cross stitch book. 126–29
Preparation, layout and cutting of lingerie. Schwebke. Sewing with the new knits. 129–
74

Linoleum block printing. *See* **Block printing**

Lions. *See* **Cats**

Livestock
Animal transport crate. Bubel. Working wood. 133–40
Goat exercise platform. Bubel. Working wood. 105–07
Pig palace. Bubel. Working wood. 121–32
Sheep shelter. Bubel. Working wood. 109–14
Small animal creep. Bubel. Working wood. 101–03

Livestock, Feeding equipment
Cattle shelters and feeders. Leavy. Successful small farms. 149–52
Feed bin. Bubel. Working wood. 141–44
Hay mangers. Bubel. Working wood. 115–20
Shelters and feeders for swine. Leavy. Successful small farms. 153–57

Locks and keys
Combination lock, padlock. Giant book of metalworking projects. 239–44
Door locksets. Rowland. Handcrafted doors & windows. 48–53
Forging a door latch. Weygers. Modern blacksmith. 61–63
Guide to super locks. Outdoor projects for home and garden. 38–45
How to install a fast-set door lock. Popular Mechanics do-it-yourself encyclopedia. Vol.
11, 1732–34
Installing a cylinder lock. Handyman. 160
Installing door locks. Spence. General carpentry. 310–11
Lock options, replacing a lock. Bragdon. Homeowner's complete manual of repair &
improvement. 168–77
Lockset repair and replacement. Nunn. Home improvement, home repair. 53–54
Repair locks. Wenn. Restoring antique furniture. 74–75
Slide-bolt-latch. Make it! don't buy it. 274–77

Locomotive models. *See* **Railroad models**

Locomotives, Toy. *See* **Railroads, Toy**

Lofts
Lofts. Built-ins. 112–19

Log carriers. *See* **Wood baskets and boxes**

Looms
Assembling and setting up Guatemalan backstrap loom. DeRodriguez. Weaving on a backstrap loom. 13–25
Backstrap loom. Bjerregaard. Techniques of Guatemalan weaving. 15–33
Backstrap loom construction. Held. Weaving. 211
Backstrap loom operation. Brown. Weaving, spinning, and dyeing book. 66–75
Backstrap loom. Newman. Contemporary Southeast Asian arts and crafts. 64–68
Back-strap loom, warp-weighted loom, Navaho loom, Kochin back-strap loom. Gilby. Free weaving. 47–63, 136–38
Bead weaving loom. Erlandsen. Bead book. 67–68
Bead weaving loom. Gill. Beadwork: the technique of stringing, threading, and weaving. 112–16
Building an upright frame loom, weaving on a multiharness loom. Make it! don't buy it. 360–63, 380–91
Cardboard loom, fabric loom, straw loom and popsicle stick loom. Linderman. Crafts for the classroom. 215–27
Constructing a frame. Tod. Joy of hand weaving. 37–39
Constructing a vertical frame. Swanson. Rigid heddle weaving. 183–86
Design and construction of Danish loom. Worst. Weaving with foot-power looms. 239–42
Design and construction of Swedish loom. Worst. Weaving with foot-power looms. 239, 243–47
Fixed-warp loom. Held. Weaving. 216–17
Floor loom, inkle loom. Abrams. Building craft equipment. 125–51
Fly shuttle. Worst. Weaving with foot-power looms. 239, 247
Four-shaft loom. Murray. Essential handbook of weaving. 73–76
Frame, backstrap, two-harness, tapestry, four-harness, jack-type, counter-balanced, and counter-marche looms. Creager. Weaving: a creative approach for beginners. 10–35
Frame looms. Murray. Essential handbook of weaving. 16–21
Frames for punch needle work. Illes. Men in stitches. 103–11
Hopi belt loom. Brown. Weaving, spinning, and dyeing book. 56–62
How to warp and thread a four-harness loom. Tod. Joy of hand weaving. 145–58
Improvised looms. Murray. Essential handbook of weaving. 11–15
Indian loom. Tod. Joy of hand weaving. 40–43
Inkle loom. Held. Weaving. 218–20
Inkle loom, frame loom, backstrap loom. Holland. Weaving primer. 11–19, 53–60, 169–72
Inkle loom operation. Brown. Weaving, spinning, and dyeing book. 46–51
Loom frame. Skowronski. Sprang; thread twisting, a creative textile technique. 13–14
Loom, warping or threading. Worst. Weaving with foot-power looms. 7–39
Looms. Lewis. Everybody's weaving book. 16–23
Looms and dressing the loom. Ickis. Weaving as a hobby. 5–36
Looms, backstrap loom weaving. Andersen. Creative exploration in crafts. 103–26
Making a frame loom. Weaving and spinning. 29–33
Making a T-D (tongue depressor) loom. Swanson. Rigid heddle weaving. 105–08
Making a two-harness table loom. Tod. Joy of hand weaving. 67–70
Making the loom, loom variations. Mattera. Navajo techniques for today's weaver. 37–52, 83–103
Making your own frame loom. Parker. Creative handweaving. 106–07
Manufactured looms. Murray. Essential handbook of weaving. 48–53

Nail frame loom. Redman. Frame-loom weaving. 16–19
Nail frame loom, simple circular loom, branch loom, tube used as a loom. Rhodes. Small woven tapestries. 115–20
Navajo loom operation. Brown. Weaving, spinning, and dyeing book. 70–105
Ojibway loom. Held. Weaving. 218
Permanent frame loom, reusable frame loom. Held. Weaving. 213–16
Pin, notched, slit-edge, stitch-edge, and spoke looms. Krevitsky. Shaped weaving. 18–31
Primitive loom, cigar box loom. Norbeck. Book of authentic Indian life crafts. 85–89
Rigid heddle. Murray. Essential handbook of weaving. 23–25
Rigid heddle loom. Swanson. Rigid heddle weaving. 8–11
Short-web tapestry loom. Held. Weaving. 217
Simple frame weaving. Encyclopedia of crafts. 38
Simple looms and frames. Seagroatt. Basic textile book. 54–56
Strip loom. Newman. Contemporary African arts and crafts. 110–21
Table top loom. Complete handyman do-it-yourself encyclopedia. 1590–94
Treadle looms. Brown. Weaving, spinning, and dyeing book. 117–65
Types of looms, dressing the loom. Black. Key to weaving. 13–52

Lorries, Toy. *See* **Trucks, Toy**

Lost-wax casting. *See* **Casting**

Love seats. *See* **Sofas**

Loudspeakers
Acoustic mini speaker. Buckwalter. Easy speaker projects. 85–90
Amplifier-record cabinet. Leavy. Bookshelves and storage units. 54–55
Bass reflex. Buckwalter. Easy speaker projects. 39–49
Bookshelf speaker. Buckwalter. Easy speaker projects. 15–20
Ceiling mounted speaker. Buckwalter. Easy speaker projects. 69–75
Corner enclosure. Buckwalter. Easy speaker projects. 21–28
Homasote baffle. Buckwalter. Easy speaker projects. 51–58
How to install car stereo speakers. Popular Mechanics do-it-yourself encyclopedia. Vol. 18, 2753–55
Nine-unit stereo speaker, speakers in end tables, bookshelf speakers, outdoor speaker in planter box. Complete handyman do-it-yourself encyclopedia. Vol. 17, 2471–77, 2505–20
Omnidirectional speaker. Buckwalter. Easy speaker projects. 59–68
Speaker cabinets. Brann. How to build kitchen cabinets, room dividers, and cabinet furniture. 77–78
Speaker cover. Burchette. More needlework blocking and finishing. 132–33
Speaker in a wall. Buckwalter. Easy speaker projects. 77–83
Speaker system cabinet. Family handyman handbook of carpentry plans/projects. 48–51
Speaker treatments. Spencer. Designing and building your own stereo furniture. 144–76
Stereo speaker elevators. Oberrecht. Plywood projects illustrated. 226–28
Television speaker. Buckwalter. Easy speaker projects. 29–37
Wells. Building stereo speakers.

Luggage
Have bag—will travel. Houck. Big bag book. 82–90

Luggage tags. *See* **Labels**

Lunch boxes
Lunch box (needlepoint). Burchette. More needlework blocking and finishing. 33–36
Lunchboxes. Parry. Stenciling. 110
Ribboned lunch box. Doherty. Family Circle book of 420 great gifts-to-make all year round for just 10¢ to $10.00. 164–65

M

Macrame
Basic cavandoli and three-dimensional knotting. Dodge. Step-by-step new macrame. 13–34
Basic knots, belt. Andersen. Creative exploration in crafts. 85–99
Boberg. Macrame.
Cavandoli samplers, simple and three colored patterns. Dodge. Step-by-step new macrame. 19–21
Introduction to macrame. Reader's Digest complete guide to needlework. 444–60
Knotting. Brown. Complete book of rush and basketry techniques. 118–28
Knotting and macrame. Parker. Beginner's book of off-loom weaving. 75–106
Knotting techniques. Andes. Far beyond the fringe. 12–157
Macrame. Dillmont. Complete encyclopedia of needlework. 365–408
Macrame. Kicklighter. Crafts, illustrated designs and techniques. 176–85
Macrame. Rose. Illustrated encyclopedia of crafts and how to master them. 285–92
Macrame. Ryan. Complete encyclopedia of stitchery. 562–85
Macrame. Torbet. Macrame you can wear. 1–64
Macrame. Waller. Knots and netting. 28–34
Macrame baskets. Meilach. Modern approach to basketry. 189–219
Macrame for disabled. Anderson. Crafts and the disabled. 115–19
Macrame hanging. Evans. Ribbonwork. 98–101
Macrame knots. Linderman. Crafts for the classroom. 244–54
Macrame knots and sampler. Held. Weaving. 222–33
Macrame seating. Meyers. Furniture repair and refinishing. 208–09
Macrame wall hangings. Casselman. Crafts from around the world. 217–23
Rouleau strips in macrame. Stearns. Macrame. 73–75
Samplers: unknotted and border outline. Dodge. Step-by-step new-macrame. 24–29
Stearns. Macrame.
Wire macrame. Newman. Wire art. 63–65

Macrame. *See also* **Knots and splices**

Magazine stands, racks, etc.
Built-in magazine and book rack. Leavy. Bookshelves and storage units. 62–64
Case for magazines, quick and simple magazine rack. Oberrecht. Plywood projects illustrated. 140–43, 192–93
Cradle magazine rack. Capotosto. Woodworking techniques and projects. 291–95
Magazine, book rack. Brann. How to build kitchen cabinets, room dividers, and cabinet furniture. 76
Magazine holder. Reader's Digest complete guide to sewing. 445
Magazine rack. Dal Fabbro. How to make children's furniture and play equipment. 89
Magazine rack. Kramer. Wirecraft. 98–99
Magazine rack. LaPlante. Plastic furniture for the home craftsman. 90–92
Magazine rack. Philbin. Cabinets, bookcases & closets. 107
Magazine rack, tilting magazine rack. Blandford. 53 space-saving built-in furniture projects. 114, 119–21, 136, 139–42
Magazine stand. DeCristoforo. Build your own wood toys, gifts and furniture. 380–83
Magazine stand. Rubin. Mission furniture. 68–69

Magazine table. Williams. Spanish colonial furniture. 72–73
Oriental-geometry. Scheuer. Designs for Holbein embroidery. 32–33
Plexiglass magazine rack. Popular Mechanics do-it-yourself encyclopedia. Vol. 14, 2209
Portsmouth magazine stand. Brann. How to build colonial furniture. 34–42
Rack for magazines. Modern general shop. Metalworking. 102–103
Stenciled magazine rack. Roda. Fabric decorating for the home. 190–91
Tree for magazines and newspapers, magazine bucket. Popular Mechanics do-it-yourself encyclopedia. Vol. 11, 1758–59
Vinyl magazine rack. Doherty. Family Circle book of 429 great gifts-to-make all year round for just 10¢ to $10.00. 5
Wall-mounted magazine rack. Oberrecht. Plywood projects illustrated. 67–70

Magnetic tape enclosures
Bookcase for paperbacks and tapes. Philbin. Cabinets, bookcases & closets. 130–31

Mail boxes
Covered bridge for newspapers. Oberrecht. Plywood projects illustrated. 63–66
Fashionable mailbox standard. Better Homes and Gardens. Step-by-step masonry & concrete. 76–77
Mail box holder. Braren. Homemade. 49
Mailbox and name plate gate. Brann. How to build outdoor projects. 49–56
Roadside mailbox rack. Brann. How to build outdoor projects. 136–38

Mailboxes, Metal
Build a mail holder. Giant book of metalworking projects. 68–69
Mailbox. Modern general shop. Metalworking. 116

Mail racks
Colonial and contemporary letter racks to organize your mail. Popular Mechanics do-it-yourself encyclopedia. Vol. 11, 1712–15
Letter and key rack. Modern general shop. Woodworking. 106
Letter holder. Cope. Plastics. 63–64
Needlepoint mailbox. Parker. Mosaics in needlepoint. 123–26
Wooden mail holder. Linsley. Decoupage on glass, wood, metal, rocks, shells, wax, soap, plastic, canvas, ceramic. 40–44

Makeup boxes. See **Cosmetics accessories**

Mantels. See **Fireplaces**

Maps
Map pocket. Lamoreaux. Outdoor gear you can make yourself. 69–73
Map reading. Popular Mechanics do-it-yourself encyclopedia. Vol. 12, 1764–67
Papier-mâché relief map. Elbert. Paperworks. 127–30
Punch needle work maps. Illes. Men in stitches. 83–101
Vinyl map case. Linsley. Great bazaar. 125
World globe. Fine woodworking techniques 3. 157–61

Marble
Marble (repair). Schuler. How to fix almost everything. 116–18
Marble tabletop repair. Marshall. How to repair, reupholster, and refinish furniture. 156

Marbeling
Marbeling panels and furniture. Oughton. Complete manual of wood finishing. 135–43

Marionettes. See **Puppets**

Marking devices
Marking out tennis, football and other pitches. Bumper book of things a boy can make. 189–90

Marquetry
Flexible veneer marquetry inlay jewelry. Sommer. Contemporary costume jewelry. 90–93
History and practice of marquetry. Fine woodworking techniques 3. 171–73
How to mount marquetry. Fine woodworking techniques 2. 178–79
Introduction to marquetry. Hobbs. Veneer craft for everyone. 147–51
Marquetry. Kicklighter. Crafts, illustrated designs and techniques. 186–95
Marquetry. Platt. Step-by-step woodcraft. 54–57
Marquetry. Rose. Illustrated encyclopedia of crafts and how to master them. 31–32
Marquetry: a difficult art made easier. Popular Mechanics do-it-yourself encyclopedia. Vol. 12, 1772–77
Marquetry boxes. Mills. The book of presents. 134
Marquetry with flexible veneers, finishing marquetry. Fine woodworking techniques 4. 204–07
Patch-pad cutting for marquetry. Fine woodworking techniques 1. 152–58
Repairing marquetry. Hayward. Antique furniture repairs. 96–97
Repairing marquetry. Wenn. Restoring antique furniture. 65–67
Straw marquetry. Coker. Craft of straw decoration. 32–34

Marquetry See also **Inlay; Pictures, Wood**

Masks
Box mask. Yoder. Sculpture and modeling for the elementary school. 155–56
Decorative cylinder masks, reversible mask, ceramic mask, half or eye mask. Lyon. Arts and crafts objects children can make for the home. 45–53
Dragon. Grainger. Creative papercraft. 81–86
Eagle mask. Gardner. Dough creations. 96–100
Face masks. Romberg. Let's discover papier-mâché. 53
Half mask; curtain mask; gauze mask; clown's make-up; paper masks. Bumper book of things a girl can make. 63–68, 76–78
Human mask. Grainger. Creative papercraft. 87–88
Making a mask. Ashurst. Collage. 103–04
Masks. Linderman. Crafts for the classroom. 92–93, 339–40
Masks and head-dresses. Tyler. Big book of soft toys. 69–77
Masks: paper bag, paper plate, elephant face, jughead, balloon, and clay forms. Yoder. Sculpture and modeling for the elementary school. 189–97
Papier-mâché mask. Kinney. How to make 19 kinds of American folk art. 15
Peters. Creative masks for stage and school.
Sleep mask. Burchette. More needlework blocking and finishing. 58–60
Tulip tree masks. Johnson. Nature crafts. 89
Woodcarving masks. Tangerman. Carving the unusual. 54–55

Masks, Decorative
Carved masks patterns. Bridgewater. A treasury of woodcarving designs. 154–76
Three-dimensional mask. Chroman. Potter's primer. 110–12

Masonry
Brickwork. Outdoor projects for home and garden. 258–61
Foundations and masonry. Bragdon. Homeowner's complete manual of repair & improvement. 534–57
How to paint masonry so it stays painted. Popular Mechanics do-it-yourself encyclopedia. Vol. 12, 1778–80

Leveling flagstones, cutting flagstone designs. Outdoor projects for home and garden. 257–58, 306–08

Masonry repairs and maintenance. Geary. Complete handbook of home exterior repair and maintenance. 205–37

Opening solid masonry for a new door or window. Time-Life Books. New living spaces. 95–97

Masonry walls. Olin. Construction. 205. 1–205. 35, 343. 1–343. 27

Pave it with bricks and sand. Outdoor projects for home and garden. 296–303

Masonry. See also **Brick construction; Concrete; Stone construction**

Matchboxes
Decorated large kitchen matchbox. Elbert. Paperworks. 83–85
Decorative borders for cards, bookmarks and table match-boxes. Gordon. Complete guide to drying and preserving flowers. 73–77
Felt covered matchboxes. Goldman. Decorate with felt. 8–11
Fireside match box. Marlow. Early American furnituremaker's manual. 18–22
Matchbox cover. Vanderbilt. Gloria Vanderbilt designs for your home. 172
Ribbon matchbooks. Coffey. Francine Coffey's celebrity sewing bee. 167
Wall hung match box. Doherty. Family Circle book of 429 great gifts-to-make all year round for just 10¢ to $10.00. 128–29

Mats. See **Door mats; Rugs; Table mats**

Mattresses
Mattress covers. McCall's sewing for your home. 35–36, 106–107, 192–93, 224

May baskets. See **Baskets**

Mazes
Making a maze. Bumper book of things a girl can make. 110–11

Measuring sticks
Guide to the right measurements, how to "enlarge" your micrometer. Popular Mechanics do-it-yourself encyclopedia. Vol. 12, 1784–85, 1828–29
Measuring fence and stop. McNair. Building & outfitting your workshop. 202–07
Two sticks (for measuring layout of big jobs) Fine woodworking techniques I. 122–25
Yardstick case. Goldman. Decorate with felt. 101

Medallions
Kaleidoscope medallions. Gardner. Dough creations. 92–94

Medicine cabinets. See **Bathrooms; Cabinets**

Megaphones. See **Loudspeakers**

Memorandum holders
Bottle gourd note box. Mordecai. Gourd craft. 84–87
Greeting cards used to make a note or card holder. D'Amato. Italian crafts. 108–11
Memo pad. LaPlante. Plastic furniture for the home craftsman. 78–79
Memo pad. Parker. Mosaics in needlepoint. 113–17
Muslin letter sorter, shopping organizer. Better Homes and Gardens easy bazaar crafts. 12, 19
Note card holder. Modern general shop. Woodworking. 105
Note holder. Blandford. 53 space-saving built-in furniture projects. 121–24

Mending. See **Clothing and dress, Mending**

Merry-go-rounds
Carousel horse. Fine woodworking techniques 4. 176–78

Merry-go-rounds, Toy
Music carousel. Cook. Decorating for the holidays. 49

Metal finishing
Antiquing copper and brass, artificial patinas. Metalcrafting encyclopedia. 43–45
Coloring by chemicals and heat. Chamberlain. Metal jewelry techniques. 113–15
Finishing damascus steel. Meilach. Decorative and sculptural ironwork. 230–33
Painting metal. Geary. Complete handbook of home exterior repair and maintenance. 152–57
Repair and care of metals. Johnson. How to restore, repair, and finish almost everything. 166–79
Reticulation. Sprintzen. Jewelry, basic techniques and design. 92–93
Rolling mill prints. Sprintzen. Jewelry, basic techniques and design. 98–99
Surface treatment of metals. Marshall. Foilcraft. 137–42
Surface treatments & finishes. Foote. Jewelry making. 60–67

Metal foil
Construction of geometric forms. Marshall. Foilcraft. 71–88
Copper foil stained glass lampshades. Duncan. Leaded glass. 175–94
Copper tooling mounted on wood, aluminum tooling on pie tins. Lyon. Arts and crafts objects children can make for the home. 153–59
Covering a molding in a repeat design. Marshall. Foilcraft. 39–41
Embossing greeting cards. Holtje. Cardcraft. 109–14
Foil plate animals. Yoder. Sculpture and modeling for the elementary school. 128–29
Foil tooling. Kicklighter. Crafts, illustrated designs and techniques. 118–23
Marshall. Foilcraft.
Working with metal foil. Metalcrafting encyclopedia. 136–44

Metal Work
Abrasive cutoff machine, portable saw pinch-hits as a cutoff machine, easy-to-make sheet-metal cutter. Popular Mechanics do-it-yourself encyclopedia. Vol. 6, 892–99
Aluminum crafting. Giant book of crafts. 175–84
Decorative rosettes and wallhooks. Weygers. Modern blacksmith. 46–51
Freezing molten metal. Sprintzen. Jewelry, basic techniques and design. 95–98
Hollow tubular frame repair. Brightman. 101 practical uses for propane torches. 118–19
Hollowing and raising. Blandford. Practical handbook of blacksmithing and metalworking. 377–402
How to drill square holes. Weygers. Recycling, use, and repair of tools. 37–39
Know-how of working sheet metal, sheet-metal brake you make of wood. Popular Mechanics do-it-yourself encyclopedia. Vol. 17, 2623–29
Lindsley. Metalworking in the home shop.
Masonite die forming. Sprintzen. Jewelry, basic techniques and design. 51–58
Measuring, holding, cutting, shaping, drilling & screwing. Blandford. Practical handbook of blacksmithing and metalworking. 311–60
Metal tubing projects: ring basket, siphon, shelf bracket, drawer pull, tool handles, bookshelf post, whistle. Popular Mechanics do-it-yourself encyclopedia. Vol. 19, 2956–59
Metalcrafting encyclopedia.
Metalwork. Capotosto. Woodworking wisdom. 108–19
Metalworking. Modern general shop. Metalworking. 1–128
Nail art, metal sculpture. Kicklighter. Crafts, illustrated designs and techniques. 196–205

Silver, pewter, brass repair, making handles and knobs. Introduction to repairing and restoring. 247–90

Smithing (forging). Rose. Illustrated encyclopedia of crafts and how to master them. 54–61

Tempering high-carbon steel. Weygers. Recycling, use, and repair of tools. 32–33

Tempering steel metal work. Brightman. 101 practical uses for propane torches. 69–72

Testing: what metal is it? Wood. Make your own jewelry. 179

Tubes and hinges. Sjoberg. Working with copper, silver and enamel. 40–42

Working with metal. Make it! don't buy it. 186–207

Working with metal.

Mice

Felt mouse. Reader's Digest complete guide to sewing. 490

Matilda mouse. Guild. Dollmaker's workshop. 46–48

Mighty mouse cat or child's toy. Woman's Day crochet showcase. 164

Mouse wedding party. American School of Needlework. Great crochet bazaar book. 131–41

Stuffed toy mouse. McCall's sewing for your home. 192

Mice. *See also* **Animals**

Microphones

Directional microphone, parabolic microphones. Complete handyman do-it-yourself encyclopedia. Vol. 11, 1658–67

Mills, Miniature

Water wheel and grist mill. Maginley. America in miniatures. 18–23

Mirrors

Adjustable hanging shop mirror. McNair. Building & outfitting your workshop. 46–52

Apple tree mirror. Christensen. Needlepoint. 51–52

Appliqued mirror frame. Gardner. Dough creations. 57–61

Authentic Lincoln reproductions of two mirrors. Popular Mechanics do-it-yourself encyclopedia. Vol. 12, 1840–45

Bargello mirror frame. Wilson. Needleplay. 126

Beveled mirror. Isenberg. How to work in beveled glass. 189–95

Blue shell mirror. Logan. Shell crafts. 149–51

Breadboard, round embroidered, square embroidered, purse sized mirrors. Doherty. Family Circle book of 429 great gifts-to-make all year round for just 10¢ to $10.00. 5, 16, 63

Butterfly mirror, Mt. Tom train mirror. Challenging projects in stained glass. 55–77

Canvas work mirror frame. Encyclopedia of crafts. 73

Carved kitchen mirror. Gottshall. Wood carving and whittling for everyone. 79–81

Carved looking glass with comb tray. Gottshall. Wood carving and whittling for everyone. 82–85

Carved walnut mirror frame. Gottshall. Wood carving and whittling for everyone. 76–78

Carved wood partridge mirror frame. Popular Mechanics do-it-yourself encyclopedia. Vol. 4, 606–07

Cheval glass (full-length swinging mirror). Capotosto. Woodworking techniques and projects. 225–32

Cloud gong on tortoiseshell lattice, mirror. Nicoletti. Japanese motifs for needlepoint 46–50

Decorative hand mirror. Coyne. Penland School of Crafts book of jewelry making. 133–48

Decoupage applied to mirrors. Davis. Step-by-step decoupage. 46

Eagle-topped frame, Mexican styled frame. Marshall. Foilcraft. 51–54

Federal mirror with eagle, stars and scallop shell. Upton. Woodcarver's primer. 90–104
Federal mirror with fruit basket panel. Upton. Woodcarver's primer. 105–20
Frame for a mirror. Christensen. Needlepoint and bargello stitchery. 94
Frame for tilting heart-shaped mirror. Popular Mechanics do-it-yourself encyclopedia. Vol. 9, 1361–62
Frame yourself (needlepoint-for mirror). Golden book of hand and needle arts. 110–11
Geometric mirror. Scheuer. Designs for Holbein embroidery. 26–27
Hand mirror. Rombert. Let's discover papier-mâché. 62
Heart shaped mirror. Vanderbilt. Gloria Vanderbilt designs for your home. 41
Lee House mirror. Daniele. Building early American furniture. 92–93
Macaroni mirror. O'Neill. Make-it-merry Christmas book. 18–21
Mahogany mirror, eighteenth century mirror. Osburn. Measured drawings of early American furniture. 26–27, 44–45
Make a mirror frame from a dinner plate. Priolo. Ceramics by coil. 44–45
Making and carving a laurel wreath mirror frame. Upton. Woodcarver's primer. 76–89
Mirror case. Christensen. Teach yourself needlepoint. 114–15
Mirror for Shaker pegboard. Moser. How to build Shaker furniture. 102–03
Mirror frame. Villiard. Art and craft of sand casting. 93
Mirror frame, plexiglass mirror ornament. Woman's Day book of gifts to make. 174–77
Mirror frame with lamp. Coyne. Penland School of Crafts book of pottery. 177–88
Mirror in shadow box. Logan. Shell crafts. 151–57
Mirror installation. Blandford. 53 space-saving built-in furniture projects. 265–67
Mirror mat on counted thread fabric. Rosenthal. Not-so-nimble needlework book. 47–48
Mirror ornament: seed tree in Pinto in Aria. D'Amato. Italian crafts. 33–38
Mirror tile installation. Burch. Tile: indoors and out, every kind and use. 119–23
Mirror with clothes hooks. Blandford. How to make your own built-in furniture. 249–51
Mirror with shelf. Brown. 44 terrific woodworking plans & projects. 130, 132–33
Mirror with shelves. Blandford. How to make your own built-in furniture. 248–49
Mirrors in needlepoint. Scobey. First easy-to-see needlepoint workbook. 68–71
Mother-of-pearl mirror frame. Casselman. Crafts from around the world. 16–18
Needlepoint hand mirror and mini hanger. Embroidery of roses. 108
Needlepoint mirror frame. Smith. Needlery. 133–35
Painted mirror frame. Sayer. Crafts of Mexico. 32–33
Painted mirror frames. Howard. New tole & folk art designs. 101–06
Pewter mirror mounts. Metal and enamel. 39–41
Pier set for your foyer. Popular Mechanics do-it-yourself encyclopedia. Vol. 14, 2162–65
Quilled silver Mylar mirror frame. Paper. 34–35
"Sampler" mirror frame (embroidered). McCall's book of America's favorite needlework and crafts. 79–80
Shell mirror. Jarnow. (Re)do it yourself. 163–68
Shell mirrors. Johnson. Nature crafts. 31–33
Shell-covered mirror. Vanderbilt. Gloria Vanderbilt designs for your home. 142–44
Super-easy glass tile mirrors, tour de force mirror, tiled mirror frame. Elbert. Shell craft. 55–61, 205–06
Three needlepoint mirror frames. McCall's book of America's favorite needlework and crafts. 136–40
Tulip-painted mirror. Evrard. Homespun crafts from scraps. 45–47
Turning a mirror frame, hand mirror, pendant mirror. Sainsbury. Craft of woodturning. 123–27, 163–66, 171
Wax intarsia hand mirror rack. Casselman. Crafts from around the world. 100–03
Wildflower design needlepoint mirror frame. Better Homes and Gardens treasury of needlecrafts. 242–44
Wreath mirror (stained glass). McCall's book of America's favorite needlework and crafts. 334

Mirrors, Silvering
Gilding, silvering, and mosaic. Duthie. Decorative glass processes. 208–13
Mirror resilvering. Patton. Furniture finishing. 209–11

Miter boxes, gages, etc.
Miter block, miter box, shooting board. Langsner. Country woodcraft. 117–18
Two miter boards, make angle blocks for miter cuts. Popular Mechanics do-it-yourself encyclopedia. Vol. 12, 1850–52, 1854–55

Mittens
Crayon-color knitted mittens. Better Homes and Gardens easy bazaar crafts. 38–39, 44
Crochet mittens. Design crochet. 105–06
Crocheted mittens, popcorn-trimmed gauntlets, girls' mittens. Woman's Day crochet showcase. 32, 73, 127
Fabric mittens. Scurlock. Muzzleloader Magazine's book of buckskinning II. 73–74
Family mittens. Favorite knitting & crochet patterns. 231–36
For his skiing, a cap and mittens. Feldman. Needlework boutique. 142–45
Fur mittens. Wilder. Secrets of Eskimo skin sewing. 47–57
Knit Aran mitts. Hollingworth. Complete book of traditional Aran knitting. 133–35
Knitted mittens. Reader's Digest complete guide to needlework. 253
Lively stitched hand warmers (crocheted). Time-Life Books. Boutique attire. 157
Mittens. Selfridge. Patchwork knitting. 152
Mittens from Lapland. Compton. Complete book of traditional knitting. 180–82
Mittens in minutes. Brown. Super sweater idea book. 192–94
Mittens (quilted). Laury. Quilted clothing. 132–33
Reversible double-thick mittens. McCall's big book of knit & crochet for home & family. 88
Stars 'n stripes mittens, child's wizard helmet and mittens. Woman's Day book of gifts to make. 92–94, 195–98
Striped knitted, two-tone knitted. Woman's Day bazaar best sellers. 26–28
Toasty mittens. Knitting techniques and projects. 61

Mobiles
Aluminum can cutouts, plantmobile, table mobile made from ping pong balls. Epple. Something from nothing crafts. 92, 155, 194–95
Animal & clown mobiles. Woman's Day book of gifts to make. 16–18, 22–23
Animal cookie mobile or poster. Elbert. Paperworks. 110–12
Baby mobile (eggs). Mills. Book of presents. 49
Baptismal mobile, wedding mobile. Hagans. All good gifts. 43–53
Bird mobile. Creative crafts yearbook: an exciting new collection of needlework and crafts. 44
Bluebird ballet (crocheted). Feldman. Needlework boutique. 29–31
Christmas mobile. Miles. Designing with natural materials. 91–94
Cornhusk angel mobile. Johnson. Nature crafts. 70–71
Crib mobile. Wargo. Soft crafts for special occasions. 32–35
Crow cats, scarecrow. Casselman. Crafts from around the world. 158–60
Designing a mobile. Marshall. Foilcraft. 62–63
Driftwood mobile. Platt. Step-by-step woodcraft. 36–37
Flowers in plastic mobile. O'Neill. Make-it-merry Christmas book. 94–95
Flying insects. Romberg. Let's discover papier-mâché. 31
Gem mobile. Meras. Vacation crafts. 107–08
Gingerbread boy jamboree (crocheted). Feldman. Needlework boutique. 18–20
Goldfish mobile. American School of Needlework. Great crochet bazaar book. 142–43
Holz. Mobiles you can make.
Honey bees mobile. Greenhowe. Making miniature toys and dolls. 80–81

Making disc mobile. Paper. 62–63
Merry-go-round, aquarium, birds, sailing ships mobiles. Tyler. Big book of soft toys. 206–19
Metal foil mobiles. Metalcrafting encyclopedia. 150–51
Metal mobiles. Yoder. Sculpture and modeling for the elementary school. 141–43
Mobiles on a base: dolly on a perch, valentine hearts, scary witch, shower of stars, Hanukkah Menorah and Lithuanian straw. Holz. Mobiles you can make. 71–91
Mobiles on a string: what am I? butterflies, floating flowers, joy and love, Jonah and the whale, silly lion, happy scarecrow, laying hen and Santa face. Holz. Mobiles you can make 49–70
Mobiles with arms: German snowflakes, pleated angel choir, birds in flight, Danish bells, angels with horns, wormy apples, Danish woven hearts, whirling wheels, paper stripe fish and ojo de Dios. Holz. Mobiles you can make. 92–117
Mourning dove in a basket. Meras. Vacation crafts. 39–40
Nautical mobiles. Tangerman. Carving the unusual. 28–33
Paper mobiles. Stephan. Creating with tissue paper. 171, 174–75
Rainbow mobile. Popular Mechanics do-it-yourself encyclopedia. Vol. 5, 696
Ring of roses, flying high birds, and beneath the waves fish mobiles. Janitch. All made from paper. 33–36
Santa Claus mobile, dove mobile. Araki. Origami for Christmas. 130–31
Seashell mobile. Evrard. Homespun crafts from scraps. 142–44
Shell mobile. Elbert. Shell craft. 68–69
Stitchery lid molules, Halloween skeleton, Santa Claus, bird, circular mobiles, Valentine, aluminum, fish. Lyon. Arts and crafts objects children can make for the home. 55–68
Valentine mobile. Perry. Holiday magic. 27–28

Moccasins
Apache moccasins. Golden book of colonial crafts. 112–17
Grainger. How to make your own moccasins.
Indian moccasins. Evrard. Twinkletoes. 72–77
Indian moccasins. Norbeck. Book of authentic Indian life crafts. 48–51
Moccasins. Clark. The make-it-yourself shoe book. 34–56
Moccasins. Whitney. American Indian clothes and how to make them. 90–100
Trail boots. Evrard. Twinkletoes. 86–88

Modeling
Clay animal, people, beads, puppet head, slab sculpture, free form fox, whistles, head, animal bank, and goofy people tray. Yoder. Sculpture and modeling for the elementary school. 17–26
Clay modeling. Rath. Splendid soft toy book. 52–57
McCullough. Clay flower techniques. Vol. 1
Modeling waxes. Marshall. Foilcraft. 135

Models
Build models like a pro, three scratch-built control-line fighters. Popular Mechanics do-it-yourself encyclopedia. Vol. 12, 1883–88
Chesneau. Scale models in plastic.
Cocktail stick models. Encyclopedia of crafts. 216
Ellis. Scale modeler's handbook.
Gordon. How to build, customize, & design plastic models.
Jackson. Modelmaker's handbook.
Model building board. Hamilton. Build it together. 62–69
Modelmaker's shop in a cabinet. Popular Mechanics do-it-yourself encyclopedia. Vol. 17, 2656–58
Price. Model-building handbook.

Models, Radio control. *See* **Radio control**

Molas. *See* **Textile craft; Applique**

Moldings
Cutting and fitting moldings. Bard. Successful wood book. 72–87
Installing cove moldings. Brightman. 101 practical uses for propane torches. 67
Installing moldings. Spence. General carpentry. 404–10
Installing moldings. Time-Life Books. New living spaces. 46–49
Making rope and other moldings. Upton. Woodcarver's primer. 48–55
Molding. Blandford. How to make early American and colonial furniture. 89–93
Moldings—the finishing touch, how to work magic with moldings. Popular Mechanics
    do-it-yourself encyclopedia. Vol. 12, 1901–09

Moldings, Repairing
Mouldings. Hayward. Antique furniture repairs. 57–63

Molds (for casting)
Linoleum block mold, wax model. Marshall. Foilcraft. 99–104
Liquid rubber moulds. Introduction to repairing and restoring. 176–77
Make a plaster mold. Priolo. Ceramics by coil. 31–33
Match-plate patterns, shad dart lure. Giant book of metalworking projects. 214
Plaster casting. Kicklighter. Crafts, illustrated designs and techniques. 232–37

Money boxes. *See* **Banks, Toy**

Mops
Scrub mop. Conner. Corncraft. 77–79

Morse code
International Morse code. Rome. Needlepoint letters and numbers. 114–16

Mosaics
Direct method, indirect method. Andersen. Creative exploration in crafts. 193–207
Methods. D'Amato. Italian crafts. 49–61
Mosaic (glass) Duthie. Decorative glass processes. 213–16
Mosaic tiles. Gardner. Dough creations. 100–05
Mosaics. Jarnow. (Re)do it yourself. 146–52
Mosaics. Kicklighter. Crafts, illustrated designs and techniques. 206–11
Mosaics. Rose. Illustrated encyclopedia of crafts and how to master them. 233–40
Mosaics from grocery seeds. Picturemaking. 54–59
Mosaics to refinish furniture. Joyner. Furniture refinishing at home. 61–71
Mosaics with natural stones. Giant book of crafts. 289–302
Pasta, grain and bean mosaics. Jarnow. (Re)do it yourself. 153–54
Paper mosaic. Linderman. Crafts for the classroom. 86–88
Ravenna mosaic. Picturemaking. 50–53
Shell mosaics. Logan. Shell crafts. 188–92
Straw mosaics. Hibbs. Straw sculpture. 80–81
Tile mosaics. Schuman. Art from many hands. 52–55

Mother's day decoration
Spoons with flowers for Mother's Day. Candlemaking and decorations. 35

Motor buses, Toy
School bus. Palmer. Making children's furniture and play structures. 128–30

Motorcycles, Toy
Three-wheel motorcycle, motorcycle, sidecar. Buckland. Toymaker's book of wooden vehicles. 60–69

Mowing machines. *See* **Lawn mowers**

Muffs
Crochet muffs. Woman's Day bazaar best sellers. 22–23, 50
Shag muffs. Holland. Weaving primer. 111–12

Mural decoration
Applying a mural. Family handyman handbook of carpentry plans/projects. 350–62
Bathroom mural, painting scenic murals. Picturemaking. 27–30
Hanging murals. Guide to wallpaper and paint. 38–41
Painting by projection. Picturemaking. 6–9

Music cabinets. *See* **Cabinets; Phonograph record cabinets**

Musical instruments
Trumpets, derders, tambourines. Hagans. All good gifts. 110–15

Mushrooms
Amanda's mushrooms. Walters. Crochet. 40
Mushrooms. Day. Complete book of rock crafting. 107–13
Mushrooms plaque. Jarvey. You can dough it! 11–13
Papier-mâché mushroom. Epple. Something from nothing crafts. 82–83

Music boxes
Musical mantelpiece. Modern general shop. Woodworking. 109

Musical instruments
Aeolian harp. Whatnot. 192
American harp, not-so-classic rosette for classical guitars, guitar binding and purfling. Fine woodworking techniques 5. 144–45, 175–79
Box musical instruments. Yoder. Sculpture and modeling for the elementary school. 152–53
Cane pipes. Johnson. Nature crafts. 47
Cigar-box ukelele, tambourine, easy-made banjo. Bumper book of things a boy can make. 46–48, 72–73, 150–51
Drum box & whistle flute. Baldwin. Old fashioned wooden toys. 38–40
Drums, bells, chimes, xylophone, shakers, rattles and banjos. Linderman. Crafts for the classroom. 314–19
Dulcimer, banjo. Horwitz. Mountain people, mountain crafts. 21–33
Dulcimers. Golden book of colonial crafts. 78–87
Flageolet, Aztec drum. Fine woodworking techniques 2. 142–45
Flute making. Adkins. Wood work. 175–83
Gourd musical instruments. Mordecai. Gourd craft. 184–97
Gourd thumb piano. Johnson. Nature crafts. 110–11
Guitar joinery, lute roses. Fine woodworking techniques I. 126–28, 170–73
Making maracas. Schuman. Art from many hands, 182–86
Shape of a violin. Fine woodworking techniques 3. 94–98
Spanish castanets. Bumper book of things a girl can make. 42–43

N

Nails
Aquarium, Inca breastplate, talisman pictures. 44 string and nail art projects. 92–96
Arsenal of specialized metal fasteners. Time-Life Books. Working with wood. 110–19
Drive the right nail. Popular Mechanics do-it-yourself encyclopedia. Vol. 13, 1954–57
Horseshoe nail projects. Metalcrafting encyclopedia. 65–73
Making nails. Blandford. Practical handbook of blacksmithing and metalworking. 112–16
Metallic designs using nails. Picturemaking. 74–77
Nail art. Kicklighter. Crafts, illustrated designs and techniques. 196–200
Nail box. McNair. Building & outfitting your workshop. 208–15
Nail panel. Metal and enamel. 54–57
Nail sculpture. Metalcrafting encyclopedia. 56–62
Nailing and nails. Waugh. Handyman's encyclopedia. 180–84
Nails. Handyman. 371–74
Nails and rivets. Make it! don't buy it. 268–73
Projects with wrought iron nails. Metalcrafting encyclopedia. 63–64
Removing nails, repairs with nails. Kinney. Complete book of furniture repair and refinishing. 26–27, 41–42
Wall sculpture. Modern general shop. Metalworking. 117

Name tags. *See* **Labels**

Napkin rings, holders, etc.
Beaded napkin ring. Hulbert. Creative beadwork. 61
Bracelets and napkin rings. Bird. Craft of Hawaiian lauhala weaving. 71–79
Bread dough napkin rings, daisy chain, felt blossom. Hetzer. Fancy folds. 122–23
Burlap napkin rings, woven napkin rings. Wargo. Soft crafts for special occasions. 94–97
Burlap placemats and napkin rings. Wargo. Soft crafts for special occasions. 94–95
Coat-hanger wire napkin holder. Kramer. Wirecraft. 64–65
Harvest mats and napkin rings. McCall's big book of country needlecrafts. 122–24
Holiday napkin rings, paper. Linsley. Great bazaar. 88–90
Laced leather napkin rings, rope napkin rings. Doherty. Family Circle book of 429 great gifts-to-make all year round for just 10¢ to $10.00. 127, 131
Metal napkin rack. Modern general shop. Metalworking. 115
Monogrammed napkin rings. Scobey. Decorating with needlepoint. 157–58.
Napkin holder. Hamilton. Build it together. 126–33
Napkin holder. Modern general shop. Woodworking. 95
Napkin holders to match tablecloths. Goldman. Decorate with felt. 38
Napkinholder with geese, napkinholder with reindeer. Lindberg. Counted cross-stitch designs for all seasons. 28–29, 92–93
Napkin ring. Metal and enamel. 52–53
Napkin ring. Mills. Book of presents. 96–97
Napkin rings. Jarvey. You can dough it! 63–65
Napkin rings. Parker. Mosaics in needlepoint. 102–04
Napkin rings. Roda. Fabric decorating for the home. 59
Napkin rings. Romberg. Let's discover papier-mâché. 48
Napkin rings. Sainsbury. Sainsbury's woodturning projects for dining. 18–24
Outdoor napkin holder. Cope. Plastics. 31
Ribbon napkin rings. Coffey. Francine Coffey's celebrity sewing bee. 75
Seashell table accessories. Johnson. Nature crafts. 37
Serviette rings. Wooldridge. Woodturning techniques. 72–74
Silver and napkin caddy. Brown. 44 terrific woodworking plans & projects. 123–26

Silverware and napkin caddy. Popular Mechanics do-it-yourself encyclopedia. Vol. 10, 1594

Tin can napkin rings. Epple. Something from nothing crafts. 182–84

Turning serviette rings. Sainsbury. Craft of woodturning. 151–58, 171–72

White scallop napkin holder, starfish napkin holder, circle-in-a-square napkin ring. Elbert. Shell craft. 172–79

Wooden napkin rings. Better Homes and Gardens easy bazaar crafts. 11, 18

Wooden teapot paper-napkin caddy. Woman's Day bazaar best sellers. 92

Napkins

Calico patchwork. Doherty. Family Circle book of 429 great gifts-to-make all year round for just 10¢ to $10.00. 16, 129

Christmas table napkins (embroidered). Creative crafts yearbook: an exciting new collection of needlework and crafts. 104–05

Cross-stitch napkins. Linsley. Great bazaar. 90–91

Floral applique napkins. Encyclopedia of crafts. 32

Flying swan. Scheuer. Designs for Holbein embroidery. 40–41

Fringed cocktail napkins. Roda. Fabric decorating for the home. 37

Hardanger napkins. Better Homes and Gardens treasury of needlecrafts. 376–78

Hardanger place mat & napkin. Better Homes and Gardens embroidery. 58–60

Hetzer. Fancy folds.

Lap naps. Coffey. Francine Coffey's celebrity sewing bee. 74

Napkins. Hagans. All good gifts. 66

Orchid folded table napkin. Paper. 123–24

Pulled thread napkin. Reader's Digest complete guide to needlework. 106

Quilted-edge napkins. Roda. Fabric decorating for the home. 219–20

Reversible napkins. Roda. Fabric decorating for the home. 63

Round breakfast napkins. Roda. Fabric decorating for the home. 51

Shadow applique-tablecloth and napkins. Better Homes and Gardens applique. 44–45

Nativity scenes. *See* **Creches**

Necklaces

African necklace. Mosesson. Jewelry craft for beginners. 41–45

Bib necklace, pendant necklace, bib. Torbet. Macrame you can wear. 94–95, 100–01, 104–05

Bird necklace. Christensen. Needlepoint. 73

Bowtie & bird necklaces. Laury. Quilted clothing. 126–27

Brass-ring necklace. Mosesson. Jewelry craft for beginners. 163–66

Button necklace. Mosesson. Jewelry craft for beginners. 46–48

Chain necklaces. Mosesson. Jewelry craft for beginners. 76–81

Cleopatra collar, instant beaded choker, sparkle chain, photograph pendant, romantic pleated collar and beaded "leather" choker. Farlie. Pennywise boutique. 97–101

Collar necklace of burlap with fringed edge. Sommer. Contemporary costume jewelry. 158

Corn, bean and squash necklaces. Connor. Corncraft. 64–65

Dangling stone necklace. Mosesson. Jewelry craft for beginners. 213–15

Egyptian crescent, Viking medallion, hammered gold band, Ecuador gold medallion, gold ribbon ruff, chaplet of leaves, butterfly and rose pendants, dogwood blossoms and stained glass medallions necklaces. Wilson. Needlework to wear. 26–39

Eight-petalled lotus necklace of turquoise and silver. Powers. Crafting turquoise jewelry. 159–61

Enameled African pendant. Mosesson. Jewelry craft for beginners. 247–249

Enameled-melon-slice necklace. Mosesson. Jewelry craft for beginners. 243–46

Enamelled necklace of shields. Mosesson. Jewelry craft for beginners. 249–52

Fabric bib with decorations. Mosesson. Jewelry craft for beginners. 52–59

Fancy fringed necklace. Farlie. Pennywise boutique. 165

Flowering branch necklace in petit point, butterfly embroidered necklace, polka-dot stuffed pansies, cross-stitch heart and macrame necklace. Wilson. Needlework to wear. 3–23

Gilded-lily brass necklace. Mosesson. Jewelry craft for beginners. 169–72

God's-eye necklaces. Sommer. Contemporary costume jewelry. 150

Going-around-in-circles necklace. Mosesson. Jewelry craft for beginners. 58–63

Hanging fish necklace with stone. Mosesson. Jewelry craft for beginners. 216–17

Indian necklaces. Stribling. Crafts from North American Indian arts. 20–50

Indian style necklace. Hulbert. Creative beadwork 53

Instructions for enamelled necklaces. Elliot. Working with copper. 98

Israeli coin necklace. Rockland. Hanukkah book. 148–50

Jeweled pendant (macrame). McCall's book of America's favorite needlework and crafts. 388–91

Jeweled silver or pewter collar. Mosesson. Jewelry craft for beginners. 217–18

Leather necklace. Sommer. Contemporary costume jewelry. 161

Locket or portrait holder. Pelisser. Jeweler's craft. 50–55

Lockets and lipstick holders. Woman's Day crochet showcase. 75

Long necklace. Torbet. Macrame you can wear. 78–79

Long three color necklace without fastener of variation. Gill. Beadwork: the technique of stringing, threading, and weaving. 50–51

Macrame cowry necklace. Logan. Shell crafts. 97–99

Macrame fringe and shell necklace. Logan. Shell crafts. 92–97

Making a necklace of twisted wire. Meyer. Rock tumbling. 76–77

Melon-slice pewter necklace. Mosesson. Jewelry craft for beginners. 173–76

A mixed-media approach to coiled body adornments. Sommer. Wearable crafts. 110–13

Modern art necklace (needle lace). Golden book of hand and needle arts. 157–58

Multicolor macrame necklace. Scharf. Butterick's fast and easy needlecrafts. 80–82

Multistrand necklace. Mosesson. Jewelry craft for beginners. 22–24

Multistrand threaded necklace. Mosesson. Jewelry for for beginners. 30–31

Necklace made of plastic rings and crochet. Scharf. Butterick's fast and easy needlecrafts. 74–77

Paper bead necklace, beadwork pendant, threaded bead jewelry, Indian bead necklace, happiness necklace, repousse fish pendant. Encyclopedia of crafts. 183–85, 190, 194, 196–97

Papier-mâché necklaces. Sommer. Contemporary costume jewelry. 175–77

Pin-money present: a necklace made of paper. Vanderbilt. Gloria Vanderbilt designs for your home. 195

Pouring and swirling a necklace. Hollander. Plastics for jewelry. 163–67

Primitive neck ornaments. Mosesson. Jewelry craft for beginners. 152–57

Prints, beads, assemblage necklaces. Sommer. Wearable crafts. 46–49

Relief painting a necklace. Hollander. Plastics for jewelry. 41–49

Rose blossom necklace. Better Homes and Gardens treasury of Christmas crafts & foods. 85

Rotationally casting a necklace. Hollander. Plastics for jewelry. 51–57

Seed necklaces. Schuman. Art from many hands. 178–82

Shell necklaces. Logan. Shell crafts. 71–78, 83–90

Silver gorget and matching earrings. Metalcrafting encyclopedia. 174

Silver helicoid neckpiece. Coyne. Penland School of Crafts book of jewelry making. 173–88

Silver necklace. Metal and enamel. 65–66

Silver torso. Coyne. Penland School of Crafts book of jewelry making. 77–108

Single-strand threaded necklace. Mosesson. Jewelry craft for beginners. 25–28

Soft silver and gold with wool necklace. Sommer. Contemporary costume jewelry. 146–48
Spice necklaces. Johnson. Nature crafts. 105
Swag necklace of clay. Mosesson. Jewelry craft for beginners. 108–11
Tatted collar necklace. Auld. Tatting; the contemporary art of knotting with a shuttle. 108–09
Three-chopper-enamelled silver necklace. Mosesson Jewelry craft for beginners. 252–54
Tin-foil necklace. Janitch. All made from paper. 43–44
Wire and metal necklaces. Mosesson. Jewelry craft for beginners. 121–34
Wire "horse rein." Newman. Wire art. 66–67
Wire-strung collar with bib. Mosesson. Jewelry craft for beginners. 70–73
Wrapped aluminum core necklace. Sommer. Wearable crafts. 102–03
Wrapped and fringed pendants with coil-button accents. Sommer. Wearable crafts. 104–05
Wrapping wool with copper foil necklace. Sommer. Contemporary costume jewelry. 148–49

Necklaces. *See also* **Jewelry**

Necklaces, Bead

Bead necklaces. Erlandsen. Bead book. 74–81
Beads on a wire chain. Mosesson. Jewelry craft for beginners. 74–76
Camelot, pink champagne, octagon beads, Apollo, Polynesian clusters, crystal lantern, tassels of the twenties, moonbean, pearl rope with tassels. Davies. Beads as jewelry. 113–36
Circle of beads on metal. Mosesson. Jewelry craft for beginners. 50–52
Crystal round and tube beads, in orbit Central Park, bugle tubes and rounds, wafer and fan beads, chunky wooden beads, circle or rounds, pink Polynesian necklaces. Davies. Beads as jewelry. 37–49
Dot and dash necklace. Gill. Beadwork: the techniques of stringing, threading, and weaving. 17–18
Feathered bead necklace. Gardner. Dough creations. 137–38
Flower string and variations—large center beads and wooden bead centers. Gill. Beadwork: the technique of stringing, threading, and weaving. 28–33
Horn and ceramic beads, look of links, crystal, rondelles and tube beads, Renaissance necklet, seventh heaven openwork necklet, stringing along with sequins, orange blossom, Victorian necklet. Davies. Beads as jewelry. 50–62
Horn ring necklace, sea urchin spine necklace, strawberry parfait, tigereye pendant, agate chip necklace, polished stones 'n links. Davies. Beads as jewelry. 99–112
Looped-wire and bead necklace. Metalcrafting encyclopedia. 166–67
Lotus blossom, regal tear drops, Egyptian circlet, Haitian seed bead neckloop, triple tier neckloop, blue bangle neckloop. Davies. Beads as jewelry. 137–49
Papier-mâché beaded necklace. Elbert. Paperworks. 107–10
Rolled paper bead necklace. Elbert. Paperworks. 38–40
Rose bead necklaces. Johnson. Nature crafts. 42–43
Seven bead necklace, night glow, cube bead chain, art deco scarabs, coffee break, cornflower necklace, cat's eye. Davies. Beads as jewelry. 85–98
Single-strand bead necklace. Mosesson. Jewelry craft for beginners. 17–21
Threaded bead necklaces. Hulbert. Creative beadwork. 14–47
Tri beads and pearls, woven necklet, Americana pie-wedge necklace, Indian basketweave, oats and pearls choker. Davies. Beads as jewelry. 63–82
Twisted seed-bead necklace. Mosesson. Jewelry craft for beginners. 32–35
Twisted wire and beads. Sommer. Contemporary costume jewelry. 32–34
Woven necklaces with beads. Holland. Weaving primer. 46–48

Necktie fasteners
Making a tie tack. Sprinzten. Jewelry, basic techniques and design. 111–16
Tie clips. Bovin. Jewelry making. 228–31

Neckties
Appliqued-ties. Better Homes and Gardens treasury of Christmas crafts & foods. 36–37
Bargello neckties. Christensen. Needlepoint and bargello stitchery. 67–70
Bargello tie. Christensen. Teach yourself needlepoint. 76–78
Batik man's tie. Anderson. Tie dyeing and batik. 88–90
Batik man's tie. Frame. Tie-dyeing and batik. 126–28
Batik ties. Tie-dye, batik and candlemaking step-by-step. 22–23
Beaded necktie. Stearns. Macrame. 48–51
Crocheted bow-ties. Woman's Day bazaar best sellers. 50
His and hers tie and scarf. Reader's digest complete guide to sewing. 492–93
Holly-berry bow tie and "embroidered" Christmas tie. Farlie. Pennywise boutique. 189–92
How to tie a tie. Speer. Put your best foot forward. 72–74
Macrame tie. Boberg. Macrame. 97
Man's necktie. Coffey. Francine Coffey's celebrity sewing bee. 108–09
Monogrammed gifts for Father's Day. Creative crafts yearbook: an exciting new collection of needlework and crafts. 116–17
Mosaic-patterned neckties. Walker. Mosaic knitting. 211–14
Neckerchief. Gehert. Rural Pennsylvania clothing. 154–56
Patchwork tie. Wooster. Quiltmaking. 134
Personalised tie. Gostelow. Cross stitch book. 110–12
Silvery-necktie. Woman's Day crochet showcase. 74
Striped tie (crocheted). Feldman. Needlework boutique. 80–81
Three-color man's tie, macrame tie. Torbet. Macrame you can wear. 92–93, 102–03
Tie rack. Cope. Plastics. 34–35
Tie rack jewelry tray. Cope. Plastics. 72

Needle cases
Embroidered mushroom needlecase. Woman's Day book of gifts to make. 97–98
Folding needlecase. Tyler. Big book of soft toys. 236–38
Folding needleholders. Woman's Day best sellers. 126
Knitting needle case. Coffey. Francine Coffey's celebrity sewing bee. 64
Korean needle case. Christmas decorations from Williamsburg's folk art collection. 17
Needle book. Fraser. Modern stitchery: stitches, patterns, free-form designing. 96–97
Needlebook. Christensen. Needlepoint and bargello stitchery. 78
Needlebook (needlepoint). Christensen. Needlepoint book. 118
Needle case. Burchette. Needlework. 83–85
Needlecase. Cane, rush and straw. 56–60
Needlecase. Fanning. Complete book of machine quilting. 269
Needlecase, pinchusion and glasses case (needlepoint). Mills. The book of presents. 36–37
Needlepoint needlecases. Creative crafts yearbook: an exciting new collection of needlework and crafts. 113

Needlepoint
All about needlepoint, designing needlepoint. McCall's big book of needlecrafts. 128–65
Ambuter. Open canvas.
Arnold. Needlepoint pattern book.
Barnes. 120 needlepoint design projects.
Blackburn. Needlepoint designs for traditional furniture

Canvas work frame. Anderson. Crafts and the disabled. 43

Canvas work. Complete guide to needlework. 24–47

Cleaning and restoration. Burchette. Needlework. 116–23

Davis. Needlework doctor.

Design workbook. Scobey. First easy-to-see needlepoint workbook. 155–86

Design from the art of Islam. Kluger. Needlepoint gallery of patterns from the past. 123–35

Designing needlepoint. Wilson. Needleplay. 136–37

Designs from the art of ancient Egypt. Kluger. Needlepoint gallery of patterns from the past. 33–47

Designs from the art of Greece and Rome. Kluger. Needlepoint gallery of patterns from the past. 65–81

Designs from the art of 17th–19th century Europe. Kluger. Needlepoint gallery of patterns from the past. 157–71

Designs from the art of the ancient Near East. Kluger. Needlepoint gallery of patterns from the past. 49–63

Designs from the art of the Byzantine Empire. Kluger. Needlepoint gallery of patterns from the past. 83–103

Designs from the art of the Middle Ages. Kluger. Needlepoint gallery of patterns from the past. 105–21

Designs from the art of the Minoans. Kluger. Needlepoint gallery of patterns from the past. 17–31

Designs from the art of the Renaissance. Kluger. Needlepoint gallery of patterns from the past. 137–55

Designs inspired by American folk art. Kluger. Needlepoint gallery of patterns from the past. 173–90

Egyptian motifs: Anubis, desert Ibex, royal leopard, lotus and buds, cloisonne lotus, twin jeweled daggers, sacred scarab, queen's panel, golden mask. Fischer. Egyptian designs in modern stitchery. 66–119

Egyptian motifs: lotus flower, Bast the cat goddess, ram's head wedjet eye, marching geese from Theban Pond, Egyptian borders, Isis kneeling, Nefertiti. Fischer. Egyptian designs in modern stitchery. 16–64

Embroidery on canvas. Marein. Stitchery, needlepoint, applique and patchwork. 83–135

Florals, animals, alphabets, art deco and a potpourri of designs. Needlework nostalgia. 22–72

Gadney. How to enter and win fabric and fiber crafts contests.

Gilbert. Needlepoint designs from Amish quilts.

Gorham. Charted designs for holidays and special occasions.

Hanley. Hope Hanley's patterns for needlepoint.

Hanley. Needlepoint.

Ireys. Encyclopedia of canvas embroidery stitch patterns.

It's the berries, flower over the bounding main and it's a birdie. Sheldon. Washable and dryable needlepoint. 98–99

Kluger. Victorian designs for needlepoint.

Kurten. Needlepoint in miniature.

Lane. Gold and silver needlepoint.

Long-stitch starburst motif for pictures or pillow. Woman's Day decorative needlework for the home. 100–01

Mushroom and butterfly motifs. Christensen. Teach yourself needlepoint. 142–43

Needlepoint. Kicklighter. Crafts, illustrated designs and techniques. 212–23

Needlepoint basics. Reader's Digest complete guide to needlework. 112–85

Needlepoint basics, string needlepoint, pillows and rug, free-form stitchery, basic needlepoint stitches. Better Homes and Gardens treasury of needlecrafts. 238–41, 288–90, 298–99, 321–23

Needlepoint for the bathroom: Lily and the frog, jogging turtles, butterflies are free, south of the border, monkey business, and snails pace. Sheldon. Washable and dryable needlepoint. 65–72

Needlepoint for the bedroom: rosebud ribbon, rosebud monogram, and butterfly looking glass. Sheldon. Washable and dryable needlepoint. 75–79

Needlepoint for the kitchen: asparagus bouquet, artichoke rose, the big carrot, hors d'oeuvre on parade. Sheldon. Washable and dryable needlepoint. 58–61

Needlepoint stitches. Christensen. Needlepoint book. 131–350

Ormond. American primitives in needlepoint.

Patterns for patches. Sheldon. Washable and dryable needlepoint. 17–30

Quickpoint rose wreath. Better Homes and Gardens treasury of needlecrafts. 248–51

Rhodes. Dictionary of canvas work stitches.

Ross. Ancient Persian designs in needlepoint.

Rubbings for needlepoint. Firestein. Rubbing craft. 70–71

Schnitzler. New dimensions in needlework.

Slater. New York Times book of needlepoint for left-handers.

Snook. Embroidery designs from the sea.

Tapestry. Dillmont. Complete encyclopedia of needlework. 196–221

Tillett. American needlework, 1776–1976: needlepoint and crewel patterns adapted from historic American images.

Treasures from the far east. Wilson. More needleplay. 92–101

Wilson. Ask Erica

Witt. Classics for needlepoint.

Needlework equipment

Frames, frame stands, hoop stands. Abrams. Building craft equipment. 106–24

Monogrammed stitchery carrier. Farlie. Pennywise boutique. 131–35

Needlework case. Burchette. More needlework blocking and finishing. 37–42

Tatting bags. Auld. Tatting; the contemporary art of knotting with a shuttle. 54–56

Nets

Butterfly net. Bumper book of things a girl can make. 58

Collingwood. Techniques of sprang.

Knotless netting or looping. Meilach. Weaving off-loom. 140–56

Knotless netting, simple looping and variations, loop and twist, cross-knit; upside-down and interconnecting. DeLeon. Basketry book. 111–15

Knotted and knotless netting and looping. Parker. Beginner's book of off-loom weaving. 158–72

Knotted netting: overhand, square, sheet bend and fisherman's knot, meshing. DeLeon. Basketry book. 115–23

Looped nets; net slings; braided nets; beaded nets. Stribling. Crafts from North American Indian arts. 51–60

Net-making and knotting, basketball net, lamp cover, fish net, pitch-back, shopping bags. Giant book of crafts. 98–123

Netting. Brown. Complete book of rush and basketry techniques. 128–32

Netting. Held. Weaving. 236–37

Netting. Longhurst. Vanishing American needle arts. 73–91

Netting and net-like fabrics. Waller. Knots and netting. 43–64

Netting and weaving in a tubular form. Parker. Beginner's book of off-loom weaving. 214–19

Single element construction. Chamberlain. Beyond weaving. 55–68

Sprang. Skowronski. Sprang; thread twisting, a creative textile technique. 13–96

Night stands. See **Tables, Bedside**

Nightgowns
Children's nightshirt made from men's undershirt. Hagans. All good gifts. 71–72
Child's nightgown. Coffey. Francine Coffey's celebrity sewing bee. 76
Clingy gown. Ruggieri. Woman's Day book of no-pattern sewing. 64
Pillowcase nightgown. Farlie. Pennywise boutique. 82–83
Pillow-slip nightie for girls. Doherty. Family Circle book of 429 great gifts-to-make all
    year round for just 10¢ to $10.00. 173
Smocked nightdress. Blandford book of traditional handicrafts. 62
Smocked nightgown, maternity dress or sundress. Fisher. Craft of smocking. 28
Smocked nightie (infant's). Benton. Sewing classic clothes for children. 86–91
Yoke nightie. Wiseman. Cuts of cloth. 24–25

Noah's ark
Noah's Ark. Baldwin. Old fashioned wooden toys. 65–68
Noah's ark. Williams. Cookie craft: no-bake designs for edible party favors and decora-
    tions. 156–61
Noah's ark, animal patterns. Hundley. Folk art toys and furniture for children. 69–77

Note holders. *See* **Memorandum holders**

Numbers
Roman numerals. Rome. Needlepoint letters and numbers. 108–09

Nursery furniture. *See* **Children's furniture**

Nut cups. *See* **Favors (for parties)**

Nutcrackers
Aluminum nutcracker. Giant book of metalworking projects. 199–202
Nut bowl with wheel cracker. Sainsbury. Sainsbury's woodturning projects for dining.
    122–25

O

Ojo de Dios
Beaded God's eye. Hulbert. Creative beadwork. 67
Eye of God. Wilson. Erica Wilson's Christmas world. 48–49
God's eyes. Meyer. Christmas crafts. 48–51
God's eyes. Rainey. Weaving without a loom. 74–75
Mexican God's eye. Linderman. Crafts for the classroom. 238–41
Star weaving—God's eyes. Weaving and spinning. 6–10
String art on dowels. Kicklighter. Crafts, illustrated designs and techniques. 341–44
Woodburned Eye of God weaving. Broadwater. Woodburning: art and craft. 88–92

Organizers
Canvas catchalls. Woman's Day book of gifts to make. 127–28
Felt wall hanging with secret pockets. Encyclopedia of crafts. 159
Flowerpot wall caddy for keys, pencils, etc. Coffey. Francine Coffey's celebrity sewing
    bee. 63
Kangaroo catchall. Reader's Digest complete guide to sewing. 489
Locker caddy, shoe cleaning caddy/car cleaning caddy, shower tote, tub tote, styro-
    foam crayon caddy, child's wall organizer, schoolbag organizer. Coffey. Francine
    Coffey's celebrity sewing bee. 92, 95, 98, 121, 131, 138
Pocket wall hanging. Rosenthal. Not-so-nimble needlework book. 37–38
Pocketed clothes hanger. Reader's Digest complete guide to sewing. 488

Wall hanging for decoration and storage. (elephant and rhino). Favorite easy-to-make toys. 226–29
Wall panel. Reader's Digest complete guide to sewing. 469
Wall things. (organizers). Better Homes and Gardens sewing for your home. 188–89, 200–01
Wall tidy. Encyclopedia of crafts. 30–31
Wheelchair pocket. Grainer. Making aids for disabled living. 70–73

Origami
Araki. Origami for Christmas.
Basic origami techniques and figures. Paper. 116–21
Bergan. Lingore paper airplane folding manual.

Ottomans. *See* **Footstools**

Outdoor lighting. *See* **Lighting, Outdoor**

Outdoor rooms
Hobby center. Marshall. Yard buildings. 109–16
Root cellar and storm shelter. Burch. Building small barns, sheds, and shelters. 166–77

Outhouses
Basic pit privy. Lane. Building in your backyard. 100–12

Ovens. *See* **Kilns**

Overnight cases. *See* **Baggage; Bags**

Owls
Black work owl. Golden book of hand and needle arts. 76–77
Cecil, the funny-faced owl. Brown. Super sweater idea book. 195–97
Embroidered owls. Mills. The book of presents. 44–45
Furry owl. Hutchings. Big book of stuffed toy and doll making. 62–64
Knitted owl pillow. McCall's big book of knit & crochet for home & family. 44
Mr. Woo—the colorful owl. Janitch. Collage; a step by step guide. 7–10
Owl. Grainger. Creative papercraft. 40–44
Owl for Father's Day. Janitch. Candlemaking and decorations. 40
"Picasso" owl on felt. Rosenthal. Not-so-nimble needlework book. 52–53
Portly owl (stuffed). Complete book of baby crafts. 156–59
Quilted owl pictures. Baldwin. Scrap fabric crafts. 96–98
Stone owl. Day. Complete book of rock crafting. 84–94
Thinking bigger/needlepoint owl. Wilson. Needleplay. 166–67

P

Package wrapping. *See* **Wrapping of packages**

Packs
Back pack. Complete handyman do-it-yourself encyclopedia. Vol. 9, 1363–71
Backpack based on the weaving of Chichicastenango. DeRodriguez. Weaving on a backstrap loom. 136–46
Backpack with sleepng bag compressor. Lamoreaux. Outdoor gear you can make yourself. 90–93
Blockbuster of a backpack. Botsford. Between thimble & thumb. 89–93

Children's backpack. Treasury of things to make. 72–74
Jiffy backpack. Baldwin. Scrap fabric crafts. 126–28
Knapsacks and haversacks. Scurlock. Muzzleloader Magazine's book of buckskinning
    II. 221–25
Needlepoint knapsack, bike pack, backpack. Doherty. Family Circle book of 429 great
    gifts-to-make all year round for just 10¢ to $10.00. 140–41, 152–58
Packing it it (backpacks and bicycle bags). Houck. Big bag book. 68–75
Ruck sack. Lamoreaux. Outdoor gear you can make yourself. 85–89
Woven backpack. Holland. Weaving primer. 41–42

Paint removers
Paint and varnish removal. Handyman. 496–500
Paint brush cleaner rack. Doherty. Family Circle book of 429 great gifts-to-make all
    year round for just 10¢ to $10.00. 125–26
Removing paint. Brightman. 101 practical uses for propane torches. 136

Paintings
Instant abstract painting. Picturemaking. 19–20
Spatter painting. Picturemaking. 21–22
Spattering to make cards. Holtje. Cardcraft. 28–31

Pajama bags
Gingham pajama bag doll. Marsten. Step-by-step dollmaking. 87–89
Kids' pajama bags (elephant and lion). American School of Needlework. Great crochet
    bazaar book. 97–100
Pelican pajama bag. Woman's Day creative stitchery from scraps. 75–77
Sweetheart nightie case of woven ribbons. Encyclopedia of crafts. 70
Wise old owl pajama bag. Coffey. Francine Coffey's celebrity sewing bee. 132

Paneling
Apply paneling. Brann. How to modernize an attic. 31–33
Hardboard wall paneling, how to work with plywood paneling, wood paneling. Popular
    Mechanics do-it-yourself encyclopedia. Vol. 12, 2054–65
Installing plywood, hardboard, fiberboard, and solid wood paneling. Spence. General
    carpentry. 383–95
Masonry panels. Wheeler. Interior painting, wallpapering & paneling. 153–63
Panel unfinished walls or old walls. Self. Working with plywood, including indoor/out-
    door projects. 275–82
Paneling. Syvanen. Interior finish: more tricks of the trade. 33–39
Paneling basement walls. Family handyman handbook of home improvement and
    remodeling. 130–35
Paneling walls. Clifford. Basic woodworking and carpentry . . . with projects. 190–93
Paneling walls. Handyman. 195–98
Panels. Wheeler. Interior painting, wallpapering & paneling. 125–50

Panoramas. *See* **Dioramas**

Pants. *See* **Slacks**

Paper
Barrett. Japanese papermaking.
Books, documents and photographs storage. Garage, attic and basement storage. 16–
    17
Hand-dyed paper. Geary. Plant prints and collages. 61–62
Handmade paper. Geary. Plant prints and collages. 56–57

Marbleized wrapping paper. Better Homes and Gardens treasury of Christmas crafts & foods. 153
Marbleizing. Elbert. Paperworks. 36–38
Marbleized paper using seaweed. Meras. Vacation crafts. 101–04
Marbling paper. Geary. Plant prints and collages. 58–60
Paper: handmade from local materials. Johnson. Nature crafts. 56–60
Papermaking. Rose. Illustrated encyclopedia of crafts and how to master them. 1–8
Paper making from wild plants. Meras. Vacation crafts. 130–33
Recycled paper. Schuman. Art from many hands. 105–07
Toale. Art of papermaking.

Paper dolls. *See* **Dolls, Paper**

Paper flowers. *See* **Flowers, Artificial**

Paper folding. *See* **Origami**

Paper hanging
How to hang wallcoverings. Scherer. Complete handbook of home painting. 151–62
How to hang wallcoverings. Wheeler. Interior painting, wallpapering & paneling. 107–20
How to hang wallpaper. Popular Mechanics do-it-yourself encyclopedia. Vol. 20, 3052–55
Removing old wallpaper and installing new. Family handyman handbook of home improvement and remodeling. 254–69
Wallpapering. Bragdon. Homeowner's complete manual of repair & improvement. 62–71
Wall papering. Handyman. 199–203
Wallpapering. Guide to wallpaper and paint. 2–37
Wallpapering. Nunn. Home paint book. 80–87
Wallpapering. Painting & wallpapering. 57–90

Paperweights
Jeweled paperweight. Hulbert. Creative beadwork. 91
Needlepoint covered stone paperweight. Parker. Mosaics in needlepoint. 93–97
Paper weight. Burchette. More needlework blocking and finishing. 51–52
Pressed flower paperweights. Creative crafts yearbook: an exciting new collection of needlework and crafts. 54
Rock paper weights. Vane. Pebble people, pets & things. 131–34
Sea biscuit paperweight. Logan. Shell crafts. 180–81
Shell filled glass paperweights. Logan. Shell crafts. 179–80
Underwater paperweight, shimmering pyramid, plaster scallop paperweight. Elbert. Shell craft. 180–83, 221–22

Paper work
Ballinger. Design with paper in art and graphic design.
Basic paper folds. Hawkesworth. Paper cutting: making all kinds of paper shapes and figures. 13–28
Decorating tissue paper: fold and dye, stencils, and printing. Stephan. Creating with tissue paper. 72–89
Decorations from pleated paper, garlands, and honey comb decorations. Stephan. Creating with tissue paper. 155–70
Decorations from two-sided paper; triangle; open-sided octadedrons; flower tree; incised triangle; circle and star; star shapes. Stephan. Creating with tissue paper. 178–91

Four seasons paperwork plaques (cut paper), paper bouquet. McCall's book of America's favorite needlework and crafts. 399–401
Free standing figures using basic structures and double curves. Grainger. Creative papercraft. 36–39
Hopf. Scherenschnitte, traditional papercutting.
Jablonski. Folk designs to color or cut.
Kozlowski. Paper cuts—Polish style.
Origami hat, paper folding and dyeing. Linderman. Crafts for the classroom. 82–86
Paper collages. Ashurst. Collage. 32–43
Paper cuts. Rockland. Hanukkah book. 97–100
Paper cutting: duplicate copies and folded designs. Stephan. Creating with tissue paper. 60–71
Paper mosaics, paper weaving, paper folding to make pop-ups. Holtje. Cardcraft. 62–93
Paper sculpture—basic technique. Anderson. Crafts and the disabled. 111–14
Paper sculpture centerpiece. Treasury of things to make. 164–67
Pied piper of Hamelin, Jason and the Golden Fleece, Brer Rabbit, Jack and the Beanstalk, Three Little Pigs, magic kilt, siege of the Alamo, Billy Goats Gruff and the troll, multi-coloured clowns, mini tree & lattice garlands. Hawkesworth. Paper cutting: making all kinds of paper shapes and figures. 27–90
Point lace paper fly cages. Whatnot. 77–78
Scrolls and medallions, leaves, aquarium figures and heraldic devices. Grainger. Creative paperwork. 23–33
Skull and crossbones, padlocks and chains, Humpty Dumpty, pool of swans, spider in a tree, merry-go-round and ladder. Hawkesworth. Paper cutting: making all kinds of paper shapes and figures. 13–28
Stretchy paper critters. Yoder. Sculpture and modeling for the elementary school. 33–38
Tissue paper on paper surfaces: posters and lettering, greeting cards, calendars, boxes, and pictures. Stephan. Creating with tissue paper. 26–39
Tissue paper picture. Holtje. Cardcraft. 99–108
Wax medallions. Stephan. Creating with tissue paper. 218
Weaving with paper. Rainey. Weaving without a loom. 9–15
Windy trees, spring placemats. Lyon. Arts and crafts objects children can make for the home. 161–91
Wycinanki: amate paper cutouts. Schuman. Art from many hands. 65–71, 154–56
Wycinanki, cut-paper folk art. Casselman. Crafts from around the world. 188–89

Papier mâché
Animals. Yoder. Sculpture and modeling for the elementary school. 61–65
Containers. Schuman. Art from many hands. 126–28
Modelling heads. Rush. Papier mâché. 73–77
Papier mâché. Elbert. Paperwork. 99–134
Papier mâché. Sommer. Contemporary costume jewelry. 172–174
Papier mâché. Giant book of crafts. 381–95
Papier mâché. Kicklighter. Crafts, illustrated designs and techniques. 224–31
Papier mâché. Rose. Illustrated encyclopedia of crafts and how to master them. 13–16
Papier mâché jewelry. Encyclopedia of crafts. 189
Papier mâché Judith wine bottle, Eleazer and the elephant. Rockland. Hanukkah book. 92–93, 104–105
Pulp papier mâché. Yoder. Sculpture and modeling for the elementary school. 73–79
Pulp, pinatas and low relief forms. Linderman. Crafts for the classroom. 98–106
Rush. Papier mâché.
Techniques. Epple. Something from nothing crafts. 66–71

Particle board
How to work with particle board. Hedden. Successful shelves and built-ins. 111–16
Working with particle board and fiberboard. Fine woodworking techniques 5. 202–07

Partitions. *See* **Room dividers**

Party decorations
Berry. How to make party and holiday decorations.
Bow garland. Wargo. Soft crafts for special occasions. 101–02
Clowning party oranges. Janitch. Candlemaking and decorations. 69–71
Daisy Maypole cake decorations. Janitch. Candlemaking and decorations. 38–39
Lacy placecards. Wargo. Soft crafts for special occasions. 75–76
Name labels for parties; bonbons, model paper hats; Maypole table decoration. 22–27
Perry. Holiday magic.
Pirate's treasure chest. Janitch. Candlemaking and decorations. 71–72
Placecard-candy dish. Wargo. Soft crafts for special occasions. 29–30
Placecards. Wargo. Soft crafts for special occasions. 133
Place cards made with shells cast in thin resin rectangles. Elbert. Shell craft. 184–85
Red and white rick-rack and gold and white rick-rack ornaments. Wargo. Soft crafts for
    special occasions. 111–14
Silk-screened party invitation. Rockland. Hanukkah book. 57–61
3-D cut ornaments. Wargo. Soft crafts for special occasions. 115–16

Patchwork
Applique and patchwork. Bakke. Sewing machine as a creative tool. 11–47
Curved piercing: drunkard's path, grandmother's fan, hands all around. MacDonald.
    Let's make a patchwork quilt—using a variety of sampler blocks. 113–15
Diamond: eight-pointed star, Virginia star. MacDonald. Let's make a patchwork quilt—
    using a variety of sampler blocks. 102–04
Dudley. Strip patchwork: quick and easy patchwork using the Seminole technique.
Envelope & Suffolk patchwork. Time-Life Books. Decorative techniques. 33–38
Fashions from bits and pieces. Time-Life Books. Boutique attire. 78–87
Four-patch blocks: flock of geese, old maid's puzzle, sawtooth, clay's choice, windmill,
    pieced star, rail fence. MacDonald. Let's make a patchwork quilt—using a variety
    of sampler blocks. 26–28
Houck. Patchwork pattern book.
Intricate piecing: log cabin, ocean waves. MacDonald. Let's make a patchwork quilt—
    using a variety of sampler blocks. 97–98
Introduction to patchwork. Cornelius. Teaching needlecraft. 81–83
Japanese sixteenth-century, sampler, Imari or tortoiseshell, arrowhead or fish-scale
    patchwork. Lane. Maggie Lane's oriental patchwork. 88–101
LaBelle. Patchworking.
Nine-patch blocks: shoofly, churn dash, Greek cross, Jacob's ladder, Ohio star. Mac-
    Donald. Let's make a patchwork quilt—using a variety of sampler blocks. 19–24
Osler. Machine patchwork.
Partical patchwork and other tricky techniques. Guth. Sewing with scraps. 59–78
Patchwork. Marein. Stitchery, needlepoint, applique and patchwork. 169–75
Patchwork. McCall's big book of needlecrafts. 41–51
Patchwork basics. Better Homes and Gardens treasury of needlecrafts. 10–55
Patchwork basics. Reader's Digest complete guide to needlework. 208–34
Patchwork for disabled person with good eyesight. Anderson. Crafts and the disabled.
    86–92
Patchworks (Indian). Bath. Needlework in America. 72–73
Patterns for knitted and Jacquard knitted patches. Chatterton. Patchwork & applique.
    123–35
Quick and easy patchwork. Better Homes and Gardens sewing for your home. 120–21

Reverse piecing: Mexican star, 54–40 or fight, crossed canoes. MacDonald. Let's make a patchwork quilt—using a variety of sampler blocks. 99–101

Seminole patchwork bag and umbrella sheath. Stribling. Crafts from North American Indian arts. 168–78

Squares, circles (yo-yos) and cathedral window. Wilson. More needleplay. 102–06

Strip patchwork for clothing and boutique sewing. Dudley. Strip patchwork: quick and easy patchwork using the Seminole technique. 93–113

Techniques and types of patchwork. Newman. Quilting, patchwork, applique and trapunto. 85–124

Twenty triangles. MacDonald. Let's make a patchwork quilt—using a variety of sampler blocks. 29

Paths. *See* Garden walks

Patios

Brick-in-sand patio, patio on the roof, roof your patio with glass. Popular Mechanics do-it-yourself encyclopedia. Vol. 14, 2090–97

Brick patios and terraces. Proulx. Plan and make your own fences and gates, walkways, walls and drives. 55–63

Building a patio. Handyman. 296–300

Building a paved patio. Day. How to build patios and decks. 57–68

Building a terrace. Harmon. Porches & terraces. 23–36

Ceramic tile patio. Burch. Tile: indoors out, every kind and use. 81–88

Circular patio to surround a tree. Porches and patios. 83

Easy way to screen in a patio. Brann. How to build patios and sundecks. 42–50

Extending a concrete patio. Outdoor projects for home and garden. 262–67

Fiberglass patio cover. Family handyman handbook of carpentry plans/projects. 418–27

Fiberglass patio cover. Outdoor projects for home and garden. 372–80

Flagstone patio. 101 do-it-yourself projects. 308–09

Flagstone-paved patio. Porches and patios. 95–97

How to build your own patio. Daniels. Decks, porches, and patios. 25–41

Masonry patios. Porches and patios. 59–73

Overhead coverings. Porches and patios. 108–15

Overhead covers. Decks and patios. 86–101

Patio builder's guide. Landis. Patios and decks. 101–23

Patio building basics. Decks and patios. 49–63

Patio paraphernalia storage. Garage, attic and basement storage. 28–29

Patio shelter. Self. Working with plywood, including indoor/outdoor projects. 223–28

Patios. Kramer. Outdoor garden build-it book. 14–58

Stone, brick, concrete, concrete slabs, and clay tile patios. Better Homes and Gardens. Deck and patio projects you can build. 60–76

Stone paving. Nickey. Stoneworker's bible. 153–65

Terrace floors: gravel, brick, slate, tile, flagstone paving block and poured; asphalt and concrete. Harmon. Porches & terraces. 69–80

Patios. *See also* Decks; Outdoor rooms; Porches

Patterns, Clothing

Adapting a sewing pattern for knitting. Time-Life books. Personal touch. 174–79

Adjusting a pattern to fit a T. Time-Life books. Exotic styling. 94–95

Adjusting patterns for perfect fit. Time-Life books. Traditional favorites. 26–27

Adjusting your pattern to you. Burns. Super sewing. 45–56

Children's patterns. Practical needlework. 103–07

Comparative analysis of pattern alteration techniques. Farmer. Concepts of fit. 31–132

Drafting basic patterns. Old. Personalized apparel. 3–110

Drafting your own basic pattern. Farmer. Concepts of fit. 133–211
Kopp. Designing apparel through the flat pattern.
Lewis. Patternless fashions.
McCunn. How to make sewing patterns.
Muka. French touch.
Pants pattern—from scratch (men). Rhinehart. How to make men's clothes. 22–45
Pattern alteration and fitting. Muka. French touch II.
Patternmaking for children's clothing. Rosen. Children's clothing. 29–92
Preliminary pattern adjustments. Time-Life books. Personal touch. 42–51
Rub-offs (rubbings on garments to duplicate patterns). Firestein. Rubbing craft. 80–81
Structural pattern modifications and developmental styling. Old. Personalized apparel.
  289–370
Styling from the basic pattern units. Old. Personalized apparel. 113–282

Pebbles. *See* **Stones, Painted**

Pedestals. *See* **Stands**

Pencil holders
Acrylic pencil holder, pen and pencil base. Cope. Plastics. 36, 68–69
Checkered pencil holder. Scobey. Decorating with needlepoint. 173–74
Crayon holder. Popular Mechanics do-it-yourself encyclopedia. Vol. 9, 1361–62
Crocheted kitty-cat pad and pencil holder, photo-trimmed, calico pencil holders.
  Woman's Day bazaar best sellers. 98–99, 119–20
Desk pen holders. Modern general shop. Woodworking. 105
Embroidered pencil case. Tyler. Big book of soft toys. 238–39
Gingham pencil holder (needlepoint). Golden book of hand and needle arts. 108–09
Oriental pencil holder. Elbert. Paperworks. 91–94
Our kids pencil holder (needlepoint). Arnold. Needlepoint pattern book. 160–61
Pen and pencil holder. Popular Mechanics do-it-yourself encyclopedia. Vol. 6, 932
Pencil cup. Burchette. More needlework blocking. 98–99
Pencil holder. Boyles. Margaret Boyles book of needle art. 28–29
Pencil holder made from a plastic bottle and yarn. Golden book of colonial crafts. 20
Pencil holder or table-top wastebasket. Christensen. Needlepoint book. 120
Pencil holders. Romberg. Let's discover papier-mâché. 61
Pencil/pen holder. Kramer. Wirecraft. 72–73
Rustic tin can & plastic spool pencil holders. Epple. Something from nothing crafts.
  167–68, 193–94
Yarn covered pens and frozen orange juice can holders. Doherty. Family Circle book
  of 429 great gifts-to-make all year round for just 10¢ to $10.00. 162–63

Pendants
Balsa core jewelry. D'Amato. Italian crafts. 91–95
Bead pendant and necklace. Auld. Tatting: the contemporary art of knotting with a
  shuttle. 103–04
Bead pendant (glued). Hulbert. Creative beadwork. 91
Beaded North American Indian pendant. Hulbert. Creative beadwork. 88
Bezel setting pendant. Sprintzen. Jewelry, basic techniques and design. 142–50
Big gold clay pendant. Mosesson. Jewelry craft for beginners. 111–14
Brass ring pendant. Mosesson. Jewelry craft for beginners. 166–69
Brass waterfall pendant. Mosesson. Jewelry craft for beginners. 188–91
Carving a soapstone mold for a pewter plique-à-jour pendant. Hollander. Plastics for
  jewelry. 107–13
Casting a metalized pendant in a wax mold. Hollander. Plastics for jewelry. 79–83
Casting a wedge for a pendant. Hollander. Plastics for jewelry. 157–61
Cedar bottle shaped pendant. Lee. Making wood and stone jewelry. 21–25

Clay pendants. Meras. Vacation crafts. 68–69
Copper pendant with abstract setting for 2 stones. Elliot. Working with copper. 71
Copper pendant with brass overlay. Elliot. Working with copper. 72
Copper pendant with swinging shape. Elliot. Working with copper. 71
Copper zodiac pendant: Aries. Elliot. Working with copper. 71
Decoupaged egg pendants. Sommer. Contemporary costume jewelry. 187–88
Embroidered burlap pendant. Sommer. Contemporary costume jewelry. 155–57
Enameling a pewter bas-relief pendant. Hollander. Plastics for jewelry. 91–98
Fashioning a slate and pewter pendant. Hollander. Plastics for jewelry. 115–19
Filagree pendants. Richards. Handmade jewelry. 101–03
Fish pendant. Powers. Crafting turquoise jewelry. 168–70
Flamingo pendant of silver and turquoise. Powers. Crafting turquoise jewelry. 162–64
Gourd pendant. Mordecai. Gourd craft. 182
Heart pendants. Laury. Quilted clothing. 128
Heat forming a pendant. Hollander. Plastics for jewelry. 27–34
Hen egg pendant. Sommer. Contemporary costume jewelry. 189
Laminated paper pendant. Romberg. Let's discover papier-mâché. 60
Making a pendant. Sprintzen. Jewelry, basic techniques and design. 10–17
Metal and leather pendants with stone. Meyer. Rock tumbling. 81–84
Metal hand pendant. Mosesson. Jewelry craft for beginners. 157–60
Metal tulip pendant. Mosesson. Jewelry craft for beginners. 183–84
Molded glass pendants. Sommer. Contemporary costume jewelry. 107–08
Necklace pendant. Auld. Tatting: the contemporary art of knotting with a shuttle. 98–100
Neckloop with pendant and matching earrings. Metalcrafting encyclopedia. 168–69
Overlay turquoise pendant. Powers. Crafting turquoise jewelry. 150–51
Paper patterns for pendants of clay. Mosesson. Jewelry craft for beginners. 104–08
Pear-shaped cloisonne pendant. Metal and enamel. 122–24
Pendant construction, silver & wood inlay. Metalcrafting encyclopedia. 201–04
Pendant money bag. Torbet. Macrame you can wear. 88–89
Potshard pendants, mini-mosaic pendant. D'Amato. Italian crafts. 58–61
Repoussé leaf pendant. Richards. Handmade jewelry. 72–74
Resin embedded sand dollar, silvery resin covered sand dollar. Elbert. Shell craft 198–99, 239–40
Rope-skipping fish, comedy and tragedy masks, anchor, harp. Marshall. Foilcraft. 65–67
Sand dollar pendant. Meras. Vacation crafts. 90–91
Scrimshaw pendant. Linsley. Custom made. 59–62
Silver cut pendant. Encyclopedia of crafts. 202
Silver pendant. Warwick. Beginning jewelry. 82–91
Silver wire pendants. Metal and enamel. 16–19
Simple pendant. Richards. Handmade jewelry. 48–57
Simple turquoise and silver pendant. Powers. Crafting turquoise jewelry. 148–49
Soft gold (lame yarn) pendant. Sommer. Contemporary costume jewelry. 143–46
Square-maze pendant of clay. Mosesson. Jewelry craft for beginners. 98–100
Summer-leaf enameled pendant. Mosesson. Jewelry craft for beginners. 255–57
Three-fish metal, brass, pewter, or silver pendant. Mosesson. Jewelry craft for beginners. 176–80
Wire and bead necklace with carved rosette pendant. Sommer. Contemporary costume jewelry. 77–79
Wire neckloop with jewelled silver pendant, cameo pendant, spiral and bead pendant. Metalcrafting encyclopedia. 169–72
Wire pendant. Metal and enamel. 9–10
Wooden bead rope with pendant. Hulbert. Creative beadwork. 40

Pendants. See also **Jewelry**

Penguins
Carving a penguin. Wiley. Woodcarving with projects. 326–28
Knitted penguins. Complete book of baby crafts. 162–64

Penny banks. *See* **Banks, Toy**

Pens, Baby. *See* **Playpens**

Pepper grinders
Pepper mill. Hodges. Woodturning handbook—with projects. 185–90
Pepper mill. Sainsbury. Sainsbury's woodturning projects for dining. 42–43
Turning pepper mills. Nish. Creative woodturning. 144–47

Perfumes
Rose oil; rose water. Johnson. Nature crafts. 43

Periscopes
Making a periscope. Warring. Balsa wood modelling. 8
Periscope. Bumper book of things a boy can make. 45–46
Super spy scope. Hodges. 46 step-by-step wooden toy projects. 101–02

Perpetual calendars. *See* **Calendars**

Pewter
Laminating earrings with pewter. Hollander. Plastics for jewelry. 168–73

Phonograph record racks
Bookcase record cabinet. Brann. How to construct built-in and sectional bookcases.
66–73
Cartridge and record organizers. Doherty. Family Circle book of 429 great gifts-to-
make all year round for just 10¢ to $10.00. 8
Fabric covered record holder. Roda. Fabric decorating for the home. 82–83
Record album bin. Oberrecht. Plywood projects illustrated. 35–37
Record rack. Hamilton. Build it together. 160–65
Record storage. Dal Fabbro. How to make children's furniture and play equipment.
126–27

Phonograph records
Record care. Popular Mechanics do-it-yourself encyclopedia. Vol. 15, 2398–400

Photography
Copy photography. Popular Mechanics do-it-yourself encyclopedia. Vol. 6, 874–76
Hand-tinting prints. Picture-making. 23–24
Hideaway home theater. Popular Mechanics do-it-yourself encyclopedia. Vol. 18,
2862–65
Hints for photographers, simple cameras can take good pictures, bring back your vacation on film, how to take good flash pictures, special effects put punch in your
pictures, frame movies with a matte box. Popular Mechanics do-it-yourself encyclopedia. Vol. 14, 2116–49
How to cure muddy prints. Popular Mechanics do-it-yourself encyclopedia. Vol. 15,
2330–33
How to make an I.D. photo. Popular Mechanics do-it-yourself encyclopedia. Vol. 10,
1523
How to mount your photo prints, add 3-D to your photo display, how to shoot in the
dark, outdoor photography, big panoramas from little pictures. Popular Mechanics
do-it-yourself encyclopedia. Vol. 13, 1930–35, 1963–66, 2006–11, 2066–68

Inexpensive lightbox. Popular Mechanics do-it-yourself encyclopedia. Vol. 11, 1723–26
Light box for viewing slides. Doherty. Family Circle book of 429 great gifts-to-make all year round for just 10¢ to $10.00. 6–7
Light studio. Geary. How to design and build your own workspace—with plans. 151–81
Load your own 35-mm film cartridges. Popular Mechanics do-it-yourself encyclopedia. Vol. 4, 596–97
Photogram. Linderman. Crafts for the classroom. 464–66
Photographing pots for juried shows. Wettlaufer. Getting into pots. 176–82
Photomontage. Popular Mechanics do-it-yourself encyclopedia. Vol. 12, 1910–11
Pictures without a camera. Giant book of crafts. 396–410
Poor man's mini-tripod, precision paper cutter, stovepipe film drier. Blackwell. Johnny Blackwell's poor man's catalog. 88–99
Slide-copy illuminator. Popular Mechanics do-it-yourself encyclopedia. Vol. 10, 1535
Trim the fat from your slide shows. Popular Mechanics do-it-yourself encyclopedia. Vol. 17, 2702–05
Underwater photography, split-screen snorkel box. Popular Mechanics do-it-yourself encyclopedia. Vol. 19, 2980–88

Pianos
Piano finish. Brumbaugh. Wood furniture finishing refinishing, repairing. 225–27
Piano finishing methods. Patton. Furniture finishing. 214–20
Rose embroidered & needlepoint piano throws. Embroidery of roses. 116–19

Picnic supplies
Fold, roll, and picnic in the park. Houck. Big bag book. 76–80
Lidded picnic basket. Wright. Complete book of baskets and basketry. 95–96
Lined picnic basket. Better Homes and Gardens treasury of Christmas crafts & foods. 106
Perky picnic pack. Botsford. Between thimble & thumb. 137–41
Picnic basket cloth. Coffey. Francine Coffey's celebrity sewing bee. 100
Picnic tote/tablecloth. Reader's Digest complete guide to sewing. 510–12
Quilted picnic set (place mat with pockets, napkin and ring). Encyclopedia of crafts. 19
Rush picnic basket. Brown. Complete book of rush and basketry techniques. 73–77

Picnic tables
Circular table and curved benches. Decks and patios. 134–35
Fold-flat picnic table, low-cost tables and benches from chimney blocks, stow away picnic table, hexagon table, octagon table. Popular Mechanics do-it-yourself encyclopedia. Vol. 14, 2150–54, 2156–61
Octagonal picnic or patio table. 101 do-it-yourself projects. 247–51
One-piece picnic tables. Porches and patios. 131–32
Patio/picnic table. Brown. 44 terrific woodworking plans & projects. 208–12
Picnic bench. Braren. Homemade. 44–45
Picnic table. Bragdon. Homeowner's complete manual of repair & improvement. 286–87
Picnic table, pine plank table. Churchill. Big backyard building book. 106–09, 167–70
Picnic table with canopy. Blandford. Constructing outdoor furniture, with 99 projects. 173–79
Picnic tables. Blandford. Constructing outdoor furniture, with 99 projects. 157–64
Picnic tables. Brann. How to built outdoor furniture. 81–95
Picnic tables and benches. Complete handyman do-it-yourself encyclopedia. Vol. 8, 13, 1195–98, 1997–98
Pine plank table. Churchill. Backyard building book II. 46–56
Trestle table and benches. Churchill. Backyard building book. 156–58
Two stowaway tables for the outdoors. Popular Mechanics do-it-yourself encyclopedia. Vol. 13, 2013–16

Picture frames
Bargello frame. McCall's big book of needlecrafts. 151
Bargello frame. Scharf,. Butterick's fast and easy needlecrafts. 184–85
Basic picture frames, building deep frames. Picturemaking. 83–88
Calico-covered sweetheart frame. Evrard. Homespun crafts from scraps. 155–59
Cardboard supports for a picture frame, etc. Elbert. Paperworks. 10–11
Carved frames. Colletti. Art of woodcarving. 107–09
Carved picture frame. Gotshall. Wood carving and whittling for everyone. 72–76
Colorful picture framing mats. Elbert. Paperworks. 65–68
Construction paper mounts. Lyon. Arts and crafts objects children can make for the home. 204
Covered picture frame. Vanderbilt. Gloria Vanderbilt designs for your home. 113
Covering a picture frame. Marshall. Foilcraft. 39
Crewel-embroidered picture frame, lace frame. Better Homes and Gardens treasury of Christmas crafts & foods. 154, 174–75
Crewel picture frame. Better Homes & Gardens embroidery. 30
Crewel picture frame. Better Homes and Gardens treasury of needlecrafts. 352
Designing and constructing picture frames. Clifford. Basic woodworking & carpentry . . . with projects. 219–24
Embroidered linen picture frame. Boyles. Needlework gifts for special occasions. 120–23
Fabric-covered mirrors or picture frames. Coffey. Francine Coffey's celebrity sewing bee. 155
Fabric-covered open-back picture frame. Roda. Fabric decorating for the home. 98–99
Flowered picture frame. Scobey. Decorating with needlepoint. 140–42
Framed photographs. Creative crafts yearbook: an exciting new collection of needlework and crafts. 60–62
Framing. Kicklighter. Crafts, illustrated designs and techniques. 124–33
Framing a picture. Christensen. Needlepoint book. 90–99
Friendship frame; busy border photo; fantasy photo; plexiglass picture frames; formal photographs. Linsley. Custom made. 36–45, 82–85, 102–10, 136–39
Glass and wood frames for sandpainting. Appel. Sand art. 76–77
How to mount and frame fine pictures, build a floater picture frame, how to repair fancy picture frames. Popular Mechanics do-it-yourself encyclopedia. Vol. 8, 1264–79
Knitted picture frames. Selfridge. Patchwork knitting. 134
Make rustic picture frames from barn siding. Popular Mechanics do-it-yourself encyclopedia. Vol. 9, 1284–85
Making picture frames. Family handyman handbook of carpentry plans/projects. 325–33
Mirror with rope frame ruffles. Design crochet. 210–13
Mounting leaf prints. Geary. Plant prints and collages. 45–47
Mounting needlepoint pictures. Burchette. Needlework. 86–89
Mounting prints and pictures. Picturemaking. 78–82
Nature's picture frames. Johnson. Nature crafts. 90–91
Padded fabric frames. Baldwin. Scrap fabric crafts. 158–60
PEG-treated slabs and blocks to mount photographs. Spielman. Working green wood with PEG. 56
Photograph on plaid fabric mat. Woman's Day book of gifts to make. 53
Picture frame. Burchette. More needlework blocking and finishing. 127–31
Picture frame. 101 do-it-yourself projects. 242–43
Picture frame. Scobey. First easy-to-see needlepoint workbook. 40–42
Picture frame clamp. McNair. Building & outfitting your workshop. 220–24
Picture frame (needlepoint). Rosenthal. Not-so-nimble needlework book. 93–94
Picture frames. Complete handyman do-it-yourself encyclopedia. Vol. 13, 1999–2008
Picture frames. Lyon. Arts and crafts objects children can make for the home. 193–99

Picture frames on ribbon. Coffey. Francine Coffey's celebrity sewing bee. 106
Picture frames, professional picture frame clamp, mat cutting guide. Brann. How to
repair, refinish, reupholster. 136–51
Picture framing. Endacott. Fine furniture making and woodworking. 84–86
Plywood frame and box, quiche pan mirror frame, rainbow picture frames. Doherty.
Family Circle book of 429 great gifts-to-make all year round for just 10¢ to $10.00.
11, 50, 178
Porcelain flowers and fantasy finish. Linsley. Great bazaar. 92, 164–67
Prints, paintings and frames. Introduction to repairing and restoring. 200–45
Recycling frames; frameless picture hanging. Kangas. By hand. 142–46
Refinishing picture frames. Joyner. Furniture refinishing at home. 72–80
Round, rectangular, square and triangular box, and interlocking paper picture frames.
Grainger. Creative papercraft. 65–74
Scrollwork mirror frame. Scobey. Decorating with needlepoint. 149–51
Seashell frame. McCall's book of America's favorite needlework and crafts. 370
Spanish frame. Egge. Recycled with flair. 84–87
Turning a small picture frame. Sainsbury. Craft of woodturning. 139–41
Turn-of-the-century portrait frames (embroidered). McCall's book of America's favorite
needlework and crafts. 77–78

Pictures
Abstract picture. Evans. Ribbonwork. 53–56
Bead picture. Hulbert. Creative beadwork. 86
Bouquet on velvet (painted). McCall's book of America's favorite needlework and
crafts. 359–60
Children's nursery pictures. Coffey. Francine Coffey's celebrity sewing bee. 124
Fabric dressing old prints. McCall's book of America's favorite needlework and crafts.
409–10
Flower basket patchwork picture. Houck. Patchwork pattern book. 40–41
Flower basket picture in cardboad. McCall's book of America's favorite needlework
and crafts. 405–06
Latch-look flowers. Baldwin. Scrap fabric crafts. 108–09
Nautical picture, clown picture, tulip picture. Goldman. Decorate with felt. 64–67, 72–
78
Paint and needle pictures. Picturemaking. 46–48
Patchwork picture: country idyll. Woman's Day book of weekend crafts. 11–13
Personalized gifts (needlepoint alphabet). Scharf, Bella. Butterick's fast and easy
needlecrafts. 186–89
Ribbon art, framed fabric and fabric art. Roda. Fabric decorating for the home. 88–91
Seaweed pictures. Geary. Plant prints and collages. 89–92
Sewing machine portraits & landscapes. Creative sewing. 87–90
Summer tapestry. Weaving and spinning. 100–01
Three-dimensional dried plant pictures. Geary. Plant prints and collages. 84
Woodland panel. McNeill. Quilting. 74–77

Pictures, Appliqued
Appliqued picture. McNeill. Quilting. 41
Appliqued portrait. Better Homes and Gardens applique. 88–89
Cat-appliqued pair, tree-appliqued hanging. McCall's big book of needlecrafts. 114–17
Country morning rooster. Baldwin. Scrap fabric crafts. 53–55
Egg basket picture. McCall's big book of country needlecrafts. 88
Egg basket picture, wall phone, and calico coffee mill applique pictures. McCall's book
of America's favorite needlework and crafts. 195–98
Fabric applique coffee mill and turn-of-the-century wall phone. McCall's big book of
country needlecrafts. 163–65

Nosegay picture, frankly fake felt flower picture and round felt flower pillow. Rosenthal. Not-so-nimble needlework book. 68–73
Quilted farm scene. Better Homes and Gardens treasury of Christmas crafts & foods. 101

Pictures, Crocheted
Bouquet of crochet, strawberry, "Love", butterfly pictures. Halliday. Decorating with crochet. 69–80

Pictures, Embroidered
Bird and heart picture. Nielsen. Scandinavian embroidery, past and present. 80–81
Bird of paradise. Encyclopedia of crafts. 104–05
Bird tree. Sayles. Step-by-step stitchery. 70–71
California poppy flower child cross-stitch framed picture, dragon blackwork framed picture, phoenix blackwork mounted picture. Gault. Needlework dragons and other mythical creatures. 69–71, 75–77, 137–39
Chinese butterflies and flowers. Silverstein. Mira Silverstein's guide to looped and knotted stitches. 86, 88–89
Christmas rose. Nielsen. Scandinavian embroidery, past and present. 72–73
Crewel embroidered butterfly. Better Homes & Gardens embroidery. 41
Crewel picture adapted from fabric. Reader's Digest complete guide to needlework. 104–05
Crewel pictures. Boyles. Margaret Boyles book of needle art. 78–83
Daisies and tiger lilies, poppies and peonies, asters in a basket, summer bouquet. McCall's book of America's favorite needlework and crafts. 62–68
Down on the farm. Great cross-stitch. 14–15
Embroider a country garden. Picturemaking. 44–46
Embroidered miniatures. Boyles. Margaret Boyles book of needle art. 102–03
Girl with garland, yarn bouquet. McCall's big book of needlecrafts. 284–85
House, squirrel and bird crewel vignettes, robin on a branch, dragonfly and Queen Anne's lace pictures, three children yarn pictures, dog pictures, two Victorian wool pictures, eight wildflower prints, strawberry picture. McCall's book of America's favorite needlework and crafts. 37–61
Jacobean-style crewel work picture, chain stitch cat, birds in a tree, crewel-work Christmas scene, free-style embroidered picture. Encyclopedia of crafts. 118–19, 130, 136, 138–41
Oval miniatures. Boyles. Needlework gifts for special occasions. 116–19
Petite floral sprays. Boyles. Margaret Boyles book of needle art. 116–17
Practice with popular patterns (embroidered). Fraser. Modern stitchery: stitches, patterns, free-form designing. 41–56
Rose pictures. Embroidery of roses. 57–74, 85–86, 110, 114
Springtime flowers, country kids, alphabet pillows. McCall's big book of country needlecrafts. 92–95, 287–90
Wild goose chase. Embroidery. 66–69

Pictures, Needlepoint
Bamse goes berry-picking. Nielsen. Scandinavian embroidery, past and present. 82–83
Bette Midler record cover. Slater. Elaine Slater's book of needlepoint projects. 124–25
Butterfly picture. Christensen. Needlepoint and bargello stitchery. 15–16
Calendar of flowers designs. Ambuter. Carolyn Ambuter's needlepoint celebrations. 42–73
Child's sketch. Slater. Elaine Slater's book of needlepoint projects. 120
Contemporary patch picture. Rosenthal. Not-so-nimble needlework book. 102–04
Crewel point mice. Wilson. Needleplay. 164–65

Dieter's motto, rainbow on the square, plaid sampler, I'm OK and you're OK, sweet raspberries, and sweet violets. Sheldon. Washable and dryable needlepoint. 42–53

Don't hurry, don't worry, dragon fly, man's box top, painting, Egyptian scarab and sun, stamp. Christensen. Teach yourself needlepoint. 112–14, 119–20, 125–26, 133–34, 139–41

Eagle, girl, king, love, nautilus, ocean, rainbow, shell, thistle, holding hands, zodiac. Smith. 100–04, 109–13, 125–32, 136–43, 166–78, 198–203

Endless knot wedding picture. Ambuter. Carolyn Ambuter's needlepoint celebrations. 30–31

Farm, interwined rainbows, car, mother & child, apple, needlepoint shop, black cat, northwest autumn, and waste knot, want knot. Christensen. Needlepoint. 63–66, 91–101, 118–52

Flying eagle. Christensen. Needlepoint and bargello stitchery. 86–87

Framed pictures and wall hangings. Scobey. Decorating with needlepoint. 104–11

Grandmother surveys the pantry, vanishing apple, "sweet dreams." McCall's big book of country needlecrafts. 141–44, 153, 244–45

Landscape in satin stitch. Picturemaking. 38–43

Mouse. Christensen. Teach yourself needlepoint. 91–92

Mushroom, oriental seasons, flowers in vase, long stitch landscape. Christensen. Teach yourself needlepoint. 100–01, 105–06, 109–10

Mushrooms. Christensen. Needlepoint and bargello stitchery. 26–32

Nantucket harbor scene. Wilson. More needleplay. 80–82

Needlepainting. Wilson. Needleplay. 168–69

Needlepoint miniatures to combine many ways. Vanderbilt. Gloria Vanderbilt designs for your home. 74–79

Needlepoint strawberries picture. Woman's Day decorative needlework for the home. 98–99

Padded picture. Burchette. More needlework blocking and finishing. 122–26

"Paint" a needlepoint bouquet. Vanderbilt. Gloria Vanderbilt designs for your home. 70–73

Pansy picture. Boyles. Margaret Boyles book of needle art. 56–61

Patriotic eagle. Needlework nostalgia. 8, 12

Pennsylvania German fractur birth record. Ambuter. Carolyn Ambuter's needlepoint celebrations. 38–39

Perforated paper JOY. Smith. Needlery. 122–24

Portrait. Slater. Elaine Slater's book of needlepoint projects. 126–27

Quiltpoint—lone star and log cabin patterns. Wilson. More needleplay. 83–85

Recapture the twenties with Clarence and Claudette. Vanderbilt. Gloria Vanderbilt designs for your home. 66–69

Red rooster in buttonhole stitch. Silverstein. Mira Silverstein's guide to looped and knotted stitches. 74–75

Rooster. Christensen. Needlepoint and bargello stitchery. 38–47

Shakespeare's winter song, Shakespeare's spring song. Wilson. Needleplay. 156–59

Silhouette. Nielsen. Scandinavian embroidery, past and present. 84–85

Spring lambs. Wilson. Needleplay. 146–47

Tiger, pussy willows, farm scene, city skyline, the moon and the coyote. Christensen. Teach yourself needlepoint. 144–46, 150–54

Treasures from the sea reproduced in needlepoint. Vanderbilt. Gloria Vanderbilt designs for your home. 147–53

Tulip-time triptych (needlepoint). Vanderbilt. Gloria Vanderbilt designs for your home. 58–60

Two-dimensional needlepoint that seems three-dimensional—optical illusions. Christensen. Needlepoint. 39–47

Victorian parrot. McCall's big book of needlecrafts. 173–74

Victorian parrot, turtledoves in a wreath, dragon of good fortune, Independence Hall, three cat portraits, red pony portrait, noble eagle, weather vanes in gros point, nature's kingdom, folk art hanging. McCall's book of America's favorite needlework and crafts. 103–30

Watermelon in blue-bordered dish, "1825", the emblem of our country, Tinkle the cat, baby in a red chair, melons and other fruit, chilly observation, and peaceable kingdom. Ormond. American primitives in needlepoint. 33–60, 103–28

Worldmap, Ukrainian wedding, three-dimensional flowers in vase. Christensen. Teach yourself needlepoint. 157–59, 165–66

Your house in needlepoint. Christensen. Needlepoint. 101–06

Pictures, Paper
"Pop up" picture. Grainger. Creative papercraft. 105–06

Pictures, Patchwork
"Still life" patchwork. McCall's big book of needlecrafts. 70–72

Pictures, Wood
Crayon on wood, felt pen on wood, watercolor on wood, shoe polish on wood, tempera on wood, pyrography. Lyon. Arts and crafts objects children can make for the home. 101–23

Inlaid veneer pictures. Complete handyman do-it-yourself encyclopedia. 1446–51

Painting on wood. Brunner. Pass it on. 79–82

Patterns for veneered pictures. Hobb. Veneer craft for everyone. 83–125

Pictures, Yarn
Tree of life yarn painting. Better Homes and Gardens treasury of Christmas crafts & foods. 140

Yarn painting. Sayer. Crafts of Mexico. 85–87

Piggy banks. *See* **Banks, Toy**

Pigs
Hog house, feeder, & fence. Braren. Homemade. 142–44, 148–49

Hog housing. Burch. Building small barns, sheds, and shelters. 202–07

Swine housing. Lytle. Farm builder's handbook, with added material for pole type industrial buildings. 85–89

Pillowcases
Blue pillow shams, pillow shams made from sheets, ruffled pillow shams, good morning pillow sham. McCall's big book of country needlecrafts. 179, 225, 245–46, 253–54

Cross-stitch pillowcases & guest towel. Better Homes & Gardens embroidery. 56–57

Embroidered baby pillowcase. Linsley. Great bazaar. 85–86

Embroidered pillowcase, machine-embroidered pillowcase. Better Homes and Gardens treasury of needlecrafts. 350–51, 386–87

Embroidered rose pillowcase. Embroidery of roses. 129–30

Embroidery patterns for pillow cases. McCall's big book of needlecrafts. 266–68

Frilled pillowcases. Practical needlework. 177

Hearts and flowers pillowcase filet trim. Svinicki. Old-fashioned crochet. 123–24

Machine-embroidered curtains & pillowcase. Better Homes & Gardens embroidery. 74–75

Neck roll cover. Coffey. Francine Coffey's celebrity sewing bee. 162

Pillowcases. Heard. Complete guide to quilting. 269–78

Pillowcases. Practical needlework. 176–77

Pillowcases from Aunt Mary's. Better Homes & Gardens embroidery. 28–29

Pillowcases with patchwork trim. Ives. Ideas for patchwork. 24–27
Plaid and white sheet bedroom ensemble. Woman's Day decorative needlework for the home. 33–34
Ruffled pillow covers. McCall's sewing for your home. 169
Standard pillowcase. Fanning. Complete book of machine quilting. 309–10
Tailored pillow sham and ruffled pillow sham. Roda. Fabric decorating for the home. 165, 168–69
Tie-dyed pillow cases. Anderson. Tie dyeing and batik. 22–23
Tie-dyed pillow case. Frame. Tie-dyeing and batik. 20–21
Tooth fairy pillowcase. Coffey. Francine Coffey's celebrity sewing bee. 77
Tooth fairy pillowcase. Roda. Fabric decorating for the home. 163–64

Pillowcases. *See also* **Bedclothes; Sheets**

Pillows
Ainu-design pillow. Casselman. Crafts from around the world. 136–37
Appliqued and quilted pillows. Laury. Treasury of needlecraft gifts for the new baby. 53–56
Baby elephant pillow. Foose. Scrap saver's stitchery book. 15–16
Backrest pillow with arms. Roda. Fabric decorating for the home. 157–59
Batik cushion. Frame. Tie-dyeing and batik. 90–93
Bedroom pillow. Fisher. Craft of smocking. 27
Boudoir pillow with ruffled cover. Roda. Fabric decorating for the home. 133–34
Box-edge pillow with cabin steps design. Loeb. Leather book. 67–77
Boxed pillow, knife-edged pillow. Heard. Complete guide to quilting. 264–68
Bull's-eye floor pillow. Roda. Fabric decorating for the home. 107–08
Burlap floor pillows with woven trim. Woman's Day decorative needlework for the home. 77–78
Children's art pillows. Laury. Treasury of needlecraft gifts for the new baby. 73–76
Chinese folk design pillow top in netting. Reader's Digest complete guide to needlework. 425
Cloth bibs and pillows (egg yolk in center). Creative crafts yearbook: an exciting new collection of needlework and crafts. 150
Clown doll and pillow top. Guth. Sewing with scraps. 57–58
Crayon friends. Foose. More scrap saver's stitchery. 44–47
Crocheted plaid pillow. Scharf. Butterick's fast and easy needlecrafts. 128, 133–34
Cushions for children. Tyler. Big book of soft toys. 242–50
Decorator pillows: pineapple, green thumb, pet, profiles, patchwork pieced, wedding and chamois. Morgan. Trapunto and other forms of raised quilting. 132–46
Diamond-shaped and rectangular bargello applique for pillows. Scharf. Butterick's fast and easy needlecrafts. 126–27, 135–36
Domino/dice pillows. Coffey. Francine Coffey's celebrity sewing bee. 101
Double-layer plaited suede pillow. Glashausser. Plaiting step-by-step. 72–81
Felt cottage cushions to stitch and glue. Woman's Day decorative needlework for the home. 75
Finishing pillow. Risinger. Innovative machine quilting. 116–20
Floor pillows. Guth. Sewing with scraps. 56–57
Florentine trapunto. D'Amato. Italian crafts. 25–28
Flossa pillow, fur and flossa pillow. Hall. Sewing machine craft book. 63–65
Geometric pillows. Reader's Digest complete guide to sewing. 466
Giant pencil pillow. Reader's Digest complete guide to sewing. 505–07
Giant size pillows. Better Homes and Gardens sewing for your home. 199–200
Good morning/good night pillow. Coffey. Francine Coffey's celebrity sewing bee. 62
Handwoven pillows. Wilson. Weaving you can use. 78–92
Herb pillow. Mills. The book of presents. 86–89
Hippo pillow. Foose. Scrap saver's stitchery book. 17–19

How to make pillows and cushions. Better Homes and Gardens sewing for your home. 123–133

Initial pillows. Reader's Digest complete guide to sewing. 458–60

Kissing corners pillow. Roda. Fabric decorating for the home. 39

Knife-edge pillow. Loeb. Leather book. 35–41

Knife-edge pillow with silk cord trim. Roda. Fabric decorating for the home. 24

Knife-edged pillow, mitered-pattern knife-edged pillow, box pillow, Turkish corner pillow, double-flange pillow, round shirred pillow, bolster pillow. Time-Life Books. Decorative techniques. 110–25

Knife-edged square pillows, boxed square cushions, boxed round cushions, ruffled round pillows, ruffled rectangular pillows, round bolsters, square bolsters. McCall's sewing for your home. 220–24

Lace pillow. Blandford book of traditional handicrafts. 36–42

Lacy collages in pillow form. Vanderbilt. Gloria Vanderbilt designs for your home. 114–17

Large shaggy pillow (hooked). Feldman. Needlework boutique. 113–14

Latch hook square in heart motif, chevron pattern, brick pattern and diagonal patches. Chatterton. Coordinated crafts for the home. 76–77, 128–29, 134–35, 168–69

Latch hook squares in patchwork and African designs. Chatterton. Coordinated crafts for the home. 128–29, 134–35, 166, 168–69

Mini-heart pillow. Woman's Day book of gifts to make. 101–04

Miniature quilt-a-pillow. MacDonald. Let's make a patchwork quilt—using a variety of sampler blocks. 37–43

Multi-triangle pillow. Loeb. Leather book. 57–65

Neck roll pillow with ruffled cover. Roda. Fabric decorating for the home. 136–37

Noble scallop and marble cone. Kinser. Sewing sculpture. 72–75

Nosegay, necktie fan pillows. Better Homes and Gardens easy bazaar crafts. 8, 17, 73, 80

Painted pillow designs. Creative sewing. 79

Patchwork cozies and chair pillow. Mills. The book of presents. 72–73

Patchwork tote or pillow: project. Hall. Sewing machine craft book. 72–73

Paw print pillows, portrait pillows, five confectionery satin pillows, hearth scene pillow, hippo pillow. Better Homes and Gardens treasury of Christmas crafts & foods. 37, 158, 209–11, 268

A pillow in Chinese braid. Dendel. Basic book of fingerweaving. 77

Pillow toys. Foose. Scrap saver's stitchery book. 46–57

Pillow village. Creative sewing. 71–74

Pillows (appliqued). Reader's Digest complete guide to sewing. 449

Pockets full of Christmas appliqued pillow. Wooster. Quiltmaking. 141

Punch-needle wall hanging and pillow. Woman's Day decorative needlework for the home. 80, 97

Purses, bags and pillows in double weave. Dendel. Basic book of fingerweaving. 88–91

Quick-change floor pillow to sew. Woman's Day decorative needlework for the home. 74

Quilted bolster cover. Roda. Fabric decorating for the home. 237

Raised cross stitch rose pillow. Rosenthal. Not-so-nimble needlework book. 117–19

Rectangular pillow with boxing. Roda. Fabric decorating for the home. 151

Ribbon pillow. Coffey. Francine Coffey's celebrity sewing bee. 83

Ribbon pillow. Wilson. Needleplay. 172

Round bolster. Roda. Fabric decorating for the home. 148–49

Ruffle border pillow, patchwork insert pillow, ribbon front pillow and piped round pillow. Roda. Fabric decorating for the home. 16–19, 21

Ruffled pillow cover. Golden book of hand and needle arts. 65

Sewing pillows. Sara. Sewing made easy. 400–06

Sitting pretty (crocheted trim). Creative crafts yearbook: an exciting new collection of needlework and crafts. 56–59
Sleepy head pillow. Vanderbilt. Gloria Vanderbilt designs for your home. 182–83
Splash of color rya pillow and shaggy sunflower pillow. Rosenthal. Not-so-nimble needlework book. 114–17
Strip patchwork pillows. Dudley. Strip patchwork: quick and easy patchwork using the Seminole technique. 80–87
Stuffed strawberry pillows, grandmother pillow, people pillows. Linsley. Custom made. 74–76, 98–99, 122–25
Throw pillow and decorations for pillows. Goldman. Decorate with felt. 68–71
Throw pillows. Jones. Fixing furniture. 171
Throwspread and bolster. Reader's Digest complete guide to sewing. 473
To construct a pillow. Sayles. Step-by-step stitchery. 77
Toy town. Complete book of baby crafts. 166–71
Velvet cushion cover. Evans. Ribbonwork. 42–43
Washcloth pillow. Rosenthal. Not-so-nimble needlework book. 25–27
Weaving a pillow cover. Thorpe. Elements of weaving. 44–94
Wedge covers. Goldman. Decorate with felt. 62–63
Wedge cushion. Goldman. Decorate with felt. 46–47
Wedge-shaped bolster. Roda. Fabric decorating for the home. 155–56
Window and pillow ensemble adapted from sheets. Woman's Day decorative needlework for the home. 120–21
Woven cushions. Evans. Ribbonwork. 86–90
Woven puff pillow or quilt. Wilson. Weaving you can use. 120–22

Pillows. *See also* **Cushions**

Pillows, Appliqued

Animal cushions, ribbon applique. Encyclopedia of crafts. 18, 20
Appliqued felt pillows. Woman's Day book of gifts to make. 161–65
Circles of felt appliques on pillow. McCall's big book of needlecrafts. 120–21
Dragon pillow, paper cutout design. Casselman. Crafts from around the world. 184–87
Easy appliqued flower pillows. Baldwin. Scrap fabric crafts. 118–20
Homespun chicken pillow. Baldwin. Scrap fabric crafts. 146–48
Moon and sun padded applique designs. Woman's Day bazaar best sellers. 143
Name pillows: project. Hall. Sewing machine craft book. 81
Owl, clamshell flower, fruit bowl, magnolia bud, star rings, twin darts, wheel of destiny. Gillies. Patterns for applique and pieced work—and ways to use them. 7–27
People pillows. Golden book of hand and needle arts. 24
Quick-and-easy heart and bird pillows. Better Homes and Gardens applique. 10–11
Quick-and-easy wall hanging and pillow. Better Homes and Gardens applique. 12–13
Quick-and-easy wildflower pillows. Better Homes and Gardens applique. 22–23
Quick-and-easy wildflower pillows, heart pillow, bird pillow, scenery pillow, swan pillow, bird pillows, floral pillows. Better Homes and Gardens treasury of needlecrafts. 78–83, 98–99, 104–07, 116–17
Quilted applique—Indian pillows. Better Homes and Gardens applique. 50–51
Reverse applique pillow. Casselman. Crafts from around the world. 148–50
Shaped applique—floral pillows. Better Homes and Gardens applique. 58–59
Sleepyhead appliqued pillows, flat-footed pillow creatures, poppy pillow. Woman's Day creative stitchery from scraps. 10–12, 37–39, 45–47
Splashes (reverse applique). Golden book of hand and needle arts. 30–31
Stitchery pillow. Andersen. Creative exploration in crafts. 56–65
Swan pillow and curtains. Better Homes and Gardens applique. 32–33
Upsilon (Greek Y appliqued on corduroy), sunburst, oriental medallion and tulip garden. Needlework nostalgia. 9, 16–17, 24, 32, 34

Pillows, Crocheted

Coming-up-roses and vine-times lavender crocheted pillows. Woman's Day decorative needlework for the home. 69–71

Crochet lion pillow. Treasury of things to make. 155–57

Doily pillows. American School of Needlework. Great crochet bazaar book. 81–85

Farm animal pillows, popcorn crochet on afghan stitch. McCall's big book of country needlecrafts. 98–104, 195–98

Floral pillow. American School of Needlework. Great crochet bazaar book. 63–64

Folding floor pillows. Great granny crochet book. 132–33

Giant multi-striped and diagonally striped pillows. Step by step to better knitting and crochet. 202–04

Irish crochet pillow sham. Halliday. Decorating with crochet. 33, 36–37

Irish crochet pillow top. Reader's Digest complete guide to needlework. 385

Owl, giraffe, patch, heart, floor, lace and Moroccan pillows. Halliday. Decorating with crochet. 82–105

Patchwork crochet cushions in squares & triangles. Chatterton. Patchwork & applique. 69–70

Pillow sampler. Edson. Creative crochet. 73–77

Pillow with filet-lace trim. Svinicki. Old-fashioned crochet. 116–17

Pillow with filet tulips insert. Svinicki. Old-fashioned crochet. 94–96

Pillows. Henderson. Woman's Day book of designer crochet. 183–89

Pink petal pillow, yellow flower pillow, uneven work pillow. Design crochet. 130–39, 206–09

Popcorn, shell, shaggy, granny and other crocheted pillows. Crochet. 90, 95, 98, 107

Portrait pillows: Mr. Snowman, Santa & Mrs. Santa. American School of Needlework. Great Christmas crochet book. 33–36

Rainbow-and-cream and honeycomb puff crocheted pillows. Woman's Day decorative needlework for the home. 67–69

Ruffled crocheted round & square pillows. Doherty. Family Circle book of 429 great gifts-to-make all year round for just 10¢ to $10.00. 37–39

Ruffled pillow. Great granny crochet book. 140–41

Santa pillow. Great granny crochet book. 88–89

Spaniel embroidered on afghan stitch pillow. McCall's big book of needlecrafts. 259–60

Spin and crochet pillows. Treasury of things to make. 113–15

Stained glass pillows, big star pillow, rose trio pillows, in-the-clover pillow. Woman's Day crochet showcase. 139–43, 151–54

Striped pillow. Halliday. Decorating with crochet. 40–44

Sun cushion. Mon Tricot. Knitting dictionary. 206–07

Sunburst and flower pillows, Victorian dog cushion, three heirloom lace pillows. McCall's book of America's favorite needlework and crafts. 236–46

Throw pillows in single crochet. Step by step to better knitting and crochet. 150–51

Toy pillows, rose wheels, rose pillow, pinwheel squares. McCall's big book of knit & crochet for home & family. 144, 228–32

Tunisian crochet cushion. Encyclopedia of crafts. 83

Very hard heart. Dittrick. Hard crochet. 120–23

Pillows, Embroidered

Art deco & strawberry pillow covers. Sayles. Step-by-step stitchery. 58–59

Blackwork corded pillow. Reader's Digest complete guide to needlework. 110

Chain stitch pillow. Better Homes & Gardens embroidery. 14

Chessie and Beatrix Potter's mouse door pillows. Wilson. Erica Wilson's Christmas world. 104–07

Chinese butterfly pillow. Boyles. Needlework gifts for special occasions. 110–15

Crewel embroidery pillow, designs from India. Casselman. Crafts from around the world. 144–47

Crewel embroidery II—introductory material (pillow). Cornelius. Teaching needlecraft. 58–70

Crewel pictures. Boyles. Margaret Boyles book of needle art. 78–83

Crewel pillow recalls early American craftsmanship. Vanderbilt. Gloria Vanderbilt designs for your home. 118–21

Cross-stitch butterfly pillow, garden pillow and patchwork pillow. McCall's big book of needlecrafts. 257, 263–66

Cross-stitch cushions. Ley. Russian & other Slavic embroidery designs. 66–69

Cushions for cat lovers. Embroidery. 76–79

Danish car pillow. Nielsen. Scandinavian embroidery, past and present. 60–61

Embroidered American Indian motifs floor pillows, chain stitch pillow, walk in the woods pillow, wildflower pillow, cross stitch floral spray, tambour work Mediterranean pillow, Middle Eastern pillow. Better Homes and Gardens treasury of needlecrafts. 329–31, 356–65, 372–74, 402–03

Embroidered, Kuwait designs. Casselman. Crafts from around the world. 138–43

Embroidered throw & floor pillows. Better Homes & Gardens embroidery. 16–18

Flowered pillows. Hana. Embroidery. 16–20

Four cross-stitch pillows worked on evenweave fabrics. Woman's Day decorative needlework for the home. 54–59

Green linen pillow. Boyles. Margaret Boyles book of needle art. 108–11

Happy Birthday pillow. Baldwin. Scrap fabric crafts. 155–57

Heracles and Achelous cross-stitch pillow. Gault. Needlework dragons and other mythical creatures. 106–09

Locomotive pillow toy. Boyles. Needlework gifts for special occasions. 128–33

Middle eastern pillow. Better Homes & Gardens embroidery. 81

Modern Danish pillow. Nielsen. Scandinavian embroidery, past and present. 66–67

Modified Falster sewing pillow. Nielsen. Scandinavian embroidery, past and present. 74–75

Mushroom pillow cover. Sayles. Step-by-step stitchery. 64–65

Norwegian eight-point star pillow. Nielsen. Scandinavian embroidery, past and present. 70–71

Nosegay pillow cross-stitched on "vanishing" canvas. Woman's Day decorative needlework for the home. 51–53

Owl door pillow. Wilson. Erica Wilson's Christmas world. 150–52

Paisley pillow cover. Sayles. Step-by-step stitchery. 74–76

Pansy pillow, chestnut leaf pillow. Lindberg. Counted cross-stitch designs for all seasons. 49–50, 66–69

Pillows. Fraser. Modern stitchery: stitches, patterns, free-form designing. 101–05

Primroses, Danish rose, anemones and pansies, wild rose pillow, sweet dreams pillow. Great cross-stitch. 20–28, 128

Reembroidered crewel print pillow. Rosenthal. Not-so-nimble needlework needlework book. 55

Rose pillows. Embroidery of roses. 84–85, 90–95, 101–02, 134–39

Small flowered pillow. Silverstein. Mira Silverstein's guide to looped and knotted stitches. 87, 90–91

Starflower pillow. Rosenthal. Not-so-nimble needlework book. 58–59

Sumatran cushion. Gostelow. Complete international book of embroidery. 270

Sunbonnet Sue pillow. Woman's Day creative stitchery from scraps. 127–29

Sunshine garden pillow. Woman's Day book of gifts to make. 205–06

Tambour work—Mediterranean pillow. Better Homes & Gardens embroidery. 80

Three flower-strewn embroidered pillows. Woman's Day decorative needlework for the home. 64–67

Tile-motif embroidered pillow. Woman's Day decorative needlework for the home. 60–63

Walk in the woods wall hanging & pillows. Better Homes & Gardens embroidery. 42–47

Wildflower pillow & crewel throw. Better Homes & Gardens embroidery. 36–39

Pillows, Knitted
Aran pillow, ridged pillow. Knitting techniques and projects. 30–31
Aran square, oblong, and bolster-shaped cushion covers. Hollingworth. Complete book of traditional Aran knitting. 136–41
Basic basketweave pillow in two colors. Walker. Mosaic knitting. 248–49
Knitted, Inca pattern, alpaca design. Casselman. Crafts from around the world. 132–35
Knitted pillow cover. Svinicki. Step-by-step spinning and dyeing. 56–57
Knitted pillow top. Doherty. Family Circle book of 429 great gifts-to-make all year round for just 10¢ to $10.00. 14–15
Knitted pillows. Better Homes and Gardens treasury of needlecrafts. 208–09
Knitted pillows. Chatterton. Scandinavian knitting designs. 167–205
Mosaic-patterned pillow cover. Walker. Mosaic knitting. 193
New pillows from old sweaters. Brown. Super sweater idea book. 172–74
Patchwork pillows. Selfridge. Patchwork knitting. 135
Pinwheel, chain, & French knot pillows. Woman's Day book of gifts to make. 105–07
Quick-knit pillows. Hubert. Weekend knitting projects. 51–53
Rainbow pillow, owl pillow, double knit pillows, reverse stripe pillow, diagonal striped pillow & popcorn pillows. McCall's big book of knit & crochet for home & family. 41, 44, 66, 92
Striped knitted pillow. Woman's Day best sellers. 144
Striped knitted pillow. Woman's Day decorative needlework for the home. 72
Sweater pillows. Brown. Super sweater idea book. 200–06
Throw pillows. Neighbors. Reversible two-color knitting. 159
Windblown snowflakes, enclosed flowers, heart motif, diamond dazzler, diamonds and stripes. Chatterton. Coordinated crafts for the home. 38–39, 52–54, 70–71, 83–84, 90–91

Pillows, Needlepoint
Aleutian pulled-work pillow. Wilson. More needleplay. 160–61
Alphabet and wedding pillows, basket and lotus pillows, home sweet home pillow, tulip pillow. McCall's big book of country needlecrafts. 44–45, 50–53, 58–60
Alphabet needlepoint pillow, needlepoint college pillow. Linsley. Custom made. 95–97, 134–35
Alphabet pillow. Slater. Elaine Slater's book of needlepoint projects. 171–84
American eagle pillow. Ambuter. Carolyn Ambuter's needlepoint celebrations. 146–47
Bargello cushion. Gostelow. Complete international book of embroidery. 107
Bargello cushions. Chatterton. Patchwork & applique. 155–87
Bargello in a contemporary mood. Boyles. Needlework gifts for special occasions. 58–61
Bargello lion pillow. Woman's Day book of weekend crafts. 46–49
Bargello on velveteen. Boyles. Margaret Boyles book of needle art. 100–01
Bargello pillow designs. Multi-stitch pillow. Giant book of crafts. 74–97
Bargello pillows. Christensen. Needlepoint and bargello stitchery. 54–59
Bargello pillows with metallic accents. Woman's Day decorative needlework for the home. 39–40
Bird pillow. Boyles. Margaret Boyles book of needle art. 84–85
Blue rust florentine pillow. Boyles. Margaret Boyles book of needle art. 34–37
Butterfly graphic. Boyles. Needlework gifts for special occasions. 40–43
Calendar of flowers designs. Ambuter. Carolyn Ambuter's needlepoint celebrations. 42–73
Carnation pillow. Boyles. Needlework gifts for special occasions. 70–73
Chinatown dragon needlepoint pillow, unicorn and griffin needlepoint pillows, enchanted land pillow, Taiyuin pillow, green dragon pillow. Gault. Needlework dragons and other mythical creatures. 24–29, 42–52, 60–63, 140–41
Chinoiserie anniversary pillow. Ambuter. Carolyn Ambuter's needlepoint celebrations. 27–29

Chrysanthemum medallion with cranes, Chrysanthemum medal, lions with "nine stars," floral diamonds in thunderbolt lattice cushions, summer grasses on lightening bolt lattice, & dandelions on lightening bolt lattice cushions. Nicoletti. Japanese motifs for needlepoint. 77–79, 94–98

Chrysanthemums within a fence, cushion, autumn grasses with butterflies, bed rest. Nicoletti. Japanese motifs for needlepoint. 105–07, 113–21

Class instruction pillow. Arnold. Needlepoint pattern book. 106–07

Clematis scrolls on checked ground cushion, peony on pine-bark lattice cushion, plum blossoms in pine-bark cartouche cushion, maple leaves on joined circle lattice, maple leaves & butterfly, chrysanthemums & butterfly cushions. Nicoletti. Japanese motifs for needlepoint. 34–36, 41–45, 59–67

Clock pillow. Ambuter. Carolyn Ambuter's needlepoint celebrations. 108–10

Designs from china willow pattern pillow. Wilson. Needleplay. 142–43

Fantasy forest, quilt lily, decisions, decisions and cozy kitty. Sheldon. Washable and dryable needlepoint. 32–39

Finishing needlepoint cushions. Burchette. Needlework. 56–61

Fireworks and anemones pillows, pillow and panel in the classic rose design. McCall's book of America's favorite needlework and crafts. 131–32, 135, 141–44

Floral fabric pillow. Slater. Elaine Slater's book of needlepoint projects. 121–23

Floral with boxed corners, butterfly with knife edge, and tulip with boxing strip. Scobey. First easy-to-see needlepoint workbook. 99–109

Florentine swag pillow. Boyles. Margaret Boyles book of needle art. 30–33

Fly stitch pillows and French stitch pillows. Orr. New needlepoint. 63–67, 88–91

Four-way bargello pillow, diagonal bargello. Christensen. Teach yourself needlepoint. 96–99

Gobelin stitch cushion cover in American Indian pattern, geometric cushion, florentine cushion cover, straight-stitch cushion in floral pattern. Encyclopedia of crafts. 40, 44–47, 162–63

Gobelin stitch pillows. Chatterton. Patchwork & applique. 189–210

Good luck pillow. Ambuter. Carolyn Ambuter's needlepoint celebrations. 32–33

Grow needlepoint vegetables. Vanderbilt. Gloria Vanderbilt designs for your home. 50–57

Heart, strawberry. Smith. Needlery. 114–16, 144–47

Irish village pillow. Slater. Elaine Slater's book of needlepoint projects. 143–46

Jacobean needlepoint pillow. Boyles. Needlework gifts for special occasions. 28–35

Kaleidoscope pillow. Wilson. Needleplay. 122–23

Lion and tiger pillows. Christensen. Needlepoint and bargello stitchery. 12–14

Love pillow. Arnold. Needlepoint pattern book. 134–35

Navajo pillows, African Kuba cushions. McCall's book of America's favorite needlework and crafts. 148–53

Needlepoint designs from Asia. Rogers.

Needlepoint I—introductory material. Cornelius. Teaching needlecraft. 115–17

Owl pillow. Arnold. Needlepoint pattern book. 98–99

Pair of floral pillows. Feldman. Needlework boutique. 121–24

"Pansies" pillow. Vanderbilt. Gloria Vanderbilt design for your home. 62–65

Pansy pillows. Wilson. Needleplay. 128–31

Patchwork and African designs. Chatterton. Coordinated crafts for the home. 124–25, 132, 138–40, 146–48 158–59, 164–65, 172–73, 176–77, 188–89, 194–95, 199, 202–05

Patchwork pillow. Arnold. Needlepoint pattern book. 154–55

Patchwork potpourri pillow. Parker. Mosaics in needlepoint. 108–13

Peking butterflies. Boyles. Needlework gifts for special occasions. 44–47

Pillows. Boyles. Margaret Boyles book of needle art. 62–70

Pillows. Scobey. Decorating with needlepoint. 74–84

Pillows (finishing). Christensen. Needlepoint book. 99–108

Plaid floor pillow and rainbow plaid pillow. Christensen. Teach yourself needlepoint. 83

Preworked needlepoint pillows. Creative sewing. 59–62

Quickpoint pillow. Christensen. Needlepoint and bargello stitchery. 22–23

Rainbow-striped pillow, half cross stitch geometric pillow, square in square continental stitch pillow. Rosenthal. Not-so-nimble needlework book. 96–101

Reversed giant cashmere pillow. Christensen. Teach yourself needlepoint. 86–87

Rosebud mini pillow, pillow with yarn cording and material backing. Orr. Now needle-point. 175–82

Sampler needlepoint pillows, bargello pillow. Woman's Day book of gifts to make. 166–74

Sampler pillow. Christensen. Teach yourself needlepoint. 128–29

Scandinavian rose, windblown snowflakes, enclosed flowers, fleur-de-lys, heart motif, diamond dazzler, diamonds and stripes. Chatterton. Coordinated crafts for the home. 26–31, 40–45, 55–59, 65–67, 72–75, 78, 85–87, 92–95

Striped sampler pillow. Christensen. Teach yourself needlepoint. 116

Textured needlepoint pillow and chair seat. Woman's Day decorative needlepoint work for the home. 41–44

Trellis pillows, latticework pillows, contour needlepoint, Aran pillows, vegetable pillows. McCall's big book of needlecrafts. 168–71, 175–83

Two delft-pattern needlepoint pillows. Woman's Day decorative needlework for the home. 46–50

Two needlepoint pillows with "patchwork" designs. Woman's Day decorative needle-work for the home. 36–39

Wildflower designs, "woven" pillows, designs with variegated yarn, quilt pattern attic windows design, chrysanthemum bargello design, bandanna design, wedding ring pillow, paper-doll sampler pillow, metal thread bargello pillow. Better Homes and Gardens treasury needlecrafts. 242–44, 256–69, 292–95

Zig zag chain pillows, wiggly chain pillows and orr weave pillows. Orr. Now needle-point. 108–11, 133–45, 163–67

Pillows, Patchwork

Baby blocks pillow, bear paw, 1000 pyramids, and Dresden plate patchwork pillows. McCall's big book of country needlecrafts. 83–85, 268–70

Chinese patchwork, mosaics, centennial patchwork and optical blocks. Needlework nostalgia. 9–10, 19–21

Clamshell, star and square pillow covers. Fairfield. Patchwork. 49, 52–53

Cushions with canvas centres. Encyclopedia of crafts. 66–69

Denim patchwork pillows. McCall's big book of needlecrafts. 56–57

Drunkard's path patchwork floor pillow. Reader's Digest complete guide to needlework. 267

Eight-pointed star pillow, Dresden plate pillow. Evrard. Homespun crafts from scraps. 65–75

Fruit basket cushion cover. Fairfield. Patchwork. 57

Mosaic patchwork pillows: elephant, cat and mouse. Foose. More scrap saver's stitch-ery. 86–87

Oddfellow's cross cushion. Houck. Patchwork pattern book. 62–63

Patchwork and quilting I and II—introductory material (pillow). Cornelius. Teaching needlecraft. 87–93

Patchwork cushions. Ives. Ideas for patchwork. 41–45

Patchwork pillow (sewn). Burns. Super sewing. 297

Patchwork pillows. Creative crafts yearbook: an exciting new collection of needlework and crafts. 20–22

Patchwork pillows. Linsley. Great bazaar. 76–77

Patchwork pillows. Woman's Day book of gifts to make. 39

Petal pillow, quilt square pillow, cherry check pillow, blue-green cross pillow. Woman's Day creative stitchery from scraps. 60–62, 133–34, 157–58

Pushover of a pillow (patchwork). Botsford. Between thimble & thumb. 64–68

Scatter cushion in pineapple pattern. Osler. Machine patchwork. 104–07
Square patchwork cushions. Chatterton. Patchwork & applique. 18–25
Star pillows. Better Homes and Gardens treasury of Christmas crafts & foods. 83–84
Tulip miniature cushion. Houck. Patchwork pattern book. 34–35

Pillows, Quilted
Birthday cushion. McNeill. Quilting. 40
Birthday pillow. Fanning. Complete book of machine quilting. 168–72
Carolina lily cushion. Houck. Patchwork pattern book. 38–39
Cathedral window cushion and pincushions. Houck. Patchwork pattern book. 30–31
Circular and square patterned satin cushions. McNeill. Quilting. 36–37
Decorative pillows. Frager. Quilting primer. 79–84
Lion's head pillow. Rosenthal. Not-so-nimble needlework book. 85–86
Pillow with borders. Wooster. Quiltmaking. 128–29
Pillows. Breckenridge. Lap quilting. 30–32
Puffed pillows. McCall's big book of needlecrafts. 56–63
Quilted cushions. McNeill. Quilting. 29
Quilted satin cushion. Encyclopedia of crafts. 25

Pillows, Smocked
Smocked pillow sham (cover). Benton. Sewing classic clothes for children. 40–45

Pillows, Woven
Framework cushion cover. Encyclopedia of crafts. 56–57
Pillows or cushions in two sizes. Brown. Weaving, spinning, and dyeing book. 171–72
Rib-weave pillow. McCall's book of America's favorite needlework and crafts. 286
Tufted pillow cover, popcorn pillow, pillow covers in pick-up weave. Holland. Weaving
    primer. 107–09, 113, 152–54
Two pillows based on work from Nebaj, woven in Coliche. DeRodriguez. Weaving on a
    backstrap loom. 98–127
Woven cushion cover. Weaving and spinning. 58–60
Woven rya pillows. Treasury of things to make. 150–51

Pinafores
Alice in wonderland style pinafore. Benton. Sewing classic clothes for children. 104–09
"Bubble" pinafore. Benton. Sewing classic clothes for children. 110–15
Child's pinafore apron. Woman's Day creative stitchery from scraps. 121–23
Pinafore. Evans. Ribbonwork. 62–69
Pinafore. Mills. The book of presents. 67
Shoulder-tie pinafore. Benton. Sewing classic clothes for children. 100–03
Toddler's gingham pinafore. Woman's Day book of gifts to make. 14–15

Piñatas
Holiday piñata. Sayer. Crafts of Mexico. 141–42
Making a piñata. Meyer. Christmas crafts. 87–93
Piñata. Romberg. Let's discover papier-mâché. 32–33
Piñatas. Coskey. Christmas crafts for everyone. 58–61

Pincushions
Beaded pincushions. Colby. Pincushions. 93–99
Cactus pincushion. Rosenthal. Not-so-nimble needlework book. 40–41
Calico, toadstool, basket, cupcake, & flower wrist pincushion. Woman's Day bazaar
    best sellers. 124–25
Cathedral window and snowball pincushions. Houck. Patchwork pattern book. 30–31,
    48–49

Chart sampler, tic-tac-toe, diamond, rectangles, Union Jack, pierced heart, tulip, fleur-de-lys and cross. Barnes. 120 needlepoint design projects. 14, 21, 27–28, 85–86, 144

Chinese cloisonne & Korean pincushions. Rogers. Needlepoint designs from Asia. 114–15, 142–43

Cockle shell and shell decorated box pincushion. Colby. Pincushions. 78–80

Crewel pincushion. Boyles. Margaret Boyles book of needle art. 86–87

Dresden plate pincushion, basket pincushions, walnut emery pincushions. Better Homes and Gardens treasury of Christmas crafts & foods. 84, 106, 175

Dressmaker's wrist and weighted pincushions. Colby. Pincushions. 59–64

Embroidered pincushions. Woman's Day book of weekend crafts. 167–71

Geometric needlepoint pincushions. Boyles. Needlework gifts for special occasions. 36–39

Hat and heart pincushions (felt). Creative crafts yearbook: an exciting new collection of needlework and crafts. 114

Heart pincushion, flowerpot pincushions, piece-of-cake pincushion. Better Homes and Gardens easy bazaar crafts. 6, 9, 16–18

Introduction to needlepoint—introductory material. Cornelius. Teaching needlecraft. 104–07

Irish crochet pincushion. Svinicki. Old-fashioned crochet. 80

Knitted covers. Colby. Pincushions. 80–83

Log cabin pincushion. Fanning. Complete book of machine quilting. 269–70

Maternity pin cushions. Colby. Pincushions. 84–89

Mattress pincushion. Colby. Pincushions. 52–54

Mountain chain pincushions. Houck. Patchwork pattern book. 14–15

Needlecase, pincushion and glasses case (needlepoint). Mills. The book of presents. 36–37

Octagonal, rectangular and hexagonal sampler pincushions. Colby. Pincushions. 54–58

Pastel bargello pincushion (needlepoint). Boyles. Needlework gifts for special occasions. 62–65

Patchwork pincushions: Three hexagonal, square pinball, stars, and hassock or footstool. Colby. Pincushions. 100–12

Pattern for pincushion (embroidered). Fraser. Modern stitchery: stitches, patterns, freeform designing. 94–96

Pincushion. Christensen. Needlepoint and bargello stitchery. 79

Pincushion. Fairfield. Patchwork. 48

Pincushion. Fowler. Can crafts. 22–23

Pincushion in willow. Maynard. Modern basketry from the start. 155–56

Pincushions. Laury. Treasury of needlecraft gifts for the new baby. 95–96

Pincushions. Morgan. Trapunto and other forms of raised quilting. 194

Pincushions & Christmas tree ornaments. Christensen. Needlepoint book. 109–10

Pincushions for decoration: stars, lifebelt, daisy or pansy, and violet or heartcase. Colby. Pincushion. 110–17

Pincushions with removable covers; pinned-on top, rectangular bolster, housewife cover, envelope cover, circular cover. Colby. Pincushions. 67–77

Pin-stuck heart cushions. Colby. Pincushions. 89–92

Pin-up cactus shaped pincushion, pretzel, smiling sun, rainbow and pinwheel pincushions. Foose. More scrap saver's stitchery. 28–34

Rectangular and square box pincushions. Colby. Pincushions. 45–52

Red heart pincushion (needlepoint). Mensinga-Biasiny. Beautiful baby clothes to crochet, knit, sew and embroider. 147–48

Scrap strip pincushion. Linsley. Great bazaar. 113–14

Smocks pincushion. Benton. Sewing classic clothes for children. 58–62

Sprigged pincushion and needlebook set (embroidered). McCall's book of America's favorite needlework and crafts. 83–84

Toe stuffers and pincushions. Burchette. Needlework. 100

Turtle & heart sachet pincushions. American School of Needlework. Great crochet bazaar book. 124–26
Using waste canvas—introductory material (cross stitch). Cornelius. Teaching needlecraft. 143–45
Valentine pincushion with pocket. Woman's Day creative stitchery from scraps. 55–56
Valentine rose (needlepoint). Needlework nostalgia. 8, 13
Victorian beaded pincushion (needlepoint). McCall's book of America's favorite needlework and crafts. 154–56
Wooden pincushion (needlepoint). Christensen. Needlepoint book. 122, 124
Zigzag chain pincushion. Orr. Now needlepoint. 107–08

Pine cones
Cone rabbits, pussy willow mice, quail family, humming birds. Meras. Vacation crafts. 35–38
Conework basket, pincushion. Whatnot. 137–39
Pine cones: spiky wooden blossoms. Johnson. Nature crafts. 126–33

Ping-pong
Ball and paddle caddy. Popular Mechanics do-it-yourself encyclopedia. Vol. 4, 509
Ping-pong paddle (repair). Schuler. How to fix almost everything. 127

Ping-pong tables
Ping pong table. Dal Fabbro. How to make children's furniture and play equipment. 146–48
Ping-pong table (repair). Schuler. How to fix almost everything. 127

Pins
Animal cracker pins. Doherty. Family Circle book of 429 great gifts-to-make all year round for just 10¢ to $10.00. 62
Brooches. Sjoberg. Working with copper, silver and enamel. 58–64
Bullion knot pin or bracelet, basket of flowers and mini sweater. Wilson. Needlework to wear. 132, 141–42
Coquina duck pin. Elbert. Shellcraft. 203–04
Enamelled penny pin. Brightman. 101 practical uses for propane torches. 113–14
Forging a fibula. Sprintzen. Jewelry, basic techniques and design. 39–45
Go-fly-a-kite pin. Mosesson. Jewelry craft for beginners. 180–83
Golden (brass) frog pin. Mosesson. Jewelry craft for beginners. 218–20
Hat and mittens lapel pin. American School of Needlework. Great crochet bazaar book. 123–24
Laminated paper pins. Romberg. Let's discover papier-mâché. 59
Lapel pins: lady bug, turtle, mouse and clown crocheted. Linsley. Great bazaar. 147–50
Leaves and diamonds pin. Pelisser. Jeweler's craft. 92–93
Macrame pin. Torbet. Macrame you can wear. 68
Metal, silver or pewter starfish pin. Mosesson. Jewelry craft for beginners. 220–22
Newspaper flower, ecology, pop top & tin can pins. Epple. Something from nothing crafts. 74–75
Picture-this pins, fabric pins. Better Homes and Gardens easy bazaar crafts, 43, 48–49
Pin construction. Bovin. Jewelry making, 221–25
Pin with stones. Pelisser. Jeweler's craft. 65–67
Plexiglas pin. Coyne. Penland School of Crafts book of jewelry making. 112–28
Silver forged pin. Coyne. Penland School of Crafts book of jewelry making. 153–67
Soldering and enameling a wire-cloisonne pewter pin. Hollander. Plastics for jewelry. 99–105

Pins. See also **Brooches; Jewelry**

Pinwheels
Pinwheel favor. Wargo. Soft crafts for special occasions. 13–16
Toy windmill. Grainger. Creative papercraft. 90

Pipe racks
New England pipe box, pipe box. Daniele. Building early American furniture. 71–72,
  122–123
Pipe cabinet. Siegele. Cabinets and built-ins. 93–96
Pipe rack and humidor. Popular Mechanics do-it-yourself encyclopedia. Vol. 9, 1353
Rack for eight pipes, pipe rack and humidor set. Doherty. Family Circle book of 429
  great gifts-to-make all year round for just 10¢ to $10.00. 50, 113

Pipes (Tobacco). *See* **Tobacco pipes**

Pitchers
Brass pitcher. Meilach. Decorative and sculptural ironwork. 252–57
Carafe. Sainsbury. Sainsbury's woodturning projects for dining. 64–67
Felt pitcher. McCall's big book of country needlecrafts. 134–35
Magic pitcher. Giant book of metalworking projects. 200–04
Pitcher spout and handle. Howell. Craft of pottery. 62–63
Pitchers. Rhodes. Pottery form. 81–88
Pottery pitchers. Campbell. Using the potter's wheel. 32–38
Raising a creamer with self-spout. Finegold. Silversmithing. 372–76
Syrup pitcher. Campbell. Using the potter's wheel. 78
Throwing a pitcher. Woody. Pottery on the wheel. 167–79

Place cards. *See* **Favors (for parties)**

Place mats. *See* **Table mats**

Plaiting. *See* **Braiding**

Plant collecting and preserving.
Preparation of dried materials for wreaths and swags. Conner. Corncraft. 124–28
Pressed and dried plants. Geary. Plant prints and collages. 65–87
Pressing and preparing the materials. Gordon. Complete guide to drying and preserv-
  ing flowers. 12–60

Plant collecting & preserving. *See also* **Flowers, Collection and preservation**

Plant stands
A—frame pot shelves, pot tree, pot shelves, and quickie shelves. Wood projects for
  the garden. 64–67
Butcher block, cart, step ladder, window box. Doherty. Family Circle book of 429 great
  gifts-to-make all year round for just 10¢ to $10.00. 78–81
Fern stand. Rubin. Mission furniture. 82
Flower pot tree. DeCristoforo. Build your own wood toys, gifts and furniture. 398–401
Fluorescent light plant stands. Braren. Homemade. 54–55
Ivy plant standard. Linsley. Fabulous furniture decorations. 113–19
Lowboy and highboy plant stand of wrought iron. Brightman. 101 practical uses for
  propane torches. 81–84
Mini plant stand. Blackwell. Johnny Blackwell's poor man's catalog. 146
Needlepoint covered wood box plant stand. Parker. Mosaics in needlepoint. 126–30
Plant stand. Kramer. Wirecraft. 102–03
Plexiglas stepladder plant stand. Popular Mechanics do-it-yourself encyclopedia. Vol.
  14, 2214–15

Shaker plant stand. 101 do-it-yourself projects. 58–59
Storage and plant stand. Waugh. Handyman's encyclopedia. 410–11
Sun fern stand. Casselman. Crafts from around the world. 32–35
Tall plant stands, plant stand with pedestal base. Egge. Recycled with flair. 108–11, 113–16
Wicker planter or fern stand. Bausert. Complete book of wicker and cane furniture making. 69–75
Wig stand planter. Hodges. Woodturning handbook—with projects. 195–212

Planters
All season window box. Blackwell. Johnny Blackwell's poor man's catalog. 78
Bargello planter. Scharf. Butterick's fast and easy needlecrafts. 140–41
Barnacle flowers and plant holder. Elbert. Shell craft. 51, 54–55
Bonsai pots. Ceramics. 32–35
Boxes for trees and shrubs. Bumper book of things a boy can make. 90–91
Brick planters. Outdoor projects for home and garden. 310–14
Cactus pots and scalloped design. Appel. Sand art. 19–29
Calico ribbon planter. Nicole. Designer accessories to make for your home. 49–52
Cedar window box wall, peg plant hangers, plywood and redwood window boxes, beaded plant hangers. Doherty. Family Circle book of 429 great gifts-to-make all year round for just 10¢ to $10.00. 82–84, 90–91, 98–102
Clothesline covered planter. Roda. Fabric decorating for the home. 221
Deck or patio planter. 101 do-it-yourself projects. 256–57
Decorative brick planters. Family handyman book of carpentry plans/projects. 469–73
Decorative planters for the bathroom. Popular Mechanics do-it-yourself encyclopedia. Vol. 10, 1464
Easy to build planter. Brann. How to build colonial furniture. 223–43
Florawood planters. Broadwater. Woodburning: art and craft. 34–36
Flower pot, planters, Aztec figurine. Villiard. Art and craft of sand casting. 75, 90–91, 94
Footed planter, stacking planter boxes. Waugh. Handyman's encyclopedia. 414–15, 422–23.
Garden seat/planter. Black and Decker power tool carpentry. 154–59
Gourd planters. Mordecai. Gourd craft. 127–38
Grow strawberries in a barrel. Popular Mechanics do-it-yourself encyclopedia. Vol. 18, 2816–17
Horizontal panel, mitered, laminated, and railroad tie planter boxes. Decks and patios. 137–45
Make a coil and slab pot inside a wooden planter. Priolo. Ceramics by coil. 42–43
Metal tile planter. Linsley. Fabulous furniture decorations. 107–22
Natural pot wraps. Johnson. Nature crafts. 19
Oak wall planter, low planter on metal legs. Egge. Recycled with flair. 101–08, 111–13
Paint bucket planters, crocheted turtle plant holder. Linsley. Great bazaar. 111–12, 142–43
Pig planter. Dodge. Step-by-step new-macrame. 55
Plant holder from paper paint pail. Linsley. Custom made. 126–27
Planter-cabinet. 77 furniture projects you can build. 123–30
Planter—cabinet plywood planter. Family handyman handbook of carpentry plans/ projects. 334–48
Planter made from strips. Scharf. Illustrated patchwork crochet. 160
Plywood planters. Popular Mechanics do-it-yourself encyclopedia. Vol. 8, 1175
Pony pull toy and planter. Brann. How to build workbenches, sawhorse tool chest and other build-it-yourself projects. 82–89
Pressed flower tin planter. Linsley. Decoupage on glass, wood, metal, rocks, shells, wax, soap, plastic, canvas, ceramic. 60–67
Raised beds, putterer's & kerfed board. Wood projects for the garden. 34–37

Raised bottle, egg carton, spray can cover, plastic pill bottle, hanging cool whip planter, plantmobile. Epple. Something for nothing crafts. 13–14, 44–45, 93–96, 119–20, 127–31, 155–58

Raised herb bed. Proulx. Plan and make your own fences and gates, walkways, walls and drives. 76–78

Rustic planters. Popular Mechanics do-it-yourself encyclopedia. Vol. 9, 1356

Serpentine planter wall. Better Homes and Gardens. Step-by-step masonry & concrete. 78–79

Sheet-metal planter, perforated metal planter. Giant book of metalworking projects. 73–74, 194–96

Shirred flower pot cover and window box cover. Roda. Fabric decorating for the home. 230–31

Simple box, multipurpose hide-a-can, vegetable, hexagonal, dowel handle, and bonsai boxes. Wood projects for the garden. 6–22

Slatted planter, grass-mat planter, cube planter. Woman's Day book of gifts to make. 70–71, 129, 137–38

Stone planters. Nickey. Stoneworker's bible. 170–72, 242–43

Strawberry barrel, pyramid & massive pot. Braren. Homemade. 98–100

Thirty-six segment redwood planter. Capotosto. Woodworking wisdom. 220–30

Tiered planter, skyscraper planter, large planter. DeCristoforo. Build your own wood toys, gifts and furniture. 386–97

Tile-covered planter. Burch. Tile: indoors and out, every kind and use. 92–93

Tin can planters. Linsley. Decoupage on glass, wood, metal, rocks, shells, wax, soap, plastic, canvas, ceramic. 67–70

Tree-size planters. Better Homes and Gardens. Deck and patio projects you can build. 85

Trellis planter, hanging cage planter, large capacity floor planter, square planter, redwood planter, octagon planter, stained planter. Popular Mechanics do-it-yourself encyclopedia. Vol. 14, 2107–15

Two tub planters for the price of one, contemporary bench-type stand, hanging wooden block planter, three-shelf room divider with built-in growing lamps, small bridge with built-in planters, wheelbarrow planter. Popular Mechanics do-it-yourself encyclopedia. Vol. 14, 2168–79

Weed pots, bud vases, planters. Spielman. Working green wood with PEG. 92–95

Windowsill planter. Evrard. Homespun crafts from scraps. 18–20

Wishing well planter. Spence. Woodworking tools, materials, processes. 592

Wood planters. Brown. 44 terrific woodworking plans & projects. 202–04

Wood planters. Kramer. Outdoor garden build-it book. 154–70

Wooden outdoor planter. Linsley. Decoupage on glass, wood, metal, rocks, shells, wax, soap, plastic, canvas, ceramic. 26–30

Wooden planter. Fischman. Decks. 84

Planters. *See also* **Flower boxes, planters, etc.; Flower pot holders**

Plants, Artificial. *See* **Flowers, Artificial**

Plaques

Coat hanger wire goldfish wall plaque. Kramer. Wirecraft. 54–56

Coffee-can plaques. Metalcrafting encyclopedia. 81–2

Concave designs on wall plaques. Elbert. Paperworks. 112–15

Coptic triptych, African. Casselman. Crafts from around the world. 152–55

Cornucopia wall plaque, medieval wall plaque, plaster relief plaque, macrame wall plaque. Encyclopedia of crafts. 210, 215, 223, 228

Decorative plaques. Zorza. Pottery: creating with clay. 94–95

Dough art on plaques. Jarvey. You can dough it! 11–57

Fall wall plaque and play dough plaque. Lyon. Arts and crafts objects children can make for the home. 18–21
Hen and chick plaque. Gardner. Dough creations. 79–84
Liberty plaque, antique auto plaque. McKellips. Practical pattern manual for woodcarving and other crafts. 99–104
Make a tile wall plaque. Priolo. Ceramics by coil. 39
Metal foil wall plaques. Metalcrafting encyclopedia. 146–49
Mezuzah. Rockland. Hanukkah book. 152
Mini picture plaques. Linsley. Great bazaar. 160–61
Oval plaques, straw pictures. Hibbs. Straw sculpture. 80
Pine bough plaque. McCall's big book of country needlecrafts. 285
Plastic bread tag, bottle cap Christmas tree, pop-top, & knick-knack plaques. Epple. Something from nothing crafts. 110–11, 145–46, 150–51, 159–60
Real scallop plaque. Elbert. Shell craft. 222–23
Shell flower plaque. McCall's book of America's favorite needlework and crafts. 370–71
Straw work plaque. D'Amato. Italian crafts. 99–100
Sunburst wall panels. Hibbs. Straw sculpture. 24
Tree plaques. Miles. Designing with natural materials. 69–71
Wall plaques. Romberg. Let's discover papier-mâché. 61
Wall plaques from assorted dry materials. Miles. Designing with natural materials. 108–10
Wire silhouettes. Newman. Wire art. 123–25
Woodburned grandma duck. Broadwater. Woodburning: art and craft. 114–18
Woodburned photoplaques. Woodburning: art and craft. 126–30

Plaques, Embroidered
Memory plaques (embroidered). Fraser. Modern stitchery: stitches, patterns, free-form designing. 99–100

Plaques, Metal
Horse wall plaques. Marshall. Foilcraft. 56
Metal cutouts, Haiti voodoo plaque. Casselman. Crafts from around the world. 118–20
Sunburst, five and eight-pointed stars, fish, owl, rooster, butterfly. Fowler. Can crafts. 133–44

Plaques, Needlepoint
Bon appetit plaques. Ambuter. Carolyn Ambuter's needlepoint celebrations. 158–67
Horn of plenty picture. Ambuter. Carolyn Ambuter's needlepoint celebrations. 126
Needlepoint name plaque. Linsley. Custom made. 31–34
Provincial birth record. Ambuter. Carolyn Ambuter's needlepoint celebrations. 124–25

Plaques, Wood
Beauty is truth, leaf and Pennsylvania Dutch plaques. Gotshall. Wood carving and whittling for everyone. 89–90
Clown plaque I, II, III, Cheshire cat plaque. DeCristoforo. Build your own wood toys, gifts and furniture. 282–91
Decoupage address plaque. Linsley. Custom made. 154–55
Farm scene plaque. Lubkemann. Carving twigs and branches. 82
Wall plaques. Egge. Recycled with flair. 99–100
Woodburned wall plaques. Brightman. 101 practical uses for propane torches. 95–96

Plaster and plastering
Farnworth. Creative work with plaster.
Interior wall plaster finish. Adams. Arco's complete woodworking handbook. 457–62
Plaster. Spence. General carpentry. 365–72
Plaster products. Olin. Construction. 218.11–218.14

Plaster work (carving)
Plaster carving. Schuman. Art from many hands. 223–24

Plastic casting
Acrylic casting. Andersen. Creative exploration in crafts. 129–46
Casting plastics. Kicklighter. Crafts, illustrated designs and techniques. 72–77
Flowers in plastic. O'Neill. Make-it-merry Christmas book. 90–95
Liquid plastic casts. Mills. Book of presents. 33–35

Plastics
Acrylics. Waugh. Handyman's encyclopedia. 371–77
How to encase shells in resin. Elbert. Shell craft. 161–72
How to work with plexiglas. Popular Mechanics do-it-yourself encyclopedia. Vol. 14, 2205–15
Internal carving plastics, plastics crafts. Kicklighter. Crafts, illustrated designs and techniques. 134–37, 238–47
Plastics. Bowie. Jewelry making. 139–47
Plastics. Rose. Illustrated encyclopedia of crafts and how to master them. 381–91
Sheet-plastic creations. Giant book of crafts. 453–64
Techniques for sewing with plastics. Time-Life Books. Novel materials. 154–69

Plate racks
Display plate rack. Blandford. 53 space-saving built-in furniture projects. 114, 116–18
Plate rack. Kramer. Wirecraft. 90–91
Plate rack. McCall's big book of country needlecrafts. 114–15
Plate rack. Rubin. Mission furniture. 105
Plate rack. Shea. Pennsylvania Dutch and their furniture. 180
Souvenir plate holder. Modern general shop. Woodworking. 109

Plates
Deep bowls and flat plates. Woody. Pottery on the wheel. 180–85
Dinner plates and side plates. Sainsbury. Sainsbury's woodturning projects for dining. 47–51
Making a plate. Finegold. Silversmithing. 309–15
Papier mâché and decoupage plate. Encyclopedia of crafts. 211
Plate liner with bluebells, plate liner with a sprig of cotoneaster, plate liner with privet motif, berry plate liner, plate liners with winter motifs. Lindberg. Counted cross-stitch designs for all seasons. 53, 62–65, 71–72, 81–82
Plates. Rhodes. Pottery form. 100–08
Plates for the Hanukkah table. Rockland. Hanukkah book. 87–90
Pottery plate. Campbell. Using the potter's wheel. 40–41
Step-by-step instructions for decorative plate using hard ground. Elliot. Working with copper. 83–84
Throwing a plate on the batt. Ceramics. 56–58

Platforms
Duckboards. Wood projects for the garden. 38–39
Elevated floor for dining or lounging. Built-ins. 104–08
Platforms, risers and cubes. Kangas. By hand. 119–23
Traveling platforms for unfinished attics. Time-Life books. Space and storage. 110–11

Playground equipment
Bunny box. Palmer. Making children's furniture and play structures. 136
Children's equipment for sandboxes, climbing, swinging and sliding. Blandford. Constructing outdoor furniture, with 99 projects. 287–300

Children's outdoor gym repair. Schuler. How to fix almost everything. 99
Folding climbing frame. Blandford. Giant book of wooden toys. 285–89
Jungle gym. Black and Decker power tool carpentry. 169–73
Jungle gym. Boeschen. Successful playhouses. 33–35
Jungle gym tree house, bouncing teeter board, merry-go-round swing, back-yard roller
 coaster, water hoop, seesaw with a new twist. Popular Mechanics do-it-yourself
 encyclopedia. Vol. 14, 2188–91, 2194–95
Modular playground set, rocker and seesaw, jungle gym with swings. 101 do-it-your-
 self projects. 337–39, 358–65
Movement explorer, pulley glide, nets. Boeschen. Successful playhouses. 21–29
Polyhedron hill. Boeschen. Successful playhouses. 105–09
Rock 'n rowboat, combination slide, seesaw and ladder. Dal Fabbro. How to make
 children's furniture and play equipment. 186–90
Seesaw. Adams. Make your own baby furniture. 150–54
Space age playhouse. Outdoor projects for home and garden. 350–55
Swing and trapeze with climbing bars; swing, ladder and seesaw, three-way ladder.
 Dal Fabbro. How to make children's furniture and play equipment. 172–78
Tapered climbing frame. Blandford. Giant book of wooden toys. 282–85
Whirling seesaw. Baldwin. Old fashioned wooden toys. 190–93

Playhouses
A-frame play shelter. Marshall. Yard buildings. 137–39
Angle house. Palmer. Making children's furniture and play structures. 122–24
Card table playhouse. Baldwin. Scrap fabric crafts. 24–27
Card table playhouse. Creative sewing. 119
Cardboard campers. Boeschen. Successful playhouses. 74–75
Carton creations. Palmer. Making children's furniture and play structures. 56–57
Castle or play station. Palmer. Making children's furniture and play structures. 62
Dice house. Palmer. Making children's furniture and play structures. 118–21
Flower-garden play house (fabric). Complete book of baby crafts. 172–75
Folding playhouse. Dal Fabbro. How to make children's furniture and play equipment.
 142–43
Forest ranger fire tower, observatory and photography darkroom, Mississippi river
 barge. Churchill. Backyard building book. 132–44
Fort in the garden. Boeschen. Successful playhouses. 36–40
Indoor playhouse, small playhouse, playhouse. Blandford. Giant book of wooden toys.
 244–59
Inflated-spaces. Palmer. Making children's furniture and play structures. 92–94
Mini-sub. Palmer. Making children's furniture and play structures. 60–61
Monster mouths. Palmer. Making children's furniture and play structures. 63
Never complete playhouse. Boeschen. Successful playhouses. 121
Outdoor playhouse and storage shed. Del Fabbro. How to make children's furniture
 and play equipment. 158–61
Panel play spaces. Palmer. Making children's furniture and play structures. 58–59
Play buildings for kids. Kentuck kamp, forest ranger fire tower, observatory and pho-
 tography darkroom, Mississippi River barge. Churchill. Big backyard building book.
 70–88
Playhouse. Stiles. Easy-to-make children's furniture. 96–100
Playhouse. Black and Decker power tool carpentry. 165–168
Playhouse. Blandford. 66 children's furniture projects. 418–28
Playhouse. Endacott. Fine furniture making and woodworking. 81–84
Playhouse. Marshall. Yard buildings. 139–42
Playhouse of tires. Boeschen. Successful playhouses. 76–77
Playhouses. Adams. Make your own baby furniture. 107–19
Play panel structure of modular cubes. Boeschen. Successful playhouses. 84–88
Playplaces. Palmer. Making children's furniture and play structures. 114–15

Pretty little playhouse, indoor playhouse. Popular Mechanics do-it-yourself encyclopedia. Vol. 14, 2200–03

Pyramid playhouse. Boeschen Successful playhouses. 72–73

Sandbox shelter. Marshall. Yard buildings. 139

Super hiding place for any playhouse (steel drum under the floor of playhouse). Lane. Building in your backyard. 135

Temporary playhouse from cardboard cartons. Lane. Building in your backyard. 121–26

Tepee, cloth playhouse. Favorite easy-to-make toys. 95–103

Tepee playhouse. Better Homes and Gardens. Sewing for your home. 191

Tree house. Marshall. Yard buildings. 142–44

Playhouses. See also **Domes, Play; Tents**

Playing card cases. See **Card cases**

Play pens.
Baby's playpen (repair). Schuler. How to fix almost everything. 132

Playpen. Adams. Make your own baby furniture. 107–119

Playpen. Blandford. 66 children's furniture projects. 106–09

Playpen. Del Fabbro. How to make children's furniture and play equipment. 40–41

Playrooms. See **Recreation rooms**

Pliers
Forging a pair of pliers. Weygers. Modern blacksmith. 80–81

Plows
Bull-tongue plow. Langsner. Country woodcraft. 191–96

Plow work. Richardson. Practical blacksmithing. Vol. 3, 256–304

Plumbing
Connecting copper pipe and copper tubing. Brightman. 101 practical uses for propane torches. 43–47

Faucets (repair). Schuler. How to fix almost everything. 69–72

How to work with plastic pipe, be your own home plumber. Popular Mechanics do-it-yourself encyclopedia. Vol. 14, 2182–85, 2216–35

Installing stainless steel sinks yourself. Family handyman handbook of home improvement and remodeling. 45–55

Loosening pipe joints. Brightman. 101 practical uses for propane torches. 132

Outdoor faucet repair. Outdoor projects for home and garden. 183–84, 200–03

Plastic pipe. Family handyman handbook of home improvement and remodeling. 111–17

Plumbing. Bragdon. Homeowner's complete manual of repair & improvement. 388–457

Plumbing. Burch. Building small barns, sheds, and shelters. 127–39

Plumbing repairs and maintenance. Nunn. Home improvement, home repairs. 99–128

Sealing unused drain. Brightman. 101 practical uses for propane torches. 127

Single-handle and two-handled faucets repair. Family handyman handbook of home improvement and remodeling. 93–107

Tapping a water line. Family handyman handbook of home improvement and remodeling. 107–11

Thawing frozen pipes. Brightman. 101 practical uses for propane torches. 123

Plywood

All about plywood. Popular Mechanics do-it-yourself encyclopedia. Vol. 15, 2244–51
Buying and cutting plywood. Stiles. Easy-to-make children's furniture. 10–13
Dealing with plywood, stacked plywood construction. Fine woodworking techniques. I. 114–15, 175–77
Fast (plywood) furniture. 77 furniture projects you can build. 319–35
How to work with plywood. Hedden. Successful shelves and built-ins. 97–109
How to work with plywood. Leavy. Bookshelves and storage units. 6–21
Plywood. Olin. Construction. 201.29–201.42
Self. Working with plywood, including indoor/outdoor projects.
16 ways to hide plywood edges. Popular Mechanics do-it-yourself encyclopedia. Vol. 14, 2238–39
Working with plywood. Leavy. Successful small farms. 82–97
Zegel. Fast furniture.

Pocketbooks. *See* **Purses**

Pokers. *See* **Fireplace equipment**

Poles

Rugged masts from thinwall conduit. Popular Mechanics do-it-yourself encyclopedia. Vol. 12, 1782–83

Polishing. *See* **Grinding and polishing**

Pomanders

Citrus pomanders. Christmas crafts book. 116
Hanging ball, paper flowers and natural material. Critchley. Step by step guide to making artificial flowers. 68–70
Light brown pierced pomander, dark brown pomander, clove studded pomander (gourd). Johnson. Nature crafts. 113–14, 116
Pomander. Mills. Book of presents. 88
Pomander bags. Doherty. Family Circle book of 429 great gifts-to-make all year round for just 10¢ to $10.00. 53
Pomander ball. Meyer. Christmas crafts 76–79
Pomander balls. Scobey. Gifts from your garden. 130–31
Pomander balls and Christmas fragrances. Johnson. Nature crafts. 146
Square and heart-shaped lavender bag, pomander. Evans. Ribbonwork. 93–97

Pompon toys

Pompon zoo. Christmas crafts book. 111–13
Wooly animals. Staples. Yarn animal book. 37–52
Wooly toys including pompon toys. Rath. Splendid soft toy book. 94–102

Pompoms

General directions. Staples. Yarn animal book. 28–36
Making a pompom. Time-Life books. Exotic styling. 86
Pompoms. Wilson. Ask Erica. 66

Ponchos

Adult poncho, beaded poncho, child's poncho. Loeb. Leather book. 91–109
Cotton mini-poncho. Jacobs. Crochet book. 77–78
Crocheted poncho, pineapple poncho. Woman's Day book of gifts to make. 149–50, 183–85
Four-square peasant poncho (sewn). Holderness. Peasant chic. 11–13
Fringed poncho. Torbet. Macrame you can wear. 98–99

Granny poncho. McCall's big book of knit & crochet for home & family. 226
Granny square poncho. Scharf. Illustrated patchwork crochet. 167
His and her fur-lined ponchos. Crochet. 27
Increased ponchos. Walker. Mosaic knitting. 214–15
Knitted sporty poncho. Knitting techniques and projects. 58
Man's and woman's poncho. Creative sewing. 18
Man's twill poncho woven in two pieces. Brown. Weaving, spinning, and dyeing book. 172–73
Mexican blanket poncho. Holderness. Peasant chic. 14–15
Multicolor full poncho. Jacobs. Crochet book. 91–92
Patchwork ponchos and capes. Selfridge. Patchwork knitting. 187–89
Poncho in linked French sennets. Dendel. Basic book of fingerweaving. 43–47
Poncho-skirt. Henderson. Woman's Day book of designer crochet. 85–87
Poncho with warp-face strips (Bolivian). Brown. Weaving, spinning, and dyeing book. 78–79
Poncho woven on a table loom. Weaving and spinning. 117–24
Quechquemitl or Mexican poncho. Brown. Weaving, spinning, and dyeing book. 75–76
Quetzquemetyl and variation. Beard. Fashions from the loom. 40–41
Reversible denim poncho. Fanning. Complete book of machine quilting. 199–203
Ruana in Osage braiding. Dendel. Basic book of fingerweaving. 68–70
Sampler square poncho. Walker. Mosaic knitting. 200
Tasseled poncho, granny-square poncho. Woman's Day crochet showcase. 51–52, 114–15
Two-strip poncho. Walker. Mosaic knitting. 195
Warp-face poncho. Brown. Weaving, spinning, and dyeing book. 189–90
Waterproof ponchos. Ruggieri. Woman's Day book of no-pattern sewing. 80
Woman's triangular poncho, long poncho for men or women. Brown. Weaving, spinning, and dyeing book. 180–82
Woven hooded poncho, long poncho cape. Beard. Fashions from the loom. 42–43
Woven poncho. Holland. Weaving primer. 154

Ponds
Dew ponds. Manners. Country crafts today. 180–83
Holding water. Campbell. Home water supply. 93–107

Pools. See **Garden pools; Swimming pools**

Popsicle sticks
Tongue depressor planters. Nicole. Designer accessories to make for your home. 53–60

Porch swings. See **Swings**

Porches
Add a screened porch, your garage can be a screened porch. Popular Mechanics do-it-yourself encyclopedia. Vol. 16, 2528–35
Adding screens to make a porch bug-proof. Porches and patios. 100–07
Building a porch. Harmon. Porches & terraces. 37–68
Doors to glass in a porch. Time-Life books. New living spaces. 20–24
Porch floors: ceramic, quarry tile, slate. Harmon. Porches & terraces. 80–81
Porch roofs. Harmon. Porches & terraces. 82–84
Porches. Adams. Arco's complete woodworking handbook. 414–18
Porches—outdoor living under a roof. Daniels. Decks, porches, and patios. 61–75
Screened-in porch. Handyman. 462–65
Spacious porch. Porches and patios. 8–29

Porches. *See also* **Decks; Patios**

Posts. *See* **Fences; Lamp posts**

Pot holders
American pieced work potholder. Fairfield. Patchwork. 20
Applique oven mit. Wilson. Needleplay. 172–73
Appliqued and quilted pot holder. Scharf. Butterick's fast and easy needlecrafts. 108–09
Appliqued pot holders: blue cat, peach pig, white hen, question mark, tulip, rainbow, hexagon beauty, diamond star, shadow box. Gillies. Patterns for applique and pieced work—and ways to use them. 62–73
Appliqued pot holders: heart, whale and tulip. Evrard. Homespun crafts from scraps. 48–60
Baker's mitt. Fanning. Complete book of machine quilting. 261–64
Barbecue or oven mitt (sewn). Burns. Super sewing. 295–96
Basic hot mitt. Morgan. Trapunto and other forms of raised quilting. 201–04
Chicken pot holder nesting on a scouring pad egg. Coffey. Francine Coffey's celebrity sewing bee. 71
Crocheted ripple band, embroidered, round pot holders, picture pot holders, gay 90's pot holders. McCall's big book of knit & crochet for home & family. 130–31, 135–36, 174–75
Crocheted sleeve for pot handles, square potholders. Woman's Day decorative needlework for the home. 143–44
Food pot holders, owl and cat hot mitts, pot holders with kitchen motifs from bygone days. McCall's big book of country needlecrafts. 161–63, 171–72
Granny potholder and popcorn stitch potholder. Great granny crochet book. 130
Heart pot holder. Linsley. Custom made. 131–33
Hot mat. Roda. Fabric decorating for the home. 55
Hot mitts. Better Homes and Gardens easy bazaar crafts. 7, 16
Hot mitts. McCall's big book of knit & crochet for home & family. 176–77
Hot mitts, hot pads. Doherty. Family Circle book of 429 great gifts-to-make all year round for just 10¢ to $10.00. 131–32, 136–38
Hot pads. Holland. Weaving primer. 86
Introduction to quilting. Cornelius. Teaching needlecraft. 84–86
Knit basket-weave & box stitch pot holders. McCall's big book of knit & crochet for home & family. 30
Leaf-shaped pot holders, hen plaque and pot holders. McCall's big book of needlecrafts. 53–54, 64
Macrame hot pad. Boberg. Macrame. 100
Maple leaf table mats and pot holder. Houck. Patchwork pattern book. 22–23
Mitt potholders. Woman's Day crochet showcase. 162–63
Mock pot holders (for decoration only). Goldman. Decorate with felt. 86–87
Oven gloves. Goldsworthy. Clothes for disabled people. 94
Oven mits. Breckenridge. Lap quilting. 55–56
Oven mits. Mills. Book of presents. 82
Padded watermelon, crocheted, bandanna, appliqued quilted fish potholders, mouse pot-handle cover. Woman's Day bazaar best sellers. 90–95
Patched pot holder and recipe-book cover. Coffey. Francine Coffey's celebrity sewing bee. 79
Patchwork and applique pot holders. McCall's book of America's favorite needlework and crafts. 209–12
Pierre the pot holder's holder. Brann. How to build workbenches, sawhorse tool chest and other build-it-yourself projects. 91–96
Pot holders. Breckenridge. Lap quilting. 54
Pot holders. Guth. Sewing with scraps. 122–23

Pot holders and bun warmers. Frager. Quilting primer. 85
Pot holder rack. Hagans. All good gifts. 60–61
Pot holder that slips over the handle of a pot. Perry. Holiday magic. 179–81
Pot holders quilted to spell "hot," salt and pepper pot holders, mason jar pot holder.
    Foose. More scrap saver's stitchery. 64–69
Quick quilted pot holders. Baldwin. Scrap fabric crafts. 56–57
Quilted pot holders. Linsley. Great bazaar. 80–82
Rose garden pot holder. Houck. Patchwork pattern book. 56–57
Sandwich pot holders. Foose. Scrap saver's stitchery book. 71–73
Square pot holder. Walker. Mosaic knitting. 198, 200
Ticktacktoe pot holder. Woman's Day book of weekend crafts. 16–17
Two chefs pot-holder dolls. Marsten. Step-by-step dollmaking. 90–93

Potato printing
Potato cuts. Bumper book of things a girl can make. 139–42
Potato printing. Mills. Book of presents. 42–43

Potpourri
Dotted-swiss potpourris. Woman's Day bazaar best sellers. 113
Dry potpourri: sweet rose, citrus mint, spice, and herb. Scobey. Gifts from your
    garden. 71–75
Moist potpourri. Scobey. Gifts from your garden. 68–70
Pot pourri. Gordon. Complete guide to drying and preserving flowers. 200–03
Potpourri. Johnson. Nature crafts. 44–45
Potpourri. McCall's big book of country needlecrafts. 42
Potpourri. Mills. Book of presents. 86–89
Potpourri. Pittaway. Traditional English country crafts and how to enjoy them today.
    180–81
Potpourri-covered deer. Better Homes and Gardens treasury of Christmas crafts &
    foods. 332
Potpourri sachets. Wiita. Dried flowers for all seasons. 33–34
Recipe for potpourri. Cook. Decorating for the holidays. 61
Sweet scented bags, pomanders and sachets. Christmas crafts book. 115–18

Potter's wheels
Make your own potter's wheel. Popular Mechanics do-it-yourself encyclopedia. Vol. 15,
    2307
Potter's wheel. Abrams. Building craft equipment. 178–91
Wheels. Harvey. Building pottery equipment. 26–71

Pottery
Anyone can make pottery. Popular Mechanics do-it-yourself encyclopedia. Vol. 5,
    746–47
Black locust weed pot. Johnson. Nature crafts. 85
Campbell. Using the potter's wheel.
Casson. Craft of the potter.
Ceramics.
Ceramics basics. Rose. Illustrated encyclopedia of crafts and how to master them.
    203–33
Chroman. Potter's primer.
Clay pinch pots, slab pots, modeling dishes on rocks. Lyon. Arts and crafts objects
    children can make for the home. 30–40
Composite pots. Zorza. Pottery: creating with clay. 92–94
Compotes. Campbell. Using the potter's wheel. 61–63
Conrad. Contemporary ceramic formulas.

Decorating bisqueware with underglaze pencils, engobes and oxides. Paak. Decorative touch. 41–44

Decorating greenware with sgraffito, slip trailing and combing, mishima inlay, added clay, stamping, incising and excising, piercing, burnishing, wax resist, engobe, and underglaze colors. Paak. Decorative touch. 1–40

Decorating with slip, oxides, burnishing, and sgraffito. Ceramics. 108–20

Decorative processes: brushwork, slip, impressed, sprigging and relief, mishima, Neritage, wax resist, and underglaze color. Dickerson. Pottery making. 73–87

Dickerson. Pottery making.

Earthenware, soft stoneware, stoneware, porcelain and raku clay body formulas. Chappell. Potter's complete book of clay and glazes. 25–106

Egyptian paste formulas. Chappell. Potter's complete book of clay and glazes. 107–11

Form and surface decoration. Troy. Salt-glazed ceramics. 78–105

Howell. Craft of pottery.

Indian pots. Stribling. Crafts from North American Indian arts. 247–67

Kriwanek. Keramos.

Make a free form coil pot, a coil pot inside a paper container. Priolo. Ceramics by coil. 9–15

Make a free-form pot with a smooth finish. Priolo. Ceramics by coil. 40–41

Making clay pots. Schuman. Art from many hands. 193–97

Ovenware and rangetop bodies & glazes. Chappell. Potter's complete book of clay and glazes. 111–15

Oxides for decoration. Zorza. Pottery: creating with clay. 123

Paddle-formed pottery, wheel-thrown pottery. Newman. Contemporary Southeast Asian arts and crafts. 191–214

Painted delft flower crocks. Better Homes and Gardens treasury of Christmas crafts & foods. 158

Photosensitized ceramics. Conrad. Contemporary ceramic techniques. 109–115

Pinch method, slab construction and coil bowls. Linderman. Crafts for the classroom. 255–71

Pinch pots, slab method, coil method. Anderson. Creative exploration in crafts. 165–89

Pots from local clay. Johnson. Nature crafts. 5–6

Potter's art. Newman. Contemporary African arts and crafts. 26–53

Pottery. Kicklighter. Crafts, illustrated designs and techniques. 248–57

Pottery step-by-step.

Pucci. Pottery.

Raku. Dickerson. Pottery making. 131–35

Raku. Howell. Craft of pottery. 129–30

Raku. Wettlaufer. Getting into pots. 158–62

Raku: clay bodies, bisque firing of glazing, and firing. Conrad. Contemporary ceramic techniques. 57–70

Raku firing and glazes. Zorza. Pottery: creating with clay. 147–54

Rhodes. Pottery form.

Riegger. Electric kiln ceramics.

Sanders. (Sunset ceramics book). How to make pottery.

Setting up a studio. Wettlaufer. Getting into pots. 104–15

Shafer. Pottery decoration.

Simple pinch pots, stick pots, slab pots. Ceramics. 15–32

Slipware. Zorza. Pottery: creating with clay. 102–04

Starting a pottery. Pittaway. Traditional English country crafts and how to enjoy them today. 29–34

Stoneware bodies, slips, stains and underglaze. Grebanier. Chinese stoneware glazes. 111–14

Storage and reconstitution of clay. Pottery step-by-step. 63

Surface slip and unlaid decoration. Pottery step-by-step. 41–47

Throwing pots in series. Wettlaufer. Getting into pots. 84–87

Tyler. Raku.
Wettlaufer. Getting into pots.
Woody. Handbuilding ceramic forms.
Woody. Pottery on the wheel.
Zorza. Pottery.

Pottery. See also **Glazes and glazing**

Pottery equipment
Clay drying boxes and storage rack. Harvey. Building pottery equipment. 22–23

Pottery kilns. See **Kilns**

Pottery making equipment
Building a potter's wheel. Sanders. (Sunset ceramics book). How to make pottery.
137–38
Constructing your own slab roller. Wettlaufer. Getting into pots. 164–68
Dry and wet clay mixers. Harvey. Building pottery equipment. 14–21
Hand tools, sponges, cut-off wire, slab cutter, rips, cut-off needle, trimming tools, glaze
and slip syringes, & banding wheel. Harvey. Building pottery equipment. 74–81
Harvey hauler. Harvey. Building pottery equipment. 170–79
Making plaster bats. Wettlaufer. Getting into pots. 170–73
Pipe rollers. Harvey. Building pottery equipment. 169
Shelves and racks. Harvey. Building pottery equipment. 164–65
Wedging board. Abrams. Building craft equipment. 192–97
Wedging table. Harvey. Building pottery equipment. 160–61
Work table. Harvey. Building pottery equipment. 162–63
Workshop layout. Harvey. Building pottery equipment. 181–89

Pottery, Repairing
Care and repair of pottery. Johnson. How to restore, repair, and finish almost every-
thing. 148–53
Pottery and porcelain. Introduction to repairing and restoring. 152–97

Potting benches. See **Garden equipment**

Potting houses. See **Garden houses, shelters, etc.**

Poultry houses
Chicken houses. Leavy. Successful small farms. 158–60
Game bird housing. Burch. Building small barns, sheds, and shelters. 193–95
Poultry house & chicken feeders, waterers, brooder, nests, egg candling light & incu-
bator. Braren. Homemade. 158–69
Poultry housing. Burch. Building small barns, sheds, and shelters. 187–93
Poultry housing. Lytle. Farm builder's handbook, with added material for pole type
industrial buildings. 76–85

Powder tables. See **Dressing tables**

Prairie schooner models
Conestoga wagon. Maginley. America in miniatures. 94–99

Printing
Brayer printing. Rainey. Weaving without a loom. 69–70
Ink platen. Abrams. Building craft equipment. 172–74
Intaglio printing. Elliot. Working with copper. 114–19

Making a linocut & printing cloth with linocuts. Dyeing & printing. 82–100
Making a monoprint. Dyeing & printing. 64–68
Oil and water prints. Holtje. Cardcraft. 52–55
Printed party papers, placemats, block-printed wall hanging, crayon-printed wall hanging, allover fabric design. Elbert. Shell craft. 258–67
Printing from the etched plate. Elliot. Working with copper. 120–21
Printing with plants: direct, offset and proof press. Geary. Plant prints and collages. 27–43
Printing with potatoes. Dyeing & printing. 60–63
Printmaking. Rockland. Hanukkah book. 100–03
Relief printing techniques. Dyeing & printing. 54–59
Stamped print, relief print, collage print, stencil print, screened print and monoprint. Linderman. Crafts for the classroom. 420–48
Styrofoam block printing, cellulose sponge printing, roll-on printing. Elbert. Paperworks. 15–28
Styrofoam prints, linoleum block prints. Holtje. Cardcraft. 13–27

Printing. See also **Block printing; Potato printing; Silk screen printing; Stencil work**

Prints
Baby footprints. Gardner. Dough creations. 145–46

Projection apparatus
Making an opaque projector. Kangas. By hand. 88–92
Roll-away projector stand. Popular Mechanics do-it-yourself encyclopedia. Vol. 15, 2342–44

Propagating frames. See **Cold frames**

Pull toys
Circus train, ducks and dachshunds that talk, buzzing bumblebee. Popular Mechanics do-it-yourself encyclopedia. Vol. 15, 2348–55
Dragonfly made of wood. Fine woodworking techniques. 111–13
Hale the whale. Popular Mechanics do-it-yourself encyclopedia. Vol. 19, 2918, 2920
Pull along wobbling dog. Blandford. Giant book of wooden toys. 161–64
Pull toy (insect). Modern general shop. Woodworking 111
Puppy pull toy, hippo pull toy, whale of a pull, spotty dog and drag a dragon. DeCristoforo. Build your own wood toys, gifts and furniture. 96–104
Roundabout (merry-go-round) with horses. Blizzard. Making wooden toys.
Toting dachshund, hopping bunny pull toy, walking ducks pull toy and dog with waggly ears. DeCristoforo. Build your own wood toys, gifts and furniture. 106–23
Waddling ducks, bobbing tortoise, hopping hare, & speedy fox. Baldwin. Old fashioned wooden toys. 10–21

Pumps
Pump to recycle waste water. Weygers. Recycling, use, and repair of tools. 18–23
Pump types and ratings. Hackleman. Water works. 83–96
Water systems handbook.

Punch needle work
Punch stitching: materials, equipment, design, color, & working the design. Illes. Men in stitches. 11–82

Punches
Center punch. Briney. Home machinist's handbook. 211–14
Hot punch from an old hammer. Make it! don't buy it. 250
Making design layouts for punches. Weygers. Recycling, use, and repair of tools. 51
Making punches. Blandford. Practical handbook of blacksmithing and metalworking. 166–72
Making punches: hand-held, miniature and washer. Weygers. Recycling, use, and repair of tools. 40–48, 52–58
Making your own punches. Sjoberg. Working with copper, silver and enamel. 72

Pup tents. *See* **Tents**

Puppet theaters
Glove puppet theatre and string puppet theatre. Anderson. Crafts and the disabled. 98–104
Magic storybook puppet theatre. Rath. Splendid soft toy book. 32–33
Puppet theater. Blandford. Giant book of wooden toys. 60–62
Puppet theatre. Blizzard. Making wooden toys. 23–25
Puppet theater. Dal Fabbro. How to make children's furniture and play equipment. 149–50
Simple cardboard theater, plywood or hardboard. Schuman. Art from many hands. 96–98
Simple puppet stage; electric puppet theatre. Bumper book of things a girl can make. 46–48, 50–51
Stage construction and painting. Flower. Puppets, methods and materials. 114–21
Store/theater. Palmer. Making children's furniture and play structures. 116–17

Puppets
Animal hand puppets. Favorite easy-to-make toys. 28–31
Big bad Bertie rabbit. Morton. Sleeve puppets. 82–90
Card puppets and stick puppets. Tyler. Big book of dolls. 78–95
Chippy the chimp. Morton. Sleeve puppets. 91–106
Cock-a-doodle-doo. Morton. Sleeve puppets. 43–52
Coco Loco the funny looking clown can step right out or sit right down. Creative crafts yearbook: an exciting new collection of needlework and crafts. 34–36
Cookie puppets, marionette nativity, goose puppet, large bunny puppet. Better Homes and Gardens treasury of Christmas crafts & foods. 226–28, 271–73
Dandy dog. Morton. Sleeve puppets. 62–72
Didgeridoo the kangaroo. Morton. Sleeve puppets. 73–81
Dolls and puppets. Hagans. All good gifts. 104–09
Felt hand-puppet family. Woman's Day creative stitchery from scraps. 13–18
Flower. Puppets, methods and materials.
Four glove puppets—the story of the three little pigs. Greenhowe. Making miniature toys and dolls. 87–93
Funny Fred. Morton. Sleeve puppets. 107–13
Gingerbread puppets and house. Linsley. Lesley Linsley's Christmas ornaments and stockings. 173–75
Glove puppet. Practical needlework. 259–60
Glove puppets. Anderson. Crafts and the disabled. 95–98
Glove puppets (penguin, frog, elephant and mouse). Gault. Crafts for the disabled. 37–46
Gourd puppet heads. Meilach. Macrame gnomes and puppets. 90–91
Hand puppets. Buxton. Craftmaking: for love or money. 118–21
Hand puppets from stockings, glove puppets, marionettes. Bumper book of things a girl can make. 44–51
Hand puppets, marionettes. Linderman. Crafts for the classroom. 109–33

Looney bird puppet. Rissell. Craftwork the handicapped elderly can make and sell. 94–95

Making shadow puppets and putting on a play. Schumann. Art from many hands. 134–43

Marionette figure, Punch and Judy show. Bumper book of things a boy can make. 96–97, 109–11

Maude and Cecil. Guild. Dollmaker's workshop. 96–98

Meilach. Macrame gnomes & puppets.

Owl puppet. Scobey. First easy-to-see needlepoint workbook. 23–25

Papier mâché hand puppet head. Elbert. Paperworks. 130–34

Papier mâché puppets. Favorite easy-to-make toys. 202–05

Papier mâché puppet heads. Meilach. Macrame gnomes and puppets. 87–89

Peter penguin, Hoolet the owl and Croaky crow. Morton. Sleeve puppets. 27–42

Pinocchio puppet. D'Amato. Italian crafts. 122-27

Punch and Judy puppet show, five fairy tale finger puppets. Greenhowe. Making miniature toys and dolls. 112–16

Puppet heads. Romberg. Let's discover papier mâché. 51–52

Puppet people: Charleston Charlotte, sugar plum fairy, and Joey the clown. Janitch. All made from paper. 76–81

Puppets. Laury. Handmade toys and games. 125–37

Puppet's head. Grainger. Creative papercraft. 97–98

Puppets, shadow puppets, glove or hand puppets, string puppets. Blandford book of traditional handicrafts. 148–67

Puppets: stick, rag doll, papier mâché, paper bag, paper cup and milk cartons, egg carton head, and dial-a-face. Yoder. Sculpture and modeling for the elementary school. 84–100

Puppets with a mouth; puppets with arms; finger puppets. Tyler. Big book of soft toys. 40–67

Santa-in-chimney. Wilson. Erica Wilson's Christmas world. 132–33

Shadow puppets. Stephan. Creating with tissue paper. 219–21

Simple newspaper puppets. Yoder. Sculpture and modeling for the elementary school. 56–60

Slimy snail. Morton. Sleeve puppets. 53–61

String puppet holding aid. Anderson. Crafts and the disabled. 43–44

Surprise clown, a stick puppet. Greenhowe. Making miniature toys and dolls. 31–33

Tell-a-story glove puppets. Creative crafts yearbook: an exciting new collection of needlework and crafts. 140–43

Washcloth puppets. Foose. Scrap saver's stitchery book. 20–24

Puppets, Crocheted

Crochet puppet pets. Favorite easy-to-make toys. 131–33

Friendly puppets. Feldman. Needlework boutique. 15–17

Lion and tree hand puppets. Crochet. 127

Santa hand puppets. McCall's book of Christmas. 162–63

Sunflower hand puppet. American School of Needlework. Great crochet bazaar book. 126–27

Puppets, Finger

Detergent-bottle puppets. Woman's Day book of gifts to make. 19–20

Father, mother, granny, baby, and dog felt finger puppets. Favorite easy-to-make toys. 22–25

Fuzzy hand puppets—koala bear and lamb. Linsley. Great bazaar. 132–37

Snow White and the Seven Dwarfs (knitted). Creative crafts yearbook: an exciting new collection of needlework and crafts. 46–48

Puppets, Knitted
Any animal puppet with variations. Staples. Yarn animal book. 178–81
Knitted glove puppets. Christmas crafts book. 110–11
Loveable monsters (knitted). Creative crafts yearbook: an exciting new collection of
    needlework and crafts. 81–83

Puppets, Wood
Italian marionettes. Schuman. Art from many hands. 88–96
Stickball, hand puppet, marionette. Peterson. Children's toys you can build yourself.
    117–26

Purse holders, racks, etc.
Handbag caddy. Roda. Fabric decorating for the home. 142–43

Purses
All aboard travel bag (needlepoint). Needlework nostalgia. 8–9, 14
Appliqued shoulder bags. Gillies. Patterns for applique and pieced work—and ways to
    use them. 95–112
Bag and belt from one knot (macrame). Time-Life books. Boutique attire. 136–41
Bag using three shades of red beads. Hulbert. Creative beadwork. 41
Bags. Henderson. Woman's Day book of designer crochet. 121–30
Bags and such, border for wooden purse, Rocky raccoon for Bermuda bag. Sheldon.
    Washable and dryable needlepoint. 100–03
Bargello evening purse. Christensen. Needlepoint and bargello stitchery. 63, 66
Basket bag with shells. Meras. Vacation crafts. 74–75
Beaded pockette. Hulbert. Creative beadwork. 60–61
Beaded shoulder bag. Torbet. Macrame you can wear. 90–91
Beaded small pockette. Hulbert. Creative beadwork. 84
Beadwork bag. Practical needlework. 130–35
Black-eyed susan purse. Christensen. Needlepoint. 49–51
Carryall (needlepoint). Feldman. Needlework boutique. 53–55
Cathedral window purses. Fairfield. Patchwork. 44
Chrysanthemum medallions on checkered ground, ivory evening bag & chrysanthe-
    mum medallions on checkered ground, blue evening bag. Nicoletti. Japanese mo-
    tifs for needlepoint. 68–71
A clever clutch (patchwork). Botsford. Between thimble & thumb. 105–09
Clutch bag, puff-quilt shoulder bag. Heard. Complete guide to quilting. 250–53
Clutch that doubles in brass (lamb suede trimmed in madras whip snake). Time-Life
    books. Novel materials. 84–93
Cobwebs and flowers evening bag. Scheuer. Designs for Holbein embroidery. 42–43
Coiled purse, coiled shoulder bag. Gault. Crafts for the disabled. 103–05
Crewel purse. Boyles. Margaret Boyles book of needle art. 104–07
Crewel shoulder; crocheted cartridge bag; placemat envelope, quilted clutch; quilted
    tea cozy shoulder bag. Doherty. Family Circle book of 429 great gifts to make all
    year round for just 10¢ to $10.00. 142–43, 146–51
Crochet barrel bag, needlepoint butterfly bag, fabric envelope bag, oriental butterfly
    bag, butterfly pouch, woven ribbon handbags, woven needlepoint bag, landscape
    bag and Queen Elizabeth's bag. Wilson. Needlework to wear. 92–105
Crochet purse. Gault. Crafts for the disabled. 76–77
Crocheted drawstring bag. Evans. Ribbonwork. 75–78
Deco clutch. Jacobs. Crochet book. 133–34
Drawstring purse, "the Maze" handbag. Woman's Day crochet showcase. 74–75, 78–
    80, 97
Duck paddle purse. Houck. Patchwork pattern book. 52–53
Easy flat money purse. Tyler. Big book of soft toys. 236

Ecuadorian saddle bag. Holderness. Peasant chic. 70–73

Embroidered purse full of Turkish treasures. Time-Life books. Exotic styling. 154–157

Evening bag. Burchette. More needlework blocking and finishing. 30–32

Evening bag with all over design of beads and sequins. Hulbert. Creative beadwork. 83–84

Evening clutch and pouch. Ruggieri. Woman's Day book of no-pattern sewing. 105

Evening purse bag. Jacobs. Crochet book. 51–52

Evening shoulder bag. Jacobs. Crochet book. 65–66

Feather purse, nosegay purse. Brock. Gladrags: redesigning, remaking, refitting all your old clothes. 232–33

Finishing a needlepoint handbag. Burchette. Needlework. 112–14

Florentine stitch purse, ribbon-woven evening bag. Encyclopedia of crafts. 60–61

Flower purse. Christensen. Teach yourself needlepoint. 154–56

Geometric needlepoint handbags. Wilson. Needleplay. 116–21

Girl's scarf & purse (embroidered). Fraser. Modern stitchery: stitches, patterns, free-form designing. 90–91

Glitter-a-little evening bags. Houck. Big bag book. 108–12

Granny square purse. American School of Needlework. Great crochet bazaar book. 26–27

Gumballs galore and pot o'gold. Sheldon. Washable and dryable needlepoint. 112–13

Handbag (repair). Schuler. How to fix almost everything. 100

Handbag. Brown. Weaving, spinning, and dyeing book. 166–67

Handbag. Hibbs. Straw sculpture. 86–87

Handbag envelope. Wargo. Soft crafts for special occasions. 142

Handbag from hexagonal patchwork. Ives. Ideas for patchwork. 76–79

Handbag or knitting bag. Ickis. Weaving as a hobby. 12–13

Handbag, placemat purse. Better Homes and Gardens easy bazaar crafts. 7, 16, 42, 47

Handbag with stripes and tapestry. Brown. Weaving, spinning, and dyeing book. 106–07

Handbag with woven-in handles. Brown. Weaving, spinning, and dyeing book. 170

Handsome handbags. Guth. Sewing with scraps. 100–07

Happy ladybug coin purse, snowflake motif and initials for coin purse. Great cross-stitch. 124–27

Hat band and bag handle (woven). Golden book of hand and needle arts. 130

Heart mini bag, fitted evening bag, posh mini totes. Woman's Day creative stitchery from scraps. 40–41, 109–11, 135–36.

Incan design purse. Dodge. Step-by-step new-macrame. 44–45

Indian beadwork bags. McCall's book of America's favorite needlework and crafts. 404–05

Initialed canvas purse. Baldwin. Scrap fabric crafts. 132–34

Instructions for the broomstick lace purse and hat. Time-Life books. Decorative techniques. 158–63

Knitted shoulder bag, belt bag. Knitting techniques and projects. 44, 60

Large Victorian pouch, blue stitch shell bag. Design crochet. 71–75, 114–16

Leather purses. Rose. Illustrated encyclopedia of crafts and how to master them. 87–94

Linen signature pouch. Gostelow. Cross-stitch book. 92–94

Long-fringed evening bag (macrame). McCall's book of America's favorite needlework and crafts. 387–88

Macrame bag, disco bag, leather shoulder bag, patchwork suede bag, suede drawstring bag. Encyclopedia of crafts. 226–27, 231, 251, 252–53

Macrame purses and a pocketbook. Boberg. Macrame. 98–99

Macrame shoulder bag. Anderson. Crafts and the disabled. 116–17

Making a pocket. Scurlock. Muzzleloader Magazine's book of buckskinning II. 65–66

Making a beaded handbag. Time-Life books. Decorative techniques. 78–83

Mermaid purse, Pegasus needlepoint clutch purse Gault. Needlework dragons and other mythical creatures. 98–99, 134–36

Monogrammed clutch purse. Linsley. Custom made. 151

Mosaic-patterned handbags. Walker. Mosaic knitting. 216–19

Motif evening purse. Svinicki. Old-fashioned crochet. 48–49

Neck purse. Fairfield. Patchwork. 40

Needlepoint rose bag. Embroidery of roses. 106–07

Nine-patch star bags. Houck. Patchwork pattern book. 24

Nonobjective metallic evening purse. Christensen. Teach yourself needlepoint. 117–18

Occasional bag. Fairfield. Patchwork. 45

Oriental patchel, rose evening purse, light-hearted tote, star-crossed tote. Great cross-stitch. 98–109

Patchwork bags. Creative crafts yearbook: an exciting new collection of needlework and crafts. 18–20

Patchwork pouch handbag. Ives. Ideas for patchwork. 73–75

Patchwork shoulder bag. Wooster. Quiltmaking. 133

Patchwork tote bag. Rosenthal. Not-so-nimble needlework book. 81–82

Personalized evening bag. Fanning. Complete book of machine quilting. 204–07

Peruvian eagle bag. Gostelow. Complete international book of embroidery. 30–31

Phulkari evening bag. Gostelow. Complete international book of embroidery. 238–39

Pocket. Gehret. Rural Pennsylvania clothing. 72–82

Poppy purse (needlepoint). Arnold. Needlepoint pattern book. 151–53

Practical purses. Houck. Big bag book. 100–07

Pre-finished bargello evening purse. Christensen. Teach yourself needlepoint. 75

Purses, bags and pillows in double weave. Dendel. Basic book of fingerweaving. 88–91

Quartet in crochet, satin-and-lace evening pouch. Woman's Day bazaar best sellers. 54–56

Quilted evening bag. Encyclopedia of crafts. 11

Quilted evening bag. Reader's Digest complete guide to needlework. 268

Quilted purse. McNeill. Quilting. 29

Ribbon clutch purse. Coffey. Francine Coffey's celebrity sewing bee. 160

Ribbon evening bag, shoulder bag. Holland. Weaving primer. 109, 138–40

Satin evening bags. Linsley. Great bazaar. 78–79

Seminole Indian patchwork purses. Hall. Sewing machine craft book. 75–79

Seminole patchwork bags. Dudley. Strip patchwork: quick and easy patchwork using the Seminole technique. 102–04

Shoulder bag. Reader's Digest complete guide to sewing. 502–03

Shoulder bag. Scobey. First easy-to-see needlepoint workbook. 110–13

Shoulder bag. Stearns. Macrame. 66–72

Shoulder bag (sewn). Burns. Super sewing. 294

Shoulder evening purse. Coffey. Francine Coffey's celebrity sewing bee. 68

Small shoulder bag (needlepoint). Gault. Crafts for the disabled. 24–25

Snow-star shoulder bag (quilted). Golden book of hand and needle arts. 38–40

Soft handbag. Coffey. Francine Coffey's celebrity sewing bee. 170

Straw braid handbag and shoulder bag. Hibbe. Straw sculpture. 96–98

Suede bag with Aztec motif. Creative crafts yearbook: an exciting new collection of needlework and crafts. 146–47

Suede evening purse. Creative crafts yearbook: an exciting new collection of needlework and crafts. 137–38

Sweater craft purse. Brown. Super sweater idea book. 188–89

Tatted purse panel. Auld. Tatting: the contemporary art of knotting with a shuttle. 97–98

Tibetan, Chinese & Mongol purses. Rogers. Needlepoint designs from Asia. 97–101, 123–30

Ultrasuede bags. Creative sewing. 15
Velvet evening bag, woven purse, oriental carpetbag, picture purse, Grandmother's purse, pillow tote, super-strong tote bag, strawberry purse, calico bandana bag, "knit" purse and matching beret, and poncho purse. Farlie. Pennywise boutique. 112–27
Velveteen and quilted clutches, canvas tote. Laury. Quilted clothing. 133–35
Veneered barn purse box. Hobbs. Veneer craft for everyone. 128–29
White-on-white drawstring pouch. Boyles. Margaret Boyles book of needle art. 112–15
Wooden purse. Christensen. Teach yourself needlepoint. 81–82
Woven purse. Krevitsky. Shaped weaving. 93–97
Woven-ribbon purse. Ruggieri. Woman's Day book of no-pattern sewing. 109
Woven shoulder bag. Weaving and spinning. 21

Purses, Children

Barn bag. Foose. Scrap saver's stitchery book. 6–7
Bassinet purse with baby doll. Linsley. Great bazaar. 144–46
Jumbo knit bag, dolly purse, monogrammed felt handbag, ribboned pocketbook and margarine container purse. Farlie. Pennywise boutique. 166–75
Lucy Locket's pocket. Laury. Treasury of needlecraft gifts for the new baby. 123–25

Puzzles

Angular puzzle, clock puzzle. Blandford. Giant book of wooden toys. 178–81
Country puzzle picture, size & shape box. Baldwin. Old fashioned wooden toys. 42–43, 47–49
Jigsaw puzzle. Blandford. Giant book of wooden toys. 59–60
Making a jigsaw puzzle. Bumper book of things a girl can make. 60–62
Picture puzzle. Elbert. Paperworks. 55–57
Puzzle boxes. Paper. 84–85
Puzzle shapes. Adams. Make your own baby furniture. 164–70
Puzzle shelves. Adams. Make your own baby furniture. 171–73
Puzzles. Laury. Handmade toys and games. 45–51
Quilter's puzzle. Better Homes and Gardens treasury of Christmas crafts & foods. 84
Simple wooden, picture, frog and rabbit, lacing boards, pegboards. Peterson. Children's toys you can build yourself. 79–95
Tiny tots puzzles. Blackwell. Johnny Blackwell's poor man's catalog. 135
Twelve-piece turtle puzzle. Hobbs. Veneer craft for everyone. 136–38
Wells. Wooden puzzles and games.

Pyrography. *See* **Wood burning**

Quill work

Indian quill work. Schumann. Art from many hands. 208–13
Indian quill work. Whitney. American Indian clothes and how to make them. 13–15
Quill work (Indian). Bath. Needlework in America. 44–53

Quilling

Method, quill work design to frame. D'Amato. Italian crafts. 111–14
Paper quilling. Paper. 28–32
Paper quilling for jewelry. Sommer. Contemporary costume jewelry. 167–71
Quilling. Kicklighter. Crafts, illustrated designs and techniques. 258–63

Quilts
ABC applique quilt. Ambuter. Carolyn Ambuter's needlepoint celebrations. 130–32
Appliqued apple quilt. Baldwin. Scrap fabric crafts. 114–17
Aunt Ellen's quilting handbook
Avery. Quilts to wear.
Baby quilt; sunbonnet Sue and overall Sam; rose quilt. Giant book of crafts. 14–15,
    124–39
Bacon. American patchwork quilts.
Barrister's block quilt. Grafton. Traditional patchwork patterns. 20–21
Basket quilt. Amish pineapple quilt, red and white quilt, plume quilt, all blue quilt.
    McCall's big book of country needlecrafts. 62–63, 75, 113-14, 154–55, 165–69,
    177–79
Bass. Applique quiltmaking.
Beyer. Quilter's album of blocks & borders.
Bleeding heart quilt. Grafton. Traditional patchwork patterns. 18–19
Bluebird quilt. Creative sewing. 67–70
Bright fancy of patchwork patterns. Time-Life books. Traditional favorites. 98–113
Bunk quilt. Roda. Fabric decorating for the home. 172
Buttercup quilt. Grafton. Traditional patchwork patterns. 22–23
Child-art crayon quilt, contemporary grandmother's flower garden quilt, quilter's quilt,
    rainbow quilt, appliqued bird quilt, lace applique quilt. Better Homes and Gardens
    treasury of needlecrafts. 58–59, 62–68, 92–93, 104–07, 126
Clarke. Kentucky quilts and their makers.
Comical quilts (animals). Better Homes and Gardens sewing for your home. 182–83
Continental quilts. Practical needlework. 175–76
Cooper. Quilters.
Cot quilt. Ives. Ideas for patchwork. 54–56
Cozy velour quilt. Foose. More scrap saver's stitchery. 70–77
Crazy quilt. McCall's big book of needlecrafts. 258–59
Cube work quilt. Grafton. Traditional patchwork patterns. 8–9
Cut glass disk quilt. Grafton. Traditional patchwork patterns. 4–5
Cyanotype quilt. Treasury of things to make. 28–31
Double Irish chain quilt. Grafton. Traditional patchwork patterns. 16–17
Dresden-plate quilt. Golden book of hand and needle arts. 46–49
Duvet cover. Osler. Machine patchwork. 102–03
Embroidered flower squares quilt, applique & embroidered flower quilts. Haraszty. Em-
    broiderer's portfolio of flower designs. 9–110
Fence rail quilt. Lewis. Mountain artisans quilting book. 82–87
Finishing quilts. Risinger. Innovative machine quilting. 104–17
Fisher. Quilting in squares.
Floral bouquet quilt. Lewis. Mountain artisans quilt book. 158–59
Flower patch quilt. Needlework nostalgia. 9, 15, 26–27, 31
Frager. Book of sampler quilts
Full moon velvet quilt. Creative sewing. 75–78
Gadney. How to enter and win fabric and fiber crafts contests.
Gingham quilt and pillow. Creative sewing. 111
Heard. Complete guide to quilting.
Hexagon, log cabin, barcarolle, and interlocking block quilts. Fairfield. Patchwork. 68–
    73
Houck. American quilts and how to make them.
Houses cot quilt. Fairfield. Patchwork. 64–65
How to make quilts. Lithgow. Quiltmaking & quiltmakers. 73–94
Interlaced-blocks quilts. Grafton. Traditional patchwork patterns. 24–25
James. Quiltmaker's handbook: a guide to design and construction.
James. Second quiltmaker's handbook: creative approaches to contemporary quilt
    design.

Kaleidoscope & Dresden plate twin bed quilts. Houck. Patchwork pattern book. 44–45, 50–51

LaBelle. Patchworking.

Lace applique quilt. Creative sewing. 39

Larsen. Patchwork quilt design & coloring book.

Linsley. America's favorite quilts.

Log cabin quilt, schoolhouse quilt, star quilt, yo-yo quilt. Better Homes and Gardens treasury of Christmas crafts & foods. 100, 104–05,107, 211

MacDonald. Let's make a patchwork quilt.

Major. Contemporary patchwork quilts.

Makris. First prize quilts.

Malone. 115 classic American patchwork quilt patterns.

Michele's quilt. Fairfield. Patchwork. 58–59

Millett. Quilt-as-you-go.

Mythical beast applique quilt. Gault. Needlework dragons and other mythical creatures. 110–33

Needlepoint quilt. Smith. Needlery. 148–65

New quilts from old blankets. Guth. Sewing with scraps. 158–73

Olser. Machine patchwork.

Paint a quilt. Encyclopedia of crafts. 153

Paintbrush batik quilt. Treasury of things to make. 41–43

Patchwork and applique quilts. McCall's book of America's favorite needlework and crafts. 164–86

Patchwork and quilting. Complete guide to needlework. 68–85

Patchwork, applique and quilting. Bath. Needlework in America. 223–81

Patchwork quilt and pillow. Creative sewing. 114

Patchwork sampler quilt, happy-home quilt, barn raising quilt and lone star quilt. McCall's big book of needlecrafts. 122–27

Penny puff quilt. Brunner. Pass it on. 32–34

Pineapple quilt. Grafton. Traditional patchwork patterns. 6–7

Puffy quilt. Treasury of things to make. 66–67

Questioning quilt (appliqued). Botsford. Between thimble & thumb. 181–89

Quick and easy patchwork quilt and shams, patchwork comforter, star pattern quilt, new-fashioned log cabin quilt, classic star of Bethlehem quilt, storm at sea quilt, easy-to-stitch windmill quilt. Better Homes and Gardens treasury of needlecrafts. 20–23, 34–39, 48–55

Quilt design, fabrics and dyes. Lithgow. Quiltmaking & quiltmakers. 26–69

Quilt repair. Schuler. How to fix almost everything. 134–35

Quilting. McCall's big book of needlecrafts. 10–31, 88–103.

Quilting basics, quilt patterns, applique designs from nature for quilts. Better Homes and Gardens treasury of needlecrafts. 42–47. 128–66

Quilting, constructing a quilting frame, basic quilting techniques, care of quilts. Reader's Digest complete guide to needlework. 236–61

Quilting frame. Brann. How to repair, refinish, reupholster. 79–95

Quilting techniques: stuffed, Italian, trapunto, applique and shadow. Wilson. More needleplay. 106–17

Rainbow, appliqued bird, lace applique, tulip basket, Aunt Mary's rose, rose wreath, blue grove, rose of Sharon, turkey tracks, Dresden plate, and appliqued sampler quilt. Better Homes & Gardens applique. 26–27, 38–39, 56–57, 70–83

Rainbow-cloud quilt. Golden book of hand and needle arts. 51–53

Ribbon border quilt. Grafton. Traditional patchwork patterns. 2–3

Rocking horse patchwork quilt. Woman's Day decorative needlework for the home. 27–29

Rocky glen quilt. Grafton. Traditional patchwork patterns. 10–11

Sewn & embroidered designs. Woman's Day prize-winning quilts, coverlets and afghans. 11–131

Simple, "grandmother's flower garden," block, box, geometric, coffin wave, and rose point patchwork quilts. Ives. Ideas for patchwork. 88–110
Square crazy quilt. Loeb. Leather book. 35–41
Starlight quilt. Grafton. Traditional patchwork patterns. 14–15
Strip patchwork for quilts. Dudley. Strip patchwork: quick and easy patchwork using the Seminole technique. 46–76
Stripy quilt. McNeill. Quilting. 45
Technique of quilting. Time-Life books. Traditional favorites. 118–23
Traditional and contemporary quilts. Better Homes and Gardens sewing for your home. 102–19
Tree of paradise quilt. Grafton. Traditional patchwork patterns. 12–13
White/blue star quilt, delectable mountains quilt, feathered star quilt, pineapple quilt, orange peel quilt, tulip quilt, oak frame, harvest sun quilt, boy and girl quilt. McCall's big book of country needlecrafts. 193–95, 227–32, 241–43, 246–51
Windmill play quilt. Mills. Book of presents. 84–85
Wooster. Quiltmaking.
Woven puff pillow or quilt. Wilson. Weaving you can use. 120–22
Youth bed quilt in double Irish chain. Houck. Patchwork pattern book. 4–5

Quilts, Historic
Clarke. Kentucky quilts and their makers.

Quilts, Infants
Alphabet cot quilt. Fairfield. Patchwork. 60–61
Alphabet coverlet. Baldwin. Scrap fabric crafts. 28–33
Appliqued crib quilt. Benton. Sewing classic clothes for children. 46–51
Baby quilt. Rosenthal. Not-so-nimble needlework book. 83–84
Baby quilt with animal appliques. Reader's Digest complete guide to needlework. 264–65
Children's quilts. MacDonald. Let's make a patchwork quilt using a variety of sampler blocks. 89
Christening quilt. McNeill. Quilting. 48
Colorwash crib quilt. Fairfield. Patchwork. 65
Crib or lap quilts—trip around the world, double Irish chain, mosaic star, biscuit patchwork, double wedding ring, and baby blocks. Houck. Patchwork pattern book. Overleaf, 3, 8–9, 26–29, 42–43
Crib quilt. Guth. Sewing with scraps. 53–54
Crib quilt. Wargo. Soft crafts for special occasions. 40–47
Crib quilt, unicorn baby quilt. McCall's big book of needlecrafts. 55–56, 117–18
Crib quilts and blankets. Frager. Quilting primer. 89–92
Crib quilts: fish in the sea, little bear, floating clown, paper dolls. 74–89
Cross-stitch baby quilt & embroidered pillow. Better Homes & Gardens embroidery. 52–55
Hinson. Quilts for babies & children.
Mama elephant quilt & pillow. Foose. Scrap saver's stitchery book. 12–15
"Me in my house" coverlet. Laury. Treasury of needlecraft gifts for the new baby. 71–73
Mrs. Mouse quilt. Mills. Book of presents. 70–71
Noah's ark appliqued quilt. Woman's Day decorative needlework for the home. 29–33
Octagonal star quilt and nap pad. Laury. Treasury of needlecraft gifts for the new baby. 66–70
Patchwork cot quilt, striped quilt, stork applique baby quilt. Encyclopedia of crafts. 9, 24, 36
Picture pram cover. Encyclopedia of crafts. 131
Quick-and-easy appliqued baby quilt. Better Homes and Gardens treasury of needlecrafts. 84–85

Quick and easy baby quilt. Better Homes and Gardens applique. 16–17
Sugar baby quilt, biscuit quilt and nap pad with decorated squares. Laury. Treasury of
    needlecraft gifts for the new baby. 151–55

Quilts, Machine
Fanning. Complete book of machine quilting.
Hawaiian quilting. Risinger. Innovative machine quilting. 148–52
Log cabin quilt. Risinger. Innovative machine quilting. 124-36
Machine piecing. Risinger. Innovative machine quilting. 49–92
Machine quilting a sheet. Fanning. Complete book of machine quilting. 147–51
Nine-patch with setting blocks pattern. Risinger. Innovative machine quilting. 34–40
Patience quilt pattern. Risinger. Innovative machine quilting. 18–25
Quilting. Bakke. Sewing machine as a creative tool. 79–104
Seminole piecing. Risinger. Innovative machine quilting. 144–48
Two Roman stripe patterns: "rail fence" and "windmill." Risinger. Innovative machine
    quilting. 25–33

Quivers
Indian arrow quivers. Latham. Leathercraft. 128–29

Quoits
Quoits. Blandford. Giant book of wooden toys. 194–95

R

Rabbits
Bartholomew bunny (stuffed needlepoint toy). Needlecraft nostalgia. 35, 41
Bean bag bunnies. Greenhowe. Making miniature toys and dolls. 82–84
Designing patterns and making a rabbit. Practical needlework. 262–64
Farmer bunny family in a carrot. Foose. More scrap saver's stitchery. 35–41
Jointed rabbit. Hutchings. Big book of stuffed toy and doll making. 120–21
Knitted rabbit, crochet rabbits. Favorite easy-to-make toys. 107–09, 126–27
Mini Easter bunnies. Creative crafts yearbook: an exciting new collection of needle-
    work and crafts. 108–10
Pompom bunny. Practical needlework. 255–57
Rabbit housing. Burch. Building small barns, sheds, and shelters. 197–201
Small bunny toy. Better Homes and Gardens treasury of Christmas crafts & foods.
    273–74
Soft sculpture rabbits. Treasury of things to make. 10–12
Stuffed needlepoint Peter rabbit and Beatrix Potter's animals. Wilson. More needle-
    play. 170–73

Rabbits. See also **Animals entries**

Racing cars. See **Automobiles, Racing**

Radiators
Easy-to-make radiator cover. Popular Mechanics do-it-yourself encyclopedia. Vol. 15,
    2386
Painting radiators. Brightman. 101 practical uses for propane torches. 137
Radiator enclosures. Dal Fabbro. How to make children's furniture and play equip-
    ment. 64–65

Radio control
Airplanes; boats; cars; helicopters; submarines. Marks. Basics of radio control modeling.
Beckman. Building and flying giant scale radio control aircraft.
McEntee. Radio control handbook.
Radio control. Jackson. Modelmaker's handbook. 254–64
Safford. Advanced radio control.
Safford. Model radio control.
Safford. Radio control hobbyist's handbook.

Radio receiving apparatus
Transistor radio receiver. Modern general shop. Electricity. 96–97

Railings
Deck railings for style and safety. Better Homes and Gardens. Deck and patio projects
   you can build. 57
Fabricating a steel stair rail. Working with metal. 91–95
Handsome wooden handrails, how to install wrought-iron railings. Popular Mechanics
   do-it-yourself encyclopedia. Vol. 15, 2387–89
Porch and step railing repairs. Nunn. Home improvement, home repair. 208–09
Wrought-iron porch railing. Lindsley. Metalworking in the home shop. 298–99

Railroad models
Frary. How to build realistic model railroad scenery.
Freight train. Williams. Cookie craft: no-bake designs for edible party favors and deco-
   rations. 105–18
Railroads. Jackson. Modelmaker's handbook. 194–226
Westcott. How to build model railroad benchwork.

Railroads, Toy
Alphabet train, old-time iron horse. Baldwin. Old fashioned wooden toys. 44–46, 87–
   96, 113–15
1887 trolley, early switching locomotive, steam locomotive and tender. Hodges. 46
   step-by-step wooden toy projects. 145–68
Freight train, water tank, passenger train, suburban station. Maginley. Trains and
   boats and planes and . . . 99–118
Locomotive. Milstein. Building cardboard toys. 57–63
Locomotive, passenger cars, track, locomotive, tender. DeCristoforo. Build your own
   wood toys, gifts and furniture. 170–83
Pull along toy train. Blandford. Giant book of wooden toys. 109–14
Steam engine, tender, coal car, box car, cattle car, auto carrier car, flat-bed car, gon-
   dola car, tanker car, caboose. Buckland. Toymaker's book of wooden vehicles.
   22–45, 47–59
Pull-along train. Mills. Book of presents. 126–27
Steam train plaque with moveable parts. Christmas crafts book. 104–05
Wood-block train. Popular Mechanics do-it-yourself encyclopedia. Vol. 19, 2919–20
Wooden steam engine. Better Homes and Gardens treasury of Christmas crafts &
   foods. 276
Wooden train, railway engine. Favorite easy-to-make toys. 151–52, 164–68

Rainwear
Come rain . . . (child's rain cape and hat). Creative crafts yearbook: an exciting new
   collection of needlework and crafts. 23–25
Raincoat and hat. Complete book of baby crafts. 122–26
Rain coat/capelet. Time-Life books. Novel materials. 158–69

Rakes. *See* **Farm equipment; Garden rakes**

Raku. *See* **Pottery**

Ramps
Build your own folding car ramps. Popular Mechanics do-it-yourself encyclopedia. Vol. 1, 142
Ramps. Russell. Walks, walls and fences. 61–62
Rocker 'car pit'. Popular Mechanics do-it-yourself encyclopedia. Vol. 15, 2390

Rasps. *See* **Files and rasps**

Rattles
Baby's rattle toys: circus bear and dancing pig. American School of Needlework. Great crochet bazaar book. 17–20
Cane rattle. Wright. Complete book of baskets and basketry. 102
Daffodil, sunflower, rose, flag, elephant's head, & humpty-dumpty rattles. Hutchings. Big book of stuffed toy and doll making. 48–57
Ice cream cone rattle. Wargo. Soft crafts for special occasions. 56–58
Match rattle. Blandford. Giant book of wooden toys. 182–86
Ring rattle. Blandford. Giant book of wooden toys. 172–73
Tin can rattle, round rattle, cigar box rattle, ratchet rattle. Bumper book of things a boy can make. 33–38
Wood rattles, ringed rattles. Fine woodworking techniques 3. 133–35

Reading stands. *See* **Bookracks; Stands**

Recipe holders
Ceramic tile recipe holder. Linsley. Great bazaar. 126–27
Colonial recipe box. Spence. Woodworking tools, materials, processes. 616
Recipe file box. Elbert. Paperworks. 137–38

Record racks. *See* **Phonograph record racks**

Recreation rooms
Porch becomes family room, 4 great ideas for family rooms, 5 great projects for a family room, bold patterns for family rooms, quick ways to spruce up the basement. Popular Mechanics do-it-yourself encyclopedia. Vol. 8, 1170–84, 1186–91
Recreation room. Marshall. Yard buildings. 117–23

Reed weaving
Weaving with a reed. Rainey. Weaving without a loom. 56–68

Refuse receptacles
Cans, glass, newspapers and discards sorting system. Garage, attic and basement storage. 18–19
Concealed sliding garbage pail. Family handyman handbook of home improvement and remodeling. 17–20
Refuse locker. 101 do-it-yourself projects. 298–300
Trash can bin. Self. Working with plywood, including indoor/outdoor projects. 219–22
Trash compressor. Family handyman book of carpentry plans/projects. 54–65
Trash containers. Blandford. Constructing outdoor furniture, with 99 projects. 340–45

Remodeling
Add a room. Family handyman handhandbook of carpentry plans/projects. 296–318
Add a room. Family handyman handbook of home improvement and remodeling. 457–538
Adding a room. Self. Working with plywood, including indoor/outdoor projects. 285–300

Adding on rooms, bathrooms, basement, attic, breezeway, kitchen remodeling. Handyman. 423–69

Converting a garage or porch. Time-Life books. New living spaces. 106–19

Garage remodeling into a family room or guest house. Popular Mechanics do-it-yourself encyclopedia. Vol. 9, 1312–21

House additions: raise the roof, "L" wing, expand over an attached garage. Popular Mechanics do-it-yourself encyclopedia. Vol. 10, 1474–86

How to enclose your deck, porch, or patio. Daniels. Decks, porches, and patios. 77–93

How to plan a room addition. Popular Mechanics do-it-yourself encyclopedia. Vol. 1, 28–29

Remodeling. Popular Mechanics do-it-yourself encyclopedia. Vol. 16, 2416–41

Remote control. *See* **Radio control**

Repoussé
Chasing. Sjoberg. Working with copper, silver and enamel. 70–71

Chasing and other surface treatments. Finegold. Silversmithing. 102–10

Chasing and raised designs (repoussé). Wood. Make your own jewelry. 94–97

Chasing and repoussé. Bowie. Jewelry making. 36–38

Craft aid for pewter and copper foil repoussé modelling. Anderson. Crafts and the disabled. 37–38

Pewter and copper repoussé modelling. Anderson. Crafts and the disabled. 105–10

Repoussé. Davis. Step-by-step decoupage. 52–54

Repoussé. Richards. Handmade jewelry. 39–40, 60–68

Repoussé and chasing. Chamberlain. Metal jewelry techniques. 103–04

Repoussé and chasing. Foote. Jewelry making. 55–56

Repoussé and chasing. Sprintzen. Jewelry, basic techniques and design. 58–62

Repoussé in copper, lead. Marshall. Foilcraft. 116–24

Revolving trays. *See* **Lazy susans**

Ribbonwork
Cachepot/basket. Wargo. Soft crafts for special occasions. 88–89, 122–24

Evans. Ribbonwork.

Gift ribbon flowers and bird. Grainger. Creative papercraft. 121–23

How to make a bow. Nicole. Designer accessories to make for your home. 28–30

Ribbon appliqued, tote bag. Stribling. Crafts from North American Indian arts. 157–64

Ribbon envelope for carrying. DeLeon. Basketry book. 87–88

Ribbon roses and poinsettia. Paper. 130–31

Trimming with flat ribbon. Time-Life books. Boutique attire. 109–10

Riding toys
Fire engine, Tin Lizzie racer, four-wheel horsey. Baldwin. Old fashioned wooden toys. 168–85, 194–98

Riding crane. Blandford. Giant book of wooden toys. 128–34

Wheeling horse. Blandford. Giant book of wooden toys. 140–46

"You-Haul" kiddie car. Popular Mechanics do-it-yourself encyclopedia. Vol. 9, 1351

Rings
Band ring with a rub over set cabochon stone. Richards. Handmade jewelry. 77–82

Basic overlay ring. Metalcrafting encyclopedia. 178–96

Basket ring. Pelisser. Jeweler's craft. 81-82

Bead rings. Hulbert. Creative beadwork. 34

Copper and silver ring. Sommer. Contemporary costume jewelry. 57

Eternity band with stones. Pelisser. Jeweler's craft. 65

Five concentric, twelve and harlequin faceted rings. Pelisser. Jeweler's craft. 37–38
Flat, channeled, double-channeled, concave, and half-round finger bands. Pelisser. Jeweler's craft. 35–36
Forming rings. Sprintzen. Jewelry, basic techniques and design. 73–74
Hand-shaped ring holders. Doherty. Family Circle book of 429 great gifts-to-make all year round for just 10¢ to $10.00. 62
Heat forming a lens-shaped ring. Hollander. Plastics for jewelry. 59–64.
How to make an etched copper ring. Elliot. Working with copper. 78–80
Illusion ring. Pelisser. Jeweler's craft. 86–87
Inlaid silver ring. Powers. Crafting turquoise jewelry. 171–74
Inlaying pewter in an enameled silver-banded ring. Hollander. Plastics for jewelry. 132–36
Layered turquoise ring. Powers. Crafting turquoise jewelry. 152–54
Making a fused ring. Sprintzen. Jewelry, basic techniques and design. 95
Making rings and ring shanks. Powers. Crafting turquoise jewelry. 110–13
Man's ring with diamonds. Pelisser. Jeweler's craft. 80
Palisander ring with plug insert. Sainsbury. Woodworking projects with power tools. 23–25
Plique-a-jour enameling a sterling silver ring. Hollander. Plastics for jewelry. 85–89
Repoussé ring. Richards. Handmade jewelry. 74–76
Ring construction. Bovin. Jewelry making. 207–17
Ring in two colors. Gill. Beadwork: the technique of stringing, threading, and weaving. 70–71
Ring with four prong crown setting and knife-edge shank. Pelisser. Jeweler's craft. 71–72
Ring with nine flowers. Gill. Beadwork: the technique of stringing, threading, and weaving. 46–49
Ring with six prong setting, box-frame setting, eternity band with stones. Pelisser. Jeweler's craft. 73–79
Rings. Sjoberg. Working with copper, silver and enamel. 48–52
Setting an oval stone. Richards. Handmade jewelry. 83–91
Silver band ring, claw setting. Metal and enamel. 70–74
Silver-plated rings. Metal and enamel. 11–13
Silver ring by lost wax or investment casting. Edwards. Lost wax casting of jewelry. 11–32
Silver rings. Giant book of crafts. 193–214
Simple forged turquoise ring. Powers. Crafting turquoise jewelry. 155–58
Table ring. Metalcrafting encyclopedia. 197–201
Winding a fiberglass filament reinforced ring. Hollander. Plastics for jewelry. 125–31
Wire ring with stone. Meyer. Rock tumbling. 79
Wooden rings. Sommer. Contemporary costume jewelry. 81–82

Rings. See Also **Jewelry**

Rivets and riveting
Riveting. Metalcrafting encyclopedia. 36–38

Roads. See **Driveways**

Robes
Bath robe. Mills. Book of presents. 68–69
Batik housecoat. Frame. Tie-dyeing and batik. 118–21
Batik kaftan. Tie-dye, batik and candlemaking step-by-step. 31–32
Bold banner caftan and traditional caftans. Blair. Banners and flags. 162–68
Border-trim robe (crocheted). Complete book of baby crafts. 64–65
Caftans. Morgan. Trapunto and other forms of raised quilting. 172–78

Chenille bedspreads (wrapped robe). Funaro. Yestermorrow clothes book. 53–54

Child's bathrobe. Step by step to better knitting and crochet. 58–60

Crocheted belted bathrobes for children. Favorite knitting & crochet patterns. 46–48

Dofuko. Lane. Maggie Lane's oriental patchwork. 74–78

Doubly dazzling kimono, flowing elegance of the caftan. Time-Life books. Exotic styling. 96–119

Dragon robe. Gostelow. Complete international book of embroidery. 258–59

Fake fur lap robe, shave sarong, man's drip dry. Doherty. Family Circle book of 429 great gifts-to-make all year round for just 10¢ to $10.00. 50, 104, 112

Hausa man's robe. Gostelow. Complete international book of embroidery. 180–81

Hooded terry robe. Reader's digest complete guide to sewing. 513–15

Kaftan, mummy moo. Wiseman. Cuts of cloth. 46–47, 54–55

Kimonos and such (quilted). Laury. Quilted clothing. 58–60, 62–72

Kirstin kaftan, kimono sleeve gown, Maid Marion's gown, hostess gown. Beard. Fashions from the loom. 82–83, 85–86

Man's caftan. Lane. Maggie Lane's oriental patchwork. 78–82

Monk's robe. Beard. Fashions from the loom. 49

Putting in a lining: a warm robe. Bradley. Design it, sew it and wear it. 92–101

Toddler robe. Great granny crochet book. 106–107

Robes. *See also* **Dresses**

Robes, Men
Man's easy-to-make short robe. Johnson. Quiltwear. 35–39

Man's kimono coat. Golden book of hand and needle arts. 57–58

Monk's robe. Holderness. Peasant chic. 83–89

Robes and caftans, three-piece robes, Joseph's "coat of many colors." Hagans. All good gifts. 79–82

Towel wrap skirt. Coffey. Francine Coffey's celebrity sewing bee. 104

Robes, Women
Contemporary caftan. Golden book of hand and needle arts. 58–60

Home comfort. Favorite knitting & crochet patterns. 83–85

Lace caftan. Creative sewing. 42

Tie-dyed kimono. Frame. Tie-dyeing and batik. 14–17

Woman's floor-length robe. Johnson. Quiltwear. 41–47

Robots
CH3-DC robot. Great granny crochet book. 58–59

Robots. Safford. Advanced radio control. 242–64

Wooden robot. Favorite easy-to-make toys. 150–51

Rocket models
Model rockets. Safford. Advanced radio control. 174–241

Stine. Handbook of model rocketry.

Rocking chairs. *See* **Chairs, Rocking**

Rocking toys
Old-fashioned rocking horse, country rocking horse. Baldwin. Old fashioned wooden toys. 162–67, 199–206

Rocker for two. Blandford. Giant book of wooden toys. 50–52

Rocking boat. Dal Fabbro. How to make children's furniture and play equipment. 162–63

Two-seater rocking camel. Fine woodworking techniques I. 145–48

Rocks. *See* **Stones, Painted**

Roofs
All about roofing farm buildings. Leavy. Successful small farms. 55–69
Applying roll roofing to a flat roof deck. Geary. Complete handbook of home exterior repair maintenance. 22–32
Asphalt shingle roofing. Alth. Do-it-yourself roofing and siding. 125–85
Be your own roofer and save half the cost, reroof with wood shakes and shingles. Popular Mechanics do-it-yourself encyclopedia. Vol. 16, 2450–58
Cornice, rake and soffit installation. Spence. General carpentry. 318–26
Framing the roof: erecting rafters. Spence. General carpentry. 217–88
How to repair a damaged roof. Popular Mechanics do-it-yourself encyclopedia. Vol. 17, 2640–41
Reroofing. Handyman. 253–58
Reroofing and minor repair. Outdoor projects for home and garden. 57–60, 73–84
Reroofing with asphalt shingles. Geary. Complete handbook of home exterior repair and maintenance. 32–63
Right roof, roofing. Burch. Building small barns, sheds, and shelters. 68–81, 91–97
River roof. Underhill. Woodwright's companion. 153–61
Roof construction. Badzinski. House construction. 82–94
Roof maintenance and repair. Nunn. Home improvement, home repair. 168–86
Roof repairs. Bragdon. Homeowner's complete manual of repair & improvement. 488–509
Roofing, reroofing. Adams. Arco's complete woodworking handbook. 319–92
Roofing your log home. Ramsey. Building a log home from scratch or kit. 197–215
Shingle roofing. Olin. Construction. 411.1–411.36
Thatching. Manners. Country crafts today. 70–82
Working with corrugated steel. Leavy. Successful small farms. 70–81

Room dividers
Adjustable divider. Philbin. Cabinets, bookcases & closets. 132–33
Beautiful walls that serve a purpose. Popular Mechanics do-it-yourself encyclopedia. Vol. 16, 2459–66
Bookcase room divider. Brann. How to construct built-in and sectional bookcases. 74–78
Buffet room-divider. Feirer. Cabinet making and millwork. 194–199
Decorative dividers. Popular Mechanics do-it-yourself encyclopedia. Vol. 8, 1190
Fabric room dividers. Better Homes and Gardens sewing for your home. 150–151
Leno room divider with willow sticks and found objects. Brown. Weaving, spinning, and dyeing book. 188–189
Louvered panels. Complete handyman do-it-yourself encyclopedia. 2192–95
Ready-made dividers, partitions from doors. Time-Life books. New living spaces. 8–11
Room divider. Leavy. Bookshelves and storage units. 59–60
Room divider. 101 do-it-yourself projects. 198–201
Room divider. Self. Working with plywood, including indoor/outdoor projects. 241–44
Room divider/modern hutch. Popular Mechanics do-it-yourself encyclopedia. Vol. 12, 1890–91
Room divider/shelves. Zegel. Fast furniture. 56–57
Room divider with storage. Philbin. Cabinets, bookcases & closets. 126–27
Room dividers. Blandford. 53 space-saving built-in furniture projects. 324–37
Room dividers. Blandford. How to make your own built-in furniture. 219–34
See-through room divider. Better Homes and Gardens step-by-step cabinets and shelves. 80–81
Simple room divider, room divider with storage. Geary. How to design and build your own workspace—with plans. 293–99

Storage room dividers. Family handyman handbook of carpentry plans/projects. 234–36
Threaded straw room dividers. Hibbs. Straw sculpture. 68–69
Three-in-one room dividers. Cary. Storage: cabinets, closets, and wall systems. 110–15
Two-sided storage divider. Philbin. Cabinets, bookcases & closets. 112–14

Rope
Plastic jump rope made from bread bags. Woman's Day book of gifts to make. 214
Rope repair. Schuler. How to fix almost everything. 141
Shallot ropes. Johnson. Nature crafts. 84
Wrapping and coil in other arts. Chamberlain. Beyond weaving. 149–69

Rubbings
Brass rubbings. Pittaway. Traditional English country crafts and how to enjoy them today. 8–14
Firestein. Rubbing craft.
Paper rubbings. Elbert. Paperworks. 12–14
Rubbings for iron-ons. Firestein. Rubbing craft. 86
Rubbings of shells and fossils. Firestein. Rubbing craft. 90

Rugs
Area rugs: Irish crochet, geometric, granny square, reversible and Indian rugs. Halliday. Decorating with crochet. 12–28
Aztec tile mat and scatter rug. Great granny crochet book. 134–35
Bargello rugs in Gobelin stitch: variations in blue and green and sun squares. Chatterton. Patchwork & applique. 210–15
Batchelder. Art of hooked-rug making.
Beatty. Hook book.
Bergama rug. Kalish. Oriental rugs in needlepoint. 102–13
Braided rag rugs. Quirke. Rug book. 50–59
Braided round rug. Roda. Fabric decorating for the home. 19–20
Braided rugs. Felcher. Complete book of rug making. 61–75
Braided rugs. Marein. Creating rugs and wall hangings. 203–08
Braided rugs. Ryan. Complete encyclopedia of stitchery. 588–93
Braided rugs. Znamierowski. Step-by-step rugmaking. 77–79
Braided rugs in different shapes. McCall's book of rugmaking. 97–104
Carty. How to make braided rugs.
Caucasian rug. Kalish. Oriental rugs in needlepoint. 33–39
Chinese dragon rug. Scobey. Decorating with needlepoint. 124–28
Chrysanthemum medallions on "braided fence" rug. Nicoletti. Japanese motifs for needlepoint. 72–76
Colorful rugs (children). Better Homes and Gardens sewing for your home. 190–91
Crochet rugs. Ryan. Complete encyclopedia of stitchery. 594–96
Crocheted and knitted rugs and wall hanging. Marein. Creating rugs and wall hangings. 179–202
Crocheted granny square and octagon and squares rugs. Chatterton. Patchwork & applique. 86–96
Crocheted or knitted checkerboard rug. Znamierowski. Step-by-step rugmaking. 75–76
Crocheted rugs. Felcher. Complete book of rug making. 140–59
Crocheted rugs. Henderson. Woman's Day book of designer crochet. 190–94
Crocheted rugs. Quirke. Rug book. 94–119
Crocheted Samarra rug, Perugia rug, petit-point nosegays rug. Woman's Day crochet showcase. 155–59
Designs for rugs or wall hangings. Scobey. Rugs & wall hangings. 179–234
Double cross stitch jute rug. Rosenthal. Not-so-nimble needlework book. 63–64

Duck paddle mat. Houck. Patchwork pattern book. 52–53
Embroidered rugs. Ryan. Complete encyclopedia of stitchery. 597–602
Embroidered rugs and wall hangings. Marein. Creating rugs and wall hangings. 163–77
Embroidered rugs (needlepoint). Felcher. Complete book of rug making. 106–39
Eternal knot, geometric, sacred mountain, double design medallion, money II, deer and crane, maze and fretwork rugs. Lane. Rugs and wall hangings. 19–24, 43–77, 107–24
Fake fur rug. Reader's Digest complete guide to sewing. 461
Felted rugs. Quirke. Rug book. 25–34
Finishing needlepoint rugs. Burchette. Needlework. 90–95
Finishing rugs. Felcher. Complete book of rug making. 199–202
Fireside cats, daisy daisy, rainbow shades. Great cross-stitch. 55–63
Fish rug. Reader's Digest complete guide to sewing. 482–83
Floorcloths. Parry. Stenciling. 108
Floral rug. Slater. Elaine Slater's book of needlepoint projects. 157–64
Flower-bed rug (embroidered) and poppy circle rug (hooked). Haraszty. Embroiderer's portfolio of flower designs. 111–19
Forest scene inlaid rug. Scobey. Decorating with needlepoint. 129–32
Gallery of patterns. Ketchum. Hooked rugs. 106–64
Geometric-pattern, intricate owl and design for love rugs (hooked). Golden book of hand and needle arts. 120–25
Geometric textured rug (hooked). Feldman. Needlework boutique. 110–11
Geometrical Kazak. Kalish. Oriental rugs in needlepoint. 40–48
Hand-hooked rugs, spaniel, rooster, woven plaid rug, trellis pattern hooked rug. McCall's big book of country needlecrafts. 46–47, 80–83, 118–19, 220–22
Hand-hooked rugs with damask floral, antique floral, Victorian rose, gourd-and-leaf, and shaded tile patterns. McCall's book of rugmaking. 1–20
Hawaiian appliqued rug. McCall's book of rugmaking. 159–60
Hooked antique floral and damask rose rugs. McCall's book of America's favorite needlepoint and crafts. 273–78
Hooked rag rugs. Quirke. Rug book. 36–50
Hooked rugs. Ryan. Complete encyclopedia of stitchery. 603–06
Hooked rugs and wall hangings. Marien. Creating rugs and wall hangings. 115–46
Hooked rugs, butterfly and arches patterns. Znamierowski. Step-by-step rugmaking. 80–85
Hooked rugs designs. Felcher. Complete book of rug making. 15–59
Hooked rugs for beginners: Godey spray, mariner's star and flat rose diamond. Beatty. Hook book. 133–38
Hooking rugs and knotting rya rugs. Rose. Illustrated encyclopedia of crafts and how to master them. 268–76
Indian rug. Slater. Elaine Slater's book of needlepoint projects. 167–70
Kaestner. Designs for needlepoint and latch hook rugs.
Kazak & Persian rugs. Rogers. Needlepoint designs from Asia. 22–25, 61–73
Knitted and crocheted rugs: yellow rose, northern lights, and cable-cord designs. McCall's book of rugmaking. 149–58
Knitted cross-over stitch sampler rug. Znamierowski. Step-by-step rugmaking. 75
Knitted rugs. Felcher. Complete book of rug making. 160–73
Knitted rugs. Quirke. Rug book. 119–30
Knitted rugs. Ryan. Complete encyclopedia of stitchery. 607–08
Knots-and-tassels floor cloth (stenciled on canvas). McCall's book of America's favorite needlework and crafts. 357–58
Knotted rugs. Ryan. Complete encyclopedia of stitchery. 609–13
Knotted rugs, rag rug. Holland. Weaving primer. 109–11
Latch hook granny rug. Woman's Day decorative needlework for the home. 122–23
Latch hook rug. Scobey. Rugmaking. 76–86

Latch hook rug in diamond-wheel pattern, triangles. Chatterton. Coordinated crafts for the home. 141–42, 149–51

Latch hook rugs. Quirke. Rug book. 136–44

Latch hooked rugs. Felcher. Complete book of rug making. 92–105

Latch hooked rugs. Scobey. Rugs & wall hangings. 163–65

Latch-hooked rugs: scarlet tanager, paisley, Victorian fruits, ABC, butterfly, Sarouk, diamond-striped, plaid, patchwork, lightning, leaf shadow, garden pathways, tropical garden, glowing embers, sunrise and bowknot designs. McCall's book of rug-making. 39–96

Latch hooked Victorian fruits, bowknot, scarlet tanager, and paisley rugs. McCall's book of America's favorite needlework and crafts. 279–84

Latchet pile rugs. Marein. Creating rugs and wall hangings. 87–93

Lesghi star rug. Kalish. Oriental rugs in needlepoint. 49–57

Loop-crochet floor cushion, six-sided rug, chain rugs, chain-stitch rug, rectangular door mat & half circle door mat. McCall's big book of knit & crochet for home & family. 255–65

Loose rough rug (grass). Wilder. Secrets of Eskimo skin sewing. 123

Lotto rug. Kalish. Oriental rugs in needlepoint. 90–101

Macrame rugs. Marein. Creating rugs and wall hangings. 209–19

Making a painted floor cloth. Quirke. Rug book. 11–21

Making a pieced carpet or rug. Quirke. Rug book. 22–25

Making a punch needle wall-to-wall rug. Illes. Men in stitches. 112–32

Marsh Arab rug. Gostelow. Complete international book of embroidery. 213

Medallion appliqued rug. Marein. Stitchery, needlepoint, applique and patchwork. 200–01

Mexican-style rug. Encyclopedia of crafts. 81

Mosaic-patterned rug. Walker. Mosaic knitting. 194–95

Mosaic tile motif crocheted rug. Woman's Day decorative needlework for the home. 123–24

Moshimer. Complete rug hooker.

Needlepoint rug. Christensen. Teach yourself needlepoint. 103–04

Needlepoint rug. Golden book of hand and needle arts. 112–13

Needlepoint rugs. Quirke. Rug book. 156–75

Needlepoint rugs. Scobey. Rugmaking. 87–103

Needlepoint rugs. Scobey. Rugs & wall hangings. 154–62

Needlepoint rugs: Greek thistle, strawberry, afghan diamonds, striped, folk art, nursery rhyme, nature's kingdom, and Peruvian designs. McCall's book of rugmaking. 105–36

Needlepoint six color rug. Gault. Crafts for the disabled. 19–21

Oriental rug. Scobey. First easy-to-see needlepoint workbook. 94–98

Oval floor mat. Jacobs. Crochet book. 166–67

Patchwork & inspiration sampler embroidered rugs. Znamierowski. Step-by-step rug-making. 62–65

Pen wiper rug. Felcher. Complete book of rug making. 76–77

Petal design braided rug. Golden book of colonial crafts. 150–52, 155–57

Pile rugs. Quirke. Rug book. 87–94

Plain weave of handspun, karakul, and rya rugs. Brown. Weaving, spinning and dyeing book. 176–79

Plaited & coiled rugs. Quirke. Rug book. 61–63

Plaited oval-shaped rag rug. Gault. Crafts for the disabled. 102–03

Pleated circle rug. Woman's Day creative stitchery from scraps. 150–53

Punch hook rugs. Quirke. Rug book. 144–55

Punch-hooked aborigine rug. Casselman. Crafts from around the world. 22–26

Punch-hooked rugs. Scobey. Rugmaking. 104–24

Punch hooking. Rissell. Craftwork the handicapped elderly can make and sell. 39–42

Punch hooking. Scobey. Rugs & wall hangings. 169–73

Punch-needle rugs: art deco diamonds, Chinese design, Venetian grille, Mexican bull-fight, graceful mallards. McCall's book of rugmaking. 21–38

Quarry-tile rug. Knitting. 103

Quick point welcome rug. Better Homes and Gardens treasury of Christmas crafts & foods. 158–59

Rag pile rugs. Marein. Creating rugs and wall hangings. 93–96

Rag rug methods. Pittaway. Traditional English country crafts and how to enjoy them today. 78–79

Rag rugs. Worst. Weaving with foot-power looms. 40–41

Repeat floral design latch hook rug. Znamierowski. Step-by-step rugmaking. 68–69

Road rug for toy cars and trucks. Foose. More scrap saver's stitchery. 26–27

Rubbing for latch-hook rug designs. Firestein. Rubbing craft. 72–73

Rug from Indian geometrics, inspiration from baskets. Wilson. More needleplay. 162–65

Rug hooking. Rainey. Weaving without a loom. 85–94

Rug making. Kicklighter. Crafts, illustrated designs and techniques. 264–79

Rug making: hooking and knotting, braiding. Reader's Digest complete guide to needlework. 462–96

Rug making techniques. Ketchum. Hooked rugs. 74–99

Rugs with spots and stripes. Kalish. Oriental rugs in needlepoint. 58–66

Rya and flossa rugs in bull's-eye and reflected shadows designs. McCall's book of rugmaking. 143–48

Rya rug. Casselman. Crafts from around the world. 83–86

Rya rug on an upright frame loom, weft-faced rug, latch hook rug, punch needle rug, braided rug. Make it! don't buy it. 364–75, 410–31

Rya rugs. Felcher. Complete book of rug making. 78–91

Rya rugs. Quirke. Rug book. 130–36

Rya rugs. Scobey. Rugs & wall hangings. 166–67

Rya rugs. Silverstein. Mira Silverstein's guide to looped and knotted stitches. 76–77

Shaker design rug to knit. Woman's Day decorative needlework for the home. 130

Shirvan rug. Kalish. Oriental rugs in needlepoint. 23–32

Simple woven rugs. Felcher. Complete book of rug making. 174–93

Small bargello rug (needlepoint). Rosenthal. Not-so-nimble needlework books. 104–06

Small oval rug (grass). Wilder. Secrets of Eskimo skin sewing. 122–23

Stone. Portuguese needlework rugs.

Tapestry and woven pile rugs. Marein. Creating rugs and wall hangings. 31–87

Tips on making needlepoint rugs. Hanley. Needlepoint. 163–65

Traditional Greek tapestry translated into needlepoint. Vanderbilt. Gloria Vanderbilt designs for your home. 80–82

Transylvanian rug. Kalish. Oriental rugs in needlepoint. 77–89

Tubular knit rug. McCall's big book of knit & crochet for home & family. 92

Tufted, wedge-woven and traditional Navajo rugs. Brown. Weaving, spinning, and dyeing book. 105–06, 108–11

Turkish knotting. Rissell. Craftwork the handicapped elderly can make and sell. 75–78

Turkish mat. Kalish. Oriental rugs in needlepoint. 114–19

Turkish needlepoint rug. Treasury of things to make. 13–15

Turkish prayer rug. Kalish. Oriental rugs in needlepoint. 67–76

Twined rugs. Marein. Creating rugs and wall hangings. 22–30

Two Aran rugs to knit. Woman's Day decorative needlework for the home. 126–29

Warm and furry prom robe (hooked). Feldman. Needlework boutique. 34–36

Weaving a rug. Znamierowski. Step-by-step rugmaking. 87–93

Weaving a rug on a frame. Tod. Joy of hand weaving. 35–39

Weaving a table mat or rug on a loom. Tod. Joy of hand weaving. 47–54

Weaving of rag rugs in plain weave. Tod. Joy of hand weaving. 110–18

Wildflower needlepoint rug, quickpoint welcome rug, fishpond rug, rag and braided rugs, rugs to knit and crochet, hooked rugs, special rug making techniques, creative rug making. Better Homes and Gardens treasury of needlecrafts. 242–47, 302–05, 414–75

Woven harvest sun rug. McCall's book of America's favorite needlework and crafts. 289–90

Woven rug. Wilson. Weaving you can use. 26–40

Woven rugs including geometric and Navajo designs. Quirke. Rug book. 63–87

Woven rugs: Navajo and harvest sun designs. McCall's book of rugmaking. 137–42

Zodiac rug. Ambuter. Carolyn Ambuter's needlepoint celebrations. 75–101

Rugs, Care

Cleaning and repairing hooked rugs. Ketchum. Hooked rugs. 99–101

Display and care. Kalish. Oriental rugs in needlepoint

Repair and care of rugs. Johnson. How to restore, repair, and finish almost everything. 130–39

Rush weaving

Cover for a flower pot. Wright. Complete book of baskets and basketry. 114

Fiber rush. Bausert. Complete book of wicker and cane furniture making. 42–54

Fiber rush. Meyers. Furniture repair and refinishing. 216–17

Making a rush chair seat. Golden book of colonial crafts. 147–49

Reseating a chair. Cane, rush and straw. 113–15

Reseating with rush. Roberts. Illustratted handbook of upholstery. 295–304

Rush reseating. Jones. Fixing furniture. 98–103

Rush seating. Blandford. Do-it-yourselfer's guide to furniture repair and refinishing. 256–62

Rush seating. Brown. Cane and rush seating. 48–63

Rush seating. Encyclopedia of crafts. 176–77

Rush seating. Meyers. Furniture repair and refinishing. 210–16

Rush seats. Blandford. Upholsterer's bible. 375–92

Rush seats. Kinney. Complete book of furniture repair and refinishing. 188–97

Rush weaving. Brann. How to repair, refinish, reupholster. 69–78

Rush weaving. Grime. Illustrated guide to furniture repair & restoration. 72–77

Rush weaving. Wright. Complete book of baskets and basketry. 106–12

Rush weaving a chair seat. Time-Life books. Repairing furniture. 69–70

Rushing. Bragdon. Homeowner's complete manual of repair and improvement. 219

Seagrass seating. Grime. Illustrated guide to furniture repair & restoration. 77–82

S

Saber saws. *See* **Saws**

Sachets

Butterfly sachet pillow. Svinicki. Old-fashioned crochet. 55–57

Circular, hanging minisachets, ribbon, pussycat, butterfly & pine tree sachets. Woman's Day bazaar best sellers. 110–12, 137

Heart and snowflake sachet bag. Great cross-stitch. 118

Muslin sachets. Doherty. Family Circle book of 429 great gifts-to-make all year round for just 10¢ to $10.00. 62–63

Needlepoint sachet. Better Homes and Gardens treasury of Christmas crafts & foods. 109

Sachet or potpourri. Meras. Vacation crafts. 140–41

Sachets. Linsley. Great bazaar. 115–16

Sachets. Mills. Book of presents. 86–89

Sachets to sew. Woman's Day decorative needlework for the home. 147
Sachets: spicey and classic Victorian. Scobey. Gifts from your garden. 76–81
Scented sachet. Wargo. Soft crafts for special occasions. 143–44
Strawberry sachets. Linsley. Custom made. 77–78
Sweetheart soap sachet. Linsley. Decoupage on glass, wood, metal, rocks, shells,
   wax, soap, plastic, canvas, and ceramic. 98–100
Useful powder sachet. Bumper book of things a girl can make. 199–201

Saddlebags
Saddle bag. Latham. Leathercraft. 138–42
Saddlebags. Scurlock. Muzzleloader Magazine's book of buckskinning II. 221

Safes
Acoustical ceiling secret compartment. Krotz. How to hide almost anything. 80
Basic baseboard. Krotz. How to hide almost anything. 28–32
The book basement. Krotz. How to hide almost anything. 55–56
Ceiling-tile secret compartment. Krotz. How to hide almost anything. 80–85
Cellar chair secret compartment. Krotz. How to hide almost anything. 62–65
Closet king. Krotz. How to hide almost anything. 32–35
Cupboard secret compartment. Krotz. How to hide almost anything. 86–89
Desk secret compartments. Krotz. How to hide almost anything. 59–60
Door jamb safe. Krotz. How to hide almost anything. 35–40
Electric plug and outlet subterfuge. Krotz. How to hide almost anything. 52–55
Elementary secret panel. Krotz. How to hide almost anything. 44–49
False closet wall. Krotz. How to hide almost anything. 97
False corner secret compartment. Krotz. How to hide almost anything. 93–94
Floor secret compartment. Krotz. How to hide almost anything. 61–67
Foot stool secret compartment. Krotz. How to hide almost anything. 60–62
Gothic wall. Krotz. How to hide almost anything. 109–13
Inset wall secret compartment. Krotz. How to hide almost anything. 94–97
Mellors model (pegged coatrack). Krotz. How to hide almost anything. 23–28
Pilaster secret compartment. Krotz. How to hide almost anything. 100–05
Pipe secret compartment. Krotz. How to hide almost anything. 65–66
Safe inside a colonial cabinet. Popular Mechanics do-it-yourself encyclopedia. Vol. 3,
   456–59
Secret panel at the back of a bookcase. Krotz. How to hide almost anything. 89–90
Secret passageways. Krotz. How to hide almost anything. 105–09
Space nook. Krotz. How to hide almost anything. 40–44
Stair kicker (secret compartment). Krotz. How to hide almost anything. 70–73
Ten places to hide your valuables. Popular Mechanics do-it-yourself encyclopedia. Vol.
   16, 2558–59
Understairs safe. Krotz. How to hide almost anything. 85–86
Wall pattern design hides secret compartment. Krotz. How to hide almost anything. 74
Wall store housing. Krotz. How to hide almost anything. 117–21
Window sill secret compartment. Krotz. How to hide almost anything. 74–79
Wood pile. Krotz. How to hide almost anything. 56–59
Wooden beam secret compartment. Krotz. How to hide almost anything. 73–74

Sailboats
Sailing dinghy. complete handyman do-it-yourself encyclopedia. Vol. 15, 2219–20

Sailboats, Toy
Sailboats. Blandford. Giant book of wooden toys. 77–82
Sailing sloop. Baldwin. Old fashioned wooden toys. 58–64

Salad utensils
Salad fork and spoon. Modern general shop. Woodworking. 107
Salad scoops. Popular Mechanics do-it-yourself encyclopedia. Vol. 11, 1654
Salad servers. Sainsbury. Sainsbury's woodturning projects for dining. 68–71

Salt and pepper shakers
Carved wooden salt and pepper shakers. Lubkemann. Carving twigs and branches. 74–75
Layered veneer salt shaker and pepper mill. Capotosto. Woodworking techniques and projects. 184–87
Pill bottle shakers. Epple. Something from nothing crafts. 115–16
Salt and pepper shakers. Cope. Plastics. 61
Salt and pepper shakers. Sainsbury. Sainsbury's woodturning projects for dining. 44–46
Salt horn. Scurlock. Muzzleloader Magazine's book of buckskinning II. 209
Salt mill. Sainsbury. Sainsbury's woodturning projects for dining. 81–88
Turning a pepper mill, salt dish. Sainsbury. Craft of woodturning. 127–33, 142–45
Wood salt and pepper shakers. Wooldridge. Woodturning techniques. 49–52

Salt boxes
Anne Leterman's salt box. Daniele. Building early American furniture. 150–51
Salt box. Shea. Pennsylvania Dutch and their furniture. 187

Salt dough. *See* **Dough**

Samplers
All about cross-stitch—introductory material. Cornelius. Teaching needlecraft. 151–53
Alphabet sampler (needlepoint). Tillett. American needlework, 1776–1976. 16–17, 126–27
Ambuter. Open canvas.
American primitive sampler. Ambuter. Carolyn Ambuter's needlepoint celebrations. 118–23
Creative stitchery sampler—moon flowers. Better Homes and Gardens embroidery. 84–86
Crewel embroidery sampler. Golden book of colonial crafts. 118–29
Crocheted sculpture—basic sampler shape. Edson. Creative crochet. 120–21
Embroidered abstract sampler, alphabet sampler. McCall's big book of needlecrafts. 250–56
Garden sampler. Boyles. Margaret Boyles book of needle art. 94–99
Geometric sampler. Slater. Elaine Slater's book of needlepoint projects. 147–50
Hieroglyph sampler. Fischer. Egyptian designs in modern stitchery. 122–35
Introduction to cross-stitch—introductory material. Cornelius. Teaching needlecraft. 140–42
Introduction to early American crewel embroidery. Cornelius. Teaching needlecraft. 42–53
Lammer. Making samplers.
Learning cross .itch—introductory material. Cornelius. Teaching needlecraft. 147–49
Learning needlepoint—introductory material. Cornelius. Teaching needlecraft. 111–14
Miniature samplers. Boyles. Needlework gifts for special occasions. 134–40
Molly Russell sampler. Tillett. American needlework, 1776–1976. 102–05
Needlepoint alphabet sampler, "stained glass" sampler. McCall's big book of needle-crafts. 166–67
Needlepoint alphabet samplers. McCall's big book of country needlecrafts. 174–75, 180–82
Needlepoint II—introductory material. Cornelius. Teaching needlecraft. 119–22

"Patchwork" flower sampler, embroidery sampler in needlepoint, alphabet sampler, memory sampler. McCall's book of America's favorite needlework and crafts. 95–102
Pegboard sampler (yarn on pegboard). Golden book of hand and needle arts. 96
Pennsylvania Dutch birth or wedding sampler. Boyles. Margaret Boyles book of needle art. 90–93
Pennsylvania Dutch wedding sampler (embroidered). Boyles. Needlework gifts for special occasions. 100–05
Perforated-paper sampler. Golden book of hand and needle arts. 102–03
Satin stitch sampler. Wilson. Needleplay. 148–49
Schoolgirl's sampler (embroidered). Boyles. Needlework gifts for special occasions. 145–49
Sentiments in stitches/animal new baby sampler. Wilson. Needleplay. 162–63
Tabby sampler. Holland. Weaving primer. 75–80
Tree of life sampler (embroidered). Feldman. Needlework boutique. 26–28

Samplers, Embroidered
Colonial sampler, "God bless our home", kindness sampler, two friendship samplers, alphabet sampler, pagoda sampler, colonial house sampler, mansion sampler. McCall's book of America's favorite needlework and crafts. 17–36
Cross-stitch samplers. Blandford book of traditional handicrafts. 77–80
Rainbow sampler, from the garden, home sweet home, where the heart is, best tradition, olde-worlde sampler, country sampler. Great cross-stitch. 131–54
Sampler. Rosenthal. Not-so-nimble needlework book. 60–62
Traditional sampler. Woman's Day book of gifts to make. 201–04

Sand blasting
Sand-blasted glass windows. Rowland. Handcrafted doors & windows. 170–75
Sand blasting. Isenberg. How to work in stained glass. 258–66
Sand blasting. Matcham. Techniques of glass engraving. 151–56
Sand blasting signs. Spielman. Making wood signs. 101–15

Sand boxes
Sand box. Dal Fabbro. How to make children's furniture and play equipment. 179–81
Sand/play center, sand pit, sand table. Boeschen. Successful playhouses. 111–14
Super sand box. Popular Mechanics do-it-yourself encyclopedia. Vol. 14, 2192–93

Sand painting
Green. Sand art book.
Making a drypainting. Stribling. Crafts from North American Indian arts. 279–92
Navajo sand paintings. Schuman. Art from many hands. 200–04
Sand art. Kicklighter. Crafts, illustrated designs and techniques. 280–87
Sand in bottles, sand painting. Meras. Vacation crafts. 55–61
Sand painting. Kinney. How to make 19 kinds of American folk art. 23–25
Sand paintings. Appel. Sand art. 57–92
Three-dimensional sand painting with a seascape design. Appel. Sand art. 69–75

Sandals
Calico corkies. Evrard. Twinkletoes. 113–16
Exercise sandals. Boyles. Margaret Boyles book of needle art. 54–55
How to embroider & attach a pair of uppers for wooden sandals. Gostelow. Mary Gostelow's embroidery book. 48–49
Leather sandals. Evrard. Twinkletoes. 101–05
Leather thongs. Evrard. Twinkletoes. 106–09
Mexican huaraches. Evrard. Twinkletoes. 60–63
Oriental straw and velvet thongs. Evrard. Twinkletoes. 135–37

Raffia runabouts. Evrard. Twinkletoes. 127–29
Sandal tops. Stearns. Macrame. 62–65
Sandals. Clark. The make-it-yourself shoe book. 84–94
Sandals. Latham. Leathercraft. 150–58
Soleless seashore sandals. Evrard. Twinkletoes. 132–34
Turkish wooden block sandals. Evrard. Twinkletoes. 117–19

Sandals, Children
Little girl's gingham party shoe. Katz. Footwear. 49

Sandals, Men
Man's pool knockabout. Katz. Footwear. 41
Slipper sandals (crocheted). Feldman. Needlework boutique. 91–92

Sandals, Women
Candy cane shoe. Katz. Footwear. 42–43
Cloth and straw espadrille. Katz. Footwear. 47
Cork clog. Katz. Footwear. 48
Fantasy disco shoe. Katz. Footwear. 51
Fiesta shoe. Katz. Footwear. 39
Gold and silver disco shoe. Katz. Footwear. 51
Market shoe. Katz. Footwear. 40–41
Needlepoint clog uppers. Katz. Footwear. 76–77
Old-fashioned needlepointed clogs. Evrard. Twinkletoes. 96–100
Peasant clogs. Evrard. Twinkletoes. 110–12
Placemat slip-on. Katz. Footwear. 46
Refurbished exercise sandals, sandal heel remake. Katz. Footwear. 106–07
Sandals (leather). Katz. Footwear. 95–97
Sandals (needlepoint straps with wooden soles). Burchette. Needlework. 96–99
Shoestring espadrilles. Feldman. Needlework boutique. 135–37
Straw T-strap festival sandal. Katz. Footwear. 46–47
Summer wedgie. Katz. Footwear. 44–45
Uppers for sandal heel remake (crocheted). Katz. Footwear. 78–79

Sandpaper
Abrasive tools: sanding blocks, spindles, abrasive board. Sainsbury. Woodworking
    projects with power tools. 132–36
Basics of belt sanding, build this disc and drum sander, sanding from start to finish.
    Popular Mechanics do-it-yourself encyclopedia. Vol. 16, 2498–508
Belt sanders. Popular Mechanics do-it-yourself encyclopedia. Vol. 2, 258–61
Block, designs. Lyon. Arts and crafts objects children can make for the home. 101,
    149–51
Inflatable drum sander, low-tech thickness sander, sanding-disc jointer, disc sander.
    Fine woodworking techniques 4. 110–13, 120–21
Pad sander know-how, mount your sander in a stand. Popular Mechanics do-it-your-
    self encyclopedia. Vol. 13, 2020–27
Sanders, sanding. Capotosto. Woodworking wisdom. 96–103, 173–84
Sanding. Make it! don't buy it. 164–67
Sanding and preparing for finish, sanding machines. Wagner. Modern woodworking.
    111–19, 269–79
Sandpaper block. Braren. Homemade. 19
Smoothing and shaping. Gladstone. Hints and tips for the handyperson. 39–42
Stroke sander. Fine woodworking techniques I. 68–73
Wooden-drum stroke sander, follow-up on stroke sanders. Fine woodworking tech-
    niqes 5. 35–41

Saunas

Building a sauna. Planning and remodeling bathrooms. 76–77
Sauna. Churchill. Big backyard building book. 89–97
Sauna bath. Complete handyman do-it-yourself encyclopedia. Vol. 15, 2265–76
Saunas. Churchill. Backyard building book. 145–53

Sawbucks

Sawbuck. Braren. Homemade. 23
Sawbuck. Brown. 44 terrific woodworking plans & projects. 203–05
Sawbuck. Bubel. Working wood. 91–93
Sawbuck. Langsner. Country woodcraft. 54–57
Sawbuck handles long logs. Popular Mechanics do-it-yourself encyclopedia. Vol. 16, 2509

Sawhorses

Sawhorse. Adams. Make your own baby furniture. 213
Sawhorse. Braren. Homemade. 13
Sawhorse. Bubel. Working wood. 87–90
Sawhorse. Waugh. Handyman's encyclopedia. 234–35
Sawhorse construction, basics, roll-around, hinged, and garden working horses. Wood projects for the garden. 47–51
Sawhorses. Fine woodworking techniques 4. 50–51
Sawhorses. Handyman. 525–26
Simple-and-easy sawhorse. Popular Mechanics do-it-yourself encyclopedia. Vol. 16, 2510–11
Wobble-free, foldaway sawhorse. McNair. Building & outfitting your workshop. 185–92
Workshop helpmates. Oberrecht. Plywood projects illustrated. 183–85

Sawing

Portable chain saw mill. Martensson. woodworker's bible. 259–63
Sawing. Capotosto. Woodworking wisdom. 122–56
Sawing by hand. Fine woodworking techniques 2. 52–55
Sawmilling. Fine woodworking techniques 3. 2–8

Saws

Band saw basics: rip fence for your band saw; jig to sharpen band saw blades; drop-on table for your band saw; bench saw; long workpiece support, wood; supersafe pusher jig; roller support; miter-gauge hold-down. Popular Mechanics do-it-yourself encyclopedia. Vol. 2, 164–70, 268–95
Basics of the band saw; jigsaw for cutting delicate stock, mitering on the table saw. Fine woodworking techniques 5. 10–19
Bench for your portable saw, circular saw blades, deburring jig, circular saw know-how. Popular Mechanics do-it-yourself encyclopedia. Vol. 5, 717–29
Bench saw dolly rolls where you want it. Popular Mechanics do-it-yourself encyclopedia. Vol. 18, 2784–85
Bow saws. Langsner. Country woodcraft. 83–84
Build a power hacksaw from washing-machine parts. Popular Mechanics do-it-yourself encyclopedia. Vol. 15, 2306–09
Carpenter's art. Time-Life books. Working with wood. 14–59
Circular saws, band saw, jigsaw, and saber saw. Wagner. Modern woodworking. 167–215
Crosscut saws. Popular Mechanics do-it-yourself encyclopedia. Vol. 6, 878–83
Hand saw, sabre saw, portable circular saw, scroll saw, band saw, table and radial-arm saw. Capotosto. Woodworking wisdom. 2–59

How to use a radial-arm saw, fine cabinet for your radial-arm saw, table extensions for a radial saw, radial saw bench with lots of storage, molding head fence for a radial saw, jacks quickly level a radial-saw table. Popular Mechanics do-it-yourself encyclopedia. Vol. 15, 2365–83

How to use a sabre saw, "table saw" from your sabre saw, bench saw basics, build the American bucksaw, compact table for a radial-arm saw. Popular Mechanics do-it-yourself encyclopedia. Vol. 16, 2482–89

Japanese saws, walking-beam saw, carbide-tipped circular saws. Fine woodworking techniques 4. 71–73, 102–09

Jeweler's saws. Popular Mechanics do-it-yourself encyclopedia. Vol. 10, 1552–54

Panel saw and storage unit, variable-taper jig, bench hook and miter, saw guide and protractor. McNair. Building & outfitting your workshop. 62–81, 174–85, 215–20

Poor man's table saw. Blackwell. Johnny Blackwell's poor man's catalog. 149

Saber, circular, radial-arm, table, scroll (jig), band, chain saws. Buckwwalter. Homeowner's handbook of power tools. 34–64, 122–34, 148–93

Saws. Underhill. Woodwright's companion. 43–56

Small saw, making a bow saw. Fine woodworking techniques 2. 51, 55

Three-wheel band saw. Giant book of metalworking projects. 229–34

Turning saw. Langsner. Country woodcraft. 86–87

Two extensions for a table saw. Popular Mechanics do-it-yourself encyclopedia. Vol. 18, 2841

Wooden bucksaw. Langsner. Country woodcraft. 84–86

Saws, Chain

Chain saw lumbering. Fine woodworking techniques 2. 2–5

Easy-build box for chain saw accessories. Popular Mechanics do-it-yourself encyclopedia. Vol. 3, 428

Keep your chain saw cutting. Popular Mechanics do-it-yourself encyclopedia. Vol. 4, 632–37

Using a chain saw. Outdoor projects for home and garden. 492–98

Saws, Sharpening

Circular saws. Fine woodworking techniques 2. 56

Oldtimer's techniques of saw-sharpening. Time-Life books. Working with wood. 56–59

Sharpening saws. Fine woodworking techniques 4. 74–76

Scarves

All in the family: caps and scarves. Feldman. Needlework boutique. 43–44

Batik scarf. Svinicki. Step-by-step spinning and dyeing. 62–63

Batique scarf. Bumper book of things a girl can make. 13–15

Braided scarf. Woman's Day book of gifts to make. 35–36

Child's cap, mittens and scarf (crocheted). Creative crafts yearbook: an exciting new collection of needlework and crafts. 132–34

Crocheted scarves with hood and pockets. Step by step to better knitting and crochet. 155–56

Crocheted scarves with style. Favorite knitting & crochet patterns 88–90

Disco scarf. Jacobs. Crochet book. 141–42

Fair Isle scarf, hat and gloves. Morgan. Traditional knitting patterns of Ireland, Scotland and England. 87–89

Fluffy boa. Fashions from the loom. 92

Fringed muffler, knit scarf, crocheted scarf. Woman's Day bazaar best sellers. 22–23, 28–29

Fringy scarf set, denim set (crocheted hats & scarves). McCall's big book of knit & crochet for home & family. 222–23, 226–27

Fuzzy-wuzzy scarf, cartwheel scarf, fluffy scarf, houndstooth scarf, popcorn-trimmed, mesh scarf, pocketed scarf, ear warmer, bulky scarf. Woman's Day crochet showcase. 22, 69–74, 77, 97–98, 171

Garter stitch knitted scarf. Reader's Digest complete guide to needlework. 285
Girl's scarf & purse (embroidered). Fraser. Modern stitchery: stitches, patterns, free-
form designing. 90–91
Hairpin crochet scarf. Encyclopedia of crafts. 90
Hand warmer muffler. Jacobs. Crochet book. 85–86
Heart-trimmed, knitted scarves. Better Homes and Gardens easy bazaar crafts. 7, 16,
40, 46
His and hers tie and scarf. Reader's Digest complete guide to sewing. 492–93
His best scarf (knit). Needlework boutique. 88–90
Hooded sweater scarf. Brown. Super sweater idea book. 182–83
Knit Aran scarf. Hollingworth. Complete book of traditional Aran knitting. 135–36
Knitted scalloped scarf. Knitting techniques and projects. 45
Knitted scarves. Chatterton. Scandinavian knitting designs. 228–31
Knitted scarves in garter stitch. Step by step to better knitting and crochet. 9
Lace scarf from Shetland. Compton. Complete book of traditional knitting. 174–75
Large batik scarf. Frame. Tie-dyeing and batik. 110–13
Long scarf (crocheted). Rosenthal. Not-so-nimble needlework book. 125
Mosaic-patterned scarf. Walker. Mosaic knitting. 192
Mufflet, bonnet scarf. Beard. Fashions from the loom. 88–89
Multicolor ski muffler. Jacobs. Crochet book. 111
Neck scarf with pockets. Coffey. Francine Coffey's celebrity sewing bee. 164
Ombre scarf (knitted). Rosenthal. Not-so-nimble needlework book. 139
Patchwork scarves. Selfridge. Patchwork knitting. 149
Rake or knit-loom scarf. Rosenthal. Not-so-nimble needlework book. 149–50
Scallop ruffle kerchief. Jacobs. Crochet book. 59–60
Scarf, ascot, bib, collar (sewn). Burns. Super sewing. 293
Scarf for children and adults. Ickis. Weaving as a hobby. 11–12
Scarf woven on a roller loom. Weaving and spinning. 111
Seed-stitch and rib-stitch hat and scarf sets. Hubert. Weekend knitting projects. 16–17
Teddy's striped scarf. Knitting. 110
Tie-dyed scarf. Svinicki. Step-by-step spinning and dyeing. 62
Tie-dyed scarves. Tie-dye, batik and candle making step-by-step. 12–13
Tie-dyed silk scarf. Frame. Tie-dyeing and batik. 30–33
Tube hat and scarf. Brown. Super sweater idea book. 183–84
Two-toned hat and scarf set. Hubert. Weekend knitting projects. 58
Woman's lacy scarf. Hubert. Weekend knitting projects. 94
Woman's tricolor crocheted, knitted man's horizontal stripe & man's vertical stripe.
Doherty. Family Circle book of 429 great gifts-to-make all year round for just 10¢
to $10.00. 58, 114–15
Woven scarf. Holland. Weaving primer. 98
Wrappings (ways to use scarves as pieces of clothing). Milinaire. Cheap chic. 153–63

Scenic models. *See* **Landscape models**

Scissors
Embroidery scissors case. Boyles. Margaret Boyles book of needle art. 88–89
Scissors caddy. Coffey. Francine Coffey's celebrity sewing bee. 159
Scissors case. Burchette. Needlework. 103–04
Scissors case. Christensen. Needlepoint. 61–62
Scissors case. Christensen. Needlepoint and bargello stitchery. 79–82
Scissors case. Parker. Mosaics in needlepoint. 92–93
Scissors case (needlepoint). Christensen. Needlepoint book. 117
Scissors case, needlepoint. Giant book of crafts. 90
Scissors operator. Grainger. Making aids for disabled living. 66–69
String and scissors caddy. Romberg. Let's discover papier mâché. 38

Sconces
Aluminum candle sconce. Woman's Day book of weekend crafts. 41
Candle sconce. Make it! don't buy it. 208–17
Candle sconce. Villiard. Art and craft of sand casting. 92
Coat hanger wire wall candle holder. Kramer. Wirecraft. 62–63
Sconce. Fowler. Can crafts. 17–19
Sconce. Modern general shop. Woodworking. 110
Sconce candleholders, pie-plate sconce. Fowler. Can crafts. 104–08
Three-arm sconce. Kauffman. Easy-to-make wooden candlesticks, chandeliers and lamps. 26–27
Wall sconce. Popular Mechanics do-it-yourself encyclopedia. Vol. 5, 706
Wall sconces with roses. Bealer. Art of blacksmithing. 310–13

Scooters
Scooter. Maginley. Toys to make and ride. 40–43
Scooter, three wheel scooter. Blandford. Giant book of wooden toys. 138–40
Scooterboards. Gould. Skateboards, scooterboards, and seatboards you can make. 41–50
Scooters from skates. Popular Mechanics do-it-yourself encyclopedia. Vol. 19, 2907

Scrap materials. *See* **Waste materials**

Scrapbooks. *See* **Albums**

Screen process printing. *See* **Silk screen printing**

Screens (furniture)
Decorative egg carton. Epple. Something from nothing crafts. 38–40
Decoupage screen. Paper. 99–102
Fabric covered folding screen. Roda. Fabric decorating for the home. 92–93
Floral embroidered screen. McCall's book of America's favorite needlework and crafts. 87–88
Floral three-panel screen. Woman's Day book of gifts to make. 210–11
Folding screen. 101 do-it-yourself projects. 236–37
Folding screen with travel posters, pivoting partition, sliding partition. Popular Mechanics do-it-yourself encyclopedia. Vol. 8, 1188
Folding screens. Parry. Stenciling. 105–08
Papered screen. Treasury of things to make. 18–19
Partition screen with handwoven panels. Make it! don't buy it. 78–85
Room-divider screen (macrame). Golden book of hand and needle arts. 142
Scrapscreen. Whatnot. 168–72
Screens and room dividers. Wilson. Weaving you can use. 60–64
Shadow applique-wall panels. Better Homes and Gardens applique. 46–47
Shirred folding screen. Roda. Fabric decorating for the home. 143
Small table screen. Elbert. Paperworks. 88–91
Swallow & willow branches, miniature screen. Nicoletti. Japanese motifs for needlepoint. 90–93
Three-panel macrame screen. Woman's Day decorative needlework for the home. 159–70
Two-way hinge for folding screen. Fine woodworking techniques 2. 105
Upholstered wooden screen. Worst. Weaving with foot-power looms. 232–38
Wallpaper-covered screen. McCall's sewing for your home. 58
Woven screen panels on a multiharness loom. Make it! don't buy it. 400–05

Screens, Wire
Aluminum oxide is a good cleaner for aluminum screens. Bragdon. Homeowner's complete manual of repair & improvement. 121
Fixing screens. Outdoor projects for home and garden. 100–07
How to repair aluminum storms and screens. Popular Mechanics do-it-yourself encyclopedia. Vol. 18, 2810–11
How to replace & patch screen wire. Nunn. Home improvement, home repair. 49–50
How to stretch a wire screen. Popular Mechanics do-it-yourself encyclopedia. Vol. 16, 2536–37
Repairing window screens. Handyman. 169
Screen weaving. Newman. Wire art. 166–67
Screens. Lewis. Cabinetmaking, patternmaking, and millwork. 390–97
Screens—installing, replacing, maintenance. Bragdon. Homeowner's complete manual or repair & improvement. 118–23
Victorian screen doors. Rowland. Handcrafted doors & windows. 90–93
Window and door screens. Adams. Arco's complete woodworking handbook. 472–76

Screwdrivers
Offset screwdriver. Modern general shop. Metalworking. 110
Screwdriver basics. Popular Mechanics do-it-yourself encyclopedia. Vol. 16, 2538–39

Screws
Using wood screws, tables of wood screw sizes, removing wood screws. Kinney. Complete book of furniture repair and refinishing. 22–26

Scrimshaw
Linsley. Scrimshaw.
Making plaster scrimshaw. Schuman. Art from many hands. 230–34
Scrimshaw. Sommer. Contemporary costume jewelry. 197–98
Scrimshaw on plaster or meat bones. Linderman. Crafts for the classroom. 354–56

Sculpture
Arch. Coyne. Penland School of Crafts book of pottery. 96–112
Cube sculptures. Sainsbury. Woodworking projects with power tools. 49–50
Gallery of wire art. Newman. Wire art. 209–34
Making it big: constructing and carving large sculptures. Fine woodworking techniques 5. 160–63
Metal and wire sculpture. Metalcrafting encyclopedia. 106–08
Metal sculpturing. Giant book of metalworking projects. 78–83
Plaster, sawdust and sand sculpture. Yoder, Sculpture and modeling for the elementary school. 101–03
Polystyrene sculpture, carving from breeze blocks, wire sculpture. Encyclopedia of crafts. 213, 220–21
Sculpt mixes: plaster and saw dust, wax and sawdust, plaster, sand and zonolite. Yoder. Sculpture and modeling for the elementary school. 111–13
Soft sculpture cubes. Better Homes and Gardens applique. 90–91
Somewhere under the rainbow. Isenberg. How to work in beveled glass. 212–13
Tissue-paper sculpture. Giant book of crafts. 427–34
Willow tree sculpture (macrame). Golden book of hand and needle arts. 143
Wood sculpture. Popular Mechanics do-it-yourself encyclopedia. Vol 20, 3118–21

Seagrass weaving. See **Rush weaving**

Seashells
Sea-scallop shell. Upton. Woodcarver's primer. 23–29
Seashell jewelry. Sommer. Contemporary costume jewelry. 183–85

Seashells. See also **Shell work**

Seaweed
Seaweed collages and notepaper. Meras. Vacation crafts. 98–104

Seeds, berries, etc.
Bean flower picture. Critchley. Step by step guide to making artificial flowers. 57–61
Collage of beans and wire. Brunner. Pass it on. 131–33
Corn kernel designs & pictures. Lyon. Arts and crafts objects children can make for the home. 18
Flowers in the sun seed picture. Janitch. Collage: a step by step guide. 40–41
Mosaics from grocery seeds. Picturemaking. 54–59
Pasta and seed collages. Ashurst. Collage. 20–25
Rooster and hen plaques (dried beans and seeds). McCall's book of America's favorite needlework and crafts. 374–76

Seesaws. See **Playground equipment**

Septic tanks
Have a trouble-free septic system. Popular Mechanics do-it-yourself encyclopedia. Vol. 17, 2575–81
Individual sewage disposal. Olin. Construction. 512.1–512.18
Making your septic tank behave. Outdoor projects for home and garden. 120–24
Sewage treatment. Bragdon. Homeowner's complete manual of repair & improvement. 454–57

Serving carts
Early American electric serving cart. Popular Mechanics do-it-yourself encyclopedia. Vol. 17, 2570–74
Kitchen storage cart. Family handyman handbook of carpentry plans/projects. 81–84
Movable buffet servers. Complete handyman do-it-yourself encyclopedia. Vol. 16, 2330–40
Patio carts. Self. Working with plywood, including indoor/outdoor projects. 259–63
Serving cart. Black and Decker power tool carpentry. 61–65
Serving cart. Spence. Woodworking tools, materials, processes. 597
Serving cart, prep and serve center. 101 do-it-yourself projects. 112–14, 220–23
Tea cart. Capotosto. Woodworking techniques and projects. 286–90
Tea carts. Alth. Making plastic pipe furniture. 83–92
Utility cart. Stevenson. How to build and buy cabinets for the modern kitchen. 243–46

Settees
Captain duck's settee. Ball. Master pieces. 104–09
Coachman's pine settee. Daniele. Building early American furniture. 220–21
Settee. Moser. How to build Shaker furniture. 172–73

Sewing
Cowan. Left-handed sewing.
Sewing desk. Moser. How to build Shaker funiture. 168–169
Tucks for ornamenting and shaping. Time-Life books. Traditional favorites. 28–31
Weller. Complete manual of rapid sewing techniques.

Sewing cases
Basket sewing box. Coffey. Francine Coffey's celebrity sewing bee. 65
Calico sewing caddy. Woman's Day bazaar best sellers. 127
Chairside sewing cabinet, cabinet for spools. Popular Mechanics do-it-yourself encyclopedia. Vol. 17, 2582–85

Dresden plate sewing pocket. Houck. Patchwork pattern book. 50–51
Embroidered sewing companion. Colby. Pincushions. 66
Housewife. Tyler. Big book of soft toys. 239–41
Needlepoint tote. Coffey. Francine Coffey's celebrity sewing bee. 81
Oogruk leather sewing kit. Wilder. Secrets of Eskimo skin sewing. 117–18
Ribbon sewing kit. Coffey. Francine Coffey's celebrity sewing bee. 73
Sewing basket. Worst. Weaving with foot-power looms. 232, 234
Sewing box. Linsley. Custom made. 6–11
Sewing caddy. Coffey. Francine Coffey's celebrity sewing bee. 125
Sewing case. Fairfield. Patchwork. 48
Sewing pocket belt. Coffey. Francine Coffey's celebrity sewing bee. 158
Super sewing box (appliqued). Botsford. Between thimble & thumb. 125–32
Wooden sewing box. Linsley. Decoupage on glass, wood, metal, rocks, shells, wax,
    soap, plastic, canvas, ceramic. 16–25

Sewing equipment
Button tin, sewing caddy, ribbon sew-help-me, scarf needlework bag. Doherty. Family
    Circle book of 429 great gifts-to-make all year round for just 10¢ to $10.00. 29,
    62, 142–43
How to build the cutting table. Vogue sewing book. 441
Mahogany sewing table. Osburn. Measured drawings of early American furniture. 38–
    39
Quilted workbasket. McNeill. Quilting. 28
Ribbon tape measure. Coffey. Francine Coffey's celebrity sewing bee. 167
Sewing center. 101 do-it-yourself projects. 202–05
Sewing table. Marlow. Classic furniture projects. 30–43
Sewing table and crafts center. Brann. How to repair, refinish, reupholster. 109–35
Shaker sewing cabinet and work cabinet. 77 furniture projects you can build. 97–100,
    121–23
Shaker sewing table. 77 furniture projects you can build. 148–51
Spool holder. Modern general shop. Woodworking. 111
Spool rack. Abrams. Building craft equipment. 161–63

Sewing machine cabinets
Heirloom sewing cabinet. 77 furniture projects you can build. 112–16
Hideaway sewing center. Better Homes and Gardens step-by-step cabinets and
    shelves. 88–9
Sewing center. Self. Working with plywood, including indoor/outdoor projects. 264–74
Sewing machine cabinet. Complete handyman do-it-yourself encyclopedia. Vol. 8,
    1174–77

Sewing rooms
Built-in sewing cabinet. Hylton. Hand crafted shelves & cabinets. 186–91
Compact sewing center. Popular Mechanics do-it-yourself encyclopedia. Vol. 12,
    1892–93
Planning a creative environment. Vogue sewing book. 438–41
Sewing and hobby center. Leavy. Bookshelves and storage units. 81–87
Sewing center for every taste and need, island unit, dual unit, dual-role unit, ideas for
    sewing built-ins. Popular Mechanics do-it-yourself encyclopedia. Vol. 17, 2586–
    601
Sewing centers. Davidson. Successful studios and work centers. 69–74
Sewing closet, sewing center storage corner, sewing storage wall. Family handyman
    handbook of carpentry plans/projects. 9–18
Sewing workshop. Geary. How to design and build your own workspace—with plans.
    221–31

Shadow boxes
Cowry display in shadow box. Logan. Shell crafts. 57–59
Framed plaque or shadow box. Miles. Designing with natural materials. 110–13
Naturalist's frame. Miles. Designing with natural materials. 117
Shadow box. Brunner. Pass it on. 127–29
Shadow box. Creative sewing. 83
Shadow boxes. Elbert. Shell craft. 30–33
Veneered shadow box. Hobbs. Veneer craft for everyone. 125–27
Window with a shadow box. Complete handyman do-it-yourself encyclopedia. Vol. 21, 3110–13

Sharpening of tools. *See* **Saws, Sharpening; Tools, Sharpening**

Shaving horses.
Holding the work: shaving horse and low bench. Fine woodworking techniques 2. 28–30
Shaving horses. Langsner. Country woodcraft. 59–66

Shawls
Bias-cut apron-shawl. Golden book of hand and needle arts. 54
Butterfly shawl. Design crochet. 148–60
Cape shawl. Rosenthal. Not-so-nimble needlework book. 35–36
Country girl knitted skirt and shawl. Favorite knitting & crochet patterns. 190–91
Crochet shawl. Gault. Crafts for the disabled. 78
Crocheted and hairpin lace shawls. Feldman. Handmade lace and patterns. 116–19
Crocheted mesh shawl, cluster stitch shawl, striped shawl. Scharf. Butterick's fast and easy needlecrafts. 84–89
Diamond-pattern crocheted shawl, lacy crocheted shawl, & one-piece triangle shawl. Woman's Day bazaar best sellers. 42–54
Evening frills. Favorite knitting & crochet patterns. 86–87
Fan shawl. Jacobs. Crochet book. 116–18
Festive shawl (hairpin lace). Feldman. Needlework boutique. 56–57
Flower-trimmed shawl (crocheted). Complete book of baby crafts. 54–55
Golden shawl (crocheted). Creative crafts yearbook: an exciting new collection of needlework and crafts. 32
Greek shawl. Gostelow. Complete international book of embroidery. 154
Gypsy shawl. Farlie. Pennywise boutique. 58
Instructions for the trapunto stole and hat. Time-Life books. Boutique attire. 122–23
Kerchief. Gehret. Rural Pennsylvania clothing. 50–56
Knitted shawl, shawl with tatted border, hairpin lace shawl. Reader's Digest complete guide to needlework. 355, 418–19, 442
Knitted shoulder wrap. Better Homes and Gardens treasury of Christmas crafts & foods. 104
Knitted triangular shawl. Knitting techniques and projects. 49
Lace and ribbon shawl, deep-fringed shawl, quilted shawl, patchwork shawl. McCall's book of America's favorite needlework and crafts. 264–70
Lacy shawl. Great granny crochet book. 122–23
Lacy shawl. Step by step to better knitting and crochet. 265
Large triangular shawl (knitted). Rosenthal. Not-so-nimble needlework book. 146–47
Leaves and vines embroidered on fabric shawl. Scheuer. Designs for Holbein embroidery. 30–31
Mesh rosette-bordered shawl. Jacobs. Crochet book. 135–36
Mexican quesquimitl (sewn). Holderness. Peasant chic. 24–26
Mohair crochet shawl, shawl in hairpin lace. Encyclopedia of crafts. 94, 97
Patchwork shawl. Ives. Ideas for patchwork. 68–72
Patchwork shawls. Scharf. Illustrated patchwork crochet. 174

Ruana (sewn). Holderness. Peasant chic. 49–51
Shawl done in the tie-dyed weaving of totonicipan. DeRodriguez. Weaving on a back-
strap loom. 128–35
Shawl from Shetland. Compton. Complete book of traditional knitting. 175–78
Shawls. Henderson. Woman's Day book of designer crochet. 65–75
Shawls. Ruggieri. Woman's Day book of no-pattern sewing. 77–78
Spider web crocheted shawl, fan-pattern crocheted shawl, diamond shawl, antique
shawl. McCall's book of America's favorite needlework and crafts. 258–64
Spider-web-lace shawl. American School of Needlework. Great crochet bazaar book.
39–40
Tasseled knitted shawl. Woman's Day book of gifts to make. 75–76
Three-color shawl. Step by step to better knitting and crochet. 180
Triangular fringed shawl. Doherty. Family Circle book of 429 great gifts-to-make all
year round for just 10¢ to $10.00. 68
Triangular fringed shawl, ruffled shawl. Woman's Day crochet showcase. 49–51
Versatile shawl (crochet). Mills. Book of presents. 8–9
Warm poncho or party shawl (sewn). Practical needlework. 108
Weave-through shawl. Rosenthal. Not-so-nimble needlework book. 76–77

Sheaths
Blackfoot dag sheath. Latham. Leathercraft. 50–55
Customize your knife sheath. Popular Mechanics do-it-yourself encyclopedia. Vol. 11,
1637–39
Knife & tomahawk sheaths. Scurlock. Muzzleloader Magazine's book of buckskinning
II. 49–50
Knife sheath making. Latham. Knifecraft. 190–221
Knife sheaths. Latham. Leathercraft. 102–25
Mountain man knife sheath. Latham. Leathercraft. 65–75
Rifle sheath. Latham. Leathercraft. 143–47
Sheath: how to design and make it. Mayes. How to make your own knives. 151–65
Sheaths for knives. Boye. Step-by-step knifemaking: you can do it! 233–47

Sheds
Equipment shed. Bubel. Working wood. 153–61
Movable shed. Braren. Homemade. 145–47
Movable shed. Leavy. Successful small farms. 132–34

Sheds. See also **Garden houses, shelters, etc.; Tool houses**

Sheets
Designer sheets. Reader's Digest complete guide to sewing. 457
Embroidered child's sheet, stenciled. Linsley. Custom made. 26–28
Embroidered rose sheet. Embroidery of roses. 129–31
Graphics from A to Z on sheets and pillows. Wilson. Needleplay. 134–35
Sheets and pillow cases. Practical needlework. 176
Sheets with patchwork trim. Ives. Ideas for patchwork. 28–31
Show-off sheets and pillow cases. McCall's sewing for your home. 54–55

Sheets. See also **Bedclothes**

Sheets, Infants
Appliqued sheets and pillowcases. Laury. Treasury of needlecraft gifts for the new
baby. 49–52

Shell work
Carving shells. Tangerman. Carving the unusual. 104–12
Collecting, cleaning, buying, sorting, oiling, etc. Logan. Shell crafts. 3–38
Etched shells. Linderman. Crafts for the classroom. 356–58
Ocean bed collage. Janitch. Collage: a step by step guide. 59, 62–63
Seashells: jewels from the sea. Johnson. Nature crafts. 24–37
Shell box, shell flowers. Whatnot. 52–62
Shell candles, shell flowers, shell dolls, etc. Meras. Vacation crafts. 70–97
Shellcraft. Kicklighter. Crafts illustrated designs and techniques. 298–305
Shell picture. Critchley. Step by step guide to making artificial flowers. 53–57
Wood-based shell sculpture. Vanderbilt. Gloria Vanderbilt designs for your home. 155–56

Shelves and racks
Adjustable and non-adjustable shelves. Handyman. 179–81
Applique shelf. Brann. How to build workbenches, sawhorse tool chest and other build-it-yourself projects. 66–70
Bird-in-hand wall rack. Daniele. Building early American furniture. 133–35
Bric-a-brac cabinet. Capotosto. Woodworking techniques and projects. 119–23
Build a cabinet for your curios. Popular Mechanics do-it-yourself encyclopedia. Vol. 8, 1154–56
Building shelves between studs. Time-Life books. Space and storage. 100–01
Cantilever shelves. Carbo. Fix-it guide for women. 107–10
Combination shelf and clothes rack. Stiles. Easy-to-make children's furniture. 23
Cookware rack. Self. Working with plywood, including indoor/outdoor projects. 256–58
Corner bric-a-brac shelf. DeCristoforo. Build your own wood toys, gifts and furniture. 371–74
Crate-style shelving. Better Homes and Gardens step-by-step cabinets and shelves. 79
Desktop display shelves. Elbert. Paperworks. 49–50
Easy-up utility shelves. Oberrecht. Plywood projects illustrated. 221–22
Entertainment center, Chinese boxes wall unit. 101 do-it-yourself projects. 206–13, 244–46
Fire surrounds. Blandford. How to make your own built-in furniture. 261–67
Fitting a shelf. Syvanen. Interior finish: more tricks of the trade. 74–76
Free-standing shelving. Self. Working with plywood, including indoor/outdoor projects. 215–18
Hole in the wall shelves. Family handyman handbook of carpentry plans/projects. 363–66
How to put up shelves that stay up, how to build wall shelves, handsome cover-up for utility shelving. Popular Mechanics do-it-yourself encyclopedia. Vol. 17, 2630–37
Hylton. Handcrafted shelves & cabinets.
Kitchen utility shelves. Shea. Pennsylvania Dutch and their furniture. 190
Nineteenth century-style étagère, Queen Anne-style corner cabinet. Taylor. How to build period country furniture. 99–102, 106–09
Organizing space with modular units. Time-Life books. Space and storage. 84–97
Overhead utility rack. Leavy. Bookshelves and storage units. 61
Perforated hardboard wall rack; wall rack for lids. Stevenson. How to build and buy cabinets for the modern kitchen. 111–12
Portable shelving. Leavy. Bookshelves and storage units. 50–51
Post-and-spar lumber rack. Fine woodworking techniques 4. 46
Rattan étagère. Alth. Rattan furniture. 119–31
Shaker shelf. Hagerty. Make your own antiques. 75
Shelf caddy. Kramer. Wirecraft. 100–01
Shelf under the window. Leavy. Bookshelves and storage units. 70–71
Shelf unit. McCall's sewing for your home. 196

Shelf units. Blandford. 66 children's furniture projects. 390–98

Shelves. Cary. Storage: cabinets, closets, and wall systems. 31–40

Shelves. Stiles. Easy-to-make children's furniture. 17–23

Shelves for a window. Family handyman handbook of home improvement and remodeling. 348–51

Shelves for blank walls. Family handyman handbook of home improvement and remodeling. 286–90

Shelves inside walls. Philbin. Cabinets, bookcases & closets. 96–97

Shelving. Blandford. How to make your own built-in furniture. 251–55

Shelving. Hedden. Successful shelves and built-ins. 81–82

Tomato ripening unit. Braren. Homemade. 40–41

Two-leaf swing-out shelves. Cary. Storage: cabinets, closets, and wall systems. 96–100

Vertical pull-out racks. Stevenson. How to build and buy cabinets for the modern kitchen. 150–62

Wall shelves; open mixing center. Stevenson. How to build and buy cabinets for the modern kitchen. 106–10

Wall/shelves, rolling shelves and ball bearing drawers, rolling shelf compartment under stairs, modular bookshelves. Family handyman handbook of carpentry plans/projects. 208–23

Zegel. Shelf book

Shelves and racks. *See also* **Bookcases; Room dividers; Storage in the home**

Shelves, Hanging

Accessory shelf, plant bracket. Doherty. Family Circle book of 429 great gifts-to-make all year round for just 10¢ to $10.00. 6–7

Appliance holder. Blackwell. Johnny Blackwell's poor man's catalog. 123

Beginners wall shelf, corner shelf. Brann. How to build colonial furniture. 244–50

Building a space saving knick-knack shelf. Clifford. Basic woodworking & carpentry . . . with projects. 197–99

Candle shelf, small hanging shelf, hanging shelves. Moser. How to build shaker furniture. 98–101

Chip-carved kitchen shelf. Casselman. Crafts from around the world. 60–66

Colonial bell shelf. Popular Mechancis do-it-yourself encyclopedia. Vol. 9, 1357

Colonial open cripboard. Platt. Step-by-step woodcraft. 26–27

Corner shelf unit. Mills. Book of presents. 132–33

Corner shelves, kitchen shelves, shelf with cabinet. Blandford. 53 space-saving built-in furniture projects. 163–67, 238–43, 285–87

Hanging canvas shelves. Favorite easy-to-make toys. 230–31

Hanging shelves. Brown. 44 terrific woodworking plans & projects. 161–63

Hanging shelves. Holland. Weaving primer. 48–49

Hanging shelves, display wall rack, Shaker shelves, hutch shelves, small shelves, shelf and clothing rack. Blandford. How to make early American and colonial furniture. 117, 120–38

Hanging shelves with ropes or chains. Zegel. Shelf book. 43–47

Hanging storage rack. 101 do-it-yourself projects. 156–57

Little shelf. Zegel. Fast furniture. 110

"Marbleized" shelf. Shea. Pennsylvania Dutch and their furniture. 181

Mirror-back wall shelf. Complete handyman do-it-yourself encyclopedia. Vol. 16, 2365–67

Painted wall shelf. Popular Mechanics do-it-yourself encyclopedia. Vol. 8, 1175–76

Plexiglas shelf and hanger. Popular Mechanics do-it-yourself encyclopedia. Vol. 14, 2212–13

Simple wall-supported items, advanced wall-supported items. Blandford. 53 space-saving built-in furniture projects. 89–161

Small wall cabinet and cupboard. Gottshall. Provincial furniture design and construction. 7–14

Tavern wall rack. Daniele. Building early American furniture. 73–74

Wall-hung storage/study unit. Better Homes and Gardens step-by-step cabinets and shelves. 82–83

Shingles

Applying shingles and shakes to roofs and walls. Spence. General carpentry. 279–84, 342–44

Shingles-finishing techniques. Scherer. Complete handbook of home painting. 145–50

Ship models (in bottles)

Ship in a bottle. Bumper book of things a boy can make. 15–19

Ships, Toy. See **Boats, Toy**

Shirts

Applique T-shirts; batik shirts, xerox transfer on shirt. Linsley. Custom made. 15–21, 140–45, 146–48

Batik shirt. Tie-dye, batik and candlemaking step-by-step. 20–21

Boy's dress shirt. Benton. Sewing classic clothes for children. 154–57

Burns. Shirt look.

Country shirt. Bradley. Design it, sew it and wear it. 16–33

Dashiki, a traditional African shirt. Schuman. Art from many hands. 21–23, 148–49

Jerseys (alterations & remodeling). Brock. Gladrags: redesigning, remaking, refitting all your old clothes. 90–109

Kangaroo shirt for a man or woman. Lane. Maggie Lane's oriental patchwork. 83–86

Man's dressy denim shirt. Doherty. Family Circle book of 429 great gifts-to-make all year round for just 10¢ to $10.00. 104–05

Nantucket whaling shirt embroidery. Wilson. More needleplay. 150–51

Pattern for apple applique shirt. Fraser. Modern stitchery: stitches, patterns, free-form designing. 80–82

Photographic color transfers from rubbings for making a T-shirt. Firestein. Rubbing craft. 77

Plains Indian war shirt, man's shirt. Scurlock. Muzzleloader Magazine's book of buckskinning II. 35–37, 78–79

Platt. T-shirting.

Seminole patchwork shirts. Laury. Quilted clothing. 96, 100

Seminole shirt. Johnson. Quiltwear. 101–06

Shirt (men's). Gehret. Rural Pennsylvania clothing. 98–124

Spider shirt. Morgan. Trapunto and other forms of raised quilting. 171

T-shirts and sweatshirts. Hagans. All good gifts. 72–74

Tie-dyed African shirt. Frame. Tie-dyeing and batik. 26–29

Tie-dyed T-shirt. Frame. Tie-dyeing and batik. 54–55

Tie-dyed T-shirt. Tie-dye, batik and candlemaking step-by-step. 8–9

Torbet. T-shirt book

Shirts, Children

Baby undershirts, decorated and dyed. Linsley. Great bazaar. 44–46

Carrot T-shirt. Creative sewing. 103

Shoe polishing equipment

Pine footstool with lift-out tray. Woman's Day book of gifts to make. 207–09

Shoeshine box. Oberrecht. Plywood projects illustrated. 238–40

Shoeshine box with drawer. Doherty. Family Circle book of 429 great gifts-to-make all year round for just 10¢ to $10.00. 130

Shoe racks
Roll-out shoe drawer. Popular Mechanics do-it-yourself encyclopedia. Vol. 17, 2651
Shoe caddy. Roda. Fabric decorating for the home. 140–41
Shoe rack. Blandford. 66 children's furniture projects. 102–04
Shoe rack. Dal Fabbro. How to make children's furniture and play equipment. 74

Shoes
Bootjack. Braren. Homemade. 48
Boots. Clark. The make-it-yourself shoe book. 77–83
Chamois light fantastics (ballet slippers). Evrard. Twinkletoes. 44–48
Fur mukluks. Evrard. Twinkletoes. 68–71
Grass roots tennis shoes. Sheldon. Washable and dryable needlepoint. 94–95
Hoot mon boots (fabric). Evrard. Twinkletoes. 34–39
Lincoln's bootjack. Popular Mechanics do-it-yourself encyclopedia. Vol. 5, 655
Mukluks. Wilder. Secrets of Eskimo skin sewing. 71–83
Shoes. Clark. Make-it-yourself shoe book. 57–76
Shoes. Gehret. Rural Pennsylvania clothing. 209–15
Sweater knit boot toppers. Brown. Super sweater idea book. 187–88

Shoes. See also **Moccasins; Sandals; Slippers**

Shoes, Children
Children's rain boots (painted). Katz. Footwear. 102
Clown sneaker (painted). Katz. Footwear. 104
Space boot. Katz. Footwear. 66–68
Three pairs of woven boots. Katz. Footwear. 68–73

Shoes, Infants
Infant deerskin booties. Katz. Footwear. 93–94
Moccasin booties (knit). Katz. Footwear. 88
Rabbit booties (knit). Katz. Footwear. 90
Three pairs of baby shoes. Katz. Footwear. 58–59

Shoes, Women
Colored (white) espadrilles (painted). Katz. Footwear. 104
Dressed-up leather clogs (painted). Katz. Footwear. 102
Espadrilles with French knots, paillettes, & appliqued. Woman's Day book of gifts to
    make. 95–96
Leather clogs. Katz. Footwear. 91–92
Mary Janes with rosette (knit). Katz. Footwear. 87
Needlepoint sneakers. Katz. Footwear. 77
Old-fashioned spats (crocheted). Katz. Footwear. 79
Platform shoe remakes. Katz. Footwear. 107
Rainbow espadrille (knit). Katz. Footwear. 86–87
Rainbow sneakers. Woman's Day crochet showcase. 99–100
Sheepskin clogs. Katz. Footwear. 92–93
Stenciled wooden clogs. Katz. Footwear. 102
Tall moccasin boots. Katz. Footwear. 97–100
Three sneaker remakes (crocheted). Katz. Footwear. 84–85
Uppers for fantasy disco shoe (knit). Katz. Footwear. 86

Shoes, Wooden
Dutch tulip kloppers. Evard. Twinkletoes. 78–80

Shopping bags. See **Bags**

Shorts
Boy's shorts. Complete book of baby crafts. 112–14
French shorts and top (knitted). Creative crafts yearbook: an exciting new collection of
 needlework and crafts. 29–30
Hiking shorts. Lamoreaux. Outdoor gear you can make yourself. 94–95
How to make shorts. Guth. Sewing with scraps. 117–19
Summer playsuit. Jacobs. Crochet book. 143–45
Three-color fringed shorts. Torbet. Macrame you can wear. 70

Show cases. *See* **Display racks**

Shower baths
Goldfish shower curtain. Foose. Scrap saver's stitchery book. 58–63
Solar shower. Calhoun. 20 simple solar projects. 138–51

Shower caps
Shower cap. Fairfield. Patchwork. 37

Shower curtains
Applique shower curtain. Giant book of crafts. 12–13
Appliqued nautical shower curtain. Roda. Fabric decorating for the home. 202–03
Floor-length shower curtain with loops. Roda. Fabric decorating for the home. 188–89
Floor-length shower curtains with shirred tiebacks. Roda. Fabric decorating for the
 home. 210–11
Ruffled shower curtain and valance. Roda. Fabric decorating for the home. 194–95
Shirred floor-length shower curtains with tiebacks. Roda. Fabric decorating for the
 home. 180–81
Shower curtains and liners. Better Homes and Gardens sewing for your home. 166–68

Shower decorations
Bridal and baby shower decorations. Berry. How to make party and holiday decora-
 tions. 123–28, 134–141
Reader's Digest shower umbrella. Epple. Something from nothing crafts. 62–63
Shower mobile. Janitch. Candlemaking and decorations. 49–52
Whimsical ornaments for baby shower. Wargo. Soft crafts for special occasions. 36–
 39

Shutters
Jute-strung shutterettes. Woman's Day decorative needlework for the home. 111–12

Sidewalks
Forming sidewalks and drives. Spence. General carpentry. 152–53
Laying a cement sidewalk. Handyman. 261–63
Soft walks. Russell. Walks, walls and fences. 56–58
Stone paving. Nickey. Stoneworker's bible. 153–65
Walk patterns, finishes & edgings. Russell, Walks, walls and fences. 32–55

Sidewalks. *See also* **Garden walks**

Siding (building)
All about siding, re-siding. Popular Mechanics do-it-yourself encyclopedia. Vol. 17,
 2680–91
Aluminum and vinyl siding installation and repairs. Alth. Do-it-yourself roofing and siding. 3–121
Aluminum siding cleaner. Popular Mechanics do-it-yourself encyclopedia. Vol. 19,
 2889

Home siding. Clifford. Basic woodworking and carpentry . . . with projects. 183–89
Home siding. Family handyman handbook of carpentry plans/projects. 282–96
Installing siding: wood, hardboard, plywood, metal and plastic. Spence. General carpentry. 327–42
Installing wood siding. Handyman. 244–47
Shingle siding. Olin. Construction 421.1—421.18
Siding. Bragdon. Homeowner's complete manual of repair & improvement. 510–17
Siding: board, plywood, shingles and shakes. Clifford. Basic woodworking & carpentry . . . with projects. 183–89
Siding installation. Geary. Complete handbook of home exterior repair and maintenance. 275–319
Taking care of your siding. Outdoor projects for home and garden. 84–88

Signs
Carved signs. Fine woodworking techniques 5. 172–74
Coat hanger wire sign holder. Kramer. Wirecraft. 58–59
Cross-stitch signs. Doherty. Family Circle book of 429 great gifts-to-make all year round for just 10¢ to $10.00. 131
Custom name plates. Brightman. 101 practical uses for propane torches. 129
Designing wood signs. Speilman. Making wood signs. 19–30
Finishing sign. Spielman. Making wood signs. 116–27
Hand-carved signs. Spielman. Making wood signs. 44–55
Lydecker. Sign carving.
Making large signs. Spielman. Making wood signs. 82–94
Methods of producing signs using foil. Marshall. Foilcraft. 59–61
Name sign. Hamilton. Build it together. 180–87
Needlepoint door signs. Better Homes and Gardens easy bazaar crafts. 14, 20
Open & closed sign. Ambuter. Carolyn Ambuter's needlepoint celebrations. 142–45
Outdoor sign. Platt. Step-by-step woodcraft. 38–43
Painting tavern signs. Howard. New tole & folk art designs. 94–97
Restoring and preserving neon signs. Kangas. By hand. 209–17
Roadside sign. Brann. How to build outdoor projects. 124–35
Routed signs. Spielman. Making wood signs. 56–74
Shop signs. Ambuter. Carolyn Ambuter's needlepoint celebrations. 148–53
Stenciled welcome sign. Evrard. Homespun crafts from scraps. 76–79

Silhouettes
Haitian silhouette designs. Schuman. Art from many hands. 186–89
Portraits from silhouettes. Picturemaking. 10–12
Silhouette. Bumper book of things a girl can make. 101–02
Silhouettes. Kicklighter. Crafts illustrated designs and techniques. 306–11
Silhouettes. McCall's big book of country needlecrafts. 245
Simple paper cut-out silhouettes. Holtje. Cardcraft. 56–62

Silk screen printing
Banzhof. Screen process printing.
Biegeleisen. Silk screen printing.
Ceramic silk screen printing. Conrad. Contemporary ceramic techniques. 117–51
Equipment for screen printing and printing on cloth. Dyeing & printing. 102–32
Flower-stained fabric. Casselman. Crafts from around the world. 87–91
Gardner. Artist's silkscreen manual.
Making a silk screen printer. Kangas. By hand. 94–97
Photographic screen printing. Dyeing & printing. 121–27
Procedure. Andersen. Creative exploration in crafts. 69–81
Rubbings for silkscreen printing. Firestein. Rubbing crafts. 75–76
Screen printing. Kicklighter. Crafts, illustrated designs and techniques. 288–97

Silk/screen. Held. Weaving. 296–98
Silk screen greeting cards. Holtje. Cardcraft. 41–51
Silk screen printing. Bumper book of things a boy can make. 53–58
Silk screen printing. Treasury of things to make. 106–09
Silk screen printing unit. Abrams. Building craft equipment. 164–71
Silk screening. Rose. Illustrated encyclopedia of crafts and how to master them. 136–44
Silk screening and glue chipping. Isenberg. How to work in stained glass. 241–57
Termini. Silkscreening.

Silversmithing
Finegold. Silversmithing.
Making a bowl. Sjoberg. Working with copper, silver and enamel. 37–40
Silversmithing. Kicklighter. Crafts, illustrated designs and techniques. 312–19
Warwick. Beginning jewelry.

Silverware
Forging flatware. Finegold. Silversmithing. 392–401

Sliverware, Storage
Carved chest for flat tableware. Gottshall. Wood carving and whittling for everyone. 66–71
Silverware and napkin caddy, tray for your best silver, colonial cutlery cupboard. Popular Mechanics do-it-yourself encyclopedia Vol. 10, 1594, 1598–600
Silverware camping caddy. Coffey. Francine Coffey's celebrity sewing bee. 99

Skateboards
Skateboard. Cope. Plastics. 67
Skateboards. Gould. Skateboards, scooterboards, and seatboards you can make. 28–31

Skates
How to keep ice skates sharp. Popular Mechanics do-it-yourself encyclopedia. Vol. 10, 1522

Skating clothes
Skate camisole and skirt. Ruggieri. Woman's Day book of no-pattern sewing. 98–99
Skating outfit. Woman's Day crochet showcase. 66–67

Skirts
Armenian skirt. Gostelow. Complete international book of embroidery. 140–41
Banded skirt. Walker. Mosaic knitting. 222–26
Basic basketweave skirt in six colors. Walker. Mosaic knitting. 251–52
Bouquet (hairpin lace skirt). Feldman. Handmade lace and patterns. 121
Breton skirt. Gostelow. Complete international book of embroidery. 98–99
Chevron crocheted skirt. Step by step to better knitting and crochet. 194–95
Chevron outfit. Step by step to better knitting and crochet. 110–12
Chevron-stitch skirt and matching top. Knitting. 91–94
Children's kilt. Benton. Sewing classic clothes for children. 160–66
Child's machine embroidered skirt. Encyclopedia of crafts. 111
Christmas entertaining skirt. Goldman. Decorate with felt. 25
Circular skirt (patchwork). Creative crafts yearbook: an exciting new collection of needlework and crafts. 22
Country girl knitted skirt and shawl. Favorite knitting & crochet patterns. 190–91
Crochet trimmed 8-gore and wrap skirts. Crochet. 31–34
Decorative panel. Slater. Elaine Slater's book of needlepoint projects. 154–56
Diamonds skirt. Scharf. Illustrated patchwork crochet. 163–64

Drafting skirt patterns. Lewis. Patternless fashions. 68–86
Dresses, skirts and tops (quilted). Laury. Quilted clothing. 90–91, 93, 94–95, 112–13
Early American patchwork skirt. Holderness. Peasant chic. 102–07
Elegant "block" skirts. Guth. Sewing with scraps. 27–34
Floor length skirt with applique. Guth. Sewing with scraps. 147–48
Four-gore skirt. Lane. Maggie Lane's oriental patchwork. 48–56
Fringed mohair dress or skirt. Knitting. 46
Fringed skirt, skirt with brushed mohair patterns. Holland. Weaving primer. 84–86, 156–57
Gathered wool and mohair skirt. Probert. Knitting in vogue. 136–37
Girl's classic skirt and top set. Hubert. Weekend knitting projects. 36–37
Girl's top and skirt. Step by step to better knitting and crochet. 96–97
Half-moon wrap skirt or cape, twelve-bandanna skirt. Wiseman. Cuts of cloth. 16–17, 42–43
Handkerchief skirt. Funaro. Yestermorrow clothes book. 48
Heart rimmed bikini and skirt. Knitting. 21–22
Heirloom mosaic skirt. Holderness. Peasant chic. 136–38
Holiday-wrap around skirt. Goldman. Decorate with felt. 39–40
Hooded coat and matching skirt. Knitting. 58
Jupon, Hawaiian applique wrap skirt, yo-yo skirt, appliqued crazy patch skirt. Heard. Complete guide to quilting. 241–248
Lace tablecloth (skirt). Funaro. Yestermorrow clothes book. 50–51
Long life for a short skirt (restyling skirts). Time-Life books. Personal touch. 98–123
Long skirt. Ley. Russian & other Slavic embroidery designs. 46–49
Making a skirt. Scurlock. Muzzleloader Magazine's book of buckskinning II. 62–63
Mother/daughter skirts. Coffey. Francine Coffey's celebrity sewing bee. 72
Moving on to skirts: a sports skirt and a straight skirt. Bradley. Design it, sew it and wear it. 73–91
Original skirts. Zukerman. Get hooked. 66–83
Patchwork party skirt, save and sew wrap-around skirt. Baldwin. Scrap fabric crafts. 123–25, 135–38
Patchwork skirts. Selfridge. Patchwork knitting. 181–85
Peasant-look evening skirt, New York skyline evening skirt, bridge party skirt and patchwork evening skirt. Farlie. Pennywise boutique. 41–57
Petticoat. Gehret. Rural Pennsylvania clothing. 45–49
Poncho-skirt. Henderson. Woman's Day book of designer crochet. 85–87
Print skirt and stole. Creative sewing. 35
Rosette-bordered skirt. Jacobs. Crochet book. 60–63
Ruffled wrap-around skirt. Farlie. Pennywise boutique. 61–63
Sampler skirt. Knitting. 67
Sarong skirt, tailored skirt, quarter circle flare skirt, peasant skirt, cocktail skirt, three panel wrap-around skirt. Beard. Fashions from the loom. 73–78
Seminole patchwork aprons and skirts. Dudley. Strip patchwork: quick and easy patchwork using the Seminole technique. 25–28
Short batik skirt. Anderson. Tie dyeing and batik. 84–87
Short batik skirt. Frame. Tie-dyeing and batik. 122–25
Silk overskirt. Farlie. Pennywise boutique. 43
Skirt alterations. Goldsworthy. Clothes for disabled people. 84–89
Skirt and stole. Holland. Weaving primer. 121
Skirt border. Slater. Elaine Slater's book of needlepoint projects. 165–66
Skirt with patchwork borders. Osler. Machine patchwork. 110–12
Skirt with patchwork trim. Ives. Ideas for patchwork. 63–68
Skirts. Crown. How to recycle old clothes into new fashions. 21–34
Skirts. Holderness. Peasant chic. 90–95
Skirts (alterations & remodeling). Brock. Gladrags: redesigning, remaking, refitting all your old clothes. 151–83

Slit skirt & sweeping skirt. Ruggieri. Woman's Day book of no-pattern sewing. 85–86
Smaland child's skirt and sweater (Sweden). Starmore. Scandinavian knitwear. 53–56
Sun-striped top and skirt. Crochet. 47
Tartan plaid skirt. Knitting. 83
Three more skirts: two circle skirts and a wrap around. Bradley. Design it, sew it and
  wear it. 119–27
Tie-dyed blouse and skirt. Anderson. Tie dyeing and batik. 32–35
Tie-dyed blouse and skirt and summer skirts. Frame. Tie-dyeing and batik. 38–47
Trapunto skirts. Morgan. Trapunto and other forms of raised quilting. 166–69
Twin-pleat skirt. Ruggieri. Woman's Day book of no-pattern sewing. 45
Victorian skirt. Wilson. Needlework to wear. 48–49, 71
Woven skirt for bulky knits. Brown. Super sweater idea book. 166
Young ballerina's ice skating skirt (knit). Feldman. Needlework boutique. 146–47

Skis
Cross-country skis—the easy way and Norwegian style. Fine woodworking techniques
  5. 152–55
How to take care of your skis. Popular Mechanics do-it-yourself encyclopedia. Vol. 17,
  2698–701
Ski bag. Coffey. Francine Coffey's celebrity sewing bee. 105
Ski repair. Schuler. How to fix almost everything. 150

Skittles
Ninepins or skittles using dolls. Tyler. Big book of dolls. 136–39
Skittles. Hagans. All good gifts. 85–86
Table skittles. Blandford. Giant book of wooden toys. 195–99

Skylights
How to install skylights. Windows and skylights. 96–111
Installation of skylights. Family handyman handbook of home improvement and remod-
  eling. 228–34
Jensen. Skylights.
Skylight installation. Brann. How to modernize an attic. 14–23
Skylight installation. Geary. How-to book of floors & ceilings. 152–58
Skylights. Popular Mechanics do-it-yourself encyclopedia. Vol. 10, 1458–61

Slacks
Breeches (men's pants). Gehret. Rural Pennsylvania clothing. 125–53
Broadfall trousers, narrow fall breeches, overalls & trousers, mountain man's trousers,
  breeches. Scurlock. Muzzleloader Magazine's book of buckskinning II. 23–32, 75–
  77
Clever guises for old pants. Time-Life books. Personal touch. 87–97
DeLynn. Secrets of how to: have the latest pant styles.
Drafting pants, slacks and shorts patterns. Lewis. Patternless fashions. 104–11
Indian pants. Lane. Maggie Lane's oriental patchwork. 54–58
Jeans (blue, pink, green or what you will). Corrigan. How to make pants and jeans that
  really fit. 99–131
Jolly juggler motif for overalls. Great cross-stitch. 88–89
Making pants or jeans. Burns. Super sewing. 264–79
Pants (alterations & remodeling). Brock. Gladrags: redesigning, remaking, refitting all
  your old clothes. 184–215
Patchwork pants. Selfridge. Patchwork knitting. 186
Simplest basic pants. Corrigan. How to make pants and jeans that really fit. 37–60
Trouser alterations. Goldsworthy. Clothes for disabled people. 28–36, 80–83
Waistbands and zippers. Corrigan. How to make pants and jeans that really fit. 61–98
Yoga tie pants and leg wraps. Wiseman. Cuts of cloth. 38–41

Slacks, Women
Altering and updating jeans. Funaro. Yestermorrow clothes book. 145–157
Evening trousers. Beard. Fashions from the loom. 79
Pants and their variations. Crown. How to recycle old clothes into new fashions. 35–44
Perfect fit. Corrigan. How to make pants and jeans that really fit. 17–36, 145–55
Pull-on pants. Ruggieri. Woman's Day book of no-pattern sewing. 88
Ribbed knit top and softly draped culottes. Time-Life book. Separates that travel. 126–29
Romaniuk. Pants: how to do your own measuring, pattern drafting, fabric selection cutting and sewing for a perfect fit.
Slacks that fit. Zukerman. Get hooked. 84–94

Sleds
Early sleigh, a Dutch sleigh. Maginley. America in miniatures. 88–93
Farm sled. McRaven. Country blacksmithing. 137
Folk art sled. Hudley. Folk art toys and furniture for children. 87–93
Indian sled. Norbeck. Book of authentic Indian life crafts. 215–16
Making bobsleds. Richardson. Practical blacksmithing. Vol. 4, 182–97
Pony cart and sleigh, dog sled. Churchill. Backyard building book II. 123–28, 136–38
Seal slider. Kinser. Sewing sculpture. 100–03
Sled for draft animals. Langsner. Country woodcraft. 181–88
Tiny tots toter. Blackwell. Johnny Blackwell's poor man's catalog. 138
Wooden sleds. Blandford. Giant book of wooden toys. 263–66

Sleds. *See also* **Toboggans**

Sleeping bags
Appliqued zoo sleeping bag and monkey tote. Better Homes and Gardens applique. 86–87
Appliqued zoo sleeping bag and monkey tote. Better Homes and Gardens treasury of needlecrafts. 156–59
Baby's sleeping bag. Mills. Book of presents. 70–71
Convertible quilt. Reader's Digest complete guide to sewing. 486
Seminole sleeping bag. Fanning. Complete book of machine quilting. 223–27
Sleeping bag. Lamoreaux. Outdoor gear you can make yourself. 138–44
Sleeping bag. Treasury of things to make. 62–63
Toddler's sleeping bag. Laury. Treasury of needlecraft gifts for the new baby. 143–45
Zoo sleeping bag. Better Homes and Gardens treasury of Christmas crafts & foods. 268–69

Slide projectors. *See* **Projection apparatus**

Slides
Indoor-outdoor slide. Dal Fabbro. How to make children's furniture and play equipment. 151–53
Indoor slide. Blandford. Giant book of wooden toys. 276–82
Outdoor slide. Dal Fabbro. How to make children's furniture and play equipment. 182–85
Outdoor slides. Blandford. Giant book of wooden toys. 293–97
Portable cardboard and dowel slide. Boeschen. Successful playhouses. 120
Stilt-house slide. Popular Mechanics do-it-yourself encyclopedia. Vol. 14, 2187

Slides and transparencies
Color slide cards. Holtje. Cardcraft. 126–29

Slingshots
Carved slingshot. Horwitz. Mountain people, mountain crafts, 50–51

Slipcovers
How to make slipcovers. McCall's sewing for your home. 24–33
How to slipcover an early American wing chair. McCall's big book of country needle-
  crafts. 25–28
Quilted chair cover. McNeill. Quilting. 49
Slip covered club chair. Roda. Fabric decorating for the home. 32–36
Slipcovers. Roberts. Illustrated handbook of upholstery. 241–51
Slipcovers. Sara. Sewing made easy. 386–400
Slipcovers for chairs and sofas. Better Homes and Gardens sewing for your home.
  135–47
Stretch-to-fit furniture throws. Brown. Super sweater idea book. 199
Studio couch cover. Roda. Fabric decorating for the home. 154–55

Slippers
Bigfeet (fabric) Evrard. Twinkletoes. 122–23
Booties (insulated). Lamoreaux. Outdoor gear you can make yourself. 105–12
Children's slippers. McCall's big book of knit & crochet for home & family. 129
Cozy slippers: hexagon boot and ribbed slippers. American School of Needlework.
  Great crochet bazaar book. 35–38
Crocheted boots. Time-Life books. Boutique attire. 160–62
Down booties (quilted). Laury. Quilted clothing. 129–31
Embroidered rose slippers. Embroidery of roses. 129
Embroidered Seminole patchwork boots. Laury. Quilted clothing. 144–45
Eskimo slippers. Great cross-stitch. 120–23
Felt slippers. Johnson. Nature crafts. 14
Furry rectangles. Evrard. Twinkletoes. 52–54
Fuzzies (knitted). Evrard. Twinkletoes. 40–43
Granny-square crocheted, fireside, moccasin, knitted bootie, dancer pomponed elf, &
  popcorn slippers. Woman's Day bazaar best sellers. 32–41
Irish fisherman slipper socks (knitted). Evrard. Twinkletoes. 89–93
Knitted lounge slippers. McCall's big book of knit & crochet for home & family. 32
Mule slippers, boat slippers, tasseled slipper boots. Woman's Day creative stitchery
  from scraps. 24–26, 51–54, 99–101
Oriental tote and slipper. Jacobs. Crochet book. 120–22
Persian carpet slippers. Evrard. Twinkletoes. 24–27
Shoes 'n' socks. Knitting techniques and projects. 66–69
Slipper boots. McNeill. Quilting. 65
Slipper socks (knit). Mills. Book of presents. 116–17
Slippers. Henderson. Woman's Day book of designer crochet. 148–51
Slippers from scraps. Crown. How to recycle old clothes into new fashions. 112–13
Slippers (leather and fur). Wilder. Secrets of Eskimo skin sewing. 58–70
Soft slippers (knitted). Rosenthal. Not-so-nimble needlework book. 144
Victorian bootikins (crocheted). Evrard. Twinkletoes. 28–31
Warm winter slippers. Johnson. Quilt-wear. 61–66
Washcloth foot wrappers. Evrard. Twinkletoes. 130–31

Slippers, Children
Child's moccasins. Woman's Day crochet showcase. 125–26
Decorated airline slippers. Katz. Footwear. 105
Furry slipper boots. Creative sewing. 103
Lion scuffies. Evrard. Twinkletoes. 124–26
Silly monster boots. Katz. Footwear. 60–61, 79

Slippers, Men
Buckled crocheted loafers. Doherty. Family Circle book of 429 great gifts-to-make all year round for just 10¢ to $10.00. 116–17
Men's comfy slippers (crocheted). Katz. Footwear. 82–83
Tweedy slippers. Woman's Day crochet showcase. 171–72

Slippers, Women
"Ballet" slippers, popcorn hot socks, loopy foot warmers, big-girl bootees. Woman's Day crochet showcase. 100–03
Beaded slippers. Farlie. Pennywise boutique. 67–68
Bedroom slippers. Burchette. Needlework. 38–41
Black Persian fabric mule. Katz. Footwear. 52–53
Boudoir slipper. Katz. Footwear. 52
Fluffy house slippers. Jacobs. Crochet book. 99–100
Pearl-trimmed lounging slippers. Farlie. Pennywise boutique. 83–84
Put your foot in your mouth. Katz. Footwear. 64–65
Quilted washable house slippers. Katz. Footwear. 54–55
"Sheepskin" slippers. Katz. Footwear. 56–57
Slippers for women. Great granny crochet book. 128
Uppers for boudoir slipper (knit). Katz. Footwear. 87
White Persian fabric mule. Katz. Footwear. 53
Winter booties. Jacobs. Crochet book. 89–91
Woven ribbon carpet slipper. Katz. Footwear. 52

Smocking
Canadian and American smocking. Time-Life books. Decorative techniques. 23–31
Fisher. Craft of smocking.
Machine smocking. Saunders. Speed sewing: 103 sewing machine shortcuts. 130–35
Smocked baby dress. Wilson. More needleplay. 144–47
Smocking. Complete guide to needlework. 86–101
Smocking. Longhurst. Vanishing American needle arts. 93–112
Smocking. Reader's Digest complete guide to needlework. 92–97
Smocking directions. Lewis. Patternless fashions. 205–07
Smocking in a honeycomb design. Time-Life books. Traditional favorites. 46–51
Traditional English smocking. Blandford book of traditional handicrafts. 51–63

Smocks
Adult's smock with patchwork decoration. Ives. Ideas for patchwork. 60–62
Child's painting smock. Evrard. Homespun crafts from scraps. 113–18
Child's smock. Anderson. Tie dyeing and batik. 44–47
Child's smock with patchwork trim. Ives. Ideas for patchwork. 57–59
Dirty-hands smock. Farlie. Pennywise boutique. 66–67
Hausa smock. Gostelow. Complete international book of embroidery. 184–85
Hobby smocks. Mills. Book of presents. 78–80
Old English smock. Wilson. Needlework to wear. 78–81
Palestinian smock. Gostelow. Complete international book of embroidery. 170–71
Smocking. Gostelow. Mary Gostelow's embroidery book. 225–28
Three little smocks (crocheted). Complete book of baby crafts. 60–61

Smokehouses
Smokehouse. Burch. Building small barns, sheds, and shelters. 208–11
Smokehouses. Braren. Homemade. 43

Snack Bars. *See* **Bars (refreshment)**

Snoods
Irish crochet snood. Svinicki. Old-fashioned crochet. 76–77

Snow craft
Snow personalities. Johnson. Nature crafts. 102–04

Snow plows
Hydraulic lift for your tractor. Popular Mechanics do-it-yourself encyclopedia. Vol. 19, 2924–27
Snow thrower purchasing and maintenance. Outdoor projects for home and garden. 206–23
Snowblowers, install a snow-melting system. Popular Mechanics do-it-yourself encyclopedia. Vol. 17, 2712–19
Snowplows. Popular Mechanics do-it-yourself encyclopedia. Vol. 18, 2724–25

Soap
Bramson. Soap.
Clam shell soap dish. Elbert. Shell craft. 46–47
Decorative soap. Linsley. Great bazaar. 42–43
Hand soap. Treasury of things to make. 128–31
Homemade soap. Black. Key to weaving. 631–32
Pressed flower soap. Linsley. Decoupage on glass, wood, metal, rocks, shells, wax, soap, plastic, canvas, ceramic. 101–02
Soap dispenser. Modern general shop. Woodworking. 108
Soap Staffordshire dogs. McCall's book of America's favorite needlework and crafts. 413–14

Sofa beds
Build your own sofa bed. Popular Mechanics do-it-yourself encyclopedia. Vol. 18, 2726–28
Sofa bed. Black and Decker power tool carpentry. 67–70
Sofa bed with built-in storage chest. Leavy. Bookshelves and storage units. 26–27

Sofas
Built in sofa. Built-ins. 84–90
Convertible sofa reupholstery. Torelli. Reupholstering for the home craftsman. 160–65
Couch. Rubin. Mission furniture. 58–60
Couches. Loeb. Leather book. 79–87
Cushioned corner lounge. Popular Mechanics do-it-yourself encyclopedia. Vol. 8, 1176–77
4-by-4 couch. Easy-to-make tables and chairs. 11–12
Frame chair and a sofa. Fine woodworking techniques 4. 153–56
Log couch. Churchill. Big backyard building book. 174–77, 180
Love seat. Alth. Making plastic pipe furniture. 138–49
Oak and leather couch. Easy-to-make tables and chairs. 14–17
Pole furniture, log couch and chair. Churchill. Backyard building book II. 54–60
Rattan love seat. Alth. Rattan furniture. 153–65
Restoring a Chesterfield sofa. Grime. Illustrated guide to furniture repair & restoration. 134–39
Sofa. Zegel. Fast furniture. 48–51
Storage couch. Hedden. Successful shelves and built-ins. 51
Studio couch and chair. Black and Decker power tool carpentry. 71–76
Upholstered Chesterfield. Restoring and reupholstering furniture. 152–63
Vinyl-covered couch, modular couch. 101 do-it-yourself projects. 88–99
Wall-to-wall cushions. Easy-to-make tables and chairs. 8–9

Soft sculpture
Baldwin. Weepeeple
Blind aid for soft toy making. Anderson. Crafts and the disabled. 46–47
Geometric shapes. Hall. Sewing machine craft book. 108–11
Hall. Soft sculpture.
Hands & dolls. Wilson. More needleplay. 142–43
Soft sculpture. Hall. Sewing machine craft book. 104–21
Soft-sculpture jam jars. Better Homes and Gardens Treasury of Christmas Crafts & Foods. 108–109
Stuffed-shirt soft sculptures to sew. Woman's Day decorative needlework for the home. 114–15

Solar energy
Calhoun. 20 simple solar projects
Guide to solar energy. Popular Mechanics do-it-yourself encyclopedia. Vol. 18, 2730–36
Solar collector anyone can build. Popular Mechanics do-it-yourself encyclopedia. Vol. 9, 1440

Solder and soldering
Hard and soft soldering. Newman. Wire art. 97–110
How to solder wiring. Popular Mechanics do-it-yourself encyclopedia. Vol. 18, 2743–45
Jewelry soldering. Chamberlain. Metal jewelry techniques. 64–70
Joining & fastening with solder. Foote. Jewelry making. 42–47
Soft soldering technique. Metal and enamel. 42–48
Soft soldering, tinning. Metalcrafting encyclopedia. 31–34
Soldering. Brightman. 101 practical uses for propane torches. 11–17
Soldering. Finegold. Silversmithing. 64–84
Soldering. Handyman. 360–66
Soldering. Introduction to repairing and restoring. 264–75
Soldering. Powers. Crafting turquoise jewelry. 75–88
Soldering and annealing. Bowie. Jewelry making. 39–48
Soldering and annealing. Richards. Handmade jewelry. 41–44
Soldering and brazing. Blandford. Practical handbook of blacksmithing and metalworking. 361–75
Soldering iron. Modern general shop. Electricity. 113–14
Soldering iron and propane torch. Buckwalter. Homeowner's handbook of power tools. 78–93
Soldering surfaces, hard soldering, soft soldering. Wood. Make your own jewelry. 77–89
Soldering technique. Kangas. By hand. 201–04
Soldering tools. Sprintzen. Jewelry, basic techniques and design. 18–23
Woodgate. Handbook of machine soldering.

Soldiers, Toy
Soft toy soldier dolls. Better Homes and Gardens easy bazaar crafts. 27, 35

Soundproofing
Sound control. Olin. Construction. 106.1–WF106.39
Sound insulation. Adams. Arco's complete woodworking handbook. 586–93
Sound insulation. Spence. General carpentry. 363–65
Soundproofing your home. Bragdon. Homeowner's complete manual of repair & improvement. 162–63

Spark screens. *See* **Fire screens**

Spats
Tassled French gaiters. Evrard. Twinkletoes. 81–85
Yankee doodle half gaiters. Evrard. Twinkletoes. 138–40

Spectacle cases
Bargello eyeglass case and checkbook cover. Christensen. Needlepoint and bargello stitchery. 72
Bargello eyeglass case (needlepoint). Boyles. Needlework gifts for special occasions. 56–57
Bargello initialed eyeglass case. Reader's Digest complete guide to needlework. 186–87
Bargello sunglasses case. Woman's Day book of weekend crafts. 159–61
Double butterfly eyeglass case. Houck. Patchwork pattern book. 24
Embroidered, leather, & needlepoint eyeglass cases. Woman's Day book of gifts to make. 110–11, 148
Eyeglass case. Breckenridge. Lap quilting. 67
Eyeglass case. Christensen. Needlepoint and bargello stitchery. 17–19
Eyeglass case. Christensen. Teach yourself needlepoint. 78–80
Eyeglass case (needlepoint). Christensen. Needlepoint book. 116–117
Eyeglass case with initials. Christensen. Teach yourself needlepoint. 110
Eyeglass cases (quilted). Laury. Quilted clothing. 142–43
Father's glass case (suede). Creative crafts yearbook: an exciting new collection of needlework and crafts. 115
Florentine eyeglasses case. Boyles. Margaret Boyles book of needle art. 26–27
Florentine stitch spectacle case. Encyclopedia of crafts. 60
Giraffe eyeglass case. Arnold. Needlepoint pattern book. 130–31
Glass cases. Burchette. Needlework. 73–74
Glasses case. Wooster. Quiltmaking. 132
Introduction to bargello—introductory material. Cornelius. Teaching needlecraft. 108–10
Knitted eyeglasses cases. Neighbors. Reversible two-color knitting. 157
Needlecase, pincushion and glasses case (needlepoint) Mills. Book of presents. 36–37
Needlepoint eyeglass case on plastic canvas (large size). Rosenthal. Not-so-nimble needlework book. 95–96
Old maid's puzzle eyeglass case. Houck. Patchwork pattern book. 48–49
Outline-quilted glass case and flower-quilted glass case. McCall's big book of needle-crafts. 52–53
Pattern for sunglasses case (embroidered). Fraser. Modern stitchery: stitches, patterns, free-form designing. 93
Quilted eyeglass case. Linsley. Great bazaar. 124
Ribbon eyeglass case. Coffey. Francine Coffey's celebrity sewing bee. 70
Roman stripe three-piece set (needlepoint). Boyles. Needlework gifts for special occasions. 67
Soft eyeglasses case. Woman's Day creative stitchery from scraps. 140–41
Stars and stripes, tulips, cherries, paisley, zebra skin, dog, pink elephant & turtle. Barnes. 120 needlepoint design projects. 22, 53, 90, 146, 158–60
Suede-cloth eyeglass case. Farlie. Pennywise boutique. 186–87
Turkish, Persian & Indian glasses cases. Rogers. Needlepoint designs from Asia. 26–28, 45–48, 93–95
Walking tall. Sheldon. Washable and dryable needlepoint. 114–15
Watermelon eyeglass case. Coffey. Francine Coffey's celebrity sewing bee. 161
Zig zag chain eyeglass case. Orr. Now needlepoint. 188–90

Spice grinders
Nutmeg grinder. Sainsbury. Sainsbury's woodturning projects for dining. 144–48

Spice racks
Bottle rack. Hamilton. Build it together. 106–11
Sliding spice rack. Feirer. Cabinetmaking and millwork. 755–57
Spice box. Marlow. Early American furnituremaker's manual. 13–17
Spice or small-parts rack. Oberrecht. Plywood projects illustrated. 229–31
Spice rack. 101 do-it-yourself projects. 148–49
Spice rack and jars. Mills. Book of presents. 130–31
Spice rack with lots of space. Family handyman handbook of home improvement and remodeling. 13
Two spice racks. Complete handyman do-it-yourself encyclopedia. Vol. 17, 2478–81

Spinning
Chadwick. Craft of hand spinning.
Distaffs. Hochberg. Handspindles. 53–56
Great wheel spinning of wool. Turner. Legacy of the great wheel. 14–65
Hand spinning. Held. Weaving. 247–67
Hand spinning, preparing wool. Chamberlain. Beyond weaving. 30–37
Making your own spindle. Svinicki. Step-by-step spinning and dyeing. 6
Scouring of fibers. Turner. Legacy of the great wheel. 103–06
Simmons. Spinning for softness and speed.
Spindle spinning of wool. Chadwick. Craft of hand spinning. 40–42
Spinning. Seagroatt. Basic textile book. 43–48
Spinning and twisting plies. Meilach. Weaving off-loom. 134–39
Spinning flax, silk, cotton, and other fibers. Turner. Legacy of the great wheel. 82–96
Spinning on a drop spindle, and a supported spindle. Hochberg. Handspindles. 41–47
Spinning on a wheel. Weaving and spinning. 131–34
Spinning on spindles and wheels. Svinicki. Step-by-step spinning and dyeing. 24–36
Spinning on the hand spindle. Crockett. Complete spinning book. 20–39
Spinning on the wheel. Crockett. Complete spinning book. 66–93
Spinning with a spindle. Weaving and spinning. 126–30
Spinning wool. Pittaway. Traditional English country crafts and how to enjoy them to-day. 51–56
Spinning your own yarns. Parker. Creative handweaving. 64–77
Wheel spinning of wool. Chadwick. Craft of hand spinning. 43–59
Wool skeining. Chadwick. Craft of hand spinning. 78–80
Worsted spinning. Teal. Hand woolcombing and spinning. 110–70

Spinning wheels
Building a spinning wheel. Crockett. Complete spinning book. 94–113
Kentucky spinning wheel. Daniele. Building early American furniture. 229–33
Kronenberg. Spinning wheel building and restoration.
Spinning wheels repair. Rodd. Repairing and restoring antique furniture. 147–49
Twisting machines. Teal. Hand woolcombing and spinning. 89–109
Upright spinning wheel. Taylor. How to build period country furniture. 160–65

Spinning wheels, Toy
Spinning wheel. Farlie. All about doll houses. 180–81
Wool wheel. Maginley. America in miniatures. 52–55

Splices. *See* **Knots and splices**

Splint weaving
Ash-splint seat. McCall's big book of country needlecrafts. 29–31
Splint. Bausert. Complete book of cane furniture making. 55–62
Splint, reed, etc., seats. Meyers. Furniture repair and refinishing. 217–21
Splint reseating. Jones. Fixing furniture. 94–98
Splint seats. Kinney. Complete book of furniture repair and refinishing. 197–202
Weaving a splint seat for a chair. Golden book of colonial crafts. 140–43
Weaving with splints. Time-Life books. Repairing furniture. 68–69
Wood split chair seats. Roberts. Illustrated handbook of upholstery. 304–14

Spoon racks
Pewter shop spoon rack. Daniele. Building early American furniture. 75–76
Spoon rack. Blandford. 53 space-saving built-in furniture projects. 109, 111, 114–15
Spoon rack. Brown. 44 terrific woodworking plans & projects. 139–41
Spoon rack. Capotosto. Woodworking techniques and projects. 85–88
Spoon rack. Marlow. Early American furnituremaker's manual. 23–29
Spoon rack. Modern general shop. Woodworking. 99
Wall boxes and spoon rack. Shea. Pennsylvania Dutch and their furniture. 189
Wooden spoon box. Mills. Book of presents. 130
Wooden wall spoon holders. Casselman. Crafts from around the world. 69–71

Spoons
Forging a punch bowl ladle. Finegold. Silversmithing. 402–14
Horn spoons. Scurlock. Muzzleloader Magazine's book of buckskinning II. 210
Love spoons in a variety of woods. Sainsbury. Woodworking projects with power tools.
    51–54
Pottery dipper. Campbell. Using the potter's wheel. 39
Spoon making. Langsner. Country woodcraft. 241–50
Turning a spoon. Sainsbury. Craft of woodturning. 148–51
Two acrylic scoops. Cope. Plastics. 22–23

Spraying apparatus
Spray booth. Abrams. Building craft equipment. 44–48

Springs
Spring repair. Kinney. Complete book of furniture repair and refinishing. 208–16

Sprinklers
Automatic lawn sprinkler installation. Outdoor projects for home and garden. 226–32
Repairing and installing underground sprinkling systems. Nunn. Home improvement,
    home repair. 214–15
Sprinkler repair. Outdoor projects for home and garden. 203

Spurs
Spur straps. Latham. Leathercraft. 92–94

Stabiles
Metal foil stabiles. Metalcrafting encyclopedia. 159

Stained glass
Challenging projects in stained glass.
Duncan. Leaded glass.
Isenberg. Crafting in glass.
Isenberg. How to work in stained glass.
Laminated stained glass panel in light box. Wood. Working with stained glass. 88–94

Leading stained glass, fusing glass, molding glass, Rose. Illustrated encyclopedia of crafts and how to master them. 241–54
Paper stained glass. Stephan. Creating with tissue paper. 222–29
Plans for a stained glass workstall and light box. Geary. How to design and build your own workspace—with plans. 192–96
Repair. Walke. All about stained glass. 232–43
Sibbett. Art nouveau stained glass pattern book.
Stained glass. Kicklighter. Crafts, illustrated designs and techniques. 320–31
Stained glass butterfly. Wood. Working with stained glass. 28–31
Stained-glass candle sculpture. Better Homes and Gardens treasury of Christmas crafts & foods. 323
Stained glass for jewelry. Sommer. Contemporary costume jewelry. 98–100
Stained glass hanging ornament. Wood. Working with stained glass. 26–27
Stained glass procedure. Andersen. Creative exploration in crafts. 223–50
Stained glass projects using liquid lead and glass stains applied with eyedroppers, art of real stained glass. Popular Mechanics do-it-yourself encyclopedia. Vol. 18, 2759–69
Walke. All about stained glass.
Window garden. Vanderbilt. Gloria Vanderbilt designs for your home. 179
Window medallion, lampshades, mobiles. Giant book of crafts. 215–29

Stained glass windows

Leaded lights. Duthie. Decorative glass processes. 30–72
Leaded window. Challenging projects in stained glass. 149–57
Rubbings for stained glass repair. Firestein. Rubbing craft. 87–89
Seashells and stained glass. Johnson. Nature crafts. 34–35
Stained glass. Duthie. Decorative glass processes. 73–126
Traditional leading: making a window. Isenberg. How to work in stained glass. 169–85
Working with glass. Rowland. Handcrafted doors & windows. 133–41

Stairs

Build steps. Brann. How to build patios and sundecks. 56–62
Building simple basement stairs. Time-Life books. Floors and stairways. 84–87
Building stairs. Day. How to build patios and decks. 133–42
Building stairs. Fine woodworking techniques 5. 192–99
Building stairways. Handyman. 470–74
Building stone steps. Proulx. Plan and make your own fences and gates, walkways, walls and drives. 117–19
Building the stairs. Russell. Garages and carports. 120–23
Circular stairways. Fine woodworking techniques 3. 216–20
Constructing railroad tie steps. Proulx. Plan and make your own fences and gates, walkways, walls and drives. 162
Construction of stairs. Adams. Arco's complete woodworking handbook. 437–49
Framing stairs. Syvanen. Interior finish: more tricks of the trade. 77–89
Garden steps. Kramer. Outdoor garden build-it book. 126–31
Garden steps: wooden, concrete, brick, railroad tie and log. Russell. Walks, walls, and fences. 62–67
Glorifying basement stairs. Family handyman handbook of home improvement and remodeling. 140–43
Glorifying basement stairs, porch steps. Family handyman handbook of carpentry plans/projects. 273–81
How to build a stairway. Brann. How to modernize an attic. 45–57
How to lay out and build stairs, how to build brick and masonry steps. Popular Mechanics do-it-yourself encyclopedia. Vol. 18, 2776–79, 2790–92
Install a stairwell to your basement. Popular Mechanics do-it-yourself encyclopedia. Vol. 2, 206–09

Installing a disappearing stair. Time-Life books. Floors and stairways. 80–81
Installing a spiral stairway. Time-Life books. Floors and stairways. 81–84
Masonry stoop and stairs. Outdoor projects for home and garden. 314–20
Opening a floor for a new stairway. Time-Life books. Floors and stairways. 76–79
Prefab stair and railing installation. Time-Life books. Floors and stairways. 88–95
Railroad tie and log steps. Russell. Walks, walls and fences. 65–66
Repairing stairs, squeaks, balustrades, and retreading. Time-Life books. Floors and
    stairways. 68–75
Spiral stairs. Spence. General carpentry. 446–47
Spiral steps. Fine woodworking techniques I. 120–21
Stair layout and installation. Spence. General carpentry. 428–48
Stair repairs. Nunn. Home improvement, home repair. 60–62, 205–06
Stairs. Balzinski. House construction. 188–91
Stairs for porches and terraces. Harmon. Porches & terraces. 85–88
Stairways and stair parts. Lewis. Cabinetmaking, patternmaking, and millwork. 417–26
Stairways and steps. Clifford. Basic woodworking and carpentry . . . with projects.
    166–71
Steps for flat and sloped sites. Porches and patios. 74–77
Stone steps. Nickey. Stoneworker's bible. 167–69
Tie garden steps, brick-and-wood steps, concrete steps. 101 do-it-yourself projects.
    264–65, 317–22

Stands
Candle stand. Marlow. Early American furnituremaker's manual. 30–36
Candle stand. Underhill. Woodwright's companion. 107–17
Colonial bookstand. Popular Mechanics do-it-yourself encyclopedia. Vol. 3, 415
Flower stand. Alth. Making plastic pipe furniture. 93–96
Hi-lo jack stand, hi-lo jack stand lamp, hi-lo jack stand floor lamp. Daniele. Building
    early American furniture. 136–41
Large round stand, small round stand, music stand. Moser. How to build Shaker furni-
    ture. 110–11
Madonna's lectern. Ball. Master pieces. 116–23
Music, lamp, shaving, tabouret. Rubin. Mission furniture. 100–01, 104, 114–15, 120
Music stand. Fine woodworking techniques 5. 146
Portable lectern. Giant book of metalworking projects. 197–98
Shaker candlestand. 77 furniture projects you can build. 145–48
Smoking stands, dictionary stand. Williams. Spanish colonial furniture. 18–19, 70–71,
    90–93
Teakettle stand. Osburn. Measured drawings of early American furniture. 30–31
Tilt-top and candle tables, hexagonal candle stand, simple round candle table and
    other candle tables, jack stand. Blandford. How to make early American & colonial
    furniture. 250–68, 283–87
Turned candle stand. Shea. Pennsylvania Dutch and their furniture. 186
Washstand with Pennsylvania Dutch designs. Midkiff. Complete book of stenciling.
    44–46
Wayside stand. Hagerty. Make your own antiques. 80–81
Whipple house washstand; elder's candle stand; retiring room stand; "sisters" work
    stand; brethren's wash stand. Daniele. Building early American furniture. 96–97,
    184–85, 186–87, 194–97, 202–03

Stars
Glitter and fabric stars. Better Homes and Gardens treasury of Christmas crafts &
    foods. 345
Large lacy star. Hibbs. Straw sculpture. 28–29
Star. Hall. Sewing machine craft book. 107

Star of David. Hibbs. Straw sculpture. 32
Star plaque. Parker. Beginner's book of off-loom weaving. 199–203
Stars including metal foil. Christmas crafts book. 36–43
Stuffed stars, eight-point needlepoint stars, Mexican clothespin stars and cross-stitch stars. Linsley. Lesley Linsley's Christmas ornaments and stockings. 27–34, 49–50, 108–11, 126–128

Stationery
All-season stationery. Perry. Holiday magic. 173–74
Decorating stationery with leaf rubbings. Burch. Making leaf rubbings. 38–39
Dried flower note. O'Neill. Make-it-merry Christmas book. 40–43
Envelopes. Holtje. Cardcraft. 11
Fabric-covered writing pad. Vanderbilt. Gloria Vanderbilt designs for your home. 110–11
Making personal notepapers. Holtje. Cardcraft. 157–60
Memo pad and writing paper holders. Elbert. Paperworks. 140–44
Natural notes. Linsley. Great bazaar. 60–61
Note paper and envelopes. Parry. Stenciling. 108–10
Oshibana and plants in "parchment," sakuragami or single ply tissue over waxed paper. Geary. Plant prints and collages. 72–77
Presstype stationery. Linsley. Custom made. 115–21
Seaweed notepaper. Meras. Vacation crafts. 98–99
Stencil designs on stationery and cards. Buxton. Craftmaking: for love or money. 68–76

Stationery holders
Cherry blossom flower child cross-stitch stationery portfolio. Gault. Needlework dragons and other mythical creatures. 64–68
Letter holder. Burchette. More needlework blocking and finishing. 95–97
Letter holder. Goldman. Decorate with felt. 97
Letter tray. Dal Fabbro. How to make children's furniture and play equipment. 87
Paper portfolios. Vanderbilt. Gloria Vanderbilt designs for your home. 186–187
Personalized stationery case. Fanning. Complete book of machine quilting. 204–07
Ribbon envelope, leather folder. DeLeon. Basketry book. 87–89

Statues
Casting lead statuary. Marshall. Foilcraft. 125

Stencil work
Basket and lotus stenciled floors, stenciled bouquet, stenciled floor pattern, bear paw stenciled floorcloth. McCall's big book of country needlecrafts. 48–50, 53–54, 91–92, 179–80
Cutting simple stencils. Paper. 23–26
Designing with bought stencils. Dyeing & printing. 70–73
Designs. Parry. Stenciling. 111–34
Homemade stencils. Dyeing & printing. 74–77
Parry. Stenciling.
Rubbing for stencils. Firestein. Rubbing craft. 74
Stencil techniques. Jarnow. (Re)do it yourself. 69–84
Stenciled dresser. Linsley. Fabulous furniture decorations. 17–26
Stenciling. Buxton. Craftmaking: for love or money. 51–67
Stenciling. Higgins. Common-sense guide to refinishing antiques. 134–36, 139
Stenciling. Howell-Koehler. Step-by-step furniture refinishing. 71–72
Stenciling. Johnson. How to restore, repair, and finish almost anything. 97–98
Stenciling. Kangas. By hand. 97–100

Stenciling. Oughton. Complete manual of wood finishing. 206–17
Stenciling paper. Elbert. Paperworks. 29–36
Stenciling walls. Family handyman handbook of home improvement and remodeling. 269–73
Stencils. Meyers. Furniture repair and refinishing. 194–95

Stepladders. *See* **Ladders**

Steps. *See* **Stairs**

Stilts
Aluminum/wood stilts. Giant book of metalworking projects. 197–200
Child's stilts. Mills. Book of presents. 137
Making a pair of stilts. Bumper book of things a boy can make. 73–74
Stilts. Blandford. Giant book of wooden toys. 260–63
Stilts. Popular Mechanics do-it-yourself encyclopedia. Vol. 14, 2199

Stockings
Child and adult hat, mitten and socks spiral knit set. Knitting. 123
Crochet socks. Walters. Crochet. 49
Executive socks. Feldman. Needlework boutique. 83–85
Heelless socks (knitted). Goldsworthy. Clothes for disabled people. 103–04
Hosiery case, needlepoint. Giant book of crafts. 88–89
Japanese tobis. Evrard. Twinkletoes. 64–67
Knitted ski socks. Woman's Day book of gifts to make. 47
Knitted sport socks. Reader's Digest complete guide to needlework. 252
Patterned socks from Scotland. Compton. Complete book of traditional knitting. 183–85
Penny loafers on bobby socks (painted). Katz. Footwear. 101
Socks with French heels & argyle socks. McCall's big book of knit & crochet for home & family. 85–87
Stockings (knit). Gehret. Rural Pennsylvania clothing. 222–37
Tabi socks (knit). Katz. Footwear. 88–89
Tabi socks (knitted—one toe). Time-Life books. Boutique attire. 162–63
Tri-color cable slipper sock (knit). Katz. Footwear. 89
Trio of sporty socks (knits). Time-Life books. Decorative techniques. 140–49
Tube socks. Selfridge. Patchwork knitting. 153

Stockings, Children
Ankle socks—decoration. Linsley. Great bazaar. 37–39
Four pair of embroidered socks. Katz. Footwear. 74–75

Stoles
Crocheted fringed stole. Woman's Day bazaar best sellers. 45
Crocheted stole. Svinicki. Step-by-step spinning and dyeing. 58
Herringbone stole. Brown. Weaving, spinning, and dyeing book. 169
Lace stole from Estonia. Compton. Complete book of traditional knitting. 163–65
Mohair and knitted worsted stole. Swanson. Rigid heddle weaving. 124–28
Mosaic-patterned stole. Walker. Mosiac knitting. 191–92
Reversible double knit ruana. Knitting. 70
Ruffled eyelet stole. Farlie. Pennywise boutique. 57
Shaped granny stole. Great granny crochet book. 124–25
Warp-face Ikat stole. Brown. Weaving, spinning, and dyeing book. 76–77
Woman's mohair stole. Hubert. Weekend knitting projects. 8–9

Stone
Carving stone. Tangerman. Carving the unusual. 104
Making artificial stone. Nickey. Stoneworker's bible. 57–62
Repair and care of stone. Johnson. How to restore, repair, and finish almost everything. 156–65

Stone carving tools
Tools. Weygers. Modern blacksmith. 46, 70–71

Stone construction
Arch construction. Nickey. Stoneworker's bible. 125–48
Building a stone retaining wall, country dry wall, flagstone walk or patio. Bragdon. Homeowner's complete manual of repair & improvement. 552–56
How to apply artificial stone. Nunn. Home paint book. 93–94
Make your own "cut stones" for wall decorations. Family handyman handbook of home improvement and remodeling. 278–86
Mortar for stone. Nickey. Stoneworker's bible. 73–80
Paving with slate flagstone. Family handyman handbook of home improvement and remodeling. 452–55
Stone trim on a house. Nickey. Stoneworker's bible. 168–70

Stone polishing. *See* **Lapidary work; Polishing and tumbling**

Stone, Painted
Day. Complete book of rock crafting.
Love stones. Linsley. Decoupage on glass, wood, metal, rocks, shells, wax, soap, plastic, canvas, ceramic. 131–33
Painted stone turtles. Woman's Day book of weekend crafts. 50–51
Painted stones. Mills. Books of presents. 90–91
Rock animal characters: fish, ladybug, owl, chicks, snail, worm, whale, dog, giraffe, cat, penguin, duck, hedgehog, alligator. Vane. Pebble people, pets & things. 33–44, 98–128, 138–45, 148–52
Rock people, basic pebble person, witch, little girl, man, old lady, monk, happy reveller, caveman, farmer, baseball player, accountant, pugilist, clown, doorman. Vane. Pebble people, pets & things. 46–88, 155–56
Rocks come to life. Yoder. Sculpture and modeling for the elementary school. 220–21

Stools
Barrel stool. Palmer. Making children's furniture and play structures. 17
Block stools, joined stool. Hagerty. Make your own antiques. 76–77, 88–89
Brazed stool. Make it! Don't buy it. 300–05
Cane a square stool. Gault. Crafts for the disabled. 86–92
Children's stools. Blandford. 66 children's furniture projects. 85–87
Cleaning stool. Feirer. Cabinetmaking and millwork. 207–08
Corded stool seat. Anderson. Crafts and the disabled. 58–61
Cricket stool. Linsley. Great bazaar. 57–59
Cricket, tabouret. Blandford. How to make early American and colonial furniture. 111, 114–21
Double- or triple-wall stool. Palmer. Making children's furniture and play structures. 18
Fanciful stool. Linsley. Fabulous furniture decorations. 144–50
Fifteenth century oak stool. Taylor. How to build period country furniture. 122–25
Folding corner stool. Dal Fabbro. How to make children's furniture and play equipment. 62
Indoor/outdoor stool, living room stool. Waugh. Handyman's encyclopedia. 402–04, 406–07
Kitchen or bar stool. 101 do-it-yourself projects. 218–19

Kitchen stool (3 legs). Shea. Pennsylvania Dutch and their furniture. 159
Library steps. Fine woodworking techniques 3. 102–04
Liquor carton stool. Palmer. Making children's furniture and play structures. 16
Little stool. Zegel. Fast furniture. 105
Mayflower stool. Daniele. Building early American furniture. 62–63
Metal step stools. Brightman. 101 practical uses for propane torches. 77–80
Milk, bicycle, studio, and bowback stools. Moser. Windsor chairmaking. 75–80
Piano stool. Blandford. 66 children's furniture projects. 193–98
Primitive camp stool. Scurlock. Muzzleloader Magazine's book of buckskinning II. 197
Rush-style stool seat. Casselman. Crafts from around the world. 170–71
Rustic slab stool. Popular Mechanics do-it-yourself encyclopedia. Vol. 18, 2793
Simple stool. Brown. 44 terrific woodworking plans & projects. 190–91
Six-part pillow footstool to sew. Woman's Day decorative needlework for the home. 73
Stool. Modern general shop. Woodworking. 100
Stool frame. Blandford. Upholsterer's bible. 429–34
Stool from one board, splayed stool, tenoned stool, peglegged stool. Blandford. How
    to make early American and colonial furniture. 95–110
Sturdy step block. Oberrecht. Plywood projects illustrated. 235–37
Swiss milking stool. Langsner. Country woodcraft. 171–74
Three and four leg stools. Wooldridge. Woodturning techniques. 75–85
3-legged stools. Wood projects for the garden. 72
Tip-proof stool. Dal Fabbro. How to make children's furniture and play equipment. 92
TV stool. Churchill. Backyard building book II. 81–84
Two-stepper, revolving stool, low foot stool, two-slat high stool. Moser. How to build
    Shaker furniture. 96–97, 118–19, 150–53
Woodburned stool. Broadwater. Woodburning: art and craft. 124–26
Young Cicero's stool, proverbial stool. Ball. Master pieces. 10–13, 98–103

Stools, Upholstered
Kitchen stool. Scobey. First easy-to-see needlepoint workbook. 90–93
Piped, buttoned and round stool seats. Blandford. Upholsterer's bible. 114–25

Storage batteries
Solar battery charger. Calhoun. 20 simple solar projects. 244–57

Storage bins. See **Bins**

Storage in the home
All-purpose storage unit. Leavy. Bookshelves and storage units. 36–37
Athletic equipment storage corner. Family handyman handbook of carpentry plans/
    projects. 30–32
Athletic equipment storage corner. Family handyman handbook of home improvement
    and remodeling. 167–70
Attic organizers. Cary. Storage: cabinets, closets, and wall systems. 128–30
Attics and basements. Garage, attic and basement storage. 68–79
Ball and bat rack. Hamilton. Build it together. 16–23
Base box or cube. Philbin. Cabinets, bookcases & closets. 115
Basement organizer. Cary. Storage: cabinets, closets, and wall systems. 121–23
Below stairs storage cabinets. Geary. How to design and build your own workspace—
    with plans. 299–300
Boxes and cubes. Geary. How to design and build your own workspace—with plans.
    284–85
Built-in storage closet, built-in storage unit, adaptable storage unit. Kangas. By hand.
    124–26, 136–38, 177–79
Carton combination. Palmer. Making children's furniture and play structures. 50–51
Corner fixtures. Blandford. How to make your own built-in furniture. 280–87

Cube. Adams. Make your own baby furniture. 28–31
Cube. DeCristoforo. Build your own wood toys, gifts and furniture. 375–79
Cubes. Cary. Storage: cabinets, closets, and wall systems. 47–48
Fishing tackle cabinet. Feirer. Cabinetmaking and millwork. 706–10
Freestanding storage wall. Leavy. Bookshelves and storage units. 33–35
Hall stand. Black and Decker power tool carpentry. 46–50
Hideaways for kitchen and laundry. Popular Mechanics do-it-yourself encyclopedia.
   Vol. 13, 1948–49
Hobby corner. Family handyman handbook of carpentry plans/projects. 24–26
Jones. Plan and build more storage space.
Lazy susan. Siegele. Cabinets and built-ins. 97–100
Living centers. Jones. Plan and build more storage space. 136–46, 163–72
Luggage and game tables, summer sports gear, winter sports equipment storage.
   Garage, attic and basement storage. 40–41, 44–47
Modular boxes. Make it! don't buy it. 40–47
Modular cubes. Philbin. Cabinets, bookcases & closets. 134–35
Modular storage cubes. Linsley. Fabulous furniture decorations. 120–27
Plaque with storage jars, canvas catchalls. Woman's Day book of gifts to make. 126–
   28
Portable built-in wall. Leavy. Bookshelves and storage units. 43–45
Roll-out storage bins to fit under the stairs. Time-Life books. Space and storage. 112–
   13
Spencer. Designing and building your own stereo furniture.
Stack of swinging trays. Popular Mechanics do-it-yourself encyclopedia. Vol. 19,
   2949–51
Stackable storage boxes, stack-and-bundle boxes. Oberrecht. Plywood projects illus-
   trated. 38–40, 60–62
Stacking boxes. Adams. Make your own baby furniture. 184–87
Stairway storage. Hedden. Successful shelves and built-ins. 48–50
Storage accessories: coat hangers, garment bags, shoe bags. Better Homes and
   Gardens sewing for your home. 170–73
Storage/appliance center. Spence. Woodworking tools, materials, processes. 606
Storage beneath the stairs. Hylton. Hand crafted shelves & cabinets. 174–81
Storage cabinet, chest for stationery or art materials. Dal Fabbro. How to make chil-
   dren's furniture and play equipment. 121–23, 128–30
Storage ideas. Popular Mechanics do-it-yourself encyclopedia. Vol. 18, 2794–808
Sunny coffee-can organizer. Evrard. Homespun crafts from scraps. 140–41
Under eave storage. Leavy. Bookshelves and storage units. 29–32
Under stairs storage. Family handyman handbook of home improvement and remodel-
   ing. 171–74
Utility room plans. Siegele. Cabinets and built-ins. 23–27

Storage walls

Adjustable shelving storage wall. In Feirer. Cabinetmaking and millwork. 652–57
Buffet storage wall, cabinet storage wall. Family handyman handbook of carpentry
   plans/projects. 224–33
Built in entertainment center. Family handyman handbook of carpentry plans/projects.
   33–35
Child's storage wall. Feirer. Cabinetmaking and millwork. 777–80
Custom entertainment center. Better Homes and Gardens step-by-step cabinets and
   shelves. 84–85
Fireplace storage walls. Family handyman handbook of carpentry plans/projects. 56–
   58
Full-function wall. Capotosto. Woodworking techniques and projects. 244–57
Full wall unit, storage in wall. Blandford. 53 space-saving built-in furniture projects.
   173–81

Hobo storage pockets. Linsley. Custom made. 22–23

Instant furniture from kitchen cabinets. Popular Mechanics do-it-yourself encyclopedia. Vol. 4, 484–87

Living room wall storage. Family handyman handbook of home improvement and remodeling. 165–67

One-wall garage-organizer. Cary. Storage: cabinets, closets, and wall systems. 124–27

Storage unit for a folding bed, food storage unit, storage hutch, divider unit desk and storage space, storage wall, free-standing storage wall. Complete handyman do-it-yourself encyclopedia. Vol. 17, 2531–52, 2572–82

Storage wall for a boy's room. Family handyman handbook of carpentry plans/projects. 134–38

Storage walls. Hedden. Successful shelves and built-ins. 45–48

Triple-wall storage unit. Palmer. Making children's furniture and play structures. 52–53

Wall systems. Cary. Storage: cabinets, closets, and wall systems. 65–75

Wall to wall bookcase with drawers. Brann. How to construct built-in and sectional bookcases. 79–95

Wall to wall bookcases. Brann. How to construct built-in and sectional bookcases. 7–26

Wall-to-wall storage. Built-ins. 61–71

Wall units. Blandford. How to make your own built-in furniture. 272–76

Stoves

Camp stove (repair). Schuler. How to fix almost everything. 33

Hood for an oven-over range. Popular Mechanics do-it-yourself encyclopedia. Vol. 13, 2018–19

How to troubleshoot your electric range. Popular Mechanics do-it-yourself encyclopedia. Vol. 15, 2391–96

Recycling old gas stoves. Kangas. By hand. 179–83

Sheet metal stove. Giant book of metalworking projects. 74–77

Stoves, Wood-burning

How to install a wood-burning stove. Popular Mechanics do-it-yourself encyclopedia. Vol. 18, 2812–15

Wood-stove surround. Better Homes and Gardens. Step-by-step masonry & concrete. 86–87

Straw work

Byelorussian straw designs. Schuman. Art from many hands. 79–82

Corn dollies: anchor, Barton turf dolly, cornucopea, Essex, Terret, Goddess Ceres, horseshoe and whip, speyside plyack, straw cockerel, Long Welsh fan in rye, oat chandelier, Okehampton mare, Oxford crown, pomanders, sea horse, straw maiden, straw rattle, Suffolk bell and Yorkshire spirals. Coker. Craft of straw decoration. 56–74

Corn dolls. Hibbs. Straw sculpture. 100–102

Crosses: St. Brigid's oat medallion, processional and three-and-four legged. Coker. Craft of straw decoration. 54–56

Egyptian fertility symbol. Hibbs. Straw sculpture. 98–99

Fringes: Montenegrin, Harnaca, Shropshire, Lancashire and North African. Coker. Craft of straw decoration. 51–54

Harvest crosses: simple woven and tied radial. Coker. Craft of straw decoration. 80–82

Hibbs. Straw sculpture.

Plaits: 4-straw plait north-east-south-west, 4-straw ribbon plait, 7-straw flat plait, 3-straw cat foot, 6-straw round, 8-straw round, group linked and 3-strand hair. Coker. Craft of straw decoration. 46–51

Rick finials: straw birds, animals, crown, and decorated oat star. Coker. Craft of straw decoration. 75–78

Straw: a golden bounty. Johnson. Nature crafts. 92–100

Straw models (wagon and horse). Coker. Craft of straw decoration. 79

Tied straw work: clove hitch knot, Scandinavian angel, tied stars, tied animals, and continental figures. Coker. Craft of straw decoration. 35–45

Traditional corn dollies. Cane, rush and straw. 126–29

Traditional 5-straw spiral weaving. Coker. Craft of straw decoration. 15

Traditional neck and variation, 5-straw flat plait, Welsh border fan, 7-straw round plait, Mordiford, working without a core, lantern and 2-straw plait in three corners. Coker. Craft of straw decoration. 16–31

Straws

Weaving with drinking straws. Rainey. Weaving without a loom. 40–41

Working with paper straws: paper straw mice. Cane, rush and straw. 121–25

String holders

Cord dispenser. Epple. Something from nothing crafts. 169–70

String box and cutter. Bumper book of things a boy can make. 31–33

Cauro. Stringcraft.

Pictures with pins.

Pictures with pins and wire, four-leaf clover, double rosette, fish, boat, butterfly, cat. Metalcrafting encyclopedia. 117–35

Pin and thread pictures. Picturemaking. 60–73

String and yarn design greeting cards. Holtje. Cardcraft. 130–34

String art. Kicklighter. Crafts, illustrated designs and techniques. 332–45

String art designs. 44 string and nail art projects. 7–90

String designs. Mobiles, earrings. Giant book of crafts. 158–72

String picture or parabola. Lyon. Arts and crafts objects children can make for the home. 140–43

String things (containers). Mills. Book of presents. 56

Stucco

Applying stucco. Better Homes and Gardens. Step-by-step masonry & concrete. 68–69

Repairing stucco. Bragdon. Homeowner's complete manual of repair & improvement. 514

Stucco. Olin. Construction. 425.1–425.20

Stucco wall finish. Spence. General carpentry. 344–45

Stuffed toys. *See* **Cloth toys; Dolls, Rag**

Styrofoam

Foam forms. Kicklighter. Crafts, illustrated designs and techniques. 112–17

Suits

Blue denim suit with leather overlays. Loeb. Leather book. 151–83

Drafting suit patterns. Lewis. Patternless fashions. 146–56

Her cardigan and pull-on skirt, his cardigan and shorts. Woman's Day crochet showcase. 115–17

White studded suit. Loeb. Leather book. 219–35

Suits, Boys

Boy's velvet suit and dress shirt. Benton. Sewing classic clothes for children. 146–57

Middy. Benton. Sewing classic clothes for children. 167–73

Suits, Children
Arctic child's two-piece suit (Lapland). Starmore. Scandinavian knitwear. 44–47
Astrakan child's all-in-one-suit (Finland). Starmore. Scandinavian knitwear. 120–23
Selbu child's pants and sweater (Norway). Starmore. Scandinavian Knitwear. 21–24

Suits, Women
Chanel suit. Crochet. 43
Chic city suit (knitted). Favorite knitting & crochet patterns. 192–94
Crocheted Victorian underwear, capelet, and skirt. Design crochet. 124–26, 172–78
Donegal tweed suit, jacket and skirt set. Design crochet. 13–17, 53–57
Five that mix and match (jacket, skirt, scarf, pants, sunsuits). Time-Life books. Separates that travel. 102–19
Go-everywhere suit. Ruggieri. Woman's Day book of no-pattern sewing. 33–35
Jacket and suit woven in twill weave or shepard's check. Tod. Joy of hand weaving. 304–06
Totally reversible look for traveling. (Tunic top, shawl, wrap coat, bag, hat—knit and crocheted.) Time-Life books. Separates that travel. 156–65
Tweed costume, embroidered suit. Woman's Day crochet showcase. 58–63
Winter sweater, skirt and hat ensemble. Jacobs. Crochet book. 112–15

Summer houses
Securing the summer home. Outdoor projects for home and garden. 34–38

Summer houses. See also **Garden houses, shelters, etc.**

Sump pumps. See **Pumps**

Sunbursts
Embroidered sun in a hoop. Rosenthal. Not-so-nimble needlework book. 53–54
Making clay suns. Schuman. Art from many hands. 161–63
Papier-mâché sun face. Casselman. Crafts from around the world. 167–69
Small, large and tailored sunbursts (tin can). Metalcrafting encyclopedia. 82–87
Smiling sun. Jarvey. You can dough it! 18–21
Sunbursts (metal foil). Metalcrafting encyclopedia. 144–45
Window sunburst. Jacobs. Crochet book. 55–58
Wooden sunburst plaque. McCall's book of America's favorite needlework and crafts. 401–02

Sundials
Build a polar sundial. Popular Mechanics do-it-yourself encyclopedia. Vol. 18, 2826–27
Slate sundial, equatorial sundial. Calhoun. 20 simple solar projects. 12–35
Spot dialling. Pittaway. Traditional English country crafts and how to enjoy them today. 92–93
Stoneman. Easy-to-make wooden sundials.
Sundials. Villiard. Art and craft of sand casting. 103–04
Sundials. Whatnot. 217–22

Surfboards
Buck board; motorized surfboard. Complete do-it-yourself encyclopedia. 294–298, 2210–17

Suspenders
Suspenders. Torbet. Macrame you can wear. 74–75

Sweaters
Angora classics, boucle for two, ski slope sweaters, Guernsey getaways & seaside specials. Favorite knitting & crochet patterns. 214–30
Aran sweaters. Morgan. Traditional knitting patterns of Ireland, Scotland and England. 60–74
Basic pullover instructions. Design crochet. 90–92
Basic T-shaped designs, T-shaped pullovers for all the family. Step by step to better knitting and crochet. 61–65, 81–82
Cardigan with beaded front. Hulbert. Creative beadwork. 85
Crocheted pale green jumper. Blandford book of traditional handicrafts. 26–27
Crocheted patchwork denim sweater. Chatterton. Patchwork & applique. 75–78
Dropped-shoulder sweater. Walker. Mosaic knitting. 200–01
Fair Isle sweaters. Morgan. Traditional knitting patterns of Ireland, Scotland, and England. 78–99
Faroe Island sweaters. Morgan. Traditional knitting patterns of Ireland, Scotland and England. 110–15
Fee. Sweater workshop.
Guernsey sweaters. Morgan. Traditional knitting patterns of Ireland, Scotland and England. 20–52
Hollingworth. Complete book of traditional Aran knitting.
Hooded sports jackets for the family. Creative crafts yearbook: an exciting new collection of needlework and crafts. 152–54
Hooded V-neck sweater (knit). Time-Life books. Sporting scene. 163
Instant sweaters: a pullover, a cardigan and a vest (sewn). Bradley, Design it, sew it and wear it. 128–39
Knit turtleneck dickey. McCall's big book of knit & crochet for home & family. 43
Knitted patch tunic. Chatterton. Patchwork & applique. 136–37
Knitted sweaters. Chatterton. Scandinavian knitting designs. 232–63
Mending sweaters. Brown. Super sweater idea book. 178–80
Mother and daughter duo (crocheted). Step by step to better knitting and crochet. 280–82
Oversweater. Walters. Crochet. 73–77
Patchwork design sweaters. Selfridge. Patchwork knitting. 164–78
Raised diamond pullover, zipped jacket, puff pattern pullover, Tyrolean sweaters, girl's snow set, flower-spray cardigans, Fair Isle set & mosaic pullover. McCall's big book of knit & crochet for home & family. 57–64, 74–77
Reversible V-necked sleeveless sweater. Neighbors. Reversible two-color knitting. 160–61
Rose bud decorated sweater and crochet sweater edging. Wilson. Needlework to wear. 138, 142
Shetland sweaters. Morgan. Traditional knitting patterns of Ireland, Scotland and England. 100–09
Skane man's or woman's sweater (Sweden). Starmore. Scandinavian knitwear. 50–52
Sweater design workshop. Brown. Super sweater idea book. 87–140
Sweater face-lifts. Brown. Super sweater idea book. 174–78
Sweater sewing. Brown. Super sweater idea book. 49–86
Sweaters (alterations & remodeling). Brock. Gladrags: redesigning, remaking, refitting all your old clothes. 56–89
Sweaters: Aran, Guernsey, Norway, and Iceland. Compton. Complete book of traditional knitting. 154–57, 167–74, 178–80
Tabards. Walker. Mosaic knitting. 209–10
Turtleneck sweaters (knit). Time-Life books. Sporting scene. 162–63
Twin turtlenecks and vests. Woman's Day bazaar best sellers. 29–30
Unplanned bias-knit reversible sweater. Walker. Mosaic knitting. 204–08
Woman's and child's picture sweater. Step by step to better knitting and crochet. 35–37
Woven sweater, drawstring sweater. Beard. Fashions from the loom. 51–52

Sweaters, Boys

Boy's hooded sweater. Jacobs. Crochet book. 150–52
Boy's shoulder-buttoned pullover. Hubert. Weekend knitting projects. 60–61
Boy's striped shawl-collared cardigan. Hubert. Weekend knitting projects. 72–73
Boy's striped sweater. Knitting. 62
Cabled outfit. Step by step to better knitting and crochet. 120–22
Father-son cardigans. Woman's Day crochet showcase. 166–68
Knitted pullover. Doherty. Family Circle book of 429 great gifts-to-make all year round
   for just 10¢ to $10.00. 172
Young man's fisherman's knit pullover. Hubert. Weekend knitting projects. 30–31
Young man's tweed zippered cardigan. Hubert. Weekend knitting projects. 34–35
Young man's wishbone cable pullover. Hubert. Weekend knitting projects. 40–41

Sweaters, Children

All-over-stripe sweater and hat, stripe-trimmed sweater and hat. Reader's Digest com-
   plete guide to needlework. 350–51
Boys and girls crayon cardigan. Crochet. 126
Children's striped pullover. Jacobs. Crochet book. 118–20
Child's cardigan, pullover. Knitting techniques and projects. 54–55, 57
Child's crocheted top. Gault. Crafts for the disabled. 80–81
Child's Fair Isle sweater. Knitting. 63
Child's hooded sweatshirt. Hubert. Weekend knitting projects. 78–79
Child's reindeer set (knitted sweater, pants & hat). McCall's big book of knit & crochet
   for home & family. 80–81
Child's sweater (knitted). Treasury of things to make. 64–65
Child's sweater with or without sleeves. Goldsworthy. Clothes for disabled people.
   100–02
Child's top, artful Aran (crocheted). Step by step to better knitting and crochet. 189–
   90, 244–45
Crocheted raglan jackets, clown cardigans, popcorn pullovers, fruit popovers. Favorite
   knitting and crochet patterns. 31–38, 42–45
Fisherman's knit turtleneck sweater and hat. Gladstone. Kids' clothes by Meredith
   Gladstone. 52–54
Flat knit turtleneck or crew neck pullovers. Gladstone. Kids' clothes by Meredith Glad-
   stone. 51–52
Garter, stockinette and multi-stitch T-shaped sweaters. Step by step to better knitting
   and crochet. 66–69
Hälsingland child's sweater (Sweden). Starmore. Scandinavian knitwear. 64–67
Her special outfit for special events (knit). Feldman. Needlework boutique. 37–38
Jumpers, knitted: a child's multicolored jumper, a child's 2-color striped jumper. Gault.
   Crafts for the disabled. 70–71
Knit sweaters. Knitting. 111–23
Removable cross-stitch Humpty Dumpty. Gostelow. Cross stitch book. 105–07
Smaland child's skirt and sweater (Sweden). Starmore. Scandinavian knitwear. 53–56
Sweater just like dad's (knit). Feldman. Needlework boutique. 41–42

Sweaters, Girls

Big apple crocheted sweater, hooded knitted sweater. Woman's Day book of gifts to
   make. 151–53, 157–60
Girl's multicolored tunic. Hubert. Weekend knitting projects. 77
Girl's Tyrolean-yoked cardigan and pullover. Hubert. Weekend knitting projects. 74–76
Kids' stuff (knitted boat-neck pullovers), candy cardigan. Favorite knitting & crochet
   patterns. 153–58

Sweaters, Infants

Granny square sweater. Scharf. Illustrated patchwork crochet. 173
Toddler's top. Step by step to better knitting and crochet. 10

Sweaters, Men

Family sweaters (knit). Mills. Book of presents. 118–19

Father-son cardigans, his-her Aran pullovers. Woman's Day crochet showcase. 166–68, 172–73

Fisherman's favorite, man about town & two's company. Favorite knitting & crochet patterns. 203–13

Garter stitch pullover, turtleneck dickey, Fair Isle pullover, belted pullover. Doherty. Family Circle book of 429 great gifts-to-make all year round for just 10¢ to $10.00. 106–107, 116–119, 121–122

How to knit the Scandanavian motifs. Time-Life books. Traditional favorites. 148–52

Jamtland man's V-necked sweater (Sweden). Starmore. Scandinavian knitwear. 83–86

Kaltimo man's sweater (Finland). Starmore. Scandinavian knitwear. 102–04

Knit sweaters. Knitting. 23–82

Man's Aran Isle crocheted sweater. Crochet. 23

Man's fisherman's cable pullover and cardigan. Hubert. Weekend knitting projects. 90–93

Man's motif pullover. McCall's big book of knit & crochet for home & family. 156

Man's patterned sweater (crocheted). Crochet. 19

Man's sand-stitch pullover. Hubert. Weekend knitting projects. 86–87

Man's striped, textured pullover. Hubert. Weekend knitting projects.

Man's T-shaped sweater, man's latticed sweater. Step by step to better knitting and crochet. 76, 116–17

Men's cardigan. Jacobs. Crochet book. 123–24

Men's ski sweater. Jacobs. Crochet book. 148–49

Pullover & socks, scenic sweater. Knitting techniques and projects. 72–79

Pullover with cables on front. Reader's Digest complete guide to needlework. 326–27

Three for the beach (crocheted T-shirts), cool and casual, sporty sweater, chunky choice, Aran sweaters, diamond duo & smoking jacket. Favorite knitting & crochet patterns. 97–109

Trøndelay man's sweater (Norway). Starmore. Scandinavian knitwear. 28–30

Young man's seed-stitch pullover. Hubert. Weekend knitting projects. 10–11

Zippered jacket (knit). Mills. Book of presents. 108–09

Sweaters, Toddlers

Infants two-colored sweatshirt. Hubert. Weekend knitting projects. 22–23

Parcheesi cardigan, "peplum" pullover, striped jumper, tiny tunic, double-breasted jacket and overalls, middy sweater. Woman's Day crochet showcase. 110–14, 118–21

Toddler sweater, hat, mittens and socks-spiral knit set. Knitting. 126

Toddler's tank top (knit). Mills. Book of presents. 110–11

Sweaters, Women

Aran-pattern pullover to knit. Reader's Digest complete guide to needlework. 315

Cape-sleeved pullover (crocheted). Crochet. 26

Cotton bobble sweater, ribbon cable sweater and popcorn pullover. Wilson. Needlework to wear. 62–65

Cotton sweater-blouse. Jacobs. Crochet book. 88–89

Crochet blouse. Goldsworthy. Clothes for disabled people. 102–03

Crocheted Aran-pattern cardigan. McCall's big book of knit & crochet for home & family. 220–22

Crocheted butterfly top, lacy look, striped comfort, touch of tapestry, comfortable cable, soft summer special, cardigan with class. Favorite knitting and crochet patterns. 52–72

Crocheted mosaic cardigan, log cabin pullover, sunflower variation jacket. Lep. Crocheting patchwork patterns. 36–46

Crocheted peach pastels, bow-tied blouse, rose shell & scroll blouse. McCall's big book of knit & crochet for home & family. 154–55, 241, 248–250

Crocheting a woman's cardigan. Reader's Digest complete guide to needlework. 394–95

Dale woman's short-sleeved sweater (Norway). Starmore. Scandinavian knitwear. 31–34

Delsbø woman's blouse (Sweden). Starmore. Scandinavian knitwear. 79–82

Delsbø woman's sweater (Sweden). Starmore. Scandinavian knitwear. 72–75

Donegal cardigan jacket, tambour bolero jacket, reversible wrap jacket and hat, blouson jacket, hooded sweater-coat. Woman's Day crochet showcase. 24–32

Double dash for a sweater. Time-Life books. Boutique attire. 148–51

Embroidered sweater. McCall's big book of needlecrafts. 259, 261

Embroidered sweater. Treasury of things to make. 132–34

Embroidery trimmed sweater. Farlie. Pennywise boutique. 78–79

Estonia woman's cardigan (Finland). Starmore. Scandinavian knitwear. 112–16

Fabric shrug. Ruggieri. Woman's Day book of no-pattern sewing. 79

Family sweaters (knit). Mills. Book of presents. 118–19

Family tree sweater. Farlie. Pennywise boutique. 47–48

Fana woman's sweater (Norway). Starmore. Scandinavian knitwear. 18–20

Fanciful sweaters. Henderson. Woman's Day book of designer crochet. 18–32

Fisherman's smock (crocheted). Step by step to better knitting and crochet. 159–60

Garter stitch with contrasting trim; basketweave knitted cardigan. Doherty. Family Circle book of 429 great gifts-to-make all year round for just 10¢ to $10.00. 72–75

Granny square cardigan with short or long set-in sleeve. Scharf. Illustrated patchwork crochet. 171

Hedin. Knit sweaters the easy way.

Hooded car coat (knit). Mills. Book of presents. 106–07

Knit sweaters. Knitting. 19–94

Knitted and crocheted sweaters. Feldman. Handmade lace and patterns. 120–123, 125

Kymi woman's cardigan (Finland). Starmore. Scandinavian knitwear. 105–08

Lacy tops. Henderson. Woman's Day book of designer crochet. 33–35

Mohair cardigan. Walters. Crochet. 56–57

Mohair evening sweater. Step by step to better knitting and crochet. 172

Mohair pastel blouson, fancy-collar pullover. Design crochet. 4–8, 47–52

Mother's top, versatile sweater, big baggy pullover, bouclé cardigan, V-neck sweaters, squares and stripes. Step by step to better knitting and crochet. 10, 12–13, 24–25, 86–87, 91–92, 137–39

Navajo sweater, sweater jacket, ribbed V-neck, zig zag rug, Chinese tunic, alpine sweater. Knitting techniques and projects. 24–27, 34, 37–38, 47, 79–80

Patchwork-motif sweater. Jacobs. Crochet book. 93–97

Patchwork pullover sweater. Scharf. Illustrated patchwork crochet. 166

Patchwork sweater (knit). Mills. Book of presents. 110–13

Refitting and redesigning sweaters. Funaro. Yestermorrow clothes book. 121–27

Shoulder sweater (knitted). Rosenthal. Not-so-nimble needlework book. 145

Side-fastening sweater (knitted or crocheted). Goldsworthy. Clothes for disabled people. 95–98

Smock sweater. Treasury of things to make. 138–39

Spring cotton sweaters. Henderson. Woman's Day book of designer crochet. 36–50

Stripe-trimmed and layered-look pullovers and hats. Crochet. 39–42

Striped pullover, bulky yarn pullover, mixed yarn pullover. Design crochet. 93–100

Striped T-top, pullover T-sweater. Great granny crochet book. 114–17

Sweaters, cardigans and jackets. Probert. Knitting in vogue. 10–129

Sweaters to coats. Zukerman. Get hooked. 116–25

Tasty turtleneck, beaded beauty, country casual & all square. Favorite knitting & crochet patterns. 159–68

Teen's bolero top. Jacobs. Crochet book. 63–64

Textured smock sweater, collared mohair pullover, cowl-neck pullover, fuzzy-wuzzy pullover/cardigan, short-sleeved boat-neck pullover, Aran pullover. Woman's Day crochet showcase. 16–23, 172–73

Tyrolean, cardigan & raspberry ripple, quilted jacket, set for success cardigan, coffee with cream. Favorite knitting & crochet patterns. 172–89

Whirlpool-motif overblouse. Jacobs. Crochet book. 73–74

Woman's bulky pullover with stripes. Hubert. Weekend knitting projects. 54

Woman's cuddly pullover with shawl collar. Hubert. Weekend knitting projects. 12–13

Woman's curly, cap sleeved tunic. Hubert. Weekend knitting projects. 65

Woman's fisherman's knit pullover. Hubert. Weekend knitting projects. 28–29

Woman's garter-stitch pullover. Hubert. Weekend knitting projects. 42

Woman's mohair cable cardigan and pullover. Hubert. Weekend knitting projects. 44–45

Woman's multi-yarn cardigan. Hubert. Weekend knitting projects. 48–49

Woman's sand-stitched pullover. Hubert. Weekend knitting projects. 84–85

Woman's spring pullover. Hubert. Weekend knitting projects. 88–89

Woman's super-easy pullover. Hubert. Weekend knitting projects. 47

Woman's textured vest. Hubert. Weekend knitting projects. 55

Woman's tweed tunic. Hubert. Weekend knitting projects. 46

Woman's warm-up cardigan. Hubert. Weekend knitting projects. 32–33

Woven granny shrug. Beard. Fashions from the loom. 90

Zippered jacket (knit). Mills. Book of presents. 108–09

Swimming accessories

After-swim cap and matching beach bag. Feldman. Needlework boutique. 132–34

Bare bikini and coverup. Time-Life books. Separates that travel. 130–36

Beach bag. Walters. Crochet. 45

Beach bag that unrolls to a coverlet. Ruggieri. Woman's Day book of no-pattern sewing. 106

Beach blanket bundle (quilted). Botsford. Between thimble & thumb. 150–55

Beach caftan, striped beach tunic, striped-sleeve beach tunic, bold-stripe beach cape, striped beach jacket. Crochet. 62–66, 70–71

Beach cover-up. Great granny crochet book. 119

Beach cover-up (sewn). Burns. Super sewing. 289–91

Beach towel with pockets. Coffey. Francine Coffey's celebrity sewing bee. 110

Beachcomber knitted cover-up. Favorite knitting & crochet patterns. 195–96

Beachcomber (robe). Ruggieri. Woman's Day book of no-pattern sewing. 96–97

Beachwear. Henderson. Woman's day book of designer crochet. 88–106

Cover-up (crocheted). Time-Life books. Sporting scene. 177

Girl's beach wrap and sun hat. Creative crafts yearbook: an exciting new collection of needlework and crafts. 26–28

Halter tops (sewn). Burns. Super sewing. 292

Roll-up beach mat. Doherty. Family Circle book of 429 great gifts-to-make all year round for just 10¢ to $10.00. 152, 158

Skirt/cape beach coverup. Reader's Digest complete guide to sewing. 504

Terry towel beach shift, poolside miniskirt and knit shirt midriff top. Farlie. Pennywise boutique. 74–76

Terry velour cape for over a bathing suit. Woman's Day book of gifts to make. 30–31

Towel chic: bandeau, wrap skirt, skirt/dress & blouse. Ruggieri. Woman's Day book of no-pattern sewing. 66–67

Swimming pools

Above ground pool installation. Outdoor projects for home and garden. 473–82, 485–88

All about vinyl liner prefab pools. Outdoor projects for home and garden. 468–73

Deck for your pool. Day. How to build patios and decks. 143–45

In-ground pool using pressurized walls. Outdoor projects for home and garden. 482–85

Open poolside shelter. Marshall. Yard buildings. 93–97

Painting your swimming pool. Scherer. Complete handbook of home painting. 121–30

Pool maintenance. Outdoor projects for home and garden. 488–91

Poolside dressing room and lounge. Marshall. Yard buildings. 99–108

10 steps to a sparkling pool, swimming pool filter you can make, diving deck gives added storage. Popular Mechanics do-it-yourself encyclopedia. Vol. 18, 2828–35

Tiling a pool. Burch. Tile: indoors and out, every kind and use. 91–92

Vacation all summer in a low-cost pool, shape up your pool, deck and activity area around pool. Popular Mechanics do-it-yourself encyclopedia. Vol. 15, 2274–84

Swings

Build an A-frame swing set. Popular Mechanics do-it-yourself encyclopedia. Vol. 1, 41–42

Build this old-time yard swing. Popular Mechanics do-it-yourself encyclopedia. Vol. 18, 2836–40

Canvas lounge swing. Kramer. Outdoor garden build-it book. 152–53

Climber swing. Peterson. Children's toys you can build yourself. 137–38

Double swing, swinging seat for two or more people. Blandford. Constructing outdoor furniture, with 99 projects. 332–40

Dowel swing. Wood projects for the garden. 73

Garden swing. Bumper book of things a boy can make. 121–22

Handwoven swing. Wilson. Weaving you can use. 77

Hanging leather and ash chair. Easy-to-make tables and chairs. 27–28

Lawn glider. Brann. How to build outdoor furniture. 96–126

Lawn or porch swing. Churchill. Backyard building book II. 109–13

Lawn or porch swing. Churchill. Big backyard building book. 218–22

Lawn swing. Complete handyman do-it-yourself encyclopedia. Vol. 8, 1191–94

Macrame swing and holder. Treasury of things to make. 168–71

Merry-go-round swing, child's swing. Popular Mechanics do-it-yourself encyclopedia. Vol. 14, 2189, 2199

Old-time porch swing. Popular Mechanics do-it-yourself encyclopedia. Vol. 15, 2285–90

Simple swing. Boeschen. Successful playhouses. 14–15

Swing. Blandford. Constructing outdoor furniture, with 99 projects. 293–94, 296–98

Swing. Blandford. Giant book of wooden toys. 289–93

Swing and frame. Adams. Make your own baby furniture. 121–31

Swing (needlepoint). Laury. Treasury of needlecraft gifts for the new baby. 102–04

Swings, strings, springs. Laury. Handmade toys and games. 91–96

Tete-a-tete swing for two. Easy-to-make tables and chairs. 29

Woven swing set for child. Wilson. Weaving you can use. 116–17

Switches, Electric. *See* **Electric switches**

T

Table decorations

Calico fruit basket, egg-citement centerpiece, ribbons and fringe, fabulous fakes: old-fashioned goodies, Victorian blue centerpiece, popcorn and cranberry bouquet. Nicole. Designer accessories to make for your home. 43–48, 139–41, 160–65, 182–85, 188–89

Bon voyage table decoration, "welcome home" table centre. Janitch. Candlemaking and decorations. 65–67

Candle wreath centerpiece. Wilson. Erica Wilson's Christmas world. 67–68

Coral strand, surrealistic seascape, cockle basket, snail in a snail, metallic sea urchins. Elbert. Shell craft. 48, 50–51, 87–89, 194–95, 241–42
Decorations for holidays. Better Homes and Gardens holiday decorations you can make. 184–202
Flower ball ornaments, festive bouquet, church scene. Araki. Origami for Christmas. 146–48
Forest centerpiece with candles. Meras. Vacation crafts. 52
Hot air balloon centerpieces. Wargo. Soft crafts for special occasions. 6–12
Japanese garden. Bumper book of things a girl can make. 134–35
Morning glories and trailing ivy. Janitch. All made from paper. 64
Mushroom-basket centerpiece. Evrard. Homespun crafts from scraps. 145–46
Sunburst centerpieces. Hibbs. Straw sculpture. 24–27
Table settings. Linsley. Custom made. 86–91
Tidbit stand. Cope. Plastics. 57
Tin can centerpieces. Metalcrafting encyclopedia. 79–80
Walnut boats in harbour. Janitch. Candlemaking and decorations. 44–45
Wineglass cascade. Janitch. Candlemaking and decorations. 62
Wood trims, festive table settings. Better Homes and Gardens treasury of Christmas crafts & foods. 332, 336–45

Table favors. *See* **Favors (for parties)**

Table games. *See* **Game boards and tables**

Table lamps. *See* **Lamps**

Table mats
Apple place mat and napkins. Coffey. Francine Coffey's celebrity sewing bee. 166
Appliqued placemats: red apple, sunny day, clown face, rainbow, hexagon beauty, star flower, pleasant paths. Gillies. Patterns for applique and pieced work—and ways to use them. 42–61
Batik place mats. Anderson. Tie dyeing and batik. 68–71
Batik place mats. Frame. Tie-dyeing and batik. 98–101
Bead trivet or table mat. Hulbert. Creative beadwork. 32
Beginning rush work (round mat & oval mat) Cane, rush and straw. 86–93, 110–13
Bird resting on a branch. Scheuer. Designs for Holbein embroidery. 38–39
Braided place mats. Golden book of colonial crafts. 154–55
Braided place mats. Roda. Fabric decorating for the home. 49
Braided place mats and napkin rings, mirror tile place mats. Better Homes and Gardens treasury of Christmas crafts & foods. 109, 345
Bread wrapper mat, circular hot mat. Lyon. Arts and crafts objects children can make for the home. 130–31, 138–39
Burlap place mats and napkin rings. Wargo. Soft crafts for special occasions. 94–95
Butterfly place mat, patchwork place mat, yo-yo place mat. Woman's Day creative stitchery from scraps. 66–68, 106–08, 148–49
Cane table mats, sisal mats. Encyclopedia of crafts. 236, 245
Child's place mat. Coffey. Francine Coffey's celebrity sewing bee. 127
Christmas placemats. Wilson. Erica Wilson's Christmas world. 70–71
Cluster stitch mat, kitchen hot mat, flower filet mat, embossed daisy mat & white rose centerpiece. McCall's big book of knit & crochet for home & family. 131–32, 180–85
Crazy-quilt patchwork place mats. Better Homes and Gardens embroidery. 70
Creatures great & small table mat and centerpiece. Wilson. More needleplay. 168–69
Crocheted place mats. Svinicki. Step-by-step spinning and dyeing. 58
Cut-out and scalloped place mat. Woman's Day decorative needlework for the home. 139

Designs from China table mat. Wilson. Needleplay. 140–41

Dishcloth weaving, colonial mats. Rissell. Craftwork the handicapped elderly can make and sell. 58–63

Doily-designed stenciled place mats, Santa place mats. Better Homes and Gardens easy bazaar crafts. 9, 18, 66, 76

Double knit place mat. Fanning. Complete book of machine quilting. 158–61

Dresden place mat (patchwork). McCall's book of America's favorite needlework and crafts. 208–09

Easy filet crochet place mats. American School of Needlework. Great crochet bazaar book. 86–87

Eat & learn place mat. McCall's big book of needlecrafts. 115

Embroidered "blue onion" place mat and napkin set, drawnwork place mat. McCall's book of America's favorite needlework and crafts. 73–77

Embroidered place mat and napkin. Woman's Day decorative needlework for the home. 134–35

Embroidered rose luncheon set. Embroidery of roses. 122–23

English patchwork place mats. Fairfield. Patchwork. 16–17

Fabric and crochet table mats, crocheted lunch mats, cutwork tablemats. Encyclopedia of crafts. 88, 102, 126

Flat, single and double-layer newspaper mat. Glashausser. Plaiting step-by-step. 45–62

Floral applique place mat, woven place mats, rag woven place mats, crochet table mats in string. Encyclopedia of crafts. 32, 41, 48–49, 76

Four place mats with pick-up patterns. Holland. Weaving primer. 150–52

Fruit-shaped vinyl, calico, "etched" plastic, patchwork, & upholstery webbing place mats. Doherty. Family Circle book of 429 great gifts-to-make all year round for just 10¢ to $10.00. 1–3, 16, 129–30

Hardanger place mat & napkin. Better Homes & Gardens embroidery. 58–60

Hardanger place mats. Longhurst. Vanishing American needle arts. 46–52, 54–55

Harvest mats and napkin rings, strawberry set, stenciled wooden mats. McCall's big book of country needlecrafts. 122–24, 133–34, 155–57

Hippo and el toro place mats. Coffey. Francine Coffey's celebrity sewing bee. 120

Holiday cloth, wreath of angels. Lindberg. Counted cross-stitch designs for all seasons. 75–78

Hot mat covers. Breckenridge. Lap quilting. 50–54

Hungarian table mat. Ley. Russian & other Slavic embroidery designs. 42–45

Instructions for embroidered place mats size 16½" by 24". Hana. Embroidery. 32

Instructions for the hairpin lace place mats. Time-Life books. Decorative techniques. 154–55

Ivy trails place mats. Janitch. Collage: a step by step guide. 75

Jute macrame place mat. Woman's Day decorative needlework for the home. 135–36

Lacy knitted place mat. Woman's Day decorative needlework for the home. 139

Lacy place mat. Woman's Day crochet showcase. 163–64

Lion placemat. Foose. Scrap saver's stitchery book. 42–45

Log cabin place mats. Breckenridge. Lap quilting. 43–44

Machine-embroidered hardanger place mats. Better Homes & Gardens embroidery. 71

Maple leaf table mats and pot holder. Houck. Patchwork pattern book. 22–23

Modern art place mats. Gostelow. Cross stitch book. 101–102

Mosaic-patterned place mats. Walker. Mosaic knitting. 219–22

Mountain chain place mats. Houck. Patchwork pattern book. 14–15

Navajo woven mat. McCall's book of America's favorite needlework and crafts. 287–88

Nosegay luncheon set, place mat motif. McCall's big book of knit & crochet for home & family. 274–75, 281

Oval pineapple place mat. American School of Needlework. Great crochet bazaar book. 58–60

Party place mats and patchwork place mats. Linsley. Great bazaar. 87, 117

Patchwork and African designs for needlepoint table mats. Chatterton. Coordinated crafts for the home. 126–27, 133, 154–55, 160–61, 178–82, 190–91, 200–01, 206–08

Patchwork place mat. Newman. Quilting, patchwork, applique and trapunto. 98–103

Patchwork place mats. Breckenridge. Lap quilting. 47–50

Patchwork place mats. Chatterton. Patchwork & applique. 17–18

Perfect place mat. Botsford. Between thimble & thumb. 171–73

Pieced and appliqued place mats. Heard. Complete guide to quilting. 260–62

Pineapple hot mat, chicken hot mat, oval hot mat, orange & green mat, orange mat & pink place mats. McCall's big book of knit & crochet for home & family. 173–74, 216–18

Place mat and coaster. Christensen. Teach yourself needlepoint. 84–85

Place mat and napkin sets (embroidered) Boyles. Needlework gifts for special occasions. 124–27

Place mat shaped as an octagon (crocheted). Feldman. Needlework boutique. 102–03

Place mats. Bird. Craft of Hawaiian lauhala. 81–93

Place mats. Hagans. All good gifts. 65

Place mats. Ley. Russian & other Slavic embroidery designs. 70–75

Place mats. Morgan. Trapunto and other forms of raised quilting. 204–05

Place mats. Selfridge. Patchwork knitting. 134

Place mats. Thorpe. Elements of weaving. 9–21

Place mats and napkins. Reader's Digest complete guide to sewing. 451

Place mats and tablecloths. Frager. Quilting primer. 70–74

Place mats, napkins and napkin rings. Laury. Treasury of needlecraft gifts for the new baby. 87–89

Place mats on counted-thread fabric, cross-stitch on ginham. Rosenthal. Not-so-nimble needlework book. 49–51

Place mats (sewn). Burns. Super sewing. 295

Pulled thread place mat and napkin. Reader's Digest complete guide to needlework. 106

Pulled-work mats. Gostelow. Complete international book of embroidery. 68–69

Quick and easy patchwork place mats, jute and linen crocheted place mats and napkin rings, spiral crocheted table toppers, country-style crocheted place mats, crazy quilt patchwork place mats, machine embroidered hardanger place mats. Better Homes and Gardens treasury of needlecrafts. 16, 200–05, 388–89

Quilted puzzle pieces place mat, Christmas star place mats, poinsettia place mat, snowflake place mat. Foose. More scrap saver's stitchery. 88–97

Red, white & blue mat, filet rose mat & leaf motif. McCall's big book of knit & crochet for home & family. 241, 246

Reverse applique table mat. Wilson. Needleplay. 183

Reversible place mats. Roda. Fabric decorating for the home. 62

Roll-up gingham place mats. Coffey. Francine Coffey's celebrity sewing bee. 84–85

Round mats and bases. Cane, rush and straw. 15–20

Scandinavian rose, windblown snowflakes, enclosed flowers, heart motif, diamonds and stripes, stars, rosette motif, snowflake, decorated rose medallion, diamonds and squares, Scandinavian stripes, trellis patterns and rose petal motif needlepoint place mats. Chatterton. Coordinated crafts for the home. 32–33, 46–47, 60–61, 79–80, 96–97, 99–100, 102, 110–11, 114, 118–20

Scandinavian table mat, round mat with medallion insets. Brown. Complete book of rush and basketry techniques. 83–85

Set of four place mats. Rosenthal. Not-so-nimble needlework book. 27

Set of place mats based on the weaving of Santiajo atitlan. DeRodriquez. Weaving on a backstrap loom. 40–62

Set of table mats. Osler. Machine patchwork. 98–99

Set the Christmas table: crocheted table runner & place mats. American School of Needlework. Great Christmas crochet book. 30–32

Simple woven design for a doily napkin or mat, blue and white breakfast set. Tod. Joy of hand weaving. 124–26

Springtime cloth, starflower place mat, cloth with chamomile and poppies, place mat and plate liner with bluebells, autumn cloth, place mat with a bough of ash. Lindberg. Counted cross-stitch designs for all seasons. 22–23, 26–27, 37–39, 51–53, 57–58, 68–70

Star doily or table mat, hardanger place mat and napkin. Better Homes and Gardens treasury of needlecrafts. 224–25, 376–78

Straw mat. Hibbs. Straw sculpture. 88

Striped place mat with coaster and round place mat. Halliday. Decorating with crochet. 120–27

Summer scenes, sophisticated table. Great cross-stitch. 31–40

Sunshine place mats. Foose. Scrap saver's stitchery book. 74–77

Synthetic straw table mat. Swanson. Rigid heddle weaving. 118–23

Table mat, buttons linked together. Blandford book of traditional handicrafts. 135

Table mat, raffia on plastic canvas. Gault. Crafts for the disabled. 22–23

Table mats. Evans. Ribbonwork. 16–17

Table mats. Geary. Plant prints and collages. 80–82

Table mats with patchwork trim & heat resistant lining. Ives. Ideas for patchwork. 46–49

Table mats with the router. Sainsbury. Woodworking projects with power tools. 78–80

Teneriffe lace medallion mat. Stillwell. Technique of teneriffe lace. 39–46

Tortoise and hare place mat and bib. Coffey. Francine Coffey's celebrity sewing bee. 139

Tray-shaped place mat, strawberry place mat. McCall's big book of needlecrafts. 269–71

Unsewn plaited table mats. Wright. Complete book of baskets and basketry. 115–16, 136

Vinyl picnic place mat with pockets. Woman's Day decorative needlework for the home. 140

Watermelon place mats and napkins. Woman's Day bazaar best sellers. 104

Weaving a table mat or rug on a loom. Tod. Joy of hand weaving. 47–54

Weiss. Crocheting placemats.

Windmill and sawtooth star table mats. Houck. Patchwork pattern book. 46–47, 54–55

Wine and white place mat and napkin (hardanger embroidered). Golden book of hand and needle arts. 83–87

Woven lace place mat. Reader's Digest complete guide to needlework. 439

Woven needlepoint canvas place mat. Woman's Day decorative needlework for the home. 136–37

Woven table runners. Svinicki. Step-by-step spinning and dyeing. 52–55

Woven table runners. Wilson. Weaving you can use. 104–11

Woven textured, scotch, plaid, and stunning table doilies. Tod. Joy of hand weaving. 122–24

Table runners

Auntie Dee's embroidered runner. Better Homes & Gardens embroidery. 64–65

Bellflower table runner, leafy table runner, table runner with poinsettia, Christmas table runner with mother and child. Lindberg. Counted cross-stitch designs for all seasons. 44–48, 59–61, 79–80, 94–95

Burlap table runner. Wargo. Soft crafts for special occasions. 92–93

Chickens in bowl. Nielsen. Scandinavian embroidery, past and present. 90–91

Christmas angels table runner & napkins. Gostelow. Cross stitch book. 102–04

Christmas candle runner. Nielsen. Scandinavian embroidery, past and present. 96–97

Colorful table runners. Wargo. Soft crafts for special occasions. 17–19

Cross-stitch runner. Better Homes & Gardens embroidery. 15

Cross-stitch table runner. Better Homes & Gardens embroidery. 6–7

Cross-stitch table runners, embroidered runner with cutwork. Better Homes and Gardens treasury of needlecrafts. 332–33, 339, 368–69
Embroidered rose table runners. Embroidery of roses. 77, 82, 97
Hand woven runners. Tod. Joy of hand weaving. 300–01
Hoj Tomtegubbar—tall Christmas elves. Nielsen. Scandinavian embroidery, past and present. 94–95
Huck embroidery table runner. Reader's Digest complete guide to needlework. 107
Patchwork points table runner. Evrard. Homespun crafts from scraps. 42–44
Patchwork table runner. Roda. Fabric decorating for the home. 56–57
Sawtooth star and rose garden table runners. Houck. Patchwork pattern book. 54–57
Specially Norweigian: counted and drawn thread table runner. Embroidery. 38–39
Star-crossed table runner, modern myths Assisi work table runner. Great cross-stitch. 51–52, 160–62
Stars and angels. Nielsen. Scandinavian embroidery, past and present. 102–03
Table runner. Ley. Russian & other Slavic embroidery designs. 60–63
Table runner, dresser scarf. Holland. Weaving primer. 100, 177–80
Table runner on a rigid heddle loom. Make it! don't buy it. 376–79
Table runner with filet insert. Svinicki. Old-fashioned crochet. 99–101
Table scarf. Brown. Weaving, spinning, and dyeing book. 165–66
Wheat pattern runner. McCall's big book of knit & crochet for home & family. 186–87

Tablecloths

Applique a centerpiece. Golden book of hand and needle arts. 25
Appliqued cloth and napkins. Vanderbilt. Gloria Vanderbilt designs for your home. 100–04
Auntie Dee's cross-stitch tablecloth. Better Homes & Gardens emboidery. 50–51
Autumn leaves tablecloth. Wilson. Erica Wilson's Christmas world. 86–89
Batik tablecloth. Anderson. Tie dyeing and batik. 78–79
Batik tablecloth. Frame. Tie-dyeing and batik. 82–85, 108–09
Batik table cover. Anderson. Tie dyeing and batik. 91–93
Blue hardanger tablecloth. Nielsen. Scandinavian embroidery, past and present. 78–79
Blue rose tablecloth. Better Homes & Gardens embroidery. 22–24
Bridge tablecloth. Roda. Fabric decorating for the home. 102–03
Card table cover. Burchette. More needlework blocking and finishing. 110–12
Chinese patchwork. Needlework nostalgia. 9, 19
Christmas, Thanskgiving or Halloween, Easter and Valentine's Day tablecloth. Goldman. Decorate with felt. 29–37
Circular patchwork table. Ives. Ideas for patchwork. 80–81
City life, wild flowers, feast of flowers, & afternoon tea tablecloths, birds and flowers Assisi work tablecloth. Great cross-stitch. 41–50, 157–60
Cloth, bibs and pillows (egg yolk in center). Creative crafts yearbook: an exciting new collection of needlework and crafts. 149–50
Crocheted and hairpin lace tablecloths. Feldman. Handmade lace and patterns. 108–09
Cross-stitch tablecloth, dorset feather-stitch tablecloth, cross-stitch design painted on a tablecloth. Encyclopedia of crafts. 127, 143, 160–61
Cutwork heirloom embroidery, cross-stitch motif tablecloths, stem stitch country-look tablecloth, run rabbit run embroidered Easter tablecloth, hen party appliqued Easter tablecloth. Embroidery. 44–61
Daisy tablecloth. Halliday. Decorating with crochet. 117–19
Danish Christmas tablecloth. Nielsen. Scandinavian embroidery, past and present. 100–01
Della Robbia tablecloth. McCall's big book of needlecrafts. 274–75
Draperies and tablecloth adopted from sheets. Woman's Day decorative needlework for the home. 118–19

Drawn thread tablecloth. Evans. Ribbonwork. 78–81

Embroidered Christmas star, patchwork star, macrame and felt disk tablecloth, felt star table skirt. McCall's book of Christmas. 48–56

Embroidered flower-ring tablecloth, appliqued strawberry circle tablecloth. McCall's book of America's favorite needlework and crafts. 69–73

Embroidered pansy cloth. Better Homes & Gardens embroidery. 25

Embroidered rose tablecloths. Embroidery of roses. 75–81, 88–89, 114–15

Embroidered tablecloth. Better Homes & Gardens embroidery. 32–33

Embroidered tablecloth. Better Homes and Gardens treasury of Christmas crafts & foods. 155–57

Embroidery in blue, traditional blue on white to match China pattern, ice crystals, stars, braided arabesque borders. Embroidery. 6–8, 12–17, 26–29

Felt tablecloth, Lapland design. Casselman. Crafts from around the world. 45–47

Floor-length round and oval tablecloths. McCall's sewing for your home. 210–11

Floral appliqued organdy. Vanderbilt. Gloria Vanderbilt designs for your home. 95–98

Flower applique tablecloth, petal patchwork tablecloth. Encyclopedia of crafts. 15, 33

Flowered tablecloth. Better Homes & Gardens embroidery. 10–11

For your game table. Feldman. Needlework boutique. 117–18

"Happy apple" embroidered tablecloth. Encyclopedia of crafts. 115

Hardanger tablecloth. Longhurst. Vanishing American needle arts. 56–57

Holiday quilted tablecloth. Baldwin. Scrap fabric crafts. 84–85

Hungarian cloth. Better Homes & Gardens embroidery. 19

Interwoven tablecloth. Jacobs. Crochet book. 172–74

Kazak card-table cover. Scobey. Decorating with needlepoint. 96–99

Lacy crocheted table cover. Step by step to better knitting and crochet. 209–10

Oval tablecloth. Roda. Fabric decorating for the home. 42

Padded table cover, TV table cover. McCall's sewing for your home. 103–05

Patchwork Christmas tablecloth. Evrard. Homespun crafts from scraps. 99–102

Patchwork table skirt, machine embroidered pomegranate cloth, layered skirt with stenciled setting, coffee break border. McCall's big book of country needlecrafts. 85–87, 116–17, 119–22, 144

Place mats and tablecloths. Frager. Quilting primer. 70–79

Quick and easy patchwork tablecloth, shadow applique tablecloth and napkins, crocheted lace tablecloth, knitted lace tablecloth, Hungarian cloth, flower embroidered tablecloths, blue rose tablecloth, embroidered pansy cloth, cross-stitch tablecloth. Better Homes and Gardens treasury of needlecrafts. 17, 110–11, 196–99, 328, 334–35, 342–47, 370–371

Quilted round tablecloth. McCall's big book of needlecrafts. 52

Quilted tablecloths. Heard. Complete guide to quilting. 262–64

Reversible bandana picnic cloth and napkins. Roda. Fabric decorating for the home. 224

Reversible, floor-length, round tablecloth. Roda. Fabric decorating for the home. 38

Round Christmas tablecloth. Coffey. Francine Coffey's celebrity sewing bee. 171

Round, floor-length tablecloth with ribbon trim. Roda. Fabric decorating for the home. 8–9

Round tablecloth. Golden book of hand and needle arts. 65

Round tablecloth with doily insert. Svinicki. Old-fashioned crochet. 85–88

Round tablecloth with embroidered or appliqued symbols, square or rectangular tablecloths. Hagans. All good gifts. 62–65

Round tablecloths. Practical needlework. 170

Shadow applique-tablecloth and napkins. Better Homes and Gardens applique. 44–45

Square cloths. Practical needlework. 169

Star of Bethlehem and French bouquet tablecloths. Houck. Patchwork pattern book. 10–11, 16

Stenciled tablecloth. Baldwin. Scrap fabric crafts. 62–63

Table linen patterns. Murray. Essential handbook of weaving. 152

Tablecloth. Ley. Russian & other Slavic embroidery designs. 80–85

Tablecloth on counted-thread fabric. Rosenthal. Not-so-nimble needlework book. 56–58

Tablecloth or wall hanging in squares and hexagons. Chatterton. Patchwork & applique. 25–35

Tablecloths to fit every table. Better Homes and Gardens sewing for your home. 156–60

Tea cloth (crocheted). McCall's book of America's favorite needlework and crafts. 249–51

Three tablecloths of appliqued organza. Woman's Day decorative needlework for the home. 132–34

Tie-dye tablecloths. Tie-dye, batik and candlemaking step-by-step. 17

Timeless tablecloth (patchwork). Botsford. Between thimble & thumb. 97–100

Trianon, sunburst, Cluny lace, shadow squares, spiderweb cloth. McCall's big book of knit & crochet for home & family. 188–95, 209, 218–19

Tucks sampler. Hall. Sewing machine craft book. 102–03

Yellow-wreathed tablecloth with daffodils, tulips, and forsythia. Lindberg. Counted cross-stitch designs for all seasons. 32–34

Tables

Acrylic plastic tabletops. Meyers. Furniture repair and refinishing. 225–26

Basic tables. Palmer. Making children's furniture and play structures. 30

Book trough table, 9-to-9 gateleg table. Capotosto. Woodworking techniques and projects. 315–23

Buffet-bed table. Popular Mechanics do-it-yourself encyclopedia. Vol. 2, 246–50

Butcher-block table, butler's table. Popular Mechanics do-it-yourself encyclopedia. Vol. 3, 463–75

Butcher-block table, butler's table kit. 101 do-it-yourself projects. 150–51, 372–73

Cable spool table. Linsley. Decoupage on glass, wood, metal, rocks, shells, wax, soap, plastic, canvas, ceramic. 53–59

Cardboard table and chair for playhouse. Boeschen. Successful playhouses. 73

Chair/table Plimoth Plantation. Daniele. Building early American furniture. 64–66

Child's stretcher table, high-back settle table, Queen Anne hunt table, Pembroke table. Gottshall. Provincial furniture design and construction. 27–34, 49–56

Console table, square table, living room table, library table, occasional table and dressing table. Williams. Spanish colonial furniture. 52–59, 64–69, 112–113

Constructing tables. Johnston. Craft of furniture making. 77–82

Covering a table with vinyl. Marshall. How to repair, reupholster, and refinish furniture. 72–74

Decoupage table. Jarnow. (Re)do it yourself. 127–30

Designing and building a table. Clifford. Basic woodworking and carpentry . . . with projects. 212–14

Dolphin mosaic table. Casselman. Crafts from around the world. 19–21

Drop leaf and gateleg tables, making cabriole legs. Fine woodworking techniques 3. 85–93, 98–101

Early American hutch table. Popular Mechanics do-it-yourself encyclopedia. Vol. 10, 1516–20

Elegant butcher-block-style tables. Oberrecht. Plywood projects illustrated. 144–48

Fabric covered parson's table. Roda. Fabric decorating for the home. 238–40

Fabric covered table. Linsley. Fabulous furniture decorations. 155–58

Farmhouse table. Langsner. Country woodcraft. 263–67

Flap table, fold-flat seat and table, corner table, gateleg flap table, lift-off table. Blandford. 53 space-saving built-in furniture projects. 146–57, 165, 168–69, 193–202

Folding tables. Blandford. How to make your own built in furniture. 283–86

Gateleg table restoration. Davis. Restoring furniture. 64–69

Gateleg table restoration. Restoring and reupholstering furniture. 54–59

Glass tile table. Burch. Tile: indoors and out, every kind and use. 126–27

Gold leaf and decoupage a table top. Giant book of crafts. 365–68

Inlay work-sunburst inlay table. Casselman. Crafts from around the world. 38–40

Knockdown tabletops, lion's paw pedestal table (round), ogee bracket feet—another way, triangular drop leaf table with rotating top. Fine woodworking techniques 4. 139–40, 170–75, 189–90

Leather patchwork parsons table. Easy-to-make tables and chairs. 49

Library table, magazine table, serving table. Rubin. Mission furniture. 64–67, 72–73

LImmer's table, cafe table with carved tablecloth, Simon's trestle table, humanoid table. Ball. Master pieces. 26–33, 42–49, 66–71, 78–83

Lining tables in cloth and leather. Wenn. Restoring antique furniture. 77–78

Ludlow candle commode. Daniele. Building early American furniture. 100–02

Millback sawbuck table (1750). Daniele. Building early American furniture. 144–47

Molded tile tabletop. Elbert. Shell craft. 232–33

Mosaic picture tabletop. Picturemaking. 56–57

Mosaic tabletops. Meyers. Furniture repair and refinishing. 222–25

Oak nesting tables. Easy-to-make tables and chairs. 61

Oval-top sawbuck table, hutch table, bench table with hutch, chair table with hutch. Shea. Pennsylvania Dutch and their furniture. 166, 173–75

Parson's table. Complete handyman do-it-yourself encyclopedia. Vol. 13, 1894–99

Parson's table. Popular Mechanics do-it-yourself encyclopedia. Vol. 3, 453

Parson's tables: building and veneering them. Fine woodworking techniques 2. 180–83

Pembroke table, round card table. Marlow. Classic furniture projects. 96–121

Pembroke table with cabriole legs, regency-style sofa table, Queen Anne side table, tripod table, Tudor-style refectory table. Taylor. How to build period country furniture. 55–65, 80–84, 95–98, 131–33

Plain table, table with drawers, drop leaf table, deep leaf table, gateleg table, swivel top table, light side table. Blandford. How to make early American and colonial furniture. 182–219

Plastic laminate tabletops; acrylic plastic tabletops; marble, stone, etc., tabletops. Meyers. Furniture repair and refinishing. 221–28

Plexiglas cube table, trisected table. Popular Mechanics do-it-yourself encyclopedia. Vol. 14, 2210–11

Quartet of nesting tables, nesting party tables, stacking tray tables. Popular Mechanics do-it-yourself encyclopedia. Vol. 13, 1958–62, 2070–77

Revolving tilting table, tier table, tilt-top box table, seat table. Blandford. How to make early American and colonial furniture. 268–83

Round table. Zegel. Fast furniture. 74–75

Round-top table, pillar-and-claw table. Fine woodworking techniques 5. 136–43

Sawbuck table, sawbuck side table, heavy sawbuck table. Blandford. How to make early American and colonial furniture. 238–50

Sawhorse craft table. Easy-to-make tables and chairs. 56–57

Settle table, wayside table, drop leaf table. Hagerty. Make your own antiques. 84–85, 86–87, 90–91

Sewing tables, tilt-top tables. Marlow. Classic furniture projects. 30–61

Shaker side tables, one-drawer, two-drawer tables, drop leaf tables and swing down table. 77 furniture projects you can build. 151–73

Shaker tables. 77 furniture projects you can build. 141–45

Simple fold down table. Geary. How to design and build your own workspace—with plans. 284, 288

Small wood or cube parquet tile table. Burch. Tile: indoors and out, every kind and use. 113

Snack tables. Popular Mechanics do-it-yourself encyclopedia. Vol. 17, 2710–11

Space-efficient corner table. Oberrecht. Plywood projects illustrated. 232–34

Stacked carton tables. Palmer. Making children's furniture and play structures. 31

Table (shell encrusted). Johnson. Nature crafts. 32
Table construction. Martensson. Woodworker's bible. 218–28
Table with drawer. Feirer. Cabinetmaking and millwork. 210–12
Tables. Lewis. Cabinetmaking, patternmaking, and millwork. 287–95
Tables that hang from walls. Built-ins. 96–101
Takedown trestle table. Blandford. How to make early American and colonial furniture. 224–29
Tile-top table, formica-top table, television table. Endacott. Fine furniture making and woodworking. 102–14
Trestle, occasional table, bedside table, splayed leg table. Marlow. Early American furnituremaker's manual. 68–74, 80–101
Trestle table, stretcher table, chair table. Moser. How to build shaker furniture. 132–35, 160–63
Two small tables, trestle-footed gateleg table, signer's table, maple table, tavern table, oval tavern table, tilt-top table. Osburn. Measured drawings of early American furniture. 22–23, 28–29, 34–35, 42–43, 52–55, 58–59, 78–79
Two-top parson's table. Waugh. Handyman's encyclopedia. 399–401
Wrought iron legs. Giant book of metalworking projects. 183–85
Wrought iron table. Modern general shop. Metalworking. 100

Tables. *See also* **Gameboards and tables**

Tables, Bedside
Bedside rack. Blandford. 53 space-saving built-in furniture projects. 273–76
Bedside table. Easy-to-make tables and chairs. 49
Bedside table. Spence. Woodworking tools, materials, processes. 609
Bedside table. Williams. Spanish colonial furniture. 56–57
Bedside table, circa 1750. Marlow. Early American furnituremaker's manual. 87–93
Bedside tables. Zegel. Fast furniture. 92
Early American night table. 101 do-it-yourself projects. 166–67
Night table. Alth. Making plastic pipe furniture. 93–96
Pair of nightstands. Oberrecht. Plywood projects illustrated. 104–10
Rattan night tables. Alth. Rattan furniture. 181–89
Scrolled-apron bedside table. Shea. Pennsylvania Dutch and their furniture. 164
Shaker bedroom table. 77 furniture projects you can build. 220–23
Small cabinet or nightstand, curly maple side table. Gottshall. Provincial furniture design and construction. 19–22, 60–62
Wallpapered night table. Linsley. Fabulous furniture decorations. 41–48

Tables, Bookcase
Bookshelf-table. Complete do-it-yourself encyclopedia. Vol. 3, 339–43

Tables, Coffee or tea
Butler table (removable tray). Capotosto. Woodworking techniques and projects. 282–85
Chimney flues and chopping block table. Easy-to-make tables and chairs. 59
Cocktail table. Brown. 44 terrific woodworking plans & projects. 164–65
Coffee table. Marlow. Early American furnituremaker's manual. 60–67
Coffee table. Williams. Spanish colonial furniture. 44–45
Coffee table. Zegel. Fast furniture. 54–55
Coffee table with plexiglas legs. Popular Mechanics do-it-yourself encyclopedia. Vol. 14, 2214–15
Coffee table (wood). Black and Decker power tool carpentry. 59–60
Coffee tables. Complete handyman do-it-yourself encyclopedia. Vol. 18, 2634–40
Coffee tables. 77 furniture projects you can build. 177–92
Egyptian-motif coffee table. Scobey. Decorating with needlepoint. 93–95

Folding coffee table and drainpipe coffee table. Alth. Making plastic pipe furniture. 63–74

Glass top coffee table, coffee table plus seats. DeCristoforo. Build your own wood toys, gifts and furniture. 343–48

Herringbone table. Easy-to-make tables and chairs. 16–17

Iron coffee table. 77 furniture projects you can build. 173–77

Large coffee table. LaPlante. Plastic furniture for the home craftsman. 115–16

Mahogony & tubing base. Easy-to-make tables and chairs. 64

Mirror-tile coffee table. Burch. Tile: indoors and out, every kind and use. 121–23

Modern accent tables. Oberrecht. Plywood projects illustrated. 96–99

Rattan coffee table. Alth. Rattan furniture. 81–96

Scalloped coffee table. Linsley. Fabulous furniture decorations. 73–79

Slab tables. Spielman. Working green wood with PEG. 62–68

Softwood coffee table. Easy-to-make tables and chairs. 13

Split chopping-block base. Easy-to-make tables and chairs. 62–64

Stool table, coffee-table slide viewer, coffee-table aquarium, coffee table for your patio. Popular Mechanics do-it-yourself encyclopedia. Vol. 6, 804–18

Tile-top table. Easy-to-make tables and chairs. 60

Trestle coffee table. Blandford. How to make early American and colonial furniture. 219–24

Trestle coffee table. Moser. How to build shaker furniture. 136–37

Trestle coffee table, pegged coffee table. 101 do-it-yourself projects. 72–79

U-shaped ash base. Easy-to-make tables and chairs. 65

Wicker and machine cane cocktail table. Bausert. Complete book of wicker and cane furniture making. 89–98

X-brace coffee tables. Palmer. Making children's furniture and play structures. 32–33

Tables, Dining

Build a mini-maxi gateleg table, classic oaken table, graceful dining set, beautiful trestle table. Popular Mechanics do-it-yourself encyclopedia. Vol. 7, 983–1000

Butterfly table—maple, Duncan Phyfe dining table. Osburn. Measured drawings of early American furniture. 48–49, 70–72

Circular pedestal table. Easy-to-make tables and chairs. 52–53

Dining room table. Alth. Making plastic pipe furniture. 97–105

Dining table. Make it! don't buy it. 108–19

Dining table. Marlow. Early American furnituremaker's manual. 75–79

Dining table. Rubin. Mission furniture. 70–71

Dining table. Williams. Spanish colonial furniture. 60–63

Dining table. Zegel. Fast furniture. 80–82

Dining table, cafe table and chairs. 101 do-it-yourself projects. 80–85, 139–43

Drop leaf table. Feirer. Cabinetmaking and millwork. 694–97

Dutch pull-out table. Fine woodworking techniques 2. 106–09

Eighteenth century-style dining table, Jacobean oval gateleg table. Taylor. How to build period country furniture. 110–13, 117–21

Fold-down table with cabinet. Black and Decker power tool carpentry. 105–07

Gateleg table. Daniele. Building early American furniture. 108–10

Hutch table. Daniele. Building early American furniture. 82–84

Knockdown buffet-table. Popular Mechanics do-it-yourself encyclopedia. Vol. 8, 1191

Pine trestle table. Easy-to-make tables and chairs. 43–45

Rectangular oak pedestal table. Easy-to-make tables and chairs. 51–52

Round dining table. Spence. Woodworking tools, materials, processes. 610

Round extension table, harvest table, splay leg drop leaf table. Moser. How to build shaker furniture. 154–59

Round table, table with a rural look. Black and Decker power tool carpentry. 87–98

Shaker hutch table. Brann. How to build colonial furniture. 75–88

Sleek dining table. Easy-to-make tables and chairs. 46–48

Space-saving dining areas. Stevenson. How to build and buy kitchen cabinets for the modern kitchen. 203–18
Trestle dining table and bench, drop leaf trestle table. Blandford. How to make early American and colonial furniture. 229–38
Trestle table. Brown. 44 terrific woodworking plans & projects. 166–70
Trestle table. Self. Working with plywood, including indoor/outdoor projects. 245–50
Trestle table and benches. Churchill. Big backyard building book. 101–06

Tables, Dough trough
Bread or dough bowl. Horwitz. Mountain people, mountain crafts. 84–86
Dough trough. Blandford. How to make early American and colonial furniture. 164–68
Dough trough. Gottshall. Provincial furniture design and construction. 57–59
Dough trough table. Shea. Pennsylvania Dutch and their furniture. 178–79
Dough troughs. Langsner. Country woodcraft. 253–61

Tables, End
Art deco table. Linsley. Fabulous furniture decorations. 67–71
Casting a small table. LaPlante. Plastic furniture for the home craftsman. 138–44
Ceramic tile table. Linsley. Fabulous furniture decorations. 168–74
Charming French provincial table, contemporary pedestal table. Popular Mechanics do-it-yourself encyclopedia. Vol. 13, 1974–80
Cherry end table. 101 do-it-yourself projects. 108–11
Comic book table. Linsley. Fabulous furniture decorations. 151–54
Cube tables, drum tables, parson's table. LaPlante. Plastic furniture for the home craftsman. 96–107
Curly maple side table. Gottshall. Provincial furniture design and construction. 60–62
End table. Kramer. Wirecraft. 96–97
End table. Zegel. Fast furniture. 54–55
End table, Girard tilt-top end table. Daniele. Building early American furniture. 79–81, 98–99
End tables. Williams. Spanish colonial furniture. 46–51
Joint table of yellow pine, occasional table. Shea. Pennsylvania Dutch and their furniture. 162–63, 167
Mirrored cube table. Linsley. Fabulous furniture decorations. 35–40
Nest of tables, contemporary end table, hexagonal commode. Spence. Woodworking tools, materials, processes. 593, 608, 611
Nested tables. Brown. 44 terrific woodworking plans & projects. 166–67
Patchwork parson's table. Scobey. Decorating with needlepoint. 87–92
Scrapwood end table, butcher-block end table. DeCristoforo. Build your own wood toys, gifts and furniture. 329–37
Side stand. Moser. How to build Shaker furniture. 140–41
Suede and tile table. Linsley. Fabulous furniture decorations. 80–84
Suede-covered parson's table. Linsley. Fabulous furniture decorations. 27–34
Tatlin's table. Ball. Master pieces. 22–25
Veneered table, white-ash end table. Capotosto. Woodworking techniques and projects. 139–46, 310–14
Wooden slat table. Linsley. Decoupage on glass, wood, metal, rocks, shells, wax, soap, plastic, canvas, ceramic. 50–53

Tables, Folding
Fold-to-wall worktable. Easy-to-make tables and chairs. 54–56

Tables, Game. *See* **Game boards and tables**

Tables, Outdoor
Duckboard tables. Wood projects for the garden. 42
Outdoor garden table. Linsley. Fabulous furniture decorations. 63–66
Outdoor table and bench. 101 do-it-yourself projects. 252–53
Patio table. Better Homes and Gardens. Deck and patio projects you can build. 78
Round top table. Brann. How to build outdoor furniture. 48–58
Tables. Blandford. Constructing outdoor furniture, with 99 projects. 129–56
Tables, and their supports, vegetable clean-up table, low table with butcher-block top, potting table. Wood projects for the garden. 52–55, 57
Tulip-covered table. Linsley. Fabulous furniture decorations. 166–67
Willow table. Johnson. Nature crafts. 16–17

Tables, Outdoor. *See also* **Picnic tables**

Tables, Picnic. *See* **Picnic tables**

Tables, Repairing
Faults in table and similar tops. Hayward. Antique furniture repairs. 81–87
Keeping hinged table leaf flat with cleats. Kinney. Complete book of furniture repair and refinishing. 69–70
Restoring tables. Salazar. Complete book of furniture restoration. 86–98
Table. Wenn. Restoring antique furniture. 51–52
Tables. Jones. Fixing furniture. 58–66
Tables. Marshall. How to repair, reupholster, and refinish furniture. 96–121
Tables. Roberts. Illustrated handbook of upholstery. 381–82
Wobbly table, crack in a tabletop. Time-Life books. Repairing furniture. 18–21, 55

Tags. *See* **Labels**

Tambourines. *See* **Musical instruments**

Tangrams
Chinese tangrams for geometric designs. Holtje. Cardcraft. 94–98

Tanks, Toy
Tank. Buckland. Toymaker's book of wooden vehicles. 70–73
Tanks and military vehicles. Ellis. Scale modeler's handbook. 66–71

Tapestries
Circle tapestry. Brown. Weaving, spinning, and dyeing book. 179–80
Crewel point tapestries. Wilson. Needleplay. 150–153
Eagle, medieval bird and grandfather clock tapestries. Halliday. Decorating with crochet. 2–11
Kilam or Middle East tapestry. Brown. Weaving, spinning, and dyeing book. 173–74
Lion tapestry. Casselman. Crafts from around the world. 199–204
Pictorial tapestry. Brown. Weaving, spinning, and dyeing book. 167–69
Rhodes. Small woven tapestries.
Roumanian-stitch spring tapestry. Wilson. Needleplay. 144–45
Tapestries. Wilson. Weaving you can use. 50–55
Tapestry patterns—offering of the heart and Victorian roses. Wilson. More needleplay. 88–91
Weaving tapestry. Murray. Essential handbook of weaving. 37–47

Tapestry, Conservation & restoration
Collecting, display and conservation of needlework. Complete guide to needlework. 190–211
Tapestry cleaning & repair. Johnson. How to restore, repair and finish almost everything. 110

Targets
Indoor target range. Blackwell. Johnny Blackwell's poor man's catalog. 110
Zeroing-in for hunting, double-duty target box. Popular Mechanics do-it-yourself encyclopedia. Vol. 12, 1768–71

Tatting
Auld. Tatting: the contemporary art of knotting with a shuttle.
Tatted medallions. Dillmont. Complete encyclopedia of needlework. 358–61
Tatting. Dillmont. Complete encyclopedia of needlework. 345–58
Tatting. Longhurst. Vanishing American needle arts. 113–33
Tatting. McCall's big book of knit & crochet for home & family. 266–75
Tatting. Preston. Needle-made laces and net embroideries. 136–47
Tatting. Reader's Digest complete guide to needlework. 413–19
Tatting. Ryan. Complete encyclopedia of stitchery. 652–85
Tatting. Waller. Knots and netting. 35–38
Tatting, tatted rings and chains. Encyclopedia of crafts. 77–78
Walker. Tatting.

Tea cozies. *See* **Teapot covers**

Tea tables. *See* **Tables, Coffee or tea**

Tea wagons
Rattan tea cart. Alth. Rattan furniture. 143–52

Teapot covers
Beehive tea cozy, crocheted. Mills. Book of presents. 12
Blue & white tea cozy. Better Homes & Gardens embroidery. 31
Cherry blossoms on diamond lattice, tea cozy. Nicoletti. Japanese motifs for needlepoint. 37–38
Cottage, place mat tea cozies. Better Homes and Gardens easy bazaar crafts. 13, 20
Cottage tea cozy (appliqued), tabby tea cozy, clam shell tea cozy (appliqued). McCall's book of America's favorite needlework and crafts. 206–08
Domed tea cozy. Morgan. Trapunto and other forms of raised quilting. 196–200
Felt tea cozy. Johnson. Nature crafts. 15
Girl applique tea cozy. Houck. Patchwork pattern book. 36–37
Hexagon tea cozy. Fairfield. Patchwork 36
Motif tea cozy. Svinicki. Old-fashioned Crochet. 46–47
Patchwork cozies and chair pillows. Mills. Book of presents. 72–73
Patchwork tea cosy, felt applique peacock tea cosy. Encyclopedia of crafts. 13, 34–35
Quilted tea cosy. Doherty. Family Circle book of 429 great gifts-to-make all year round for just 10¢ to $10.00. 150
Quilted tea cosy. McNeill. Quilting. 37
Quilted tea cozy. Woman's Day bazaar best sellers. 92
Quilted tea cozy and potholder. Evrard. Homespun crafts from scraps. 61–64
Rectangular tea cozy/toaster cover. Morgan. Trapunto and other forms of raised quilting. 194–95
Tea and coffee cosies. Breckenridge. Lap quilting. 56–57
Tea cosies. Whatnot. 94–97
Tea cozy. Burchette. More needlework blocking and finishing. 134–37

Tea cosy. Osler. Machine patchwork. 96–97
Tea cozy. Roda. Fabric decorating for the home. 44–45
Tea cosy foundation. Bumper book of things a girl can make. 232–33
Tea cozy (sewn). Vanderbilt. Gloria Vanderbilt designs for your home. 105–06
Tea or coffee cozy. Christmas crafts book. 107–08
Tea-party tea cozy. Better Homes and Gardens treasury of Christmas crafts & foods. 213
Wadded quilting tea cosy. Blandford book of traditional handicrafts. 94

Teapots
Dents, restoring spout, handles. Introduction to repairing and restoring. 173, 260, 276–77
Jug and teapot. Pottery step-by-step. 34–36
Making a teapot. Zorza. Pottery: creating with clay. 89–92
Non-drip teapot stand. Bumper book of things a boy can make. 138–39
Teapot. Campbell. Using the potter's wheel. 84–85
Teapot pouring stand. Grainger. Making aids for disabled living. 74–79
Teapot with clay or cane handles. Ceramics. 98–104
Teapots. Rhodes. Pottery form. 135–42
Teapots with different type lids. Wettlaufer. Getting into pots. 68–74
Teapots with side, overhead, or bamboo handle. Campbell. Using the potter's wheel. 56–59
Throwing a teapot. Woody. Pottery on the wheel. 159–66
Thrown teapot. Howell. Craft of pottery. 43–44

Teepees. *See* **Tents**

Teeter-totters. *See* **Playground equipment**

Telephone stands
Early American gossip bench. Popular Mechanics do-it-yourself encyclopedia. Vol. 9, 1365–66
Plexiglass telephone stand. Popular Mechanics do-it-yourself encyclopedia. Vol. 14, 2211
Telephone shelf. Blandford. 53 space-saving built-in furniture projects. 342, 345–46
Telephone stand and stool. Rubin. Mission furniture. 98–99
Telephone table. Black and Decker power tool carpentry. 51–54
Telephone table. LaPlante. Plastic furniture for the home craftsman. 93–95
Wall-mounted telephone cabinet. Make it! don't buy it. 94–107

Telescopes
Turn your camera lens into a telescope. Popular Mechanics do-it-yourself encyclopedia. Vol. 18, 2846–47

Television cabinets & stands
Corner TV stand. Blandford. 53 space-saving built-in furniture projects. 202–05
Home video center. Oberrecht. Plywood projects illustrated. 134–39
Stereo/TV stand. Spence. Woodworking tools, materials, processes. 602
Television cabinet. Philbin. Cabinets, bookcases & closets. 128–29
Television table. Endacott. Fine furniture making and woodworking. 110–14
TV and stereo cabinet. 101 do-it-yourself projects. 100–05
TV cabinet-bookcase. Complete handyman do-it-yourself encyclopedia. Vol. 3, 348–50
TV hi-fi console. 77 furniture projects you can build. 116–21
TV—hi-fi console cabinet. Family handyman handbook of carpentry plans/projects. 52–55
TV table. Churchill. Backyard building book II. 84–86

Tennis
Multipatterned flower. Scheuer. Desings for Holbein embroidery. 78–79
Restring your own tennis racket. Popular Mechanics do-it-yourself encyclopedia. Vol. 18, 2831–53
Shirt converted for playtime. Time-Life books. Sporting scene. 102–11
"Sunshine" tennis raquet cover. Sheldon. Washable and dryable needlepoint. 96–97
Tennis cap and racket cover (crocheted). Feldman. Needlework boutique. 138–40
Tennis dress (crocheted). Time-Life books. Sporting scene. 174–75
Tennis racquet cover. Burchette. More needlework blocking and finishing. 66–69
Tennis racket cover. Coffey. Francine Coffey's celebrity sewing bee. 107
Tennis racquet cover. Parker. Mosaics in needlepoint. 119–23
Tennis racquet cover. Scobey. First easy-to-see needlepoint workbook. 36–39
Tennis racquet cover and tote. Roda. Fabric decorating for the home. 116–21

Tents.
Card table tent with appliques, "Nomad tent." Hagans. All good gifts. 93–103
Dowel tent. Palmer. Making children's furniture and play structures. 78–82
Garden hose tent. Palmer. Making children's furniture and play structures. 82–83
Indian teepee. Creative crafts yearbook: an exciting new collection of needlework and crafts. 90–91
Lean-to. Scurlock. Muzzleloader Magazine's book of buckskinning II. 233–35
Mongolian yurt. Boeschen. Successful playhouses. 62–64
Portable pavilion. Creative sewing. 94
Play wigwam. Mills. Book of presents. 60–61
Tipi (tepee). Boeschen. Successful playhouses. 64–67
Tipi, wigwam. Norbeck. Book of authentic Indian life crafts. 198–205
Two-person tent. Lamoreaux. Outdoor gear your can make yourself. 145–51

Terraces. *See* **Decks; Outdoor rooms; Patios; Porches**

Terrariums
Canopy terrarium. Challenging projects in stained glass. 87–103
Christmas terrarium. Meyer. Christmas crafts. 81–86
Glass-house terrarium. 101 do-it-yourself projects. 328–29
How to make a dried terrarium. Miles. Designing with natural materials. 129–31
Jar terrariums, terrarium lamp. Epple. Something from nothing crafts. 29–37
Make a Tiffany-style terrarium. Popular Mechanics do-it-yourself encyclopedia. Vol. 18, 2858–59
Pagoda and green terrariums. McCall's book of America's favorite needlework and crafts. 332–34
Plexiglas terrarium. Popular Mechanics do-it-yourself encyclopedia. Vol. 14, 2210
Stained glass terrarium, multifaceted terrarium with hinged lid. Wood. Working with stained glass. 15–25
Terrarium. Treasury of things to make. 78–81
Terrarium case with lid and cabinet. La Barge. Pet house book. 132–42
Terrarium table. Appel. Sand art. 107–09
Terrariums and a landscape design. Appel. Sand art. 29–36
Tom Thumb-size greenhouse. Doherty. Family Circle book of 429 great gifts-to-make all year round for just 10¢ to $10.00. 94

Testing instruments. *See* **Electric testers**

Tetherball
Pole tennis. Blandford. Giant book of wooden toys. 298–301
Tetherball. Popular Mechanics do-it-yourself encyclopedia. Vol. 14, 2199

Textile craft
Mola. Treasury of things to make. 143–45
Textile design. Rose. Illustrated encyclopedia of crafts and how to master them. 301–07

Textile fabrics, Care
Fine linens, cottons, embroidery and lace repair. Johnson. How to restore, repair, and finish almost everything. 111–14

Textile painting
Fabric painting. Seagroatt. Basic textile book. 81–83
Fabric painting. Treasury of things to make. 75–77
Hammered leaf prints. Geary. Plant prints and collages. 51–52
Painted and printed fabrics. Sommer. Wearable crafts. 13–28
Painting and stenciling with dyes. Time-Life books. Boutique attire. 70–73
Painting on cotton cloth—Senufo style. Contemporary African arts and crafts. 89–96
Painting on fabric. Howard. New tole & folk art designs. 121–28
Plant pictures on cloth. Geary. Plant prints and collages. 78
Printed fabric. Better Homes and Gardens treasury of Christmas crafts & foods. 17
Printing on cloth. Geary. Plant prints and collages. 49–52
Scrap printing on fabric, lino block printing, screen printing on fabric. Encyclopedia of crafts. 154–57
Stenciling on cloth. Dyeing & printing. 78–80
Stenciling on fabrics. Midkiff. Complete book of stenciling. 50–51
Tie-and dye, printing and painting. Murray. Essential handbook of weaving. 149–51
Velvet painting. Brunner. Pass it on. 76–78

Textile painting. *See also* **Silk screen painting**

Theaters, Toy
Miniature theater. Elbert. Paperworks. 152–57

Tie-Dyeing. *See* **Dyes and dyeing**

Tigers. *See* **Cats**

Tiles
Burch. Tile: indoors and out, every kind and use.
Laying tiles. Kramer. Outdoor garden build-it book. 27
Many pattern possibilities of tile. Porches and patios. 88–94
Patted-on floral tile and landscape. Gardner. Dough creations. 106–10
What you should know about tiling walls. Popular Mechanics do-it-yourself encyclopedia. Vol. 18, 2869–74

Tiles. *See also* **Floors, Tile**

Tiles, Ceramic
Backup board for ceramic tile. Popular Mechanics do-it-yourself encyclopedia. Vol. 20, 3049–51
Ceramic tile finishes. Olin. Construction. 442.1–442.24
How to set ceramic tile. Nunn. Home paint book. 87–92
Installing ceramic tile. Family handyman handbook of home improvement and remodeling. 248–54
Installing ceramic tile. Waugh. Handyman's encyclopedia. 61–64
Tiles. Chroman. Potter's primer. 52–54

Timing devices
Three-minute hourglass. Hodges. Woodturning handbook with projects. 173–76

Tin cans
Gems from junk. Popular Mechanics do-it-yourself encyclopedia. Vol. 18, 2875–80
Tin-can crafting. Metalcrafting encyclopedia. 74–95
Tin can punching. Metal and enamel. 20–22
Tin can tower. Metalcrafting encyclopedia. 99
Working with cans. Fowler. Can crafts. 4–13

Tin foil. *See* **Metal foil**

Toads. *See* **Frogs and toads**

Toast racks
Toast rack. Sainsbury. Sainsbury's woodturning projects for dining. 39–41

Tobacco boxes
Tobacco canteen. Scurlock. Muzzleloader Magazine's book of buckskinning II. 221
Tobacco jar and lid. Wooldridge. Woodturning techniques. 39–43
Tobacco pouches. Burchette. More needlework blocking and finishing. 100–02

Tobacco pipes
Carved pipe. Kinney. How to make 19 kinds of American folk art. 27–29
Cherry wood pipe; making a pipe rack. Bumper book of things a boy can make. 78–
    80, 129–30
Corncob pipes. Johnson. Nature crafts. 72
Peace pipes. Norbeck. Book of authentic Indian life crafts. 136–40

Toboggans
Dog-powered toboggan. Churchill. Backyard building book II. 89–91
Making a toboggan. Bumper book of things a boy can make. 93–94
Toboggan. Dal Fabbro. How to make children's furniture and play equipment. 164–65
Toboggan repair. Schuler. How to fix almost everything. 164

Tole painting
Hauser. Priscilla Hauser book of tole and decorative painting.
Howard. New tole & folk art designs.
Painting on wood & tinware, special finishing techniques. Buxton. Craftmaking: for love
    or money. 17–150

Tomahawks
Tomahawk. Villiard. Art and craft of sand casting. 78

Tongs
Blacksmith's tongs. Make it! don't buy it. 251
Charcoal tongs. Modern general shop. Metalworking. 105
Forging blacksmiths' tongs. Weygers. Modern blacksmith. 65–66
Forging fireplace tongs. Weyger. Modern blacksmith. 58
Forging a pair of tongs. McRaven. Country blacksmithing. 65–67
Making light and heavy tongs. Blandford. Practical handbook of blacksmithing and
    metalworking. 201–06
Small tongs. Scurlock. Muzzleloader Magazine's book of buckskinning II. 229–30
Veneered toast tongs. Hobbs. Veneer craft for everyone. 127–28

Tool boxes, racks, etc.
Big and little tool boxes. Hamilton. Build it together. 8–15
Cabinetmaker's tool cabinet. Fine woodworking techniques 5. 63–65
Carpenter's tool box. Braren. Homemade. 14
Carpenter's tool box. Shea. Pennsylvania Dutch and their furniture. 176
Contemporary toolbox. Popular Mechanics do-it-yourself encyclopedia. Vol. 19, 2896–98
Drill bit holder; paintbrush cleaner rack; wall hung board for tools. Doherty. Family Circle book of 429 great gifts-to-make all year round for just 10¢ to $10.00. 124–25
Garden tool organizer. Family handyman handbook of carpentry plans/projects. 405–14
Garden tool organizer. Outdoor projects for home and garden. 422–30
Handy tool tote. Oberrecht. Plywood projects illustrated. 207
Handyman's tool toter. Handyman. 524–25
Hanging tool caddy made from upholstery webbing. Rissell. Craftwork the handicapped elderly can make and sell. 68–69
Joiners' tool case, bigfoot tool rack. Fine woodworking techniques 4. 40–41, 48
Open tool racks, tool locker, whetstone case, garden tool racks. Blandford. 53 space-saving built-in furniture projects. 355–67, 371–74
Parts bin, parts/tool cabinet. Giant book of metalworking projects. 223–26
Satellite electric tool caddy, portable tool and fixture rack. McNair. Building & outfitting your workshop. 87–97, 117–27
Sawhorse tool chest. Brann. How to build workbenches, sawhorse tool chest and other build-it-yourself projects. 57–64
Small household tool box. Wagner. Modern woodworking. 13–19
Tool cabinet, tote box for portable tools. Brown. 44 terrific woodworking plans & projects. 113–20
Tool cabinets. Fine woodworking techniques 2. 26–27
Tool cabinets, portable tool box, sawhorse tool box. Blackwell. Johnny Blackwell's poor man's catalog. 9, 11
Tool caddy from scraps. Popular Mechanics do-it-yourself encyclopedia. Vol. 4, 510
Tool carrying case. Geary. How to design and build your own workspace—with plans. 116–17
Tool chest. Stiles. Easy-to-make children's furniture. 72–76
Tool hanger. Mills. Book of presents. 74–75
Tool panel organizer. Modern general shop. Metalworking. 114
Tool racks. Blandford. How to make your own built-in furniture. 316–21
Tool storage. Braren. Homemade. 60
Tote box and multiuse carpenter's box. Wood projects for the garden. 70–71
Tote box for nails and tools. Syvanen. Interior finish: more tricks of the trade. 123
Wall cabinet for tools. Leavy. Bookshelves and storage units. 46–48
Woodburned tool carryall. Broadwater. Woodburning: art and craft. 135–39

Tool houses
Backyard storage shed. Boeschen. Successful playhouses. 128–39
Barn storage shed, outdoor garden storage shed. Self. Working with plywood, including indoor/outdoor projects. 170–75, 193–203
Build storage into a fence. Popular Mechanics do-it-yourself encyclopedia. Vol. 8, 1199–1201
Chalet storage building, family bank, Irish shanty. Churchill. Big backyard building book. 149–65
Gambrel roofed storage barn, outdoor equipment shed, storage building kit. Family Handyman handbook of carpentry plans/projects. 428–56
Garden shelters. Outdoor projects for home and garden. 321–71
Gardener's all purpose building. Marshall. Yard buildings. 67–73

Hand-hewn log shed. Lane. Building in your own backyard. 88–91
House-frame shed. Lane. Building in your backyard. 83–87
Little red barn shed. Complete handyman do-it-yourself encyclopedia. Vol. 9, 1280–88
Portable storage building. Burch. Building small barns, shed, and shelters. 184–85
Pole-frame shed. Lane. Building in your backyard. 66–82
Storage gazebo. Popular Mechanics do-it-yourself encyclopedia. Vol. 14, 2110–11
Storage/guest house. Marshall. Yard buildings. 47–58
Storage shed. 101 do-it-yourself projects. 278–81
Tool shed. Braren. Homemade. 58–59
Tool shed. Family handyman handbook of carpentry plans/projects. 388–98
Toolshed. Marshall. Yard building. 39–46
Tool shelter. Burch. Building small barns, sheds, and shelters. 180–81
Woodsheds. Burch. Building small barns, sheds, and shelters. 181–84

Tools

Albers. How to use woodworking tools effectively and safely.
Antique tools: a buyer's guide to many you can use. Fine woodworking techniques I. 65–67
Arbor press, drill-press vise, pulley pullers, steel anvil. Giant book of metalworking projects. 234–41, 245
Bealer. Tools that built America.
Bench clamp. Abrams. Building craft equipment. 175–77
Branding tools for identification. Brightman. 101 practical uses for propane torches. 126
Clubs, mauls, and mallets. Langsner. Country woodcraft. 73–79
Eight fine tools you can make: calipers, lathe chisels, two-faced sander, bench hook, handles, shooting board, V-block, bead former. Popular Mechanics do-it-yourself encyclopedia. Vol. 17, 2670–72
Forging a crowbar, center punch, one-point stonecarving tool. Weyger. Modern blacksmith. 46
Froes (club). Langsner. Country woodcraft. 160–61
Hand planes. Fine woodworking techniques I. 46–55
Handtools of arts and crafts.
Improved screw chuck, dial indicator, making your own machines, shaper cutters and fences, abrasive planer. Fine woodworking techniques 4. 90–101, 117–20
Improving planes, restoring Bailey planes, router tables, jointer, shaper, old-fashioned turners, gauges you can make yourself. Fine woodworking techniques 3. 26–30, 32–35, 50–53, 79–85, 140–41
Leaf rake repair. Schuler. How to fix almost everything. 136
Machinist's jack, brass mallet, setup tool, parallel bars, angle plate, sine bar. Briney. Home machinist's handbook. 214–25, 231–38, 244–56
Making insets. Weygers. Recycling, use, and repair of tools. 95–100
Making spikes, screwdrivers, a crowbar, holdfast, jaws, hammers, a set, fullers, swages, bottom tools, and stakes. Blandford. Practical handbook of blacksmithing and metalworking. 172–80, 192–99, 206–25
Making tool handle ferrules and shoulders. Weygers. Recycling, use, and repair of tools. 16–17
Milling cutters, augers and drills. Weygers. Modern blacksmith. 67–69
Planemaker's float, pair of panel-raising planes. Fine woodworking techniques 5. 58–62
Planing. Waugh. Handyman's encyclopedia. 207–11
Poor man's mini plane. Blackwell. Johnny Blackwell's poor man's catalog. 145
Poor man's sanders. Blackwell. Johnny Blackwell's poor man's catalog. 147
Router. Buckwalter. Homeowner's handbook of power tools. 109–21
Router rail, Japanese planes, modern wooden plane, set of carving gouges. Fine woodworking techniques 4. 52–53, 64–69, 77–79

Sander, use and maintenance. Buckwalter. Homeowner's handbook of power tools. 65–77

Scratch beader, marking gauge. Fine woodworking techniques 2. 50–51

Self. Woodworking tools and hardware.

Self-lubricating oilstone. Popular Mechanics do-it-yourself encyclopdedia. Vol. 17, 2610–11

Spatula made from a section of coil spring. Weyger. Modern blacksmith. 59–60

Storage for molding cutters. Popular Mechanics do-it-yourself encyclopedia. Vol. 12, 1900

T-bar auger, wrecking bar. McRaven. Country blacksmithing. 105, 108

Tool handles. Langsner. Country woodcraft. 89–99

Tool maintenance and storage. Gladstone. Hints and tips for the handyperson. 2–23

Tool sharpening, cleaner, finder, & brander. Braren. Homemade. 61–64

Trip-hammer and its use & upsetting. Weygers. Recycling, use, and repair of tools. 89–94, 101–02

Tune up your power tools, stands for your power tools, roll-away stand holds router and drill. Popular Mechanics do-it-yourself encyclopedia. Vol. 15, 2310–23

U-build bearings, U-build pulleys, motor mounts, speed reducer, eccentric, drill stand, spring winder, drum sander, etc. Blackwell. Johnny Blackwell's poor man's catalog. 4–34

Use of woodworking tools. Blandford. Do-it-yourselfer's guide to furniture repair and refinishing. 105–32

Wooden mallet. Fine woodworking techniques 4. 11

Wooden wedges. Langsner. Country woodcraft. 100–104

Woodworking tools. Huckleberry. How to make your own wooden jewelry. 33–52

Workshop tool to fit bandsaw or disc sander for making wood discs. Popular Mechanics do-it-yourself encyclopedia. vol. 7, 1001

Tools, Sharpening
Albers. How to use woodworking tools effectively and safely.

How to keep cutting edges sharp. Popular Mechanics do-it-yourself encyclopedia. Vol. 17, 2608–09

How to sharpen, Japanese blades (traditional sharpening methods), slow-speed sharpening. Fine woodworking techniques 5. 45–52

How to sharpen tools on your radial-arm saw. Popular Mechanics do-it-yourself encyclopedia. Vol. 15, 2384–85

Professional methods for sharpening drill bits. Time-Life Books. Working with wood. 76–79

Sharpening a shaper to a fine cutting edge. Time-Life Books. Working with wood. 102–07

Sharpening tool edges. Weygers. Recycling, use, and repair of tools. 106–07

Sharpening your tools. Handyman. 38–41

Whetstones: how novaculite is quarried and finished; sharpening. Fine woodworking techniques 2. 36–41

Tools, Sharpening. See also **Saws, Sharpening**

Toothpicks
Candle or toothpick holder. Fowler. Can crafts. 112–14

Stockade toothpick holder. Lubkemann. Carving twigs and branches. 76–79

Toothpick dispenser. Cope. Plastics. 52–53

Tops
Gyroscopic top. Giant book of metalworking projects. 207–09

Spinning top. Blandford. Giant book of wooden toys. 156–59

Spinning top. Modern general shop. Woodworking. 111–12

Spinning tops. Baldwin. Old fashioned wooden toys. 22–24

Totem poles
Box totem pole. Yoder. Sculpture and modeling for the elementary school. 154–55
Pumpkin totem pole. Johnson. Nature crafts. 88–89
Totem pole bags. Yoder. Sculpture and modeling for the elementary school. 71
Totem poles. Norbeck. Book of authentic Indian life crafts. 123–28

Towel bars
Folding towel rails, bathroom towel rack. Blandford. 53 space-saving built-in furniture projects. 226–28, 287–91
Handy cabinet-towel rack for bathroom wall. Family handyman handbook of home improvement and remodeling. 88–91
Ship's ladder towel rack. Roda. Fabric decorating for the home. 207
Three attractive towel racks. Popular Mechanics do-it-yourself encyclopedia. Vol. 19, 2906
Towel bar. Make it! don't buy it. 264–67
Towel and paper holders. Kangas. By hand. 193–94
Towel rack. Brown. 44 terrific woodworking plans & projects. 136–37
Towel rack. Doherty. Family Circle book of 429 great gifts-to-make all year round for just 10¢ to $10.00. 6–7

Towels
Applique bath towels. Reader's Digest complete guide to sewing. 518–19
Bunny bath towel. Roda. Fabric decorating for the home. 196
Checkerboard beach towel. Reader's Digest complete guide to sewing. 508–09
Cross-stitch hand towels. Wilson. Erica Wilson's Christmas world. 91–92
Cross-stitch pillowcases & guest towel. Better Homes & Gardens embroidery. 56–57
Decorator and embroidered tea. Linsley. Great bazaar. 47–48, 158–59
Guest hand towel. Coffey. Francine Coffey's celebrity sewing bee. 156
Guest towels with filet insert. Svinicki. Old-fashioned crochet. 96–98
Kitchen hand towel. Coffey. Francine Coffey's celebrity sewing bee. 165
Show kitchen towel. Jacobs. Crochet book. 171–72
Tie-dyed hand towel. Frame. Tie-dyeing and batik. 22–25

Towels, Infant
Hooded bath towels. Laury. Treasury of needlecraft gifts for the new baby. 43–47

Toys
Bamboo squirt gun, sky pierces, teaching/learning toys, rattlin' roller. Hodges. 46 step-by-step wooden toy projects. 97–101, 137–44, 217–19
Beach toys. Thiebault. Kites and other wind machines. 82–85
Boomerangs. Warring. Balsa wood modelling. 6–7
Box toys and characters. Yoder. Sculpture and modeling for the elementary school. 146–52
Cane ball. Wright. Complete book of baskets and basketry. 135
Christmas tree bagatelle. Greenhowe. Making miniature toys and dolls. 85–86
Crib gym. Scobey. First easy-to-see needlepoint workbook. 26–30
Elephant with nodding head, rolling drum push or pull toy, push or pull ferris wheel, pinwheel pull toy. DeCristoforo. Build your own wood toys, gifts and furniture. 124–43
Escaping robber, somersaulting clown, sand engine. Blizzard. Making wooden toys. 15–17, 20–22, 26–29
Eskimo toys and personal things. Wilder. Secrets of Eskimo skin sewing. 111–17
Felt jump rope handles. Coffey. Francine Coffey's celebrity sewing bee. 129
Four pop-up toys. Greenhowe. Making miniature toys and dolls. 58–62
Gadget board for playpen. Adams. Make your own baby furniture. 158–63
Geometric toy. Blandford. Giant book of wooden toys. 57–59

Giant dice. Great granny crochet book. 62
Hammer and peg game, swinging hammer and peg game. Blandford. Giant book of wooden toys. 174–78
Hide'n seek gingerbread toy (crocheted). Feldman. Needlework boutique. 21–22
Interlocking panel and logs paper constructional toys. Grainger. Creative papercraft. 95–96
Jacob's ladder. Warring. Balsa wood modelling. 5
Knitted toys. Selfridge. Patchwork knitting. 136–45
Ladder box. Dal Fabbro. How to make children's furniture and play equipment. 154–55
Magic tortoise move about a garden. Greenhowe. Making miniature toys and dolls. 100–01
A me-tree. Palmer. Making children's furniture and play structures. 133
Milk carton toys. Woman's Day book of gifts to make. 24–27
Noah's ark. Blandford. Giant book of wooden toys. 68–72
Papier-mâché tumble toy. Elbert. Paperworks. 124–27
Play table. Dal Fabbro. How to make children's furniture and play equipment. 139
Pony pull toy and planter. Brann. How to build workbenches, sawhorse tool chest and other build-it-yourself projects. 82–89
See-saw, Margery Daw swinging weight toy. Greeenhowe. Making miniature toys and dolls. 16–21
Soft sculpture rabbits. Treasury of things to make. 10–12
Solar hitchhiker. Calhoun. 20 simple solar projects. 234–43
Three wooden toys. Woman's Day book of weekend crafts. 98–101
Toy town (pillows). Complete book of baby crafts. 167–71
Whimsy diddling. Underhill. Woodwright's companion. 87–93
Windmill. Blizzard. Making wooden toys. 49–55

Toys, Storage
Circus-wagon toy box. Popular Mechanics do-it-yourself encyclopedia. Vol. 19, 2914–16
Mobile toy box. Blandford. Giant book of wooden toys. 88–89
Modular toy box/stacking units. Waugh. Handyman's encyclopedia. 424–26
Portable storage wagon. Stiles. Easy-to-make children's furniture. 106–09
Shaker toy chests. 77 furniture projects you can build. 90–92
Toy bag. Favorite easy-to-make toys. 222–25
Toy box. Blandford. 66 children's furniture projects. 91–92
Toy box. Zegel. Fast furniture. 106–07
Toy box house. Favorite easy-to-make toys. 169–75
Toy box made from cradle. Adams. Make your own baby furniture. 34–42
Toy boxes. Popular Mechanics do-it-yourself encyclopedia. Vol. 3, 430–32
Toy chest. Hundley. Folk art toys and furniture for children. 102–06
Toy chest and bench. Dal Fabbro. How to make children's furniture and play equipment. 124–25
Toy crate. Hamilton. Build it together. 46–53
Toy shelves. Adams. Make your own baby furniture. 178–83
Toy storage unit. Stiles. Easy-to-make children's furniture. 102–03
Toy truck. Blandford. 66 children's furniture projects. 220–28, 262–76
Train toy bag and flower toy bag. Laury. Treasury of needlecraft gifts for the new baby. 146–50
Treasured playthings (toy storage). Houck. Big bag book. 91–96
Versatile toy bag. Complete book of baby crafts. 165
War chest. Churchill. Backyard building book II. 78–81

Toys, Wooden
Mexican painted animals. Sayer. Crafts of Mexico. 116–19

Tractors, Toy
Farm tractor and wagon, road grader, large farm tractor, grain wagon, farm combine. Hodges. 46 step-by-step wooden toy projects. 169–203
Garden tractor and cart, pickup truck, tractor and trailer, hay wagon. Maginley. Trains and boats and planes and . . . 47–56
Toy tractors. Endacott. Fine furniture making and woodworking. 79–80
Tractor and tipper trailer. Blandford. Giant book of wooden toys. 119–24
Tractor, farm trailer, disk, plow. Buckland. Toymaker's book of wooden vehicles. 103–14
Tractor, mini tractor. Maginley. Toys to make and ride. 70–79, 84–87

Trailers
Bike trailer. Blackwell. Johnny Blackwell's poor man's catalog. 45
Boating trailer maintenance. Popular Mechanics do-it-yourself encyclopedia. Vol. 3, 373–80
Trailer. Giant book of metalworking projects. 219–21
Trailer for your garden tractor, tent trailer. Popular Mechanics do-it-yourself encyclopedia. Vol. 19, 2928–36
Two-wheeled cart or farm trailer, trailer hitch. McRaven. Country blacksmithing. 136, 138–41

Trains, Toy. *See* **Railroads, Toy**

Transoms
Installing a transom. Time-Life Books. New living spaces. 25

Traps
Rat bait stations. Braren. Homemade. 170–71

Trapunto
Florentine trapunto. D'Amato. Italian crafts. 25–28
Morgan. Trapunto and other forms of raised quilting.
Mounting for framing. Morgan. Trapunto and other forms of raised quilting. 152–54
Three dimensional forms—trapunto and stuffing. Newman. Quilting, patchwork, applique and trapunto. 193–234
Trapunto. Hall. Sewing machine craft book. 94–95
Trapunto. Mansfield. Clothing construction. 377–79
Trapunto. Risinger. Innovative machine quilting. 99–103
Trapunto for appliques, pendants and buttons. Sommer. Wearable crafts. 65–69

Trash Cans. *See* **Refuse receptacles; Waste baskets**

Tray stands
Butler's tray table. Complete handyman do-it-yourself encyclopedia. Vol. 19, 2865–71

Trays
Bed tray. Blandford. 66 children's furniture projects. 350–56
Butterfly serving tray. Scobey. Decorating with needlepoint. 154–56
Cheese tray. Popular Mechanics do-it-yourself encyclopedia. Vol. 9, 1353
Chippendale tray (painted). McCall's book of America's favorite needlework and crafts. 344–46
Colonial tray stand. Spence. Woodworking tools, materials, processes. 596
Cracker and butter dish. Sainsbury. Sainsbury's woodturning projects for dining. 101–04
Cracker tray. Modern general shop. Woodworking. 94
Decorative tray holder to hand trays on the wall. Perry. Holiday magic. 179–81

Decoupage serving trays. Elbert. Paperworks. 77–79
Early American tray. Modern general shop. Woodworking. 101
Easy storage for trays. Family handyman handbook of home improvement and remodeling. 13
Etched copper tray. Metalcrafting encyclopedia. 54–55
Fancy wooden tray. Popular Mechanics do-it-yourself encyclopedia. Vol. 11, 1653
Foilcraft tray. Marshall. Foilcraft. 54–56
Folding snack server. Popular Mechanics do-it-yourself encyclopedia. Vol. 19, 2944–47
Garden tray hanger. Scobey. Decorating with needlepoint. 152–53
Gold-leafed dragon box and bird tray. McCall's book of America's favorite needlework and crafts. 363–66
Hors d'oeuvre tray. Campbell. Using the potter's wheel. 72–73
Hors d'oeuvre tray. Hodges. Woodturning handbook—with projects. 194–97
Making a tray. Finegold. Silversmithing. 315–29
Oval tray and baskets. Cane, rush and straw. 34–40
Party tray. Linsley. Custom made. 92–94
Petite fours dish. Sainsbury. Sainsbury's woodturning projects for dining. 136–39
Plexiglass tray. Woman's Day book of gifts to make. 212–13
Rectangular trays. Nish. Creative woodturning. 128–31
Rope edged trays. Grainger. Creative ropecraft. 113–18
Serving tray. Modern general shop. Woodworking. 112
Serving tray. Williams. Spanish colonial furniture. 16–17
Spanish blackwork tray cloth. Encyclopedia of crafts. 142
Table tray used as a bread basket, letter tray, or object holder. Kramer. Wirecraft. 78–79
Tea tray in willow. Maynard. Modern basketry from the start. 151–52
Tie-dyed tray cloth. Frame. Tie-dyeing and batik. 48–49
Tile-lined tray and stand. Treasury of things to make. 116–21
Tray sling. Roda. Fabric decorating for the home. 64
Trays. Blandford. 66 children's furniture projects. 96–100
Trays and plates. Romberg. Let's discover papier-mâché. 42
TV trays. Self. Working with plywood, including indoor/outdoor projects. 283–84
Twin server. Modern general shop. Woodworking. 107
Victorian butler's tray. Black and Decker power tool carpentry. 55–58
Wine-labeled, see-through, jigsaw puzzle, armchair lapboard, bulletin board, herb inlaid, & picture frame. Doherty. Family Circle book of 429 great gifts-to-make all year round for just 10¢ to $10.00. 2–3, 10–12, 14, 128, 130, 191

Tree houses
Ground-level house in a grove of trees. Lane. Building in your backyard. 150–51
Indoor treehouse, living treehouse. Boeschen. Successful playhouses. 41–44
Simple, wood frame, and treeless treehouses. Boeschen. Successful playhouses. 10–18
Tower fort. Boeschen. Successful playhouses. 19–21
Treehouses on a trunk or among the branches. Lane. Building in your backyard. 152–57

Trees, Miniature
Bouquet garni tree. Mills. The book of presents. 48
Christmas tree. Williams. Cookie craft: no-bake designs for edible party favors and decorations. 122–24
Flower tree. Stephan. Creating with tissue paper. 183
Jesse tree. Hagans. All good gifts. 126–31
Lonepine, curled wood pyramid, and flowering trees. Christmas crafts book. 14–17
Pear in a partridge tree. Elbert. Shell craft. 62–64
Standing tree. Gardner. Dough creations. 115–19

Stylized tree. Hibbs. Straw sculpture. 72–73, 104
Table centerpiece. Christmas crafts book. 33–34
Topiary tree. Heard. Complete guide to quilting. 279
Topiary tree. Meras. Vacation crafts. 51
Topiary tree. Wiita. Dried flowers for all seasons. 74–75

Trellises
Fencelike structures—trellises, arbors and pergola. Proulx. Plan and make your own
    fences and gates, walkways, walls and drives. 41–45
Free standing trellis. Brann. How to build patios and sundecks. 77–91
Garden pergola. Kramer. Outdoor garden build-it book. 183
Grape, apple, vine-crop, watermelon, tomato, A-frame, folding; interwoven, portable,
    dowel door, and free standing screen trellises. Wood projects for the garden. 23–
    33
Side trellis. Brann. How to build outdoor projects. 75–78
Trellis. 101 do-it-yourself projects. 270–71
Trellis made from plastic 6-pack holders. Epple. Something from nothing crafts. 107–
    08
Trelliswork. Kramer. Outdoor garden build-it book. 178

Trick toys
"Magic" belt holder. Cope. Plastics. 73
Pop-in trick toy. Blandford. Giant book of wooden toys. 181–82
Sliding block. Blandford. Giant book of wooden toys. 191–92

Tripods
Aluminum tripod. Giant book of metalworking projects. 212–13

Trivets
Aluminum trivet. Woman's Day book of weekend crafts. 40
Bargello trivet. Christensen. Teach yourself needlepoint. 74–75
Bead trivet or table mat. Hulbert. Creative beadwork. 32
Clay trivets. Chroman. Potter's primer. 55
Clothespin trivets. Woman's Day book of gifts to make. 130–32
Dinner mats. Sainsbury. Sainsbury's woodturning projects for dining. 15–16
Flower trivet in cast plastic. O'Neill. Make-it-merry Christmas book. 93
Freeform trivets. Wargo. Soft crafts for special occasions. 98–100
Kitchen trivet. Hamilton. Build it together. 32–39
Matchstick, edge grained, laced leather, cork, dowel. Doherty. Family Circle book of
    429 great gifts-to-make all year round for just 10¢ to $10.00. 4, 124, 127, 129,
    134
Needlepoint coasters and trivets. Burchette. Needlework. 52–53
Openwork trivet. Gardner. Dough creations. 112–13
Owl trivet. Modern general shop. Metalworking. 100–01
Table trivets made from corks or clothespins. Better Homes and Gardens easy bazaar
    crafts. 11, 19
Tile trivet. Modern general shop. Woodworking. 108
Trivet. Zegel. Fast furniture. 111
Trivets. Fowler. Can crafts. 26–27
Wooden trivet from a solid block. Popular Mechanics do-it-yourself encyclopedia. Vol.
    2, 277

Trucks, Toy
Big hauler truck and trailer. Hodges. 46 step-by-step wooden toy projects. 203–16
Bulldozer. Peterson. Children's toys you can build yourself. 47–48
Cab, log carrier, moving van, sand carrier. DeCristoforo. Build your own wood toys,
    gifts and furniture. 148–61

Dump truck. Milstein. Building cardboard toys. 45–49
Fuel oil truck, moving van, garbage truck, parcel delivery truck, delivery van, lumber truck, tractor & flatbed hauler, tractor and semi-trailer, tractor and tandem trailers, tractor & open trailer, dump truck, rock hauler, dump trailer & tractor, road grader, double drum roller. Maginley. Trains and boats and planes and . . . 14–26, 66–98
Pull along truck. Blandford. Giant book of wooden toys. 115–18
Push truck. Blandford. Giant book of wooden toys. 102–04
Sand digger, 6-wheel lorry. Blizzard. Making wooden toys. 30–34, 56–59
Soft-sculpture truck. Woman's Day creative stitchery from scraps. 30–34
Steam shovel. Peterson. Children's toys you can build yourself. 49–53
Tipping truck. Blandford. Giant book of wooden toys. 134–37
Toy dump truck. Popular Mechanics do-it-yourself encyclopedia. Vol. 7, 1059
Toy van. Endacott. Fine furniture making and woodworking. 76–79
Two toy trucks. Fine woodworking techniques 3. 108–09
Wooden truck with blocks. Favorite easy-to-make toys. 159–63
Wrecker, semi-tractor, flat-bed trailer, enclosed trailer, tanker trailer, auto carrier trailer, dump truck, earth mover, road roller, dozer, grader. Buckland. Toymaker's book of wooden vehicles. 78–82, 88–102, 115–42

Trunks. *See* **Chests**

Tumbling barrels

Building your own rotary tumbler. Hyde. Complete book of rock tumbling. 35–45
Equipment for tumbling. Meyer. Rock tumbling. 33–49
Fletcher. Rock and gem polishing.
Tumbling slabs and preforms. Hyde. Complete book of rock tumbling. 95–103
Using tumbler for burnishing finished jewelry. Hyde. Complete book of rock tumbling. 149–51
Vibrating tumblers. Hyde. Complete book of rock tumbling. 46–56

Turkeys

Bag sculpture turkey. Yoder. Sculpture and modeling for the elementary school. 71–72

Turning. *See* **Lathes; Wood turning**

Turtles

Painted stone turtles. Woman's Day book of weekend crafts. 50–51
Rock turtle. Day. Complete book of rock crafting. 21–42
Shell turtles. Logan. Shell crafts. 171
Terrance the turtle. Feldman. Needlework boutique. 23–25
Tillie turtle. Guild. Dollmaker's workshop. 44–45
Yoyo turtle. Creative sewing. 102

Typewriter stands

Typewriter desk. Williams. Spanish colonial furniture. 116–17
Typing table. Blandford. 53 space-saving built-in furniture projects. 292–96

U

Umbrellas

Case for your recorder. Tyler. Big book of soft toys. 239
Foul-weather bench to store umbrellas and rain shoes or boots. Capotosto. Woodworking techniques and projects. 109–13
Rainy day hat and umbrella. Farlie. Pennywise boutique. 130–31
Readers Digest shower umbrellas. Epple. Something for nothing crafts. 62–63

Seminole patchwork umbrella sheath. Stribling. Crafts from North American Indian arts. 177
Umbrella cover. Burchette. More needlework blocking and finishing. 74–78
Umbrella repair. Schuler. How to fix almost everything. 168–69
Umbrella stand. Alth. Making plastic pipe furniture. 75–82
Umbrella stand. Blandford. 53 space-saving built-in furniture projects. 350–53
Umbrella stand. Goldman. Decorate with felt. 120–21
Umbrella stand. Rubin. Mission furniture. 61
Umbrella stand. Zegel. Fast furniture. 112
Wooden cube boot and umbrella stand. Woman's Day book of gifts to make. 135–36

Upholstery
Arm and wing chairs. Blandford. Upholsterer's bible. 165–78
Basic course in upholstery. Popular Mechanics do-it-yourself encyclopedia. Vol. 19, 2990–3001
Blandford. Upholsterer's bible.
Elementary upholstery. Meyers. Furniture repair and refinishing. 167–81
Fabric selection. McDonald. Modern upholstering techniques. 64–77
McDonald. Upholstery repair and restoration.
Methods of springing and suspension. McDonald. Modern upholstering techniques. 33–49
Nesovich. Reupholstering at home.
Parker. Upholstering for everyone.
Removing upholstery. Blandford. Upholsterer's bible. 357–64
Repairing and reupholstering. Brann. How to repair, refinish, reupholster. 16–45
Repairing vinyl upholstery. Roberts. Illustrated handbook of upholstery. 95
Reupholstering for a new look. Time-Life Books. Repairing furniture. 97–133
Reupholstering furniture. Marshall. How to repair, reupholster, and refinish furniture. 162–97
Reupholstering furniture. Restoring and reupholstering furniture. 79–173
Reupholstery. Johnson. How to restore, repair, and finish almost everything. 114–23
Reupholstery. Jones. Fixing furniture.
Roberts. Illustrated handbook of upholstery.
Torelli. Reupholstering for the home craftsman.
Upholstering. Blandford. Do-it-yourselfer's guide to furniture repair and refinishing. 247–55
Upholstering a drop-in seat, simple upholstery repairs. Encyclopedia of crafts. 170–73
Upholstery. Blandford. 53 space-saving built-in furniture projects. 65–79
Upholstery. Blandford. How to make your own built-in furniture. 159–66
Upholstery. Hilts. Popular Mechanics complete book of furniture. 265–99
Upholstery and plastic laminates. Wagner. Modern woodworking. 317–31

Upholstery. *See also* **Cushions; Names of specific pieces of furniture**

V

Valances
Bargello valance. Scobey. Decorating with needlepoint. 115–18
Bathtub cornice. Roda. Fabric decorating for the home. 212
Cornice cover and draperies to sew. Woman's Day decorative needlework for the home. 107–09
Fabric covered cornice. Roda. Fabric decorating for the home. 2–4
How to make decorative valances and cornices. McCall's sewing for your home. 132–36, 139–41
Mirror-cloth valance (India). Casselman. Crafts from around the world. 12–15
Tasseled valance. Crochet. 110

Valentines
Lace paper valentines. Elbert. Paperworks. 60–62
Lacy quilted heart. Better Homes and Gardens treasury of Christmas crafts & foods. 104
Mosaic valentine box. Jarnow. (Re)do it yourself. 154–55
Valentine boxes, designs, 3-D valentine. Lyon. Arts and crafts objects children can make for the home. 92–95
Valentine keepsake card. Encyclopedia of crafts. 113
Valentine surprise. Linsley. Custom made. 100–01
Valentines. Perry. Holiday magic. 32–35

Valentine's day decorations
St. Valentine's day decorations. Better Homes and Gardens holiday decorations you can make. 190–92
Saint Valentine's ring. Janitch. Candlemaking and decorations. 30–32
Valentine place card, wall hanging, and table decorations. Berry. How to make party and holiday decorations. 15–21
Valentine's day decorations. Perry. Holiday magic. 27–32

Vanities. *See* **Dressing tables**

Vases
Bud vase (for wet, dry display). DeCristoforo. Build your own wood toys, gifts and furniture. 309–13
Bud vases. Sainsbury. Sainsbury's woodturning projects for dining. 11–14
Cluster vase. Woman's Day book of gifts to make. 69
Dough vase. Gardner. Dough creations. 73–74
Flattened vase. Campbell. Using the potter's wheel. 82–83
Jars and vases. Rhodes. Pottery form. 43–48
Making a large vase. Ceramics. 22
Mexican and oriental flower cart vase. Wooldridge. Woodturning techniques. 53–63
Pebble and sand vases, spool bud vase. Epple. Something from nothing crafts. 27–28, 189–90
Pine vases. Woman's Day bazaar best sellers. 105
Rolled clay cylinder vase with shell design. Elbert. Shell craft. 227–28
Sculpted flower "vase." McCall's book of America's favorite needlework and crafts. 340
Three-dimensional vase. Dodge. Step-by-step new macrame. 33–34
A thrown cylindrical vase. Howell. Craft of pottery. 49–54, 66
Thrown form. Coyne. Penland School of Crafts book of pottery. 157–72
Two tone vase with tripod legs. Wooldridge. Woodturning techniques. 43–49
Vase. Design crochet. 201
Vases. Romberg. Let's discover papier-mâché. 37
Vases and geometric design. Appel. Sand art. 43–56
Vine-wrapped vases. Johnson. Nature crafts. 79
Watchband and vase (woven). Golden book of hand and needle arts. 131
Weed pots, bud vases. Spielman. Working green wood with PEG. 92–95

Vegetables
Peas-in-pod toy. Woman's Day creative stitchery from scraps. 115–17
Vegetable string, Italy. Casselman. Crafts from around the world. 163–66
Veggies in a basket. McCall's big book of country needlecrafts. 135–37

Veneers and veneering

Hammer veneering, leather on wood, how to mount marquetry, veneering parsons tables. Fine woodworking techniques 2. 172–83

Hobbs. Veneer craft for everyone.

Hobbs. Veneering simplified.

Invisible mending for veneer. Time-Life Books. Repairing furniture. 46–49

Laminating wood veneers. Kicklighter. Crafts, illustrated designs and techniques. 138–43

Patching with veneer, repairing veneered surfaces. Marshall. How to repair, re-upholster, and refinish furniture. 49–52, 57–71

Problems with veneer. Hayward. Antique furniture repairs. 88–93

Real veneer. Krenov. Impractical cabinetmaker. 36–47

Repair veneer. Higgins. Common-sense guide to refinishing antiques. 155

Repairing veneer. Jones. Fixing furniture. 71–72

Repairing veneer. Kinney. Complete book of furniture repair and refinishing. 59–66

Repairing veneer. Savage. Professional furniture refinishing for the amateur. 66–69

Restoring veneering. Learoyd. Conservation and restoration of antique furniture. 71–83

Shop-built vacuum press to bend and glue veneers, oyster-shell veneering. Fine woodworking techniques 3. 36–41, 174–75

Veneer. Waugh. Handyman's encyclopedia. 377–87

Veneering. Blandford. Do-it-yourselfer's guide to furniture repair and refinishing. 171–85

Veneering. Blandford. How to make early American and colonial furniture. 70–77

Veneering. Brumbaugh. Wood furniture finishing, refinishing, repairing. 94–132

Veneering. Frid. Tage Frid teaches woodworking. 118–45

Veneering. Grime. Illustrated guide to furniture repair & restoration. 57–66

Veneering. Rose. Illustrated encyclopedia of crafts and how to master them. 24–30

Veneering. Taylor. How to build period country furniture. 19–28

Veneering: beautiful wood on a budget. Popular Mechanics do-it-yourself encyclopedia Vol. 20, 3044–48

Veneers. Johnson. How to restore, repair, and finish almost everything. 56–61

Veneer buffet. Egge. Recycled with flair. 131–37

Venetian blinds

Repair and maintenance. Bragdon. Homeowner's complete manual of repair & improvement. 131

Venetian blind repair. Schuler. How to fix almost everything. 170–71

Ventilators

Cool your attic to cool your house. Popular Mechanics do-it-yourself encyclopedia. Vol. 1, 120–24

How to install a roof-top ventilator. Outdoor projects for home and garden. 14–18

Ventilators. Geary. Complete handbook of home exterior repair and maintenance. 246–49

Vests

Aran waistcoat. Morgan. Traditional knitting patterns of Ireland, Scotland and England. 71–72

Bargello vest. Woman's Day book of gifts to make. 188–92

Beach bolero. Walters. Crochet. 40–41

Bolero. Torbet. Macrame you can wear. 96–97

Bolero and cowboy tie. Woman's Day bazaar best sellers. 46–47

Bolero vest with passementerie trim. Time-Life Books. Decorative techniques. 73–75

Braid-trimmed vest and head scarf. Knitting 55

Chevron jacket (sleeveless). McNeill. Quilting. 61

Crazy quilt Victorian vest. Johnson. Quiltwear. 95–100
Crochet vest. Mills. Book of presents. 14
Embroidered vest. Ley. Russian & other Slavic embroidery designs. 50–55
Fair Isle pullover. Morgan. Traditional knitting patterns of Ireland, Scotland and England. 81–82
Fair Isle pullover (knit). Mills. The book of presents. 104–05
Fair Isle waistcoat. Morgan. Traditional knitting patterns of Ireland, Scotland and England. 78–80
Fringed chamois vest. Time-Life Books. Decorative techniques. 70–72
Garter yoke pullover and sleeveless vest. Knitting. 35
Granny square vest. American School of Needlework. Great crochet bazaar book. 28–30
His and hers patchwork vests. Scharf. Illustrated patchwork crochet. 161–62
Knitted sleeveless sweater. Simmons. Spinning for softness and speed. 69–71
Lined hunter's vest. Lamoreaux. Outdoor gear you can make yourself. 112–20
Macrame vest. Boberg. Macrame. 102
Man's or woman's tabard waistcoat. Goldsworthy. Clothes for disabled people. 98–100
Mississippi river boat gambler vest. Christensen. Teach yourself needlepoint. 162–64
Nomad's vest. Knitting. 78
Painted waistcoat. Encyclopedia of crafts. 148–49
Paisley arrangement embroidered vest. Scheuer. Designs for Holbein embroidery. 60–61
Patchwork vest. Vanderbilt. Gloria Vanderbilt designs for your home. 188–89
Patchwork vest and striped patchwork vest. McCall's big book of needlecrafts. 72–73
Pattern for Indian design. Fraser. Modern stitchery: stitches, patterns, free-form designing. 84–85
Poetic vest (birds fly over the rainbow), cache coeur. Knitting techniques and projects. 22–24, 36
Quilted vest. Fanning. Complete book of machine quilting. 174–76
Suede waistcoat. Encyclopedia of crafts. 250
Swirling wave suede vest. Wilson. Needlework to wear. 76
Tabard. Holland. Weaving primer. 88
Tabard top, vest with pockets, gypsy vest, seamless vest, belted vest. Beard. Fashions from the loom. 53–58
Telemark bolero. Gostelow. Complete international book of embroidery. 72–73
Tie vest. Wiseman. Cuts of cloth. 52–53
Tunic. Beard. Fashions from the loom. 81
Vest in afghan stitch. Golden book of hand and needle arts. 9
Vest with ball fringe. Guth. Sewing with scraps. 149
Vests. Brown. Weaving, spinning, and dyeing book. 182
Vests. Loeb. Leather book. 111–23
Vests (quilted). Laury. Quilted clothing. 28–45, 61, 69
Waistcoat from Austria. Compton. Complete book of traditional knitting. 158–63
Wallpaper-motif vest. Slater. Elaine Slater's book of needlepoint projects. 136–39
Woven checkerboard vest. Better Homes and Gardens treasury of Christmas crafts & foods. 107
Woven vests and boleros. Krevitsky. Shaped weaving. 70–75

Vests, Children
Child's bolero. Evans. Ribbonwork. 68–71
Child's vest. Coffey. Francine Coffey's celebrity sewing bee. 123
Child's vest. Torbet. Macrame you can wear. 82–83
Child's waistcoat of crocheted squares. Gault. Crafts for the disabled. 112–13
Drummer boy vest, pioneer girl vest. Creative sewing. 115
Good news cable. Favorite knitting & crochet patterns. 149–52
Her special outfit for special events (hairpin lace). Feldman. Needlework boutique. 37, 39–40

Ming vest. Great cross-stitch. 91–94
"Shearling" vest (knitted). Woman's Day bazaar best sellers. 69
Versatile vest. Knitting techniques and projects. 56
Vest for toddlers. Great granny crochet book. 102–03
Victorian vest. Doherty. Family Circle book of 429 great gifts-to-make all year round for just 10¢ to $10.00. 174

Vests, Men
Baltic man's slip-over (Finland). Starmore. Scandinavian knitwear. 95–96
Fair Isle classic & two's company. Favorite knitting & crochet patterns. 201–02, 209–10
Fair Isle favorite & Tunisian vest. Favorite knitting & crochet patterns. 91–96
Fair Isle pullover. Doherty. Family Circle book of 429 great gifts-to-make all year round for just 10¢ to $10.00. 118–19
Holly-berry vest. Farlie. Pennywise boutique. 188–89
Man's patchwork vest. Reader's Digest complete guide to needlework. 262
Man's vest. Scurlock. Muzzleloader Magazine's book of buckskinning II. 80–81
Man's waistcoat. McNeill. Quilting 52–53
Men's simple indoor/outdoor vest. Johnson. Quiltwear. 21–25
Ruska man's slip-over (Finland). Starmore. Scandinavian knitwear. 99–101
Shetland vest, sleeveless sweater. Step by step to better knitting and crochet. 227–28, 254–55
Simple slip stitch pattern vests. Step by step to better knitting and crochet. 142–44
Vest for a man. Scobey. First easy-to-see needlepoint workbook. 117–25
Waistcoat (men's vest). Gehret. Rural Pennsylvania clothing. 157–65

Vests, Women
Afghan stitch vest. Design crochet. 35–39
Bargello stitch bolero. Christensen. Needlepoint and bargello stitchery. 24–25
Cable-patterned waistcoats, lady's evening waistcoat, lady's tabard. Hollingworth. Complete book of traditional Aran knitting. 95–100, 123–31
City vest (knitted). Favorite knitting & crochet patterns. 169–71
Country vest, evergreen vest, cap-sleeved vest, fuzzy vest, crisscross vest, tie-front chenille vest. Woman's Day crochet showcase. 41–48
Crazy patchwork waistcoat. Osler. Machine patchwork. 100–01
Crocheted cluster-trimmed bolero. Doherty. Family Circle book of 429 great gifts-to-make all year round for just 10¢ to $10.00. 58–59
Daffodil waistcoat. McNeill. Quilting. 53
Embroidered tunic. Silverstein. Mira Silverstein's guide to looped and knotted stitches. 96–97
Jacquard top. Walters. Crochet. 64–65
Kesakuu woman's sleeveless top (Finland). Starmore. Scandinavian knitwear. 97–98
Lacy vest. Henderson. Woman's Day book of designer crochet. 51–53
Long vest, casual vest (knitted). Step by step to better knitting and crochet. 10, 15–16
Mother and daughter vest and hat set. Crochet. 30
Multi-use macrame vest. Time-Life Books. Boutique attire. 142–47
Needlepoint vest. Smith. Needlery. 179–84
Patchwork-on-patchwork tunic. Farlie. Pennywise boutique. 84–85
Quilted flowered scarf vest. Doherty. Family Circle book of 429 great gifts-to-make all year round for just 10¢ to $10.00. 68–69
Quilted vest decorated with roses. Wilson. Needlework to wear. 140
Sleeveless jacket in Chinese braid. Dendel. Basic book of fingerweaving. 78–79
Sleeveless vest (crocheted). Rosenthal. Not-so-nimble needlework book. 127
Sporty suede cloth jerkin. Farlie. Pennywise boutique. 80–82
Tabard. Great granny crochet book. 118
Tabard top. Wilson. Needlework to wear. 77

Tweedy-look tunic, patchwork vest, sleeveless jacket, classic mohair slipover. Step by step to better knitting and crochet. 160–61, 182–83, 259–61, 276–77

Vest, popcorn vest. Design crochet. 102–04, 179–83

Woman's curly, cap-sleeved vest. Hubert. Weekend knitting projects. 64

Woman's knitted vest. Woman's Day bazaar best sellers. 29–30

Woman's nubby, long vest. Hubert. Weekend knitting projects. 59

Woman's patterned sweaters and hats. Crochet. 19–22

Woman's puff-trimmed, tie-front and curly vests. Hubert. Weekend knitting projects. 66–71

Woman's side-closing double-padded vest, whitework tabard vest, string quilted vest, Nora's rainbow vest, Rachel's machine-appliqued vest, warm padded vest with Seminole trim, velvet evening vest, sampler vest. Johnson. Quiltwear. 27–34, 51–53, 73–85, 107–22, 129–35

Woodland waistcoat (vest). Walters. Crochet. 56

Vises

Bench vises. Langsner. Country woodcraft. 119–21

C-clamp vise. Blackwell. Johnny Blackwell's poor man's catalog. 143

Dogs, bench rest, holdfast, miter block, etc. Langsner. Country woodcraft. 116

Leg vise. Fine woodworking techniques 2. 31

Portable mechanic's vise. McNair. Building & outfitting your workshop. 136–44

Shoulder vise and clamping dogs, wooden vise. Fine woodworking techniques 4. 44–45

W

Wagon models. *See* **Prairie schooner models**

Wagons

Carriage building. Complete guide to blacksmithing. 153–222

Wagons, Toy

Children's express wagon (repair). Schuler. How to fix almost everything. 66

Chore wagon. Maginley. Toys to make and ride. 58–63

Double-duty wagon. Baldwin. Old fashioned wooden toys. 186–89

Folk art wagon. Hundley. Folk art toys and furniture for children. 78–86

Horses and wagon. Fine woodworking techniques 4. 189

Painted wagon. Jarnow. (Re)do it yourself. 109

Toy-tote wagon, express wagon. DeCristoforo. Build your own wood toys, gifts and furniture. 222–37

Wagon. Blandford. Giant book of wooden toys. 99–102

Wagon. Dal Fabbro. How to make children's furniture and play equipment. 170–71

Yard wagon. Blandford. Giant book of wooden toys. 104–09

Walks. *See* **Garden walks; Sidewalks**

Wallboard

All about hardboard. Popular Mechanics do-it-yourself encyclopedia. Vol. 9, 1398–1403

Gypsum board. Spence. General carpentry. 372–82

Gypsumboard repairs. Nunn. Home improvement, home repair. 30–35

How to patch holes in drywall. Popular Mechanics do-it-yourself encyclopedia. Vol. 7, 1058

How to work with plasterboard. Popular Mechanics do-it-yourself encyclopedia. Vol. 14, 2180–81

Using gypsum wallboard. Handyman. 185–94

Wall hangings
Animals and abstract designs. Villiard. Art and craft of sand casting. 72–102
Bargello & macrame hanging. Boyles. Margaret Boyles book of needle art. 50–53
Batik wall hanging: garden and St. Francis. Tie-dye, batik and candlemaking step-by-step. 26–30
Bead hanging. Hulbert. Creative beadwork. 42
Camel and rider, licheenut, dragon and butterflies, Mongolian archer, and regal eagle hangings. Lane. Rugs and wall hangings. 25–42, 78–106, 124–33
Christmas wall hangings. Better Homes and Gardens holiday decorations you can make. 100–13
Churn dash wall hangings. Houck. Patchwork pattern book. 58–59
Creating a wall hanging. Heard. Complete guide to quilting. 200–11
Decorative panels. Geary. Plant prints and collages. 77–78
Designs for rugs or wall hangings. Scobey. Rugs & wall hangings. 179–234
Diagonal wall hanging. Hall. Sewing machine craft book. 98–99
Door hangings with appliques. Hagans. All good gifts. 39–40
Fabulous fakes: peppermint and cherries jubilee. Nicole. Designer accessories to make for your home. 144–51
Festival banner (felt cut out designs). Casselman. Crafts from around the world. 192–93
Finishing wall hangings. Burchette. Needlework. 101–02
Flower wall hanging. Goldman. Decorate with felt. 18–19
Fon applique hanging. Gostelow. Complete international book of embroidery. 188
Glittery picture beaded wall hanging. Hulbert. Creative beadwork. 58–59
Have a heart pockets, woven name banner. Linsley. Custom made. 54–58, 72–73
Heraldic banner in Mexican double weave. Dendel. Basic book of fingerweaving. 85
Hooked abstract wall hanging. Reader's Digest complete guide to needlework. 495
Indian brave and squaw beaded wall hanging. Hulbert. Creative beadwork. 57
Lace panels and stitchery panels. Laury. Treasury of needlecraft gifts for the new baby. 62–65
Leaf rubbings as wall hangings. Burch. Making leaf rubbings. 32–35
Macro-lace wallhanging. D'Amato. Italian crafts. 39–48
Medallion wall hanging. Hall. Sewing machine craft book. 100–01
Miniature stitcheries, bargello pictures and hangings, Navajo needlepoint wall hanging, miniature quilts. Scharf. Butterick's fast and easy needlecrafts. 165–78
Mount hangings on dowels. Auld. Tatting; the contemporary art of knotting with a shuttle. 118
Oriental wall hanging (hooked). Feldman. Needlework boutique. 115–16
Painted wall piece, shadow box wall piece, odds & ends wall piece. Egge. Recycled with flair. 90–98
Peach pit special, country kitchen arrangements, pheasant and pods. Nicole. Designer accessories to make for your home. 84–89, 96–98
Punch-needle wall hanging and pillow. Woman's Day decorative needlework for the home. 80, 98
Reindeer corral. Casselman. Crafts from around the world. 207–08
Ring wall panel, miniature picture frames made from aluminum can bottoms. Epple. Something from nothing crafts. 11–13, 162–64
Round-wire wall decorations. Metalcrafting encyclopedia. 177
Rubbing for wall hanging. Firestein. Rubbing craft. 83–84
Rya wall hanging. Svinicki. Step-by-step spinning and dyeing. 49–52
Schoolhouse block wall hanging, home sweet home banner. Better Homes and Gardens treasury of Christmas crafts & foods. 100, 104, 208–09
Sculptured banner. Blair. Banners and flags. 154–57
Square wooden bead hanging. Hulbert. Creative beadwork. 62
Stitchery wallhangings. Lyon. Arts and crafts objects children can make for the home. 69–79

Stitchery with shells & beads. Better homes & gardens embroidery. 82–83
Strip patchwork wall hanging. Dudley. Strip patchwork: quick and easy patchwork using the Seminole technique. 87–91
Taaniko wall hanging. Smith. Taaniko, Maori hand-weaving. 55–67
Tablecloth or wall hanging in squares and hexagons. Chatterton. Patchwork & applique. 25–35
Tie-dyed: fireworks and sewn hanging. Tie-dye, batik and candlemaking step-by-step. 14–16
Tie-dyed wall hanging. Anderson. Tie dyeing and batik. 28–31
Tie-dyed wall hanging. Frame. Tie-dyeing and batik. 34–35
Turning your rug into a wall hanging. Scobey. Rugmaking. 132–33
Wall hanging. Evans. Ribbonwork. 13–15
Wall hanging. McCall's sewing for your home. 105–06
Wall hanging with crocheted appliques. Scharf. Butterick's fast and easy needlecrafts. 155–57
Wall hangings. Fairfield. Patchwork. 76–77
Woven cross and bead embroidered wall hanging. Hulbert. Creative beadwork. 68–69
A woven panel to wear or to hang. Dendel. Basic book of fingerweaving. 30–32
Yarn painting—Huichol Indians of Mexico. Casselman. Crafts from around the world. 194–98

Wall hangings, Appliqued
Applique and stitchery—wall hanging. Better Homes and Gardens applique. 60–61
Applique banner. Rockland. Hannukkah book. 106–09
Appliqued and quilted window wall hanging, sunset wall hanging, garden scene, staircase scene, machine appliqued creche banner, festive rejoice banner, silhouette in white, sewing machine, reverse applique, appliqued portrait, butterfly wall panel. Better Homes and Gardens treasury of needlecrafts. 69, 82–83, 94–97, 100–03, 114–15, 118–24, 160–61, 167
Appliqued garden scene. Better Homes and Gardens applique. 28–29
Appliqued staircase scene. Better Homes and Gardens applique. 30–31
Blossoms in a bowl wall hanging. Rosenthal. Not-so-nimble needlework book. 73–74
Cut-through applique wall hanging. Reader's Digest complete guide to needlework. 266
Dahomey wall hanging. Casselman. Crafts from around the world. 224–25
Felt bouquet—appliqued wall hanging. McCall's big book of needlecrafts. 118–19
Foxy wall hanging. Woman's Day creative stitchery from scraps. 78–80, 97–98
Goose wall hanging. Better Homes and Gardens easy bazaar crafts. 55, 62–63
Hearth and farm primitive "paintings," boat wall hanging, eight vegetable banners. McCall's book of America's favorite needlework and crafts. 192–195, 199–202
Lace applique—butterfly wall panel. Better Homes and Gardens applique. 55
Quilted applique silhouette wall hanging. Better Homes and Gardens applique. 52–53
Quilted sunflower. Encyclopedia of crafts. 16
Reverse applique—wall hanging. Better Homes and Gardens applique. 62–66
Reverse applique wall hanging. Encyclopedia of crafts. 26
San blas bird (mola). Golden book of hand and needle arts. 32–33
Winter in Waitsfield, country Christmas, lazy day wall hanging, vegetable banners. McCall's big book of country needlecrafts. 76–80, 96–97, 139–41

Wall hangings, Crocheted
Beaded wall hanging. Halliday. Decorating with crochet. 128–32
Cupid panel. McCall's book of America's favorite needlework and crafts. 247–49
Irish crochet wall hanging. Svinicki. Old-fashioned crochet. 78–79
New York skyline wall hanging. Jacobs. Crochet book. 161–62
Op-art bedspread/wall hanging. Jacobs. Crochet book. 156–59
Patchwork hanging. Design crochet. 160–68

Picture wall hangings: window view and rocket ship. American School of Needlework. Great crochet bazaar book. 41–47

Rainbow window hanging. American School of Needlework. Great crochet bazaar book. 88–90

Three kings lace assemblage. McCall's book of America's favorite needlework and crafts. 253–54

Wall hangings. Henderson. Woman's Day book of designer crochet. 195–202

Wall hangings, Embroidered
Butterfly wall hanging. Sayles. Step-by-step stitchery. 68–69

Crewel embroidery I—introductory material (sampler wall hanging). Cornelius. Teaching needlecraft. 54–57

Dancing clown. Sheuer. Designs for Holbein embroidery. 54–55

Danish handcraft guild amager embroidery plaque. Nielsen. Scandinavian embroidery, past and present. 108–09

Danish sunflowers wall hanging. Nielsen. Scandinavian embroidery, past and present. 62–63

Do not tread on me, George Washington driving the chariot of state, whale paisley, tea chop, John Hewson bouquet, Shaker tree of life, Boston tea party. Tillett. American needlework, 1776–1976. 34–45, 50–53, 58–61, 82–85, 106–09.

Eastern-looking cross stitch wall hanging. Encyclopedia of crafts. 42–43

Machine embroidered wall hanging. Better Homes & Gardens embroidery. 72–73

Machine embroidery and applique hanging. Creative sewing. 86

Metal thread work—embroidered panel. Better Homes & Gardens embroidery. 78–79

Oriental cranes. Boyles. Needlework gifts for special occasions. 92–99

Rose-in-bloom wall hanging, woolwork wreath. McCall's big book of needlecrafts. 272–73, 280–83

Rustic wall hanging. Better Homes & Gardens embroidery. 8–9

Walk in the woods—wall hanging & pillows. Better Homes & Gardens embroidery. 42–47

Walk in the woods wall hanging, machine embroidered tulips with bulbs, moon flowers sampler, angels worked in metal thread, stitchery with shells and beads. Better Homes and Gardens treasury of needlecrafts. 356–61, 390–91, 397–401, 404–05

Wall hanging. Ley. Russian & other Slavic embroidery designs. 56–59

Wall hanging with yellow tulips, wallhanging with purple tulips and apple blossom, pink tulips wall hanging, wall hanging with a sprig of hairy greenwood. Lindberg. Counted cross-stitch designs for all seasons. 17–21, 24–25, 30–31, 40–41

Wedding wall hanging. Nielsen. Scandinavian embroidery, past and present. 92–93

Wall hangings, Knitted
Concentric squares knitted hanging. Woman's Day decorative needlework for the home. 102–03

Interlocking knitted wall hanging. Knitting techniques and projects. 29

Maze wall hanging. Neighbors. Reversible two-color knitting. 166–70

Mosaic-patterned wall hanging. Walker. Mosaic knitting. 192–93

Patchwork wall hangings. Selfridge. Patchwork knitting. 131–32

Wall hangings, Macrame
Bull's head. Anderson. Crafts and the disabled. 118–19

Butterfly, lion with plants, poppies, and dandelions wall hangings. Dodge. Step-by-step new macrame. 46–53

Chinese priest cords. Casselman. Crafts from around the world. 229–33

Karakul wall hanging. Svinicki. Step-by-step spinning and dyeing. 61

Macrame wall hangings. Scharf. Butterick's fast and easy needlecrafts. 158–64

Microme hanging (very small thread macrame). Golden book of hand and needle arts. 144–45

Tan and brown baobob tree and elephant. Dodge. Step-by-step new-macrame. 38–40

Wall hangings, Needlepoint
Abstract Gobelin stitch wall hanging. Nielsen. Scandinavian embroidery, past and present. 76–77
Bless this house hanging. Ambuter. Carolyn Ambuter's needlework celebrations. 36–37
Cat wall hanging. Christensen. Needlepoint and bargello stitchery. 34–36
Confederate flag, crazy horse and General Custer, heart flag, spirit of '76, stenciled fruit. Tillet. American needlework, 1776–1976. 62–81
Dragon in the sea needlepoint wall hanging, phoenix wall hanging. Gault. Needlework dragons and other mythical creatures. 30–41, 53–59
General Washington and his lady, Martha Washington's needlepoint, Martha Washington's ballgown, bicentennial medallion, Benjamin Franklin's bouquet, patchwork quilt. Tillett. American needlework, 1776–1976. 18–21, 22–25, 128–130, 26–29, 30–33, 46–49, 131–33, 18–33, 46–49, 54–57.
Hanukka needlepoint wall hanging. Rockland. Hanukkah book. 73–77
Irises on basketwork lattice, "flaming drum" wallhanging. Nicoletti. Japanese motifs for needlepoint. 20–22
The naturalist tapestry. Ambuter. Carolyn Ambuter's needlepoint celebrations. 168–69
Personification of the River Jordan wall hanging. Parker. Mosaics in needlepoint. 97–102
Rainbow wall hanging. Slater. Elaine Slater's book of needlepoint projects. 141–42
Small tent stitch landscape hanging. Encyclopedia of crafts. 71
Washday, American rose, sailor's farewell, united we stand, Clementine's bouquet, mules in the pasture, eagles all over. Tillet. American needlework, 1776–1976. 86–89, 94–101, 110–25.

Wall hangings, Patchwork
Calico house portrait. Evrard. Homespun crafts from scraps. 80–82
Child's sail-away wall hanging. Evrard. Homespun crafts from scraps. 128–32
Patchwork wall decorations. Scharf. Butterick's fast and easy needlecrafts. 151–53
Patriotic wall hanging. McCall's big book of needlecrafts. 127

Wall hangings, Quilted
"Field of light" wall hanging. McNeill. Quilting. 68–70
Grandmother's fan panel and shoo fly wall hanging. Houck. Patchwork pattern book. 20–21
Organic wall hanging. Golden book of hand and needle arts. 41–42
Overall Sam wall-hanging. Breckenridge. Lap quilting. 64–66
"Rising sun" wall hanging. McNeill. Quilting. 64
Triangles wall hanging. McNeill. Quilting. 71–73

Wall hangings, Wood
Carved wall decorations. Colletti. Art of woodcarving. 109–10

Wall hangings, Trapunto
Chinese fish and "twenty-five-cent" eagle. Morgan. Trapunto and other forms of raised quilting. 15–59

Wall hangings, Wood
Curled wood wall hanging. Christmas crafts book. 20–21
Driftwood panel. Platt. Step-by-step woodcraft. 32–33
Lobster shack. Platt. Step-by-step woodcraft. 34–35

Wall hangings, Woven
Banners and hangings, belled hanging, decorative hangings, bold textured wall hanging, tapestry wall hanging. Holland. Weaving primer. 43–44, 86, 88, 98–100, 105–07, 138
Ethnic wall rug. Wilson. Weaving you can use. 26–31
Indian weaving. Encyclopedia of crafts. 58
Leno wall hanging. Brown. Weaving, spinning, and dyeing book. 87–88
Small wall hanging. Lewis. Everybody's weaving book. 120–26
Snowy owl and abstract wall hangings. McCall's book of America's favorite needlework and crafts. 290–92
Three-dimensional wall hanging. Brown. Weaving, spinning, and dyeing book. 174–75
Twist of inkles. Golden book of hand and needle arts. 132
Wall hanging based on Nebaj weaving. DeRodriguez. Weaving on a backstrap loom. 78–97
Woven wall coverings. Wilson. Weaving you can use. 42–49

Wallpaper
Protecting and cleaning wallpaper. Guide to wallpaper and paint. 47
Removing wallpaper. Guide to wallpaper and paint. 44–47
Wall papering with leaves. Geary. Plant prints and collages. 82–84

Wallpaper. See also **Paper hanging**

Wallets
Colonial wallet, colonial purse, Indian parfleche. Scurlock. Muzzleloader Magazine's book of buckskinning II. 216–20
Leather wallet and fob. Encyclopedia of crafts. 249
Wallet and credit card case. Christensen. Teach yourself needlepoint. 132
Wallet repair. Schuler. How to fix almost everything. 173

Walls
All about sheathing. Popular Mechanics do-it-yourself encyclopedia. Vol. 17, 2620–22
Brick screening wall. 101 do-it-yourself projects. 310–13
Brick walls. Proulx. Plan and make your own fences and gates, walkways, walls and drives. 67–75
Building a retaining wall. Proulx. Plan and make your own fences and gates, walkways, walls and drives. 113–14
Building a stone retaining wall, country dry wall. Bragdon. Homeowner's complete manual of repair & improvement. 552–55
Building and repairing stone walls. Proulx. Plan and make your own fences and gates, walkways, walls and drives. 81–103
Building block walls. Better Homes and Gardens. Step-by-step masonry & concrete. 54–59
Building concrete, brick and stone walls. Russell. Walks, walls, and fences. 77–98
Building log walls. Ramsey. Building a log home from scratch or kit. 131–61
Building retaining walls. Russell. Walks, walls and fences. 98–103
Building walls with railroad ties. Proulx. Plan and make your own fences and gates, walkways, walls and drives. 159–62
Capping a brick wall with concrete. Outdoor projects for home and garden. 270–71
Construction of walls. Clifford. Basic woodworking and carpentry . . . with projects. 135–47
Corduroy-block privacy screen. Better Homes and Gardens. Step-by-step masonry & concrete. 82–83
Erecting brick walls. Better Homes and Gardens. Step-by-step masonry & concrete. 60–65
Exterior walls repair. Nunn. Home improvement, home repair. 187–93

Four fool-proof ways to cover walls with fabric. McCall's sewing for your home. 213–17

How to build retaining walls. Popular Mechanics do-it-yourself encyclopedia. Vol. 16, 2446–49

How to build walls. Chamberlain. Fences, gates & walls. 72–129

How to open a wall. Clifford. Basic woodworking and carpentry . . . with projects. 147–49

How to remove a bearing wall. Popular Mechanics do-it-yourself encyclopedia. Vol. 2, 242–45

How to remove a wall. Brann. How to modernize a kitchen. 53–56

Installing cement block, brick and stone walls. Kramer. Outdoor garden build-it book. 85–104

Installing dry walls and wainscoting. Family handyman handbook of home improvement and remodeling. 235–48

Make your own pass-through. Family handyman handbook of home improvement and remodeling. 25–29

Masonry walls. Decks and patios. 103–16

Pass through opening in wall. Family handyman handbook of carpentry plans/projects. 92–95

Repairing walls, building new walls and improving old ones. Bragdon. Homeowner's complete manual of repair & improvement. 18–25, 30–45

Retaining walls. Complete handyman do-it-yourself encyclopedia. Vol. 17, 2527–30

Roll-away window wall. Rowland. Handcrafted doors & windows. 180–83

Terraced stone walls. Outdoor projects for home and garden. 308–09

Wall construction, exterior wall construction, interior walls. Bodzinski. House construction. 58–65, 75–82, 140–59

Wall framing. Spence. General carpentry. 195–211

Wall framing, wall sheathing. Adams. Arco's complete woodworking handbook. 273–81, 298–301

Walls, Interior

"Brick" (plastic) walls. Handyman. 203–06

Build partitions. Brann. How to modernize an attic. 24–29

Fabric covered walls—double faced carpet tape. Roda. Fabric decorating for the home. 74

Fabric covered walls—fiberboard. Roda. Fabric decorating for the home. 85

Fabric covered walls—paste. Roda. Fabric decorating for the home. 127–28

Fabric covered walls—shirred. Roda. Fabric decorating for the home. 28–29

Fabric covered walls—staple. Roda. Fabric decorating for the home. 184–85

How to decorate or repair any kind of wall. Carbo. Fix-it guide for women. 70–87

Lattice strips installed over a painted wall. Popular Mechanics do-it-yourself encyclopedia. Vol. 10, 1462

Opening up walls. Philbin. Cabinets, bookcases & closets. 89

Putting up and tearing down walls. Time-Life Books. New living spaces. 27–57

Wall and ceiling repair. Gladstone. Hints and tips for the handyperson. 66–71

Wall stenciling. Parry. Stenciling. 79–92

Wardrobes

Children's wardrobe. Blandford. 66 children's furniture projects. 368–75

Wardrobe. Brann. How to build kitchen cabinets, room dividers, and cabinet furniture. 73–75

Wardrobe. Dal Fabbro. How to make children's furniture and play equipment. 104–06

Wardrobe. Williams. Spanish colonial furniture. 120–21

Wardrobes. Rubin. Mission furniture. 108–09

Wastebaskets
Carved wood wastebasket. Gottshall. Wood carving and whittling for everyone. 37–39
Child's wastebasket. Goldman. Decorate with felt. 110
Covered drum wastebasket. Roda. Fabric decorating for the home. 185
Egg carton wastebasket. Yoder. Sculpture and modeling for elementary school. 205–06
Executive's wastebasket, file 13. Oberrecht. Plywood projects illustrated. 41–45, 56–59
Needlepoint cover for a waste basket. Burchette. Needlework. 115
Upholstered wooden wastebasket. Worst. Weaving with foot-power looms. 230–33
Wastebasket. Dal Fabbro. How to make children's furniture and play equipment. 88
Wastebasket. Scobey. First easy-to-see needlepoint workbook. 57–62
Wastebasket. Zegel. Fast furniture. 112
Wastebasket repair. Schuler. How to fix almost everything. 174
Wastepaper basket. Wright. Complete book of baskets and basketry. 90
Wastepaper basket. Rubin. Mission furniture. 119
Waste paper basket in cane using a manufactured base. Maynard. Modern basketry from the start. 131–32
Wastepaper box. Williams. Spanish colonial furniture. 20–21

Waste materials
Casting found objects. Sprintzen. Jewelry, basic techniques and design. 88–90
Christmas decorations. Cook. Decorating for the holidays. 51–57
Collages from waste materials. Ashurst. Collage. 62–67
Egg carton creations: animal, tulip toy and crown. Yoder. Sculpture and modeling for the elementary school. 199–208
Evrard. Homespun crafts from scraps.
Flowers. Metalcrafting encyclopedia. 115
Flowers. Wilkinson. Flower fabrication. 147–67
Jewelry from found objects. Mosesson. Jewelry craft for beginners. 258–76
Kampmann. Creating with found objects.
Laury. Handmade toys and games.
Making furniture from scrap material. 77 furniture projects you can build. 343–60
Metal sculptures. Metalcrafting encyclopedia. 105
Modern wall sculpture. Metalcrafting encyclopedia. 97–98
Play with light candleholder. Metalcrafting encyclopedia. 116
Rock critters, sea shell characters, styrofoam, drinking straw, spaghetti and string sculpture, marble and pine cone animals. Yoder. Sculpture and modeling for the elementary school. 219–32
Unusual sculpture from scraps and waste pieces. Tangerman. Carving the unusual. 34–37
What to do with fabric scraps and glue. Guth. What to do with fabric scraps and glue. 181–92
Wood mosaic, toys, building blocks. Yoder. Sculpture and modeling for the elementary school.

Watch straps
Cavandote watch band. Dodge. Step-by-step new-macrame. 36–37
Rosebud and striped watchband. Great cross-stitch. 116
Sporty bargello watchband. Farlie. Pennywise boutique. 185–86
Watch strap (five beads wide). Gill. Beadwork: the techniques of stringing, threading, and weaving. 174–76
Watchband. Parker. Mosaics in needlepoint. 117–19
Watchband and vase (woven). Golden book of hand and needle arts. 131
Woven watch band. Weaving and spinning. 75–76

Watches
Watch encased in a decorated eggshell. Sommer. Contemporary costume jewelry. 190–91

Water heaters
How to install a solar water heater. Popular Mechanics do-it-yourself encyclopedia. Vol. 18, 2739–42
How to insulate a round water heater. Nunn. Home improvement, home repair. 95–96
How to troubleshoot a water heater, how to get hot water from the sun. Popular Mechanics do-it-yourself encyclopedia. Vol. 9, 1411–18
Water heater maintenance. Nunn. Home improvement, home repair. 137–38

Water wheel models
Water wheel and grist mill. Maginley. America in miniatures. 18–23

Watering cans
Brass watering can. Lindsley. Metalworking in the home shop. 290–91
Watering can. Make it! don't buy it. 230–37

Waterproofing
Keeping your basement dry. Handyman. 234–38
Wet basement control. Family handyman handbook of home improvement and remodeling. 119–30

Weapons
Means of making weapons. Bealer. Art of blacksmithing. 341–412

Weather vanes
Americana (galloping horse) fabric weather-vane. Baldwin. Scrap fabric crafts. 152–54
Cupola/weathervane with eagle. Woodworking techniques and projects. 214–24
Needlepoint horse weathervane. Smith. Needlery. 185–87
Reindeer weather vane. Golden book of colonial crafts. 94–95
Simple weather vane. Thiebault. Kites and other wind machines. 90–92
Stallion, bull, whale weather vanes. Hagerty. Make your own antiques. 99–102
Weathercock. Lindsley. Metalworking in the home shop. 297
Weather vane. Make it! don't buy it. 316–21
Weather vane. Marshall. Foilcraft. 50

Weatherstripping. *See* **Insulation (heat)**

Weaving
Adding new materials: dried plants, beads, suede and chamois, feathers and found objects. Weaving and spinning. 66–70
Anderson. Guatemalan textiles today.
Backstrap loom weaving. Anderson. Guatemalan textiles today. 70–152
Barrett. Boundweave.
Beard. Fashions from the loom.
Beginning tablet weaving. Weaving and spinning. 71–76
Beveridge. Warp/weft/sett.
Bjerregaard. Techniques of Guatemalan weaving.
Bowen. Four-harness weaving.
Brocading. Bjerregaard. Techniques of Guatemalan weaving. 34–92
Bronson patterns. Black. Key to weaving. 337–60
Brostoff. Professional handweaving on the fly-shuttle loom.
Brown. Weaving, spinning, and dyeing book.
Collingwood. Techniques of tablet weaving.

Complex twill patterns. Windeknecht. Color-and-weave. 69–105
Crackle weave or jamtlandsvav patterns. Black. Key to weaving. 307–10
Creager. Weaving.
Dendel. Basic book of fingerweaving.
Double cloth weave. Swanson. Rigid heddle weaving. 158–82, 192–215
Double weave. Murray. Essential handbook of weaving. 120–31
Easy weaving on a box loom, meat carton loom. Lyon. Arts and crafts objects children can make for the home. 125–39
Eight harness twills and large checks. Windeknecht. Color-and-weave. 106–29
Finger weaving. Weaving and spinning. 11–16
Finger weaving & braiding. Meilach. Weaving off-loom. 114–21
Fingerweaving and plaiting. Parker. Beginner's book of off-loom weaving. 120–28
Finger weaving, spool weaving and frame weaving. Linderman. Crafts for the class-room. 227–40
First experiments. Seagroatt. Basic textile book. 49–63
Frames, boards, cardboard, hoops and other objects. Meilach. Weaving off-loom. 48–99
Free form tapestry. Weaving and spinning. 97–101
Free-style weaving. Parker. Beginner's book of off-loom weaving. 33–74
Gadney. How to enter and win fabric and fiber crafts contests.
Gilby. Free weaving.
Gilmurray. Weaving tricks.
Handweaving. Make it! don't buy it. 336–59
Heddle jig, flat shuttle, rug shuttle. Abrams. Building craft equipment. 152
Held. Weaving.
Inkle weaving: belts, bands and straps. Golden book of hand and needle arts. 126–33
Inkle weaving on a loom. Weaving and spinning. 82–88
Lewis. Everybody's weaving book.
Log cabin and colour and weave patterns. Murray. Essential handbook of weaving. 112–13
Log cabin, shadow weave, and related effects patterns. Windeknecht. Color-and-wave. 144–55
Mattera. Navajo techniques for today's weaver.
Mexican double weaving. Dendel. Basic book of fingerweaving. 80–84
More pattern drafts. Murray. Essential handbook of weaving. 114–19
Murray. Essential handbook of weaving.
Nature weavings. Johnson. Nature crafts. 80–83
O'Connor. Twill of your choice.
Off-loom weaving. Parker. Beginner's book of off-loom weaving. 11–18
Overshoot patterns. Black. Key to weaving. 226–87
Overshot patterns. Murray. Essential handbook of weaving. 105–11
Patches as decoration, pockets, appliques, yokes, sleeves, and cuffs. Krevitsky. Shaped weaving. 45–58
Pattern drafts. Murray. Essential handbook of weaving. 78–80
Pattern weaving. Murray. Essential handbook of weaving. 96–104
Patterns for pattern weaves. Windeknecht. Color-and-weave. 156–74
Patterns on eight shafts. Murray. Essential handbook of weaving. 132–40
Phillips. Weaver's book of fabric design.
Plain weaves—finger manipulated patterns. Black. Key to weaving. 105–59
Plain weaves—loom controlled patterns. Black. Key to weaving. 53–104
Plain weaving patterns. Windeknecht. Color-and-weave. 15–29
Plaited designs for strip weaving. Striblings. Crafts from North American Indian arts. 115–21
Redman. Frame-loom weaving.
Rhodes. Small woven tapestries.
Sculptural fiber forms. Meilach. Weaving off-loom. 100–13
Selvages. Murray. Essential handbook of weaving. 77

Smith. Taaniko, Maori hand-weaving.
Space hangings. Wilson. Weaving you can use. 65
Sprang. Held. Weaving. 233–36
Supporting forms for off-loom weaving. Parker. Beginner's book of off-loom weaving. 107–19
Sutton. Structure of weaving.
Tablet and shuttle for tablet weaving. Weaving and spinning. 72–73
Tablet weaving. Encyclopedia of crafts. 51
Tapestry sampler. Weaving and spinning. 34–47
Tapestry techniques. Parker. Creative handweaving. 141–49
Tapestry weaves. Black. Key to weaving. 447–528
Tapestry weaving. Rainey. Weaving without a loom. 78–83
Tartan weaves. Black. Key to weaving. 408–47
Thorpe. Elements of weaving.
Three-dimensional shaped weaving. Krevitsky. Shaped weaving. 93–101
Tod. Joy of hand weaving.
Treadle-loom weaving. Anderson. Guatemalan textiles today. 153–75
Twill patterns. Black. Key to weaving. 160–225
Twill patterns. Windeknecht. Color-and-weave. 30–69
Twining, coiling, and weaving in the round. Parker. Beginner's book of off-loom weaving. 129–57
Variations and extensions on twill threadings. Black. Key to weaving. 287–307
Weaves and ways to use them. Meilach. Weaving off-loom. 20–47
Weaving. Bronson. Early American weaving and dyeing. 9–103
Weaving a small head scarf or table cover. DeRodriguez. Weaving on a backstrap loom. 26–39
Weaving equipment. Murray. Essential handbook of weaving. 54–58
Weaving in the round on a ring or loop. Parker. Beginner's book of off-loom weaving. 210–14
Weaving into scrim, cotton mesh, and burlap. Rainey. Weaving without a loom. 16–28
Weaving on a basic loom, inkle loom, and four-harness loom. Parker. Creative handweaving. 89–140
Weaving on a four harness loom including patterns. Ickis. Weaving as a hobby. 47–69
Weaving on a frame. Rainey. Weaving without a loom. 49–55
Weaving on a loom. Rose. Illustrated encyclopedia of crafts and how to master them. 276–82
Weaving on a pencil. Rainey. Weaving without a loom. 29–33
Weaving on a roller loom. Weaving and spinning. 102–11
Weaving on a simple loom. Weaving and spinning. 17–20
Weaving on a table loom. Weaving and spinning. 112–15
Weaving on a two-harness loom. Tod. Joy of hand weaving. 58–65
Weaving on a two-harness loom including patterns. Ickis. Weaving as a hobby. 37–46
Weaving on cardboard. Rainey. Weaving without a loom. 42–48
Weaving on primitive looms. Newman. Contemporary African arts and crafts. 105–21
Weaving process for Ikat. Newman. Contemporary Southeast Asian arts and crafts. 68–89
Weaving with metal. Sprintzen. Jewelry, basic techniques and design. 177–80
Weft-faced and warped-faced effects. Windeknecht. Color-and-weave. 175–85
Wire weaving. Newman. Wire art. 68
Worst. Weaving with foot-power looms.
Wrapping, finger weaving. Krevitsky. Shaped weaving. 33–44

Weaving, Card
Card weaving. Brown. Weaving, spinning, and dyeing book. 32–41
Card weaving. Chamberlain. Beyond weaving. 169–183
Card weaving. Held. Weaving. 241–44
Weaving on a cardboard loom. Schuman. Art from many hands. 199–200

Weaving, Repairing
Fine-drawn patch. Goldsworthy. Mend it! a complete guide to clothes repair. 34–36
Rewoven patch. Goldsworthy. Mend it! a complete guide to clothes repair. 36–39

Wedding anniversary decorations
Silver & golden anniversary decorations. Berry. How to make party and holiday decorations. 158–63
Silver wedding anniversary candles. Janitch. Candlemaking and decorations. 57–58

Wedding clothes
Bridal headdresses. Couldridge. The hat book. 96–107
Bridal headpieces. Morgan. Trapunto and other forms of raised quilting. 186–90
Bridal parasol. Wargo. Soft crafts for special occasions. 64–68
Silk wedding dress. Laury. Quilted clothing. 110–11
Wedding dress. Treasury of things to make. 96–97
Wedding gown. Woman's Day crochet showcase. 53–58

Wedding decorations
Bell garland. Wargo. Soft crafts for special occasions. 77–78
Bridal flowers. Wilkinson. Flower fabrication. 169–81
Bridal procession. Janitch. Candlemaking and decorations. 45–47
Rice bag. Wargo. Soft crafts for special occasions. 71–72
Silk and dried flowers wedding bouquet. Wiita. Dried flowers for all seasons. 44–46
Wedding wreath. Wargo. Soft crafts for special occasions. 69–70

Welding
Brazing and welding. Make it! don't buy it. 284–99
Faggot and angular welds. Blandford. Practical handbook of blacksmithing and metalworking. 116–22
Forge welding. Meilach. Decorative and sculptural ironwork. 86–88
Pattern welding steel. Meilach. Decorative and sculptural ironwork. 216–18
Welding. Brightman. 101 practical uses for propane torches. 27–38
Welding of Damascus steel. Meilach. Decorative and sculptural ironwork. 222–24
Welding, welding table, welding cart. Giant book of metalworking projects. 84–109

Wells
Building a dry well, creating underground drainage. Bragdon. Homeowner's complete manual of repair & improvement. 475, 504
Deep well and shallow well. Hackleman. Waterworks. 104–13, 115
Water systems handbook.
Wells: contractors, location, dug, bored, washed, driven, drilled. Campbell. Home water supply. 50–62

Wells, Ornamental
Wishing well. Complete handyman do-it-yourself encyclopedia. 1759–62

Wheelbarrows
Bicycle wheelbarrow. Blackwell. Johnny Blackwell's poor man's catalog. 70
Repair. Outdoor projects for home and garden. 204–05
Toy wheelbarrow. Better Homes and Gardens treasury of Christmas crafts & foods. 250–51
Wheelbarrow. Langsner. Country woodcraft. 163–69

Wheelbarrows, Miniature
Scarecrow and the wheelbarrow. Isenberg. Crafting in glass. 164–70
Wheelbarrow. Fowler. Can crafts. 153–57

Wheels
Metal tires. Richardson. Practical blacksmithing. Vol. 4, 41–100

Whistles
Bird whistle. Encyclopedia of crafts. 219
Slide whistle. Popular Mechanics do-it-yourself encyclopedia. Vol. 19, 2958–59
Willow whistles. Underhill. Woodwright's companion. 88–91

Whittling. *See* **Carving; Wood carving**

Wicker furniture
Duncan. How to buy and restore wicker furniture.
Restoring wicker furniture. Saunders. Collecting and restoring wicker furniture. 88–108
Wicker chair. Bausert. Complete book of wicker and cane furniture. 76–88

Wigwams. *See* **Tents**

Wind chimes
Beer bottle windchimes. Epple. Something from nothing crafts. 19–21
Hanging pieces of clay. Chroman. Potter's primer. 56–58
Shell wind chimes. Logan. Shell crafts. 177–79
Wind chimes. Kramer. Wirecraft. 92–93

Windmills
Windmill, wind generator, & a wind motor. Churchill. Big backyard building book. 110–28
Windmill, wind generator, wind motor. Churchill. Backyard building book. 85–103

Window hangings
Batik door and window decoration. Rockland. Hanukkah book. 64–68
Caged parrot. Challenging projects in stained glass. 78–91
Capture a tide pool, crystal madeleines. Elbert. Shell craft. 198–202
Dazzling window dressings. Better Homes and Gardens holiday decorations you can make. 159–65
Eggbeater window hanging. Svinicki. Old-fashioned crochet. 57–58
Four window plaques (stained glass). McCall's book of America's favorite needlework and crafts. 331
Kitchen utensils window hanging. Svinicki. Old-fashioned crochet. 58–59
Leaded window medallion. Wood. Working with stained glass. 32–41
Macrame window screen. Reader's Digest complete guide to needlework. 460
Man in the moon. Isenberg. How to work in beveled glass. 206–07
Needle lace window hanging. Golden book of hand and needle arts. 155–57
Stained glass hanging ornament, leaded window medallion. Wood. Working with stained glass. 26–41
Stained glass window hanging, Santa Claus and wreath window hangings. Popular Mechanics do-it-yourself encyclopedia. Vol. 5, 700–01, 708
Stained glass window ornaments, hanging hearts. Linsley. Great bazaar. 96–97, 151–53
Suncatchers and other creative shapes. Isenberg. How to work in stained glass. 219–25
Window screens made from inkle bands, casement cloth, casement cloth with wrapped warps. Holland. Weaving primer. 41–43, 86, 94–98

Window screens. *See* **Screens, Wire**

Window seats
Bay window seat. Burch. Tile: indoors and out, every kind and use. 118–19
Window recess seat. Blandford. 53 space-saving built-in furniture projects. 188–92
Window seat. Marlow. Classic furniture projects. 62–79
Window seat. 101 do-it-yourself projects. 106–07

Window shades.
Batik blind. Encyclopedia of crafts. 150
Covered blinds, seven ways to make window shades. McCall's sewing for your home. 138, 150–53
Fabric covered window shade with dowel pull. Roda. Fabric decorating for the home. 149–50
How to make shades: Austrian shades, Roman shades, roller shades. Better Homes and Gardens sewing for your home. 60–67
Knitted lace window shade. Knitting techniques and projects. 32
Macrame hanging or window blind. Woman's Day decorative needlework for the home. 104–06
Macrame Roman window blind. Woman's Day decorative needlework for the home. 171–73
Pennsylvania Dutch shade trim. Scobey. Decorating with needlepoint. 121–22
Quick-and-easy window shade. Better Homes and Gardens applique. 14
Roller blinds. Practical needlework. 161–64
Roman blinds. Practical needlework. 164–65
Roman shade. Scobey. First easy-to-see needlepoint workbook. 76–80
Room dividers. Reader's Digest complete guide to sewing. 444
Sailboat shade. Reader's Digest complete guide to sewing. 484
Sliding fabric panels. Better Homes and Gardens sewing for your home. 73
Stenciled window shade. Midkiff. Complete book of stenciling. 52–53
Threaded-straw window beautifier. Hibbs. Straw sculpture. 68
Window coverings; slat blinds, warp/screen. Wilson. Weaving you can use. 56–59
Window shade decorated with pictures. Elbert. Paperworks. 82–83
Window shades. Parry. Stenciling. 96
Woven window blind. Weaving and spinning. 28

Window shutters. *See* **Shutters**

Windows
Cornices and columns. McCall's sewing for your home. 219–20
Double-hung and casement windows. Clifford. Basic woodworking and carpentry . . . with projects. 158–62
Faceted glass windows. Rowland. Handcrafted doors & windows. 164–69
Filigree window panels. Capotosto. Woodworking techniques and projects. 178–83
How to add a dormer. Popular Mechanics do-it-yourself encyclopedia. Vol. 1, 116–18
How to install windows. Windows and skylights. 65–85
How to remove a window. Brann. How to build kitchen cabinets, room dividers, and cabinet furniture. 52
Installing new aluminum windows, rejuvenating old windows, inside storm windows, installing combination storm and screen windows. Family Handyman handbook of home improvement and remodeling. 327–47
Installing storm windows and replacing broken windows. Handyman. 149–57
Installing windows. Burch. Building small barns, shed, and shelters. 99–104
Installing windows. Ramsey. Building a log home from scratch or kit. 162–68
Installing wood and metal windows. Spence. General carpentry. 291–314

Lambrequin. McCall's sewing for your home. 218–19
Maintaining and repairing windows. Windows and skylights. 86–95
Making a window where there was none. Time-Life Books. New living spaces. 88–91
Making windows. Rowland. Handcrafted doors & windows. 106–41
Moyer. Solar heat-n-grow window.
Painting, reglazing, cord replacement, window shades. Waugh. Handyman's encyclopedia. 200–02, 225–27, 278–82
Potted plant. Isenberg. How to work in beveled glass. 210–11
Putting in a new window. Time-Life Books. New living spaces. 98–101
Repairing screens, replacing a glass pane, curtain rod & venetian blind repair. Carbo. Fix-it guide for women. 100–05
Replacing a window pane. Brightman. 101 practical uses for propane torches. 73–75
Sash and window frames. Lewis. Cabinetmaking, and millwork. 410–15
Sash joiner. Underhill. Woodwright's companion. 141–49
Sheet metal window grates. Rowland. Handcrafted doors & windows. 176–79
Storm window. LaPlante. Plastic furniture for the home craftsman. 77–78
Window casing. Syvanen. Interior finish: more tricks of the trade. 63–67
Window installation. Brann. How to modernize an attic. 11–13
Window repairs. Nunn. Home improvement, home repair. 45–48
Window repairs & replacement, storm windows, drapery hardware, window shade installation. Bragdon. Homeowner's complete manual of repair & improvement. 106–31
Window treatment. McCall's sewing for your home. 60
Wood windows, aluminum windows. Olin. Construction. 202.9–202.17, 214.1–214.17

Windows, Repairing
How to replace a broken window pane. Popular Mechanics do-it-yourself encyclopedia. Vol. 20, 3068–69
Repairs to windows. Wood finishing and refinishing. 113–15
Windows and doors. Gladstone. Hints and tips for the handyperson. 59–66

Wine cradles
Making oval wine cradles. Cane, rush and straw. 48–54
Wine cradle. Wright. Complete book of baskets and basketry. 96–97

Wine making
Wayside wines process and recipes. Pittaway. Traditional English country crafts and how to enjoy them today. 182–91

Wine racks
Burlap wine rack holder. Linsley. Fabulous furniture decorations. 132–35
Bottle tote. Cane, rush and straw. 64–67
Patio wine rack. Popular Mechanics do-it-yourself encyclopedia. Vol. 14, 2109
Poor man's bubbly rack. Blackwell. Johnny Blackwell's poor man's catalog. 126
PVC wine rack. Kangas. By hand. 188–90
Simple wine rack. Oberrecht. Plywood projects illustrated. 218–20
Steel wine rack. 101 do-it-yourself projects. 332–33
Three novel wine racks. Popular Mechanics do-it-yourself encyclopedia. Vol. 20, 3070–73
Wall wine rack. Capotosto. Woodworking wisdom. 329–32
Wine & cheese rack. Spence. Woodworking tools, materials, processes. 603
Wine in waiting. Garage, attic and basement storage. 56–59
Wine rack. Family handyman handbook of carpentry plans/projects. 110–15
Wine rack. Kramer. Wirecraft. 89
Wine rack. Mills. The book of presents. 138–39

Wine rack. 77 furniture projects you can build. 210–16
Wine rack. Waugh. Handyman's encyclopedia. 405
Wine racks. Zegel. Shelf book. 103–06

Wire
Braiding and twisting. Sprintzen. Jewelry, basic techniques and design. 183–87
Coloring wires. Newman. Wire art. 38–39
Filigree. Newman. Wire art. 152–53, 155
Geometical designs with fine wire. Elliot. Working with copper. 99–105
Kramer. Wirecraft.
Spiralling. Metalcrafting encyclopedia. 29
Weaving into wire. Rainey. Weaving without a loom. 34–39
Wire armature. Newman. Wire art. 186–206
Wire dolls. Tyler. Big book of dolls. 67–77
Wire sculpture—athletes and musicians. Lyon. Arts and crafts objects children can
   make for the home. 147
Wire sculpture. Elliot. Working with copper. 106
Wire sculpture. Encyclopedia of crafts. 221
Wire sculpture: tissue-covered, tightly wound, outline, screen wire, bas-relief. Yoder.
   Sculpture and modeling for the elementary school. 121–28, 130–32, 134–39

Wiring, Electric. *See* Electric wiring

Witches
Flying witch. Bumper book of things a girl can make. 18–20
Halloween is coming witch table decoration. Creative crafts yearbook: an exciting new
   collection of needlework and crafts. 120–21
Kitchen witch. Baldwin. Scrap fabric crafts. 58–61
Kitchen witch. Guild. Dollmaker's workshop. 113–14
Knitted witch. Tyler. Big book of dolls. 64–67
Miss Witch. Kinser. Sewing sculpture. 79–81

Wood baskets and boxes
Brass log basket. Lindsley. Metalworking in the home shop. 289
Build a woodbox. Popular Mechanics do-it-yourself encyclopedia. Vol. 8, 1228
Canvas log carrier. Roda. Fabric decorating for the home. 115
Firewood crib. Oberrecht. Plywood projects illustrated. 93–95
Log basket. Brown. Complete book of rush and basketry techniques. 81–82
Log basket. Wright. Complete book of baskets and basketry. 116–17
Log box. Brown. 44 terrific woodworking plans & projects. 130–31, 134
Log carrier (sewn). Burns. Super sewing. 296–97
Log holder. Giant book of metalworking projects. 195–97
Log tote and cradle. 101 do-it-yourself projects. 330–31
Lumber and materials storage rack, scrap lumber bin. McNair. Building & outfitting
   your workshop. 81–87, 97–108
Storage chest for logs. Traister. All about chimneys. 150–51
Stovewood holder, wood box. Braren. Homemade. 25–26
Wood box. Moser. How to build Shaker furniture. 104–05
Wood box. Williams. Spanish colonial furniture. 82–83

Wood bending
Bending. Frid. Tage Frid teaches woodworking. 2–26
Bending. Platt. Step-by-step woodcraft. 62–63
Bent laminations. Fine woodworking techniques I. 183–86
Bent wood repair. Marshall. How to repair, reupholster, and refinish furniture. 152–54

Fixtures for steambending, bending with ammonia. Fine woodworking techniques 5. 188–91

How to put a bend in wood. Popular Mechanics do-it-yourself encyclopedia. Vol. 20, 3088–93

Laminating and bending wood. Wagner. Modern woodworking. 310–15

Restoring the curves of bentwood. Time-Life Books. Repairing furniture. 56–57

Steam bending, hot-pipe bending. Fine woodworking techniques 2. 162–71

Wood burning

Basic procedures and burn strokes. Broadwater. Woodburning: art and craft. 12–26

Black duck oval plaque (pattern). Broadwater. Woodburning: art and craft. 29–30

Book shelves, picture frames, switch plates, drawers, doors, chairs, salad bowls, kitchen cabinets. Brightman. 101 practical uses for propane torches. 99–103

Butterfly pattern. Broadwater. Woodburning: art and craft. 27–29

Patterns for woodburning. Broadwater. Woodburning: art and craft. 67–72

Pharoah pattern. Broadwater. Woodburning: art and craft. 32–33

Plan your own woodburning designs. Broadwater. Woodburning: art and craft. 75–88

Puppy pattern. Broadwater. Woodburning: art and craft. 30–32

Pyrography picture. Lyon. Arts and crafts objects children can make for the home. 110–13

Rubbings for woodburning. Firestein. Rubbing craft. 60–61

Woodburning. Sommer. Contemporary costume jewelry. 86–87

Wood burning. See also **Pyrography**

Wood carving

Beiderman. Beginner's handbook of woodcarving.

Caricaturing animals. Tangerman. Carving the unusual. 14–24

Carved shells, chip carving. Fine woodworking techniques 3. 152–56

Carving. Blandford. How to make early American and colonial furniture. 77–83

Carving. Frid. Tage Frid teaches woodworking. Vol. 2, 40–56

Carving details on furniture. Taylor. How to build period country furniture. 33–41

Carving in balsa. Warring. Balsa wood modelling. 40–44

Carving lab, chain-saw carving, relief carving, ball and claw feet, cockleshell for corner cupboard. Fine woodworking techniques 2. 146–59

Carving letters. Adkins. Wood book. 184–85

Carving thick bark. Tangerman. Carving the unusual. 98–101

Carving wood. Linderman. Crafts for the classroom. 319–23

Chip carving candle and base. D'Amato. Italian crafts. 80–84

Colletti. Art of woodcarving.

Craft figures or maypole. Tangerman. Carving the unusual. 46–47

Ethnic or national carving. Tangerman. Carving the unusual. 38–45

Expert's bird-carving secrets. Popular Mechanics do-it-yourself encyclopedia. Vol. 3, 340–43

Hand-carved signs. Spielman. Making wood signs. 44–55

Hand shaping, carving fans, gothic tracery, lute roses. Fine woodworking techniques I. 160–73

Lubkemann. Carving twigs and branches.

Makonde wood and ivory process. Newman. Contemporary African arts and crafts. 286–91

Nuts, pits and gourds. Tangerman. Carving the unusual. 90–97

Platt. Step-by-step woodcraft.

Processes; wood. Newman. Contemporary Southeast Asian arts and crafts. 178–86

Scenes, panel of flowers, birds and insects. Tangerman. Carving the unusual. 66–80

Set of carving gouges. Fine woodworking techniques 4. 77–79

Stylizing humans. Tangerman. Carving the unusual. 24–27

Upton. Woodcarver's primer.

Wiley. Woodcarving with projects.
Wood carved picture, carving in the round. Lyons. Arts and crafts objects children can make for the home. 121–23
Wood carving. Blandford. Do-it-yourselfer's guide to furniture repair and refinishing. 233–45
Woodcarving. Kicklighter. Crafts, illustrated designs and techniques. 346–61
Wood sculpture. Rose. Illustrated encyclopedia of crafts and how to master them. 320–26
Wood sculpture. Treasury of things to make. 44–45
Wood whittling: rocker, little hanging shelf. Brunner. Pass it on. 83–88
Zimmerman. Carving horses in wood.

Woodcarving, patterns
Animal forms. Bridgewater. A treasury of woodcarving designs. 154–86
Atlas. Tangerman. Carving flora and fables in wood. 79–85
Beowulf vs. Grendel. Tangerman. Carving flora and fables in wood. 91–97
Campfire and coffee pot, wayside philosopher, liberty plaque, antique auto. McKellips. Practical pattern manual for woodcarving and other crafts. 84–89, 99–104
Circles. Bridgewater. A treasury of woodcarving designs. 57–85
Elf. Tangerman. Carving flora and fables in wood. 105–11
Flower panel carving. Carving flora and fables in wood. 23–28, 32–38, 42–48
Forest clowns, grapes and vines, clockmaker, roses, Bacchus, mare and colt, birds in grapes, daisies. McKellips. Practical pattern manual for woodcarving and other crafts. 47–77
Heavenly kingdom, grace in motion, truth shall make you free, horse, musical composition. McKellips. Practical pattern manual for woodcarving and other crafts. 27–45
Heracles vs. the Nemean lion. Tangerman. Carving flora and fables in wood. 86–90
Intaglio carving. Tangerman. Carving flora and fables in wood. 29–31
Lines. Bridgewater. A treasury of woodcarving designs. 27–56
Little mermaid. Tangerman. Carving flora and fables in wood. 54–66
McKellips. Practical pattern manual for woodcarving and other crafts.
Mini mallards. Blackwell. Johnny Blackwell's poor man's catalog. 131
Odysseus vs. the Cyclops. Tangerman. Carving flora and fables in wood. 98–104
Pine tree. Tangerman. Carving flora and fables in wood. 49–53
Plant forms. Bridgewater. A treasury of woodcarving designs. 122–51
Thor and his hammer. Tangerman. Carving flora and fables in wood. 74–78
Twined forms. Bridgewater. A treasury of woodcarving designs. 88–119
Unicorn. Tangerman. Carving flora and fables in wood. 112–18
Whittle simple flowers. Tangerman. Carving flora and fables in wood. 20–22

Wood carving, Projects
Christmas elf. Gottshall. Wood carving and whittling for everyone. 134–38
Indian. Gottshall. Wood carving and whittling for everyone. 138–43
Painted cutouts. Firestein. Rubbing craft. 56–59
Spread eagle. Gottshall. Wood carving and whittling for everyone. 95–96
Squirrel, elephant. Colletti. Art of woodcarving. 63–69, 74–79

Wood, Drying. *See* **Kilns**

Wood finishing
Basics of wood staining. Popular Mechanics do-it-yourself encyclopedia. Vol. 18, 2770–71
Choosing a finish. Johnson. How to restore, repair, and finish almost everything. 46–55
Fine finishes for furniture. Popular Mechanics do-it-yourself encyclopedia. Vol. 20, 3094–99

Finishes. Blandford. 53 space-saving built-in furniture projects. 80–88
Finishes. Taylor. How to build period country furniture. 42–47
Finishing. Blandford. How to make your own built-in furniture. 323–32
Finishing. Feirer. Cabinetmaking and millwork. 785–833
Finishing. Frid. Tage Frid teaches woodworking. Vol. 2, 172–210
Finishing materials. Fine woodworking techniques 3. 178–91
Finishing: stain, dyes and pigments, sanding, tung oil. Fine woodworking techniques 2. 186–97
Finishing wood. Bard. Successful wood book. 117–28
Finishing wood. Philbin. Cabinets, bookcases & closets. 65–77
French polishing. Fine woodworking techniques 4. 201–10
French polishing, oil/varnish mix. Fine woodworking techniques I. 130–33
Furniture finishing. Roberts. Illustrated handbook of upholstery. 386–93
Give unpainted furniture a custom look. Popular Mechanics do-it-yourself encyclopedia. Vol. 13, 2039–44
How to finish wood. Clifford. Basic woodworking & carpentry . . . with projects. 230–45
Notes on clear finishes, coloring with penetrating oils, lacquer finishing, fumed oak finish. Fine woodworking techniques 5. 212–25
Oughton. Complete manual of wood finishing.
Raising grain on wood. Brightman. 101 practical uses for propane torches. 128
Rosmaling techniques and designs. McCall's big book of country needlecrafts. 273–81
Sanding, staining, and finishing. Haynie. Cabinetmaking. 72–78
Spray finishing. Martensson. Woodworker's bible. 281–83
Varnish basics. Popular Mechanics do-it-yourself encyclopedia. Vol. 19, 3033
Wood finishing. Clifford. Basic woodworking and carpentry . . . with projects. 230–42
Wood finishing. Make it! don't buy it. 162–83
Wood finishing. Modern general shop. Woodworking 50–57
Wood finishing. Wagner. Modern woodworking. 121–49
Wood finishing and refinishing.

Wood finishing. See also **Floors; Furniture, Refinishing**

Wood Pictures. See **Inlay; Marquetry; Pictures, Wood**

Wood turning
Bolection turning, hollow turning, tips from the turning conference. Fine woodworking techniques 3. 127–32, 138–40
Five basic spindle laminations, turning for figure, inlaid turnings, hand-carved turnings. Fine woodworking techniques 5. 104–10, 118–19
Hodges. Woodturning handbook.
Hogbin. Wood turning.
Nish. Creative woodturning.
Sainsbury. Craft of woodturning.
Sainsbury. Woodworking projects with power tools.
Spindle turning, faceplate turning. Frid. Tage Frid teaches woodworking. Vol. 2, 58–110
Spindle turning, small turned boxes, turning spalted wood, laminated turning. Fine woodworking techniques 2. 120–45
Turning. Blandford. How to make early American and colonial furniture. 83–89
Turning. Platt. Step-by-step woodcraft. 58–61
Turning thin spindles (lacemaker's bobbins). Fine woodworking techniques 4. 192–93
Turning tools. Albers. How to use woodworking tools effectively and safely. 132–53
Woodturning. Blandford. Do-it-yourselfer's guide to furniture repair and refinishing. 219–33
Wood turning. Rose. Illustrated encyclopedia of crafts and how to master them. 17–24
Woolridge. Woodturning techniques.

Woodworking

Black light makes some woods glow, harvesting green wood, PEG for the woodworker. Fine woodworking techniques 3. 9–19

Briney. Home machinist's handbook.

Cabinet for a router. Popular Mechanics do-it-yourself encyclopedia. Vol. 17, 2602–07

Clamping wide boards, unwinding lumber, surfacing wide boards. Fine woodworking
techniques 4. 7, 11

Frid. Tage Frid teaches woodworking. Vol. 2

How to use a router. Popular Mechanics do-it-yourself encyclopedia. Vol. 16, 2468–79

Lumber sawing support, shooting board, router guides, auxiliary table set, feather
boards, problem-solving water level. McNair. Building & outfitting your workshop.
127–36, 151–74, 192–202

Making dowels, wooden plugs and dutchmen. Upton. Woodcarver's primer. 71–75

Pin router, homemade overhead and pin routers, wood jointer. Fine woodworking techniques 5. 23–34

13 bonus tricks for your jointer, mobile stand for a 6-in. jointer. Popular Mechanics
do-it-yourself encyclopedia. Vol. 10, 1582–87

Turnings without screw holes. Fine woodworking techniques 4. 88–89

Working with wood. Bard. Successful wood book. 95–116

Woodcraft. Kicklighter. Crafts, illustrated designs and techniques. 362–69

Woodworking shop. Geary. How to design and build your own workspace—with plans.
45–119

Wool

Selection, handling, washing, scouring, sicking, carding, and combing of wool. Turner.
Legacy of the great wheel. 65–81

Teal. Hand woolcombing and spinning.

Washing and carding wool. Hochberg. Handspindles. 59–61

Workbenches

Apartment workshop. Handyman. 522–24

Basic workbench with shelves, base-cabinet workbench. Oberrecht. Plywood projects
illustrated. 73–78, 171–79

Basic workbench, workbench fit for a pro, tailgate workbench, build a shop inside a
bench, cabinet bench for a small shop. Popular Mechanics do-it-yourself encyclopedia. Vol. 20, 3124–41

Carver's bench. Tangerman. Carving the unusual. 13

Child's size bench. Brann. How to build workbenches, sawhorse tool chest and other
build-it-yourself projects. 19–21

Child's workbench and tool caddy. 101 do-it-yourself projects. 340–43

Compact workbench or shop workbench. Family handyman handbook of carpentry
plans/projects. 253–64

Constructing a work bench. Johnston. Craft of furniture making. 73–76

Easy workbench. Family handyman handbook of home improvement and remodeling.
179–82

Foldaway work bench. Brann. How to build workbenches, saw horse tool chest, and
other build-it-yourself projects. 23–38

Fold-down work table. Nunn. Home improvement, home repair. 10

Folding bench. Blandford. 53 space-saving built-in furniture projects. 367–71

Hobby bench. Blandford. 66 children's furniture projects. 399–407

Making a workbench. Platt. Step-by-step woodcraft. 24–25

Old-world workbench. 101 do-it-yourself projects. 194–97

Poor man's workbench, fold-down workbench. Blackwell. Johnny Blackwell's poor
man's catalog. 6–7, 11

Sawhorse becomes a workbench. Popular Mechanics do-it-yourself encyclopedia. Vol.
16, 2512–13

Shop workbench. 77 furniture projects you can build. 252–56

Six-foot workbench. Brann. How to build workbenches, sawhorse tool chest and other build-it-yourself projects. 7–19

Small workbench. Fine woodworking techniques 2. 25

Softwood work bench, double-top workbench. Fine woodworking techniques 4. 42–43, 46–47

Standard workbench. Brown. 44 terrific woodworking plans & projects. 109–13

Super workbench. Leavy. Bookshelves and storage units. 56–58

Table top workbench. Brann. How to build workbenches, sawhorse tool chest and other build-it-yourself projects. 42–56

Tool cabinet and workbench, light-duty workbench, heavy-duty workbench, butcher block type top, heavy-duty automobile workbench. Geary. How to design and build your own workspace—with plans. 46–54, 188–89, 266–68

Tool cabinet-workbench. Self. Working with plywood, including indoor/outdoor projects. 236–40

Tool cabinet workbench. Nunn. Home improvement, home repair. 8

Work areas. Jones. Plan and build more storage space. 147–55

Workbench. Braren. Homemade. 15

Workbench. Complete handyman do-it-yourself encyclopedia. Vol. 21, 3174–95

Work bench. Fine woodworking techniques I. 40–45

Workbench. Hamilton. Build it together. 172–179

Workbench. Waugh. Handyman's encyclopedia. 319–25

Workbench. Zegel. Fast furniture. 108–09

Workbench ways to hold wood. Fine woodworking techniques 3. 22–25

Workbenches. Blandford. How to make your own built-in furniture. 311–13

Workbenches. Langsner. Country woodcraft. 107–21

Workshops

Assembled workshop. Brann. How to build workbenches, sawhorse tool chest and other build-it-yourself projects. 39–41

Automobile workshop. Geary. How to design and build your own workspace—with plans. 262–76

Craft workshops. Geary. How to design and build your own workspace—with plans. 182–211

Dust collection system. Fine woodworking techniques. Vol. 2, 22–24

Hobby centers. Popular Mechanics do-it-yourself encyclopedia. Vol. 10, 1454–57

How to lay out your workshop. Popular Mechanics do-it-yourself encyclopedia. Vol. 20, 3142–43

McNair. Building & outfitting your workshop.

Setting up a small shop, return-air dust collection. Fine woodworking techniques 4. 18–32, 38–39

Shop organizer, clever shop tips, woodworking tips, "eggs" hold small parts. Popular Mechanics do-it-yourself encyclopedia. Vol. 17, 2659–68, 2709

Stand for your propane torch. Popular Mechanics do-it-yourself encyclopedia. Vol. 19, 2905

Storage. Blandford. How to make your own built-in furniture. 314–16

Woodworking and shop areas. Davidson. Successful studios and work centers. 95–114

Workmate workshop. Oberrecht. Plywood projects illustrated. 118–21

Workshop. Marshall. Yard buildings. 75–83

Workshop basics. Garage, attic and basement storage. 52–55

Wrapping of packages

Accordion wraps, basket gift wraps, napkin wraps, package characters, newspaper trims, rippled trims. McCall's book of Christmas. 142–48

Bags of fun (gift pouches). Creative crafts yearbook: an exciting new collection of needlework and crafts. 98

Decorative bows, swirl, butterfly and sunburst. Paper. 127–28
Fabric wrappings, ribbons and bows, and trims. O'Neill. Make-it-merry Christmas book.
    110–13
Gift-wrap art: cutouts make each package a mini-collage. Vanderbilt. Gloria Vanderbilt
    designs for your home. 174–75
Holly-printed wrapping paper. Meyer. Chrismas crafts. 25–28
Origami gift wrappings. Araki. Origami for Christmas. 142–45
Presenting your presents. Mills. The book of presents. 140–43
Recycled paper wrappings. O'Neill. Make-it-merry Christmas book. 106–09
Roll-on printing gift wrap paper. Elbert. Paperworks. 28–29
Roth. Creative gift wrapping.

Wreaths
Advent wreath. Hagans. All good gifts. 123–25
Advent wreath. Meyer. Christmas crafts. 9–14
Advent wreaths. Coskey. Christmas crafts for everyone. 24–30
Angel and Santa wreaths. Foose. More scrap saver's stitchery. 116–21
Autumn wreaths. Scobey. Gifts from your garden 135–36
Baby's breath Christmas wreath. Wiita. Dried flowers for all seasons. 90–91
Bent wire, single wire, flat and wicker wreaths. Miles. Designing with natural materials.
    73–77
Birds and berries holiday wreath. Sheldon. Washable and dryable needlepoint. 84–85
Bouquet garni wreath. Johnson. Nature crafts. 51
Bow Christmas wreath. Coffey. Francine Coffey's celebrity sewing bee. 149
Braided bread dough wreath. O'Neill. Make-it-merry Christmas book. 62–65
Braided corn husk wreath. Giant book of crafts. 259–60
Braided satin, gold doily, necktie, pinecone. Better Homes and Gardens easy bazaar
    crafts. 68, 72–74, 76, 80
Bread dough wreath. McCall's book of Christmas. 104
Calico bow wreath. O'Neill. Make-it-merry Christmas book. 102–05
Christmas card wreath, woodlands pinecone heart and pinecone Christmas wreath.
    Evrard. Homespun crafts from scraps. 87–88, 92–98
Christmas patchwork wreath. Breckenridge. Lap quilting. 87–89
Christmas wreath. Christensen. Needlepoint. 84–88
Christmas wreath. Fowler. Can crafts. 21–22
Christmas wreath. Great granny crochet book. 84
Christmas wreath. Scobey. First easy-to-see needlepoint workbook. 139–43
Christmas wreath crocheted with rug yarn, braided Christmas wreath. American
    School of Needlework. Great Christmas crochet book. 29, 37
Christmas wreath. Wargo. Soft crafts for special occasions. 104–06
Christmas wreaths made from cones, pods, seeds and bracts. Meras. Vacation crafts.
    43–49
Clothespin wreath. Linsley. Great bazaar. 98–99
Coffee dough wreath. Woman's Day book of weekend crafts. 83–84
Cornhusk wreath with Osage oranges. Johnson. Nature crafts. 65
Cranberry wreath. Johnson. Nature crafts. 145
Crepe paper flowers and wreath, quickpoint rose wreath, Christmas star wreath, soft
    sculpture holly wreath, lace wreath, quilted wreath, cornhusk flower wreath, Della
    Robbia wreath, crazy quilt wreath, needlepoint wreath. Better Homes and Gardens
    treasury of Christmas crafts & foods. 32, 85–86, 109, 141, 155, 333–35
Crocheted Christmas wreath. Henderson. Woman's Day book of designer crochet.
    203–04
Cross-stitch rose wreaths. Better Homes & Gardens embroidery. 26–27
Della Robbia needlepoint wreath. Better Homes and Gardens treasury of needlecrafts.
    306–09
Door wreath in kru coast and round braids. Dendel. Basic book of fingerweaving. 102–
    07

Dough art wreath. Rissell. Craftwork the handicapped elderly can make and sell. 96–98

Dream wreath and excelsior wreath. Berry. How to make party and holiday decorations. 105–07

Dried herb wreaths. Johnson. Nature crafts. 87

Fabric holly wreath. Baldwin. Scrap fabric crafts. 74–75

Felt Della Robia wreath, holly wreath with pom-pon berries, felt "Balsam fir" wreath, three-toned green holly wreath, walnut and pinecone wreath, feather wreath, dried wheat and apple spray, seashell wreath, stained-glass flowers and fruit or dove and holly, calico wreath. McCall's book of Christmas. 20–33

Flower wreath. Critchley. Step by step guide to making artificial flowers. 66–68

Golden yarrow wreath. Wiita. Dried flowers for all seasons. 76–77

Gypsophila, witch's broom, double pinecone, country plaid, Victorian blue, and popcorn and cranberry wreaths. Nicole. Designer accessories to make for your home. 61–63, 72–73, 102–04, 136–38, 177–80, 186–87

Holiday greenery: decorating with native materials. Johnson. Nature crafts. 134–37

Holiday wreaths. McCall's big book of country needlecrafts. 285–87

Hospitality wreath. Baldwin. Scrap fabric crafts. 110–13

Man-made foliage wreaths. Cook. Decorating for the holidays. 16–21

Miniature wreaths. O'Neill. Make-it-merry Christmas book. 34–40

Miniature wreaths in shadow boxes. Cook. Decorating for the holidays. 36–37

More than a dozen dried wreaths. Miles. Designing with natural materials. 34–53

Nativity wreath. Cook. Decorating for the holidays. 5–6

Nature's rope (vine wreaths). Johnson. Nature crafts. 74–78

Nut wreath. Cook. Decorating for the holidays. 60

Padded calico wreath. Wilson. Erica Wilson's Christmas world. 66

Pine cone and linoleum paste wreaths. O'Neill. Make-it-merry Christmas book. 22–26

Pine cone wreath. Wiita. Dried flowers for all seasons. 83–85

Pine cone wreaths. Johnson. Nature crafts. 130–31

Poinsettia, persimmon, white swan, and crane wreaths. Araki. Origami for Christmas. 134–36

Puff-heart felt wreath, pompon wreath. Woman's Day bazaar best sellers. 130–32

Puff quilt wreath. Heard. Complete guide to quilting. 278

Rosemary and yarrow wreath. Johnson. Nature crafts. 86

Roundup of holiday wreaths. Better Homes and Gardens holiday decorations you can make. 114–19

Shell wreath. Johnson. Nature crafts. 33

Spanish moss wreath. Johnson. Nature crafts. 144

Spicy kitchen wreath. Johnson. Nature crafts. 147

Spiral wreath. Hibbs. Straw sculpture. 108

Straw, blue cone ruscus, flower wall garland wreaths. Christmas crafts book. 11–13, 21

Straw Christmas ring. Coker. Craft of straw decoration. 78

Weed wreath. Wiita. Dried flowers for all seasons. 72–74

Welcome wreath. Gordon. Complete guide to drying and preserving flowers. 205–09

Wreaths, swags, and roping. Conner. Corncraft. 129–41

Yo-yo wreath & ornament, woodland animals Christmas tree skirt or wreath. Wilson. Erica Wilson's Christmas world. 72–79

Yo-yo wreath (cloth). Foose. Scrap saver's stitchery book. 119

Wrenches

Forging wrenches. Richardson. Practical blacksmithing. Vol. 3, 33–35

Forging wrenches. Weygers. Modern blacksmith. 72–73

Tap wrench. Modern general shop. Metalworking. 109

XYZ

Yachts
Fiddleheads and billetheads. Upton. Woodcarver's primer. 134–40
Stern transom carvings for yachts. Upton. Woodcarver's primer. 120–28
Yacht trailboards. Upton. Woodcarver's primer. 129–33

Yardsticks. *See* **Measuring sticks**

Yarn
Huichol Indian yarn paintings. Schuman. Art from many hands. 150–53
Lorant. Yarns for textile crafts.
Spinning your own yarn. Brown. Weaving, spinning, and dyeing book. 212–44
Yarn printing ikat. Held. Weaving. 290–96
Yarns, threads and fibers. Lewis. Everybody's weaving book. 24–30

Yokes
Hauling yoke. Langsner. Country woodcraft. 177–79
Poke. Langsner. Country woodcraft. 205–07

Yo-yos
Yo-yo. Blandford. Giant book of wooden toys. 152–53

Zippers
Zipper (repair). Schuler. How to fix almost everything. 181

Zodiac
Carving the zodiac signs. Colletti. Art of woodcarving. 84–106
Signs of the zodiac in string work. 44 string and nail art projects. 57–84